Integrated Mathematics **1**

Authors

Senior Authors

Rheta N. Rubenstein

Timothy V. Craine

Thomas R. Butts

Kerry Cantrell

Linda Dritsas

Valarie A. Elswick

Joseph Kavanaugh

Sara N. Munshin

Stuart J. Murphy

Anthony Piccolino

Salvador Quezada

Jocelyn Coleman Walton

McDougal Littell
A HOUGHTON MIFFLIN COMPANY
Evanston, Illinois • Boston • Dallas

Authors

Senior Authors

Rheta N. Rubenstein   Associate Professor of Education, University of Michigan at Dearborn, Dearborn, Michigan

Timothy V. Craine   Professor and Chair, Department of Mathematical Sciences, Central Connecticut State University, New Britain, Connecticut

Thomas R. Butts   Professor of Mathematics Education, University of Texas at Dallas, Dallas, Texas

Kerry Cantrell   Mathematics Teacher and Divisional Technology Coordinator, Marshfield High School, Marshfield, Missouri

Linda Dritsas   Mathematics Coordinator, Fresno Unified School District, Fresno, California

Valarie A. Elswick   Mathematics Consultant and former Mathematics Teacher, Roy C. Ketcham Senior High School, Wappingers Falls, New York

Joseph Kavanaugh   Academic Head of Mathematics, Scotia-Glenville Central School District, Scotia, New York

Sara N. Munshin   Middle School Mathematics Specialist, Los Angeles Unified School District, Los Angeles, California

Stuart J. Murphy   Visual Learning Specialist, Evanston, Illinois

Anthony Piccolino   Associate Professor of Mathematics, Montclair State University, Upper Montclair, New Jersey

Salvador Quezada   Mathematics Teacher, Theodore Roosevelt High School, Los Angeles, California

Jocelyn Coleman Walton   Educational Consultant, Mathematics K-12, and former Mathematics Supervisor, Plainfield High School, Plainfield, New Jersey

All authors contributed to the planning and writing of the series. In addition to writing, the Senior Authors played a special role in establishing the philosophy of the program, planning the content and organization of topics, and guiding the work of the other authors.

Field Testing   The authors give special thanks to the teachers and students in classrooms nationwide who used a preliminary version of this book. Their suggestions made an important contribution to its development.

ISBN: 0-618-07394-9   5 6 7 8 9 10-VJM-08 07 06 05 04

Editorial Advisers and Reviewers

Carol A. Andrews   Mathematics Teacher, Greece Arcadia High School, Rochester, New York

John G. Balzano   Mathematics Teacher, Johanna Perrin Middle School, Fairport, New York

Janet M. Burt   Mathematics and Science Supervisor, Clinton Central School, Clinton, New York

Barbara P. Chamberlain   former Mathematics Teacher, Shorecrest High School, Seattle, Washington

Gerlena R. Clark   Mathematics Consultant, Jefferson City, Missouri

John Fourcroy   Mathematics Teacher, Lindhurst High School, Marysville, California

Charles V. Kruger   Mathematics Teacher, Eden Valley-Watkins High School, Eden Valley, Minnesota

Terry Wozny   Mathematics Educator, Port Washington School District, Port Washington, Wisconsin

Manuscript Reviewers

Cheryl Avalos   Mathematics Consultant, Los Angeles County Office of Education, Los Angeles, California

Joan C. Countryman   Head of School, Lincoln School, Providence, Rhode Island

Deborah K. Jenkins   Mathematics Department Head, Pershing High School, Detroit, Michigan

Cesar Larriva   Doctoral Student, Department of Education, Stanford University, Stanford, California

Les Leibovitch   Mathematics Teacher, Van Nuys Middle School, Mathematics and Science Magnet, Sherman Oaks, California

Karen S. Norwood   Assistant Professor, Department of Mathematics and Science Education, North Carolina State University, Raleigh, North Carolina

Jeri P. Philbrick   Mathematics Department Chairperson, Oxnard High School, Oxnard, California

Matthias Vheru   Secondary Mathematics Teacher, Locke High School/Los Angeles Unified School District, Los Angeles, California

Program Consultants

Joel L. Arougheti   Mathematics Supervisor, High School of Art and Design, New York, New York

Sandrea Assam   Assistant Principal for Math Instruction, Andrew Jackson High School, Queens, New York

William H. Harris   Coordinator of Mathematics and Science, City School District of Troy, Troy, New York

Samuel Johnson, Jr.   Director of Personnel, San Mateo Union High School District, San Mateo, California

Euclid Mejia   Principal, George Washington High School, New York, New York

Richard P. Stucky   Coordinator of Mathematics and Technology, Shoreline School District, Seattle, Washington

Barbara Griggs Wells   UCLA Site Director, Mathematics Diagnostic Testing Project, UCLA, Los Angeles, California

Welcome to Integrated Mathematics!

Course Goals

This new program has been written to prepare you for success in college, in careers, and in daily life in the 21st century.

It helps you develop the ability to:

- ➤ **Explore and solve mathematical problems**
- ➤ **Think critically**
- ➤ **Work cooperatively with others**
- ➤ **Communicate ideas clearly**

Mathematical Topics

You can learn more with *Integrated Mathematics* because the mathematical topics are integrated. Over a three-year period, this program teaches all the essential topics in the *Algebra 1/Geometry/Algebra 2* sequence, plus many other interesting, contemporary topics. (see the Topic Spiraling Chart on page xiii)

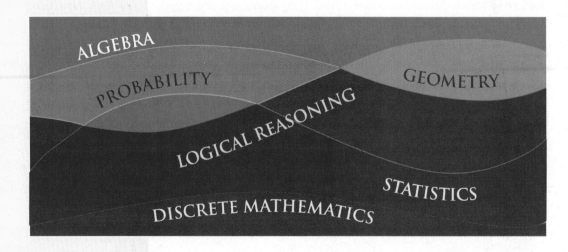

ALGEBRA

PROBABILITY

GEOMETRY

LOGICAL REASONING

STATISTICS

DISCRETE MATHEMATICS

Course Structure

➤ Algebra and Geometry are taught in each of the three years.

➤ Topics from Logical Reasoning, Measurement, Probability, Statistics, Discrete Mathematics, and Functions are interwoven throughout.

➤ Topics are spiraled throughout the course, so that you continually build on what you have learned.

Advantages of this Program

Integrated Mathematics develops clear understanding of topics and strong problem solving skills by helping you:

➤ **Get actively involved in learning**

➤ **Study meaningful mathematics**

➤ **See connections among different branches of mathematics**

➤ **Try a wide variety of types of problems, including real-world applications and long-term projects**

➤ **Use calculators and computers**

➤ **Get Internet support at our Web site, www. mcdougallittell.com**

Contents

Unit 1   Exploring and Communicating Mathematics

Unit Project
Images   1

1-1 Communicating with Diagrams   3
Interpreting data in tables, graphs, and concept maps.

1-2 Investigating Patterns   10
Finding and evaluating variable expressions for numerical,
algebraic, and geometric patterns. Everyday applications.

1-3 Patterns with Powers   19
Using exponents to represent repeated multiplication.
Making conjectures about exponents in powers of 10.

1-4 Writing and Evaluating Expressions   26
Evaluating numerical and variable expressions by using the
order of operations.

1-5 Modeling the Distributive Property   31
Applying the distributive property to calculations, variable
expressions, and geometric relationships.

1-6 Working Together on Congruent Polygons   37
Exploring how a square can be cut into congruent polygons
in different ways.

1-7 Exploring Quadrilaterals and Symmetry   44
Exploring perimeters and symmetries of four-sided figures.
Using writing to explore ideas and to communicate.

Review and Assessment   **Checkpoint**   **30**
                                          Review and Assessment   **51**

Unit 2   Using Measures and Equations

Unit Project
Magnitude   54

2-1 Numbers and Estimates   57
Estimating populations, distances, and probabilities.
Deciding if quantities are discrete or continuous.

2-2 Using Negative Numbers   64
Evaluating numerical and algebraic expressions using
positive and negative numbers in everyday situations.

2-3 Exploring Scientific Notation   71
Converting numbers between decimal and scientific notation. Using scientific notation to estimate and compute.

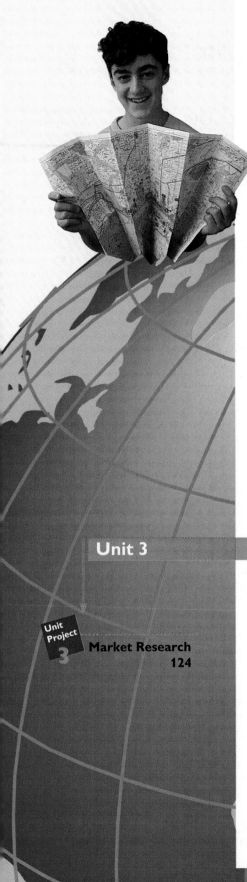

2-4 Estimating Measures: Length and Area 79
Estimating lengths, distances on maps, and areas. Using geometric notation for lines, segments, and lengths.

2-5 Exploring Angle Relationships 85
Investigating geometric ideas using manipulatives. Applying angle relationships, including angles formed by intersecting lines, in circles, and in triangles.

2-6 Expressions for Measures 93
Writing expressions for measures of geometric figures. Simplifying these expressions by multiplying, using the distributive property, and grouping like terms.

2-7 Solving Equations: Balancing 99
Using algebra tiles to solve equations by balancing. Using equations to model and solve problems about areas and angle measures.

2-8 Solving Equations: Undoing 105
Solving equations by undoing operations and simplifying. Modeling and solving problems with equations.

2-9 Square Roots and Cube Roots 111
Estimating and evaluating rational and irrational square roots and cube roots in everyday contexts.

Review and Assessment   **Checkpoint 78, 98**
Review and Assessment 120

Unit 3	Representing Data

Unit Project 3 Market Research 124

3-1 Using Matrices and Graphs 127
Exploring how to display and interpret real-world data using matrices, spreadsheets, and graphs.

3-2 Mean, Median, and Mode 135
Analyzing data sets to identify typical values, outliers, and ranges. Using equations with data.

3-3 Inequalities and Intervals 143
Using number lines and inequality symbols to display and compare real-world data.

3-4 Histograms and Stem-and-Leaf Plots 150
Using histograms, frequency tables, and stem-and-leaf plots to display and interpret data.

3-5 Box-and-Whisker Plots   158
Displaying and comparing the medians, quartiles, ranges, and extremes of data sets.

3-6 Choosing a Data Display   164
Choosing an appropriate type of graph to display a given data set and explaining that choice.

3-7 Analyzing Misleading Graphs   170
Recognizing when data displays give a misleading impression of a set of data.

Review and Assessment   **Checkpoint   149**
                                 Review and Assessment   177

Unit 4   Coordinates and Functions

Unit Project 4 Animation   180

4-1 Coordinates for Locations   183
Using coordinate systems to solve real-world problems about locations in different settings.

4-2 Introduction to Coordinate Geometry   190
Exploring coordinate geometry. Finding areas of right triangles and other polygons drawn on a coordinate plane.

4-3 Translations   197
Translating figures on a coordinate plane. Recognizing translational symmetry in everyday objects.

4-4 Rotations   202
Rotating figures on a coordinate plane and on polar graph paper. Recognizing rotational symmetry in geometric figures and everyday objects.

4-5 Scatter Plots   211
Collecting real-world data and analyzing it. Interpreting scatter plots and making predictions.

4-6 Graphs and Functions   218
Recognizing graphs and everyday relationships that represent functions. Identifying control variables and dependent variables. Graphing functions.

4-7 Functions and Equations   225
Exploring ways to represent functions. Using tables, equations, and technology to graph some basic functions.

Review and Assessment   **Checkpoint   210**
                                 Review and Assessment   235

Unit 5   Equations for Problem Solving

Unit Project
Community Service
238

5-1 Modeling Problem Situations   241
Using spreadsheets, tables, graphs, equations, and technology to model situations and solve problems. Describing everyday situations that could be modeled by equations.

5-2 Opposites and the Distributive Property   247
Simplifying variable expressions. Solving equations that involve opposites, like terms, or the distributive property. Writing and solving equations for real-world situations.

5-3 Variables on Both Sides   255
Using algebra tiles to solve equations with variables on both sides. Using these equations to model situations.

5-4 Inequalities with One Variable   261
Exploring how to rewrite simple inequalities. Solving and graphing inequalities, and using them to model situations.

5-5 Rewriting Equations and Formulas   270
Rewriting algebraic and geometric equations and formulas to make them easier to use in problem solving situations.

5-6 Using Reciprocals   275
Using reciprocals to solve equations. Using reciprocals to rewrite equations for calculator use.

5-7 Area Formulas   280
Using manipulatives to explore formulas for the area of a parallelogram, a triangle, and a trapezoid. Using these area formulas to solve problems.

5-8 Systems of Equations in Geometry   289
Solving pairs of two-variable equations using substitution. Solving real-world problems using systems of equations.

Review and Assessment   **Checkpoint   269**
                              Review and Assessment   295

Unit 6   Ratios, Probability, and Similarity

Unit Project
Advertising   298

6-1 Ratios and Rates   301
Writing ratios in simplest form. Solving everyday problems with ratios. Comparing unit rates.

6-2 Investigating Probability   306
Exploring how likely it is that an event will happen, both experimentally and theoretically.

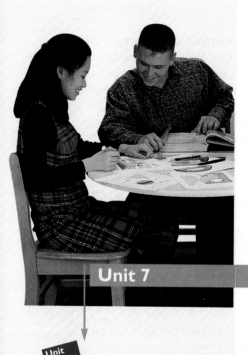

6-3 Solving Proportions 314
Modeling and solving problems with proportions.

6-4 Sampling and Making Predictions 321
Investigating and modeling some sampling techniques.
Making estimates based on samples and margins of error.

6-5 Similar Polygons 328
Exploring the properties of similar polygons. Modeling
everyday situations with similar figures and scale drawings.

6-6 Dilations 337
Enlarging or reducing a figure without changing its shape.

6-7 Sine and Cosine Ratios 343
Investigating right triangle ratios. Using these ratios and
technology to model and solve real-world problems.

Review and Assessment   **Checkpoint 320**
                               Review and Assessment 352

Unit 7   Direct Variation

Unit
Project
7 **Sports Design 356**

7-1 Direct Variation, Slope, and Tangent 359
Exploring three relationships that involve constant ratios.
Applying these relationships in everyday settings.

7-2 A Direct Variation Model 367
Using direct variation models to represent real-world situations and to make predictions. Finding the slope of a line.

7-3 Circumference and Arc Length 375
Experimenting to find pi. Finding circumferences of circles
and arc lengths in geometric and real-world shapes.

7-4 Direct Variation with $y = kx$ 383
Recognizing the characteristics of a direct variation graph
or equation. Graphing lines with negative slopes.

7-5 Using Dimensional Analysis 392
Using the strategy of dimensional analysis with rates and
conversion factors to solve everyday problems.

7-6 Areas of Circles and Sectors 400
Exploring the area of a circle. Using the formulas for the
areas of circles and sectors to solve problems.

Review and Assessment   **Checkpoint 382**
                               Review and Assessment 409

Unit 8 — Linear Equations as Models

Unit Project 8 Breakthroughs **414**

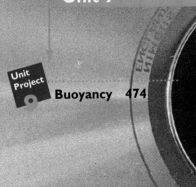

8-1 Linear Growth and Decay 417
Modeling linear growth and decay using tables, graphs, and the slope-intercept form of an equation for a line.

8-2 Linear Combinations 425
Using linear combinations and the standard form of an equation for a line to model everyday situations. Graphing these equations. Finding the intercepts of a line.

8-3 Horizontal and Vertical Lines 433
Investigating the slopes of horizontal and vertical lines. Writing and graphing equations for such lines.

8-4 Writing Equations for Lines 439
Writing an equation for a line using two points or the slope and one point. Using equations to solve problems.

8-5 Graphing Systems of Linear Equations 447
Solving problems by finding the point where two lines intersect. Recognizing systems of equations with no solutions.

8-6 Graphing Linear Inequalities 455
Exploring the graphs of inequalities in a coordinate plane. Using graphs of inequalities in everyday situations.

8-7 Systems of Linear Inequalities 463
Solving real-world problems by writing and graphing systems of linear inequalities.

Review and Assessment **Checkpoint 438, 454**
Review and Assessment 470

Unit 9 — Reasoning and Measurement

Unit Project 9 Buoyancy **474**

9-1 The Pythagorean Theorem and Reasoning 477
Investigating the relationship among the lengths of the sides of a right triangle, and using this relationship to solve problems. Using inductive and deductive reasoning.

9-2 Investigating Properties of Square Roots 486
Exploring, simplifying, and multiplying square roots. Solving equations and problems involving square roots.

9-3 If-Then Statements and Converses 492
Writing if-then statements and their converses, and deciding whether they are true or false. Using the zero-product property and the converse of the Pythagorean theorem.

9-4 Geometric Probability 500
Using lengths and areas to find theoretical and experimental geometric probabilities.

9-5 Surface Area of Space Figures 507
Using models to find the surface areas of prisms, cylinders, and pyramids. Finding surface areas of everyday objects.

9-6 Volumes of Prisms and Cylinders 515
Finding the volumes of prisms and cylinders. Solving problems using volume formulas.

9-7 Volumes of Pyramids and Cones 523
Finding the volumes of pyramids and cones. Applying volume formulas to real-world situations.

9-8 Similar Figures: Area and Volume 530
Finding and comparing corresponding lengths, areas, and volumes of similar figures using ratios.

Review and Assessment

Checkpoint 499, 522
Review and Assessment 540

Unit 10   Quadratic Equations as Models

Unit Project 10 Trajectories 544

10-1 Reflections 547
Exploring reflections in the real world and in a coordinate plane. Drawing the mirror image of an object.

10-2 Transforming Parabolas 555
Using technology to explore the graphs of parabolas and how they are transformed by different operations.

10-3 Factors and Intercepts 562
Drawing a parabola from its equation. Using algebra to find a parabola's intercepts. Solving problems with these methods.

10-4 Working with Powers 568
Exploring and using the rules of exponents.

10-5 Factored Form and x-Intercepts 576
Using algebra tiles to factor and multiply algebraic expressions. Using factors to find x-intercepts.

10-6 Expanded Form and Line of Symmetry 583
Using algebra tiles to multiply binomials. Exploring the features of a parabola whose equation is in standard form.

10-7 Using Factors to Sketch $y = x^2 + bx + c$ **591**
Using algebra tiles to factor trinomials. Using the vertex, line of symmetry, and intercepts to graph a parabola.

10-8 Solving Quadratic Equations 598
Solving quadratic equations and real-world problems by factoring, graphing, and using the quadratic formula.

Review and Assessment   **Checkpoint   567, 590**
Review and Assessment   607

Student Resources

Technology Handbook 611 • Extra Practice 620
Toolbox 640 • Tables 666 • A-1 Domain and Range 670
A-2 Slope and y-Intercept 672 • Glossary 674
Index 682 • Credits 692 • Selected Answers 1

Integrated Mathematics   Topic Spiraling

This chart shows how mathematical strands are spiraled over the three years of the *Integrated Mathematics* program.

	Course 1	Course 2	Course 3
Algebra	Linear equations Linear inequalities Multiplying binomials Factoring expressions	Quadratic equations Linear systems Rational equations Complex numbers	Polynomial functions Exponential functions Logarithmic functions Parametric equations
Geometry	Angles, polygons, circles Perimeter, circumference Area, surface area Volume Trigonometric ratios	Similar and congruent figures Geometric proofs Coordinate geometry Transformational geometry Special right triangles	Inscribed figures Transforming graphs Vectors Triangle trigonometry Circular trigonometry

Statistics, Probability	Analyzing data and
	  displaying data
	Experimental and
	  theoretical probability
	Geometric probability
		Sampling methods
		Simulation
		Binomial distributions
			Variability
			Standard deviation
			z-scores

Logical Reasoning	Conjectures Counterexamples If-then statements	Inductive and deductive reasoning Valid and invalid reasoning Postulates and proof	Identities Contrapositive and inverse Comparing proof methods
Discrete Math	Discrete quantities Matrices to display data Lattices	Matrix operations Transformation matrices Counting techniques	Sequences and series Recursion Limits

What Students are Saying...

Who has the **BEST IDEAS** about how mathematics should be taught? **Students** and **teachers**, of course! That is why preliminary versions of this book were tried out by thousands of students in hundreds of different CLASSROOMS NATIONWIDE. The suggestions from these students and their teachers have been incorporated into this book.

Here is what some of the students who have already studied this course have said.

I like math much more now. I can see that it's not just finding a right answer. The thought process is really important.

I liked working with other students on the projects and explorations. It's good practice for working on project teams in our future jobs.

Your Ideas are Important!

Get Involved

This course may be different from ones you have taken before. This is not a year to sit back and just listen. In this course you will be

➤ TALKING about mathematics

➤ working *together* to explore ideas

➤ gathering **DATA**

➤ looking for *patterns*

➤ making and testing **predictions**.

Your ideas and viewpoints are important. Sharing them with others will help everyone learn more. So don't hold back. Jump right in and get involved.

x^2

My friends and I were so interested in what we were learning that we started talking about math outside of class. I've never done that before.

After doing the explorations, I was able to understand why things worked. Me, the kid who couldn't do math! I'll never think of myself that way again.

............................➤

Guide to Your Course

The next ten pages will give you an overview of the organization of your book and a preview of what you will be learning in the course. They will help you get off to a good start.

I was used to working alone. Now I realize that I can learn more by working with other students. I have much more respect for their ideas.

XV

Unit Projects

Each unit begins with a project that sets the stage for the mathematics you will be *learning* in the unit. The project gives you a chance to begin DOING mathematics right away. Don't expect to be able to finish the project immediately, though. As you study the unit, you will gradually develop the skills and the **INFORMATION** that you will need to complete it. The first three pages of each unit help you get started.

Project Theme

Each project has a theme, like animation, that relates the mathematics of the unit to careers and to daily life.

Getting Started

Here are some ideas to use when you make your flip book.

☞ Use a pad of paper or cut several sheets of paper to a convenient size.

☞ Use graph paper and a coordinate grid to keep track of the positions of your drawings.

☞ Make the first drawing on the last piece of paper. The next drawing should be slightly different.

☞ If you can see through the paper that you use, you can trace the previous drawing, then make changes to the new one.

☞ You will need to use a series of small changes to show movement. Experiment to see how many drawings are needed to show a movement.

Working on the Unit Project

Your work in Unit 4 will help you create your flip book.

Related Exercises:
Section 4-1, Exercise 36
Section 4-2, Exercise 27
Section 4-3, Exercises 32-34
Section 4-4, Exercises 25, 26
Section 4-5, Exercise 31
Section 4-6, Exercise 26
Section 4-7, Exercise 47

Alternative Projects p. 4-54

Can We Talk — Animation

> Have you seen any animated movies? If so, which ones?

> Do you have a favorite animated television show? If so, which one?

> Have you noticed any differences between animation in movies and animation in television shows? Describe the differences.

> Do you think it would be easier to make an animated cartoon of a car moving or of a person walking? Why?

> How could you show the path of an arrow being shot into the air toward a target?

> Suppose you want to show the motion of someone sledding down a hill. How could the background move instead of the sled?

> What would the path of a basketball be when it is thrown toward the hoop? Is there more than one possible path?

> How do objects slow down and speed up in animated movies? How do you think you could show this in a flip book?

Starting the Project

At the beginning of each unit, there is a description of the project, hints for getting started, and questions to get you thinking and talking about the project.

Working on the Unit Project

In each section of the unit, there are exercises to help you complete your work on the project as you study the unit.

Completing the Unit Project

Now you've completed the unit. You can finish the project and present your results. You are ready to look back over what you have learned.

Completing the Unit Project

> Now you are ready to finish your flip book.

> Complete your drawings. Put the pages in order and make sure that they are all the same size. Clip or staple the pages together.

> Write a script to narrate while the pages are being flipped.

Look Back

Describe how you used a coordinate system when making the drawings for your flip book. Did you have any problems making the flip book? If so, describe how you solved them.

Alternative Projects

Project 1: Making a Map

Create a map of the neighborhood around your school or of the neighborhood in which you live. Use a coordinate system and make a map key by listing the coordinates for the locations of the places on the map. Include a scale on your map.

Project 2: Recognizing Functions in Science

Read about the scientific research on global warming. Write a report on the latest findings. Discuss the evidence for global warming and what might be causing it. Include data tables and graphs with your report. Use the phrases "is a function of," "control variable," and "dependent variable" to describe the data.

Project 3: Collecting and Graphing Data

Collect data that can be displayed in a scatter plot. Write a report and include:

➤ the method(s) you used to gather the data

➤ a summary of the data

➤ a scatter plot of the data

➤ the type of correlation the scatter plot shows and the reasons for it

➤ several questions that can be answered by using the scatter plot

● Tropical forest
○ Former tropical forest area

Unit Projects

Explorations

Explorations are an important part of this course. They will help
you DISCOVER, UNDERSTAND, and CONNECT mathematical ideas. In the Explorations, you will be measuring, gathering
data, looking for **patterns**, and making generalizations.
You will be working with others and *sharing your ideas*.

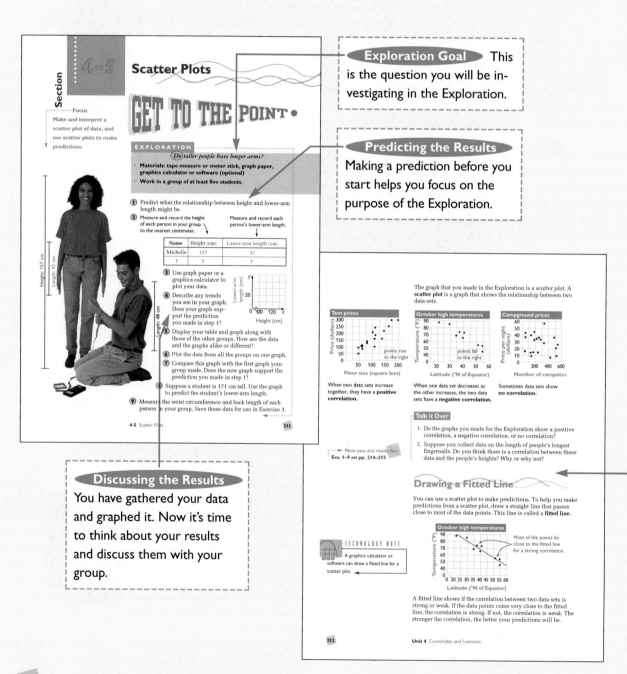

Section 4-5

Scatter Plots

GET TO THE POINT

Focus
Make and interpret a
scatter plot of data, and
use scatter plots to make
predictions.

EXPLORATION

Do taller people have longer arms?

- Materials: tape measure or meter stick, graph paper,
  graphics calculator or software (optional)
- Work in a group of at least five students.

① Predict what the relationship between height and lower-arm
length might be.

② Measure and record the height
of each person in your group
to the nearest centimeter.

Measure and record each
person's lower-arm length.

Name	Height (cm)	Lower-arm length (cm)
Michelle	157	42
?	?	?

③ Use graph paper or a
graphics calculator to
plot your data.

④ Describe any trends
you see in your graph.
Does your graph sup-
port the prediction
you made in step 1?

⑤ Display your table and graph along with
those of the other groups. How are the data
and the graphs alike or different?

⑥ Plot the data from all the groups on one graph.

⑦ Compare this graph with the first graph your
group made. Does the new graph support the
prediction you made in step 1?

⑧ Suppose a student is 171 cm tall. Use the graph
to predict the student's lower-arm length.

⑨ Measure the wrist circumference and back length of each
person in your group. Save these data for use in Exercise 3.

4-5 Scatter Plots   **211**

Exploration Goal This
is the question you will be investigating in the Exploration.

Predicting the Results
Making a prediction before you
start helps you focus on the
purpose of the Exploration.

The graph that you made in the Exploration is a *scatter plot*. A
scatter plot is a graph that shows the relationship between two
data sets.

Tent prices
points rise
to the right
Floor size (square feet)

When two data sets increase
together, they have a **positive
correlation.**

October high temperatures
points fall
to the right
Latitude (°N of Equator)

When one data set decreases as
the other increases, the two data
sets have a **negative correlation.**

Campground prices
Number of campsites

Sometimes data sets show
no correlation.

Talk it Over

1. Do the graphs you made for the Exploration show a positive
correlation, a negative correlation, or no correlation?

2. Suppose you collect data on the length of people's longest
fingernails. Do you think there is a correlation between these
data and the people's heights? Why or why not?

▸ Now you are ready for:
Exs. 1–9 on pp. 214–215

Drawing a Fitted Line

You can use a scatter plot to make predictions. To help you make
predictions from a scatter plot, draw a straight line that passes
close to most of the data points. This line is called a **fitted line.**

TECHNOLOGY NOTE
A graphics calculator or
software can draw a fitted line for a
scatter plot.

October high temperatures
Most of the points lie
close to the fitted line
for a strong correlation.
Latitude (°N of Equator)

A fitted line shows if the correlation between two data sets is
strong or weak. If the data points come very close to the fitted
line, the correlation is *strong*. If not, the correlation is *weak*. The
stronger the correlation, the better your predictions will be.

212   **Unit 4** Coordinates and Functions

Discussing the Results
You have gathered your data
and graphed it. Now it's time
to think about your results
and discuss them with your
group.

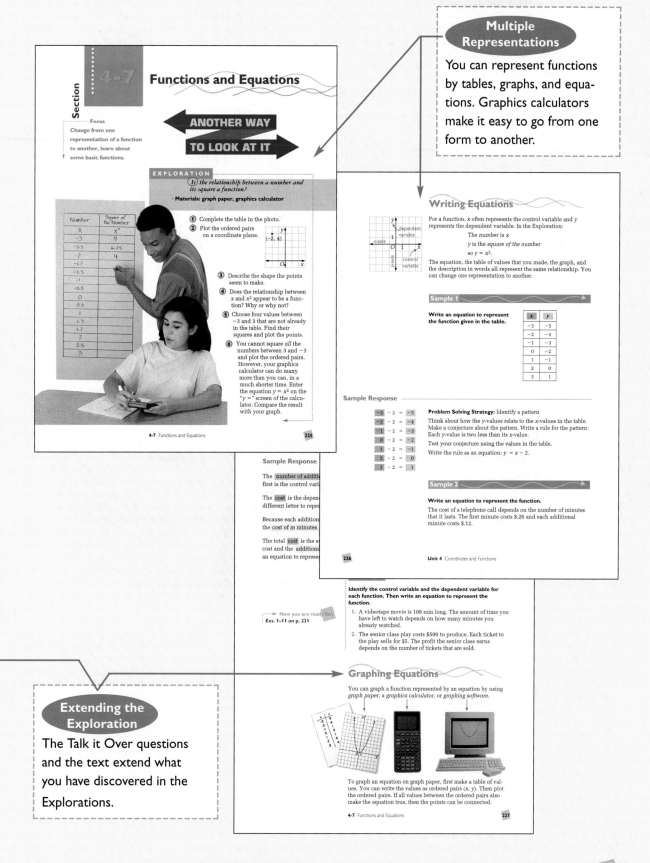

Section 4-7

Functions and Equations

← ANOTHER WAY TO LOOK AT IT →

Focus
Change from one representation of a function to another, learn about some basic functions.

EXPLORATION

Is the relationship between a number and its square a function?

Materials: graph paper, graphics calculator

Number	Square of the Number
X	X²
-3	9
-2.5	6.25
-2	4
-1.7	
-1.5	
-1	
-0.5	
0	
0.5	
1	
1.5	
1.7	
2	
2.5	
3	

① Complete the table in the photo.
② Plot the ordered pairs on a coordinate plane.
③ Describe the shape the points seem to make.
④ Does the relationship between x and x^2 appear to be a function? Why or why not?
⑤ Choose four values between −3 and 3 that are not already in the table. Find their squares and plot the points.
⑥ You cannot square *all* the numbers between 3 and −3 and plot the ordered pairs. However, your graphics calculator can do many more than you can, in a much shorter time. Enter the equation $y = x^2$ on the "$y =$" screen of the calculator. Compare the result with your graph.

4-7 Functions and Equations   **225**

Writing Equations

For a function, x often represents the control variable and y represents the dependent variable. In the Exploration:

The *number* is x

y is the *square of the number*

so $y = x^2$.

The equation, the table of values that you made, the graph, and the description in words all represent the same relationship. You can change one representation to another.

Sample 1

Write an equation to represent the function given in the table.

x	y
−3	−5
−2	−4
−1	−3
0	−2
1	−1
2	0
3	1

Sample Response

−3	− 2	=	−5
−2	− 2	=	−4
−1	− 2	=	−3
0	− 2	=	−2
1	− 2	=	−1
2	− 2	=	0
3	− 2	=	1

Problem Solving Strategy: Identify a pattern

Think about how the y-values relate to the x-values in the table. Make a conjecture about the pattern. Write a rule for the pattern: Each y-value is two less than its x-value.

Test your conjecture using the values in the table.

Write the rule as an equation: $y = x − 2$.

Sample 2

Write an equation to represent the function.

The cost of a telephone call depends on the number of minutes that it lasts. The first minute costs $.26 and each additional minute costs $.12.

Unit 4 Coordinates and Functions

Sample Response

The number of additio... first is the control var...

The cost is the depen... different letter to repr...

Because each additio... the cost of m minutes...

The total cost is the s... cost and the additiona... an equation to represe...

226

Now you are ready for
Exs. 1–11 on p. 231

Identify the control variable and the dependent variable for each function. Then write an equation to represent the function.

1. A videotape movie is 108 min long. The amount of time you have left to watch depends on how many minutes you already watched.

2. The senior class play costs $500 to produce. Each ticket to the play sells for $5. The profit the senior class earns depends on the number of tickets that are sold.

Graphing Equations

You can graph a function represented by an equation by using *graph paper*, a *graphics calculator*, or *graphing software*.

To graph an equation on graph paper, first make a table of values. You can write the values as ordered pairs (x, y). Then plot the ordered pairs. If all values between the ordered pairs also make the equation true, then the points can be connected.

4-7 Functions and Equations   **227**

Explorations

Section Organization

This book has been written to help you UNDERSTAND mathematics and to see the many different ways it can be applied. The organization of the material within sections is patterned after the **way that you learn**: Ideas are introduced. You **EXPLORE** them, **think** about them, and TALK about them with other students. You check that you understand them by working through some SAMPLE PROBLEMS. Before going on, you pause and **look back** at what you have learned.

Focus This is what you will be doing in the lesson.

Application A problem situation helps you think about the purpose of the mathematics you will be studying.

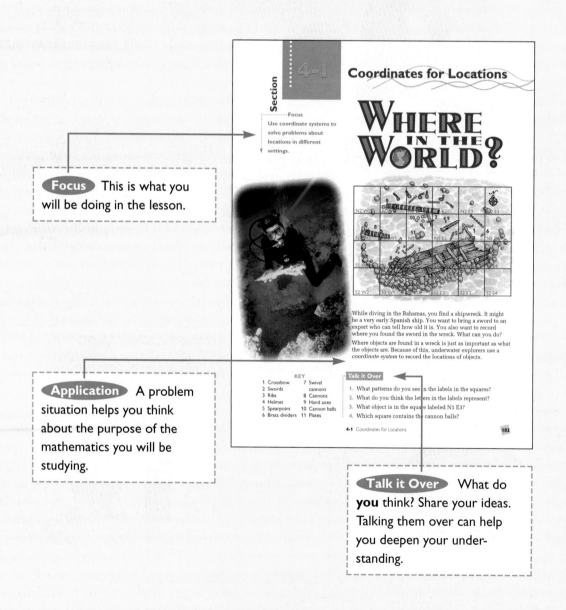

Section 4-1

Focus
Use coordinate systems to solve problems about locations in different settings.

Coordinates for Locations

WHERE IN THE WORLD?

While diving in the Bahamas, you find a shipwreck. It might be a very early Spanish ship. You want to bring a sword to an expert who can tell how old it is. You also want to record where you found the sword in the wreck. What can you do?

Where objects are found in a wreck is just as important as what the objects are. Because of this, underwater explorers use a *coordinate system* to record the locations of objects.

KEY
1 Crossbow
2 Swords
3 Ribs
4 Helmet
5 Spearpoint
6 Brass dividers
7 Swivel cannons
8 Cannons
9 Hand axes
10 Cannon balls
11 Plates

Talk it Over

1. What patterns do you see in the labels in the squares?
2. What do you think the letters in the labels represent?
3. What object is in the square labeled N1 E3?
4. Which square contains the cannon balls?

4-1 Coordinates for Locations — 183

Talk it Over What do **you** think? Share your ideas. Talking them over can help you deepen your understanding.

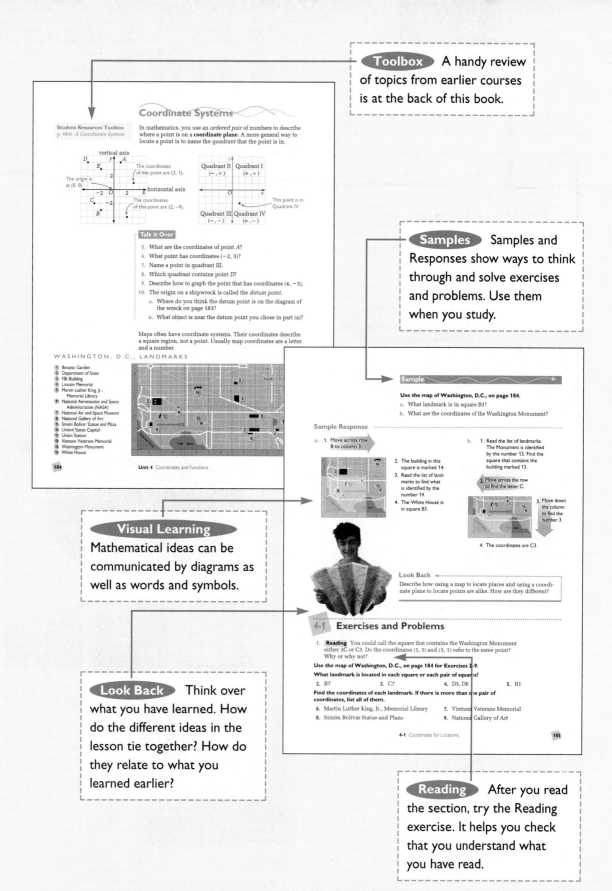

Toolbox A handy review of topics from earlier courses is at the back of this book.

Samples Samples and Responses show ways to think through and solve exercises and problems. Use them when you study.

Visual Learning Mathematical ideas can be communicated by diagrams as well as words and symbols.

Look Back Think over what you have learned. How do the different ideas in the lesson tie together? How do they relate to what you learned earlier?

Reading After you read the section, try the Reading exercise. It helps you check that you understand what you have read.

Section Organization

Exercises and Problems

Each section has a wide variety of exercises and problems.
Some **PRACTICE** and **EXTEND** the concepts and
skills you have learned. Others apply the concepts to everyday
situations and **explore connections** to other subject areas
and to careers. The problems help you sharpen your **THINKING**
and **problem solving skills**.

Here are some of the types of exercises and problems you will see
in the course.

Practicing and Extending

These exercises build on the
ideas in the Talk it Over questions and the Sample on the
preceding pages.

Connections to...

Sometimes math shows up
where you don't expect it —
in social studies, science, art,
literature, music, sports.

Use the diagram of Washington, D.C., at the left.

NW | NE / SW | SE   U.S. Capitol

10. What is the *origin* in the coordinate system of Washington, D.C.?
11. In which direction from the Capitol is 3rd St. NE?
12. How do the four quadrants of Washington, D.C., compare with the four quadrants on a coordinate plane?
13. Which quadrant on a coordinate plane would contain G St. SW?

connection to SOCIAL STUDIES

Coordinates locate places on Earth. The grid lines on Earth are
lines of latitude and longitude. Places are identified by latitude
first, then longitude.

The prime meridian is a line of longitude.
The equator is a line of latitude.

The vertical axis is a line from the North Pole to the South Pole passing through Greenwich, England. This line is called the *prime meridian*.

The equator is the horizontal axis.

Melbourne has latitude 38° south and longitude 145° east. You write 38 S, 145 E.

Use the map above for Exercises 14–25.
Estimate the latitude and longitude of each city.

14. Cairo, Egypt   15. Quito, Ecuador   16. Tokyo, Japan

186 Unit 4 Coordinates and Functions

What city is near each location?

17. 1 S, 37 E   18. 52 N,
20. About how many degrees west of Delhi
21. About how many degrees south of Los A
22. What line of longitude do you think is o meridian on the other side of Earth?
23. Name two cities on the map that have a latitude. What is their latitude?
24. **Research** Find the latitude and longitu
25. **Writing** Describe how using latitude a locate places on Earth is similar to using to locate points.

connection to ART

Chuck Close is an artist in New York who m
photographs. He divides the photograph and
uses a grid system to locate each square. Sor
the one on this painting.

26. **a.** Describe the grid system that Chuck Close used for this painting.
   b. How is his grid system similar to a coordinate plane? How is it different?
27. **Open-ended** Do you think this method could be used to make very small paintings? Explain why or why not.
28. An illness has reduced Chuck Close's mobility. For this painting, he used a chair that can move sideways and up and down to work on different areas of the painting.
   Describe how the movements of the chair are related to locating a point on a coordinate plane.

Both th the painting have a horizontal axis.

4-1 Coordinates for Locations   187

Review/Preview

These exercises at the end of
each section help you keep
skills alive and get ready for
the next section.

FAN COSTS

Review **PREVIEW**

The display shows the fan costs
for selected items at a basketball
game. *(Section 3-6)*

34. a. Interpret the information
shown in the display.

   b. Do you think this is the best
way to display the information?
Explain why or why not.

35. Quadrilateral *ABCD* has two
pairs of parallel sides and at
least one right angle. *(Section 1-7)*

   a. Make an accurate sketch of
quadrilateral *ABCD*.

   b. What is the special name for
quadrilateral *ABCD*?

Program	$3	$5	$6	$5
Soda	$1.50	$3	$2.75	$2.25
Hot dog	$2.50	$4	$3.25	$2.25
Cap	$18	$18	$18	$16
Average ticket price	$48.10	$52.84	$86.82	$40.76
	San Francisco	Chicago	New York	Dallas

 Working on the Unit Project

---

connection to **LITERATURE**

In *The Hunt for Red October*, Soviet submarine captain Ramius reads his
orders and learns that he is to participate in a tracking drill with another
submarine.

> 17   **THE HUNT FOR RED OCTOBER**
>
> Ramius chuckled. "The boys in the attack submarine directorate still have
> not figured out how to track our new drive system. Well, neither will the
> Americans. We are to confine our operations to grid square 54–90 and the
> immediately surrounding squares. That ought to make Viktor's task a bit
> easier." ... "He will have a fair chance of locating us, I think. The exercise is
> confined to nine squares, forty thousand square kilometers. We shall see
> what he has learned since he has served with us."

29. How does Ramius identify a grid square?

30. How does Ramius know that there are only nine squares that might
contain the submarine?

31. What do you think the numbers of the squares surrounding grid square
54-90 could be? Explain your reasoning.

Ongoing **ASSESSMENT**

There were about 10,000 Anasazi people living in Chaco Canyon,
New Mexico, about 1000 years ago. They suddenly disappeared.
Archaeologists are trying to understand why.

Archaeologists use coordinate systems to record locations of objects.
As they dig deeper, the relationships of the locations can be clues to
the daily life in lost civilizations.

32. **Open-ended** Describe how you could put a coordinate system
on the sketch of the room. Where would you put the origin? the
axes? Use your system to give the coordinates of the firepit.

KEY
F firepit
FP misc. floor pit
MB mealing bin
PH posthole
N wall niche

33. **Writing** Archaeologists also record an object's depth beneath surface
level. Describe how coordinates could identify the depth of an object.

188   **Unit 4** Coordinates and Functions

189

Ongoing Assessment

These problems pull together
the different things you have
studied in the section. They
give you a chance to show
what you have learned.

Open-ended Problems

There is more than one right
answer to these questions.

Writing
Problems that
ask you to put your thoughts
into words help you think and
express your ideas clearly.

Review and Assessment

With this book you **REVIEW** and **ASSESS** your progress as you go along. In each unit there are one or two Checkpoints for self-assessment, plus a thorough Unit Review and Assessment at the end.

Assessment Matches Learning

The Checkpoint and unit Review and Assessment questions are like the ones in the text and the Exercise and Problem sets.

Topic Overview To give you an overview of the unit, the summary is organized by math topic strands.

Technology

In this course you will see many different ways that **CALCULATORS** and **COMPUTERS** can make exploring ideas and solving problems easier.

Graphing Technology helps you understand the relationships among equations and their graphs.

Spreadsheets make it easy to create tables of data.

*The following text appears within the figure:*

EXPLORATION

(How) can you find other functions whose graphs are parabolas?

- **Materials: graphics calculators or graphing software**
- **Alternative approach:** Make a table of values for each function and sketch the parabola on graph paper.
- **Work in a group of four students.**

① Using a standard viewing window, graph the function $y = x^2$.

② On the same axes, graph the function $y = x^2 + 4$. Describe the relationship between the graphs of the two functions.

③ Repeat step 2 comparing the graph of $y = x^2$ with the graph of $y = x^2 - 4$.

④ Repeat step 2 comparing the graph of $y = x^2$ with the graph of $y = (x + 4)^2$.

⑤ Repeat step 2 comparing the graph of $y = x^2$ with the graph of $y = (x - 4)^2$.

⑥ Summarize your findings by answering these questions.

a. How is the graph of $y = x^2$ translated when a number is added to or subtracted from x^2?

b. How is the graph of $y = x^2$ translated when a number is added to or subtracted from x *before* it is squared?

▶ Now you are ready for:
Exs. 1–16 on pp. 558–560

556   **Unit 10** Quadratic Equations as Models

Section 5-1

Modeling Problem Situations

WHAT ARE THE

Focus
Use a table, graph, or equation to model situations and solve problems.

Would you pay $142 for a portable CD player in 1990, when 3,186,000 players were sold?

The graph shows the cost of CD players from 1990–1997. Graphs, tables, functions, equations, or inequalities that describe a situation are called **mathematical models.** Using mathematical models is called **modeling.**

Cost of a Portable CD Player

Bar graph with Cost (dollars) on vertical axis (0, 50, 100, 150) and Year (1990–1997) on horizontal axis.

Sample 1

Model and solve this situation. A portable CD player costs $85, including tax. You already have $11 and can save $5 per week. After how many weeks can you buy the player?

Sample Response

Method ❶ Model the situation using a table.

Number of weeks	Total saved ($) $11 + 5 \times$ (no. of weeks)
0	11
1	$11 + 5(1) = 16$
2	$11 + 5(2) = 21$
3	$11 + 5(3) = 26$
•	•
•	•
13	$11 + 5(13) = 76$
14	$11 + 5(14) = 81$
15	$11 + 5(15) = 86$

After 15 weeks, more than $85.

Method ❷ Model the situation using a spreadsheet.
Add $5 for each week.

Savings Table

	A	B
	Number of Weeks	**Total saved <dollars>**
1		
2	0	11
3	1	5 + B2
4	2	5 + B3
5	3	5 + B4
•	•	•
•	•	•
15	13	5 + B14
16	14	5 + B15
17	15	5 + B16

You can buy the player the week that the total saved is at least $85.
You can buy the player after 15 weeks.

5-1 Modeling Problem Situations   241

Exploring and Communicating Mathematics

If you were driving in Morocco and you saw this sign, you would probably know what to do even without knowing how to read the Arabic word. The image of a red octagon means **STOP** to many people around the world. When you travel, international symbols and signs can help you find your way around and follow local rules.

The radiating lines represent a type of headdress and show the importance of the sun in Native American culture.

The base of the symbol represents Mother Earth and emphasizes the relationship between nature and Native American people.

symmetry

A graphic artist may create many designs before one is chosen as a logo for a team or an organization.

Larry DesJarlais, Jr., a North Dakota Chippewa and faculty member at the Institute of American Indian Arts, designed this logo for the Smithsonian Institution's National Museum of the American Indian National Campaign. The geometric shapes and symmetry in his design form the image and have special meaning.

Design a Logo

Your group project is to create a team logo to identify your math class. Your work in this unit will help you choose various shapes, patterns, math symbols, numbers, and words to use in your logo.

You will put your logo on a book cover to fit your math book. On the inside flap of the front cover, you will describe your group's design and explain why you included each design element.

The **images and colors** on flags often tell a story about the history or geography of a country.

symbols

The motto of Brazil is "Order and Progress."

Blue and white are the colors of Portugal, an important country in Brazil's history.

There is one star for every state in Brazil, and one to represent the territories.

The green background represents the land of Brazil.

The constellation is one seen over the capital city of Rio de Janiero.

The gold represents the minerals found in the soil.

BRAZIL

sports

Team recognition is important on the playing field. Sports organizations use logos and colors to identify their team and sport. How can you use these logos to tell which sport each team plays? What other information do the logos show?

Getting Started

For this project you should work in a group of three students. Here are some ideas to help you get started.

☞ As a group, describe what materials to use and where you will get them. Can you use any recycled materials?

☞ Measure the cover of your math book. Think about the size and position of your logo.

☞ It may be a good idea to fit a blank cover on your book and then mark the area where you want to put your logo.

☞ Book covers can be made in many ways. Which methods do you know? Which method protects the book the best?

Will you center your design?

Will you have one large logo or a repeating pattern of many small logos?

Other than on the front, where else on your cover could you place the logo?

Working on the Unit Project

Your work in Unit 1 will help you design your logo.

Related Exercises:

Section 1-1, Exercise 37
Section 1-2, Exercise 47
Section 1-3, Exercise 45
Section 1-4, Exercise 42
Section 1-5, Exercise 41
Section 1-6, Exercise 32
Section 1-7, Exercise 36

Alternative Projects p. 50

Can We Talk — IMAGES

➤ Describe some famous logos. What shapes or images did the designers use? Why do you think those images were used?

➤ What logos can you recognize just by their shape, color, or style of print? Why do you think you remember these images?

➤ What feelings do lighthouses, rocks, and doves communicate? What organizations might use these symbols?

➤ Does your school have a symbol that is used on stationery or official documents? If so, how do the parts of that logo represent your school?

➤ What do you think these international symbols mean? Why do you think these symbols were created?

➤ What do the symbols and colors on the United States flag represent? Why do you think these images were chosen?

Communicating with Diagrams

Make statements about information presented in tables, graphs, and concept maps.

What Do You Say?

seven

English

sô bảy

paqallqo

satt

Vietnamese

Aymara

Punjabi

tallimat malɣuk

eéjè

What do you think these people are saying? They are saying the number "7" using different languages. More than 4000 languages and dialects are spoken in the world today. Because there are so many languages, people often need diagrams instead of language to communicate.

Yoruba

Inuit

Talk it Over

1. You see these signs along a road. What do you think they mean?

   a.   b.   c.   d.

2. You see these signs in an airport. What do you think they mean?

   a.   b.   c.   d.

American Sign Language

Tables and Graphs

Tables and graphs are two ways you can show mathematical information. A table shows data numerically. A graph shows data visually. They can tell you different things about the same information.

Sample

The table and the graph show the total number of people in the world who speak each language, and the number for whom the language is their native language.

a. What are two things you can learn from the table?

b. What are two things you can learn from the graph?

c. Invent a question that is more easily answered from the table than from the graph. Explain how to find the answer.

d. Invent a question that is more easily answered from the graph than from the table. Explain how to find the answer.

Speakers (millions)

LANGUAGE	Native	Total
Mandarin	885	1075
Hindi	375	496
Spanish	358	425
English	347	514
Arabic	211	256
Bengali	210	215
Portuguese	178	194
Russian	165	275
Japanese	125	126
German	100	126

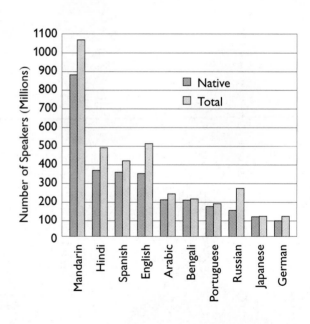

Sample Response

There are many possible answers. Examples are given.

a. Mandarin is spoken by more people than any other language. ← Compare all the totals.

Spanish is the native language of more people than English. ← Compare the numbers from two countries.

b. Mandarin has the most non-native speakers.

There are relatively few non-native speakers of Bengali, Portuguese, and Japanese.

Which "total" bar extends the farthest beyond the "native" bar?

c. "How many non-native speakers of Arabic are there?"

Think of a question about the numbers in the table.

To answer, subtract the data values in the row for Arabic. There are 45 million non-native speakers of Arabic.

d. "Which three languages have the greatest numbers of non-native speakers?"

Think of a question about the differences in bar heights in the graph.

To answer, look at how far the gold bars extend beyond the blue bars. This represents the numbers of non-native speakers. Mandarin, English, and Hindi have the greatest number of non-native speakers.

The Sample asks *open-ended questions.* There are many ways to answer an open-ended question correctly.

Concept Maps

A **concept map** is a visual summary that helps you remember the connections between ideas. You can organize ideas in a concept map to help you think about what you know.

> **Talk it Over**
>
> **3.** What ideas do you think the person who made this concept map has learned?
>
> **4.** List some ideas you might put in a concept map about road signs.

Look Back

Why do you think information is sometimes presented using tables, graphs, and concept maps?

1-1 Exercises and Problems

Reading **Match each number with the sign for it.**

1. 6   **2.** 9   **3.** 33

4. 100   **5.** 1000

BY THE WAY...

The signs for 100 and 1000 are based on the Roman numerals C and M.

How would you show these numbers in sign language? Explain your reasoning.

6. 8   **7.** 108   **8.** 1008

You see these signs in a building. What do you think they mean?

9.   **10.**   **11.**   **12.**

You see these signs along a road. What do you think they mean?

13.   **14.**   **15.**   **16.**

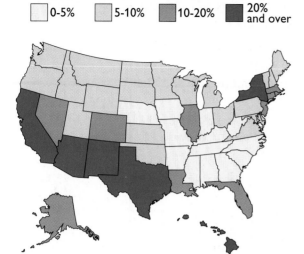

Percent Speaking Language other than English at Home

0-5%	5-10%	10-20%	20% and over

Number of people five and older who speak a language other than English at home, from the 1990 census, and percent change since 1980:

State	Non-English	Pct. Change	State	Non-English	Pct. Change
Ala.	107,866	61.6	Mont.	37,020	–1.0
Alaska	60,165	32.4	Neb.	69,872	0.7
Ariz.	700,287	38.9	Nev.	146,152	102.6
Ark.	60,781	55.7	N.H.	88,796	–0.6
Calif.	8,619,334	73.6	N.J.	1,406,148	28.3
Colo.	320,631	13.3	N.M.	493,999	10.0
Conn.	466,175	11.3	N.Y.	3,908,720	18.5
Del.	42,327	39.3	N.C.	240,866	86.5
D.C.	71,348	49.9	N.D.	46,897	–30.6
Fla.	2,098,315	73.5	Ohio	546,148	5.3
Ga.	284,546	112.9	Okla.	145,798	29.2
Hawaii	254,724	11.3	Ore.	191,710	47.1
Idaho	58,995	24.1	Pa.	806,876	5.8
Ill.	1,499,112	22.7	R.I.	159,492	8.6
Ind.	245,826	17.1	S.C.	113,163	58.5
Iowa	100,391	9.1	S.D.	41,994	–15.0
Kan.	131,604	27.9	Tenn.	131,550	59.9
Ky.	86,482	43.2	Texas	3,970,304	39.7
La.	391,994	2.1	Utah	120,404	27.9
Maine	105,441	–6.6	Vt.	30,409	–3.1
Md.	395,051	62.4	Va.	418,521	89.5
Mass.	852,228	21.0	Wash.	403,173	52.1
Mich.	569,807	1.5	W.Va.	44,203	14.2
Minn.	227,161	7.9	Wis.	263,638	4.9
Miss.	66,516	50.6	Wyo.	23,809	–11.5
Mo.	178,210	27.4			

REPORT SHOWS U.S. RESIDENTS SPEAKING MANY LANGUAGES AT HOME

WASHINGTON – Americans increasingly are speaking Spanish, Chinese, Korean or Vietnamese, but not English. The trend reflects the rise of immigration into the United States.

A new Census Bureau report shows that one in seven U.S. residents, 14 percent, spoke a language other than English at home in 1990, up from 11 percent in 1980.

Nationally, Spanish was spoken by more than half of the 31.8 million U.S. residents who didn't routinely converse in English. The next most common languages were French, German, Italian, Chinese and Tagalog, a language of the Philippines. Languages with the biggest increases were Spanish, Chinese, Tagalog, Korean and Vietnamese.

For Exercises 17–22, answer each question and tell whether you used the article, the map, or the table.

17. What is the main point of the article?

18. Which state has the largest number of people who speak a language other than English in the home?

19. Which state has the smallest number of people who speak a language other than English in the home?

20. In how many states do more than 20% of the people speak a language other than English in the home?

21. Which state had the greatest percent change from 1980 to 1990 in the number of people speaking a language other than English in the home?

22. About how many people routinely speak Spanish in the home?

23. **Writing** What are two things you can learn from the table?

24. **Writing** What are two things that are shown more clearly in the map than in the table?

25. **Open-ended** What is another appropriate title for the article?

Reading Use the table and the graph on page 4.

26. Which language has more non-native speakers, Arabic or Portuguese? Did you use the table or the graph?

27. What is an appropriate title for the table and the graph?

28. a. Find out how many students in your math class speak a language other than English at home. What languages do they speak?

   b. Find out how many students in your math class study a language other than English at school. What languages do they study?

   c. **Open-ended** Show the information from parts (a) and (b) in a way that others will understand. Use tables, graphs, or other diagrams.

29. **Research** Make a chart that shows you, your parents, your grandparents, your great-grandparents, and so on. How far back can you go? Why do you think this chart is sometimes called a *tree diagram?*

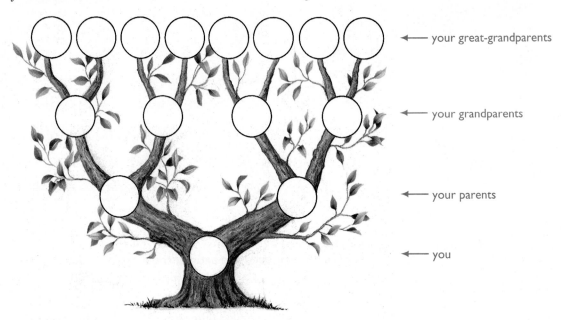

← your great-grandparents

← your grandparents

← your parents

← you

30. **Open-ended** Make a concept map about the musicians and music you like to listen to.

31. **Open-ended** Give an example of a situation that is better described with a graph than with a table or words.

Student Resources Toolbox
p. 658 *Perimeter*

Find the perimeter of each rectangle. *(Toolbox Skill 17)*

32.
```
      5
  ┌────────┐
3 │        │ 3
  └────────┘
      5
```

33.
```
          6
   ┌──────────────┐
 2 │              │ 2
   └──────────────┘
          6
```

34.
```
       4
  ┌────────┐
  │        │
4 │        │ 4
  │        │
  └────────┘
       4
```

Use the Toolbox at the back of this book. *(Toolbox, pp. 640–665)*

35. List three topics in the Toolbox that you think you do not need to study.

36. List three topics in the Toolbox that you think you may need to study.

 Working on the Unit Project

37. Find some symbols without words that are understood internationally. Sketch three examples.

United States

Australia

Spain

Investigating Patterns

Express yourself

"If you want to plant kudzu, drop it and run," say many farmers in the southeastern United States. Kudzu grows so fast that people call it the "mile-a-minute" vine. Kudzu does not grow quite that fast, but it can grow up to 12 in. per day.

You can use a table to show how fast kudzu grows.

Days	1	2	3	4	...	d
Length of kudzu vine (inches)	12	24	36	48	...	$12d$

variable

This means $12 \times d$

variable expression

BY THE WAY...

Kudzu was brought to the United States from Japan in 1876. By 1943 there were 20,000 people in The Kudzu Club. They held kudzu rallies to support the introduction of the plant.

Variable Expressions

A **variable** is a letter used to represent one or more numbers. In the table, d represents the number of days the kudzu grows. The **variable expression** $12d$ represents the length of the kudzu vine after d days.

To avoid confusing the variable x and the times sign $\times$, you write multiplication in algebra in other ways.

raised dot	*parentheses*	*no symbol*
$12 \cdot 2$	$(12)2$ or $12(2)$ or $(12)(2)$	$12d$

Peter earns $12 an hour. Write a variable expression for the amount he earns in _h_ hours.

Sample Response

Look for a pattern.

12(1) ⟵ If Peter works 1 hour, he earns $12.

12(2) ⟵ If Peter works 2 hours, he earns $24.

12*h* ⟵ If Peter works *h* hours, he earns 12*h* dollars.

Talk it Over

1. How are the variable expressions for the length of kudzu and the amount of money Peter earns alike? How are they different?

2. Describe a situation that could be represented by the expression 4*x*. Be sure to tell what *x* represents.

Sample 2

A row of triangles is built with toothpicks. Write a variable expression for the perimeter of Shape _n_.

Shape 1	Shape 2	Shape 3

  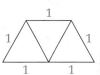

Sample Response

Problem Solving Strategy: Identify a pattern

Sketch a few more shapes.

Shape 4	Shape 5	Shape 6

  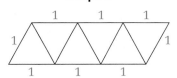

Sample response continued on next page.

11

Make a table of the perimeters.

Shape number	1	2	3	4	5	6	n
Perimeter	3	4	5	6	7	8	?

Look for a pattern. The perimeter is 2 more than the shape number.

An expression for the perimeter of Shape n is $n + 2$.

Evaluating Variable Expressions

When you evaluate a variable expression, you substitute numbers for the variables and find the result.

Sample 3

Suppose a kudzu vine grows 12 in. a day. How long is the vine after each number of days?

a. 7   **b.** 30   **c.** 365

Sample Response

Write the variable expression first.

a. $12d$

$12(7)$ ← Substitute 7 for d.

84

After a week, the kudzu is 84 in. long.

b. $12d$

$12(30)$ ← Substitute 30 for d.

360

After a month, the kudzu is 360 in. long.

c. $12d$

$12(365)$ ← Substitute 365 for d.

4380

After a year, the kudzu is 4380 in. long.

Talk it Over

3. Sample 2 shows triangles made from toothpicks. How many toothpicks would you need to build a row of a million triangles?

4. Evaluate each expression when $a = 3$ and $b = 7$.

    a. $5a$ **b.** $\dfrac{b}{14}$

    c. ab **d.** $6a + b$

······► Now you are ready for:
Exs. 1–25 on pp. 14–16

x-tile

1 1

x

x

Whose rectangle has a greater perimeter?

- **Materials: ten algebra tiles, called "x-tiles"**
- **Work with another student.**

1 Make rectangles by placing the x-tiles next to each other. One of you should make long rectangles. One of you should make tall rectangles.

long

x x x
1 ▭▭▭ 1
x x x

tall

x
1 ▭ 1
1 ▭ 1
1 ▭ 1
x

2 Find a variable expression for the perimeter of each rectangle.

perimeter of long

$\underbrace{x + x + x + x + x + x}_{6x} + \underbrace{1 + 1}_{2}$

perimeter of tall

$\underbrace{x + x}_{2x} + \underbrace{1 + 1 + 1 + 1 + 1 + 1}_{6}$

3 Put your results in a table.

Perimeter		
Number of x-tiles	**Long rectangles**	**Tall rectangles**
1	?	?
2	?	?
3	$6x + 2$	$2x + 6$
4	?	?
5	?	?

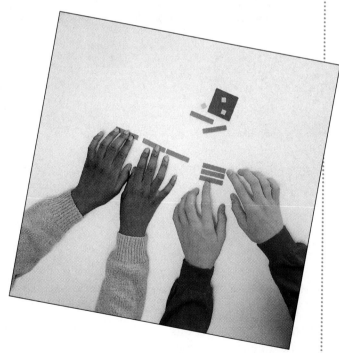

4 Which type of rectangle do you think has a larger perimeter, a long rectangle or a tall rectangle? Why?

······► Now you are ready for:
Exs. 26–47 on pp. 16–18

Look Back ◄

What are the advantages of using a variable expression instead of a table to show how something changes?

Exercises and Problems

1. **Reading** What do variables represent?

2. **a.** The Jacksons rent an apartment for $500 a month. How much rent do they pay in 6 months? in 12 months?

   b. Write a variable expression for the amount they pay in *m* months.

3. **a.** There are 24 hours in one day. How many hours are there in 7 days? in 365 days?

   b. Write a variable expression for the number of hours in *d* days.

4. **a.** You pay for some groceries with a $20 bill. How much change do you get if your groceries cost $18? $16.95?

   b. Write a variable expression for the change you get when you buy *g* dollars worth of groceries.

Draw Shapes 4 and 5 in each pattern. Make a table of the perimeters of the shapes. Then write a variable expression for the perimeter of Shape *n*.

5.　　　**Shape 1**　　　**Shape 2**　　　　　**Shape 3**

6.　　**Shape 1**　　　**Shape 2**　　　　　**Shape 3**

Write a variable expression for each phrase.

7. the price *p* plus the sales tax *t*

8. multiply the rate *r* by the time *t*

9. the number of parents *p* plus the number of teachers *t*

10. 55 times the distance *d*

11. How are the variable expressions you wrote in Exercises 7 and 9 alike? How are they different?

Match each word phrase with the correct variable expression.

12. el producto de 5 y un número *k*

13. la suma de un número *k* y 5

14. un número *k* menos 5

15. un número *k* dividido por 5

A. $\frac{k}{5}$

B. $k - 5$

C. $5k$

D. $k + 5$

For Exercises 16–18, use the article.

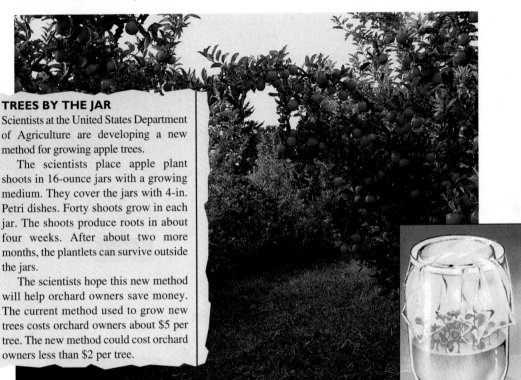

TREES BY THE JAR

Scientists at the United States Department of Agriculture are developing a new method for growing apple trees.

The scientists place apple plant shoots in 16-ounce jars with a growing medium. They cover the jars with 4-in. Petri dishes. Forty shoots grow in each jar. The shoots produce roots in about four weeks. After about two more months, the plantlets can survive outside the jars.

The scientists hope this new method will help orchard owners save money. The current method used to grow new trees costs orchard owners about $5 per tree. The new method could cost orchard owners less than $2 per tree.

16. Make a list of five number facts from the article.

17. Use information from the article to write three variable expressions. Explain what your variable expressions represent.

18. **Writing** Write a letter to an orchard owner about this new method. Use variable expressions to explain how much money the orchard owner can save using the new method.

19. Suppose kudzu really grew a mile a minute. It would cover 5280 ft every minute.

  a. Write a variable expression for the length (in feet) of a kudzu vine after *m* minutes.

  b. How many feet long would the kudzu vine be after one day?

20. In 1999, dogs in the United States bit 8 mail carriers per day. The Postal Service estimated that dog-bite incidents cost the Postal Service about $69,500 per day in medical costs and other related costs.

   a. Write two variable expressions based on this information.

   b. About how many mail carriers are bitten by dogs in one year?

   c. About how much money does the Postal Service spend each year on dog-bite incidents?

Evaluate each variable expression when $p = 4$ and $t = 40$.

21. $p + t$ **22.** pt **23.** $\dfrac{t}{p}$ **24.** $0.5t + p$

25. Which of the variable expressions in Exercises 21–24 is greatest when $p = 2$ and $t = 10$? Which is greatest when $p = 0.2$ and $t = 10$?

Use the expressions from the table you made in the Exploration on page 13.

26. Make a table showing the perimeters of the rectangles when $x = 2$.

27. Make a table showing the perimeters of the rectangles when $x = \dfrac{1}{2}$.

28. For what value of x are the perimeters of the long rectangles equal to the perimeters of the tall rectangles?

29. **Writing** Explain how knowing the value of x helps you decide whether the long or the tall rectangles have greater perimeters.

Write a variable expression for the perimeter of each shape.

30.

31.

32.

33. **Using Manipulatives** Use x-tiles to make these shapes.

   a. Write variable expressions for the perimeters of Shapes A and B.

   b. Find a value for x so that Shape A has a larger perimeter than Shape B.

   c. Find a value for x so that Shape B has a larger perimeter than Shape A.

   d. Find a value for x so that the perimeters of the two shapes are equal.

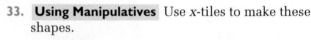

Letters are sometimes used to show patterns in a poem. Lines that rhyme are indicated with the same letter.

There once was a finicky **ocelot**	*a*
Who all the year round was **cross a lot**	*a*
Except at **Thanksgiving**	*b*
When he enjoyed **living**	*b*
For he liked to eat cranberry **sauce a lot.**	*a*

—*Eve Merriam*

34. **Writing** Eve Merriam has written several "Animalimericks" like this one. The rhyme scheme of a limerick is *aabba*. Write a limerick that uses mathematical terms.

35. **Research** Shakespeare wrote over 150 sonnets with the rhyme scheme *abab cdcd efef gg*. Find one and write out its pairs of rhyming words.

36. How is the use of variables to describe rhyme schemes different from the use of variables in mathematical expressions?

Variables are sometimes used to write general rules. Look for a pattern in the examples. Write the pattern using the given number of variables.

37. Use one variable.

$$1 \cdot 16 = 16$$
$$1 \cdot 23.5 = 23.5$$
$$1 \cdot \frac{2}{3} = \frac{2}{3}$$
$$1 \cdot 2 = 2$$

38. Use two variables.

$$5 \cdot 3 = 3 \cdot 5$$
$$8.24 \cdot 6.81 = 6.81 \cdot 8.24$$
$$\frac{3}{8} \cdot \frac{4}{7} = \frac{4}{7} \cdot \frac{3}{8}$$
$$1 \cdot 2 = 2 \cdot 1$$

39. Use three variables.

$$\frac{3}{7} + \frac{2}{7} = \frac{3 + 2}{7}$$
$$\frac{2.4}{10} + \frac{5.6}{10} = \frac{2.4 + 5.6}{10}$$
$$\frac{1}{3} + \frac{2}{3} = \frac{1 + 2}{3}$$

40. Use four variables.

$$\frac{3}{5} \cdot \frac{4}{7} = \frac{3 \cdot 4}{5 \cdot 7}$$
$$\frac{3.6}{9.1} \cdot \frac{10.8}{13.9} = \frac{3.6 \cdot 10.8}{9.1 \cdot 13.9}$$
$$\frac{1}{2} \cdot \frac{3}{4} = \frac{1 \cdot 3}{2 \cdot 4}$$

Ongoing **ASSESSMENT**

41. **Open-ended** Using *x*-tiles and 1-tiles, make two different shapes whose perimeters are equal no matter what value you choose for *x*.

x-tile	1-tile
$1 \;\underset{x}{\overset{x}{\blacksquare}}\; 1$	$1 \;\underset{1}{\overset{1}{\square}}\; 1$

Use the U.S. Census Bureau information below.
(Section 1-1)

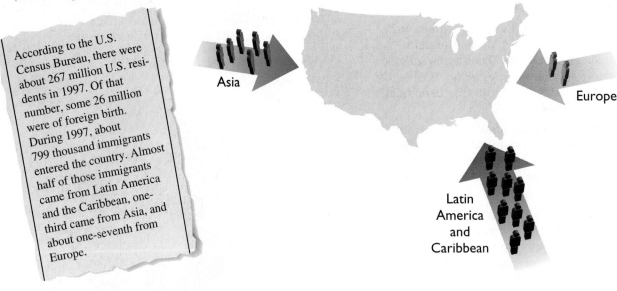

According to the U.S. Census Bureau, there were about 267 million U.S. residents in 1997. Of that number, some 26 million were of foreign birth. During 1997, about 799 thousand immigrants entered the country. Almost half of those immigrants came from Latin America and the Caribbean, one-third came from Asia, and about one-seventh from Europe.

Asia

Europe

Latin America and Caribbean

42. Which bar graph shows the information from the U.S. Census Bureau?

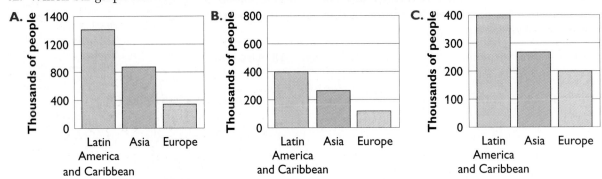

A. Thousands of people — 1400, 1200, 800, 400, 0 — Latin America and Caribbean, Asia, Europe

B. Thousands of people — 800, 600, 400, 200, 0 — Latin America and Caribbean, Asia, Europe

C. Thousands of people — 400, 300, 200, 100, 0 — Latin America and Caribbean, Asia, Europe

Use the Toolbox at the back of this book. *(Toolbox, pp. 640–665)*

43. Study a topic from the Toolbox that you need to review.

Calculate each repeated multiplication.

44. $7 \times 7 \times 7 \times 7$ **45.** $9 \cdot 9 \cdot 9 \cdot 9 \cdot 9$ **46.** $(0.5)(0.5)(0.5)$

Working on the Unit Project

47. To begin to think about a logo for your math class, list some words that you think of when someone says "mathematics."

Patterns with Powers

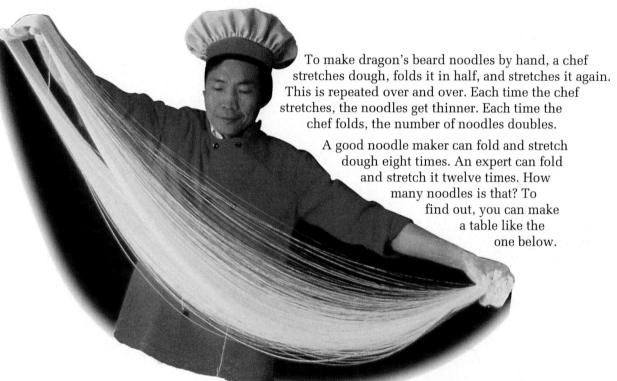

Flour Power

Use exponents to express repeated multiplication, evaluate powers of variables, and make conjectures.

To make dragon's beard noodles by hand, a chef stretches dough, folds it in half, and stretches it again. This is repeated over and over. Each time the chef stretches, the noodles get thinner. Each time the chef folds, the number of noodles doubles.

A good noodle maker can fold and stretch dough eight times. An expert can fold and stretch it twelve times. How many noodles is that? To find out, you can make a table like the one below.

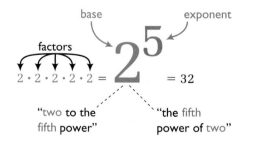

$$ \underbrace{2 \cdot 2 \cdot 2 \cdot 2 \cdot 2}_{\text{factors}} = 2^5 = 32 $$

base · exponent

"two to the fifth power" · "the fifth power of two"

Number of folds	Repeated multiplication	Written as a power of two	Number of noodles
1	2	2^1	2
2	$2 \cdot 2$	2^2	4
3	$2 \cdot 2 \cdot 2$	2^3	8
4	$2 \cdot 2 \cdot 2 \cdot 2$	2^4	16
5	$2 \cdot 2 \cdot 2 \cdot 2 \cdot 2$	2^5	32

Numbers multiplied together are called **factors.** When the same number is repeated as a factor, you can rewrite the product as a **power** of that number. The repeated factor is the **base,** and the number of times it appears as a factor is the **exponent.**

Sample 1

Write the product as a power. Then write how to say it.

a. $2 \cdot 2 \cdot 2 \cdot 2 \cdot 2 \cdot 2 \cdot 2 \cdot 2$

b. $2 \cdot 2 \cdot 2 \cdot 2 \cdot 2 \cdot 2 \cdot 2 \cdot 2 \cdot 2 \cdot 2 \cdot 2 \cdot 2$

Sample Response

a. The repeated factor is 2, so the base is 2.

The factor appears 8 times, so the exponent is 8.

The product is 2^8. ⟵———"Two to the eighth power."

b. The repeated factor is 2, so the base is 2.

The factor appears 12 times, so the exponent is 12.

The product is 2^{12}. ⟵———"Two to the twelfth power."

8 factors

$$2 \cdot 2 \cdot 2 \cdot 2 \cdot 2 \cdot 2 \cdot 2 \cdot 2 \qquad 2^8$$

The repeated factor is 2.

Talk it Over

1. A good noodle maker can fold and stretch dough 8 times. Use repeated multiplication to find the number of noodles.

2. An expert noodle maker can fold and stretch dough 12 times. Use the exponent key on a calculator to find the number of noodles.

3. Which method do you prefer to use, repeated multiplication or the exponent key? Why?

4. If the expert noodle maker's noodles are each about 5 ft long, how many miles would the noodles cover if they were laid end to end? (*Hint:* There are 5280 ft in 1 mi.)

Evaluating Powers of Variables

You can use a variable as the base of a power.

$$x \cdot x = x^2$$

"x squared"

can represent the
area of a square
with sides of length x

$$y \cdot y \cdot y = y^3$$

"y cubed"

can represent the
volume of a cube
with sides of length y

Area $= x^2$

Volume $= y^3$

TECHNOLOGY NOTE

The exponent key on a calculator may be labeled x^y or y^x or ∧. You enter the base, press the key, and then enter the exponent.

To evaluate powers of variables, you substitute a value for the variable and then simplify.

Sample 2

Write an expression for the area covered by the tiles.

Evaluate your expression for each value of x.

a. $x = 5$ b. $x = 10$

Sample Response

The tiles have areas x^2, x, and 1.

The total area they cover is $x^2 + x + 1$ square units.

a. $x^2 + x + 1$ ◄——— Write the expression.

$5^2 + 5 + 1$ ◄——— Substitute 5 for x.

$25 + 5 + 1$

31

The tiles cover 31 square units when $x = 5$.

b. $x^2 + x + 1$ ◄——— Write the expression.

$10^2 + 10 + 1$ ◄——— Substitute 10 for x.

$100 + 10 + 1$

111

The tiles cover 111 square units when $x = 10$.

······► Now you are ready for:
Exs. 1–27 on pp. 23–24

Conjectures about Powers of Ten

Powers of ten show an interesting pattern.

$10^3 = 1000$ ◄——— 1 with three zeros

$10^4 = 10,000$ ◄——— 1 with four zeros

$10^5 = 100,000$ ◄——— 1 with five zeros

$10^6 = 1,000,000$ ◄——— 1 with six zeros

Talk it Over

5. a. A **conjecture** is a guess based on your past experiences. Make a conjecture about the number of zeros you need to write out 10^9.

   b. Test your conjecture by using a calculator to find the decimal notation for 10^9.

6. a. Make a conjecture about the number of zeros you need to write out 10^n.

   b. Use your conjecture to predict the number of zeros you need to write out 10^{100}.

BY THE WAY...

The nine-year-old nephew of American mathematician Edward Kasner invented the name "googol" for 10^{100}.

7. Look at the products of powers of ten. What patterns do you see in the exponents?

$$10^4 \cdot 10^1 = (10 \cdot 10 \cdot 10 \cdot 10) \cdot (10) = 10^5$$

$$10^3 \cdot 10^2 = (10 \cdot 10 \cdot 10) \cdot (10 \cdot 10) = 10^5$$

$$10^2 \cdot 10^3 = (10 \cdot 10) \cdot (10 \cdot 10 \cdot 10) = 10^5$$

$$10^1 \cdot 10^4 = (10) \cdot (10 \cdot 10 \cdot 10 \cdot 10) = 10^5$$

$$10^0 \cdot 10^5 = (10 \cdot 10 \cdot 10 \cdot 10 \cdot 10) = 10^5$$

8. Write each product as a power of ten.

   a. $10^5 \cdot 10^3 = (10 \cdot 10 \cdot 10 \cdot 10 \cdot 10) \cdot (10 \cdot 10 \cdot 10) = 10^?$

   b. $10^6 \cdot 10^2 = 10^?$

   c. $10^8 \cdot 10 = 10^?$

9. Make a conjecture about multiplying powers of ten.

10. Write each quotient as a power of ten.

    a. $\dfrac{10^5}{10^3} = \dfrac{10 \cdot 10 \cdot 10 \cdot 10 \cdot 10}{10 \cdot 10 \cdot 10} = \dfrac{10 \cdot 10}{1} = 10^?$

    b. $\dfrac{10^6}{10^2} = \dfrac{?}{?} = 10^?$

    c. $\dfrac{10^8}{10} = 10^?$

11. Make a conjecture about dividing powers of ten.

Counterexamples

Not all conjectures are true. A **counterexample** is an example that shows that a statement is false.

| Sample 3 |

Larry makes a conjecture that x^2 is greater than x for all values of x. Find a counterexample.

Sample Response

The number 0 is a counterexample, because 0^2 is *not* greater than 0.

The number 1 is a counterexample, because 1^2 is *not* greater than 1.

Numbers between 0 and 1 are also counterexamples:

$$\text{If } x = \frac{1}{2}, \text{ then } x^2 = \frac{1}{2} \cdot \frac{1}{2} = \frac{1}{4}.$$

For numbers like these, x^2 is less than x.

Larry's conjecture is false.

Unit 1 Exploring and Communicating Mathematics

Look Back

How can you rewrite these expressions?

$$n + n + n + n$$

$$n \cdot n \cdot n \cdot n$$

How can you rewrite repeated addition? How can you rewrite repeated multiplication?

······▶ **Now you are ready for:**
Exs. 28–45 on pp. 24–25

1-3 Exercises and Problems

1. **Reading** What are three other ways of writing 2^5?

Write the product as a power. Then write how to say it.

2. $2 \cdot 2 \cdot 2 \cdot 2 \cdot 2 \cdot 2$

3. $4 \cdot 4 \cdot 4$

4. $5 \cdot 5 \cdot 5 \cdot 5 \cdot 5$

5. $x \cdot x \cdot x$

6. $y \cdot y$

7. $z \cdot z \cdot z \cdot z \cdot z \cdot z$

Write using exponents.

8. two to the fifth

9. five squared

10. three to the seventh

11. seven cubed

12. y to the fourth

13. x to the sixth

14. To show 1,000,000 using sign language, you strike the sign for 1000 (fingertips in an "M" shape) into the palm twice. Explain how this sign is similar to power notation.

Arrange from smallest to largest. Explain your reasoning.

15. 4^5, 4^4, 4^6, 4^3

16. 2^{10}, 6^{10}, 4^{10}, 3^{10}

17. $\left(\frac{1}{2}\right)^3$, $\left(\frac{1}{2}\right)^2$, $\left(\frac{1}{2}\right)^4$, $\left(\frac{1}{2}\right)^5$

18. 0^5, 0^7, 0^6, 0^8

19. $(0.1)^2$, $(0.3)^2$, $(0.4)^2$, $(0.8)^2$

20. A chain letter tells you to send copies to five friends.

   a. Complete the table showing the number of letters sent during each round.

   b. Write an expression for the number of letters sent during round n.

Round	1	2	3	4	5	6	7	8	9	10
Number of letters	5	25	125	625	?	?	?	?	?	?

   c. Guess which round will send out more than a billion letters. Check your guess using a calculator.

Write an expression for the area covered by each group of tiles. Evaluate each expression when $x = 7$.

21.

22.

23.

Write an expression for the area covered by each group of tiles.

24.

25.

26.

27. Sketch the next square that follows the pattern in Exercises 24–26. Write an expression for the area.

Write each expression as a power of ten.

28. $10^8 \cdot 10^7$

29. $10^6 \cdot 10^6$

30. $10^{17} \cdot 10$

31. $10^{473} \cdot 10^{27}$

32. $\dfrac{10^8}{10^7}$

33. $\dfrac{10^6}{10^6}$

34. $\dfrac{10^{17}}{10}$

35. $\dfrac{10^{473}}{10^{27}}$

36. Complete this conjecture about multiplying powers of ten.
$$10^a \cdot 10^b = 10^?$$

37. Complete this conjecture about dividing powers of ten.
$$\frac{10^a}{10^b} = 10^? \text{ when } a \text{ is greater than } b$$

38. According to the pattern on page 22, $10^0 \cdot 10^5 = 10^5$. Make a conjecture about the value of 10^0. Check your conjecture using a calculator.

39. Write as a power of ten.

   a. $10^5 \cdot 10^5 \cdot 10^5$

   b. $10^3 \cdot 10^5 \cdot 10^7$

   c. $10^2 \cdot 10^5 \cdot 10^8$

   d. Complete this conjecture about multiplying three powers of ten:
$$10^a \cdot 10^b \cdot 10^c = 10^?$$

40. Samuel writes this statement: "$x^2 + x^5 = x^7$ for all numbers."

   a. Give a counterexample to Samuel's statement.

   b. Is there any value of x that makes the statement true?

   c. Rewrite Samuel's statement so it is true.

41. **Writing** Imagine that you are explaining to a friend over the telephone how to work with powers of ten.

   a. Write what you would say about multiplying powers together.

   b. Write what you would say about dividing powers.

   c. Read what you have written to a family member or a friend. If the person does not understand, rewrite your explanation.

Review **PREVIEW**

42. Latex paint comes in two sizes of cans, small and large. *(Section 1-2)*

   a. Write a variable expression for the cost of *s* small cans.

   b. Write a variable expression for the cost of *l* large cans.

   c. Evaluate the expressions in parts (a) and (b) for $s = 5$ and $l = 3$.

43. You will review polygons later in this chapter. Write three sentences about polygons based on this concept map. *(Section 1-1)*

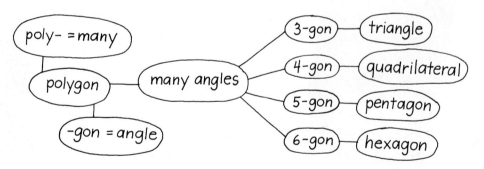

44. Find the average of these test scores: 93, 85, 85.

 Working on the Unit Project

45. **a.** Your knowledge of mathematics will be growing this year. Look through this book for ideas about what you will be learning.

   b. Think about including in your logo a pattern of numbers or geometric shapes that suggests growth.

   c. Sketch one of your ideas.

Writing and Evaluating Expressions

Left to Right → MAY BE WRONG

Talk it Over

1. Marlene wants to find the average of three test scores: 84, 75, and 75. What is a reasonable guess for her average?

2. Marlene enters 84 **+** 2 **×** 75 **÷** 3 **=** on a calculator and gets 2150. What did the calculator do?

3. Marlene knows that 2150 is not her test average. She borrows a graphics calculator from Ron. She enters
   84 **+** 2 **×** 75 **÷** 3 **ENTER** on the graphics calculator and gets 134. What did the graphics calculator do?

4. Marlene knows that 134 is not her test average either. Explain how she can use the parenthesis keys on her graphics calculator to find her test average. What is it?

5. Some calculators do not have parenthesis keys. Find a keystroke sequence that gives the correct average but does not use parentheses.

Ron's graphics calculator follows the **order of operations,** a set of rules people agree to use so an expression has only one answer. In algebra, the order of operations is not always from left to right.

ORDER OF OPERATIONS

Parentheses ←——— Simplify inside parentheses.

Exponents ←——— Calculate any powers.

Multiplication and **D**ivision ←——— Do these as they appear from left to right.

Addition and **S**ubtraction ←——— Do these as they appear from left to right.

Watch Out!
Multiplications are not done before divisions. Multiplications and divisions are done as they appear, from left to right.

Sample 1

Calculate according to the order of operations.

$48 + (12 - 8)^2 \div 8$

Sample Response

$48 + (12 - 8)^2 \div 8$

$48 + 4^2 \div 8$ ←——— Do operations in parentheses first.

$48 + 16 \div 8$ ←——— Do exponents next.

$48 + 2$ ←——— Do division.

50 ←——— Do addition.

Sample 2

Insert parentheses to make each statement true.

a. $4 + 16 \div 2 + 3 \times 5 = 20$

b. $4 + 16 \div 2 + 3 \times 5 = 59$

Sample Response

Problem Solving Strategy: Guess and check

Add parentheses in different ways and calculate.

a. $(4 + 16) \div 2 + 3 \times 5 = 25$ ←——— Try parentheses around first pair.

$4 + (16 \div 2) + 3 \times 5 = 27$ ←——— Try parentheses around second pair.

$4 + 16 \div (2 + 3) \times 5 = 20$ ←——— This answers part (a).

b. $(4 + 16 \div 2) + 3 \times 5 = 27$ ←——— Try parentheses around first three.

$4 + (16 \div 2 + 3) \times 5 = 59$ ←——— This answers part (b).

1-4 Writing and Evaluating Expressions

Write an expression for the area covered by the tiles. Evaluate the expression when $x = 5$.

Sample Response

There are 4 x^2-tiles, 8 x-tiles, and 4 1-tiles.

An expression for the area is $4x^2 + 8x + 4$.

$4x^2 + 8x + 4$

$4 \cdot 5^2 + 8 \cdot 5 + 4$ ◄――― Substitute 5 for x.

$4 \cdot 25 + 8 \cdot 5 + 4$ ◄――― Do exponent first.

$100 + 40 + 4$ ◄――― Do all multiplications from left to right.

144 ◄――― Do all additions from left to right.

When $x = 5$, the tiles cover an area of 144 square units. This answer makes sense, because the tiles form a square. The square is 12 units on each side when $x = 5$. The area is $12 \cdot 12$, or 144 square units.

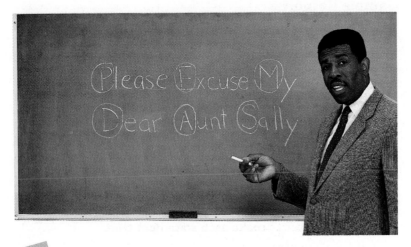

Look Back ◄

This teacher uses the phrase shown in the photograph to help students remember the order of operations. Explain how this phrase might help you.

1-4 Exercises and Problems

1. **Reading** Why do people agree on an order of operations?

2. **Open-ended** Draw a silly picture showing what happens when someone does not follow the correct "order of operations" for a nonmathematical task.

Calculate according to the order of operations.

3. $3 + 4 \cdot 5$

4. $4 \div 2 + 5$

5. $2^4 - 3$

6. $4 + 6^3$

7. $12 \div 2^2$

8. $7^5 \cdot 10$

9. $10 - 4 + 9 - 3$

10. $2 + 4^2 \cdot 3$

11. $10^3 + 36 \div 4$

12. $135 \div 3^3 - 4$

13. $17 \cdot 3 - 2^3$

14. $15 - 125 \div 5^2$

15. $15 - 3(4 - 2)$

16. $15 - (4 - 2)^3$

17. $15 + (4^3 - 2)$

18. $[(12 - 4) \cdot 2 + 11] \div 3$

19. $35 + 5[(16 + 12) \div 4]$

20. $(35 + 5)[16 + (12 \div 4)]$

Write out the keystrokes you could use on a calculator with parentheses to calculate each expression.

21. $\dfrac{15 - 3}{4 + 2}$

22. $\dfrac{15 - 3(4 - 2)}{2^2 - 1}$

Insert parentheses to make each statement true.

23. $48 \div 4 + 8 - 4 + 2 = 14$ **24.** $48 \div 4 + 8 - 4 + 2 = 8$ **25.** $48 \div 4 + 8 - 4 + 2 = 2$

Insert parentheses in the expression $6 \cdot 5^2 - 7 + 9$ to get each answer.

26. a number less than 125

27. a number between 125 and 150

28. a number between 150 and 175

29. a number greater than 175

30. **Open-ended** Write an expression using at least three different operations whose correct answer you can find by doing operations from left to right.

31. **Open-ended** Write an expression using at least three different operations whose correct answer you cannot find by doing operations from left to right.

Using Manipulatives **For each group of tiles, do these things.**

a. Write a variable expression for the perimeter.
b. Write a variable expression for the area.
c. Evaluate the expression when $x = 7$.

32.   **33.**   **34.**

Ongoing **ASSESSMENT**

35. **Writing** Juanita wants to buy a calculator. Her teacher recommends that she buy one that follows the order of operations. Write a plan for how she might test a calculator to see if it follows the order of operations.

Review **PREVIEW**

Show each conjecture is false by finding a counterexample. *(Section 1-3)*

36. $x^2 + x = x^3$

37. $x^2 \cdot x^4 = x^8$

Tell whether each word phrase can be represented by the variable expression $d + 7$. Write *Yes* or *No*. *(Section 1-2)*

38. 7 more than d dinosaurs

39. 7 times a number of dogs

40. d days plus the number of days in a week

41. **a.** Evaluate the expressions $2x + 3$ and $2(x + 3)$ for three values of x.

   b. For each expression, what operations did you use? In what order?

   c. Which expression is larger? Why?

Working on the Unit Project

42. Magazines, newspapers, and telephone yellow pages are good places to find logos.

    a. Trace or cut out five different logos. Tape each logo to a separate piece of paper.

    b. Draw arrows to point out features of the logos that you think convey meaning about the product or service.

    c. Do the same with one of your sketches for your math logo.

Moray Wheels
ADAPTIVE SCUBA ASSOCIATION

Unit 1   **CHECKPOINT**

Language used at home	1980	1990
Mon-Khmer	16,000	127,000
French Creole	25,000	188,000
Hindi	130,000	331,000
Vietnamese	203,000	507,000
Thai	89,000	206,000

The table shows languages that had great increases in speakers in the United States between 1980 and 1990.   **1-1**

  1. **Writing** Write three statements based on the information in the table.

  2. **Writing** Explain why Mon-Khmer is at the top of the table and Thai is at the bottom.

Evaluate each variable expression when x = 4 and y = 7.   **1-2**

  3. $3x$ **4.** $y + 17$ **5.** $5y - x$

Write as a power of ten.   **1-3**

  6. $10^3 \cdot 10^5$ **7.** $10 \cdot 10^{17}$ **8.** $\dfrac{10^9}{10^2}$

Evaluate when x = 9.

  9. $x^2 + 1$ **10.** $x^2 + x$ **11.** $x^4 + x + 1$

Calculate according to the order of operations.   **1-4**

  12. $36 \div 3^2 + 7 \cdot 4 + 2^4 - 11 + 6 \div 2$

Modeling the Distributive Property

················Focus

Use the distributive property to simplify calculations, rewrite expressions, and combine like terms.

Combination Plate

Alicia is buying a sandwich and a drink for herself and the same meal for three friends. How can she figure out how much it will cost?

Ben's

Alicia's

Talk it Over

1. What does Alicia do to figure out the cost? What does Ben do?

2. Find the answers Alicia and Ben get. What do you notice?

3. If the sandwich costs $2.25 and the drink costs $.75, whose method would you use? Why?

4. Ben uses mental math to find the cost of four sandwiches. Complete his work.

   He thinks of $2.95 as $3 − $.05.

   $4 \cdot 2.95 = 4(3 − 0.05) = 4(3) − 4(0.05) = \underline{\ ?\ } − \underline{\ ?\ } = \underline{\ ?\ }$

5. Describe a way to use mental math to find the cost of four drinks.

   $4 \cdot 0.89 = \underline{\ ?\ }$

Find each product using mental math.

a. 7(108)   b. 15(98)

Sample Response

a. Think of 108 as 100 + 8.

   $7(108) = 7(100 + 8) = 7 \cdot 100 + 7 \cdot 8 = 700 + 56 = 756$

b. Think of 98 as 100 − 2.

   $15(98) = 15(100 - 2) = 15 \cdot 100 - 15 \cdot 2 = 1500 - 30 = 1470$

Illustrate the expression 3(x + 2) using algebra tiles. Rewrite the expression without parentheses.

Sample Response

A rectangle of width 3 and length $(x + 2)$ has area $3(x + 2)$.

Imagine pulling the rectangle apart. What are the areas of the two smaller rectangles?

The area of the left group is $3x$. The area of the right group is 6.

The algebra tiles show that $3(x + 2) = 3 \cdot x + 3 \cdot 2 = 3x + 6$.

When you rewrite a product as a sum or a difference, you are using a mathematical rule called the *distributive property*.

DISTRIBUTIVE PROPERTY

For all numbers a, b, and c:

$a(b + c) = ab + ac$

$a(b - c) = ab - ac$

·····▶ **Now you are ready for:**
Exs. 1–21 on pp. 34–35

Combining Like Terms

When you add expressions, each expression is a **term** in the sum.

variable term   variable term   constant term

$$3x^2 \quad + \quad 2x \quad + \quad 4$$

coefficient of x^2 coefficient of x

The numerical part of a variable term is called a **coefficient.**

Terms with the same variable part are called **like terms.** You use the distributive property in reverse to **combine like terms.**

variable parts are the same: $\quad 5x^2 + 3x^2 \longrightarrow (5+3)x^2 \longrightarrow 8x^2$

variable parts are the same: $\quad 5x + 3x \longrightarrow (5+3)x \longrightarrow 8x$

Talk it Over

6. How is the distributive property used in combining like terms?

7. What do you think terms with different variable parts are called?

Sample 3

Simplify $5(x + 4) - 3x$.

Sample Response

$5(x + 4) - 3x$

$5 \cdot x + 5 \cdot 4 - 3x \quad \longleftarrow$ Use the distributive property.

$5x + 20 - 3x$

$5x - 3x + 20 \quad \longleftarrow$ Group like terms together.

$2x + 20 \quad \longleftarrow$ Combine like terms.

Look Back

How can you use the distributive property to rewrite a product as a sum? to rewrite a sum as a product?

Show examples that use numbers and examples that use variable expressions.

▶ **Now you are ready for:**
Exs. 22–41 on pp. 35–36

Exercises and Problems

Rewrite each product as a sum or difference. Do not calculate.

1. $2(300 + 50)$ **2.** $5(100 - 2)$ **3.** $5(40 + 8)$ **4.** $4(1000 - 150)$

Find each product using mental math.

5. $5(205)$ **6.** $9(397)$ **7.** $7(4\frac{6}{7})$ **8.** $3(1006)$

Use the distributive property to find each sum or difference mentally.

9. $479 \cdot 7 + 479 \cdot 3$ **10.** $280 \cdot 40 - 80 \cdot 40$

11. $250 \cdot 17 - 250 \cdot 7$ **12.** $64 \cdot 32 + 64 \cdot 68$

13. The four walls of a room are to be painted.

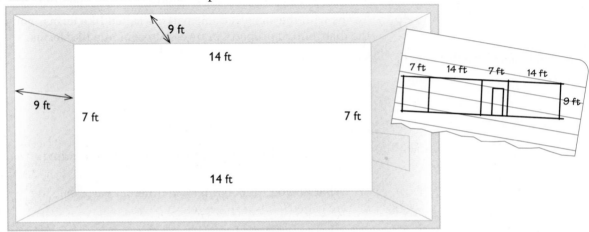

a. Explain how you could find the total area of the four walls.

b. Complete this extension of the distributive property:

$$a(b + c + d + e) = \underline{\ ?\ } + \underline{\ ?\ } + \underline{\ ?\ } + \underline{\ ?\ }$$

Write two expressions for the area covered by the tiles, one with parentheses and one without parentheses.

14.

15.

Use the distributive property to rewrite each expression without parentheses.

16. $2(l + w)$ **17.** $3(2a - b)$ **18.** $\frac{1}{3}(3x^2 - 12x)$ **19.** $\frac{1}{5}(20t^2 + 5)$

20. **Writing** When Hector did Exercises 16 and 17, he wrote

$$2(l + w) = 2l + w$$

$$3(2a - b) = 6a - b$$

Explain his mistakes and how to correct them.

21. A tile design with area $x^2 + 2x + 1$ is used four times. The new area is $4(x^2 + 2x + 1)$. Use the distributive property to rewrite this expression without parentheses. Show how your answer matches the design.

Insert parentheses to make the statement true.

22. $3x + 2 = 3x + 6$

23. $6x + 6x + 1 = 12x + 6$

Combine like terms. If you cannot, explain why.

24. $3y + 5y$ **25.** $3z^2 + 5z + 3$ **26.** $4x + 2x^3 + 3x$

27. $7 + 3(y + 4) + 6y$ **28.** $6y + 3(y + 4) - 7$ **29.** $6(y + 7) + 3(y + 4)$

30. **Writing** Alexandra writes these statements:

$$5x^2 + 3x^2 = 8x^4$$
$$2x^2 + 4x = 6x^3$$

Explain her mistakes and how to correct them.

31. **Group Activity** Have each member of your group start with a different number and follow the steps.

    1) Starting number: ___?___

    2) Add 8.

    3) Multiply by 3.

    4) Subtract 12.

    5) Multiply by $\frac{1}{3}$.

    6) Ending number: ___?___

a. Make a table showing starting and ending numbers.

b. What pattern do you notice?

c. Suppose the starting number is x. Write a variable expression for every step along the way. Simplify each expression as much as possible.

d. If the starting number is x, what is an expression for the ending number?

e. If the ending number is y, what is an expression for the starting number?

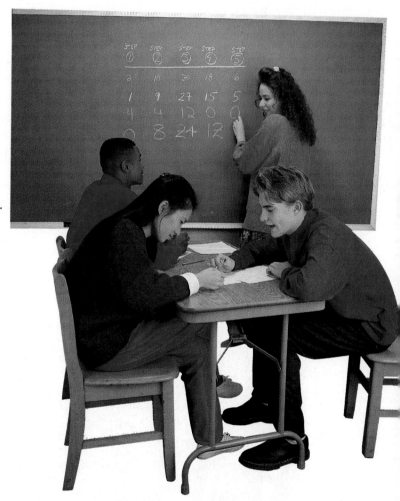

32. Writing Explain how the distributive property can be used to perform some calculations mentally.

Evaluate each expression when $x = 9$. *(Section 1-4)*

33. $x^2 + 2x + 1$ **34.** $4x^2 + 4x + 1$ **35.** $9x^2 + 12x + 4$

Write as a power of ten. *(Section 1-3)*

36. $10 \cdot 10$ **37.** $10^7 \cdot 10^3$ **38.** $\dfrac{10^7}{10^3}$

Write two expressions for the perimeter of each figure, one with parentheses and one without parentheses. *(Section 1-2)*

39.   **40.**

 Working on the Unit Project

41. Find three different logos for the same kind of product, company, or organization. How are the logos alike? How are they different?

Working Together on Congruent Polygons

MATCHED SETS

People often work together on projects like painting a mural. You may be surprised at how much you can do when you work with other people.

Mural Revival in L.A.

The Los Angeles Conservation Corps organizes teams of young people to clean up and care for neighborhoods across Los Angeles. Over 1200 students participate each year in the *Clean and Green* program, planting and caring for trees, setting up recycling programs, and painting murals.

The Los Angeles Conservation Corps logo symbolizes helping hands and resembles the recycle logo.

Through community service, these students develop leadership skills and the ability to work with others.

In the photograph, students work with a Creative Solutions mural team to combat graffiti, learn art techniques, and explore the history of public art.

EXPLORATION

How many ways can you divide a square into four identical pieces?

- **Materials: dot paper or graph paper**
- **Work with another student.**

① Use a square made with 25 dots.

② Divide the square into four pieces that have the same size and shape. Use only straight lines that connect dots.

③ Draw as many different designs as you can, each in its own square.

④ Stop after five minutes.

1. How many designs did you and your partner find in five minutes?

2. Were you surprised at the number you found?

3. Compare these two designs. Do you think they should be considered the same or different? Explain.

Congruent Figures

Two figures that have the same size and shape are called **congruent.** If you can slide, turn, or flip a figure so it covers another figure exactly, then the two figures are congruent.

slide

turn

flip

4. What movement will show that the blue shape is congruent to the red shape?

a.   b.   c.

5. Are the shaded shapes in question 3 congruent?

Can you work with others to find new ways to divide the square?

- **Materials: dot paper or graph paper**
- **Work in a group of four students.**

(1) Use a square made with 25 dots that measures 4 in. on each side.

(2) Start with all your pencils in the center of the square.

(3) Choose a leader to follow. Copy the leader's movements in your part of the square.

(4) Choose a new leader and make another design. Repeat.

(5) Stop after ten minutes.

(6) Shade one piece in each design you made.

(7) Tape your designs to a wall next to the other groups' designs. ◀·············

Talk it Over

6. In the Exploration, how many different shaded pieces did the class find?

7. Do you think the class has found all the possible pieces?

········▶ **Now you are ready for:**

Exs. 1–12 on p. 41

8. How would you describe the shapes of the shaded pieces?

Describing Polygons

The straight-sided shapes you shaded in the Explorations are **polygons**.

3-gon	4-gon	5-gon	6-gon	7-gon	8-gon
triangle	quadrilateral	pentagon	hexagon	heptagon	octagon

To name polygons, write a different letter at each **vertex** (corner) and list consecutive vertices in order. (*Vertices* is the plural of *vertex*.) Each **side** of the polygon is named with two consecutive vertices. Two sides that have the same length are called **congruent sides**.

The ≅ symbol means "is congruent to."

quadrilateral *ABCD* ≅ quadrilateral *EFGH*

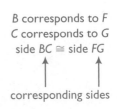

B corresponds to *F*
C corresponds to *G*
side *BC* ≅ side *FG*

corresponding sides

In congruent polygons, matching vertices are called **corresponding vertices** and matching sides are called **corresponding sides**.

When you name congruent polygons, list the corresponding vertices in the same order.

Sample

a. **Name the congruent polygons.**
b. **Name three pairs of congruent sides.**

Sample Response

a. quadrilateral *JKLM* ≅ quadrilateral *PQRS*

b. side *JK* ≅ side *PQ*; side *KL* ≅ side *QR*; side *LM* ≅ side *RS*

You can use tick marks or letters on diagrams, or written statements near the diagrams, to indicate congruent sides.

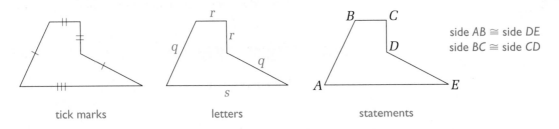

side *AB* ≅ side *DE*
side *BC* ≅ side *CD*

tick marks   letters   statements

Look Back

······► Now you are ready for:
Exs. 13–32 on pp. 41–43

Why is it helpful to name congruent polygons by listing corresponding vertices in order?

Exercises and Problems

What kind of movement *(slide, turn, or flip)* **shows that the blue polygon is congruent to the red polygon?**

1.   **2.**   **3.**

Are the letters congruent? If so, what kind of movement *(slide, turn, or flip)* **shows this?**

4. u n **5.** b d **6.** p q

For Exercises 7–11, use the designs with four congruent pieces that you made in the Explorations.

7. List some ways in which working in a group helped you in the Explorations.

8. Draw a triangle, square, and rectangle that you found in the Explorations. What other names of polygons do you know?

9. **Open-ended** Choose one of your designs. Cut out the four congruent pieces and rearrange them into a shape that is not a square. Tape your design to a separate piece of paper.

10. **Group Activity** Choose one of your designs and make an 8 in. by 8 in. version. Color your design. Join it to the squares made by your classmates to create a large mural.

11. Describe the congruent shapes you see in the quilt at the right. What slides, turns, or flips would you use to show they are congruent?

12. Choose one of your Exploration designs and repeat it to create a quilt pattern. You may want to flip or turn some of the squares for variety. Color your design.

13. Cut out two congruent polygons from the Exploration designs. Tape them to a piece of paper and label the vertices. Name the corresponding vertices. List three pairs of congruent sides.

14. Graphic Design Arrange four congruent polygons in a way that expresses one of these words: *order, disorder, danger, fun*. Explain why your design expresses the word.

Here are some examples.

order

disorder

danger

fun

15. **Reading** What are some ways to show that sides of a polygon have the same length?

Mark congruent lengths by using tick marks.

16.

17.

18.

Mark congruent lengths by using letters. Then write a variable expression for the perimeter of the polygon.

19.

20.

21.

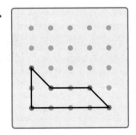

Name the congruent polygons. Then list three pairs of corresponding sides.

22.

23.

24.

Ongoing **ASSESSMENT**

25. **Group Activity** Organize the polygons that you found in the Explorations based on the number of sides of each polygon.

Review **PREVIEW**

Rewrite without parentheses. *(Section 1-5)*

26. $5(2x + 3)$

27. $6(y^2 - 3y + 4)$

Evaluate according to the order of operations. *(Section 1-4)*

28. $6 - 3 \cdot 2$

29. $8 \div 4 - 2$

Write a variable expression for the perimeter of each polygon. *(Section 1-2)*

30.

31.

Working on the Unit Project

32. Find a logo that includes congruent pieces. Describe the slides, turns, or flips that show the pieces are congruent.

Why do you think congruent pieces are used in the logo?

The recycle logo uses three congruent arrow shapes.

A turn moves one arrow onto another.

The cycle of arrows represents an endless reuse of materials.

Find out what a Möbius Strip is. Is the recycle logo an example?

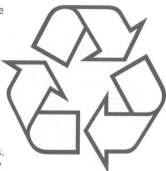

Exploring Quadrilaterals and Symmetry

Section 1-7

Focus

Build quadrilaterals from congruent triangles and write expression for their perimeters, find lines of symmetry, and communicate ideas through writing.

PUTTING IT TOGETHER

EXPLORATION

What kinds of quadrilaterals can you make with two congruent triangles?

- **Materials: paper, scissors, ruler**
- **Work in a group of four students.**

① Use a ruler to draw two congruent triangles.

Each of you should create a different kind of triangle: *equilateral, isosceles, scalene,* and *right.*

② Cut out your triangles and write the lengths of the sides on the front and back.

Equilateral triangles have three sides the same length.

Isosceles triangles have two sides the same length.

Scalene triangles have no sides the same length.

Right triangles have one right angle.

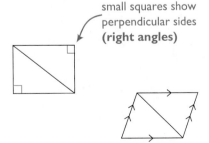

small squares show perpendicular sides **(right angles)**

Arrows show parallel sides

③ Make as many different polygons as you can by joining your two triangles so that congruent edges match.

④ Draw each polygon you make. Use right angle marks to show **perpendicular** sides. Use arrows to show **parallel** sides.

⑤ Record the perimeter of each polygon you make.

⑥ Write a summary of the findings of your group. Include answers to these questions:

How does the type of triangle you use affect the number of different polygons you can make? How does it affect the number of different perimeters you get?

In the Exploration, you may have made these special quadrilaterals:

parallelogram   **kite**   **rhombus**   **rectangle**   **square**

tick marks show sides
with same length

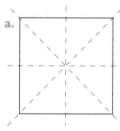

If you can fold a polygon so that
one half matches the other, the
polygon has **symmetry.**
The fold line is called a **line
of symmetry.**

Talk it Over

1. What are some features of a parallelogram?

2. What are some features of a kite?

3. Is a rhombus a parallelogram? Is a rhombus a kite?

4. Which of your polygons have no lines of symmetry?

5. Which of your polygons have one line of symmetry?

6. Which of the polygons that you made have two lines of symmetry?

Sample

Draw the lines of symmetry for each polygon.

a.   b.   c.

Sample Response

a.   b.   c.

► Now you are ready for:
Exs. 1–20 on pp. 47–48

NOTES ON EXPLORATION
My triangels were 2 inchs, 4 inchs, and 5 inchs and I got shapes with different perimters like 12, 14 and 18 inchs. That's all I got. When Sondra used triangels like 3, 4, 5 she got perimters like 14, 16, 18 which are all in a row maybe 'cause 3, 4, 5 are all in a row?

REPORT ON EXPLORATION

I made quadrilaterals by joining two congruent triangles together. My triangles had edges of length 2, 4, and 5 inches. I got parallelograms and kites. Only three perimeters were possible: 12 inches, 14 inches, and 18 inches.

When Sondra used triangles with 3, 4, and 5 inch edges, she got other shapes, including a rectangle. Her perimeters were 14, 16, and 18 inches.

Sondra's rectangle

Personal Writing

A good way to explore a problem is to write down your ideas. At first, do not worry about making it look good.

Jot down notes and ideas.

Describe the steps you try.

Write about patterns you notice.

List unanswered questions.

You can fix spelling and grammar later.

Communicating With Others

Writing or speaking to others requires more careful work. Others may expect to see words, symbols, and diagrams used in conventional ways.

Describe the problem or activity.

Use standard mathematical words that others will understand.

Organize your ideas and results clearly.

Include labeled drawings with appropriate symbols.

Talk it Over

7. In the first writing sample, the writer uses nonstandard spelling and grammar. Give some examples.

8. In the second writing sample, the writer uses mathematical words correctly. Give some examples.

9. There is an idea in the first writing sample that is not developed in the second sample. What is it? Discuss how it could be developed.

10. Compare the use of diagrams in the two writing samples.

Look Back

In the Exploration, was everyone in your group able to make shapes with symmetry? Explain why or why not.

▶ **Now you are ready for:**
Exs. 21–36 on pp. 48–49

Exercises and Problems

Exercises 1–6 are based on the Exploration. The table shows the results from one group's work.

1. Name the type of triangle that each student used.

2. Who was able to make the greatest number of different perimeters from two congruent triangles?

3. What perimeters can you make if you build quadrilaterals from two triangles with sides of length 5, 6, and 7?

	Sides of triangles	Perimeters made
Jeanine	4 4 4	16
Alain	4 5 5	18, 20
Helen	3 5 6	16, 18, 22
Duane	3 4 5	14, 16, 18

4. Make a quadrilateral using two equilateral triangles with sides of length a, a, and a. Draw a diagram. Write a variable expression for its perimeter.

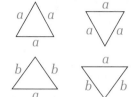

5. Make two different quadrilaterals using two isosceles triangles with sides of length a, b, and b. Draw diagrams. Write variable expressions for their perimeters.

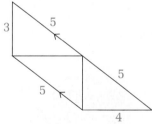

6. Make three different quadrilaterals using two scalene triangles with sides of length a, b, and c. Draw diagrams. Write variable expressions for their perimeters.

7. A quadrilateral with one pair of parallel sides is called a *trapezoid*.

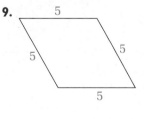

You can make a trapezoid by joining three congruent triangles.

   a. Draw two other trapezoids that you can make with the triangles shown.

   b. Find the perimeter of each of your trapezoids.

What name best describes each quadrilateral?

8.

9.

10.

11.

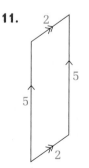

Draw all lines of symmetry for each figure or write *no symmetry*.

12.

13.

14.

15.

16. How many lines of symmetry does a circle have?

17. **Open-ended** List some things you see every day that have symmetry.

Write what you know about each figure, based on the marks and labels in the diagram.

18.

19.

20.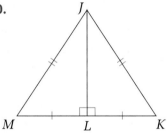

Writing Do some personal writing about each activity. Include drawings if they are helpful.

21. Make three congruent scalene triangles with sides of length a, b, and c. Build three different trapezoids with them. Draw and label the diagrams. Then write a variable expression for the perimeter of each trapezoid.

22. You can create different rectangles with the same perimeter. Choose at least three different perimeters and use toothpicks to make rectangles with these perimeters. How does the number of toothpicks affect the number of rectangles you can make?

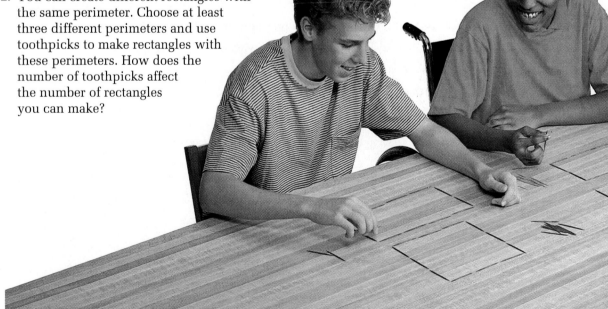

23. List some numbers that are the sum of two or more consecutive numbers. (For example, **7** = 3 + 4 and **26** = 5 + 6 + 7 + 8.) What counting numbers cannot be expressed as the sum of two or more consecutive numbers?

Writing For Exercises 24 and 25, write an answer that someone younger than you could understand.

24. How do you find the average of a set of numbers?

25. Can you draw a triangle with no line of symmetry? exactly one line of symmetry? exactly two lines of symmetry? exactly three lines of symmetry? Use diagrams to explain your answers.

26. Choose a problem from an earlier section of this unit. Write a letter to a friend explaining how you worked on the problem.

27. Explain how to predict the perimeters of the polygons you can make from two congruent triangles if you know the lengths of the sides of the triangles. You may want to use the variable expressions you wrote in Exercise 6.

Ongoing ASSESSMENT

28. **Open-ended** Draw a quadrilateral with the given number of lines of symmetry, if possible. If the quadrilateral has a special name, write it.

   a. exactly one   **b.** exactly two

   c. exactly three   **d.** exactly four

Review PREVIEW

29. Draw one of the polygons you built in the Exploration and label the vertices. Show all the congruent sides in some way. *(Section 1-6)*

Combine like terms. *(Section 1-5)*

30. $a + c + b + c + c$ **31.** $a + b + a + b$

Write each power of ten as a number and in words. *(Section 1-3)*

32. 10^2 **33.** 10^3 **34.** 10^6 **35.** 10^9

 Working on the Unit Project

36. Find some logos that have symmetry and others that do not. Why do some companies use symmetry in their logos?

Completing the Unit Project

➤ Now you are ready to make your book cover. Your group can work together to make one cover to display or three individual versions of your group's logo design.

➤ On the inside flap of your book cover, explain what the patterns, symbols, numbers, and shapes in your logo represent. Tell why you think your design identifies your math class.

➤ You may want to make an enlargement of your logo to display on a poster in your classroom. You may decide to make a bookmark showing a smaller version of your logo.

Look Back ◄

Think about how your group worked together on the project. What would you recommend to a group just starting to work on this project to improve their teamwork or their results?

Alternative Projects

Project 1: The Fibonacci Sequence

The list of numbers 1, 1, 2, 3, 5, 8, 13, 21, . . . is called the *Fibonacci* sequence. Describe this number pattern. Research the Fibonacci sequence and write a report about it. Describe how this pattern is displayed in nature.

Project 2: Create a Polygon Pattern

Regular polygons are shapes that have equal sides and equal angles. The triangle, square, and hexagon shown are regular polygons. Create a few patterns using these shapes. What kinds of patterns can you build with just one type of polygon? with two types? with all three types? Sketch the patterns you make. Describe the symmetry of each design. Shade the polygons with different colors. How can the use of color affect the symmetry of your design?

The table shows the numbers of United States residents 5 years old and over who speak a language other than English at home. 1-1

Language	1980	1990
Spanish	11,549,000	17,339,000
French	1,572,000	1,703,000
German	1,607,000	1,547,000
Italian	1,633,000	1,309,000
Chinese	632,000	1,249,000
Tagalog	452,000	843,000
Polish	826,000	723,000
Korean	276,000	626,000
Vietnamese	203,000	507,000
Portuguese	361,000	430,000

1. Which languages were spoken by fewer U.S. residents in 1990 than in 1980?

2. Explain why a bar graph of this data might be hard to read.

3. **Open-ended** What are three things you can learn from the table?

Write a variable expression for each amount. 1-2

4. 4 more than a number

5. your share of the rent in a 4-person apartment whose monthly rent is x dollars

6. the distance traveled by a car in four hours at an average speed of x miles per hour

7. Yoshi's car gets 21 miles per gallon of gasoline.

   a. How many miles can Yoshi drive on a tank of 12 gal of gasoline?

   b. Write a variable expression for the number of miles Yoshi can drive on a tank of x gallons of gasoline.

8. Complete the table of perimeters for the rectangles.

Write as a power of ten. 1-3

9. $10^7 \cdot 10^4$

10. $\dfrac{10^7}{10^4}$

11. $10^7 \cdot 10^4 \cdot 10$

12. a. Give a counterexample to the statement $10^a + 10^b = 10^{a+b}$.

    b. Are there any values of a and b that make the original statement true? If so, give an example.

    c. Rewrite the original statement so it is true.

Calculate according to the order of operations. 1-4

13. $10^3 + 48 \div 3 + 25$ **14.** $[(10 - 6) \cdot 3 + 12] \div 4$

Use the distributive property to find each sum or product mentally. 1-5

15. $374 \cdot 6 + 374 \cdot 4$ **16.** $7 \cdot 198$

Combine like terms, if possible.

17. $5x^2 + 3x + 7x^2$ **18.** $5x^2 + 3x + 7$ **19.** $5x^2 + 3x + 7x$

20. **Writing** Amy made a mistake when she rewrote this expression: $4 + 6(3x + 12) = 30x + 120$. Explain her mistake and how to correct it.

Use the diagram at the right. 1-6

21. Name two congruent polygons.

22. What kind of movement (or combination of movements) shows the trapezoids are congruent: *slide, turn,* or *flip*?

23. List three pairs of congruent sides.

24. Draw the shape a rubber band would make if placed around all three trapezoids together. Name the shape.

25. **Open-ended** Use variables to express the lengths of the sides of the shape in Question 24. Write an expression for the perimeter.

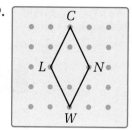

For Questions 26–29, do these things. 1-7

a. List all pairs of sides that are perpendicular.

b. List all pairs of sides that are parallel.

c. Tell what special name is given to the shape.

26.   **27.**   **28.** 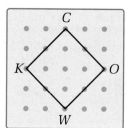   **29.**

30. **Self-evaluation** Make a list of four important ideas in this unit that you think will be the most useful to you. Explain why they are important.

31. **Group Activity** Work with another student. Use x-tiles and 1-tiles.

   a. Make several different rectangles with a perimeter of $4x + 8$.

   b. Sketch the rectangles you make. Label them to show why the perimeter is $4x + 8$.

   c. Give your partner a different variable expression and challenge your partner to find more than one kind of rectangle with that perimeter. (Be sure it can be done before you give the challenge.)

IDEAS AND (FORMULAS) $= x^2$

ALGEBRA

➤ You can use variables to describe some patterns. *(p. 10)*

➤ You evaluate a variable expression by substituting numbers for the variables and following the order of operations. *(pp. 12, 27)*

➤ You can use exponents to write expressions involving repeated multiplication. *(p. 19)*

➤ When you multiply powers of ten, add the exponents. *(p. 22)*

➤ When you divide powers of ten, subtract the exponents. *(p. 22)*

➤ The distributive property allows you to rewrite a product as a sum or difference. *(p. 32)*

$$a(b + c) = ab + ac$$
$$a(b - c) = ab - ac$$

➤ Like terms have the same variable part. Like terms can be combined. *(p. 33)*

GEOMETRY

➤ Congruent figures have the same size and shape. If you can slide, turn, or flip one shape onto another so that the shapes match, they are congruent. *(p. 38)*

➤ Some special names of polygons are triangle, quadrilateral, pentagon, hexagon, heptagon, and octagon. *(p. 39)*

➤ A shape has symmetry when it can be folded so that one half matches the other. The fold line is the line of symmetry. *(p. 45)*

➤ **Reasoning** Conjectures are statements based on experience. You can show that a conjecture is false by finding a counterexample. *(pp. 21, 22)*

⋯⋯⋯Key Terms

- **concept map** (p. 5)
- **evaluate** (p. 12)
- **power** (p. 19)
- **conjecture** (p. 21)
- **distributive property** (p. 32)
- **like terms** (p. 33)
- **quadrilateral** (p. 39)
- **congruent sides** (p. 40)
- **equilateral** (p. 44)
- **right triangle** (p. 44)
- **parallel** (p. 44)
- **rhombus** (p. 45)

- **variable** (p. 10)
- **substitute** (p. 12)
- **base** (p. 19)
- **counterexample** (p. 22)
- **term** (p. 33)
- **congruent** (p. 38)
- **vertex** (p. 40)
- **corresponding vertices** (p. 40)
- **isosceles** (p. 44)
- **right angle** (p. 44)
- **parallelogram** (p. 45)
- **symmetry** (p. 45)

- **variable expression** (p. 10)
- **factor** (p. 19)
- **exponent** (p. 19)
- **order of operations** (p. 26)
- **coefficient** (p. 33)
- **polygon** (p. 39)
- **side** (p. 40)
- **corresponding sides** (p. 40)
- **scalene** (p. 44)
- **perpendicular** (p. 44)
- **kite** (p. 45)
- **line of symmetry** (p. 45)

2

Using Measures and Equations

Did you know that Americans eat about 100 acres of pizza each day? That is enough pizza to carpet just about all the floors in all 110 stories of Chicago's Sears Tower. In order to understand the magnitude of very large or very small counts and measures, you can relate them to something whose size you know.

Magnitude

Magnitude is size:

How **far**? How **deep**?
How **strong**? How **loud**?
How **fast**?

$$1.86 \times 10^5 \text{ mi/s}$$

Writers of songs and stories often make comparisons to help you understand measures . . . the corn is as HIGH as an elephant's eye . . . as *light* as a feather . . . so **HOT** you can fry an egg on it . . . so **noisy** I can't hear myself think!

compare

Iowa - Corn Capital of the World

Theme Poster Contest

Your group project is to create a poster that presents interesting numerical facts in ways that make them easier to understand.

Your poster should have a theme. You may choose a topic from another class or from any field that you like.

When it is finished, your poster should display four numerical facts presented in interesting ways, four questions that can be answered using the numerical facts, and an equation that can be solved to find another interesting fact.

To decide how well you explained magnitudes, hold a class contest. Display all the posters in your classroom. The class will judge all the posters on standards you have chosen in advance.

←—If all Earth's water fit inside a one gallon jug, the available fresh water would equal just over a tablespoon, which is less than 0.5% of the total.

Sun   ⊙— Earth

How **much** of the world's oxygen do the rain forests in Brazil produce?

How SMALL is the amoeba you read about in biology class?

Scientists put magnitude········ in perspective:

. . . if the SUN were the size of a basketball, EARTH would be the size of a *grain of sand* . . .

astronomy

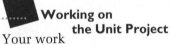

Unit Project 2

Here are some ideas to help you get started on your project.

☞ With the whole class, create an evaluation sheet for the posters. Be sure to rate how well they help people understand the magnitude of each fact on the display. Decide whether you want to rate other factors such as interest level, humor, or creativity.

☞ Work in a group of three students to create your theme poster.

☞ With your group, choose a theme for your poster. Brainstorm topics that use very small and very large numbers. You could look at your school from the microscopic level and from miles away.

☞ Discuss how you might add interest to your poster by using three-dimensional elements, such as a roll-out number line or different-sized measuring cups.

Can We Talk

Magnitude

➤ Favorite pizza toppings include curry in Pakistan, eel and squid in Japan, shrimp and pineapple in Australia, and coconut in Costa Rica. What three toppings do you think are the most popular in the United States?

➤ Americans eat about 251,800,000 pounds of pepperoni a year. This is roughly the same weight as 21,000 elephants! Make another comparison to describe this amount.

➤ In 1997, 83.8 million tons of paper was thrown away in the United States. What are some comparisons you can make to help you understand how big 83.8 million tons is?

➤ Suppose the distance from your home to your school were the length of a one-foot ruler. What would model the distance from your home to the nearest shopping mall?

➤ About how long would it take you to walk from one end of your town or city to the other?

Working on the Unit Project

Your work in Unit 2 will help you create your theme poster.

Related Exercises:

Section 2-1, Exercise 42
Section 2-2, Exercise 63
Section 2-3, Exercise 55
Section 2-4, Exercise 29
Section 2-5, Exercise 40
Section 2-6, Exercise 39
Section 2-7, Exercise 37
Section 2-8, Exercise 32
Section 2-9, Exercises 55–57

Alternative Projects p. 119

Numbers and Estimates

figures in the CROWD

Focus

See different ways that numbers are used and tell whether an estimate of a population or distance is reasonable or likely.

Talk it Over

1. Without counting, guess whether the number of people in the photograph is in the *tens, hundreds, thousands,* or *millions.*

2. Describe a method for estimating the number of people.

3. Use your method to estimate the number of people.

4. How does your estimate compare with your guess in question 1?

5. Can you use your method to estimate the number of hairs on your head? the size of an audience in a theater with you? a city population? How?

You see many types of numbers used in everyday life. Negative numbers are used for cold temperatures. Decimals are used to identify library books. Numbers can be used to identify, order, count, and measure. For example:

A wheelchair racer wearing the number 806 finishes first out of about 8 wheelchair racers in a 800 m race.

Numbers used for identifying and ordering are exact.

IDENTIFY
The number 806 identifies the racer.

ORDER
The number *first* tells you in what position the racer finished.

Numbers used as counts and measures can be estimates.

COUNT
The number 8 tells you about how many racers there were.

MEASURE
The number 800 in the phrase *800 m* tells you the length of the race.

6. Give some examples of how a fraction, a decimal, and a negative number are used in your everyday life.

For questions 7–9, tell whether each number could be *estimated*, or whether it must be *exact*. Give a reason for your choice.

7. a student's school identification number

8. the population of a state capital

9. the length of time it takes to read a book

10. Look at the size of the group in the photograph on page 57. About how many groups of this size would make a total of one billion people?

11. Guess whether the number of math books that could be stacked in your classroom is in the *hundreds, thousands, millions,* or *billions*. Then explain how you could estimate this number.

The world's population in 1998 was about 5.9 billion.

The air distance from New York City to Seattle, Washington, is 2409 mi.

The maximum legal capacity of the Pasadena Rose Bowl is 93,000.

The population of the United States in 1998 was about 270 million.

The population of New York City in 1998 was about 7.4 million. It was the largest city in the United States at that time.

Estimating by Making Comparisons

Sometimes you cannot see what you want to count or measure. You need to estimate by making comparisons using facts like those at the left.

Sample 1

Estimate whether each value is in the *hundreds, thousands, millions,* or *billions*.

a. the population of Los Angeles, California

b. attendance at the Super Bowl

Sample Response

Use facts from your experience or the list above to help you estimate.

a. Los Angeles is a very large city, like New York City. Its population is probably in the millions.

b. The Super Bowl is held in large stadiums, such as the Rose Bowl, and is generally well attended. Attendance at the Super Bowl is probably in the thousands.

12. Suppose you want to know what percent of the world's population in 1998 was the United States' population. What two facts can help you find this number? Are they included in the list of facts on page 58?

13. Estimate whether the air distance in miles from Portland, Maine, to Portland, Oregon, is in the *hundreds, thousands, millions,* or *billions.*

······► **Now you are ready for:**
Exs. 1–18 on pp. 60–61

Estimating Probabilities

You can use your experience to help you estimate the probability that an event will happen. The probability of an event happening is a number from 0 to 1.

Sample 2

Writing Use a number anywhere on the scale below to estimate the probability that it will rain during your school's next outdoor sports event. Give a reason for your answer.

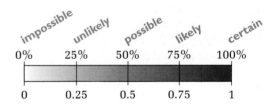

Sample Response

Use facts from your experience to help you estimate.

Meilin's answer:

"It doesn't rain much here in Los Angeles. I estimate a 25% chance of rain."

Jason's answer:

"Our school has a track meet tomorrow. The weather report said that the probability of rain tomorrow is 60%."

14. Use the scale in Sample 2. Estimate the probability that it will rain during your school's next outdoor sports event. Give a reason for your answer.

15. Use the weather map. Is the probability of rain in the Northwest more likely to be 0.1 or 0.8?

Discrete and Continuous Quantities

Continuous → Quantities that are measured are **continuous,** such as the temperature of water as it is heated from 60°F to boiling. As water is heated, it does not jump in temperature from 60°F to 61°F. It takes on every temperature between 60°F and 61°F.

Discrete → Quantities that are counted are **discrete,** such as the number of people entering a library. If you were counting, there would not be a person between the 60th person and the 61st person.

Talk it Over

Classify each quantity as *continuous* or *discrete*.

16. the water level in a sink as it is being filled

17. the speed of a car driven from your home to a shopping mall

18. the goals scored during each soccer game of the season

19. Classify each quantity in questions 16–18 as a *count* or *measure*.

Look Back

Describe how you could estimate the number of people in a crowded room if you were in the room. Then describe how you could do the estimating if you were nowhere near the room.

······➤ Now you are ready for:
Exs. 19–42 on pp. 62–63

2-1 Exercises and Problems

1. **Career** Medical technicians use *petri dishes* to grow bacteria.

   a. Without counting any bacteria, guess whether the number of bacteria in the petri dish is in the *tens, hundreds, thousands,* or *millions.*

   b. Describe a method for estimating the number of bacteria.

   c. Use your method to estimate the number of bacteria.

   d. How does your estimate compare with your guess in part (a)?

For Exercises 2–4, guess whether each number is in the *hundreds, thousands, millions,* or *billions*. Then estimate each number. Describe your method.

2. the number of printed letters, numbers, and symbols on this page

3. the number of photographs in this textbook

4. the number of tennis balls that would fill a bathtub

5. **Writing** Write one or two sentences about your school using numbers to identify, order, count, and measure. Tell the category of each number.

Estimate whether each value is in the *hundreds, thousands, millions,* or *billions*.

6. the population of Chicago, Illinois

7. the air distance in miles from Washington, D.C., to Seattle, Washington

8. the population of Mexico City, Mexico

9. the number of people in the crowd for Martin Luther King's "I have a dream" speech

10. the attendance at a sold-out rock concert

connection to **GEOGRAPHY**

Reading **For Exercises 11–16, use the facts on page 58.**

11. In 1998, was the population of North America and South America *more than* or *less than* 300 million?

12. Is the air distance from San Francisco, California, to Salt Lake City, Utah, *more than* or *less than* 1500 mi?

13. Is it *reasonable* or *unreasonable* to say that the population of Los Angeles, California, in 1998 was about 10 million? Explain.

14. Is it *reasonable* or *unreasonable* to say that the population of Europe in 1998 was about 3 billion? Explain.

15. In 1998, the population of China was about 21% of the world's population. What was the approximate population of China in 1998?

16. About what percent of the world's population in 1998 was the United States' population?

17. If 10 adults are standing in an elevator and a sign says "maximum capacity 4000 lb," should they be concerned?

18. **Research** Estimate the number of freshmen in your school. Do some research to check your estimate.

BY THE WAY...

On August 28, 1963, Martin Luther King, Jr., gave his "I have a dream" speech in Washington, D.C. He later received the Nobel Prize for Peace for his role in the civil-rights movement.

2-1 Numbers and Estimates

Writing Use a number anywhere on the scale below to estimate the probability of each event. Give a reason for your answer.

19. You will have pizza for breakfast on some day this year.

20. It will rain one day next week.

21. You will find a new friend this month.

22. A woman will win the next presidential election in the United States.

23. The sun will rise tomorrow.

24. Cats will learn to fly in the year 2020.

For Exercises 25–28, classify each quantity as *continuous* or *discrete*.

25. the population of your school

26. the height above the ground of a wheelchair being rolled up a ramp

27. the amount of fuel in a taxi's gasoline tank

28. the number of pieces of fruit sold at a market each day

29. **Open-ended** Give your own examples of one quantity that is continuous and one quantity that is discrete.

connection to **BUSINESS EDUCATION**

Many store products are identified by a number called a *Uniform Product Code* (UPC). A UPC is printed on a package in two ways: as a number and as a set of vertical lines called a *bar code*.

Stores use scanners to read bar codes. A computer connected to the scanner calculates the check digit to be sure that the other digits scanned accurately. The computer also searches its files for the price of the product and subtracts the item from the inventory.

7 26284 12501 6

broadly classifies the product

identifies the manufacturer

gives information about the product

the check digit

Here is how the computer finds the check digit for the UPC shown above, 7 26284 12501 6.

1. Add the digits in the odd positions. ⟶ $7 + 6 + 8 + 1 + 5 + 1 = 28$

2. Multiply the answer in step 1 by 3. ⟶ $28 \cdot 3 = 84$

3. Add the digits in the first five even positions. ⟶ $2 + 2 + 4 + 2 + 0 = 10$

4. Add the results of steps 2 and 3. ⟶ $84 + 10 = 94$

5. Subtract the units digit of the answer in step 4 from the number 10. ⟶ $10 - 4 = 6$ ⟵ The result is the check digit.

Calculate the value of the check digit. Is the check digit shown correct? Write *Yes* or *No*.

30.

9 780395 421697 9

31.

0 24182 18145 5

32.

0 70735 95500 5

33. **a.** **Research** Find UPCs on three different grocery-store items from one manufacturer.

   b. What is the code that identifies this manufacturer?

   c. Using a check digit of 2, make up a valid UPC for a product made by this manufacturer.

34. **Writing** Describe how bar codes can help a store manager be sure there are enough items in the store to meet customers' needs.

35. **Open-ended** Every half hour for six hours record a number you see being used. Tell whether the number is used for *identifying, ordering, counting,* or *measuring.* Also tell whether the quantity is *discrete* or *continuous.* What types of numbers appear most often?

36. Make a concept map that summarizes the ideas you have learned in this section. *(Section 1-1)*

Write the prime factorization of each number. *(Toolbox Skill 7)*

37. 42   **38.** 36   **39.** 98   **40.** 125

41. Graph the numbers 4, −7, 3, 0, −5, and 7 on a number line. What do you notice about 7 and −7? *(Toolbox Skill 2)*

Working on the Unit Project

42. **Research** Look in books, magazines, and newspapers for interesting numerical facts about the topic you choose for your theme poster. Write down at least 10 facts. Be sure to include counts, measurements, and percents.

Using Negative Numbers

PLUSES *and* minuses

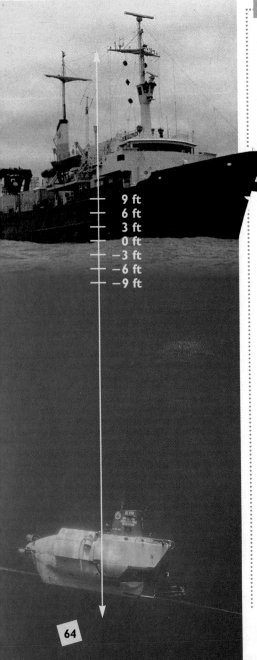

9 ft
6 ft
3 ft
0 ft
−3 ft
−6 ft
−9 ft

Talk it Over

1. Describe how negative numbers are used in the photo of Atlantis II and DSV Alvin. What are two other uses of negative numbers?

2. Where on the vertical number line at the left would you place −8?

3. The **absolute value** of a number is its distance from zero on a number line. You write *the absolute value of −3* as $|-3|$. An absolute value is a positive number or zero.

$$|-3| = 3 \qquad |0| = 0 \qquad |3| = 3$$

3 and −3 are located three units from 0. The absolute value of 3 is 3 and the absolute value of −3 is also 3.

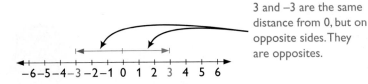

−6 −5 −4 −3 −2 −1 0 1 2 3 4 5 6

a. Read aloud and simplify $|12|$.

b. Read aloud and simplify $|-4|$.

4. What two numbers have an absolute value of 10?

5. Two numbers are **opposites** if they are the same distance from zero on a number line, but on opposite sides of zero.

3 and −3 are the same distance from 0, but on opposite sides. They are opposites.

−6 −5 −4 −3 −2 −1 0 1 2 3 4 5 6

What is the opposite of 7? of −2? of 0?

6. The number −5 is read *negative 5* or *the opposite of 5*. How can the number −12 be read?

7. The +/− key on a calculator gives the opposite of the number on the display. What is the result of pressing this key if the display shows 15? if the display shows −27?

(Do) *you remember how to operate with negative numbers?*

- **Materials: calculators**
- **Work with another student.**

Set A	Set B
a) 12 + 8	**a)** −12 + (−8)
b) 6 + 7	**b)** −6 + (−7)

Set C	Set D
a) −12 + 8	**a)** 12 + (−8)
b) −6 + 7	**b)** 6 + (−7)

① Use a calculator to simplify each expression in Sets A−D.

② Look for patterns in step 1 to figure out the rules your calculator follows to find the sum of two numbers when one or both are negative.

Set E	Set F
a) 42 − 25	**a)** −14.9 − 6.4
b) 42 + (−25)	**b)** −14.9 + (−6.4)

Set G	Set H
a) 12.3 − (−34.9)	**a)** −6 − (−4)
b) 12.3 + 34.9	**b)** −6 + 4

③ Compare the expressions in Set E. Discuss how they are alike and how they are different. Use a calculator to simplify each expression in Set E. How do the results compare?

④ Repeat step 3 for Sets F−H.

⑤ Use the results of steps 3 and 4. Replace the _?_ with the correct word.

> Subtracting a number gives the same result as adding the _?_ of that number.

Set J	Set K
a) 6 · 3	**a)** (−6)(−3)
b) 50 · 5	**b)** (−50)(−5)

Set L	Set M
a) (−6)(3)	**a)** 6 · (−3)
b) (−50)(5)	**b)** 50 · (−5)

⑥ Use a calculator to simplify each expression in Sets J−M.

⑦ Look for patterns in step 6 to figure out the rules that the calculator follows to find the product of two numbers when one or both are negative.

⑧ Replace multiplication with division in each expression in Sets J−M. Use a calculator to simplify each expression.

⑨ Look for patterns in step 8 to figure out the rules that the calculator follows to find the quotient of two numbers when one or both are negative.

Talk it Over

Now you are ready for:
Exs. 1–32 on pp. 67–69

Simplify.

8. −15 + 15 **9.** 8 + (−8) **10.** −200 + 200

11. What do you think is the sum of any pair of opposites?

Evaluating Algebraic Expressions Involving Negative Numbers

You need to be careful with negative numbers when you evaluate expressions. You may want to use parentheses to do this.

Sample 1

The expression $-x$ is read *the opposite of x*. Evaluate $-x$ for each value of x.

a. $x = 1.3$ b. $x = -5$ c. $x = 0$

Sample Response

Substitute.

a. $-x = -(1.3) = -1.3$

Ask yourself, what is the opposite of 1.3?

b. $-x = -(-5) = 5$

c. $-x = -(0) = 0$

Sample 2

Evaluate each expression for the given values of the variables.

a. $-x + 4$ when $x = -9$

b. $m^2 + 2n$ when $m = -8$ and $n = -12$

Sample Response

a. $-x + 4 = -(-9) + 4$ ← Substitute -9 for x.

         $= 9 + 4$ ← Simplify.

         $= 13$

       Substitute -8 for m and -12 for n.

b. $m^2 + 2n = (-8)^2 + 2(-12)$

         $= 64 + (-24)$ ← $(-8)^2 = (-8)(-8) = 64$

         $= 40$

TECHNOLOGY NOTE

Use this key sequence to calculate $(-8)^2$ on a calculator:

8 [+/−] [x^2] → 64

Talk it Over

12. Evaluate $-1 \cdot x$ when $x = 1.3$, $x = -5$, and $x = 0$. Compare the results with those in Sample 1. What do you observe? Generalize your observations.

13. Suppose the expression in part (b) of Sample 2 were $m^2 - 2n$. What would the answer be?

14. Which of the samples so far can you do using mental math? Which would you prefer to do with a calculator? Why?

The type of wax you put on cross-country skis depends on the temperature of the snow. Suppose the snow is fine-grained and its temperature is −4°F. Is this the correct wax to use?

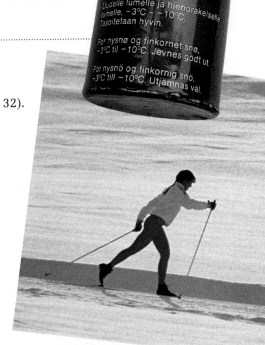

Sample Response

Find the equivalent Celsius temperature for a temperature of −4°F. To convert a Fahrenheit temperature (F) to the equivalent Celsius temperature (C), use the expression $\frac{5}{9}(F - 32)$.

$\frac{5}{9}(F - 32) = \frac{5}{9}(-4 - 32)$ ⟵ Substitute −4 for F.

$= \frac{5}{9}(-36)$ ⟵ First work inside the parentheses. Then multiply.

$= -20$ ⟵ Recall: $\frac{5}{9} \cdot \frac{-36}{1} = -20$

A temperature of −4°F is equivalent to a temperature of −20°C. The wax shown is for a temperature between −3°C and −10°C. This is not the correct wax to use.

Look Back

Summarize how to do operations with negative numbers.

⋯▶ **Now you are ready for:**
Exs. 33–63 on pp. 69–70

2-2 Exercises and Problems

Find the absolute value and the opposite of each number.

1. −17   **2.** 2.34   **3.** $-\frac{1}{2}$ **4.** $6\frac{2}{3}$ **5.** −3,785,200

Reading For Exercises 6–11, tell whether each statement is *True* or *False*. If the statement is false, give a counterexample.

6. The opposite of every positive number is negative.

7. The opposite of every negative number is negative.

8. The absolute value of a positive number is always negative.

9. The absolute value of a negative number is always positive.

10. The absolute value of zero is zero.

11. $|x| = x$ for every value of x.

12. Predict what you will get if you enter 8 [+/−] [+/−] on a calculator. Then try it. What does this tell you about the opposite of the opposite of a number?

Use the result of step 5 of the Exploration on page 65. Replace each ? with the correct number.

13. $86 - 53 = 86 +$?   **14.** $-19 - (-25) = -19 +$?

Student Resources Toolbox
p. 640 *Integers*

Simplify.

15. $|-18|$ **16.** $|0|$ **17.** $|24|$

18. $-17.4 + (-2)$ **19.** $-48 + 29$ **20.** $16 - (-4.5)$

21. $-120 - 60$ **22.** $5.78 + (-2.4)$ **23.** $12 \cdot (-2.5)$

24. $-7.2 \div (-8)$ **25.** $-9 \div 2$ **26.** $(-100)(-21)$

27. **Writing** You can do many calculations faster in your head than on a calculator. Which of the expressions in Exercises 18–26 do you think you can do as easily in your head as on a calculator? Pick two of them and explain how you could simplify them in your head.

connection to **GEOGRAPHY**

DEATH VALLEY

For Exercises 28–30, use the diagram. The elevations in the diagram are given in relation to sea level.

28. Find the difference between the elevation of Telescope Peak and the elevation of the lowest point in Death Valley.

29. Official temperatures are no longer recorded at Furnace Creek. Instead, they are measured at the Death Valley park headquarters nearby. What is the difference in elevation between these two sites?

30. It is estimated that temperatures in Death Valley are 3°F to 5°F cooler for every 1000 ft you go up.

    a. Estimate what the temperature on Telescope Peak might have been when the record high temperature was recorded at Furnace Creek. Give your answer as a range of temperatures.

    b. The average temperature in Death Valley in the month of January is 52.0°F. Estimate the average temperature on Telescope Peak in the month of January. Give your answer as a range of temperatures.

31. A contestant on a television game show has a score of −$200 and then correctly answers a question worth $500. What is the contestant's new score?

32. Timmy is playing a card game with his grandfather. Timmy has a score of −15 and his grandfather has a score of 45. A score of 500 wins. How many points does Timmy need in order to win?

Simplify. Show every step.

33. $3 + 18 \div 2 \cdot (-3)$

34. $14 - 5(-7 + 9)$

35. $-9 \div 2 \cdot 10 \div 3$

36. $2.4 + (0.6)(-0.2) - 6$

37. $\dfrac{-20 - 5}{2}$

38. $\dfrac{-9 + 15}{3 \cdot (-2)}$

Evaluate each expression for the given values of the variables.

39. $-n$ when $n = 12.5$

40. $-p + 1.8$ when $p = -3.2$

41. $k + k$ when $k = -8$

42. $xy + 3$ when $x = -5$ and $y = 10$

43. $\dfrac{a + b}{2}$ when $a = -9$ and $b = 3$

44. $-4.9t + at$ when $t = 10$ and $a = 50$

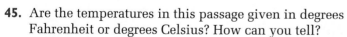

connection to **LITERATURE**

In Jack London's *To Build a Fire*, a logger's life is endangered by the extreme temperature in the Yukon.

> **To Build a Fire**
>
> At the man's heels trotted a dog, a big native husky, the proper wolf dog....The animal was depressed by the tremendous cold....Its instinct told it a truer tale than was told to the man by the man's judgment. In reality, it was not merely colder than fifty below zero....It was seventy-five below zero. Since the freezing point is thirty-two above zero, it meant that one hundred and seven degrees of frost obtained. The dog did not know anything about thermometers....But the brute had its instinct....The dog had learned fire, and it wanted fire...

45. Are the temperatures in this passage given in degrees Fahrenheit or degrees Celsius? How can you tell?

46. Write each temperature in this passage using symbols instead of words.

47. How many degrees below freezing is the temperature?

48. Convert the temperatures in this passage to the other temperature scale as in Sample 3.

Here are two formulas to convert temperatures between Celsius (*C*) and Fahrenheit (*F*).

$$C = \frac{5}{9}(F - 32) \qquad F = \frac{9}{5}C + 32$$

Copy and complete the table of equivalent temperatures.

	°**F**	°**C**
49. Normal body temperature	98.6	?
50. Temperature at which water freezes	32	?
51. Average night temperature on the moon's surface	?	−153
52. Record low temperature for Antarctica (recorded on July 21, 1983)	?	−89.2

53. **Open-ended** Choose two temperatures that you come across in your daily life to add to your table in Exercises 49–52. Write the temperatures in degrees Fahrenheit and degrees Celsius.

Ongoing **ASSESSMENT**

54. **Group Activity** There is one very cold temperature where the temperature in degrees Fahrenheit equals the temperature in degrees Celsius. Work with another student using trial and error to find this temperature.

Review **PREVIEW**

For Exercises 55–57, estimate whether each value is in the *hundreds, thousands, millions,* or *billions*. (Section 2-1)

55. the population of California

56. the number of people at a World Series game

57. the distance in miles from New York City to Phoenix, Arizona

58. Replace each ? with the correct term. (Section 1-3)

In the power 10^{31}, 10 is the ? and 31 is the ?. The number 31 in 10^{31} tells you that 10 is used as a ? 31 times.

Write each expression as a power of ten. (Section 1-3)

59. $10^2 \cdot 10^{12}$ **60.** $10^{15} \cdot 10^{25}$ **61.** $\dfrac{10^{20}}{10^5}$ **62.** $\dfrac{10^{36}}{10^9}$

Working on the Unit Project

63. **Group Activity** Share the facts you have collected with your group. Do your facts include a negative number? If not, discuss whether one can reasonably be found in a fact about your theme. Plan to include a negative number on your theme poster if you can.

Exploring Scientific Notation

SHORThand for Numbers

Focus

Read and write numbers in scientific notation and recognize whether a result in scientific notation on a calculator is reasonable.

EXPLORATION

(What) *do negative powers of 10 mean?*

- **Materials: scientific calculators**
- **Work in a group of two or three students.**

① Copy the table onto your paper.

② Use the power key, y^x or x^y, on your calculator to complete the decimal column.

③ Complete the last lines of the fraction column.

④ Look for patterns in the data in the table. Write down the observations made by people in your group.

⑤ Make conjectures about the relationship between the exponent of a power of 10 and the equivalent decimal or fraction.

Talk it Over

1. a. How many zeros are there in the decimal notation for the power 10^6?

   b. How many zeros are there to the right of the decimal point in the decimal notation for 10^{-6}?

   c. How many decimal places are there in the decimal notation for 10^{-6}?

2. The power 10^{-6} can be written as the fraction $\dfrac{1}{1,000,000}$ or $\dfrac{1}{10^6}$. Write 10^{-12} as a fraction in two different ways.

Scientific Notation

Light travels about five trillion, nine hundred billion miles in a year! Scientists work with very small and very large numbers that have many digits. To save space and make it easier to compare numbers, scientists write them in a shorter form called **scientific notation.**

$$5,900,000,000,000 = 5.9 \times 10^{12}$$

a number that is at least one but less than 10 ⟶

⟵ a power of 10

multiplied by

Sample 1

Write each number in scientific notation.

a. the number of seconds in a week: 604,800

b. the thickness of a piece of paper in inches: 0.0039

Sample Response

a. The leading digit is 6. It is in the hundred thousands' place.

$604,800 = 6.048$ hundred thousands

$$= 6.048 \times 100,000$$

$$= 6.048 \times 10^5$$

b. The first digit that is not zero is 3. It is in the thousandths' place.

$0.0039 = 3.9$ thousandths

$$= 3.9 \times 0.001$$

$$= 3.9 \times 10^{-3}$$

Sample 2

Write each number in decimal notation.

a. the average radius of Earth in meters: 6.38×10^6

b. the thickness of a wire on a computer chip in meters: 3×10^{-6}

Sample Response

$6.38 \times 10^6 = 6.38 \times 1,000,000$

a. $6.38 \times 10^6 = 6,380,000$

Multiplying by 1,000,000 moves the decimal point 6 places to the right.

$3 \times 10^{-6} = 3 \times 0.000001$

b. $3 \times 10^{-6} = 0.000003$

Multiplying by 0.000001 moves the decimal point 6 places to the left.

····▶ Now you are ready for:
Exs. 1–26 on pp. 75–76

Talk it Over

Write each number in scientific notation. Explain your steps.

3. 34,000   **4.** 0.00000219

Write each number in decimal notation and read it in words.

5. 9.3×10^6 **6.** 4.8×10^{-4}

Is each expression written in scientific notation? If not, write it in scientific notation.

7. 0.4×10^{15} **8.** 12.7×10^{-6}

Scientific Notation on a Calculator

Results found by calculators and computers are often in scientific notation. Calculator displays have a limited number of digits. When a result is too big, some calculators display the result in scientific notation without showing the base 10.

Sample 3

An audio CD contains about 3.46 million bits of information for each second of recording time. About how many bits are needed for a six-minute song?

Sample Response

Multiply by the number of seconds in six minutes.

360 $\times$ 3,460,000 $=$ ⟶ **1.2456 09** ◀—— This means
$1.2456 \times 10^9 = 1,245,600,000.$

Check Estimate to see if the calculator result is reasonable.

$360 \cdot 3.46 \text{ million} \approx 400 \cdot 3,000,000$ ◀—— Round each number to the leading digit. The symbol $\approx$ means "is approximately equal to."

Write each number in scientific notation. $\approx (4 \times 10^2)(3 \times 10^6)$

$\approx 12 \times 10^8$ ◀—— Use the product of powers rule.
$10^2 \cdot 10^6 = 10^{2+6} = 10^8$

Watch Out!
Do more than add the powers of ten to see if a result is reasonable. Look at the product of the leading digits too.

$\approx 1.2 \times 10^9$

The power of ten is the same for 1,200,000,000 and 1,245,600,000. ✔ The calculator result is reasonable.

About 1.25 billion bits on a CD are needed for a six-minute song.

distance from the sun to Pluto = 4 billion miles

Light travels four times this distance in one day.

Sample 4

Light travels about 5.9×10^{12} mi in a year. About how far does light travel in a day?

Sample Response

Divide by the number of days in a year.

5.9 [EE] 12 [÷] 365 [=] ⟶ | 1.6164 10 |

↑
This means
$1.6164 \times 10^{10} = 16{,}164{,}000{,}000.$

Check Estimate to see if the calculator result is reasonable.

$$\frac{5.9 \times 10^{12}}{365} \approx \frac{6 \times 10^{12}}{4 \times 10^2} \quad\longleftarrow\quad \text{Write numbers in scientific notation and round to the leading digit.}$$

$$\approx \frac{6}{4} \times \frac{10^{12}}{10^2}$$

$$\approx 1.5 \times 10^{10} \quad\longleftarrow\quad \frac{10^{12}}{10^2} = 10^{12-2} = 10^{10}$$

The power of ten is the same for 15,000,000,000 and 16,164,000,000. ✔

The calculator result is reasonable.

Light travels about 16 billion miles in a day.

Talk it Over

9. In Sample 3, suppose you want to know how many bits of information are on a particular CD. What other information do you need?

Replace each ? with the correct power of ten.

10. $0.5(1.25 \times 10^6) \approx (5 \times 10^{-1})(1 \times 10^6)$

$$\approx 5 \times 10^{-1+6}$$

$$\approx 5 \times \underline{\ ?\ }$$

11. $\dfrac{2.3 \times 10^3}{76{,}000} \approx \dfrac{2 \times 10^3}{8 \times 10^4}$

$$\approx 0.25 \times 10^{3-4}$$

$$\approx 0.25 \times \underline{\ ?\ }$$

$$\approx 2.5 \times \underline{\ ?\ }$$

12. What do you get when you enter 10 [yˣ] 4 [=] on your calculator? What do you get when you enter 10 [EE] 4? Why are the results different?

TECHNOLOGY NOTE

Some calculators and computers use a letter E between the decimal and the exponent.

| 1.6164 E10 |

E stands for exponent.

RULES OF EXPONENTS

In Unit 1 you worked with these rules of exponents.

Product of Powers Rule: $10^a \cdot 10^b = 10^{a+b}$

Quotient of Powers Rule: $\dfrac{10^a}{10^b} = 10^{a-b}$

In the Exploration you discovered these rules of exponents.

Zero Exponent Rule: $10^0 = 1$

Negative Exponent Rule: $10^{-n} = \dfrac{1}{10^n}$

Look Back

You have now worked with powers of ten with exponents that are positive integers, negative integers, or zero.

Choose values for a, b, and n that are positive integers. Give an example of the product of powers rule, the quotient of powers rule, and the negative exponent rule.

Now you are ready for: Exs. 27–55 on pp. 76–78

2-3 Exercises and Problems

1. **Reading** A number written in scientific notation has a specific form. What is that form?

2. **a.** Describe two methods for finding the decimal notation for 10^7.

   b. Write 10^7 in decimal notation.

3. **a.** Describe a method for finding the decimal notation for 10^{-7}.

   b. Write 10^{-7} in decimal notation.

Tell whether each power of 10 is *less than*, *greater than*, or *equal to* 1.

4. $10^3 \underline{\ ?\ } 1$

5. $10^0 \underline{\ ?\ } 1$

6. $10^{-8} \underline{\ ?\ } 1$

7. $10^1 \underline{\ ?\ } 1$

8. $10^{-1} \underline{\ ?\ } 1$

9. $10^{-10} \underline{\ ?\ } 1$

10. Use the results of Exercises 4–9. Describe how you can use the exponent of a power of 10 to tell whether the number is greater than or less than 1.

Write each number in exponential notation using a base of 10.

11. 10,000,000,000

12. 0.0001

13. 1

14. 0.0000001

15. Write each answer to Exercises 12 and 14 as a fraction with an exponent.

Write each number in scientific notation.

16. average radius of the sun: 695,000,000 m

17. an erg (a unit of energy): 0.0000000239 Cal

18. sound intensity of a normal conversation: 0.000001 W/m²

19. mass of propellant in a space shuttle solid rocket booster: 503,600 kg

For Exercises 20–26, use the diagram below. Write each number in decimal notation.

20. the diameter of a cell

21. the length of a pygmy shrew

22. the height of Mount Everest

23. the length of a common dolphin

24. the length of an ant

25. the length of a blue whale

cell
1×10^{-5} m

blue whale
(longest mammal)
2.6×10^1 m

Mount Everest
8.850×10^3 m

ant
4.2×10^{-3} m

Eastern
gray squirrel
2.5×10^{-1} m

| 10^{-5} | 10^{-4} | 10^{-3} | 10^{-2} | 10^{-1} | 10^0 | 10^1 | 10^2 | 10^3 |

paramecium
2.10×10^{-4} m

pygmy shrew
(smallest mammal)
4×10^{-2} m

common dolphin
2.2×10^0 m

soccer field
1×10^2 m

26. **Writing** About how many times larger than a common dolphin is a blue whale? Describe how the exponents of the powers of 10 help you make this type of comparison.

Match each key sequence with the correct calculator display.

27. 10 y^x 5 =

A. 50

E. 5 –10

28. 5 EE 10

B. 10 –5

F. –50

29. 10 y^x 5 +/– =

C. 100000

G. 0.00001

30. 5 EE 10 +/–

D. 5 10

Simplify. Write each answer in scientific notation.

31. $120(1.2 \times 10^8)$

32. $0.3(2.8 \times 10^6)$

33. $70(5.4 \times 10^{-9})$

34. $\dfrac{8.86 \times 10^7}{300}$

35. $\dfrac{7.2 \times 10^4}{36}$

36. $\dfrac{5.7 \times 10^2}{2000}$

37. **Writing** Explain how you could find the product $(3.4 \times 10^{15})(1.2 \times 10^{23})$ without using a calculator. Then write a key sequence you could use to find the product using a scientific calculator.

For Exercises 38–40, make a reasonable estimate of each answer. Then calculate a more precise answer. Write each answer in scientific notation, in decimal notation, and in words.

38. The United States Postal Service prints about 109.6 million stamps each day. How many stamps are printed in one year? in five years?

39. In 1999, Americans consumed about 634 hot dogs every second of the day in the United States. How many hot dogs were eaten in one day? in one year?

40. The United States Bureau of Engraving and Printing prints about 37 million new bills each day. How many new bills are printed in one year? in 10 years?

41. Light travels approximately 9.5×10^{15} m in one year. About how far does light travel in one day? in one minute? in one second?

42. **Chemistry** A scientist uses 1.2×10^{-5} L of an enzyme for one chemical reaction. The scientist wants to mix enough for 140 reactions. How much of the enzyme does the scientist need? Write your answer in scientific notation.

Sales of CD Recordings (1999)

Sales (millions): United States ≈ 940, United Kingdom ≈ 180, Japan ≈ 260

For Exercises 43–46, use the graph. Write each answer in scientific notation and in decimal notation.

43. About how many compact discs were sold in each country in 1999?

44. Suppose the average cost of a compact disc in the United States was $15 in 1999. About how much money was paid for compact discs in the United States in 1999?

45. About how many more compact discs were sold in the United States than in Japan in 1999?

46. About how many times more compact discs were sold in the United States than in the United Kingdom in 1999?

Ongoing **ASSESSMENT**

47. **Open-ended** Look through some newspapers and magazines. Find some examples of numbers that are written in scientific notation or that can be written more compactly using scientific notation.

Review **PREVIEW**

Simplify. *(Section 2-2)*

48. $|-1.8|$ 49. $-8 - 40$ 50. $-9.4 + 6.2$ 51. $-2 + 3(-4 + 6)$

Replace each ? with the correct number. *(Table of Measures, page 666)*

52. 2 ft = _?_ in.   53. 8 mm = _?_ cm   54. 6 m = _?_ cm

2 Working on the Unit Project

55. a. Group Activity Check your group's facts. Is any number so large that you should write it in scientific notation? Is any number so small that it has a negative exponent when written in scientific notation? If not, brainstorm some facts about your theme that would include very large or very small numbers.

b. Research Have each person in the group research one of the facts. Write the number in decimal notation and in scientific notation.

Unit 2 CHECKPOINT 1

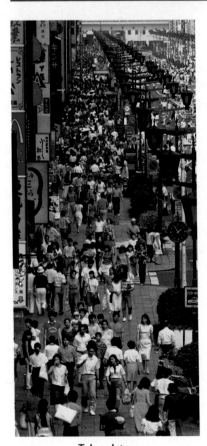

Tokyo, Japan

1. **Writing** Write about how you could estimate the number of kernels of popped popcorn that will fill a shoe box.

2. Estimate the number of people in the photograph. **2-1**

3. Tell whether the population of Tokyo, Japan, is in the *hundreds, thousands, millions,* or *billions.*

4. Is the population of Tokyo a continuous or discrete quantity?

5. **Writing** Use a number anywhere on the scale below to estimate the probability that it will snow in your city or town in February. Give a reason for your answer.

Evaluate each expression for the given values of the variables. **2-2**

6. $-a + b^2$ when $a = 9$ and $b = -4$

7. $xy + x$ when $x = -7$ and $y = -3$

Write each number in scientific notation. **2-3**

8. 0.000345   9. 26,710,000

10. Simplify $2500(3.2 \times 10^8)$. Write your answer in decimal notation.

Estimating Measures: Length and Area

Section

Focus
Estimate lengths, distances on a map, and areas.

MEASURING UP

Marisa Fuentes has students in her mathematics class from many different cultures. Some of the students are used to United States customary units of length. Others are used to metric units of length.

She had her students work in groups to make guides to units in these two systems of measurement.

GUIDE TO U.S. CUSTOMARY UNITS OF LENGTH

1 in. The length of the upper section of a thumb

1 ft The length of a shoe

1 yd The length of a step

1 mi The distance a person could walk in 20 minutes

GUIDE TO METRIC UNITS OF LENGTH

1 mm The thickness of the tip of a sharpened pencil

1 cm The width of a person's little fingertip

1 m The length of a big step

1 km The distance a person can walk in 12 minutes

Talk it Over

For questions 1–4, tell which length in each pair is greater.

1. 1 in., 1 mm
2. 1 in., 1 cm
3. 1 ft, 1 m
4. 1 mi, 1 km

5. Which length is greater, 1 yd or 1 m? How do you know?

6. The prefixes used in the metric system stand for powers of ten. For example, the prefix *milli-* means one thousandth, which is 10^{-3}.

   a. What does *centi-* mean? Which power of ten does it stand for?

   b. What does *kilo-* mean? Which power of ten does it stand for?

7. Estimate the length of 100 copies of this textbook laid end to end.

8. Estimate the height of the door to your classroom.

9. What units of length might a hairdresser, a carpenter, and a runner be good at estimating?

Estimating on a Map

Map scales and grid lines can help you estimate long distances and large areas.

Use the map to estimate the distance from Los Angeles to New York City to the nearest hundred miles.

Sample Response

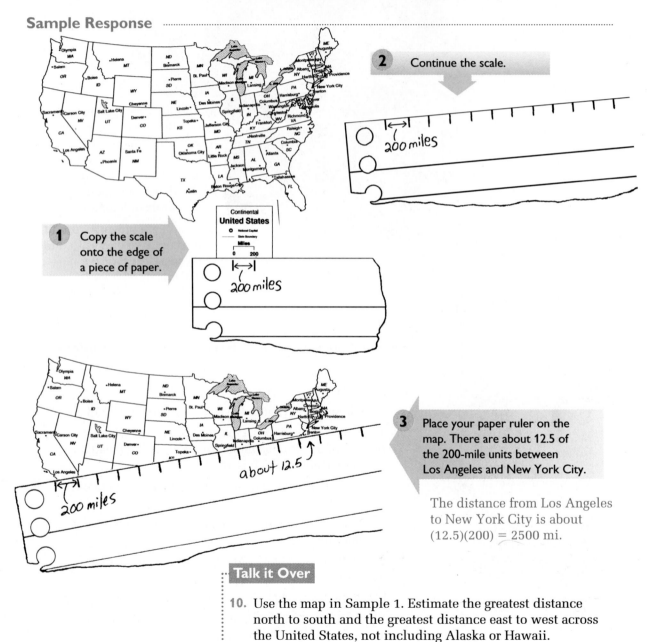

2 Continue the scale.

200 miles

1 Copy the scale onto the edge of a piece of paper.

Continental
United States
○ National Capital
— State Boundary
Miles
0   200

200 miles

3 Place your paper ruler on the map. There are about 12.5 of the 200-mile units between Los Angeles and New York City.

about 12.5

200 miles

The distance from Los Angeles to New York City is about $(12.5)(200) = 2500$ mi.

Talk it Over

10. Use the map in Sample 1. Estimate the greatest distance north to south and the greatest distance east to west across the United States, not including Alaska or Hawaii.

Use the map in Sample 1. Estimate the area of the state of Utah.

Sample Response

Problem Solving Strategy: Break the problem into parts

1 Make a sketch of Utah.

2 Draw a dashed line to split Utah into two rectangular areas.

3 Use the scale at the bottom of the map to estimate the dimensions of Utah. Then label your sketch.

4 Find each rectangular area.

Area of Utah = Area A + Area B

Use the formula
Area = length × width.

$$\approx (180)(80) + (300)(300)$$

$$\approx 14{,}400 + 90{,}000$$

$$\approx 104{,}400$$

Student Resources Toolbox
p. 658 *Perimeter, Area, Volume*

5 You can think about the units this way:

$$\text{mi} \times \text{mi} = \text{mi}^2.$$

The area of Utah is approximately 104,400 mi².

Talk it Over

11. Describe another method you could use to estimate the area of Utah in Sample 2.

12. a. About how many grid squares does the Great Salt Lake cover?

    b. Each grid square is 20 mi on a side. Use your answer to part (a) to estimate the area of the Great Salt Lake.

This photograph of the Great Salt Lake was taken by a satellite from a distance of 475 mi.

Symbols

The **line** shown is identified as $\overleftrightarrow{XY}$ or $\overleftrightarrow{YX}$. It goes on forever in two directions.

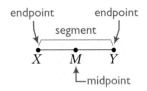

The part of the line with **endpoints** X and Y is the **segment** identified as $\overline{XY}$ or $\overline{YX}$. The symbol XY means **the length of $\overline{XY}$.**

Point M on $\overline{XY}$ is called the **midpoint** of $\overline{XY}$ because it divides the segment in half. Every segment has a midpoint, but a line does not.

Segments with equal measures are congruent segments. In the diagram, $\overline{XM} \cong \overline{MY}$.

Talk it Over

13. Explain what each of the symbols $\overleftrightarrow{AB}$, $\overline{AB}$, and AB represents in this diagram.

14. Estimate QP in inches.

Look Back

Give an everyday example of needing an exact length and an example of needing only an estimated length. Explain why the needs are different.

2-4 Exercises and Problems

1. **Reading** How does the information about lines and segments above lead you to the conclusion that you can measure a segment but not a line?

For Exercises 2–4, estimate each measure in both customary and metric units.

2. the width of this textbook

3. the length of each side of quadrilateral $QRST$

4. the length of your bedroom

5. a. **Research** Find out the lengths of the upper sections of the thumbs of at least five people, including one adult. (Measure to the nearest $\frac{1}{8}$ in.)

   b. Is there a length that appears most often?

   c. Whose length is the closest to one inch?

   d. Suppose the length of the upper section of your thumb is not exactly one inch. How could you use your measurement to estimate lengths in inches?

The map shows Australia.

6. Estimate the distance from Perth to Sydney.

7. Is 3500 km a reasonable estimate of the distance from Melbourne to Brisbane? Explain.

8. Estimate the area of Western Australia.

9. Each grid square is about 500 km on a side. Use the grid on the map to estimate the area of Australia.

10. **Writing** Roberto was reading about Australia. The magazine article said that the Great Sandy Desert and the Great Victoria Desert together covered 300,000 km². Roberto decided that the reported area was not reasonable, and that there must be a misprint in the article. Do you *agree* or *disagree*? Why?

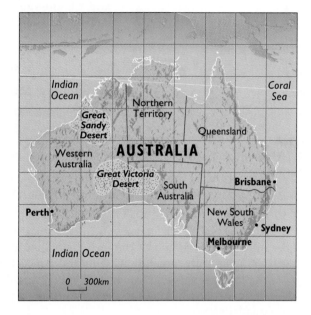

Average marriage ages

United States
Switzerland
Australia
Dominican Republic
Egypt

0   5   10   15   20   25   30
Age in years

■ bride   ■ groom

Use the double bar graph. Name each country described. Use the age scale to estimate the measure of each bar for that country.

11. the country where the average age of brides and grooms is the same

12. the country where the average age of grooms is less than the average age of brides

13. the country with the greatest difference between the average age of grooms and the average age of brides

14. Midori wants to cover one of her bedroom walls with posters. The wall is 10 ft wide by 8 ft high. She plans to use only posters that are 2 ft by 3 ft.

   a. What is the area of the wall? of a poster? Can Midori completely cover the wall without overlapping any posters? Why or why not?

   b. How many posters can Midori fit on her wall without any overlap if she buys only posters that are oriented vertically? horizontally?

   c. What combination of vertical and horizontal posters will fit on the wall and cover the most space without any overlap?

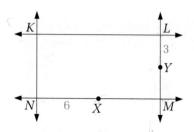

In the diagram, *KLMN* is a rectangle. *X* is the midpoint of $\overline{NM}$ and *Y* is the midpoint of $\overline{LM}$. For Exercises 15–19, tell whether each statement is *True* or *False*.

15. $XM = 6$ **16.** $KN = 2 \cdot YM$ **17.** $KL = \frac{1}{2} \cdot XM$

18. $\overline{KL}$ is perpendicular to $\overline{NM}$ **19.** $\overleftrightarrow{KN}$ is parallel to $\overleftrightarrow{LM}$

20. Find the perimeter of rectangle *KLMN*.

21. **Open-ended** Write four statements, like the ones in Exercises 15–19, that are true about the diagram.

22. **Using Manipulatives** You will need a ruler and scissors.

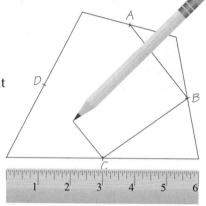

a. Use a ruler to draw any quadrilateral. Connect the midpoints of the sides to form quadrilateral *ABCD*. What type of quadrilateral does *ABCD* appear to be?

b. Cut out the quadrilateral you drew in part (a) and then cut off the four triangles. Compare the total area of the four triangles to the area of quadrilateral *ABCD* by arranging the four triangles on top of it. Then compare the area of quadrilateral *ABCD* to the area of the original quadrilateral.

Ongoing **ASSESSMENT**

23. **Open-ended** Draw an eight-sided figure that has a perimeter of 42 cm. Use dot paper or graph paper if necessary. What is the area of the figure? Is your answer an estimate or is it exact? Explain.

Review **PREVIEW**

24. One angstrom is equal to 1×10^{-10} m. What is the length in meters of 2500 angstroms? Write your answer in scientific notation and in decimal notation. *(Section 2-3)*

Name each quadrilateral. *(Section 1-7)*

25.   **26.**   **27.**

28. Define the terms *acute angle, right angle,* and *obtuse angle.* (*Hint:* Use the glossary.)

 Working on the Unit Project

29. Decide on an interesting way to help people understand the magnitude of each of your numerical facts except for the percent. You may want to compare a length or an area with something in your school.

Exploring Angle Relationships

You can get a moped
license at age 14 in Iowa, but
in California you have to wait
until age 16. The circle graph
shows the percentage of states
having each age requirement.
To make a circle graph, you use
geometry.

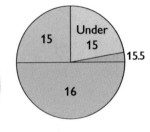

**Required Age for Moped
Licenses in the U.S. in 1996**

A **ray** is a part of a line.
The symbol for ray OZ is $\overrightarrow{OZ}$.
You write the endpoint first.

It starts at one point
(the *endpoint*).

It extends forever
in one direction.

An **angle** is the figure
formed when two rays meet
at a common endpoint.

The common endpoint
is called the **vertex.**

The angle YOZ can be named in these ways: $\angle O$, $\angle YOZ$, $\angle ZOY$,
or $\angle 1$. You can identify an angle by its vertex alone when only
one angle has that vertex. Otherwise, use three letters or a number. Be sure that the middle letter names the vertex.

Talk it Over

Use the circle graph above.

1. Name three rays.

2. Name three angles.

3. Name $\angle 3$ in two
   other ways.

4. For each angle, point O is
   called the ? .

5. Can any of the angles be named $\angle O$? Why or why not?

6. A **central angle** is an angle, such as $\angle YOZ$, with its vertex at
   the center of a circle. Name two other central angles.

The measure of an angle is the number of degrees from one ray to the other. Many angles have special names and special relationships based on their angle measures.

The measure of ∠WOX is 90°.
You write ∠WOX = 90°.
∠WOX is a **right angle**.

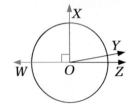

The measure of ∠WOZ is 180°.
You write ∠WOZ = 180°.
∠WOZ is a **straight angle**.

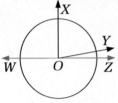

The measure of ∠WOY is between 90° and 180°.
∠WOY is an **obtuse angle**.

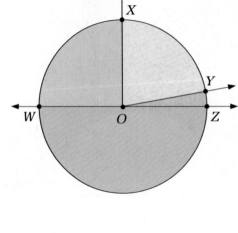

The measure of ∠YOZ is between 0° and 90°.
∠YOZ is an **acute angle**.

Two angles whose measures add up to 90° are called **complementary angles**.
∠XOY and ∠YOZ are complementary angles.

Two angles whose measures add up to 180° are called **supplementary angles**.
∠WOY and ∠YOZ are supplementary angles.

Talk it Over

7. Which combination of age groups in the circle graph has an obtuse central angle?

8. a. Which two parts of the circle graph together total one fourth of the circle?

   b. An entire circle has a measure of 360°. What is the angle measure of one fourth of a circle?

   c. What is the relationship between the central angles of the sectors in part (a)?

Unit 2 Using Measures and Equations

Estimate to sketch each angle.

a. $\angle A = 90°$ b. $\angle B = 45°$ c. $\angle C = 135°$

Sample Response

a. A 90° angle can be formed by sketching intersecting horizontal and vertical lines.

b. Sketch a 90° angle. The measure of a 45° angle is half the measure of a 90° angle.

c. A 135° angle measures 45° more than a 90° angle.

······▶ Now you are ready for:
Exs. 1–18 on pp. 89–90

Talk it Over

Explain how you could estimate to sketch each angle.

9. $\angle Q = 60°$ 10. $\angle R = 75°$ 11. $\angle P$ is an obtuse angle.

Special Angle Relationships

Angles with equal measures are **congruent angles**.

You can mark the angles the same way to show that they are congruent.

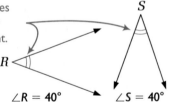

$\angle R = 40°$ $\angle S = 40°$

$\angle R \cong \angle S$

Watch Out!
How long you draw the rays does not affect the measure of an angle.

Two angles formed by intersecting lines and facing in opposite directions are called **vertical angles**.

Angles 1 and 3 are vertical angles.

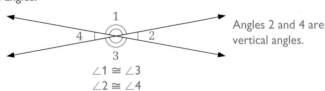

Angles 2 and 4 are vertical angles.

$\angle 1 \cong \angle 3$
$\angle 2 \cong \angle 4$

The results of Exercise 13 on page 90 lead you to a special angle relationship. Vertical angles have equal measures.

The angles of a triangle also have a special relationship.

How are the angles of a triangle related?

- **Materials: rulers, protractors, scissors**
- **Work in a group of three students.**

An **acute triangle** is a triangle with three acute angles.

1 **Student 1:** Use a ruler to draw a large acute triangle.

An **obtuse triangle** is a triangle with one obtuse angle.

Student 2: Use a ruler to draw a large obtuse triangle.

A **right triangle** is a triangle with one right angle.

Student 3: Use a ruler to draw a large right triangle.

2 Cut out your triangle. Turn it so that its longest side is at the bottom. Number the angles as shown. Then turn the triangle over so that the numbers are face down.

3 Make a fold perpendicular to the longest side of the triangle and passing through the opposite vertex.

4 Unfold the triangle. Find the point where the fold line intersects the longest side. Label it *F*.

5 Fold each vertex of the triangle to meet point F. Leave the triangle folded.

6 With your group, make a conjecture about the sum of the measures of angles 1, 2, and 3. How can you test your conjecture?

7 Share your conjecture with the class. Did any groups find counterexamples to your conjecture?

Find the unknown angle measure in each figure.

a.

b.

Sample Response

a. The Exploration shows that the sum of the measures of the angles of a triangle is 180°.

$$x = 180 - (30 + 20)$$ ← Subtract the sum of the known angle measures from 180.

$$= 180 - 50$$

$$= 130$$

The measure of the angle is 130°.

b. A straight angle measures 180°.

$$x = 180 - 100$$ ← Subtract the known angle measure from 180.

$$= 80$$

The measure of the angle is 80°.

SPECIAL ANGLE RELATIONSHIPS

∠1 ≅ ∠3
∠2 ≅ ∠4

Vertical angles have equal measure.

∠5 + ∠6 + ∠7 = **180°**

The sum of the measures of the angles of a triangle is 180°.

Look Back ◄

In this section, you learned the two special angle relationships shown above. Summarize other facts about angles that you learned or reviewed in this section.

····► Now you are ready for:
Exs. 19–40 on pp. 91–92

2-5 **Exercises and Problems**

1. **Reading** Describe three different ways to name an angle.

2. Suppose you are a carpenter building a house. What is the probability that you will use a 90° angle in your work? a 30° angle? Use a number on the scale to estimate.

For Exercises 3–9, use the circle graph.

3. Name each ray.

4. Name a right angle.

5. Name two acute angles.

6. Name three obtuse angles.

7. Name ∠*NOL* another way.

8. **a.** Estimate the measure of the angle for each region.

   b. Estimate the percent of sales for the South region.

   c. There were 886,000 new privately owned one-family houses sold in 1998. Estimate the number of houses sold in the South region.

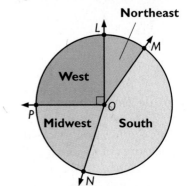

1998 Sales of New Privately Owned One-Family Houses in Regions of the United States

Student Resources Toolbox
pp. 653–656   *Percent*

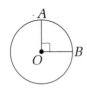

9. In the figure, ∠*AOB* is a central angle of circle *O*.

   a. Are ∠*AOB* and ∠*LOP* in the diagram above complementary or supplementary?

   b. Does the measure of ∠*AOB* equal the measure of ∠*LOP*? Why or why not?

10. ∠*A* and ∠*B* are complementary angles. Find the measure of ∠*B*.

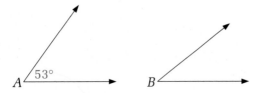

11. ∠*C* and ∠*D* are supplementary angles. Find the measure of ∠*D*.

12. Use the figure in Exercise 11. Name ∠*E* in two other ways.

13. **a.** Use a ruler to draw two intersecting lines. Number the angles as shown. Your angle measures do not have to match the ones in the diagram.

   b. Look at the angles and estimate their measures. Make conjectures about the relationships between the measures of the angles.

   c. Measure the angles with a protractor or trace and fold your diagram to test your conjectures.

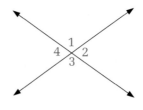

Without using a protractor, estimate to sketch each angle. Then describe how you estimated each angle.

14. ∠*T* is an acute angle.   15. ∠*Q* = 22°   16. ∠*V* = 70°   17. ∠*G* = 120°

18. Use a protractor to measure each angle you sketched in Exercises 15–17. For which angle did you make the most accurate sketch? the least accurate sketch? How could you improve your ability to make a freehand sketch of an angle?

In the diagram, $\overleftrightarrow{AD}$, $\overleftrightarrow{GB}$, and $\overleftrightarrow{EH}$ are straight lines. Replace each __?__ with the name of another angle.

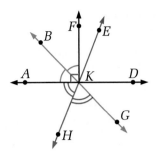

19. $\angle BKF \cong \underline{\ ?\ } \cong \underline{\ ?\ }$

20. $\angle GKH \cong \underline{\ ?\ } \cong \underline{\ ?\ }$

Use the diagram for Exercises 19 and 20. Find the measure of each angle without estimating or using a protractor.

21. $\angle BKF$ **22.** $\angle GKH$ **23.** $\angle EKF$

24. **Using Manipulatives** In the Exploration, you learned a relationship among the three angles of any triangle. Here you will explore a relationship between the acute angles of a right triangle.

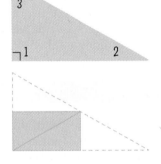

a. Use a ruler to draw three large right triangles. Cut them out. Then position the triangles and number their angles as shown.

b. Fold the vertex of $\angle 2$ and the vertex of $\angle 3$ to meet the vertex of $\angle 1$.

c. Make a conjecture about the relationship between the acute angles of a right triangle. Then measure to test your conjecture.

For Exercises 25–27, write and solve an equation to find each unknown angle measure.

25.   **26.**   **27.**

28. Tell whether the triangle in Exercise 25 is *acute, right,* or *obtuse.*

29 TECHNOLOGY Use geometric drawing software.

Alternative Approach Work in a group of three students and use rulers and protractors. Share responsibility for part (a). Have each student do parts (b) and (c). Compare results with each other in part (d).

a. Draw a large quadrilateral, a large pentagon, and a large hexagon. The figures do not have to have equal sides.

b. Measure the angles of each figure. Find the sum of the measures of the angles for each figure.

c. Compare the sums of the measures of the angles for each figure in part (b). What pattern do you see?

d. Use the pattern suggested by part (c) to predict the sum of the measures of the angles of a polygon with seven sides (a *heptagon*). How can you test your prediction?

30. Group Activity Work in a group of three students.

   a. Have each person in the group use a ruler to draw an isosceles triangle. One triangle should be acute, one triangle should be obtuse, and one triangle should be right.

   b. Write a conjecture about the angles opposite the sides of equal length in your triangle. Mark the sides and angles on your sketch to illustrate your conjecture.

   c. Measure the angles of your triangle to test your conjecture.

   d. Do you think that your conjecture is true for all isosceles triangles? Compare your conjecture with others in your group.

   e. Suppose your conjecture in part (b) is true. What does this lead you to believe about the angles of an equilateral triangle? Sketch and mark an equilateral triangle to indicate the relationships between the sides and between the angles.

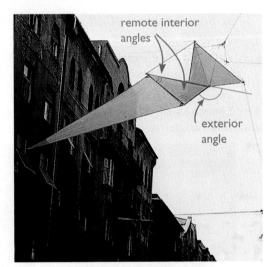

> **BY THE WAY...**
>
> In the summer, the strength of the sun's ultraviolet rays is less during the first two and the last two hours of the day. During these hours, the sun is less than 30 degrees up from the horizon, and the sun's rays pass through more air.

Ongoing **ASSESSMENT**

An *exterior angle* of a triangle is an angle formed outside the triangle by extending one side of the triangle. An exterior angle is associated with a pair of angles inside the triangle called *remote interior angles*.

31. Writing Write a procedure for exploring the relationship between an exterior angle of a triangle and its remote interior angles. You may want to use the Exploration and Exercises 13, 24, 29, and 30 as samples.

Kite sculpture in Budapest, Hungary

Review **PREVIEW**

Describe in words what each symbol means. *(Section 2-4)*

32. $\overline{AB}$ **33.** JK **34.** $\overleftrightarrow{RS}$ **35.** PQ

Name the property shown. *(Toolbox Skill 1)*

36. $12 \cdot 9 = 9 \cdot 12$ **37.** $23 + (15 + 9) = (23 + 15) + 9$

Simplify. *(Section 1-5)*

38. $4(x + 2)$ **39.** $6a + 5 + 2a + 1$

Working on the Unit Project

40. Some of your numerical facts are percents. Choose one to show in a circle graph. Tell what the whole circle represents, and tell the measure of the central angle you are using for your percent.

Student Resources Toolbox
pp. 661–663 *Data Displays*

Expressions for Measures

Simplify expressions for measures of geometric figures by multiplying and combining like terms.

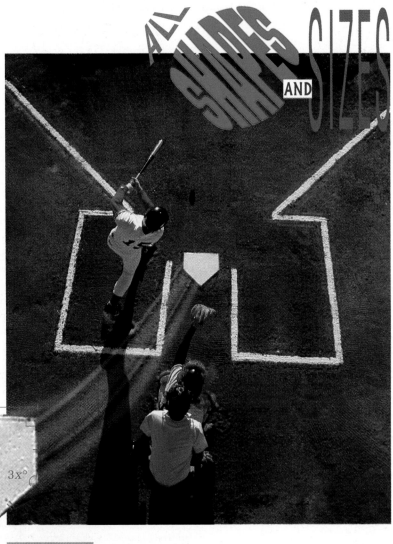

ALL SHAPES AND SIZES

Talk it Over

1. In baseball, home plate is a pentagon like the one shown. Write and simplify an expression for the sum of the angles of home plate.

2. Write and simplify an expression for the perimeter of home plate.

Variable expressions are sometimes used to represent measures of geometric figures. To work with these measures, you need to know how to multiply and add variable expressions.

2-6 Expressions for Measures

93

Write and simplify an expression for the area of each figure or pair of figures.

a.

$A = 4x^2$ $A = 4x^2$

b.

$5x$

$2y$

Sample Response

Problem Solving Strategy: Use a formula

a. $\text{Area} = 2 \cdot 4x^2$ ◀──── Total area $= 2 \times$ area of each square

$= (2 \cdot 4)x^2$ ◀──── Group numerical factors.

$= 8x^2$

b. $\text{Area} = 2y \cdot 5x$ ◀──── Area of a rectangle $=$ length $\times$ width

Student Resources Toolbox
p. 640 *Properties*

$= (2 \cdot 5)(y \cdot x)$ ◀──── **Rearrange factors. Group** coefficients **and group** variable factors.

$= 10xy$ ◀──── This could be written 10*yx*, but variable factors are usually written in alphabetical order.

Write and simplify an expression for the volume of the box.

$4b$

$3b$

b

Sample Response

Problem Solving Strategy: Use a formula

Volume of a box $=$ length $\times$ width $\times$ height

$= 4b \cdot 3b \cdot b$ ◀──── The *b* on the end has a coefficient of 1.

$= (4 \cdot 3 \cdot 1)(b \cdot b \cdot b)$

$= 12b^3$

Student Resources Toolbox
p. 659 *Volume*

Unit 2 Using Measures and Equations

3. Suppose the area of each square in part (a) of Sample 1 were $9y^2$ instead of $4x^2$. What would be the simplified expression for the area?

4. Write and simplify an expression for the combined volume of the four boxes.

$V = x^3$

$V = 8x^3$

$V = x^3$

$V = 3x^3$

Like Terms with Two Variables

You add like terms involving two variables, such as $-5xy$ and $9xy$, the same way you add other like terms.

Sample 3

Simplify.

   a. $-5xy + 9xy$ b. $8x^3 + 7xy - 5x^3 + 3xy + 2x$

Sample Response

a. $-5xy + 9xy = (-5 + 9)xy$ ⟵ Use the distributive property.

          $= 4xy$

b. $8x^3 + 7xy - 5x^3 + 3xy + 2x = (8x^3 - 5x^3) + (7xy + 3xy) + 2x$ ⟵ Group like terms.

                $= 3x^3 + 10xy + 2x$

::: Talk it Over

Tell whether the terms in each pair are like terms.

5. $5x^2$ and $5x^3$ 6. $-8a$ and $17a$ 7. $7wz$ and $7w$

8. Tell whether $3x^2 + 7x - 9y$ can be simplified. If so, simplify it. If not, tell why not.
:::

Look Back ⟵

You need like terms in order to do some operations. Which operations require like terms? Which operations do not?

Exercises and Problems

1. Reading How is the distributive property used to simplify expressions?

Write and simplify an expression for the perimeter of each rectangle.

2.

$2m + 1.4n$

$m + n$

3.

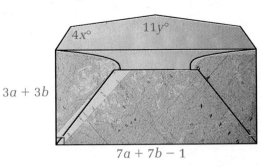

$4x°$ $11y°$

$3a + 3b$

$7a + 7b - 1$

4. Write and simplify an expression for the sum of the measures of the labeled angles in the figure in Exercise 3.

5. This is a pattern that you can use to make a box of any size. The size and proportions of the box depend on the values of x, y, and z. Write and simplify an expression for the area of the pattern.

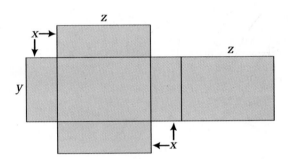

z

z

x

y

x

Simplify if possible. If it is not possible to simplify, explain why not.

6. $(13y)(13z)$ **7.** $5(6m^2)$ **8.** $(-8a)(6a)$ **9.** $(8a)(5c)$ **10.** $6(7n^3)$

11. $5h + 11k + 3hk + 9h + 4hk$ **12.** $5a^2 + 4ab + 3b^2$

13. $m^3 + 4n + 10m^3$ **14.** $4x^3 + 7x^2 + 3x + x^3 + 10x^2$

15. $-7x + 9xy + 7x - 7xy$ **16.** $-3w^3 + 11w + 9w^2 - w + 4w^3$

17. $8cf + 6c^2 + 3 - 6f - 6c^2$ **18.** $7xy + 9x^3 + 2x - 5y$

Write and simplify an expression for each measure.

19. the area of a rectangle with dimensions $9y$ and $5z$

20. the area of a rectangle with dimensions 4 and $a + 2$

21. the volume of a box with dimensions $10c$, $5c$, and $3c$

Match each expression with the figure whose area or volume it represents.

22. $2y^2$

23. $(2y)^2$

24. $2y^3$

25. $(2y)^3$

A. y y

y y

B. y y

y y y y

C. $2y$

$2y$

D. $2y$

$2y$

$2y$ $2y$

The diagram at the right is a floor plan of a Japanese house. In traditional Japanese architecture, the shape of each room is based on a rectangular mat called a *tatami.*

The tatami may be used as a floor covering, as a bed, and as a cushion for sitting. The length of a tatami is usually twice its width.

For Exercises 26–29, let w = the width of a tatami. Write and simplify an expression in terms of w for each measure.

26. the perimeter of Parlor 1   27. the perimeter of Parlor 2

28. the area of Parlor 1   29. the area of Parlor 2

30. The actual size of a tatami has varied slightly over the years. Suppose the width of a tatami is 96 cm. What is the total area of the house shown above in square meters?

31. **Research** The size and shape of a tatami are important in Japanese architecture. What measures and shapes are important in the architecture of other cultures?

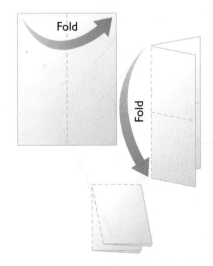

32. **Using Manipulatives** Take any rectangle of paper.
    a. Fold the paper as shown.
    b. Without measuring, predict: Is the perimeter of the small rectangle *one fourth* or *one half* of the perimeter of the big rectangle?
    c. Let l = the length of the big rectangle. Let w = the width of the big rectangle. Write an algebraic expression for the perimeter of the big rectangle and for the small rectangle.
    d. **Writing** Explain how the results of part (c) help you answer the question in part (b).

33. Use the diagram and the variables in Exercise 32(c). Use algebra to prove that the area of the small rectangle is one fourth of the area of the big rectangle.

Ongoing **ASSESSMENT**

34. **Open-ended** Draw and label a rectangle with perimeter $12x$, a rectangle with area $12x^2$, and a box with volume $12x^3$. The variable x does not have to represent the same value in each figure.

Review **PREVIEW**

35. Estimate to sketch a 40° angle. Then describe how you estimated. *(Section 2-5)*

Model each expression using algebra tiles. *(Section 1-3)*

36. $2x$ **37.** $x + 3$ **38.** $2x + 4$

Working on the Unit Project

39. **Group Activity** Show your group the circle graph you made for Exercise 40 in Section 2-5. Discuss your ideas for expressing your other numerical facts. Agree on at least four facts to illustrate on your theme poster. Include a very large number and a very small number in scientific notation, a measurement, and a percent.

Unit 2   CHECKPOINT 2

1. **Writing** Describe how you estimate distances on a map, how you estimate areas on a map, and how you estimate angle measures.

For Exercises 2–4, use the map of Tanzania, a country in Africa.   2-4

2. Estimate the distance from Tabora to Arusha.

3. Is 450 km a reasonable estimate of the distance from Mwanza to Dar es Salaam? Explain.

4. Use the grid on the map to estimate the area of Tanzania. Each grid square is 300 km on a side.

For Exercises 5–7, use triangle *ABC*.

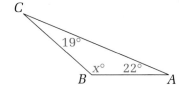

5. Estimate the length of each side of triangle *ABC* in both customary and metric units.

6. Suppose X is the midpoint of $\overline{AC}$. Is it *True* or *False* that $AX = 2 \cdot XC$? Explain.

7. Write and solve an equation to find the unknown angle measure in the triangle.   2-5

8. Estimate to sketch a 15° angle. Then describe how you estimated.

Simplify.   2-6

9. $(2y)(7y)(y)$ **10.** $2c^3 - 9c^2 - 7c + 7c^3$

11. $-7mn + 5m + 4mn - 4n$ **12.** $11a + 7b - 4a + b$

Solving Equations: Balancing

GO FLY A KITE

BY THE WAY...

The record for the largest kite ever flown was set September 7, 1997. The area of the kite was 7319 ft^2, which is about nine tenths the area of a baseball diamond.

$x + 2 = 5$

A mathematical statement in which one expression equals another is an **equation.**

Your knowledge of arithmetic facts tells you that x must represent 3 in the equation.

Sometimes streamers or tassels are added to kites. To keep both sides of the kite balanced in flight, the amount added to the right side must equal the amount added to the left side.

In mathematics the equals sign works like the balance line of the stunt kite, or the pivot point of a balance scale. The equals sign tells you that the expression on the right side of it has the same value as the expression on the left side.

A value of a variable that makes an equation true is a **solution** of the equation. The process of finding solutions is called **solving an equation.**

x + 2 = 5

One way to solve an equation is to make changes to both sides until the variable is alone on one side and the solution is alone on the other side. The changes you make must keep the equation in balance.

You can use algebra tiles to help you solve equations like $x + 2 = 5$.

Sample 1

Solve the equation $2x + 3 = 11$.

Sample Response

Use algebra tiles to model the equation.

$2x + 3 = 11$

To get the x-tiles alone on one side, first take away three 1-tiles from both sides.

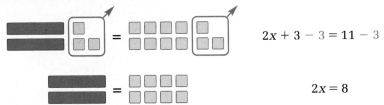

$2x + 3 - 3 = 11 - 3$

$2x = 8$

To see what a single tile alone equals, divide each side into two identical groups.

$\dfrac{2x}{2} = \dfrac{8}{2}$

There is one x-tile by itself in each group. It equals four 1-tiles.

$x = 4$

Check

Substitute 4 for x in the original equation.

$2x + 3 = 11$

$2(4) + 3 \stackrel{?}{=} 11$

$8 + 3 \stackrel{?}{=} 11$

$11 = 11$ ✔   The solution is 4.

When you make the same change to both sides of an equation, you change the form of the equation, but not the solution. Equations that have the same solution are called **equivalent equations**. The original equation $2x + 3 = 11$ and the new equation $x = 4$ are equivalent.

Solve the equation $3x - 4 = 11$.

Sample Response

Use algebra tiles to model the equation.
The red tiles show numbers subtracted.

$$3x - 4 = 11$$

To get the x-tiles alone on one side, add four 1-tiles
to both sides. Then you can remove four pairs of
tiles from the left side, because they add up to zero.

$$3x - 4 + 4 = 11 + 4$$

$$3x = 15$$

To see what a single tile alone equals, divide
each side into three identical groups.

$$\frac{3x}{3} = \frac{15}{3}$$

There is one x-tile by itself in
each group. It equals five 1-tiles.

$$x = 5$$

Check

$$3x - 4 = 11$$

Substitute 5 for x in
the original equation.

$$3(5) - 4 \stackrel{?}{=} 11$$

$$15 - 4 \stackrel{?}{=} 11$$

$$11 = 11 \checkmark \qquad \text{The solution is 5.}$$

Talk it Over

1. Is 23 a solution of the equation $2w + 18 = 28$? Explain.

2. Are $15n - 8 = 22$ and $5n = 10$ equivalent equations? Explain.

**Tell how to get the variable alone on one side of each equation.
Then solve.**

3. $t + 9 = 54$ 4. $39 = 6b$ 5. $6r - 10 = 212$

Student Resources Toolbox
pp. 645–647 *Solving One-Step
Equations*

Problem Solving Strategy: Use an Equation

You can write and solve equations to find unknown measures. Some of the equations will use special angle relationships.

Sample 3

Find the value of x on the kite.

Sample Response

Problem Solving Strategy: Use an equation

$$x + x + 90 = 360$$ ← The angles form a complete circle. An entire circle has a measure of $360°$.

Simplify the left side of the equation. → $$2x + 90 = 360$$

$$2x + 90 - 90 = 360 - 90$$ ← To get $2x$ alone on one side and keep the equation balanced, subtract 90 from both sides.

$$2x = 270$$

$$\frac{2x}{2} = \frac{270}{2}$$ ← To get x alone and keep the equation balanced, divide both sides by 2.

$$x = 135$$

The value of x is 135.

Look Back

What do you think are the most important ideas about equation solving for you to remember? Give at least three ideas.

2-7 Exercises and Problems

1. **Using Manipulatives** Suppose ▬▬ represents x and □ represents 1.

   a. What equation does the diagram at the right illustrate?

   b. Show how to solve the equation for ▬▬ using the model in part (a).

   c. Show how to solve for x using the equation you wrote in part (a).

   d. Show how to solve $2x - 1 = 3$ using algebra tiles.

2. **Reading** It takes one more step to solve the equation in Sample 3 than it does to solve the equations in Samples 1 and 2. What is the extra step?

3. **Reading** What would happen to the balance scale shown on page 99 if you removed the two smaller weights from the left-hand pan? Describe two ways to restore the balance.

Solve.

4. $h - 7 = 48$

5. $8p = 56$

6. $0 = 16n$

7. $4a + 13 = 25$

8. $18g - 30 = 6$

9. $8 + 5x = 33$

10. $26 = 4b - 2$

$4b - 2 = 26$

11. $m + m + 7 = 15$

12. $6 + 5 + a = 18$

Two students gave the two different solutions shown for each equation. Decide which is the correct solution. Explain the mistake that may have led to the other solution.

13. $w + 6 = 17$ 23, 11

14. $x + x - 40 = 100$ 70, 140

15. $5h - 10 = 20$ 14, 6

16. $9 + 3x = 30$ 3, 7

Write and solve an equation to find each unknown measure.

17. One dimension of a rectangular lot is 330 ft. The area of the lot is 217,800 ft². What is the other dimension of the lot?

18. There is 1008 ft² of floor space in the Reboulets' house. They are planning to build a rectangular addition. The length of the addition will be 18 ft. There will be 1170 ft² of floor space in the Reboulets' house when they are done. How wide will the addition be?

Match each figure with an equation that describes a relationship among the angle measures. (*Note:* **There may be more than one answer, or repeated answers.**)

19.

20.

21.

A. $2x + 240 = 360$

B. $2x + 60 = 180$

C. $2x + 60 = 360$

D. $2x + 90 = 180$

Write and solve an equation to find each unknown measure in each figure. (*Note:* **The sum of the measures of the angles of a quadrilateral is 360°.**)

22.

23.

24.

perimeter = 78 in.

25.

perimeter = 116 cm

When polygons form a pattern that covers a plane without gaps or overlaps, the pattern is called a *tessellation*.

Islamic Star Pattern

The sum of the measures of the angles at any vertex not on the boundary is 360°.

$$\angle 1 + \angle 2 + \angle 3 + \angle 4 = 360°$$

For Exercises 26 and 27, write and solve an equation that describes a relationship among the angle measures in each tessellation.

boundary

26.

Midwest Amish

27.

Navajo

28 TECHNOLOGY Use geometric drawing software.

Alternative Approach Use a ruler and a protractor.

Draw a tessellation using a triangle whose angles are all 60° and a parallelogram whose angles are 60°, 120°, 60°, and 120°.

Ongoing **ASSESSMENT**

29. **Writing** Suppose you are helping a friend learn algebra. Explain the difference between simplifying an expression and solving an equation. Give an example of each.

Review **PREVIEW**

Simplify if possible. If not, explain why not. *(Section 2-6)*

30. $8(-4x^3)$ **31.** $10n^3 + 5n^2 + n$ **32.** $-8a^3 + 12ab + 3a^3 + 4a - 9ab$

Simplify. *(Section 2-2)*

33. $-7 + 6$ **34.** $-12 - 4$ **35.** $(-3)(-1.6)$ **36.** $-20 \div 0.4$

Working on the Unit Project

37. **Writing** Write four mathematical questions that can be answered using the facts included on your display. Write one question for each fact.

2-8

Solving Equations: Undoing

Focus
Use equations to solve a variety of real-life problems.

Can you solve this number puzzle?

If you divide a number by 3 and subtract 64, you get 76. What is the number?

You could solve this puzzle using mental math, by working backward. The steps can be shown in a flow chart.

Read the puzzle again and

break it into steps.

If you divide a number by 3…

…and subtract 64…

…you get 76. What is the number?

Start with the unknown number.

Divide by 3.

Subtract 64.

76

In order to solve it, you could work backward, undoing each operation.

420   That gives me 420.

Multiply by 3.   Undo dividing by 3 by multiplying by 3.

Add 64.   Undo subtracting 64 by adding 64. That makes 140.

Start with 76.

The same kind of thinking can help you solve an equation. The method is called *solving by undoing* or *solving by inverse operations*. In Sample 1, the number puzzle is written as an equation and solved.

2-8 Solving Equations: Undoing

Solve $\frac{x}{3} - 64 = 76$.

Sample Response

Method ❶ Undo the operations. Remember that your goal is to get x alone on one side of the equation.

$$\frac{x}{3} - 64 = 76$$

$$\frac{x}{3} - 64 + 64 = 76 + 64 \quad \longleftarrow \quad \begin{array}{l} \text{Undo subtraction of } 64. \\ \text{Add } 64 \text{ to both sides.} \end{array}$$

$$\frac{x}{3} = 140$$

$$3 \cdot \frac{x}{3} = 3 \cdot 140 \quad \longleftarrow \quad \begin{array}{l} \text{Undo division by } 3. \\ \text{Multiply both sides by } 3. \end{array}$$

$$x = 420$$

Check $\frac{x}{3} - 64 = 76$

Substitute 420 for x in the original equation. $\longrightarrow$ $\frac{420}{3} - 64 \overset{?}{=} 76$

$$140 - 64 \overset{?}{=} 76$$

$$76 = 76 \; ✔$$

The solution is 420.

Method ❷ Once you know how to solve equations by undoing, you can use a calculator to undo the operations. Start with 76 and work backward to x.

$$\frac{x}{3} - 64 = 76$$

76 [+] 64 [ENTER] [×] 3 [ENTER] $\rightarrow$ 420

Check $\frac{x}{3} - 64 = 76$

Substitute 420 for x and work forward. $\longrightarrow$ 420 [÷] 3 [−] 64 [ENTER] $\rightarrow$ 76

The solution is 420.

Talk it Over

1. **a.** Explain how to solve $-49 = 4n + 7$ using Method 1 from Sample 1. Then solve.

   b. How is solving $-49 = 4n - 7$ different from solving $-49 = 4n + 7$?

2. Describe a calculator key sequence you could use to solve the equation in question 1(a). Then solve using a calculator.

Marcus left his bicycle at a repair shop to have seven spokes replaced. When he got home he found the phone message shown. How much did each spoke cost?

Marcus!
The bike shop called—your bike is ready. Total bill is $9.94. The labor charge is $7.49 (they said it took about 2 hours).

Sample Response

Problem Solving Strategy: Use an equation

Choose a variable to represent a number you do not know.

Let c = the cost of each spoke.

$$\text{Cost of spokes} + \text{cost of labor} = \text{total bill}$$

$7c$ = the cost of seven spokes. $\longrightarrow$ $7c + 7.49 = 9.94$

$$7c + 7.49 - 7.49 = 9.94 - 7.49 \longleftarrow$$ Undo addition of 7.49.
Subtract 7.49 from both sides.

$$7c = 2.45$$

$$\frac{7c}{7} = \frac{2.45}{7} \longleftarrow$$ Undo multiplication by 7.
Divide both sides by 7.

$$c = 0.35$$

The cost of each spoke is $0.35.

Simplifying before Solving

Sometimes you have to simplify one or both sides of an equation before you begin to solve the equation by undoing.

For her theme poster project, Michelle bought 3.25 yd of fluorescent blue nylon, and 2.5 yd of hot pink nylon. The price per yard was the same for both colors. The total cost for the fabric was $40.02. What was the cost per yard of the nylon?

Sample Response

Problem Solving Strategy: Use an equation

Let n = the cost per yard of nylon.

$3.25n$ = the cost of the blue nylon

$2.5n$ = the cost of the hot pink nylon

$$\text{Total cost} = \text{cost of blue} + \text{cost of pink}$$

$$40.02 = 3.25n + 2.5n \longleftarrow$$ Combine like terms to simplify the right side of the equation.

$$40.02 = 5.75n$$

$$\frac{40.02}{5.75} = \frac{5.75n}{5.75}$$

$$6.96 = n \qquad \text{The cost per yard of the nylon is \$6.96.}$$

2-8 Solving Equations: Undoing

2-8 Exercises and Problems

1. **Reading** When you solve equations by undoing, you try to get the equation in a particular form. What is that form?

Solve.

2. $2x + 8 = 26$

3. $6h - 117 = -21$

4. $9h - 3h = 15$

5. $-7a - 1 = 13$

6. $\frac{m}{2} + 7 = 9$

7. $\frac{a}{3} - 2 = 1.5$

8. $-50 = 18c + 7c$

9. $17 = 0.05x - 60$

10. $-3.6y + 70 = -2$

11. $-37 = \frac{k}{6} - 19$

12. $7.49 = 0.75x + 1.39x$

13. $12 = 15 + 36d$

14. **Open-ended** Write and solve three number puzzles similar to the one at the beginning of this section. At least one puzzle should have a negative solution and at least one should have a decimal solution.

For Exercises 15–19, write and solve an equation to find each unknown value.

15. When Hanako Sakata had her car repaired, the total bill was $255.50. The bill included a cost of $150.50 for parts and a separate charge for labor. The charge for labor was $35 per hour. How many hours of labor were included in the bill?

16. Rudy bought a can of three tennis balls and a new grip for his racquet. The grip cost $7.49. The items cost $9.38 in all. How much did each tennis ball cost?

17. Michelle bought a case of motor oil and a quart of transmission fluid for $11.97. The transmission fluid sells for $1.29 per quart. There are twelve quarts of oil in a case. How much did one quart of oil cost?

18. Jason Mills bought pencils and erasers to lend to his students taking the SAT (Scholastic Assessment Test). He bought the same number of pencils as erasers. The pencils cost $.29 each and the erasers cost $.14 each. He spent $10.32 in all. How many of each did he buy?

19. Angelica bought equal amounts of two different fabrics to make costumes. The price per yard for each fabric is shown in the photograph. The total cost was $33.88. How many yards of each fabric did Angelica buy?

$3.99/yd.

$4.48/yd.

Women have made many contributions in mathematics and science. In their roles as writers and lecturers, they have combined communication skills with their knowledge of mathematics and science.

For Exercises 20–23, use the time line. Write and solve an equation to find each unknown year.

20. Emilie du Châtelet wrote a physics textbook called *Institutions de Physique*. Let $y =$ the year this book was published. By doubling that year and then subtracting 1721, you get the year that her translation of the *Principia* was published.

21. Mary Fairfax Somerville wrote many books, including a book about chemistry and physics called *Molecular and Microscopic Science*.

    a. Let $y =$ the year this book was published. By dividing that year by 3 and then adding 1208, you get the year her book *The Mechanism of the Heavens* was published.

    b. Use your answer to part (a) to find out how old Mary Somerville was when *Molecular and Microscopic Science* was published.

22. Women were not allowed to get university degrees in Russia in 1863. Sonya Kovalevsky went to Germany to get her Ph.D. in mathematics. Let $y =$ the year she got her Ph.D. By tripling that year and then adding the year Winifred Merrill got her Ph.D., you get 7508.

23. a. **Research** Find the year of another important event in the life of a female mathematician. You may choose a mathematician from the time line or another female mathematician.

    b. **Writing** Using a variable to represent the year you found, write a puzzle relating the year you found to a year in the time line.

    c. Write an equation to represent the puzzle you wrote in part (b). Then solve the equation to check that the solution is the correct year.

    d. **Group Activity** Share your puzzle with a classmate. (Do not share the equation.) Solve your classmate's puzzle and compare results.

1700

1750

1800

1850

1900

1950

Emilie du Châtelet
(1706 – 1749) Wrote the only French translation of Newton's *Principia*, published in 1759.

Mary Fairfax Somerville
(1780 – 1872) Wrote *The Mechanism of the Heavens*, a translation of Laplace's *Mécanique céleste* with added commentary, published in 1831.

Ada Byron Lovelace
(1815 – 1852) Considered to be the first person to write about how computers are programmed, in a paper published in 1843.

Sonya Kovalevsky
(1850 – 1891) Became a mathematics lecturer at the University of Stockholm, and thus the first female lecturer in Sweden, in 1883.

Winifred Edgerton Merrill
(1862 – 1951) Was the first woman to receive a doctorate in Mathematics from an American university (Columbia) in 1886.

Emmy Noether
(1882 – 1935) Barred from academic work by the Nazis, she came to the United States to be a professor of mathematics at Bryn Mawr in 1933.

	Cal/min
Basketball	12.5
Cross-country skiing	11.7
Dancing	10.5
Walking (5mi/h)	9.3
Tennis (singles)	7.1

24. **a.** Write a formula for the number of Calories Jason uses while dancing for any number of minutes, x.

    b. How long should he dance to use 190 Calories?

25. Suppose Jason plans to spend equal amounts of time playing basketball and playing tennis. How much time should he allow for each if he wants to use 400 Cal?

Ongoing ASSESSMENT

26. **Group Activity** Work in a group of three students.

    a. Write a five-question quiz on Sections 2-7 and 2-8. At least one question should involve a problem solving situation. At least one question should involve geometry.

    b. Make enough copies of your group's quiz for students in another group. Have them take the quiz.

    c. Collect and correct the quizzes. Write a summary of any errors that were made by more than one student.

Review PREVIEW

27. **a.** What equation does the diagram below illustrate? *(Section 2-7)*

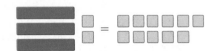

    b. Show how to solve for ▮▮▮▮ using the model in part (a).

Write each number in decimal notation. *(Section 2-3)*

28. 6.3×10^7 29. 1.8×10^{-5}

Replace each __?__ with the correct number. *(Section 1-3)*

30. $11^2 = \underline{?} \times \underline{?} = \underline{?}$ 31. $7^3 = \underline{?} \times \underline{?} \times \underline{?} = \underline{?}$

 Working on the Unit Project

32. **a.** You should still have some numerical facts that are not yet included on your theme poster. Write an equation that someone else could solve to find one of these numerical facts. For example, to find the number of legs on a butterfly, solve the equation $5x - 11 = 19$.

    b. Solve the equation you wrote in part (a) to be sure the solution matches the fact.

Square Roots and Cube Roots

·······Focus

Find square roots and
cube roots and distinguish
a rational number from
an irrational number.

GETTING TO THE

ROOT

OF THE PROBLEM

Talk it Over

1. In the diagram, some squares are drawn on dot paper. The first square has an area of one square unit. Use the diagram to complete the table below.

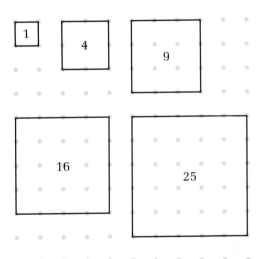

Area of square	1	4	9	16	25
Length of side	1	2	?	?	?

2. What is the length of each side of a square with an area of 36 square units? 49? 64? 100? 400?

When you use the area of a square to find the length of a side of the square, you undo the squaring of a number. This process is called *finding a square root*.

The **square root** of a number is one of two equal factors of the number. Every positive number has both a positive and a negative square root.

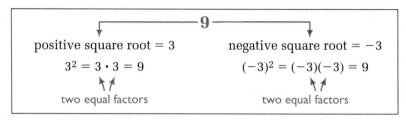

positive square root = 3

$3^2 = 3 \cdot 3 = 9$

two equal factors

negative square root = −3

$(-3)^2 = (-3)(-3) = 9$

two equal factors

The symbol $\sqrt{}$ stands for the *nonnegative* square root of a number.

$\sqrt{9} = 3$

The symbol $-\sqrt{}$ stands for the negative square root.

$-\sqrt{9} = -3$

The symbol $\pm\sqrt{}$ stands for both square roots.

$\pm\sqrt{9} = 3$ or -3

plus-or-minus

TECHNOLOGY NOTE

See page 611 of the Technology Handbook for help with finding square roots on a calculator.

When you use the **INV** **x²** on a calculator you will only get the positive square root or zero.

Talk it Over

For questions 3–6, use the diagram. Suppose that *AB* is 1 unit.

3. Is *BC* greater than, less than, or equal to 1? How do you know?

4. Is *BC* greater than, less than, or equal to 2? How do you know?

5. What can you say about *BD*?

6. What can you say about *PQ*?

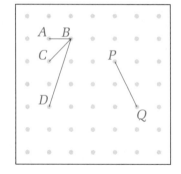

7. In the diagram, some squares are drawn on dot paper and labeled with their areas. Estimate the length of a side of each square and complete the table below.

Area of square	2	5	8	10	13
Estimated length of side	?	?	?	?	?

8. Use your calculator to find the square root of each area in question 7 to the nearest hundredth.

9. Compare the results of questions 7 and 8. Should they be about the same? Are they about the same? Explain.

Unit 2 Using Measures and Equations

Types of Numbers

When you use a calculator to find a square root, you may see any of these kinds of displays.

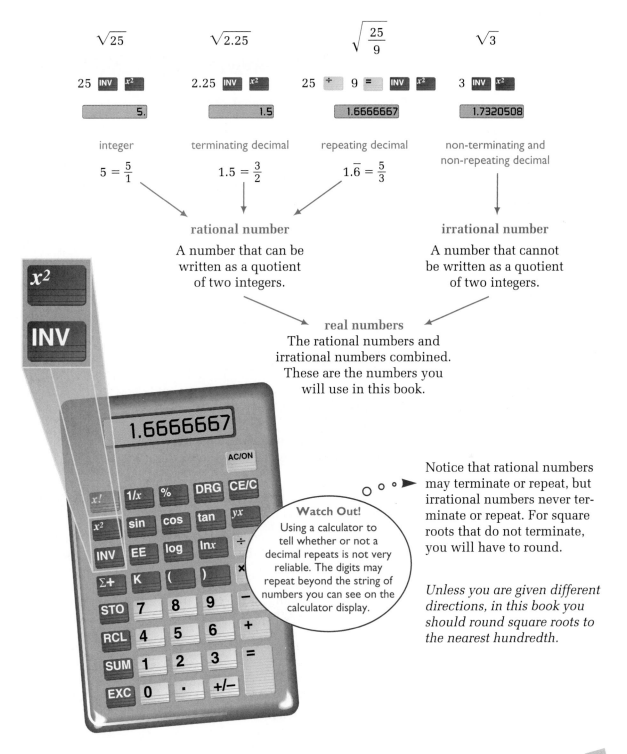

$$\sqrt{25} \qquad \sqrt{2.25} \qquad \sqrt{\frac{25}{9}} \qquad \sqrt{3}$$

25 [INV] [x^2]   2.25 [INV] [x^2]   25 [÷] 9 [=] [INV] [x^2]   3 [INV] [x^2]

    5.   1.5   1.6666667   1.7320508

integer   terminating decimal   repeating decimal   non-terminating and non-repeating decimal

$$5 = \frac{5}{1} \qquad 1.5 = \frac{3}{2} \qquad 1.\overline{6} = \frac{5}{3}$$

rational number
A number that can be written as a quotient of two integers.

irrational number
A number that cannot be written as a quotient of two integers.

real numbers
The rational numbers and irrational numbers combined. These are the numbers you will use in this book.

Watch Out!
Using a calculator to tell whether or not a decimal repeats is not very reliable. The digits may repeat beyond the string of numbers you can see on the calculator display.

Notice that rational numbers may terminate or repeat, but irrational numbers never terminate or repeat. For square roots that do not terminate, you will have to round.

Unless you are given different directions, in this book you should round square roots to the nearest hundredth.

Estimating Square Roots

Numbers that have square roots that are integers are **perfect squares.** The areas of the squares shown in the diagram on page 112 are perfect squares. Perfect squares may help you estimate square roots.

Sample 1

Estimate $\sqrt{51}$ within a range of two integers.

Sample Response

Find the two perfect squares closest to 51 on either side of it. They are 49 and 64. Write an inequality.

$$49 < \ \ 51 \ \ < 64 \ \ \longleftarrow \text{Read as } \textit{51 is between 49 and 64.}$$

$$\sqrt{49} < \sqrt{51} < \sqrt{64}$$

$$7 < \sqrt{51} < 8$$

$\sqrt{51}$ is a number between 7 and 8.

········► Now you are ready for:
Exs. 1–17 on p. 116

Cube Roots

$2^3 = 2 \cdot 2 \cdot 2 = 8$

three equal factors

The **cube root** of a number is one of three equal factors of the number. For example, the cube root of 8 is 2.

$\sqrt[3]{8} = 2$

A **perfect cube** is a number whose cube root is an integer. The number 8 is a perfect cube.

You can think of finding the cube root of a number as undoing the cubing of the number.

The symbol $\sqrt[3]{\ }$ stands for the cube root of a number. *The cube root of 8 is written* $\sqrt[3]{8}$.

Talk it Over

10. Find the volume of a cube with edge length 3 cm.

11. Find the edge length of a cube with volume 8 cm³.

Solving Square Root and Cube Root Equations

Sample 2

The area of a square is 15 m². Find the length of a side of the square.

Sample Response

Problem Solving Strategy: Use a formula

$$A = s^2 \longleftarrow \text{Area} = (\text{length of side})^2$$

Substitute 15 for A. $\longrightarrow$ $15 = s^2$

Undo the squaring. $\longrightarrow$ $\pm\sqrt{15} = s$

$3.87 \approx s \longleftarrow$ Find the positive square root: 15 **INV** x^2

Watch Out!
A length must be positive, so only the positive square root of 15 makes sense here.

The length of a side of the square is about 3.87 m.

3 in.

Sample 3

The volume of a cube is 27 in.³. Find the length of an edge of the cube.

3 in.

3 in.

Sample Response

Problem Solving Strategy: Use a formula

$$V = s^3 \longleftarrow \text{Volume} = (\text{length of side})^3$$

Substitute 27 for V. $\longrightarrow$ $27 = s^3$

Undo the cubing. $\longrightarrow$ $\sqrt[3]{27} = s$

$3 = s \longleftarrow$ 27 **INV** y^x 3 **=**

The length of an edge of the cube is 3 in.

Look Back

Describe the connection between a square and a square root, and between a cube and a cube root. Include an example about area and volume that shows the relationship between these measurements: 3 ft, 9 ft², 27 ft³.

▶ Now you are ready for:
Exs. 18–57 on pp. 117–118

Exercises and Problems

1. **Reading** How is $\sqrt{16}$ different from $\pm\sqrt{16}$?

2. **Writing** Suppose you were not given the area of each square outlined in the diagram at the bottom of page 112. Describe how you could use the dotted lines in the squares to find the area of each square.

Find the square roots of each number.

3. $\dfrac{1}{81}$
4. 0.25
5. $\dfrac{100}{9}$
6. 0.0001

Tell whether each number is rational or irrational.

7. $8.\overline{3}$
8. $\sqrt{10}$
9. $\dfrac{22}{7}$
10. 3.625
11. 50

Estimate each square root within a range of two integers. Then use a calculator to find each square root.

12. $\sqrt{7}$
13. $\sqrt{21}$
14. $\sqrt{111}$
15. $\sqrt{38}$

connection to **PHYSICS**

16. The photograph at the right describes the velocity of an object at the end of a slope.

    a. Find the velocity of a speed skier when the skier reaches the bottom of a ski slope that is 115 m high.

    b. **Open-ended** Look at the formula. What does the speed of the skier depend on? Explain.

Suppose that the skier starts at rest.

Suppose there is no friction as he goes down the incline.

Then at the end of the slope, the skier's velocity in meters per second will be $v = \sqrt{19.6h}$.

height h in meters

17. The photograph below describes the motion of an object traveling along the ground. Suppose a car starts at rest and then accelerates at 20 ft/s². How many seconds will it take the car to travel a distance of 100 ft?

Suppose that the car travels some distance at a constant rate of acceleration a.

Then the time in seconds that it will take to travel the distance is $t = \sqrt{\dfrac{2s}{a}}$.

distance s

Estimate each cube root within a range of two integers. Then use a calculator to find each cube root.

18. $\sqrt[3]{38}$

19. $\sqrt[3]{90}$

20. $\sqrt[3]{110}$

21. $\sqrt[3]{1300}$

For Exercises 22–27, choose the letter of the point on the number line that matches each number.

22. $\sqrt{40}$

23. $\sqrt[3]{500}$

24. $\sqrt{98}$

25. $\sqrt[3]{98}$

26. $\sqrt{75}$

27. $\sqrt[3]{300}$

Rewrite the numbers in order from least to greatest.

28. $7, \sqrt{43}, 6.1, \sqrt{71}, \sqrt{86}, 8.8, \sqrt{14}, \sqrt{35}$

29. $3, \sqrt{48}, \sqrt[3]{48}, 18, \sqrt{700}, \sqrt[3]{1100}, \sqrt{169}, \sqrt[3]{14}$

30. **a.** Find $\sqrt[3]{-8}$, $\sqrt[3]{-27}$, and $\sqrt[3]{-1}$. What do you notice about your answers?

   b. Can you find $\sqrt{-4}$? Explain.

31. Both the square root and the cube root of 1 are integers. The next such number is 64. What is the next number whose square root and cube root are both integers? How many numbers like this exist from 1 to 1000?

Each measurement is the area of a square. Find the length of a side of each square.

32. 49 m^2

33. 225 cm^2

34. 169 in.^{2}

35. 118 ft^2

36. The length of a side of a square is an integer. The area of the square is between 50 square units and 150 square units. What are the possible lengths for a side of the square?

Each measurement is the volume of a cube. Find the length of an edge of each cube.

37. 64 cm^3

38. 216 m^3

39. 350 in.^{3}

40. 0.008 ft^3

41. The length of an edge of a cube is an integer. The volume of the cube is between 500 cubic units and 900 cubic units. What are possible lengths of an edge of the cube?

Career **For Exercises 42–45, use the information below.**

Doctors sometimes need to know a patient's body-surface area in order to decide what dose of medicine to prescribe. The formula below gives body-surface area (in square meters) for a given height (in inches) and a given weight (in pounds).

$$\text{Body-surface area} = \sqrt{\frac{\text{height} \times \text{weight}}{3131}}$$

42. Calculate the body-surface area of a person who is 72 in. tall and weighs 170 lb.

43. Calculate your own body-surface area.

44. Use your answer to Exercise 43. Imagine a square with the same area as your body-surface area. What would be the length of a side of the square?

45. Why do you suppose a doctor would want this formula to give answers in square meters instead of square inches or square feet?

46. Use the bar graph. Suppose a cube has the same volume as each dam. What is the length of a side of each cube?

Ongoing **ASSESSMENT**

47. **Group Activity** Work with another student. Do parts (a) and (b) by yourself. Then work together for part (c).

   a. Make a list of 6 numbers between 1 and 1000.

   b. Graph the square root and the cube root of each number on the same number line.

   c. Exchange number lines. (Do not share your list.) Figure out the numbers on each other's list.

Review **PREVIEW**

Solve. *(Section 2-8)*

48. $3x + 2.7 = 5.4$ **49.** $\frac{n}{4} - 9 = 7$ **50.** $11 = -2.4a + 6.2$

51. 36 is what percent of 144? *(Toolbox Skill 12)*

52. Find 24% of 150. *(Toolbox Skill 14)*

53. 231 is 55% of what number? *(Toolbox Skill 15)*

54. Draw a bar graph. *(Toolbox Skill 22)*

Large Dams of the World

Volume (Millions of cubic meters)

- Tarbela (Pakistan): 105.57
- New Cornelia Tailings (United States): 209.5
- Pati (Argentina): 238.18
- Chapetón (Argentina): 296.2
- Syncrude Tailings (Canada): 540

Powerful Dams of the World

Dam	Itaipu (Brazil-Paraguay)	Grand Coulee (United States)	Guri (Venezuela)	Tucurui (Brazil)
Planned power capacity in megawatts	12,600	10,830	10,300	8000

Working on the Unit Project

55. Choose one of the facts going on your theme poster that could be expressed as an area. Suppose you express the fact as the area of a square. What would be the length of a side of the square?

56. Choose one of the four facts for your theme poster that could be expressed as a volume. Suppose you express the fact as the volume of a cube. What would be the length of an edge of the cube?

57. Compare the area and volume you chose in Exercises 55 and 56 with some areas and volumes that you know, such as the area of the United States or the volume of your school. Plan to include these comparisons on your theme poster.

Completing the Unit Project

Now you are ready to make your theme poster. Keep in mind how the poster will be judged as you make your display.

➤ Show at least four facts including a count, a measurement, and a percent. One number should be very large and one very small.

➤ For each fact write one question that can be answered using the information on your poster.

➤ Write an equation that can be solved to find another fact.

Be sure to include these details.

➤ Use a circle graph to illustrate the percent.

➤ Express your very large and very small numbers in decimal notation and in scientific notation.

➤ Describe at least one fact in terms of area or volume.

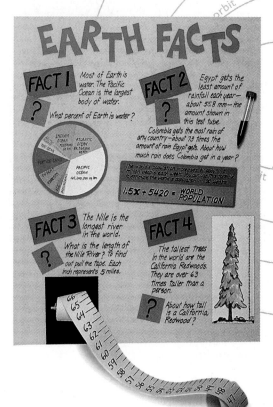

EARTH FACTS

FACT 1
?
Most of Earth is water. The Pacific Ocean is the largest body of water.
What percent of Earth is water?

FACT 2
?
Egypt gets the least amount of rainfall each year—about 55.8 mm—the amount shown in this test tube.
Colombia gets the most rain of any country—about 73 times the amount of rain Egypt gets. About how much rain does Colombia get in a year?

The world's population increases by about 1.6 million people each week. You can use this formula to estimate the world's population in 20 years.

$$1.5x + 5420 = \text{WORLD POPULATION}$$

FACT 3
?
The Nile is the longest river in the world.
What is the length of the Nile River? To find out pull the tape. Each inch represents 5 miles.

FACT 4
?
The tallest trees in the world are the California Redwoods. They are over 63 times taller than a person.
About how tall is a California Redwood?

Look Back ◄

What did you learn from this project that will help you make sense of numbers that you read and hear about in everyday life?

Alternative Projects

Project 1: Redesigning a Room

Make plans to redesign a classroom in your school to make it more efficient or more attractive. Plan an arrangement of desks and workstations. Estimate how many desks will fit in the redesigned room. Write a paragraph giving your reasons for redesigning the room. Explain why your design is an improvement.

Project 2: Conducting an Interview

Numerals, fractions, and decimals are sometimes written differently in other countries. Research some of the differences. Interview people who have been to other countries to find out if they noticed any other ways numbers are written. Report your findings to your class.

1. Guess whether the number of spaces between words on this page is in the *hundreds, thousands, millions,* or *billions.* Then estimate the number. Describe your method.   2-1

2. Estimate whether the population of Moscow, Russia, is in the *hundreds, thousands, millions,* or *billions.*

3. **Writing** Use a number anywhere along the scale at the right to estimate the probability that you will see a movie this week. Give a reason for your answer.

4. Is your distance from home as you travel to school *continuous* or *discrete*?

Evaluate each expression when $a = -4$ and $b = 3$.   2-2

5. $|a|$

6. $-a + b$

7. $\dfrac{a + 7}{b}$

8. $a^2 - ab$

Write each expression in decimal notation.   2-3

9. 10^{-8}

10. 10^0

Write each number in scientific notation.

11. 715,100,000

12. 0.00906

13. Simplify $\dfrac{6.13 \times 10^3}{2,000,000}$. Write the answer in scientific notation, in decimal notation, and in words.

14. The distance from Mercury to the sun is 5.79×10^{10} m. The distance from Neptune to the sun is about 78 times this distance.

   a. Make a reasonable estimate of the distance from Neptune to the sun. Write the answer in scientific notation.

   b. Calculate a more precise estimate of the distance from Neptune to the sun. Write the answer in decimal notation.

The map shows Canada.   2-4

15. Estimate the distance from Winnipeg to Fort Smith.

16. Is 1000 km a reasonable estimate of the distance from Yellowknife to Whitehorse? Explain.

17. Estimate the area of the Fort Smith region.

18. Use the grid on the map to estimate the area of the mainland of Canada. Each grid square is 1500 km on a side.

In the diagram, *M* is the midpoint of $\overline{RT}$. Tell whether each statement is *True* or *False*.

19. *RT* is about 4 cm.

20. $RT = 2 \cdot MT$

21. *M* is the midpoint of $\overleftrightarrow{RT}$.

For Questions 22–25, use this diagram of a camera lens that shows   2-5
how rays of light pass through the center of the lens.

22. Name a pair of supplementary angles.

23. Name an angle congruent to $\angle DCE$.

24. Name a pair of vertical angles.

25. Suppose $\angle ACD = 128°$.

    a. Find the measure of $\angle ACB$.

    b. Find the measure of $\angle BCE$.

26. Estimate to sketch a 100° angle.
Then describe how you estimated.

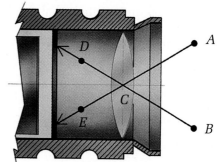

27. **Open-ended** Describe what you have learned   2-1, 2-4, 2-5
about measurement in this unit. Be sure to include
the following points.

   ➤ why you need to estimate measurements

   ➤ methods for estimating measurements

   ➤ the need for accurate measurements

Simplify.   2-6

28. $8mn - 4m + 2mn + 9m$ **29.** $-8k^3 - 14 + 6k^3 - k^2$ **30.** $8(12a^2)$

31. Write and simplify an expression
for the area of the rectangle.

Write and solve an equation to find each unknown value.   2-5, 2-7, 2-8

32.

33.

Solve.

34. $t - 7 = 98$ **35.** $\frac{n}{5} + 35 = 25$ **36.** $56 = 6x + 8x$

37. Ilana Meyers plans to buy a pad of paper and a pen for each
person scheduled to attend a peer counseling workshop. Each
pad of paper costs $1.39 and each pen costs $.49. Ilana has
$45.12. How many people can she buy supplies for?

Unit 2 Review and Assessment   121

38. Lorenzo Walker paid $8.51 for eight containers of yogurt and a loaf of bread. The bread cost $2.19. How much did each container of yogurt cost?

39. Is $\sqrt{16}$ *rational* or *irrational*?　　　**40.** Find the square roots of 121.　　　2-9

41. Estimate $\sqrt[3]{72}$ within a range of two integers.

42. The area of a square is 150 ft². Find the length of a side of the square.

43. The volume of a cube is 81 mm³. Find the length of an edge of the cube.

44. **Self-evaluation** Describe as much as you can about each figure. Use as many terms and symbols that you have learned in this unit as you can. Which figure do you know the most about? Which figure do you need to study more?

45. **Group Activity** Work with another student. You will need rulers and protractors.

a. Have each person draw a large triangle. Measure the angles of the triangle and measure the sides in inches. Write the measurements on a separate piece of paper.

b. Label one angle of the triangle $x°$. Use the angle measurements to write an expression in terms of $x°$ for each of the other angles. Label the triangle with your expressions.

c. Exchange triangles. Write and solve an equation to find the measure of each angle of the triangle you receive.

d. Compare your results with the actual measurements.

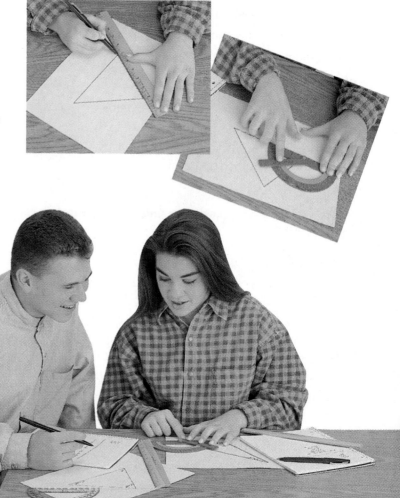

IDEAS AND (FORMULAS)= X^2

ALGEBRA

➤ Subtracting a number gives the same result as adding the opposite of that number. *(p. 65)*

➤ $10^{-n} = \dfrac{1}{10^n}$, and $10^0 = 1$. *(p. 75)*

➤ When you simplify algebraic expressions involving addition and subtraction, you can only combine like terms. *(p. 95)*

➤ To solve an equation, you get the variable alone on one side. You must keep the equation balanced as you do this. *(p. 100)*

➤ To solve a two-step equation, undo the operations that were performed on the variable, but in the opposite order. *(p. 105)*

➤ By knowing some perfect squares, you can estimate square roots. *(p. 114)*

➤ You can solve square root equations and cube root equations by undoing the squaring and cubing. *(p. 115)*

GEOMETRY

➤ You can estimate some numbers by doing an informal count or by making comparisons to facts you know. *(p. 58)*

➤ You can estimate lengths, distances, and areas using common guides for length and scales on maps. *(pp. 79–81)*

➤ An entire circle has a measure of 360°. *(p. 86)*

➤ Vertical angles have equal measures. *(p. 87)*

➤ The sum of the measures of the angles of a triangle is 180°. *(p. 88)*

STATISTICS & PROBABILITY

➤ The probability of an event is a number from 0 to 1, where 0 means impossible and 1 means certain. *(p. 59)*

Key Terms

- **continuous** (p. 60)
- **opposites** (p. 64)
- **line, $\overleftrightarrow{XY}$** (p. 82)
- **length of a segment** (p. 82)
- **ray, $\overrightarrow{OZ}$** (p. 85)
- **central angle of a circle** (p. 85)
- **complementary angles** (p. 86)
- **vertical angles** (p. 87)
- **right triangle** (p. 88)
- **solving an equation** (p. 99)
- **rational number** (p. 113)
- **perfect square** (p. 114)

- **discrete** (p. 60)
- **scientific notation** (p. 72)
- **endpoint** (pp. 82, 85)
- **midpoint** (p. 82)
- **angle, $\angle YOZ$** (p. 85)
- **right angle** (p. 86)
- **supplementary angles** (p. 86)
- **acute triangle** (p. 88)
- **equation** (p. 99)
- **equivalent equations** (p. 100)
- **irrational number** (p. 113)
- **perfect cube** (p. 114)

- **absolute value, $|x|$** (p. 64)
- **$\approx$** (p. 73)
- **segment, $\overline{XY}$** (p. 82)
- **congruent segments** (p. 82)
- **vertex of an angle** (p. 85)
- **straight angle** (p. 86)
- **congruent angles** (p. 87)
- **obtuse triangle** (p. 88)
- **solution** (p. 99)
- **square root, $\pm\sqrt{}$** (p. 112)
- **real number** (p. 113)
- **cube root, $\sqrt[3]{}$** (p. 114)

One day you may wake up to find that your favorite station has changed its tune overnight! The style of music played by a radio station changes as new sounds develop and tastes change. In the past, the station you listen to now may have broadcast Swing music to your grandparents or Motown sounds to your parents.

Representing Data

Market researchers survey people's tastes. They may ask you about your favorite TV shows or your spending habits. Their analysis of this information helps retailers decide where to advertise, what products to sell, and where to locate stores.

Tastes and fashions have changed over the years. Car manufacturers, hair stylists, and clothes designers are among the people who try to predict and shape future trends. What do you think will be fashionable in the next decade?

1900   1910   1920   1930   1940

Plan a Music Store

Your project is to develop a business brochure that presents your plan for a music store in your area. A business brochure, also known as a *prospectus*, is designed to interest investors in financially supporting your business.

Your group will need to research the musical tastes of your customers before deciding on the formats and music that you will stock. The data you collect will help you decide what is typical of your customers.

Plan to include graphs and other data displays in your brochure to show the results of your market research and support your decisions.

Malls around the country are changing their marketing focus to meet the needs of the consumers in their community. When research showed that the Hispanic community was more than five times as large as any other population near an Arizona mall, stores in the mall updated their merchandising focus. Special events, such as a festival for the Mexican holiday of Cinco de Mayo, are also held at the mall to celebrate Hispanic heritage.

950 .... 1960 .... 1970 .... 1980 1990

125

Unit Project 3

Getting Started

For this project you should work in a group of three students. Here are some ideas to help you get started.

☞ Decide on a name for your music store. Will you include a logo on your brochure that represents your store?

☞ You will need to find out which songs and music artists are the most popular. How can you find this information?

☞ Musical tastes depend on many factors, including age and cultural background. How can you find out which groups purchase the most music recordings in your area?

☞ Throughout this unit you will be gathering data and completing research. How will you organize this information? Can you use a computer to create a database?

Can We Talk

MARKET RESEARCH

➤ What is your favorite type of music? Do your friends like the same music? What type of music do your parents like? your grandparents?

➤ How many different styles of music can you think of? For each style that you list, can you name a popular solo artist or group?

➤ What type of products do you think would be advertised on a radio station that plays jazz? country-western music? heavy metal music? Explain your reasoning.

➤ Which music groups do you think will be popular next year? Why? Can you make predictions based on what sold well in the past?

➤ Do you buy cassettes or compact discs most often? Do you buy music videos? Do you think your buying habits are typical of teenagers?

➤ What type of music recording is the most expensive? Does the price of a recording prevent people from buying it?

➤ How has the packaging for compact discs changed since they were first introduced? Why was it changed?

Working on the Unit Project

Your work in Unit 3 will help you collect and organize data for your brochure.

Related Exercises:
Section 3-1, Exercise 31
Section 3-2, Exercises 35, 36
Section 3-3, Exercise 28
Section 3-4, Exercise 25
Section 3-5, Exercise 27
Section 3-6, Exercise 24
Section 3-7, Exercise 34

Alternative Projects p. 176

Using Matrices and Graphs

TABLE THAT... THOUGHT

Use matrices and graphs to display and interpret data.

EXPLORATION

(How) *can you use tables and graphs to understand data?*

• **Work in a group of at least five students.**

The student government in your school wants to set up a new organization for volunteering. Your group's task is to gather information on student interest in various types of volunteer work.

Which types of volunteer work most interest you? Write a "1" next to your first choice and a "2" next to your second choice.

Hospital _____

Work with elderly _____

Big Brother/Big Sister _____

Homeless shelter _____

Tutoring _____

Recycling _____

Animal shelter _____

Student Resources Toolbox
pp. 661–663 *Data Displays*

① Use a survey like the one shown. Collect responses from everyone in your class.

② Organize the data from all the surveys in a table.

③ Based on the data you collected, which type of volunteer work do you think would be the most popular? With your group, come to an agreement on the most popular volunteer activity. Support your choice with one or more graphs.

④ Compare your results with other groups.

⑤ Save your data to use in Exercise 6 on page 131.

Displaying Data in a Matrix

A table that displays data that belong to more than one category is an example of a *matrix*. The matrix below shows data from City Year, a community service organization of 17–23 year olds.

In a **matrix,** numbers are arranged in *rows* and *columns*. The number of rows and columns, in that order, are the **dimensions** of the matrix. (The plural of matrix is *matrices*.)

City Year Participants' Education Level, 1998–2000

Category labels →

	1998	1999	2000
Did not complete high school	16%	16%	17%
High school graduate	42%	46%	53%
Some college	25%	23%	18%
College graduate	16%	15%	12%

The number 17% is in the first row, third column. In 2000, 17% of the participants had not completed high school.

4 rows

3 columns

The dimensions of the matrix are 4 × 3 (read "4 by 3").

BY THE WAY...

Alan Khazei and Michael Brown launched the Boston-based City Year in 1988, with the goal of providing a diverse group of young people a chance to work together in service to others.

Talk it Over

1. What number is in the third row, second column of the matrix? What does this number represent?

2. When you give the dimensions of a matrix, do you count the row and the column of category labels?

3. Is the table you made in step 2 of the Exploration a matrix? If so, what are its dimensions?

Graphs can help you compare sets of data, observe trends, draw conclusions, and support a point of view.

Sample 1

These line graphs display data from the City Year Participant Education matrix above. Use each line graph to describe a trend for the three-year period 1998–2000.

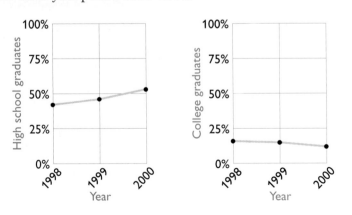

Student Resources Toolbox
pp. 653–656 *Percent*

The graphs show that the percent of City Year participants who were high school graduates steadily increased over the three-year period while the percent of participants who were college graduates steadily decreased.

Talk it Over

4. The percent of City Year participants who were high school graduates was higher in 2000 than in 1998 or 1999. Does that mean there were a greater number of high school graduates participating in City Year in 2000 than in 1998 or 1999? Explain.

5. Do you think it is easier to see the trends described in Sample 1 by looking at the graphs or by looking at the data displayed in the matrix? Explain your choice.

······▶ **Now you are ready for:**
Exs. 1–14 on pp. 131–132

Spreadsheets

In a spreadsheet, columns are lettered and rows are numbered.

Computer **spreadsheet** software stores information in matrices. The spreadsheet matrix below shows the financial support received by a non-profit organization during each of three years.

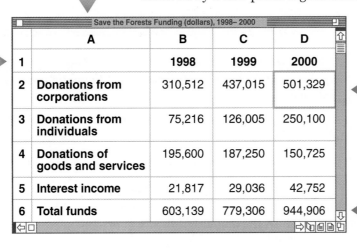

	A	B	C	D
		1998	**1999**	**2000**
1				
2	**Donations from corporations**	310,512	437,015	501,329
3	**Donations from individuals**	75,216	126,005	250,100
4	**Donations of goods and services**	195,600	187,250	150,725
5	**Interest income**	21,817	29,036	42,752
6	**Total funds**	603,139	779,306	944,906

Save the Forests Funding (dollars), 1998– 2000

Each position in a spreadsheet is called a **cell**. The number 501,329 is in cell D2.

You can enter the formula D2 + D3 + D4 + D5 in cell D6. The software finds the sum of the numbers in cells D2 to D5.

Talk it Over

6. Which row and which column of the spreadsheet contain the category labels for the matrix?

7. What number is in cell C5? Which cell contains the number 195,600? What does each number represent?

8. In which other cells could you enter formulas like the formula in cell D6? What are some advantages of entering a formula, rather than a number, in a spreadsheet cell?

Computer software can create graphs from data in a spreadsheet. These graphs display the Save the Forests Funding data shown on page 129.

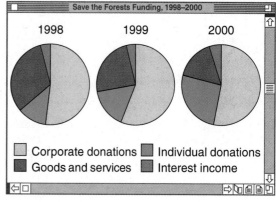

Talk it Over

9. Which rows of the spreadsheet does the bar graph represent?

10. Does each circle graph represent a *row* or a *column* of the spreadsheet?

Sample 2

Writing Use the Save the Forests Funding graphs. Which graph better supports the statement below? Explain your choice.

The amount of support from goods and services has decreased.

Sample Response

State your choice. ⟶ The bar graph. The bars represent the dollar amounts of each type of funding. The bars for goods and services get shorter, so the amount of this type of support has decreased.

Explain how the graph supports the statement.

Since the circle graph does not show the dollar amounts, it does not show that the *amount* of support in goods and services has decreased.

Explain why you did not use the other graph to support the statement.

······► Now you are ready for:
Exs. 15–31 on pp. 133–134

Look Back ◄

What are some advantages of presenting data in a matrix? in a graph?

1. **Reading** Use the City Year Participant Education matrix on page 128. Suppose that a column is added for the year 2001. What will the dimensions of the new matrix be?

For Exercises 2–5, use the matrix and the *stacked bar graph*.

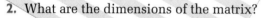

Gasoline Prices, 1999		
	Base price ($/gallon)	Tax ($/gallon)
United States	0.78	0.38
Japan	1.32	1.95
Turkey	0.97	2.33
France	0.76	3.26
Norway	1.31	3.39

2. What are the dimensions of the matrix?

3. What does the number in the third row, second column represent?

4. Explain how the stacked bar graph shows the total price of a gallon of gasoline in each country.

5. The data in the matrix could also be displayed in a double bar graph. Do you think a *double bar graph* or a *stacked bar graph* is better for this type of data? Give a reason for your choice.

6. **a.** Display the data you collected in the Exploration in a stacked bar graph.

   b. Suppose the new student organization plans to sponsor only three volunteer activities in its first year. Which three activities should they offer? Use your graph in part (a) to support your answer.

7. Use the tide table.

   a. Describe two patterns in the tide data that are shown in the tide table.

   b. There are actually two high tides and two low tides each day. Predict the times of the other high and low tides on Friday.

8. **Research** A tide table is an example of an everyday matrix. Find at least three more examples of everyday matrices. For each example that you find, tell what kind of graph (if any) you could use to display the information in the matrix.

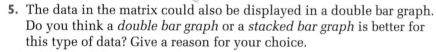

TIDE TABLE–AUG.

	High tide	Low tide
Friday	4:46 A.M.	11:00 A.M.
Saturday	5:35 A.M.	11:55 A.M.
Sunday	6:25 A.M.	12:51 P.M.
Monday	7:16 A.M.	1:42 P.M.
Tuesday		

Florence Nightingale (1820–1910) used data displays to convince the British government to reform military health care. This display is based on data collected during and after the Crimean War (1854–56).

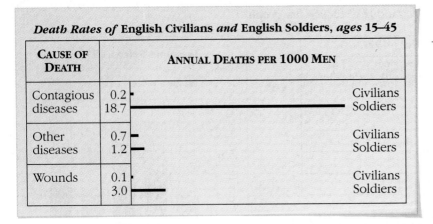

Death Rates of English Civilians *and* English Soldiers, *ages 15–45*

CAUSE OF DEATH	ANNUAL DEATHS PER 1000 MEN	
Contagious diseases	0.2	Civilians
	18.7	Soldiers
Other diseases	0.7	Civilians
	1.2	Soldiers
Wounds	0.1	Civilians
	3.0	Soldiers

BY THE WAY...

Florence Nightingale is well known for her role in the history of nursing. She was equally interested in statistics, and made important contributions to this new field of study.

9. Display the data in the second column in a matrix like the ones in this section. Be sure to include row and column category labels, and a title.

10. **Writing** A graph like the one above appeared in a report of the Royal Commission on the Health of the Army, formed in 1857. Write a part of the report, explaining the conclusions that can be drawn from the graph.

Use the matrix and the multiple line graph.

11. a. Which type of music recording is the most popular regardless of the year?

b. Did you use the *matrix* or the *graph* to answer part (a)?

12. Which type of music recording is the least popular but maintains steady sales? Use the graph to explain your answer.

13. a. Use the graph to compare the values of the shipments of different types of music recordings in 1998.

b. Use the graph to describe how the value of music video shipments changed from 1996 to 1999.

c. For parts (a) and (b), you had to read the graph in different ways. How were they different?

14. Use the graph to write three statements comparing the values of shipments of cassette singles and compact disc singles from 1996 to 1999.

Value of Music Shipments (millions of dollars)

		1996	1997	1998	1999
⬤	**Albums (LPs and EPs)**	36.8	33.3	34.0	31.8
	Cassette singles	189.3	133.5	94.4	48.0
	Compact disc singles	184.1	272.7	213.2	222.4
	Music videos	236.1	323.9	508.0	376.7

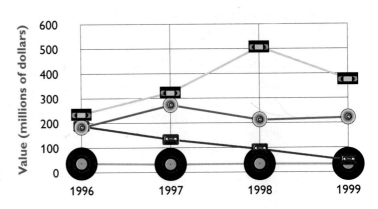

Business Use the spreadsheet and the bar graph.

	A	B	C	D	E
		1997	1998	1999	2000
1					
2	Investment income	93.1	100.9	715.4	618.7
3	Expenses	106.4	127.4	413.6	412.5
4	Net income or loss	−13.3	−26.5	301.8	206.2

Mutual Money Fund: Financial Data (millions of dollars)

15. What number is in cell D4? In which cell is the number 127.4? What does each number represent?

16. Write a formula that will calculate the value in cell E4 from the values in cells E2 and E3.

17. Which row(s) of the spreadsheet does the graph display?

18. How does the graph show profits and losses?

The five breeds shown in the pictograph and the circle graph represent about one-third of all dogs registered in the United States in 1999.

Writing Which graph better supports each statement? Explain your choice.

U.S. Dog Registrations Top Five Breeds, 1999

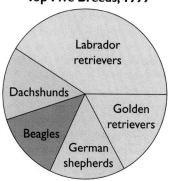

U.S. Dog Registrations: Top Five Breeds, 1999

Labrador retriever	🐕🐕🐕🐕🐕🐕🐕🐕🐕🐕🐕🐕🐕🐕🐕🐕🐕
Golden retriever	🐕🐕🐕🐕🐕🐕
German shepherd	🐕🐕🐕🐕🐕🐕
Dachshund	🐕🐕🐕🐕🐕
Beagle	🐕🐕🐕🐕🐕

Each 🐕 represents 10,000 dogs registered.

19. Of the top five breeds, the beagle has the smallest number of dogs registered.

20. Of the top five breeds, the two breeds with about the same number of registered dogs are the dachshund and the beagle.

21. The number of registered beagles and Labrador retrievers is about half the number of dogs registered from the top five breeds.

22. Suppose you enter the City Year Participant Education matrix on page 128 in a spreadsheet so that the data for 1998 are in cells B2 through B5. Write a formula for B6 to show that all 1998 participants are accounted for.

23. **Writing** Use the Save the Forests Funding graphs on page 130. Which graph better supports the statement below? Explain your choice.

> The portion of funds that comes from donations from individuals has increased each year.

Ongoing **ASSESSMENT**

24. **Open-ended** Suppose you have to show a group of fifth-grade students how to display information in a graph. You want the students to take part in the demonstration. Your materials are self-stick removable notes, felt-tipped markers, and graph paper or poster board.

Describe your demonstration. Include these parts:

➤ an introduction: Why do we use graphs?

➤ a survey question that the students can easily answer

➤ a method for displaying the results of the question with your materials

➤ a conclusion

Review **PREVIEW**

25. The area of a square is 196 m². Find the length of a side of the square. *(Section 2-9)*

Use a number anywhere along the scale to estimate the probability of each event. *(Section 2-1)*

26. You will do some volunteer work this year.

27. School will be closed because of a snowstorm at least once this year.

impossible	unlikely	possible	likely	certain
0%	25%	50%	75%	100%
0	0.25	0.5	0.75	1

Solve each equation. *(Sections 2-7, 2-8)*

28. $3x - 8 = 13$

29. $\frac{x}{6} = -5$

30. $\frac{x}{4} + 10 = 12$

Working on the Unit Project

31. **a.** **Research** Follow the popularity of a song or a group using data from the last several months. You may want to use magazines such as *Billboard, Entertainment Weekly,* and *Variety.*

b. Choose a format to display the data you collected.

c. **Writing** Describe any trends you notice in the data you collected.

Mean, Median, and Mode

The MEDIAN *is the message.*
I'm in the MODE *for math.*
But, what does it all MEAN?

---Focus

Find values that are typical
of a data set, identify data
values that are not typical
of a data set, and use
equations to find missing
data values.

Nutritionists recommend a diet that is low in fat. You can read
package labels to find the approximate fat content of many foods.

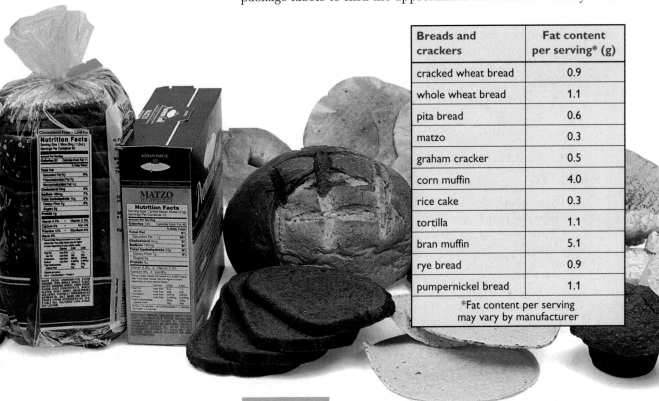

Breads and crackers	Fat content per serving* (g)
cracked wheat bread	0.9
whole wheat bread	1.1
pita bread	0.6
matzo	0.3
graham cracker	0.5
corn muffin	4.0
rice cake	0.3
tortilla	1.1
bran muffin	5.1
rye bread	0.9
pumpernickel bread	1.1
*Fat content per serving may vary by manufacturer	

Talk it Over

1. What do you notice about the numbers in the table?

2. Does one value appear more often than any other?

3. Are any of the values very different from the others?

4. How many grams of fat per serving do you think is most
   typical of the types of breads and crackers listed?

Three values that may be typical of a data set are the *mean,* the
median, and the *mode.* Which value is "most typical" may
depend upon the type of data, and it may be a matter of opinion.

Find the mean, the median, and the mode of the fat-per-serving data set on page 135.

Sample Response

Mean: Find the sum of all the data. Then divide by the number of data items.

$$0.9 + 1.1 + 0.6 + 0.3 + 0.5 + 4.0 + 0.3 + 1.1 + 5.1 + 0.9 + 1.1$$

$$\frac{15.9}{11} = 1.4\overline{45}$$

There are 11 data items.

To the nearest tenth, the mean is 1.4 g.

Median: List the data in order from least to greatest. Then find the middle number. *Note:* When the number of data items is even, the median is the *mean* of the *two* middle numbers.

Method ❶ Move by pairs from both ends of the data to the middle number. The median is 0.9 g.

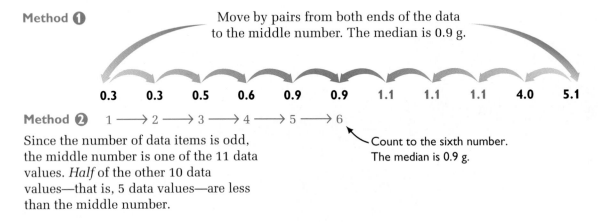

| 0.3 | 0.3 | 0.5 | 0.6 | 0.9 | 0.9 | 1.1 | 1.1 | 1.1 | 4.0 | 5.1 |

Method ❷ 1 ⟶ 2 ⟶ 3 ⟶ 4 ⟶ 5 ⟶ 6

Since the number of data items is odd, the middle number is one of the 11 data values. *Half* of the other 10 data values—that is, 5 data values—are less than the middle number.

Count to the sixth number. The median is 0.9 g.

Mode: Find the number(s) that appear most often. *Note:* A data set may have more than one mode, or it may have no mode.

The value 1.1 appears three times. All other values appear one or two times. The mode is 1.1 g.

Talk it Over

5. Explain why the mean of the data in Sample 1 is greater than the median and the mode.

6. Will the mean be greater than the median and the mode for any data set? Give examples to support your answer.

7. Do you think the *mean,* the *median,* or the *mode* is the most typical of the data in Sample 1? Give a reason for your choice.

TECHNOLOGY NOTE

Many calculators and computer software packages can find the mean of a data set, and can sort data from smallest to largest.

Outliers and Range

Data values that are much larger or much smaller than the other values in a data set are called **outliers,** because they lie outside most of the other values. Outliers are *not* typical of the data set.

The difference between the smallest and largest numbers in a data set is called the **range** of the data set.

Sample 2

a. **Which values in the data set in Sample 1 are outliers? Explain.**

b. **What is the range of the data set in Sample 1?**

Sample Response

A *line plot* helps you picture the outliers and the range. In a **line plot,** you show each data value as an x above its position on a number line.

a. Most of the values are clustered near 1.

The outliers are far away from the other values. The outliers are 4.0 and 5.1.

b. 0.3   **5.1 − 0.3 = 4.8**   5.1

To find the range, subtract the smallest number from the largest number. — The range is 4.8.

Talk it Over

8. Which breads are associated with the outliers in the fat-per-serving data set? What advice would you give to someone trying to eat a low-fat diet?

9. Replace the data for bran and corn muffins with data for breads that are lower in fat:

English muffin: 1.1 g of fat per serving

Bagel: 1.4 g of fat per serving

a. Does the new data set have any outliers? What is the range of the new data set?

b. Find the mean, the median, and the mode of the new data set. Which one is most affected by the change in the data?

····► Now you are ready for:
Exs. 1–17 on pp. 139–141

Lin's test scores are 87, 86, 89, and 88. There is one more test in the grading period. Lin wants her mean test score to be 90. What score must she get on the last test? Explain your method.

Sample Response

Method ❶

Problem Solving Strategy: Guess and check

Lin's first four scores are less than 90, so her last test score must be greater than 90.

Try a number larger than 90, such as 95.

Find the mean of the scores:

$$\frac{87 + 86 + 89 + 88 + 95}{5} = \frac{445}{5} = 89$$

The mean is less than 90.

Try a number larger than 95, such as 100.

$$\frac{87 + 86 + 89 + 88 + 100}{5} = \frac{450}{5} = 90$$

Lin's mean test score will be 90 if her last test score is 100.

Method ❷

Problem Solving Strategy: Work backward

In order to have a mean of 90 on 5 tests, the sum of the five test scores must be

$$90 \cdot 5 = 450.$$

The sum of the first four scores is

$$87 + 86 + 89 + 88 = 350.$$

So the last test score must be

$$450 - 350 = 100.$$

Lin's mean test score will be 90 if her last test score is 100.

Method ❸

Problem Solving Strategy: Use an equation

Let $x =$ Lin's last test score.

1 Write the mean of her five test scores in terms of x.	$\dfrac{\text{sum of five scores}}{5} = \dfrac{87 + 86 + 89 + 88 + x}{5} = \dfrac{350 + x}{5}$
2 Write an equation.	$\dfrac{350 + x}{5} = 90$ ◄——— The mean is 90.
3 Solve the equation.	$5 \cdot \dfrac{350 + x}{5} = 5 \cdot 90$ ◄——— Multiply both sides by 5.
	$350 + x = 450$
	$350 + x - 350 = 450 - 350$ ◄——— Subtract 350 from both sides.
	$x = 100$ ◄——— Lin's mean test score will be 90 if her last test score is 100.

······► Now you are ready for:
Exs. 18–36 on pp. 141–142

Look Back ◄——

How are the ideas of mean, median, and mode alike? How are they different? Can you think of everyday uses of these words that can help you remember which is which?

Exercises and Problems

1. **Writing** Explain how to find the median of 23, 15, 12, 17, 43, and 56.

2. **Reading** Change the data set in Sample 1 so that it has more than one mode.

3. Is it possible for a data set to have no mode? Explain.

Find the mean, the median, and the mode(s) of each data set. What number(s) do you think is (are) most typical of the set? Give a reason for your choice.

4. Times of swimming trials (in seconds): 66, 58.9, 61.1, 69, 53.5, 64.3, 53.5, 51.1, 55.2, 54.8

5. Attendance at school assemblies: 143, 125, 122, 144, 146, 121, 123, 122, 126, 146, 144, 122, 153, 144

6.

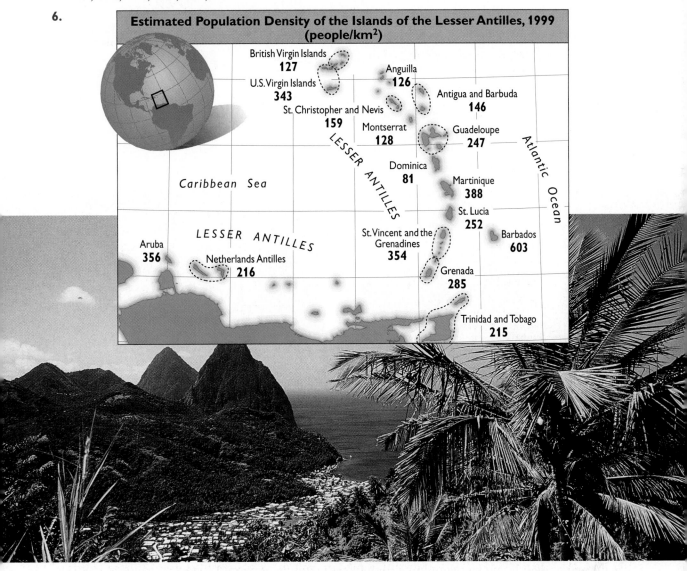

Estimated Population Density of the Islands of the Lesser Antilles, 1999 (people/km²)

British Virgin Islands **127**

U.S. Virgin Islands **343**

St. Christopher and Nevis **159**

Anguilla **126**

Antigua and Barbuda **146**

Montserrat **128**

Guadeloupe **247**

Dominica **81**

Martinique **388**

St. Lucia **252**

Barbados **603**

St. Vincent and the Grenadines **354**

Grenada **285**

Trinidad and Tobago **215**

Aruba **356**

Netherlands Antilles **216**

Caribbean Sea

LESSER ANTILLES

Atlantic Ocean

7. Find the outlier(s), if any, for each of the data sets in Exercises 4–6.

8. Find the range of each of the data sets in Exercises 4–6.

9. The sizes of 14 shirts sold at a souvenir stand are XS, S, M, S, XL, M, XL, XL, L, XL, S, L, L, and M. Is it possible to find the *mean,* the *median,* or the *mode* of this data? Explain.

10. **Astronomy** An *astronomical unit* is about 93,000,000 mi.

    a. Write this number in scientific notation.

    b. **Research** Find the definition of astronomical unit in a dictionary. Does the definition use a *mean,* a *median,* or a *mode*?

Use these data: Maria's test scores are 78, 25, 82, 96, 91, and 82.

11. Find the mean of Maria's test scores.

12. Use the grading scale. What grade will Maria receive if her grade is the mean of her scores? if it is the median? the mode?

13. a. Give a reason to use the mean for Maria's grade.

    b. Give a reason to use the median for Maria's grade.

    c. Do you think the *mean* or the *median* is more typical of Maria's original scores? Why?

14. a. Which one of Maria's scores is an outlier?

    b. Suppose Maria's teacher decides to drop each student's lowest grade. What effect will this have on the mean of Maria's scores? on the median? on the mode?

GRADING SCALE	
Score	Grade
90–100	A
80–89	B
70–79	C
60–69	D
0–59	F

Salaries For Exercises 15–17, use the salary data.

AD PROS   LUNCH FARE

15. a. Find the mean, the median, and the mode(s) of the salaries at Ad Pros and of the salaries at Lunch Fare.

    b. Which company would you think has higher salaries if you knew only the means of the salaries? if you knew only the medians? the modes?

16. **Open-ended** If you were applying for a job at Lunch Fare, would it be most helpful to know the *mean,* the *median,* or the *mode* of the salaries? Explain your choice.

17 TECHNOLOGY Use spreadsheet software to create the matrix shown below. Use the *copy* or *fill down* command.

Alternative Approach Create the matrix with pencil and paper.

a. Create a matrix that displays the Ad Pros salaries and the results of adding $1000 and $5000 to each Ad Pros salary. Show the mean, the median, and the range of each salary data set.

Enter the salaries from smallest to largest.

	A	B	C	D
		Salary	Salary + 1000	Salary + 5000
1				
2		20,000	= B2 + 1000	
3		23,000		
4		25,000		
5		25,000		
6		26,000		
7	mean			
8	median			
9	range			

Ad Pros Salaries

In column C enter formulas that add $1000 to the salaries in column B. In column D enter formulas that add $5000 to the salaries in column B.

In each column enter formulas for the mean, the median, and the range of the salaries in that column.

b. What effect does adding $1000 to each salary have on the mean? on the median? on the range?

c. What effect does adding $5000 to each salary have on the mean? on the median? on the range?

d. What effect do you think adding n dollars to each salary will have on the mean? on the median? on the range? Test your guesses for at least three more values of n.

e. Revise the matrix in part (a) to display the results of *multiplying* each Ad Pros salary by some factor n (choose at least five values for n). Describe the effect this has on the mean, the median, and the range.

Solve each equation.

18. $\dfrac{8 + x}{7} = 12$

19. $\dfrac{a + 15}{3} = -6$

20. $\dfrac{-9 + 2n}{5} = 11$

Use a problem solving strategy such as *Guess and check, Work backward,* or *Use an equation.*

21. Helen bowled six games. Her mean score was 153. What was the total score for the games? How did you find the answer?

22. Dan bowls in a league. His average score for last season was 159. In the first two games of the new season, he scored 138 and 143. What must he score on a third game in order to have an average of 159 for the first three games of the new season?

23. Maggie has a mean of 88 on the first nine tests of the grading period. In order to receive an A, her mean score must be 90 or higher. There is one test remaining in this grading period. Is it possible for Maggie to receive an A? Why or why not?

BY THE WAY...

Ancient Egyptians played a game, similar to bowling, that used pins and balls made of stone. Two other early versions of bowling are *ula maike* (Polynesian) and *bocci* (Italian).

Open-ended Find two different data sets that fit each description. Include at least four or five data values.

24. The median is 36.　　**25.** The mean is 36.　　**26.** The mode is 18 and the mean is 12.

27. In 1998, the median age (in years) of the population of the United States was 35.2. Does this imply that in 2008, the median age will be 55.2? Why or why not?

28. **Using Manipulatives** Break five pieces of uncooked spaghetti into three pieces each. Do not try to make all the pieces the same length. Line up the pieces in order from shortest to longest.

    a. Without measuring the pieces, find the median and the mode. Explain how you found them.

    b. Is it possible to find the mean without measuring the pieces? Explain.

Ongoing **ASSESSMENT**

29. **Open-ended** In a newspaper or magazine, find an article that uses the word "average." Do you think that the word means the *mean,* the *median,* the *mode,* or none of these? Give a reason for your answer.

Review **PREVIEW**

30. Would you use a *matrix* or a *graph* to display the fuel-economy ratings for city and highway driving for six different cars? Explain. *(Section 3-1)*

Write each product as a power. *(Section 1-3)*

31. $3 \cdot 3 \cdot 3 \cdot 3 \cdot 3 \cdot 3 \cdot 3$　　　　**32.** $x \cdot x \cdot x$

Show each pair of integers on a number line. Then compare the integers using > or <. *(Toolbox Skill 2)*

33. 3 and -5　　　　　**34.** -2 and -4

Working on the Unit Project

35. a. **Research** Find the prices of at least 25 different recordings. Keep track of the type of music (for example, rock, classical, country) and the format of each recording (for example, cassette, CD, LP).

    b. Find the mean, the median, and the mode of all the price data.

    c. Find the mean, the median, and the mode of the prices of each of the different types of music. Which type has the largest mean?

    d. Find the mean, the median, and the mode of the prices of each of the different musical formats. Which format has the largest mean?

36. Suppose you ask 25 people to name their favorite type of music. Could you find the *mean,* the *median,* or the *mode* of their answers? Explain.

Inequalities and Intervals

.... Focus

Use inequalities to describe number line graphs.

The number line graph shows data on world records set since 1900 in the men's long jump.

August 5, 1901
7.61 m
Peter O'Conner
(Great Britain)
at Dublin

October 27, 1931
7.98 m
Chuhei Nambu
(Japan)
at Tokyo

August 30, 1991
8.95 m
Mike Powell
(United States)
at Tokyo

7.5 m

1901 1921 1924 | 8 m | 1925 1928 1928 1931 | 1935 1960 1961 1961 1962 1964 1964 1965, 1967 | 8.5 m | 1968 1991 | 9 m

Men's Long Jump Records

Talk it Over

1. Does the scale on the number line measure distance or years?

2. Estimate the record distance for 1935.

3. In which years was the record broken more than once? In which years did a record jump match the existing record?

4. Describe the lengths of record long jumps set by men after 1991.

5. Describe the lengths of all long jumps made in competition by men before October 27, 1931.

6. In which year was the *increase* in the record the greatest? the smallest? How can you use the graph to answer these questions?

BY THE WAY...

The first known long jump record was 7.05 m, set by Chionis of Sparta in 656 B.C.

Student Resources Toolbox
p. 641 *Comparing Integers*

a. **Write an inequality to describe any record long jump set by a man after August 30, 1991.**

b. **Graph the inequality on a number line.**

Sample Response

a. Let r = the length of a record long jump set by a man after August 30, 1991.

The graph on page 143 shows that on August 30, 1991, Mike Powell set a long jump record of 8.95 m, so

r is *greater than or equal to* 8.95 m.

In symbols, write $r \geq 8.95$.

b. Graph all values equal to or greater than 8.95.

A closed circle shows that 8.95 is on the graph.

Shade the number line to the right of 8.95.

On July 16, 1961, Iolanda Balas of Romania set her twelfth consecutive women's high jump record. Her record of 1.91 m stood for over a decade, until October 4, 1971.

a. Write an inequality to describe the height of all high jumps made in competition by women before October 4, 1971.

b. Graph the inequality on a number line.

Sample Response

a. Let j = the height of a high jump made in competition by a woman before October 4, 1971.

Then j is *greater than* 0 m and j is *less than or equal to* 1.91 m.

Write $j > 0$ and $j \leq 1.91$ You can write these two inequalities

or $0 < j \leq 1.91$.   as a **combined inequality.**

One way to read the combined inequality is,

   "j is *greater than* 0 and *less than or equal to* 1.91."

You can also read it as,

   "0 is less than j and j is less than or equal to 1.91."

b. The combined inequality $0 < j \leq 1.91$ helps you see that j is between 0 and 1.91 on the number line.

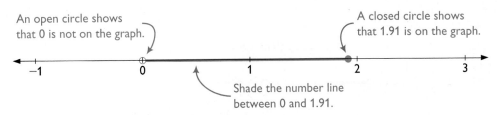

An open circle shows that 0 is not on the graph.

A closed circle shows that 1.91 is on the graph.

Shade the number line between 0 and 1.91.

Talk it Over

7. In the inequality $r \geq 8.96$ in Sample 1, why is the symbol $\geq$ used instead of the symbol $>$? Compare the meanings of the symbols $>$ and $\geq$, and the symbols $<$ and $\leq$.

8. In Sample 2, the simple inequality $j > 0$ is "turned around" when it appears in the combined inequality $0 < j \leq 1.91$. Explain why the inequalities $j > 0$ and $0 < j$ have the same meaning.

9. Does every point on the graph in Sample 1 represent a possible long jump record? Does every point on the graph in Sample 2 represent a past high jump record? Explain.

BY THE WAY...

Prehistory is the period of human history for which no written records exist. Prehistory includes the Stone Age, the Bronze Age, and the Iron Age.

Intervals

The graphs of the inequalities in Samples 1 and 2 are *intervals* of the number line. Each statement below refers to an interval, as shown in the graph. Each interval is also described by an inequality.

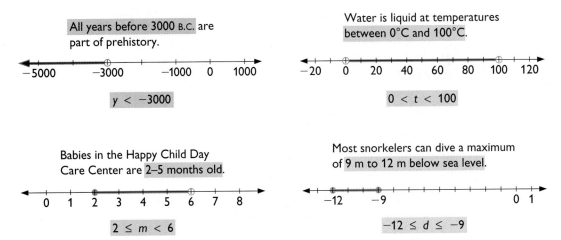

All years before 3000 B.C. are part of prehistory.

$y < -3000$

Water is liquid at temperatures between 0°C and 100°C.

$0 < t < 100$

Babies in the Happy Child Day Care Center are 2–5 months old.

$2 \leq m < 6$

Most snorkelers can dive a maximum of 9 m to 12 m below sea level.

$-12 \leq d \leq -9$

Intervals of a number line are continuous. Data such as the record long jumps are discrete. When discrete data are displayed in a line plot, they lie inside a continuous interval of the number line.

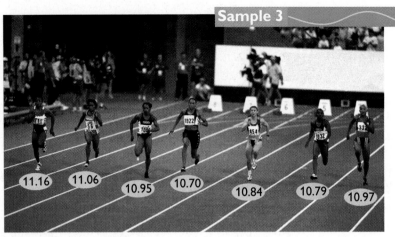

11.16 11.06 10.95 10.70 10.84 10.79 10.97

The photograph shows the finishing time (in seconds) of each runner of the 100 m final in the 1999 Women's World Track and Field Event held in Saville, Spain.

a. Make a line plot of the finishing times.

b. Write an inequality to describe the shortest interval of the number line that contains all the finishing times.

Sample Response

a.

Let t = the finishing time of a runner.
Then $10.70 \leq t \leq 11.16$.

b. The finishing times are in the interval of the number line that includes the points 10.70 and 11.16 and all the points between them.

Look Back

Think of and describe a real-world situation that involves data that lie in a interval. Write an inequality to describe the shortest interval that contains the data. Graph the inequality on a number line.

3-3 Exercises and Problems

1. Use the graph on men's long jump records on page 143.

   a. Estimate the men's long jump records set in 1960 and 1967.

   b. Write an inequality to describe the shortest interval that contains all the men's long jump records set from 1960 to 1967.

Match each graph with the correct inequality.

2.
   −3 −2 −1 0 1 2 3

3. −3 −2 −1 0 1 2 3

4. −3 −2 −1 0 1 2 3

A. $-2 < x < 2$

B. $-2 < x \leq 2$

C. $x \leq 2$

Graph each inequality on a number line. Then write each inequality in words.

5. $0 \leq x < 8$

6. $x > 3\frac{2}{3}$

7. $-1.6 \leq x \leq 1.1$

8. Reading Explain why each open or closed circle was used on the four graphs at the bottom of page 145.

Write and graph an inequality to describe the interval referred to in each statement.

9. The surface temperature of sea water may range from −2°C to 30°C.

10. Johanna has at least $80 in her savings account.

11. The measure of an obtuse angle is between 90° and 180°.

Driving **Write and graph an inequality to describe the allowable driving speeds as shown by each sign.**

12.

SCHOOL

SPEED LIMIT

20

WHEN CHILDREN
ARE PRESENT

13.

MAXIMUM

55

MINIMUM

40

For Exercises 14–16, use the matrix of data on women's hammer throw records set during the 1990s.

14. a. Write an inequality to describe the length of any record hammer throw made by a woman since 1999.

   b. Graph the inequality on a number line.

15. a. Complete the increase column.

   b. Make a line plot of the data in the increase column.

   c. Write an inequality to describe the shortest interval that contains all the increase data.

   d. What is the range of the data in the increase column? How is the range related to the shortest interval of the number line that contains all the data?

16. Career A sports statistician uses sports data to observe trends and make predictions.

Do you think a sports statistician would be more interested in knowing the mean of the data in the *distance* column or of the data in the *increase* column? Explain your answer.

17. Look at the inequalities you wrote in Exercises 9–13. Tell if the quantity each inequality describes is *discrete* or *continuous*.

BY THE WAY...

Mihaela Melinte of Romania set two of the 1999 records on the same day.

increase = new record − old record

0.02 = 66.86 − 66.84

Women's Hammer Records		
Year	Record (meters)	Increase (meters)
1994	66.84	
1995	66.86	0.02
1995	67.08	0.22
1995	68.14	1.06
1995	68.16	0.02
1997	69.00	0.84
1997	69.58	0.58
1997	71.22	
1997	73.10	
1997	73.14	
1999	75.29	
1999	75.97	
1999	76.07	

For Exercises 18 and 19, do these things.

a. **Open-ended** Describe a real life situation that fits each graph.

b. **Write an inequality to describe each graph.**

18.
    $2\frac{1}{2}$

19.

20. a. Write a description of this graph in words and in symbols.

    b. Which is easiest for you to understand, the *description in words*, the *description in symbols*, or the *graph*?

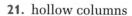

connection to **SCIENCE**

For Exercises 21–23, do these things.

a. **Draw a number line graph to show the temperature interval(s) for each snow crystal shape.**

b. **Write one or more inequalities to describe your graph.**

21. hollow columns

22. sector plates

23. dendrites

Below −8°F
Hollow columns

−8°F to 3°F
Sector plates

3°F to 10°F
Dendrites

10°F to 14°F
Sector plates

14°F to 21°F
Hollow columns

21°F to 25°F
Needles

25°F to 32°F
Thin plates

Ongoing **ASSESSMENT**

24. **Writing** Write a summary of the main ideas of this section. Which ideas are new to you? How has your understanding of inequalities changed since you first learned about them?

Review **PREVIEW**

25. Find the mean, median, and mode of this data set. *(Section 3-2)*

    Number of nations participating in Winter Olympic Games held from 1924 to 1998:
    16, 25, 17, 28, 28, 30, 32, 30, 36, 37, 35, 37, 37, 49, 57, 64, 67, 72

26. Find the square roots and the cube root of 225. *(Section 2-9)*

27. Make a bar graph of the data on home runs. *(Toolbox Skill 22)*

Number of Home Runs Made in World Series Games

10 Gehrig
10 Jackson
12 Berra
18 Mantle
11 Snider
15 Ruth

Working on the Unit Project

28. **Research** Find the prices of seven different recordings. Make a line plot of the prices. Write an inequality to describe the shortest interval of the number line that contains all the prices.

Unit 3 CHECKPOINT

Quiz	Grade
1	74
2	73
3	68
4	75
5	81
6	84
7	84
8	92

1. **Writing** Suppose the table shows your grades. In a letter to your parents, describe how your grades have improved. Include at least one graph or display, and the mean, the median, and the mode of the grades.

2. In 1978–1979, men earned 52% of the bachelor's degrees, and women earned 48%. In 1988–1989, men earned 47% and women earned 53%. In 1998–1999, men earned 44% and women earned 56%.

   a. Organize the bachelor's degree data in a matrix.

   b. Use your matrix to describe a trend in the data.

   c. Give a reason for using three circle graphs instead of a matrix to present the data.

3-1

3. Each photograph shows the age (in months) when the baby first walked.

   3-2

   a. Find the mean, the median, and the mode of the data set. Which number(s) would you call most typical of the set? Explain your choice.

   b. Find the range and the outlier(s), if any, of the data set.

   c. Suppose there is an error in the data set. The baby labeled "18" walked at 11 months. Is the *mean*, the *median*, or the *mode* most affected by correcting the error?

4. Lisa's mean score in chemistry on the first four tests is 86. There are two tests remaining in the grading period. What scores does she need on the last two tests in order to have a mean of at least 90?

Write and graph an inequality to describe the interval referred to in each statement.

3-3

5. The diameters of Native American tipis range from 8 ft to 40 ft.

6. Water freezes in temperatures at or below 32°F.

Histograms and Stem-and-Leaf Plots

Focus

Use histograms, frequency tables, and stem-and-leaf plots to display data.

BEHIND BARS

TV stations, magazines, and newspapers often report the number of viewers or readers in different age groups:

"*Galaxy* magazine is most popular with readers age 20 to 24."

Talk it Over

1. Which interval of the number line would you use to represent "readers age 20 to 24"? Explain your choice.

2. Write an inequality to describe the interval you chose.

Histograms

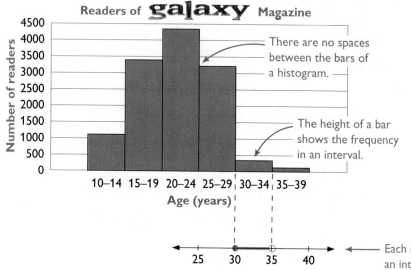

There are no spaces between the bars of a histogram.

The height of a bar shows the frequency in an interval.

This graph, called a *histogram,* shows how many people in various age groups read *Galaxy,* a science magazine.

A **histogram** is a bar graph that shows how many data items occur in each of one or more intervals. The number of data items in an interval is a **frequency.**

Each age group corresponds to an interval of the number line.

Use the histogram shown on page 150 to make two statements about the ages of *Galaxy* magazine's readers.

Sample Response

Here are two possible statements based on the histogram:

➤ Most of *Galaxy* magazine's readers are in their teens and twenties.

➤ About 500 readers are in their thirties.

Talk it Over

3. Use the histogram to estimate the total number of *Galaxy* readers of ages 10–19 years.

4. Compare the histogram to the bar graphs in Section 3-1. How are they alike? How are they different?

5. Why are there no spaces between the bars of a histogram?

Frequency Tables

Sometimes you want to display the exact number of data items in an interval. This **frequency table** shows the exact number of *Galaxy* magazine readers in each age group used in the histogram on page 150.

Readers of

galaxy

Magazine

Age group	Frequency
10–14	1110
15–19	3398
20–24	4344
25–29	3215
30–34	332
35–39	112

Number of

galaxy

copies sold each week

256	311	275	342	312
246	298	281	302	294
331	300	250	241	277
234	274	314	298	325
259	258	235	297	321

Talk it Over

6. Does either the histogram or the frequency table show how many readers of *Galaxy* magazine are 24 years old? Explain.

7. How close was your estimate in question 3?

8. A newsstand owner keeps track of how many copies of *Galaxy* magazine are sold each week. The table at the left shows the data from the last 25 weeks.

   a. What is the range of the data?

   b. What intervals would you use to display the data in a histogram with five bars?

   c. Make a frequency table for the data using the intervals you chose in part (b).

┄┄┄➤ Now you are ready for:
Exs. 1–9 on pp. 154–155

Stem-and-Leaf Plots

To display every number in a data set and still organize the data in intervals, you can use a *stem-and-leaf plot*. Separate each piece of data into two parts, a *stem* and a *leaf*.

The leaf is the last digit on the right.

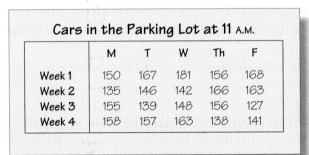

1 5 2

The stem is the remaining digit or digits.

Sample 2

Cars in the Parking Lot at 11 A.M.					
	M	T	W	Th	F
Week 1	150	167	181	156	168
Week 2	135	146	142	166	163
Week 3	155	139	148	156	127
Week 4	158	157	163	138	141

In order to decide if the high school needs a bigger parking lot, a town manager's assistant gathered the data shown in the matrix.

Make a stem-and-leaf plot of the data.

Sample Response

1 Use a vertical line to separate the stems from the leaves.

2 To the left of the line, list the stems in order from smallest to largest.

Cars in the Parking Lot at 11 A.M.

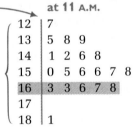

```
12 | 7
13 | 5  8  9
14 | 1  2  6  8
15 | 0  5  6  6  7  8
16 | 3  3  6  7  8
17 |
18 | 1
```

3 Write the leaf of each data value to the right of its stem. List the leaves for each stem in order from smallest to largest.

This row contains the numbers 163, 163, 166, 167, and 168.

Talk it Over

9. The number 156 appears twice in the parking-lot data set. Does it appear twice in the stem-and-leaf plot? Explain.

10. Describe how to use a stem-and-leaf plot to find the median of the data. What is the median of the parking-lot data?

11. Suppose the parking lot in Sample 2 contains 180 parking spaces. Should the lot be made bigger? Why or why not?

Unit 3 Representing Data

Making a Histogram from a Stem-and-Leaf Plot

A stem-and-leaf plot contains the information you need to make a histogram.

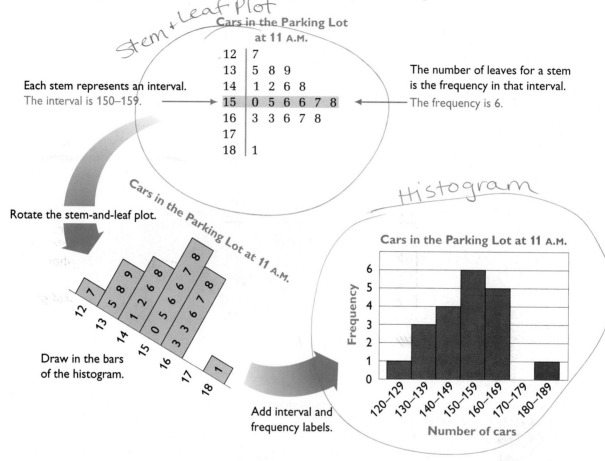

Stem + Leaf Plot

Cars in the Parking Lot at 11 A.M.

12	7
13	5 8 9
14	1 2 6 8
15	0 5 6 6 7 8
16	3 3 6 7 8
17	
18	1

Each stem represents an interval.
The interval is 150–159.

The number of leaves for a stem is the frequency in that interval.
The frequency is 6.

Rotate the stem-and-leaf plot.

Cars in the Parking Lot at 11 A.M.

Draw in the bars of the histogram.

Add interval and frequency labels.

Histogram

Cars in the Parking Lot at 11 A.M.

Talk it Over

12. Compare the stem-and-leaf plot and the histogram made from the same data. How are they alike? How are they different?

13. Can you make a stem-and-leaf plot from either a frequency table or a histogram? Can you make a histogram from a frequency table? Explain your answers.

Look Back

Does a *histogram*, a *frequency table*, or a *stem-and-leaf plot* give you the most detailed information about a data set? Give a reason why you might *not* want to use a stem-and-leaf plot to display a data set.

······▶ Now you are ready for:
Exs. 10–25 on pp. 155–157

Exercises and Problems

1. **Reading** Look at the *Galaxy* magazine readers histogram on page 150.

   a. How would the histogram change if the intervals 10–19, 20–29, and 30–39 were used instead of the intervals shown?

   b. Give a reason why the publisher of *Galaxy* magazine might want to display the data with the intervals in part (a).

---

connection to **GEOGRAPHY**

Use the United States population histograms.

Southern States Population

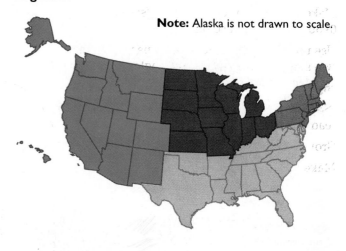

Note: Alaska is not drawn to scale.

Midwestern States Population

Northeastern States Population

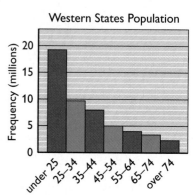

Western States Population

2. Make two statements about the populations in all four regions.

3. Why do you think that in each region, "under 25" is the age group with the greatest frequency?

4. Make a statement about the population of your state's region as compared to the populations of the other regions.

5. Estimate the total number of people living in your region.

6. About what percent of the population of your region is 35–64 years old?

7. Sales The manager of a school store collected data on the amount of money spent by customers during one day. Make a histogram of the data using the intervals shown in the frequency table.

Amount (dollars)	Number of transactions
0.01 – 5.00	102
5.01 – 10.00	76
10.01 – 15.00	30
15.01 – 20.00	6
20.01 – 25.00	15
over 25	11

8. a. On graph paper, draw all the rectangles with perimeter 60 and with sides whose lengths are integers.

   b. Find the area of each rectangle.

   c. Make a histogram of the areas. Use intervals 0–50, 51–100, and so on.

   d. Use the histogram you made in part (c) to make two statements about the rectangles.

9. **Using Manipulatives** Use index cards or self-stick, removable notes.

   a. **Research** Ask at least 20 people how many magazines each one has read this month. Write each response on a separate card or note.

   b. Group the cards or notes into intervals.

   c. Make a histogram of the data you collected.

Draw a pair of axes on a large piece of paper. On the horizontal axis, write the intervals you chose in part (b).

Then put each card or note in place above the interval in which it belongs. Do not overlap the notes.

   d. What is the frequency of the data in each of your intervals?

   e. **Writing** Does your histogram give more detailed information than the Readers of *Galaxy* Magazine histogram on page 150? Explain.

10. The parking lot described in Sample 2 is also used at night. For four weeks, cars are counted at 8 P.M.

   a. Make a stem-and-leaf plot of the data.

   b. **Writing** Describe two differences between the data for 8 P.M. and the data for 11 A.M. based on the stem-and-leaf plots.

Cars in the Parking Lot at 8 P.M.

	M	T	W	Th	F
Week 1	12	14	36	35	14
Week 2	45	15	17	13	49
Week 3	51	53	146	149	35
Week 4	28	135	146	24	26

**For Exercises 11–17, use the table on precipitation (rain, snow, sleet, and hail).
The regional color-code matches the one used in the map on page 154.**

AVERAGE NUMBER OF DAYS OF PRECIPITATION PER YEAR

West   Midwest   South   Northeast

Albany, NY	134	Detroit, MI	135	Norfolk, VA	115
Albuquerque, NM	61	Duluth, MN	134	Oklahoma, OK	82
Atlanta, GA	115	Great Falls, MT	101	Omaha, NE	98
Atlantic City, NJ	112	Hartford, CT	127	Philadelphia, PA	117
Bismarck, ND	96	Houston, TX	104	Phoenix, AZ	36
Boise, ID	90	Indianapolis, IN	125	Pittsburgh, PA	154
Boston, MA	126	Kansas City, MO	104	Portland, ME	128
Buffalo, NY	169	Little Rock, AR	104	Portland, OR	152
Burlington, VT	154	Los Angeles, CA	35	Providence, RI	124
Cheyenne, WY	99	Louisville, KY	124	Reno, NV	51
Chicago, IL	126	Miami, FL	129	Salt Lake City, UT	90
Cleveland, OH	156	Milwaukee, WI	125	Seattle-Tacoma, WA	156
Columbia, SC	109	Mobile, AL	122	Sioux Falls, SD	97
Concord, NH	125	Mt. Washington, NH	209	Spokane, WA	113
Denver, CO	89	Nashville, TN	119	Wichita, KS	86
Des Moines, IA	107	New Orleans, LA	114	Wilmington, DE	116

11. a. Make one stem-and-leaf plot of all the data.

   b. What is the median number of days of precipitation in one year?

12. Which four cities have the fewest days of precipitation? What do these cities have in common?

13. Which cities have more than 160 days of precipitation per year? What do these cities have in common?

14. Predict which of the four regions has the least number of days of precipitation per year.

15. Group Activity Work in a group of four students.

   a. Make four stem-and-leaf plots, one for each region.

   b. Describe three ways in which the stem-and-leaf plot for the southern cities differs from the stem-and-leaf plot for the western cities.

   c. Writing Do the stem-and-leaf plots your group made in part (a) support the prediction you made in Exercise 14? Explain your answer.

   d. Do you think the precipitation in Norfolk is typical or unusual for its region? How is this shown on the stem-and-leaf plot?

BY THE WAY...

In 1990 the world record for the greatest rainfall in one year was still held by Cherrapunji, India, where almost 87 ft of rain fell from August 1, 1860 to July 31, 1861.

16. **a.** Make a histogram from the stem-and-leaf plot for the midwestern cities.

    b. Find the median number of days of precipitation for the midwestern cities.

    c. **Writing** Is it possible to find the median from the histogram? Explain.

17 TECHNOLOGY Use a graphics calculator or spreadsheet software to make a histogram for the data for the northeastern cities. What intervals are shown on the histogram?

Ongoing ASSESSMENT

18. **Writing** Compare the stem-and-leaf plots you made in Exercise 15 with the four United States population histograms on page 154. Write about the possible relationship, if any, between the amount of precipitation in a region and its population. Use the displays to support your position.

Review PREVIEW

Write and graph an inequality to describe the interval referred to in each statement. *(Section 3-3)*

19. United States citizens must be at least 18 years old in order to vote.

20. The average global temperature may rise 2°F to 9°F by 2050.

Draw an angle with each measure. *(Toolbox Skill 16)*

21. 130°   22. 40°   23. 90°

24. The scoreboard shows the total points earned in one season by each member of the North High wrestling team. Find the median, the range, and the outliers of the data. *(Section 3-2)*

NORTH HIGH WRESTLING TEAM

202   97 103 109 156   82 148 194 163

187 279 224 181 194 199 187 170 187

Working on the Unit Project

25. **a.** **Research** Make a list of all the radio stations that broadcast in your area. Record each station's call letters, its number, whether it is AM or FM, and its category (such as country, top 40, classical, oldies, gospel, news/talk, and so on).

    b. Use several types of data displays to look at different aspects of the information you collected in part (a). How can you use your displays to help you plan what to sell in your music store?

Box-and-Whisker Plots

GOING TO EXTREMES

**Test Scores
Integrated Math Class**

68	78	93	79
72	88	44	79
75	92	71	89
75	88	73	80
66	100	75	82

After giving a test to his Integrated Math students, LaSalle Johnson used a *box-and-whisker plot* to see how their scores are grouped.

A **box-and-whisker plot** shows the median and the range of a data set. You can use box-and-whisker plots to compare how data are grouped in two sets.

Sample 1

Make a box-and-whisker plot of the test-score data shown above.

Sample Response

Step 1 Write the scores in order from lowest to highest.

Step 2 Find the median, the *extremes,* and the *quartiles* of the ordered data set.

The **lower extreme** is the lowest score.

The median divides the data set into two halves.

The **upper extreme** is the highest score.

The **lower quartile** is the median of the lower half of the data.

The **upper quartile** is the median of the upper half of the data.

44 66 68 71 72 | 73 75 75 75 78 | 79 79 80 82 88 | 88 89 92 93 100

72.5   78.5   88

Step 3 Graph the five values below a number line.

Step 4 Draw a box from the lower quartile to the upper quartile. Draw a vertical line through the median.

40 50 60 70 80 90 100

box   whisker

Step 5 Draw line segments, or whiskers, from the box to the extremes.

Talk it Over

1. **a.** What is the difference between the lower quartile and the lower extreme? the upper extreme and the upper quartile?

   b. How are these ranges shown on the box-and-whisker plot?

2. **a.** About what percent of the scores are greater than the upper quartile? less than the lower quartile?

   b. Will the percents you found in part (a) change if the number of scores in the data set changes? Why or why not?

3. **a.** About what percent of the scores are greater than the lower quartile *and* less than the upper quartile?

   b. How are these scores shown on the box-and-whisker plot?

   c. Will the percent you found in part (a) change if the number of scores in the data set changes? Why or why not?

4. Why do you think the term *quartile* is used to describe the numbers that determine one end of each whisker?

Sample 2

Under one number line, LaSalle Johnson made box-and-whisker plots for the test scores in his two algebra classes. Write at least three statements comparing the scores of the two classes.

Test Scores: Algebra Classes

Sample Response

Here are three possible statements:

Class I has a greater median. This means that the top half of Class I generally scored higher than the top half of Class II.

Class I has a greater range, but the middle 50% of Class I's scores are closer together.

Test Scores: Algebra Classes

Class I's lower quartile is greater than Class II's median. This means that about 75% of the students in Class I scored higher than half the students in Class II.

5. Do you need to know the exact values of the medians, the ranges, and the lower quartiles to make the statements in Sample 2? Explain.

6. Explain how the box-and-whisker plots show that the middle 50% of Class I's scores are closer together than the middle 50% of Class II's scores are.

7. Estimate the lower quartile for each class. Write a statement comparing the classes' scores based on the lower quartiles.

Look Back

What are the five numbers that determine a box-and-whisker plot? How do you find them?

3-5 Exercises and Problems

1. **Reading** The second paragraph on page 158 describes two pieces of information that a box-and-whisker plot shows. Name at least four *other* pieces of information shown by a box-and-whisker plot. In which part of the section are these ideas presented?

Kim's class collected data by asking students the ages of their brothers and sisters.

Use the data from Kim's class.

2. Tell how to find the median of the data.

3. Tell how to find the lower quartile.

4. What are the extremes of the data?

5. **a.** Make a box-and-whisker plot of the data.

   b. About what percent of the ages are greater than or equal to 11?

   c. About what percent of the ages does each whisker represent?

6. Suppose you chose an age at random from Kim's data. Is it more likely that the age is *greater than* the upper quartile or *less than* the upper quartile?

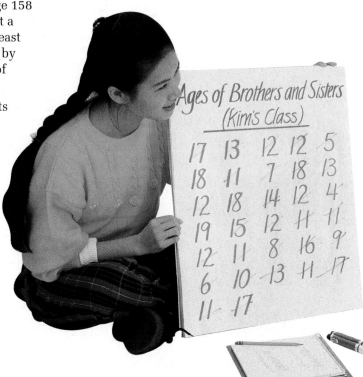

Ages of Brothers and Sisters (Kim's Class)

17 13 12 12 5
18 11 7 18 13
12 18 14 12 4
19 15 12 11 11
12 11 8 16 9
6 10 13 11 17
11 17

Jared's class also collected data by asking students the ages of their brothers and sisters.

Use the data from Kim's and Jared's classes.

7. **a.** Use the plot you made for part (a) of Exercise 5. Add a box-and-whisker plot for the data from Jared's class.

   b. Use your plots to make two statements comparing the data sets.

   c. Give an example of a statement about Jared's data set that is shown more clearly in the plot for his class than in the chart for his class.

   d. **Writing** Claudia says that the plots show that Jared's classmates have brothers and sisters who are generally older than Kim's classmates' brothers and sisters. Do you agree? Why or why not?

8. **a.** Jared collected four more pieces of data: 5, 24, 18, and 21. Include these in his data set. Find the new extremes, quartiles, and median. Compare them to the original extremes, quartiles, and median.

   b. Suppose Jared drew a box-and-whisker plot for the new data set. How would it differ from the original plot for his class?

9. **a.** Find the difference between the lower quartile and the lower extreme in Kim's data set.

   b. Find the difference between the lower quartile and the lower extreme in Jared's data set.

   c. Compare the numbers you found in parts (a) and (b). How are they shown on the box-and-whisker plot?

10. **a.** How many pieces of data are there in Kim's data set?

    b. How many pieces of data are there in Jared's original data set?

    c. Is there a relationship between the size of a data set and the size of a box-and-whisker plot of the data? Explain.

Ages of Brothers and Sisters
(Jared's Class)

10	17	21	22
22	24	24	14
22	2	17	18
18	19	5	25
14	23	24	17
21	21	20	20

Car Repairs **For Exercises 11–15, use the box-and-whisker plots below.**

Costs of Car Repairs (dollars)

11. About how much is the median cost of repairs for a Facet? for a Traveler?

12. Does the *Facet* or the *Traveler* have a greater range of repair costs?

13. About what percent of the repairs of a Facet cost between $250 and $350?

14. A report says that more than half the repairs of a Facet cost more than any repair done on a Traveler. Do the box-and-whisker plots support the report? Why or why not?

15. Peggy Quinn's car is a Facet. The cost of repairing her car is about $300. She thinks this is higher than most repair costs for a Facet. Is she right? Explain.

16. **Writing** Explain how the word *quartile* is used in this newspaper report on standardized test scores.

17. **Writing** The lower extreme, lower quartile, median, upper quartile, and upper extreme of a data set are called the *five-number summary* of the data set. Do you think a *five-number summary* or a *box-and-whisker plot* gives more information about a data set? Explain your choice.

18. **a.** Where would the outliers of a data set be located on a box-and-whisker plot?

    b. By looking at a box-and-whisker plot, can you tell whether or not the data set has any outliers? Explain.

19. **Open-ended** Make up a data set for the box-and-whisker plot shown on this graphics calculator screen. Include at least 15 items of data. Tell why your data set fits the plot.

Scores Up 20 Points at Martin L. King, Jr., H. S.

Principal Yolanda Johnson reports that the SAT scores of this year's class are 20 points higher than last year's and 14 points above the national average. In fact, 150 students are in the upper quartile for the nation.

20. Use scores from your own mathematics quizzes and tests as data.

   a. Find and record the median and the quartiles of your scores.

   b. The next time you get a test or quiz result, add the score to your data set and repeat part (a). Continue until you have added at least three more scores to your data set. Each time, compare your results with your earlier results. Keep notes about any changes you observe.

   c. **Writing** Report on your results. Your report should include these things.

      ➤ a box-and-whisker plot for each data set under the same number line

      ➤ any changes in the median and the quartiles of your data when you added a score

      ➤ any differences in finding the median and the quartiles with an odd or even number of scores

Use the Volunteer Network histogram that shows how many members volunteer for each range of hours during one week. *(Section 3-4)*

21. About how many Network members volunteer for 4 or more hours per week?

22. Which interval has the greatest frequency? What does this mean in terms of the data?

23. What else do you need to know in order to make a stem-and-leaf plot for this data set?

Simplify. *(Section 1-5)*

24. $4a + 5a - 3b - 9b$ **25.** $-2x^2 + 5x^2$

26. An oceanographer records the height of the tide over 24 h. Should the oceanographer display the data with a *bar graph* or a *line graph*? *(Section 3-1)*

Volunteer Network

Frequency vs Hours per week (0–1.9, 2–3.9, 4–5.9, 6 or more)

 Working on the Unit Project

27. **Group Activity** Work in a group of four students. Have each member of the group ask at least eight people how many music recordings they bought in the last year. Keep track of the age of each person asked.

   a. Combine all the data and make a box-and-whisker plot.

   b. Divide the data into two groups: the answers from people under 20 years old and the answers from people 20 years old and over. Make a box-and-whisker plot for each group.

   c. Compare the plots you made in part (b). Which group usually buys more recordings? Which group has a greater range?

Choosing a Data Display

EVERY PICTURE Tells a STORY

After helping with hazardous-waste disposal at a recycling center, Rafael did some research on trash. He used four different graphs to display data that he found in an almanac.

RECYCLING OF SELECTED ITEMS

Percent (y-axis): 0, 10, 20, 30, 40, 50, 60
Items (x-axis): Glass, Tires, Cans, Paper

He used a **bar graph** to compare data in groups like paper, glass, and so on, which cannot be put in numerical order.

SPACE USE IN LANDFILLS

Other man-made materials
Plastic
Metal
Glass
Paper
Organic material

He made a **circle graph** that shows the division of a whole into parts, for data on the volume of each type of trash in a landfill.

NUMBER OF LANDFILLS

0   20   40   60   80   100

Western states

Southern states

He chose a **box-and-whisker plot** to compare the range and the grouping of data from two different regions.

RECYCLING BY STATE*

Number of states (y-axis): 0, 10, 20, 30
*Data for two states is unknown.
Percent of trash recycled (x-axis): 0–9, 10–19, 20–29, 30 or more

He grouped data on percent of trash recycled into intervals and then used a **histogram** to show the frequency in each interval.

Talk it Over

1. Suppose you were given the exact percent of trash recycled by each state. Choose another type of display for the data and describe what it could show.

2. Could the landfill data be displayed in another type of graph? If so, describe the graph.

3. Name other types of graphs that could be used to compare the amount of trash that each person produces in the southern and western regions of the United States.

Sample 1

a. Make three statements about the data shown in the line graph on the number of women in Japan's Local Assembly.

b. **Writing** Explain why a line graph is a good choice for the data.

Sample Response

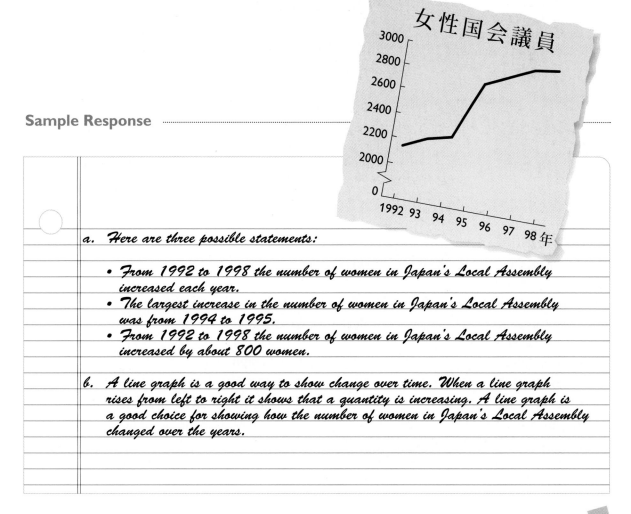

女性国会議員

3000
2800
2600
2400
2200
2000
0

1992 93 94 95 96 97 98 年

a. *Here are three possible statements:*

- *From 1992 to 1998 the number of women in Japan's Local Assembly increased each year.*
- *The largest increase in the number of women in Japan's Local Assembly was from 1994 to 1995.*
- *From 1992 to 1998 the number of women in Japan's Local Assembly increased by about 800 women.*

b. *A line graph is a good way to show change over time. When a line graph rises from left to right it shows that a quantity is increasing. A line graph is a good choice for showing how the number of women in Japan's Local Assembly changed over the years.*

What type of graph is a good choice for displaying each data set? Explain your choice.

a. the middle 50% of the scores of 200 college entrance exams

b. the number of books 15 students borrowed from a library one year

c. how much the members of the junior class spend on lunch on a typical day

Sample Response

Some possible choices are:

a. a box-and-whisker plot, because the box shows the middle 50% of a data set. Also, a box-and-whisker plot helps you make sense of a large data set by turning it into a simple picture that shows the median, the quartiles, and the range.

b. a stem-and-leaf plot, since the data set is small. Since a stem-and-leaf plot shows each number in the data set, you can make exact comparisons, and you can find the mean, median, mode, range, or outliers of the data set.

c. a histogram or a stem-and-leaf plot, since you can group the lunch costs in intervals like $0–1.49 and $1.50–2.99. If the junior class is very large, use a histogram. If the class is small (under 50 students), you could use a stem-and-leaf plot.

Look Back ←

Choose a graph from another section in this unit. Is there another way to display the same information? If so, describe it and explain the strengths of each display. If not, explain why the graph should not be changed.

3-6 Exercises and Problems

1. **Reading** Make a statement about the data shown in each graph on page 164.

For Exercises 2–6, choose the letters of all the statements that describe each type of graph.

2. circle graph

   a. shows each number in the data set

   b. shows parts of a whole

   c. shows outliers

   d. uses the whole circle to represent the total and sectors to represent the parts

3. bar graph

   a. can represent positive and negative data

   b. shows the mean of the data set

   c. can be used for data that cannot be put in numerical order

   d. shows the range of the data set

4. box-and-whisker plot

  a. shows the median and the quartiles of the data set

  b. shows the range of the data set

  c. shows each number in the data set

  d. shows the mean of the data set

5. stem-and-leaf plot

  a. shows each number in the data set

  b. shows trends over time

  c. shows the mean of the data set

  d. groups the data in intervals

6. histogram

  a. has spaces between the bars

  b. is a picture of the numbers in a frequency table

  c. can be used for data that can be put into intervals

  d. shows each number in the data set

7. Write three statements similar to the ones in Exercises 2–6 to describe a line graph.

For Exercises 8–11, do these things:

a. Make a statement about the data in each display.

b. Writing Explain why this type of display was chosen for the data.

8.

9.

10.

How People Traveled to Work One Year

Toronto
Car 63%
Walk, bicycle 6%
31%
Train, bus, etc.

Hong Kong
Car 3%
Train, bus, etc. 62%
Walk, bicycle 35%

11. Number of Times Running Club Members Ran in October

```
0 | 4  6  6  7  8  8  8
1 | 0  1  3  5  5  8  9
2 | 0  1
3 | 0
```

12. Find the mean, the median, and the mode of the data in Exercise 11. Which, if any, of these numbers are displayed in the stem-and-leaf plot?

For Exercises 13 and 14, tell what type of graph you think is a good choice for displaying each data set. Explain your choice.

13. The data below describe land use in Mexico.

Growing food 13%

Raising animals 39%

Forest 22%

Other 26%

14. In the table, the states are grouped by the dates they became states of the United States.

15. A preschool director wishes to compare the ages of the children in two classes. The director wants to display the ages of the oldest and the youngest child in each class, and the median of the ages. What type of display could the director use?

16. A coach wants to show that the members of the swim team practice from 45 to 80 minutes per day. What type of display could the coach use? Give two possible answers.

Years	Number of states added
1775–1799	16
1800–1824	8
1825–1849	6
1850–1874	7
1875–1899	8
1900–1924	3
1925–1949	0
1950–1974	2

17. a. Which type of data display do you think shows the outliers of a data set most clearly? Give a reason for your choice.

b. Which type of data display do you think hides the outliers of a data set? Give a reason for your choice.

18 TECHNOLOGY Use spreadsheet or statistical graphing software.

Alternative Approach Use graph paper and work with another student.

a. Choose one of the data sets given in Exercises 13 and 14. Make the type of graph you chose for the data set.

b. Graph the same data, using another type of graph. If you are using software, display both graphs next to each other on the screen.

c. Describe the differences between the graphs you made in parts (a) and (b). Which graph do you think displays the data better? Explain your choice.

19. **Writing** Find examples of at least two types of graphs in newspapers or magazines. For each graph, tell whether or not it is a good choice for the data that it displays. Explain why or why not.

20. Make a box-and-whisker plot of the data on the map of South America. *(Section 3-5)*

21. Each grid square on the map of Lake Titicaca is 20 km on a side. Estimate the area of the lake. *(Section 2-4)*

Forest Land in South America, 1994 estimates
(thousands of square miles)

172 VENEZUELA
205 COLOMBIA
60 ECUADOR
31 FRENCH GUIANA
64 GUYANA
58 SURINAME
327 PERU
224 BOLIVIA
2143 BRAZIL
50 PARAGUAY
64 CHILE
4 URUGUAY
197 ARGENTINA
0 FALKLAND ISLANDS

BOLIVIA
Lake Titicaca
PERU

Use the bar graph at the right. *(Section 3-1)*

22. Which store sold more cassettes? How many more?

23. Tell whether the statement "Record Place sold about twice as many cassettes as Music City" is *True* or *False*.

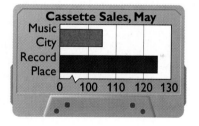

Cassette Sales, May

Music City
Record Place

0   100   110   120   130

Working on the Unit Project

24. a. **Research** Now you should have data on prices of recordings, types of radio stations, and the number of recordings people buy. What else do you want to know before completing a plan for a music store? Conduct a survey, collect data from magazines and newspapers, or contact local music organizations for information.

    b. **Open-ended** Choose a type of graph or display for each data set you have collected. Experiment with different types of displays.

Analyzing Misleading Graphs

····Focus

Recognize when graphs do
not give an accurate picture
of a data set.

All three line graphs below display the same data on median
family income, which is shown in the table.

Median Family Income in the United States (dollars)

Year	1992	1993	1994	1995	1996	1997	1998
Income	36,573	36,959	38,782	40,611	42,300	44,568	46,737

Graph A

Graph B

Graph C

Talk it Over

1. Do you think the graphs give different pictures of how
median family income changed from 1992 to 1998? If so,
how would you describe the change shown by each graph?

2. a. How far apart (in dollars) are the scale marks on the vertical axis in Graph A? in Graph B? in Graph C?

   b. How far apart (in years) are the scale marks on the horizontal axis in Graph A? in Graph B? in Graph C?

   c. How do the scales affect the way the data look?

3. By what percent did median family income increase from
1992 to 1998? Which graph do you think shows this most
clearly? Explain.

TECHNOLOGY NOTE

If you use a graphics
calculator or graphing software
to draw a graph, you can change the
way the graph looks by changing the
values you enter for the window
variables. See Technology
Handbook, p. 613.

As the graphs above show, a *change in the scale* of a graph
changes how the graph looks and it may make the graph
misleading. A *misleading graph* may lead the viewer to draw a
false conclusion about the data.

The graph on the next page shows how a *gap in the scale* can
also change how a graph looks.

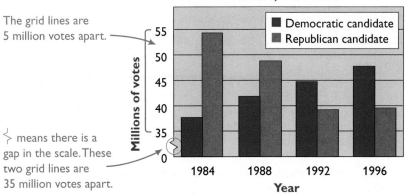

United States Presidential Election Results, 1984–1996

The grid lines are 5 million votes apart.

⋛ means there is a gap in the scale. These two grid lines are 35 million votes apart.

Millions of votes

55
50
45
40
35
0

1984   1988   1992   1996

Year

■ Democratic candidate
■ Republican candidate

Sample

Writing Do you think the bar graph above gives an accurate picture of the 1984 election results? Explain.

Sample Response

Answer the question.

No.

The Democratic candidate received a little less than 38 million votes, and the Republican candidate received a little less than 55 million votes. The Republican received about 17 million more votes than the Democrat.

◀ Write about what the numbers say.

The graph is misleading because the bar for the Republican is more than twice as long as the bar for the Democrat. It looks as if the Republican received over twice as many votes as the Democrat.

◀ Write about how the graph looks.

Graphics Calculators at South High School

Number of calculators

500
400
300
200
100
0

1999   2000

425

213

Talk it Over

4. Use the graph at the left. Compare the number of graphics calculators at South High School in 2000 to the number in 1999.

5. Compare the length and width of the "bar" for the 2000 data with the length and width of the "bar" for 1999. Then compare the areas of the "bars." What do you find?

6. Do you think the graph gives an accurate picture of the change in the number of graphics calculators from 1999 to 2000? If not, how could you make the graph less misleading?

Look Back ◀

Suppose you want to decide whether or not a graph is misleading. Describe three things to look for in the graph.

Exercises and Problems

Reading Use the table and graphs on median family income on page 170.

1. Which graph would you use to convince someone that incomes rose steeply in the period 1992–1998? Explain your choice.

2. Between which two years did median family income rise the most? Which graph makes it easiest to find this information? Why?

Reading Use the graph on presidential election results on page 171.

3. A newspaper article says the graph shows that the 1996 election was much closer than the 1984 election. Do you agree or disagree? Why?

4. Suppose you redrew the graph to make it less misleading. How would the heights of the bars for 1984 compare on your new graph?

For Exercises 5–9, use the bar graph.

Record Single Jumps

For Exercises 5–7, tell whether each statement is *True* or *False*.

5. The men's record is more than twice the frog's record.

6. The kangaroo's record is about two and a half times the women's record.

7. The women's record differs from the frog's record by about 8 ft.

8. **Writing** Do you think the graph gives an accurate picture of how far the frog jumped compared to the kangaroo? Explain.

9. **a.** Use the graph to estimate the length of each record jump. Can you estimate the length to the nearest *inch* or to the nearest *foot*?

   b TECHNOLOGY Use statistical graphing or spreadsheet software.
   Alternative Approach Use paper and pencil.

   Draw a graph that gives an accurate picture of the record jumps. How is your graph different from the original graph?

BY THE WAY...

At the 1986 Calaveras Jumping Jubilee in Angels Camp, California, Rosie the Ribiter set an American record of 21 ft $5\frac{3}{4}$ in. for the longest triple jump by a frog.

Use Graph A, Graph B, and the table.

Graph A

Number of Hurricanes, 1886–1992

Graph B

Number of Hurricanes, 1886–1992

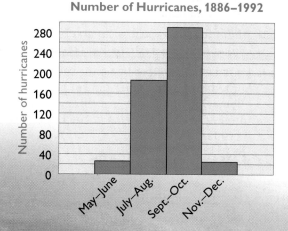

Number of Hurricanes, 1886–1992	
January	0
February	0
March	1
April	0
May	3
June	23
July	35
August	151
September	193
October	97
November	21
December	3

10. Both histograms display the data in the table. Do you think they give different pictures of the data? If so, how are they different?

11. Describe two pieces of information shown in the table but not in the histograms.

12. How many hurricanes occurred from 1886 through 1992? Do you think it is easier to use *Graph A* or *Graph B* to estimate the total? Explain.

13. Could the hurricane data be graphed using smaller-sized intervals than the ones used in Graph A? Why or why not?

14. Why can the hurricane data be shown in histogram form?

15. Choose the letter of the graph that better supports each statement.

a. There were more hurricanes in fall than in summer.

b. There were more hurricanes in September than in October.

c. May and December had the same number of hurricanes.

16. **Open-ended** Write a question that can be answered by reading Graph A but not by reading Graph B.

Use the television graph.

17. Describe two ways in which the graph shows that the number of cable television systems in the United States rose from 1975 to 1995.

18. About how many times greater is the number of cable television systems in 1995 than in 1975?

19. Let x be the number of cable systems in the United States in 1985. Choose the letter of the expression that is the best estimate of the number of cable systems in the United States in 1995.

   a. x^2 **b.** $x + 5,000,000$

   c. $5x$ **d.** x^3

20. Suppose the pictures of televisions represent cubes.

   a. Find the volume of each cube.

   b. About how many times greater is the volume of the cube for 1985 than the volume of the cube for 1975?

   c. About how many times greater is the volume of the cube for 1995 than the volume of the cube for 1975?

21. **Writing** Do you think the graph gives an accurate picture of the growth in the number of cable systems from 1975 to 1995? Explain.

Cable Systems in the United States, 1975–1995

Number of systems (millions)

Ongoing **ASSESSMENT**

22. **Group Activity** Work in a group of four students. Use the table and the graph shown below for parts (a)–(e).

Federal Funding of Public Education Elementary and Secondary Schools

School year	Amount (thousands of dollars)	Percent of all public education funds
1988–1989	11,902,001	6.2
1989–1990	12,700,784	6.1
1990–1991	13,776,066	6.2
1991–1992	15,493,330	6.6
1992–1993	17,261,252	7.0
1993–1994	18,341,483	7.1
1994–1995	18,582,157	6.8
1995–1996	19,104,019	6.6
1996–1997	20,081,235	6.6

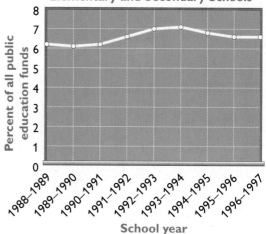

Federal Funding of Public Education Elementary and Secondary Schools

a. Describe the change in federal funding of public education that the graph shows.

b. Choose a different scale for the vertical axis. Redraw the graph so that it gives a different picture of the data. Describe the change in federal funding of public education as shown by your graph.

c. Make a graph showing the *amount* of federal funding for the school years 1988–1989 through 1996–1997. How is the new graph different from the graph shown on page 174?

d. In the period 1993–1994 to 1995–1996, the *amount* of federal funding for education went up. In the same period, the *percent* of public education funds that came from the federal government went down. Explain how both of these statements can be true.

e. **Writing** Write a report that presents the results of parts (a)–(d).

Review **PREVIEW**

What type of graph is a good choice for displaying each data set? Explain your choice. *(Section 3-6)*

23. lengths of long jumps made in a varsity track and field meet

24. number of visitors to a museum each day of one month

25. ages of students in a graduating high school class

Write each number in scientific notation. *(Section 2-3)*

26. 700,000

27. 23,400,000

28. 0.006

29. 0.0000461

Graph each point on a coordinate plane. *(Toolbox Skill 21)*

30. $A(5, 3)$

31. $B(-2, 4)$

32. $C(0, 4)$

33. $D(-3, -5)$

Working on the Unit Project

34. Use the data you have collected about the prices of recordings of different types of music on cassette, CD, and so on.

a. Draw two graphs of the same data. Use one graph to show that cassettes, CDs, and so on have very different prices, and the other to show that cassettes, CDs, and so on have very similar prices.

b. Which graph would you use to convince customers to buy one form of recording instead of another? Explain your choice.

TECHNOLOGY NOTE

If you use a graphics calculator or graphing software, use the first year of each school year for the *x*-value. For 1988–1989, use 1988, and so on.

Completing the Unit Project

Now you are ready to make your business brochure. You may want to use color or visual designs to make your brochure more attractive.

The plan you present in your brochure should include a summary of your market research. Include the percentage of your merchandise devoted to each music style and each format. To support your figures, describe the consumers in your store's area.

Include graphs and other data displays in your brochure. You may want to use a spreadsheet or other graphics software.

Look Back

Were the results of your research about popular styles and formats of music what you expected? Describe how your ideas about what is typical changed during the project.

Alternative Projects

Project 1: Supporting an Opinion

One movie critic claims that the titles of popular movies in the 1970s were very short (*Jaws*, *Star Wars*) compared to the titles of older movies (*Casablanca*, *Gone with the Wind*). Gather data and decide if you agree or disagree. Include these points in your report.

➤ how you decided what "popular" means in this case

➤ how you chose your data sets

➤ a summary of the data sets, including their means, medians, or modes

➤ the process you used to make a decision

➤ the conclusion that your data supports

Project 2: Analyzing a Process

Find out how data are collected for making a Top Ten music, movie, or book list. Who supplies the data? Are any formulas used?

Write a summary of how the list is determined. Suggest how changes in the process could produce different results.

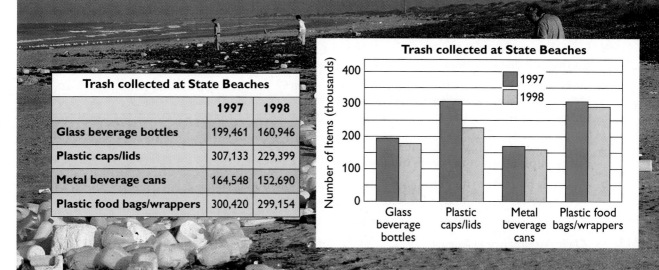

Trash collected at State Beaches

	1997	1998
Glass beverage bottles	199,461	160,946
Plastic caps/lids	307,133	229,399
Metal beverage cans	164,548	152,690
Plastic food bags/wrappers	300,420	299,154

Use the matrix and the double bar graph.   3-1

1. What are the dimensions of the matrix?

2. What does the number in the second row, first column of the matrix represent?

3. a. **Open-ended** Write two statements comparing the numbers of items collected on state beaches in 1997 and 1998.

   b. For each statement that you wrote for part (a), tell whether it is better supported by the *matrix* or the *graph*.

Use these scores on a magazine's "Are You Interesting?" quiz: 3-2
18, 23, 28, 26, 22, 30, 26, 18, 27, 18, 28

4. Find the mean, the median, and the mode of the scores. Which number would you call most typical of the data set?

5. What is the range of the scores?

6. Is a score of 30 an outlier? Explain why or why not.

7. Suppose five friends take the quiz. The mean of four friends' scores is 25.5. A score of 26 is rated FASCINATING. What must the fifth score be for the mean of the five scores to be FASCINATING?

For Exercises 8 and 9, write and graph an inequality   3-3
to describe the interval referred to in each statement.

8. Laurie Chin was driving 35 mi/h when she entered a freeway on-ramp. She accelerated and merged with traffic when driving 55 mi/h.

9. In New Jersey you must be at least 17 years old to take a road test at a driver testing center.

10. a. Use the histogram to make two statements   3-4
      about the sales of video cassette recorders.

    b. What is *not* shown in the histogram? Give two examples.

VCR Sales at Hunt's Store

11. a. Make a stem-and-leaf plot of the data for the first day of school.

b. Find the median of the data for the first day of school.

c. Make a general statement about the class sizes on the first day of school.

Homeroom Class Sizes

First Day of School					Last Day of School				
15	23	38	12	56	20	23	35	22	56
26	14	23	34	34	26	25	23	27	51
23	17	30	23	24	20	22	35	26	29
51	43	26	28	17	23	56	29	33	26
67	29	31	26	21	28	27	23	25	21

12. a. Make a box-and-whisker plot for each data set shown above. Put both plots under the same number line.   3-5

b. Use your plots to write two statements comparing the homeroom class sizes on the first day of school and the last day of school.

Explain why each type of display was chosen for the data.   3-6

13.   **Daily Attendance in August**

14.   **Sara's Monthly Spending**

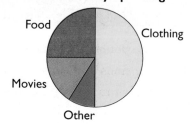

15. What type of graph would you use to display changes in the minimum wage over the last ten years? Explain your choice.

16. The graph shows the same data as the Questions 1–3. Compare the two graphs. Describe how this graph gives a misleading impression of the data.   3-7

17. **Writing** Onika made a concept map about circle graphs. Describe three ideas that you see in her map.

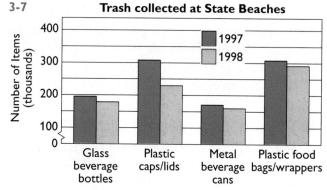

Trash collected at State Beaches

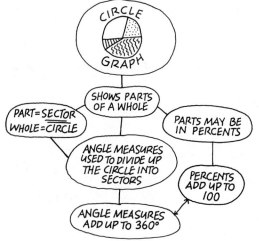

18. **Self-evaluation** You may have seen some of the data displays in this unit in other classes. Which were new to you? How have your ideas about displaying data changed?

19. **Group Activity** Work in a group of five students. Pass a sheet of paper around the group. Each student writes about a method of displaying data, saying why the method is useful. Discuss the ideas. Make a presentation about at least two types of displays.

IDEAS AND (FORMULAS) $= x^2$ $_5P_5$

➤ You can use a matrix to organize and display data that belong to more than one category. *(p. 128)*

➤ Graphs can help you compare sets of data, observe trends, draw conclusions, and support a point of view. *(p. 128)*

➤ Computer spreadsheet software stores information in matrices. *(p. 129)*

➤ The mean, the median, and the mode are three values that may be considered typical of a data set. *(p. 135)*

➤ You can use a line plot to help you picture the outliers and the range of a data set. *(p. 137)*

➤ You can use a histogram to show the frequency of data that are grouped in intervals. *(p. 150)*

➤ Stem-and-leaf plots allow you to display every number in a data set and still organize the numbers in intervals. *(p. 152)*

➤ You can use box-and-whisker plots to compare how data are grouped in two data sets. *(p. 158)*

➤ You can use a bar graph to display data in categories that can not be put in numerical order. *(p. 164)*

➤ Circle graphs show the division of a whole into parts. *(p. 164)*

➤ A misleading graph may lead the viewer to make a false conclusion about the data. *(p. 170)*

DISCRETE **3!** MATH
$3 \cdot 2 \cdot 1 =$ $_5P_5$

➤ When discrete data are displayed on a line plot, they lie inside a continuous interval of the number line. *(p. 145)*

ALGEBRA $) x^2$
$(\times$

➤ To solve an equation with a fraction in it, begin by multiplying both sides of the equation by the denominator of the fraction. *(p. 138)*

➤ An algebraic inequality can be graphed as an interval on a number line. *(p. 145)*

Key Terms

- **matrix** (p. 128)
- **cell** (p. 129)
- **mode** (p. 136)
- **line plot** (p. 137)
- **interval** (p. 145)
- **frequency table** (p. 151)
- **lower quartile** (p. 158)

- **dimensions** (p. 128)
- **mean** (p. 136)
- **outliers** (p. 137)
- **$\leq, \geq$** (p. 144)
- **histogram** (p. 150)
- **stem-and-leaf plot** (p. 152)
- **upper quartile** (p. 158)

- **spreadsheet** (p. 129)
- **median** (p. 136)
- **range** (p. 137)
- **combined inequality** (p. 144)
- **frequency** (p. 150)
- **box-and-whisker plot** (p. 158)
- **extremes** (p. 158)

unit 4

ANIMATION

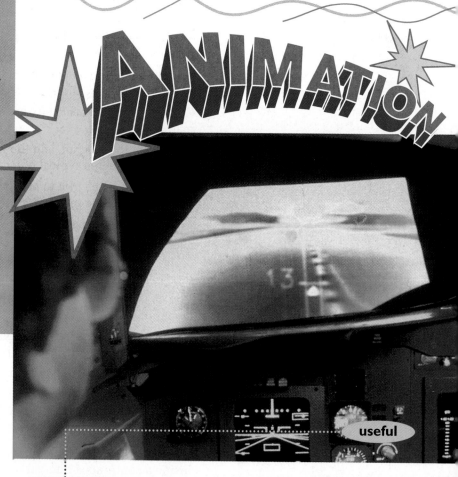

How can a single drawing of Bart Simpson turn into a moving picture? The smooth movements of cartoon characters are actually a series of drawings that appear to move when shown one after another. *Animation* is the process of making the drawings.

Pilots use this system to practice takeoffs.

useful

entertaining

Coordinates were used to create the animated dinosaurs in Jurassic Park.

Animation is useful as well as entertaining. Engineers use animation to simulate the flight of a new airplane design before building the airplane. Some animated programs help people learn to drive. Others help doctors practice surgery before they perform it.

Making a Flip Book

Your project is to create an animated flip book. The pages of a flip book contain pictures. Each picture is slightly different from the one before it. When you flip through the pages quickly, you see a short story showing motion.

To create a flip book, you will need to solve some of the same problems an artist or a computer programmer solves when creating animated drawings.

You will need to keep track of the location of the figures in your drawing. The movements may include slides and turns. They may follow the paths of graphs of functions. You may be able to write equations for the movements in your flip book.

$$y = -2x^2 + 2$$

Motions that repeat can be used to animate a figure. When a person or an animal is shown walking, the same leg and arm motions are shown again and again, while the background changes.

Computer programmers use equations of lines and curves that look like the motion they want to show.

An equation can describe the path of a bounced object. Using equations to define the paths of objects that are bounced or thrown makes many computer games possible.

Unit Project 4

Getting Started

Here are some ideas to use when you make your flip book.

☞ Use a pad of paper or cut several sheets of paper to a convenient size.

☞ Use graph paper and a coordinate grid to keep track of the positions of your drawings.

☞ Make the first drawing on the last piece of paper. The next drawing should be slightly different.

☞ If you can see through the paper that you use, you can trace the previous drawing, then make changes to the new one.

☞ You will need to use a series of small changes to show movement. Experiment to see how many drawings are needed to show a movement.

Can We Talk

Animation

➤ Have you seen any animated movies? If so, which ones?

➤ Do you have a favorite animated television show? If so, which one?

➤ Have you noticed any differences between animation in movies and animation in television shows? Describe the differences.

➤ Do you think it would be easier to make an animated cartoon of a car moving or of a person walking? Why?

➤ How could you show the path of an arrow being shot into the air toward a target?

➤ Suppose you want to show the motion of someone sledding down a hill. How could the background move instead of the sled?

➤ What would the path of a basketball be when it is thrown toward the hoop? Is there more than one possible path?

➤ How do objects slow down and speed up in animated movies? How do you think you could show this in a flip book?

Working on the Unit Project

Your work in Unit 4 will help you create your flip book.

Related Exercises:

Section 4-1, Exercise 36
Section 4-2, Exercise 27
Section 4-3, Exercises 32–34
Section 4-4, Exercises 25, 26
Section 4-5, Exercise 31
Section 4-6, Exercise 26
Section 4-7, Exercise 47

Alternative Projects p. 4-54

Focus
Use coordinate systems to
solve problems about
locations in different
settings.

Coordinates for Locations

WHERE IN THE WORLD?

While diving in the Bahamas, you find a shipwreck. It might
be a very early Spanish ship. You want to bring a sword to an
expert who can tell how old it is. You also want to record
where you found the sword in the wreck. What can you do?

Where objects are found in a wreck is just as important as what
the objects are. Because of this, underwater explorers use a
coordinate system to record the locations of objects.

KEY

1	Crossbow	7	Swivel cannons
2	Swords	8	Cannons
3	Ribs	9	Hand axes
4	Helmet	10	Cannon balls
5	Spearpoint	11	Plates
6	Brass dividers		

Talk it Over

1. What patterns do you see in the labels in the squares?

2. What do you think the letters in the labels represent?

3. What object is in the square labeled N1 E3?

4. Which square contains the cannon balls?

Coordinate Systems

Student Resources Toolbox

p. 660 *A Coordinate System*

In mathematics, you use an *ordered pair* of numbers to describe where a point is on a **coordinate plane.** A more general way to locate a point is to name the *quadrant* that the point is in.

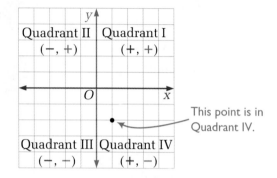

Talk it Over

5. What are the coordinates of point *A*?

6. What point has coordinates $(-2, 3)$?

7. Name a point in quadrant III.

8. Which quadrant contains point *D*?

9. Describe how to graph the point that has coordinates $(4, -3)$.

10. The origin on a shipwreck is called the *datum point.*

    a. Where do you think the datum point is on the diagram of the wreck on page 183?

    b. What object is near the datum point you chose in part (a)?

Maps often have coordinate systems. Their coordinates describe a square region, not a point. Usually map coordinates are a letter and a number.

WASHINGTON, D.C., LANDMARKS

1. Botanic Garden
2. Department of State
3. FBI Building
4. Lincoln Memorial
5. Martin Luther King, Jr., Memorial Library
6. National Aeronautics and Space Administration (NASA)
7. National Air and Space Museum
8. National Gallery of Art
9. Simón Bolívar Statue and Plaza
10. United States Capitol
11. Union Station
12. Vietnam Veterans Memorial
13. Washington Monument
14. White House

Use the map of **Washington, D.C.,** on page 184.

a. What landmark is in square B3?

b. What are the coordinates of the Washington Monument?

Sample Response

a. 1. Move across row B to column 3.

2. The building in this square is marked 14.

3. Read the list of landmarks to find what is identified by the number 14.

4. The White House is in square B3.

b. 1. Read the list of landmarks. The Monument is identified by the number 13. Find the square that contains the building marked 13.

2. Move across the row to find the letter C.

3. Move down the column to find the number 3.

4. The coordinates are C3.

Look Back

Describe how using a map to locate places and using a coordinate plane to locate points are alike. How are they different?

4-1 Exercises and Problems

1. **Reading** You could call the square that contains the Washington Monument either 3C or C3. Do the coordinates (1, 3) and (3, 1) refer to the same point? Why or why not?

Use the map of Washington, D.C., on page 184 for Exercises 2–9.

What landmark is located in each square or each pair of squares?

2. B7

3. C7

4. D5, D6

5. B1

Find the coordinates of each landmark. If there is more than one pair of coordinates, list all of them.

6. Martin Luther King, Jr., Memorial Library

7. Vietnam Veterans Memorial

8. Simón Bolívar Statue and Plaza

9. National Gallery of Art

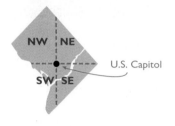
NW | NE
SW | SE
U.S. Capitol

Use the diagram of Washington, D.C., at the left.

10. What is the *origin* in the coordinate system of Washington, D.C.?

11. In which direction from the Capitol is 3rd St. NE?

12. How do the four quadrants of Washington, D.C., compare with the four quadrants on a coordinate plane?

13. Which quadrant on a coordinate plane would contain G St. SW?

connection to **SOCIAL STUDIES**

Coordinates locate places on Earth. The grid lines on Earth are lines of latitude and longitude. Places are identified by latitude first, then longitude.

The prime meridian is a line of longitude.

The equator is a line of latitude.

The vertical axis is a line from the North Pole to the South Pole passing through Greenwich, England. This line is called the *prime meridian*.

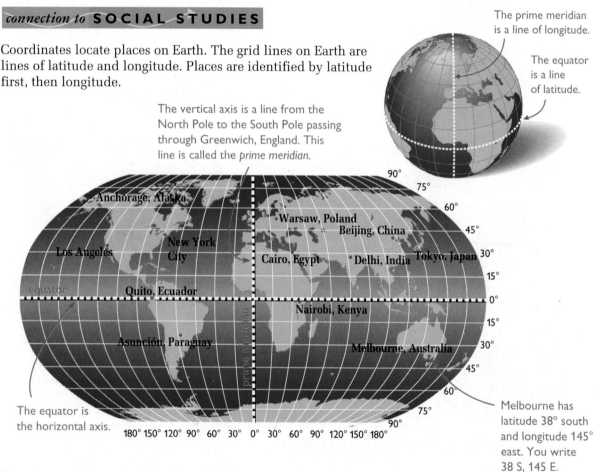

The equator is the horizontal axis.

Melbourne has latitude 38° south and longitude 145° east. You write 38 S, 145 E.

180° 150° 120° 90° 60° 30° 0° 30° 60° 90° 120° 150° 180°

Use the map above for Exercises 14–25.

Estimate the latitude and longitude of each city.

14. Cairo, Egypt

15. Quito, Ecuador

16. Tokyo, Japan

What city is near each location?

17. 1 S, 37 E   **18.** 52 N, 21 E   **19.** 34 N, 118 W

20. About how many degrees west of Delhi is Asunción?

21. About how many degrees south of Los Angeles is Melbourne?

22. What line of longitude do you think is opposite the prime meridian on the other side of Earth?

23. Name two cities on the map that have about the same latitude. What is their latitude?

24. **Research** Find the latitude and longitude of your city or town.

25. **Writing** Describe how using latitude and longitude to locate places on Earth is similar to using a coordinate plane to locate points.

> **BY THE WAY...**
>
> In Australia, summer vacation is in December and January. Because it is south of the equator, Australia has winter in June.

---

connection to **ART**

Chuck Close is an artist in New York who makes large paintings from small photographs. He divides the photograph and his canvas into tiny squares and uses a grid system to locate each square. Some of the grids are diagonal like the one on this painting.

26. a. Describe the grid system that Chuck Close used for this painting.

   b. How is his grid system similar to a coordinate plane? How is it different?

27. **Open-ended** Do you think this method could be used to make very small paintings? Explain why or why not.

28. An illness has reduced Chuck Close's mobility. For this painting, he used a chair that can move sideways and up and down to work on different areas of the painting.

   Describe how the movements of the chair are related to locating a point on a coordinate plane.

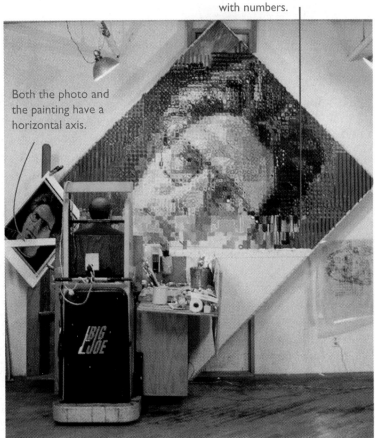

Each axis is labeled with numbers.

Both the photo and the painting have a horizontal axis.

In *The Hunt for Red October,* Soviet submarine captain Ramius reads his orders and learns that he is to participate in a tracking drill with another submarine.

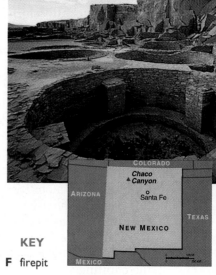

> 17　　　　　　**THE HUNT FOR RED OCTOBER**
>
> Ramius chuckled. "The boys in the attack submarine directorate still have not figured out how to track our new drive system. Well, neither will the Americans. We are to confine our operations to grid square 54–90 and the immediately surrounding squares. That ought to make Viktor's task a bit easier." … "He will have a fair chance of locating us, I think. The exercise is confined to nine squares, forty thousand square kilometers. We shall see what he has learned since he has served with us."

29. How does Ramius identify a grid square?

30. How does Ramius know that there are only nine squares that might contain the submarine?

31. What do you think the numbers of the squares surrounding grid square 54-90 could be? Explain your reasoning.

Ongoing **ASSESSMENT**

There were about 10,000 Anasazi people living in Chaco Canyon, New Mexico, about 1000 years ago. They suddenly disappeared. Archaeologists are trying to understand why.

Archaeologists use coordinate systems to record locations of objects. As they dig deeper, the relationships of the locations can be clues to the daily life in lost civilizations.

32. **Open-ended** Describe how you could put a coordinate system on the sketch of the room. Where would you put the origin? the axes? Use your system to give the coordinates of the firepit.

KEY

F　firepit
FP　misc. floor pit
MB　mealing bin
PH　posthole
N　wall niche

33. **Writing** Archaeologists also record an object's depth beneath surface level. Describe how coordinates could identify the depth of an object.

The display shows the fan costs for selected items at a basketball game. *(Section 3-6)*

34. a. Interpret the information shown in the display.

b. Do you think this is the best way to display the information? Explain why or why not.

35. Quadrilateral *ABCD* has two pairs of parallel sides and at least one right angle. *(Section 1-7)*

a. Make an accurate sketch of quadrilateral *ABCD*.

b. What is the special name for quadrilateral *ABCD*?

FAN COSTS

	San Francisco	Chicago	New York	Dallas
Program	$3	$5	$6	$5
Soda	$1.50	$3	$2.75	$2.25
Hot dog	$2.50	$4	$3.25	$2.25
Cap	$18	$18	$18	$16
Average ticket price	$48.10	$52.84	$86.82	$40.76

Working on the Unit Project

A computer screen is made up of tiny points of light called *pixels.* Programmers use coordinates to identify which pixels to light when creating artwork. Different computers have different numbers of pixels.

pixel (0, 0)

pixel (4, 2)

pixel (1, 8)

36. Writing If you turn off the pixel at (4, 2) and turn on the one directly below it, it will look as if the pixel moved down.

a. Describe how you could make the pixel "fall" to the bottom of the screen.

b. How do the coordinates of the pixel change as it "falls"?

c. Suppose you want to put a falling image in your flip book. Use your answers to parts (a) and (b) to describe how to do this.

Introduction to Coordinate Geometry

SHAPING UP

EXPLORATION

How can you describe a shape?

- **Materials: graph paper, ruler**
- **Work with a partner.**

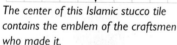

The center of this Islamic stucco tile contains the emblem of the craftsmen who made it.

(1) Describe the shape of the star tile in words.

(2) List the coordinates of the corners of the tile in the order that they are connected by line segments.

(3) What are some advantages of describing a shape in words (as you did in step 1)? What are some advantages of describing a shape with coordinates (as you did in step 2)?

(4) **a.** Draw any polygon on graph paper. Don't let your partner see it.

b. Use words or coordinates to describe your polygon to your partner.

c. Have your partner draw the polygon using only your description.

d. Compare your partner's drawing with your original polygon. How could you improve your description?

Drawing figures on a coordinate plane is one part of *coordinate geometry*. When you analyze a shape on a coordinate plane, find its area, or compare it to another shape, you use coordinate geometry.

For each set of points, follow these steps.

➤ **Plot the points on a coordinate plane. Connect the points in order and connect the last point to the first.**

➤ **Write the specific name of the polygon you formed.**

➤ **Explain how you know what it is.**

a. $A(5, 1)$, $B(2, 1)$, $C(2, -2)$

b. $D(3, 1)$, $E(1, 3)$, $F(-2, 3)$, $G(-3, -1)$, $H(-1, -3)$, $J(2, -3)$

Sample Response

a. The polygon is an isosceles right triangle because. . .

The polygon has three sides.

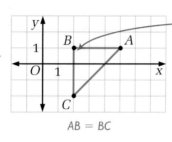

$\angle B$ is a right angle formed by the horizontal and vertical segments.

AB = BC

b. The polygon is a hexagon because. . .

The polygon has six sides.

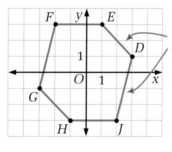

The sides are not the same length.
The polygon is not a regular hexagon.

Talk it Over

$\triangle ABC$ means "triangle ABC."

1. How do you know that $\triangle ABC$ in Sample 1 is isosceles and not equilateral?

2. Are any sides of hexagon $DEFGHJ$ congruent? If so, which?

Finding Areas of Right Triangles

Remember that a rectangle is made up of two congruent right triangles.

You can use that fact to find the area of a right triangle on a coordinate plane.

Find the area of right triangle XYZ.

Sample Response

Problem Solving Strategy: Use a diagram

Insert helping lines
to build a rectangle.

Label point W.

length
5.5

width: 4

Area of △ $= \frac{1}{2} \times$ Area of ▱

$= \frac{1}{2} lw$

$= \frac{1}{2} (5.5)(4)$

$= 11$

The area of △XYZ is 11 square units.

Talk it Over

3. How do you know that figure $WXYZ$ in Sample 2 is a rectangle?

4. How is the width 4 related to the coordinates of X and Y?

5. How is the length 5.5 related to the coordinates of Y and Z?

6. a. Plot the points $R(-1, -4)$, $S(-8, -4)$, and $T(-8, -1)$ on a coordinate plane. Connect the points in order. Connect the last point to the first.

   b. Find the area of the right triangle you formed.

▶ Now you are ready for:
Exs. 1–11 on p. 194

Finding Areas of Other Polygons

You can use what you know about the areas of rectangles and right triangles to find the areas of other polygons drawn on a coordinate plane.

Find the area of trapezoid *LMNP*.

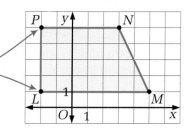

Remenber that a **trapezoid** is a quadrilateral with one pair of parallel sides.

Sample Response

Problem Solving Strategy: Break the problem into parts

To find the area of the trapezoid, you can solve the simpler problems of finding the areas of a rectangle and a right triangle.

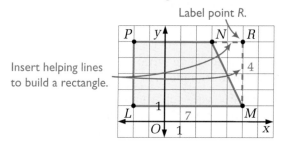

First find the area of rectangle *LMRP*.

Label point *R*.

Insert helping lines to build a rectangle.

Use $A = lw$.

Area of [figure] = 7(4) = 28

Next find the area of △*NMR*.

Insert a helping line to build another rectangle.

Label point *S*.

Area of rectangle *NSMR* = 4(2) = 8

Area of [triangle] = $\frac{1}{2}$ (8) = 4

Then subtract.

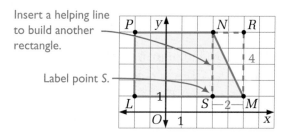

Area of [figure] = area of [figure] − area of [triangle]

= 28 − 4

= 24

The area of trapezoid *LMNP* is 24 square units.

Talk it Over

7. Sample 3 uses the area formula to find the area of rectangle *NSMR*. Describe another method for finding this area.

8. Try Sample 3 another way. Divide the trapezoid into rectangle *LSNP* and right triangle *NSM*. Explain how to use these polygons to find the area of trapezoid *LMNP*.

Look Back

Plot the points $K(-6, -3)$, $L(-2, -3)$, and $M(-4, 3)$ on a coordinate plane. Connect the points in order. Connect the last point to the first. Describe the polygon. Explain how you know what it is. Explain how to find the area of the polygon.

► **Now you are ready for:**
Exs. 12–27 on pp. 194–196

4-2 Exercises and Problems

Suppose you had to draw each shape on graph paper. For each shape, tell whether you would prefer to use coordinates or a description in words. Explain your choice.

1. a square   **2.** a circle   **3.** a parallelogram

4. **Writing** Draw a scalene right triangle on a coordinate plane. Then write directions that someone else could follow to draw the same triangle.

5. **Reading** Suppose all the sides of the hexagon in Sample 1 were congruent. Does this mean that all the angles must be congruent? Explain why or why not.

Follow these steps for Exercises 6–9.

➤ **Plot the points on a coordinate plane. Connect the points in order and connect the last point to the first.**

➤ **Write the specific name of the polygon you formed.**

➤ **Explain how you know what it is.**

6. $A(-1, -1)$, $B(0, 2)$, $C(4, -1)$ **7.** $M(0, 4)$, $N(3, 0)$, $P(6, 0)$, $Q(7, 5)$, $R(2, 6)$

8. $H(1, 3)$, $J(5, 3)$, $K(7, -2)$, $L(-2, -2)$ **9.** $S(0, 3)$, $T(-8, 3)$, $U(-8, -5)$, $V(0, -5)$

Find the area of each polygon. Describe the method you used.

10.

11.

12.

13.

14.

15.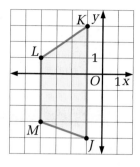

16. **Using Manipulatives** Work with another student.

    a. Choose one of the polygons in Exercises 10–15. Create a human-sized version of the polygon with a long piece of string. (Use the photographs on pages 192 and 193 as a guide.)

    b. Have your partner guess which polygon you chose.

    c. Switch places and repeat the process.

17. Four students are making flags out of checkered cloth for a school play. Which student has the most cloth left over?

Albert

Calvin

Beatrice

Deanna

18. **Open-ended** On a coordinate plane, create two different triangles with area 20 square units.

19. **Group Activity** Each person in the group should make a different rectangle.

    a. Draw a rectangle on a coordinate plane. List the coordinates of the vertices of the rectangle and find the area of the rectangle.

    b. Double each coordinate. Graph the new rectangle. Find its area.

    c. Compare the areas of the original rectangle and the new rectangle. How are they related?

    d. Did everyone in the group get the same result in part (c)? Make a generalization about the results.

20. a. The vertices of a rectangle are $A(-6, 2)$, $B(-6, -3)$, $C(1, 2)$ and D. What are all the possible coordinates of D?

b. The vertices of a parallelogram are $W(-3, -10)$, $X(-3, 6)$, $Y(9, 6)$, and Z. What are all the possible coordinates of Z?

Ongoing **ASSESSMENT**

21. **Open-ended** Design an interesting polygon with at least six sides on a coordinate plane. Find the area of the polygon using rectangles, squares, and right triangles.

Review **PREVIEW**

Simplify each expression. *(Sections 1-4, 1-5)*

22. $3(6) + 10 - (-3)(7)$

23. $(17 + (-3)) \div 7 - (-11)$

24. $4(x - 3) + 5x$

25. $3a(5 + b) - 6a$

26. a. The coordinates of point A are $(4, 3)$. Graph point A. *(Section 4-1)*

b. What are the coordinates of a point that is 5 units below point A? Label this point B on your graph.

c. What are the coordinates of a point that is 6 units to the left of B? Label this point C on your graph.

d. Draw $\triangle ABC$. What type of triangle is it?

Working on the Unit Project

27. The diagrams below show a flip book sequence of parallelograms.

a. Describe the motion the flip book shows. Which coordinates of the parallelograms change in the sequence? Which do not change?

b. Find the areas of the parallelograms. Is one area larger than the others? If so, which one?

c. *True* or *False?* All parallelograms with sides of the same length have the same area.

> **BY THE WAY...**
>
> Computer programmers use coordinate geometry when developing software that creates artwork, drawings, and animation on a computer.

Ready?

here it goes...

going...

ta da!

Translations

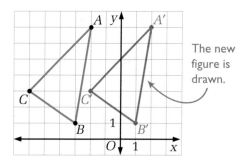

Translate figures on a coordinate plane and recognize translational symmetry.

FROM HERE

TO THERE

When you ride on an escalator, only your location or position changes. You do not turn around, grow, shrink, or change shape. Escalators just slide you from place to place. Another name for a slide is a *translation*. A **translation** moves an object without changing its size or shape and without turning it or flipping it.

Here is a translation of △*ABC* on a coordinate plane.

Each vertex slides the same distance in the same direction.

The new vertices are labeled with *primes*.

The new figure is drawn.

Talk it Over

1. Look at each vertex of △*ABC*. How far did it move? In what direction did it move?

2. Are the coordinates of every point of △*ABC* changed?

3. What are the coordinates of *B* and *B'*? How are the coordinates alike?

Find the coordinates of each vertex of △DEF after the translation:

6 units right and 2 units down

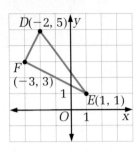

Sample Response

Translate each vertex.
Then draw the triangle.

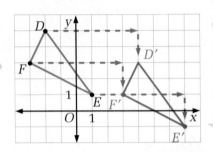

1 First, F moves 6 units right.

2 Then F moves 2 units down.

An arrow (→) that means "goes to" can be used to represent a translation in symbols.

The translation is written this way: $\triangle DEF \rightarrow \triangle D'E'F'$

$D(-2, 5) \rightarrow D'(4, 3)$ $E(1, 1) \rightarrow E'(7, -1)$ $F(-3, 3) \rightarrow F'(3, 1)$

The coordinates of each vertex after the translation are $D'(4, 3)$, $E'(7, -1)$, and $F'(3, 1)$.

Talk it Over

4. Suppose you change only the first coordinates of the points of a shape. What is the direction of the translation?

5. Suppose you change only the second coordinates of the points of a shape. What is the direction of the translation?

Translational Symmetry

Some computer software lets you choose the background pattern for the screen or a fill pattern for a drawing.

1. You select a simple pattern like the squares shown.

2. The computer translates this pattern again and again until it covers the screen or drawing.

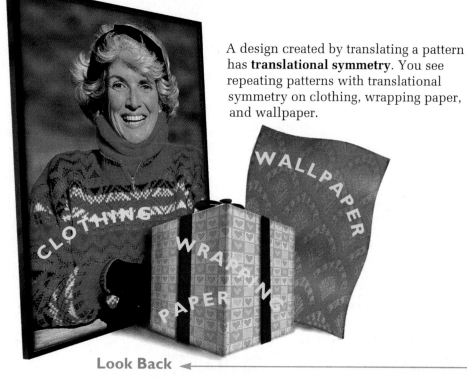

A design created by translating a pattern has **translational symmetry**. You see repeating patterns with translational symmetry on clothing, wrapping paper, and wallpaper.

Look Back

How do the coordinates of the vertices of a polygon change for each of these translations?

a. a number of units right or left

b. a number of units up or down

c. a number of units right or left *and* a number of units up or down

4-3 Exercises and Problems

1. **Reading** Is a translation most like a *flip*, a *slide*, or a *turn*? Explain your choice.

Find the coordinates of each vertex of △TDE after each translation.

2. 3 units down

3. 2 units left

4. 1 unit right and 2 units down

5. 5 units left and 4 units up

Tell whether each picture shows a translation. If it does, describe how the vertices moved.

6.

7.

8.
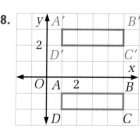

9. Translate △*JKL* 4 units left and 3 units up. What are the coordinates of each vertex after the translation?

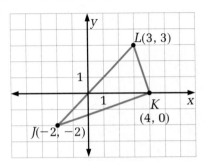

10. Translate parallelogram *PQRS* 5 units right. What are the coordinates of each vertex after the translation?

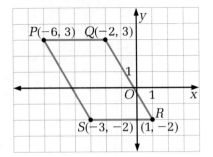

The traditional and modern designs of many cultures display translational symmetry.

Tell whether each design has translational symmetry.

11.

Hopi

12.

The Netherlands

13.

Indonesia

14.

Zaire

15. **Open-ended** Create a design. Use your design to make a pattern with translational symmetry.

Cup from the Kuba culture of Zaire.

Use this information for Exercises 16–22.

Another way to describe a translation is to show the change in the coordinates (x, y) of any point. For example, a translation of 2 units right and 1 unit down is written $(x, y) \rightarrow (x + 2, y - 1)$.

Write the coordinates of *P'* after each translation of *P*(4, 5).

16. $(x, y) \rightarrow (x + 1, y + 3)$

17. $(x, y) \rightarrow (x - 3, y + 2)$

18. $(x, y) \rightarrow (x, y + 1)$

19. $(x, y) \rightarrow (x - 2, y)$

Describe each translation by showing the change in the coordinates (x, y) of any point.

20. 1 unit left
21. 4 units right, 6 units down
22. 1 unit left, 2 units up

23. Research In the game of chess, a king may move in any direction but only one square at a time. Find out what rules control the movement of the other pieces used in chess. For each chess piece, describe a move as a translation.

 Ongoing **ASSESSMENT**

24. a. Copy the boat on graph paper. Find its area.

b. Writing Suppose you want to tell a friend how to show the boat sailing across the grid. Describe to your friend how the coordinates of the boat change as it moves.

c. Does the area of the boat change as it moves? Explain your answer.

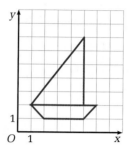

Review **PREVIEW**

25. a. Plot the points $W(0, 0)$, $X(3, 3)$, $Y(6, 0)$, and $Z(3, -3)$. Connect them in order and connect Z to W. *(Section 4-2)*

b. Write the specific name of the polygon you formed. Explain how you know what it is.

Solve each equation. *(Sections 2-7, 2-8)*

26. $x + 7 = 18$
27. $3a + 15 = -32$
28. $2g - 9 = -26$

Find the measure of each angle in the diagram at the right. *(Section 2-5)*

29. $\angle ACD$
30. $\angle ACB$
31. $\angle 1$

 Working on the Unit Project

32. The pictures show a person dropping to the ground with a parachute. How do the coordinates of the parachute change as it approaches the ground?

33. Open-ended Draw a cartoon figure on a coordinate plane. Sketch two movements of the figure. Describe how the coordinates of the figure change as the figure moves.

34. Decide what your flip book will show. What types of motions will it use? Write a short description of your plan for the flip book.

Rotations

······· Focus

Recognize rotations of figures on a coordinate plane, rotate figures on polar graph paper, and recognize rotational symmetry.

center of rotation

Transformations

translation

rotation

The gymnast is turning or *rotating* around the horizontal bar. A turn around a point is called a **rotation.** The point is called the **center of rotation.** Wheels, doors, and clothes dryers also rotate. A center of rotation may be at the center of an object, as on a wheel. It may also be at some other point *on* or *off* the object.

Rotating and translating are two ways to *transform* an object. A **transformation** describes a change made to an object or its position.

Place a piece of paper on your desk. Press one finger down on the paper to create a center of rotation. Rotate the paper.

1. When you rotate the paper, does it change size or shape?

2. What information does someone need in order to copy a rotation? Give directions for copying your rotation.

The *direction* of a rotation may be *clockwise* (↻) or *counterclockwise* (↺). The *amount of turn* of a rotation may be stated in degrees.

complete turn
360°

half-turn
180°

quarter-turn
90°

Sample 1

The graphs show rotations of △ABC around the origin. Describe the direction and the amount of the rotation of each graph.

a.

b.

c.

Sample Response

a.
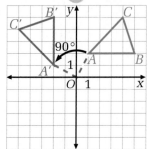

② Measure ∠AOA′.

① Draw lines from the center of the rotation to corresponding points on each figure (OA and OA′).

90° counterclockwise

b.

180°

c.
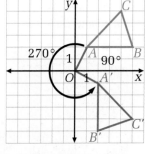

270° counterclockwise

4-4 Rotations

203

3. Why is the direction of turn not included in the description of a 180° rotation?

4. a. Name a clockwise rotation that gives the same results as a rotation of 90° counterclockwise.

   b. Name a clockwise rotation that gives the same results as a rotation of 270° counterclockwise.

ROTATIONS

To describe a rotation, you need to tell:

➤ the amount of turn, as a fraction or in degrees

➤ the direction—clockwise or counterclockwise

➤ the location of the center of rotation

Drawing Rotations

It is easier to draw rotations on a special type of graph paper called *polar graph paper*.

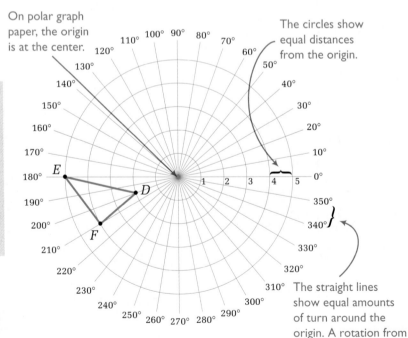

On polar graph paper, the origin is at the center.

The circles show equal distances from the origin.

The straight lines show equal amounts of turn around the origin. A rotation from one line to the next is 10°.

Rotate △DEF 60° counterclockwise around the origin.

Sample Response

Move each vertex along its circle:

direction—counterclockwise

amount of turn—60° is 6 · 10°, so move six lines

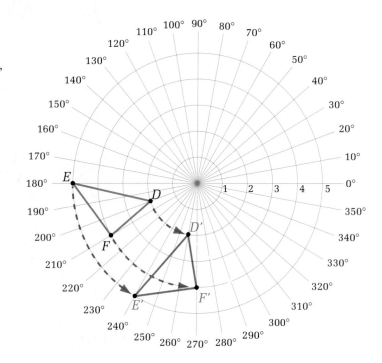

Then draw the rotated triangle.

Rotational Symmetry

Every object looks the same after a 360° rotation around its center. Some objects look the same after a rotation of less than 360°. If so, they have **rotational symmetry.** To describe rotational symmetry, tell how many degrees the object must rotate in order to look the same way it did before the rotation.

A square has 90°, 180°, and 270° rotational symmetry.

original   30°   60°   90°   120°   150°   180°   210°   240°   270°   300°   330°   original

Tell whether or not each figure has rotational symmetry. If it does, describe the symmetry.

"Tomo" is Japanese for "friend."

a.   友

b.

c.   72°

Sample Response

a. No. The character must rotate 360° in order to look the way it did before the rotation.

b. Yes. This design has 180° rotational symmetry.

c. Yes. The starfish has 72°, 144°, 216°, and 288° rotational symmetry.

Look Back

How are translational symmetry and rotational symmetry alike? How are they different?

4-4 Exercises and Problems

1. a. Describe the rotation that occurs when a tree falls.

   b. Describe the rotation that occurs when a pair of scissors is used.

   c. Describe another rotation that you have observed in your life.

2. **Reading** What are two types of transformations? How are they alike?

The graphs show rotations around the origin. Describe the direction and the amount of the rotation in each graph.

3.

4.

5.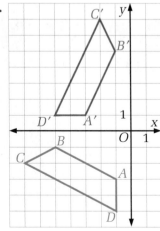

Copy each figure on polar graph paper. Draw each indicated rotation of the figure around the origin.

6. a. 50° counterclockwise

  b. 180° clockwise

7. a. 60° clockwise

  b. 120° counterclockwise

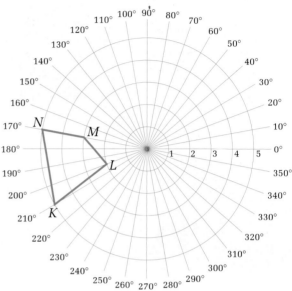

8. Career A pilot can plot the location of an airplane using its distance from a radio tower and its clockwise rotation from north on a magnetic compass.

  a. What are the coordinates of airplane *B*?

  b. What are the coordinates of airplane *C*?

  c. **Writing** Describe how this system of locating airplanes and the method of locating points on polar graph paper are alike and how they are different.

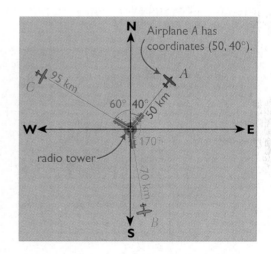

Airport runways are numbered by their clockwise rotation from north. To determine a runway number, follow these steps:

(1) Find the clockwise rotation from north.

(2) Divide by 10°.

(3) Round the quotient to the nearest whole number.

For example, a runway with a clockwise rotation of 32° from north is named "runway 3."

What is the number of the runway at each location?

  9. 10° north of east

  10. 13° south of west

  11. 48° east of south

Tell whether each design has rotational symmetry. If it does, describe the symmetry.

12.   13.

14.   15.

In Exercises 16–18, what type(s) of symmetry does each design have? Copy the pattern that repeats and describe the transformation.

Designs with many types of symmetry are created by people all over the world. These are from India, Panama, Mexico, and the United States.

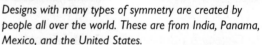

16.   17.

18.

19. **Open-ended** Create a design. Use your design to make a pattern with rotational or translational symmetry, or both.

20. **Using Manipulatives** Create at least three paper snowflakes. Cut out at least one snowflake each from a circle (as shown), a square, and an equilateral triangle. Describe the rotational symmetries in your favorite snowflake.

1. Fold the paper in half,   2. then fold into thirds.   3. Cut some designs out of the edges,   4. then unfold.

21. **Research** What shape does the nut on a fire hydrant have? What rotational symmetry does this nut have? Why do you think this shape was chosen?

Ongoing **ASSESSMENT**

22. **Group Activity** Work in a group of four students.

    a. Describe the rotational symmetry of a regular pentagon, hexagon, octagon, and 9-gon.

    b. Look for a pattern in your results. Then create a method for describing the rotational symmetry of any regular polygon.

Review **PREVIEW**

23. Translate $\overline{AB}$ 2 units to the right and 3 units down. Draw $\overline{A'B'}$. What are the coordinates of each point after the translation? *(Section 4-3)*

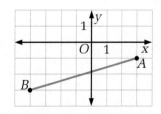

24. Make a graph to show the data. *(Section 3-6)*

RESULTS OF A POLL THAT ASKED:

"Which day of the week do you think is the worst?"	Answer	SUN	MON	TUE	WED	THU	FRI	SAT	Don't Know
	%	3.8	62.2	5.1	6.0	2.0	3.9	2.4	14.6

Working on the Unit Project

25. Imagine making a flip book for each situation. Would you use a *translation* or a *rotation* to show each movement?

   a. a snail creeping along the ground

   b. an elevator arrow switching from "up" to "down"

26. **Open-ended** Describe a movement that could be shown by each transformation.

   a. translation   **b.** rotation

Unit 4   CHECKPOINT

1. **Writing** Choose two uses of coordinate systems. Write a paragraph describing how they are alike and how they are different.

Jo's flip book shows the Little Dipper and the Big Dipper.

2. a. Graph the points $A(-17, -6)$, $B(-14, -7)$, $C(-13, -8)$, $D(-10.5, -10)$, $E(-6, -11)$, $F(-7, -13)$, and $G(-10, -12)$ on a coordinate plane. Connect the points to form the Big Dipper. Connect G to D to complete the bowl.   **4-1**

   b. What quadrant contains the Big Dipper?

   c. Describe the shape of the bowl of the Big Dipper.

3. What name is used for the location of the North Star on the coordinate plane?

4. Find the area of the bowl of the Little Dipper.   **4-2**

5. Translate the Little Dipper 2 units to the left and 4 units down. What are the coordinates of each point after the translation?   **4-3**

6. Jo's flip book shows a rotation of the Little Dipper around the North Star. Describe the direction and the amount of the rotation.   **4-4**

The Little Dipper

Tell whether each pattern has *translational symmetry*, *rotational symmetry*, or *no symmetry*.

7.

Guatemala

8.

Denmark

9.

United States

4-5

Focus

Make and interpret a scatter plot of data, and use scatter plots to make predictions.

Scatter Plots

GET TO THE POINT•

EXPLORATION

Do taller people have longer arms?

- **Materials: tape measure or meter stick, graph paper, graphics calculator or software (optional)**
- **Work in a group of at least five students.**

① Predict what the relationship between height and lower-arm length might be.

② Measure and record the height of each person in your group to the nearest centimeter.

Measure and record each person's lower-arm length.

Name	Height (cm)	Lower-arm length (cm)
Michelle	157	42
?	?	?

③ Use graph paper or a graphics calculator to plot your data.

④ Describe any trends you see in your graph. Does your graph support the prediction you made in step 1?

⑤ Display your table and graph along with those of the other groups. How are the data and the graphs alike or different?

⑥ Plot the data from all the groups on one graph.

⑦ Compare this graph with the first graph your group made. Does the new graph support the prediction you made in step 1?

⑧ Suppose a student is 171 cm tall. Use the graph to predict the student's lower-arm length.

⑨ Measure the wrist circumference and back length of each person in your group. Save these data for use in Exercise 3.

Height: 157 cm

Length: 42 cm

Length: 48 cm

The graph that you made in the Exploration is a *scatter plot*. A **scatter plot** is a graph that shows the relationship between two data sets.

Tent prices

October high temperatures

Campground prices

When two data sets increase together, they have a **positive correlation.**

When one data set decreases as the other increases, the two data sets have a **negative correlation.**

Sometimes data sets show **no correlation.**

> **Talk it Over**
>
> 1. Do the graphs you made for the Exploration show a positive correlation, a negative correlation, or no correlation?
>
> 2. Suppose you collect data on the length of people's longest fingernails. Do you think there is a correlation between these data and the people's heights? Why or why not?

······► **Now you are ready for: Exs. 1–9 on pp. 214–215**

Drawing a Fitted Line

You can use a scatter plot to make predictions. To help you make predictions from a scatter plot, draw a straight line that passes close to most of the data points. This line is called a **fitted line.**

TECHNOLOGY NOTE

A graphics calculator or software can draw a fitted line for a scatter plot.

October high temperatures

Most of the points lie close to the fitted line for a strong correlation.

A fitted line shows if the correlation between two data sets is strong or weak. If the data points come very close to the fitted line, the correlation is *strong*. If not, the correlation is *weak*. The stronger the correlation, the better your predictions will be.

212   **Unit 4** Coordinates and Functions

The table shows the piston displacement and horsepower (hp) of nine similarly powered cars. What horsepower do you predict for a 3200 cc engine?

Car	A	B	C	D	E	F	G	H	I
Displacement (cc)	2389	1836	3405	3535	1840	2977	2986	1998	2164
Horsepower	155	134	300	310	140	270	220	119	130

Sample Response

Make a scatter plot of the data. Draw a fitted line. Then predict.

3 The point where the line meets the vertical axis is the prediction.

1 From the 3200 mark on the horizontal axis, draw a vertical line to the fitted line.

2 Then draw a horizontal line to the vertical axis.

A 3200 cc engine in a similarly powered car should have about 270 hp.

Talk it Over

3. In the Sample, can you be certain that a 3200 cc engine will have 270 hp? Why or why not?

4. Use the scatter plot in the Sample to predict the displacement of an engine in a similarly powered car that has 200 hp.

5. A fitted line must lie close to the points on a scatter plot, but there is not one correct placement. Decide whether each line is appropriate as a fitted line for the scatter plot. Explain your decisions.

a.

b.

Watch Out!

A correlation between two sets of data does *not* necessarily mean there is a cause-and-effect relationship.

Suppose there is a positive correlation between the number of students who go to their school's basketball games and the number of games won. Here are some conclusions you might make.

➤ Stronger student support causes the team to win more often.

➤ The team's success causes more students to attend games.

➤ Something else, such as a new gymnasium causes both attendance to rise and the team to win.

Look Back

Do you think that the scatter plots you made in the Exploration show a strong or a weak correlation between height and lower-arm length? How did you decide?

▸ **Now you are ready for:**
Exs. 10–31 on pp. 215–217

4-5 Exercises and Problems

1. Use the graph you made in the Exploration.

   a. Suppose two people have the same height and different lower-arm lengths. How would this look on the graph?

   b. Suppose two people have different heights and the same lower-arm length. How would this look on the graph?

2. TECHNOLOGY Use a graphics calculator or graphing software.

   a. Plot the data that you collected in the Exploration using the statistics menu of the calculator. Does it look like the graph that you drew in Step 3 of the Exploration? If not, change the range until it does. What is the range that you need to use?

   b. Use the *linear regression* feature to find a fitted line for the data. *Trace* along the line until you find the point with x-coordinate 171. What is the y-coordinate of the point?

   c. Explain what the y-coordinate that you found in part (b) represents. How is it related to the prediction that you made in Step 8 of the Exploration?

3. Use one of the data sets that you collected in Step 9 of the Exploration.

   a. What kind of correlation, if any, do you think that there is between the data set and height? Why?

   b. Test your prediction by making a scatter plot. (Put height on the horizontal axis.)

   c. Describe the correlation shown by the scatter plot. Does your scatter plot support your prediction? Explain.

BY THE WAY...

In his first year as a professional basketball player, Shawn Bradley wore number 76 for the Philadelphia 76ers. He is 7 ft 6 in. tall. Can you predict his lower-arm length?

4. What types of manufacturers might need to know about the relationships between heights and arm lengths? Why might they need this information?

State whether each scatter plot shows a *positive correlation*, a *negative correlation*, or *no correlation*.

5.

6.

7.

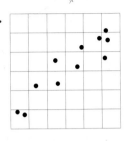

8. Choose one of these titles for each of the scatter plots in Exercises 5–7. Explain your choice.
   a. Number of Cars vs. Number of Traffic Lights in a City 5
   b. Amount of Time Spent Working vs. Amount of Leisure Time
   c. Temperature vs. Winter Coat Sales 7
   d. Shoe Size vs. Amount of Savings 6

9. **Open-ended** Make up your own title for each scatter plot in Exercises 5–7. Be sure your titles reflect the relationships shown in the scatter plots.

10. **Reading** Use diagrams to describe how to use a fitted line to make predictions from a scatter plot.

11. **Writing** A newspaper claims there is a strong correlation between the weather on the day of an election and voter turnout. What do you think the newspaper means? Could the newspaper use a scatter plot to support its claim? If so, what would be on each axis?

12. This graph shows a strong negative correlation.

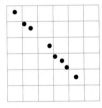

This graph shows a weak negative correlation.

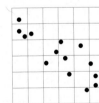

a. Draw a graph that shows a strong positive correlation. Draw another graph that shows a weak positive correlation.

b. When you look at a scatterplot, you can decide two things: *a positive or a negative* correlation, and *a strong or a weak* correlation. Which type of decision do you think is easier to make?

TECHNOLOGY NOTE

If you use a graphics calculator to find a fitted line for a data set, you can get a measure of how strong the correlation is.

The calculator will produce a number called "*r*". The closer *r* is to 1 or −1, the stronger the correlation.

Make a scatter plot for each relationship. State whether each scatter plot shows a *positive correlation*, a *negative correlation*, or *no correlation*.

City	Latitude (°N)	Average precipitation (in.)	Annual range of average temperatures (°F)	Average temperature in January (°F)	Average number of days of rain per year
Anchorage, AK	61	15.2	45.1	13	115
Austin, TX	30	31.5	35.6	49.1	83
Bismarck, ND	47	15.4	63.7	6.7	96
Charleston, WV	38	42.4	41.6	32.9	151
Grand Rapids, MI	43	34.4	49.4	22	143
Honolulu, HI	21	23.5	7.5	72.6	100
Los Angeles, CA	34	12.0	13	56	36
Madison, WI	43	30.8	55	15.6	118
Minneapolis, MN	45	26.4	61.9	11.2	115
Olympia, WA	47	51.0	25.8	37.2	164
San Francisco, CA	38	19.7	13.7	48.5	63
Tampa, FL	28	46.7	22.3	59.8	107

13. the latitude and the average precipitation

14. the annual range of average temperatures and the average temperature in January

15. the average precipitation and the days of rain per year

For Exercises 16–21, use the scatter plots you made for Exercises 13–15.

16. **Using Manipulatives** Use a piece of uncooked spaghetti to represent a fitted line in each of the scatterplots. Which scatter plot shows the strongest correlation? the weakest correlation?

17. Predict the average temperature in January in a city with an annual range of average temperatures of 30°F.

18. Which do you think is greater: the probability that a city with an average precipitation of 13 in. has an average of 80 days of rain per year or the probability that it has an average of 170 days of rain per year?

19. Predict the average precipitation of a city with 40 days of rain per year.

20. Does your graph prove that there is a cause-and-effect relationship between the annual range of average temperatures and the average temperature in January? Explain why or why not.

21. Use the scatter plot that you made for Exercise 13. Which of these conclusions, if any, can you make?

   a. The graph shows that cities that are further north have more rain.

   b. The graph shows that cities that have more rain are further north.

   c. The graph shows that latitude and rain are not related.

   d. The graph shows that cities that are further south have more rain.

Research In a reference book such as an almanac, find two data sets that relate to each other like the ones in this section. The data could be about population, entertainment, sports, geography, social issues, government, sales, and so on.

a. Make a scatter plot of the data you collect.

b. What kind of correlation does the scatter plot show?

c. Write a question that can be answered by using the scatter plot.

Ongoing ASSESSMENT

23. **Group Activity** Collect data from 10 students in your class about the number of sweet snacks they eat in a week and the number of salty snacks they eat in a week.

a. What kind of correlation do you predict your data will show? Why?

b. Make a scatter plot of the data. Draw a fitted line, if possible. Does your scatter plot show the correlation you expected? Explain.

c. Compare your scatter plot with the plots of several other students. How are they alike and how are they different? Do all the scatter plots show the same correlation?

Review PREVIEW

Give the number of degrees in each type of rotation. (Section 4-4)

24. half-turn   25. quarter-turn   26. whole turn

Graph each inequality on a number line. (Section 3-3)

27. $a \geq -3$ 28. $x \leq 5$ 29. $-2 < c \leq 7$

30. Savannah earns $5.75/h as a receptionist in a beauty shop. Tell how much she earns for each number of hours she works. (Section 1-2)

a. 3 hours   b. 7 hours   c. x hours

Working on the Unit Project

31. **Research** Read about how animation is created and used. As you read, you may want to take notes about animation ideas to help you as you make your flip book.

Suggested Bibliography

Laybourne, Kit. *The Animation Book*. New York: Crown Publishers, 1979.

Andersen, Yvonne. *Make Your Own Animated Movies*. Boston: Little, Brown and Company, 1970.

Platt, Richard. *Film*. (Eyewitness Guides Series). London: Dorling Kindersley Limited, 1992, pp. 50–53.

Graphs and Functions

Focus
Understand what a function is, identify control variables and dependent variables, draw graphs of functions, and recognize functions.

THIS DEPENDS ON THAT

Talk it Over

1. What does this graph show?

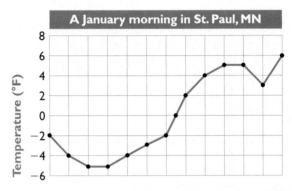

A January morning in St. Paul, MN

Temperature (°F) vs. Time of day

2. Estimate the highest and the lowest temperatures. At what time did each happen?

3. During what interval(s) of time did the temperature increase? When did it decrease?

4. Does the temperature depend on the time of day?

5. Does the time of day depend on the temperature?

The dependent variable is usually put on the vertical axis.

dependent variable

control variable

Dependent and Control Variables

The graph shows information about two variables: time of day and temperature. The temperature *depends* on what time of day it is. The temperature is called the **dependent variable.** The time of day is called the **control variable.** (The control variable is sometimes called the *independent variable.*)

Identify the dependent variable and the control variable in each situation.

a. Cal volunteers to wrap gifts for a charity. He uses different amounts of wrapping paper to wrap boxes of different sizes.

b. Mai earns $4.50 per hour in a hardware store. When she works different numbers of hours, she earns different amounts of money.

Sample Response ....

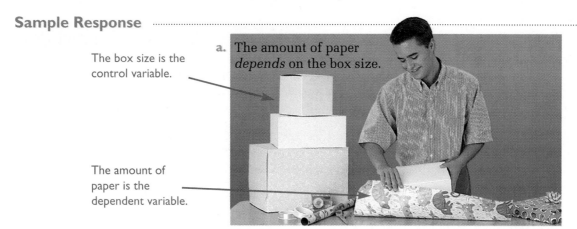

a. The amount of paper *depends* on the box size.

The box size is the control variable.

The amount of paper is the dependent variable.

b. The amount of money earned *depends* on the number of hours worked.

The number of hours is the control variable.

The amount of money earned is the dependent variable.

Talk it Over

6. Suppose you graph Cal's box sizes and amounts of paper. Which variable would you plot on the horizontal axis? Why?

7. Identify the dependent variable and the control variable: When riding a Ferris wheel, you are at different heights from the ground at different times during the ride.

Functions

A **function** is a relationship in which there is *only one* value of the dependent variable for each value of the control variable. For example, in the graph on page 218, for each time of day, there is only one temperature. You can say "the temperature is a function of the time of day."

A function can be represented many ways: in words, in symbols, with a table of values, or with a graph.

Sample 2

At a week-long charity rummage sale, the price of each item is half the previous day's price. Draw a graph of the price of an $8 item during the sale. Does the graph represent a function?

Sample Response

First make a table of values.

Then draw a graph.

To find each day's price, multiply the previous day's price by $\frac{1}{2}$.

The original price is $8.

The price depends on the day of the sale. So the day of the sale is the control variable.

TECHNOLOGY NOTE

You can also use spreadsheet software to make a table.

Use the "fill down" command for the cells in column B.

	A	B
1	Day	Price
2	1	8
3	2	= 0.5 * B2

Day of sale	Price (dollars)
1	8
2	$\frac{1}{2}(8) = 4$
3	$\frac{1}{2}(4) = 2$
4	$\frac{1}{2}(2) = 1$
5	$\frac{1}{2}(1) = 0.50$
6	$\frac{1}{2}(0.50) = 0.25$
7	$\frac{1}{2}(0.25) = 0.13$

Plot the price on the vertical axis.

Plot the day of the sale on the horizontal axis.

For each day of the sale, the item has only one price. So the graph represents a function.

Vertical-Line Test for Functions

You can tell if a graph represents a function by looking at it. For each value of the control variable, there should be only one value of the dependent variable. This means that no two points on a graph of a function lie directly above one another.

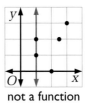

not a function

To test whether a graph represents a function, imagine drawing vertical lines through the graph. If two or more points of the graph lie in the same vertical line, then the graph does not represent a function. This test is called the *vertical-line test*.

Sample 3

Tell whether each graph represents a function.

a.

Times and distances of track team members

time / distance

b.

Triangle *ABC*

c.

Sound waves

Sample Response

Use the side of a pencil as a vertical line. Slide the pencil across the page to check if two or more points lie in the same vertical line. You can also imagine drawing vertical lines through each graph.

a.

Times and distances of track team members

time / distance

b.

Triangle *ABC*

c.

Sound waves

Many points of the graph lie on the same vertical line.

The graph does not represent a function.

Many points of the graph lie on the same vertical line.

The graph does not represent a function.

No two points of the graph lie on the same vertical line.

The graph represents a function.

Look Back

In Sample 2 the relationship is a function. How can you tell from the table? How can you tell from the graph?

Exercises and Problems

1. **Reading** Complete the statement. The control variable is usually put on the ? axis and the dependent variable is usually put on the ? axis.

For Exercises 2–4, describe each situation using the phrase "is a function of." What is the dependent variable? the control variable?

2. Felicia Ramiro owns a carpet cleaning business. She charges different prices for cleaning carpets of different sizes.

3. **Sports** Michael practices running the 100 m dash every day. The faster he runs, the shorter his time.

4. Students in a driver's education class study the night before a written test. Students who study longer earn better scores.

5. **Marine Biology** The table shows the length of a lemon shark at various ages.

   a. Identify the dependent variable and the control variable.

   b. Graph the data.

   c. Does the graph represent a function? Explain.

   d. Estimate the shark's length at age 6.

   e. Estimate the shark's age when its length was 149 cm.

| Length of a lemon shark ||
Age (years)	Length (cm)
1	50
2	62
3	86
4	93
5	107
7	126
8	140
10	156
11	161
12	169

6. Use the situation described in Sample 2. Suppose you want to buy an item originally priced at $20. Graph the function. How is the graph similar to the one in Sample 2? How is it different?

Choose the most reasonable graph for each situation.

7. Bob's earnings at a sub shop are a function of how many hours he works.

8. An oven is turned on and set for a certain temperature. The temperature of an oven is a function of the length of time the oven has been on. (A thermostat maintains the temperature.)

a.

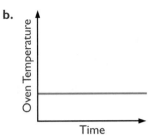

b.

c.

Draw a graph of each situation. Tell whether the graph represents a function. Explain.

9. The Ecology Club has a bake sale every year. This year they raised $240. They decide to try to raise 1.5 times the amount they raised the previous year for the next three years.

10. Linda Lee teaches five art classes that have 23, 26, 21, 29, and 24 students. She buys a drawing pad for each student, plus 4 extras for each class.

11. Use these two graphs.

Graph A

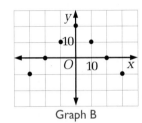
Graph B

a. Use Graph A. If someone asks you what y is when $x = 10$, how many answers can you give?

b. Use Graph B. If someone asks you what y is when $x = 10$, how many answers can you give?

c. **Writing** Which graph represents a function? Explain your choice.

12 TECHNOLOGY Use geometric drawing software.

Alternative Approach Work in a group of three students using graph paper and rulers.

a. Draw six different rectangles that are twice as long as they are wide.

b. Find the perimeter and area of each rectangle. Make a table of your results.

c. Use your table to make three graphs:
➤ length as a function of width
➤ perimeter as a function of width
➤ area as a function of width

d. How are the graphs alike? How are they different?

Width	Length	Perimeter	Area
?	?	?	?
?	?	?	?
?	?	?	?
?	?	?	?
?	?	?	?
?	?	?	?

Tell whether each graph represents a function. Explain your answer.

13.

14.

15.

16. **Open-ended** Think of a situation that involves two quantities, one of which depends on the other. Describe the situation as a function. Identify the dependent variable and the control variable. Draw a graph of the function.

Review **PREVIEW**

17. Draw a scatter plot that shows a strong positive correlation. *(Section 4-5)*

Give the reciprocal of each number. *(Toolbox Skill 9)*

18. 4

19. -4

20. $\frac{1}{2}$

21. $-\frac{3}{8}$

Evaluate each expression when $x = -2$, $x = 0$, and $x = 3$. *(Sections 1-4, 2-2)*

22. $-5x^2$

23. $|x| + 8$

24. $-x$

25. $\frac{1}{x}$

Working on the Unit Project

26. Start making the drawings for your flip book. Draw on graph paper to make sure the positions of your drawings are consistent. Keep track of the types of translations and rotations you use.

BY THE WAY...

The movie *Jaws* starred a white shark. Because it is difficult and dangerous to get near a white shark, not much is known about them. They are about 120 cm long at birth, and the maximum confirmed length of a white shark is 6 m.

Functions and Equations

Section 4-7

Focus
Change from one representation of a function to another, learn about some basic functions.

ANOTHER WAY TO LOOK AT IT

EXPLORATION

Is the relationship between a number and its square a function?

- **Materials: graph paper, graphics calculator**

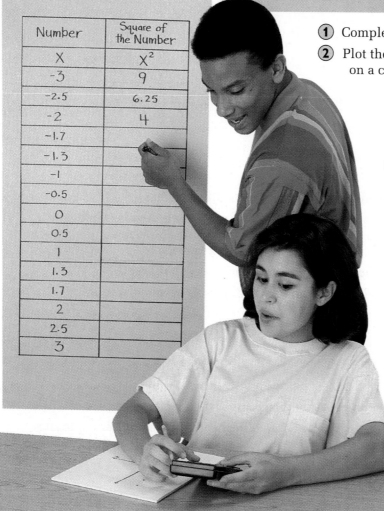

Number	Square of the Number
X	X^2
-3	9
-2.5	6.25
-2	4
-1.7	
-1.3	
-1	
-0.5	
0	
0.5	
1	
1.3	
1.7	
2	
2.5	
3	

1 Complete the table in the photo.

2 Plot the ordered pairs on a coordinate plane.

$(-2, 4)$

3 Describe the shape the points seem to make.

4 Does the relationship between x and x^2 appear to be a function? Why or why not?

5 Choose four values between -3 and 3 that are not already in the table. Find their squares and plot the points.

6 You cannot square *all* the numbers between 3 and -3 and plot the ordered pairs. However, your graphics calculator can do many more than you can, in a much shorter time. Enter the equation $y = x^2$ on the "$y =$" screen of the calculator. Compare the result with your graph.

Writing Equations

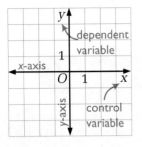

For a function, x often represents the control variable and y represents the dependent variable. In the Exploration:

> The *number* is x
>
> y is the *square of the number*
>
> so $y = x^2$.

The equation, the table of values that you made, the graph, and the description in words all represent the same relationship. You can change one representation to another.

Sample 1

Write an equation to represent the function given in the table.

x	y
-3	-5
-2	-4
-1	-3
0	-2
1	-1
2	0
3	1

Sample Response

$-3 - 2 = -5$
$-2 - 2 = -4$
$-1 - 2 = -3$
$0 - 2 = -2$
$1 - 2 = -1$
$2 - 2 = 0$
$3 - 2 = 1$

Problem Solving Strategy: Identify a pattern

Think about how the y-values relate to the x-values in the table. Make a conjecture about the pattern. Write a rule for the pattern: Each y-value is two less than its x-value.

Test your conjecture using the values in the table.

Write the rule as an equation: $y = x - 2$.

Sample 2

Write an equation to represent the function.

The cost of a telephone call depends on the number of minutes that it lasts. The first minute costs \$.26 and each additional minute costs \$.12.

Sample Response

The number of additional minutes after the first is the control variable. Represent it by m.

The number of additional minutes is m.

The cost is the dependent variable. Use a different letter to represent it.

The total cost in dollars of the telephone call is c.

Because each additional minute costs $.12, the cost of m minutes is $.12 times m.

The cost of the additional minutes is $0.12m$.

The total cost is the sum of the first minute's cost and the additional minutes' costs. Write an equation to represent the function.

Then $c = 0.26 + 0.12m$.

••••► **Now you are ready for:**
Exs. 1–11 on p. 231

Talk it Over

Identify the control variable and the dependent variable for each function. Then write an equation to represent the function.

1. A videotape movie is 108 min long. The amount of time you have left to watch depends on how many minutes you already watched.

2. The senior class play costs $500 to produce. Each ticket to the play sells for $5. The profit the senior class earns depends on the number of tickets that are sold.

Graphing Equations

You can graph a function represented by an equation by using *graph paper*, a *graphics calculator*, or *graphing software*.

To graph an equation on graph paper, first make a table of values. You can write the values as ordered pairs (x, y). Then plot the ordered pairs. If all values between the ordered pairs also make the equation true, then the points can be connected.

4-7 Functions and Equations

Graph each equation.

Carmella burns 5 Calories per minute when she rides her bicycle.

a. $y = |x|$

b. The equation $y = 5x$ gives the number of Calories (y) that Carmella burns in x minutes.

Sample Response

➤ Make a table to find the coordinates of several points.

➤ Choose both positive and negative values for x. Some easy values to evaluate are −1, 0, and 1. Use other values to show the shape of the graph better.

➤ Graph the ordered pairs and connect them.

a. Make a table.

$y = |x|$		
x	y	(x, y)
−3	$|-3| = 3$	$(-3, 3)$
−2	$|-2| = 2$	$(-2, 2)$
−1	$|-1| = 1$	$(-1, 1)$
0	$|0| = 0$	$(0, 0)$
1	$|1| = 1$	$(1, 1)$
2	$|2| = 2$	$(2, 2)$
3	$|3| = 3$	$(3, 3)$

If x is negative, then its absolute value is the opposite of x.

If x is positive or zero, its absolute value is itself.

Plot the points and connect them.

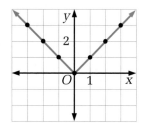

The shape of the graph is a V.

b. Make a table.

$y = 5x$		
x	y	(x, y)
−1	$5(-1) = -5$	$(-1, -5)$
0	$5(0) = 0$	$(0, 0)$
1	$5(1) = 5$	$(1, 5)$
2	$5(2) = 5$	$(2, 10)$

Plot the points and connect them.

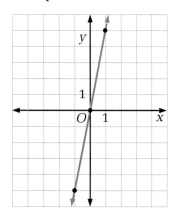

The shape of the graph is a line.

TECHNOLOGY NOTE

If you use a graphics calculator or software to graph the equation, be sure that the graph screen settings include all the x- and y-values from your table.

······▶ Now you are ready for:
: Exs. 12–20 on pp. 231–232

Talk it Over

3. All the points on the line in Sample 3(b) make the equation true, but only the points in the first quadrant model the situations. Why is this?

4. Choose a point on the graph in Sample 3(b) that is between two of the plotted points. Find its coordinates. Does this ordered pair make the equation true?

5. Elena made this chart to help her remember which axis to use. Complete the chart.

horizontal axis	$\underline{?}$ axis
x	y
$\underline{?}$ variable	dependent variable

Shapes of Graphs

The U-shaped graph of the squaring function in the Exploration is called a **parabola**. In Sample 3 you saw a function whose graph is a line and another function whose graph is V-shaped. Other functions have special shapes when they are graphed.

Sample 4

Graph each equation.

a. $y = x$

b. $y = \dfrac{1}{x}$

Sample Response

Make a table to find the coordinates of several points. Graph the ordered pairs and connect them.

a. Make a table.

$y = x$		
x	y	(x, y)
-3	-3	$(-3, -3)$
-2	-2	$(-2, -2)$
-1	-1	$(-1, -1)$
0	0	$(0, 0)$
1	1	$(1, 1)$
2	2	$(2, 2)$
3	3	$(3, 3)$

Plot the points and connect them.

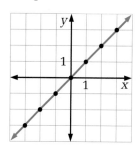

The shape of the graph is a line.

4-7 Functions and Equations

b. Make a table.

$y = \frac{1}{x}$		
x	y	(x, y)
-3	$-0.\overline{3}$	$(-3, -0.\overline{3})$
-2	-0.5	$(-2, -0.5)$
-1	-1	$(-1, -1)$
-0.5	-2	$(-0.5, -2)$
-0.25	-4	$(-0.25, -4)$
0	—	—
0.25	4	$(0.25, 4)$
0.5	2	$(0.5, 2)$
1	1	$(1, 1)$
2	0.5	$(2, 0.5)$
3	$0.\overline{3}$	$(3, 0.\overline{3})$

Remember that $\frac{1}{-2}$ is the same as $-\frac{1}{2}$.

Use fractional values of x to see the shape of the graph better.

Plot the points and connect them.

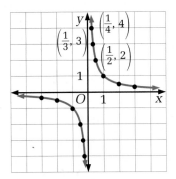

The shape of the graph is two curves. This graph is called a **hyperbola.**

Talk it Over

6. The function $y = x$ is called the *identity function*. Why do you think this function has this name?

7. The function $y = \frac{1}{x}$ is called the *reciprocal function*. Why do you think this function has this name?

SOME BASIC FUNCTIONS

Equation	$y = x^2$	$y = |x|$	$y = x$	$y = \frac{1}{x}$
Words	squaring function	absolute value function	identity function	reciprocal function
Graph	shape: parabola	shape: V	shape: line	shape: hyperbola

Look Back

Suppose you are given a function described by an equation. How can you represent it with a table? with a graph?

Now you are ready for: Exs. 21–45 on pp. 232–233

Exercises and Problems

1. **Reading** What are three different ways to represent a function?

Write an equation to represent each function.

2.

x	y
−3	−1
−2	0
−1	1
0	2
1	3
2	4
3	5

3.

x	y
−3	−1.5
−2	−1
−1	−0.5
0	0
1	0.5
2	1
3	1.5

4.

x	y
−3	−14
−2	−13
−1	−12
0	−11
1	−10
2	−9
3	−8

5. **Commissions** Rehema Strong works at a shoe store. Her weekly base pay is $350. She also receives a 4.5% commission on her total sales.

   a. Identify the control variable and the dependent variable.

   b. Write an equation to represent the situation.

   c. One week Rehema Strong sold $5348 worth of shoes. Find her total pay for the week.

Write an equation to represent each function. Tell what your variables represent.

6. **Health** An estimate of normal systolic blood pressure depends on a person's age. A general guideline estimates that normal blood pressure is 110 more than one half a person's age.

7. Use the photo. Sound travels at an average rate of 1000 ft/s.

8. On a summer day, the temperature at 3 A.M. is about 16°F less than the temperature at 3 P.M.

9. A group of people plan to rent a vacation cottage for $800. The amount of money each person pays depends on the number of people who go on vacation at the cottage.

10. The number of times a cricket chirps per minute depends on the air temperature. The number of chirps is thirty less than seven times the temperature in degrees Celsius.

11. **Writing** Think of a real life situation that the equation $y = 1.25x$ could represent. Describe the situation in words and tell what x and y represent.

12. The amount of change received from a $20 bill depends on the total cost of the items bought.

   a. Identify the control variable and the dependent variable.

   b. Write an equation to represent the situation.

   c. What limits are there on the values of the dependent variable? the control variable?

The time that the sound of thunder takes to reach you...

...depends on how far you are from the lightning that created the thunder.

TECHNOLOGY **Use a graphics calculator or graphing software.**

Match each equation with its graph.

13. $y = -4x - 1$

14. $y = \dfrac{3}{x}$

15. $y = -3x^2$

A.

B.

C.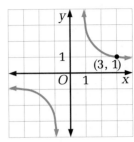

Write each function as an equation. Then graph the function.

16. Your age 25 years from now depends on your current age.

17. A worker earns \$5.30 per hour. The worker's gross pay depends on the number of hours worked.

18. The area of a circle depends on the length of its radius. The area is about 3.14 times the square of the radius.

19. A car travels at an average rate of 30 mi/h. The number of miles traveled depends on the number of hours the car traveled.

20. The length of a rectangle is two less than three times the width.

21. **Consumerism** A 5% sales tax is charged on some items. The total cost of taxable items depends on the total price of the items before the tax.

   a. What is the total cost of a taxable bracelet that costs \$4.99 before tax?

   b. What is the total cost of an item that costs x dollars before tax?

   c. Write an equation to represent the function.

   d. Graph the equation in part (c).

   e. Plot the values from part (a) on the same coordinate plane you used in part (d). Does this point appear to be on your graph? (Extend your graph if necessary.)

For Exercises 22–37, use the summary of basic functions on page 230.

Name the basic function that has each shape.

22. parabola

23. V-shaped

24. line

25. hyperbola

State whether the graph of each function includes the origin.

26. $y = |x|$

27. $y = \dfrac{1}{x}$

28. $y = x^2$

29. $y = x$

In which quadrant(s) is the graph of each equation?

30. $y = x$

31. $y = x^2$

32. $y = \dfrac{1}{x}$

33. $y = |x|$

For each function, make a conjecture about the shape of its graph. Test your conjecture by graphing the function.

34. $y = -2x^2$

35. $y = 6x - 3$

36. $y = \dfrac{1}{x} + 5$

37. $y = 4|x|$

38. **a.** Make a table of widths x and lengths y for rectangles with area 60 m². Find at least six rectangles.

   b. Use your table to make a graph.

   c. What shape does the graph seem to have?

   d. Use the formula for the area of a rectangle to write an equation that shows the length as a function of the width.

x	y
60	1
30	2
?	?

39. **a.** Graph the equation $y = -x$.

   b. How do you know that it is a function?

   c. **Writing** What name would you give to the function you graphed? Why?

40. **Writing** Investigate the function $y = x^3$. Include:

   ➤ a graph of the function

   ➤ the name you would give to this function

   ➤ a comparison of the graph to the other basic graphs in the section

BY THE WAY...

The word "function" was first used to describe a mathematical relationship by Gottfried Leibniz (1646–1716). He also introduced the terms "constant," "variable," and "coordinates."

41. Draw a graph that does not represent a function. *(Section 4-6)*

Solve each equation. Check each solution. *(Section 2-7)*

42. $2t + 6 = 48$

43. $3n + 5 = 17$

44. $7x \div 3 = -9$

 Working on the Unit Project

45. Suppose you want your flip book to show a spaceship landing, then taking off again.

   a. **Open-ended** Which graph would you use to show the path of the spaceship?

absolute value

parabola

hyperbola

   b. Find the coordinates of five points on the graph that you chose.

   c. Make five separate diagrams of the spaceship, using the points that you found in part (b).

   d. Cut out the diagrams and make a 5-page flip book with them.

Completing the Unit Project

➤ **Now you are ready to finish your flip book.**

➤ **Complete your drawings. Put the pages in order and make sure that they are all the same size. Clip or staple the pages together.**

➤ **Write a script to narrate while the pages are being flipped.**

Look Back

Describe how you used a coordinate system when making the drawings for your flip book. Did you have any problems making the flip book? If so, describe how you solved them.

Alternative Projects

......**Project 1:** Making a Map

Create a map of the neighborhood around your school or of the neighborhood in which you live. Use a coordinate system and make a map key by listing the coordinates for the locations of the places on the map. Include a scale on your map.

......**Project 2:** Recognizing Functions in Science

Read about the scientific research on global warming. Write a report on the latest findings. Discuss the evidence for global warming and what might be causing it. Include data tables and graphs with your report. Use the phrases "is a function of," "control variable," and "dependent variable" to describe the data.

Tropical forest

Former tropical forest area

......**Project 3:** Collecting and Graphing Data

Collect data that can be displayed in a scatter plot. Write a report and include:

➤ the method(s) you used to gather the data

➤ a summary of the data

➤ a scatter plot of the data

➤ the type of correlation the scatter plot shows and the reasons for it

➤ several questions that can be answered by using the scatter plot

1. **Open-ended** Use graph paper to make a map of your classroom. Put yourself at the origin. Mark the locations of desks, windows, and classroom "landmarks" on the plan. Give coordinates of the locations.

4-1

2. The Yoruba of Nigeria stencil *adire* cloth with geometric designs like this one. A coordinate system has been placed on the design.

   a. Find the coordinates of points A, B, and C.

   b. Which quadrant contains point B?

3. a. Plot the points $W(-2, 2)$, $X(4, 2)$, $Y(2, -3)$, and $Z(-4, -3)$ on a coordinate plane. Connect the points in order and connect Z to W.

4-2

   b. Write the specific name of the polygon you formed.

   c. Find the area of $WXYZ$.

4. Translate quadrilateral $PQRS$ 3 units left and 4 units up. What are the coordinates of each vertex after the translation?

4-3

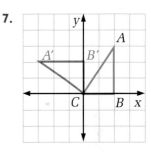

The graphs show rotations of △ABC around the origin. Describe the direction and the amount of the rotation in each graph.

4-4

5.

6.

7.

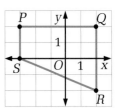

Tell whether each pattern has *translational symmetry*, *rotational symmetry*, or *no symmetry*.

8.

Japan

9.

Panama

10.

United States

Use the data in the table.

4-5

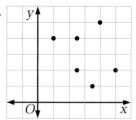

TYPE OF BALL	Approximate diameter (cm)	Average weight (g)
baseball	7.6	145
billiard	6.4	163
field hockey	7.6	160
golf	4.3	46
handball	4.8	65
softball, large	13	279
softball, regular	9.8	187

11. Make a scatter plot of the data. Draw a fitted line.

12. Is there a *positive correlation*, a *negative correlation*, or *no correlation* between the diameter and weight of the balls?

13. Predict the weight of a sports ball with diameter 5.5 cm.

14. Predict the diameter of a sports ball with weight 175 g.

Tell whether each graph represents a function.

4-6

15.

16.

17.

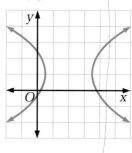

18. You have $30. You buy some tapes on sale for $3.50 each. The money you have left depends on how many tapes you buy.

   a. Identify the dependent variable and the control variable.

   b. Describe the situation using the phrase "is a function of."

   c. Write an equation to represent the function.

   d. Draw a graph of the function.

19. Write an equation to represent the function in the table.

20. Graph $y = -2x + 3$ on a coordinate plane.

21. Graph $y = x^2 - 3$ on a coordinate plane. Describe its shape.   4-7

22. **Writing** Identify at least three different uses of coordinates and explain how they are helpful in each situation.

23. **Self-evaluation** Think back to your work on this unit. Which section did you like working on best? Explain what you liked about it.

x	y
-3	-1
-2	0
-1	1
0	2
1	3
2	4
3	5

24. **Group Activity** Your school is planning an International Festival. You are helping to plan it. Here are some variables that you might consider:

   ➤ the amount of space available   ➤ the size of the booths   ➤ the costs of materials

Use two variables from the list (or use other variables) that are related.

   a. Identify the control variable and the dependent variable.

   b. Make a table of possible values for these variables. Explain why you think your values are reasonable.

   c. Use your table to make a graph of the function.

   d. Use your graph to make a recommendation for the festival plans.

IDEAS AND (FORMULAS) = x^2 $_5P_5$

ALGEBRA $)x^2$
$(x$

➤ The control variable is put on the horizontal axis of a graph, and the dependent variable is put on the vertical axis. *(p. 218)*

➤ You can represent a function in words, as an equation, with a table of values, or with a graph. *(pp. 220, 226)*

➤ A vertical-line test shows if a graph represents a function. *(p. 221)*

➤ In a function, x often represents the control variable, and y often represents the dependent variable. *(p. 226)*

➤ Some basic functions have distinct shapes of graphs and equations. *(p. 230)*

GEOMETRY ▸

➤ Polygons can be described using coordinates. *(p. 191)*

➤ You can find the areas of some geometric figures on a coordinate plane using the areas of rectangles and right triangles. *(p. 193)*

➤ A translation moves an object without rotating or flipping it. *(p. 197)*

➤ When you translate or rotate an object, its size and shape do not change. *(pp. 197, 203)*

➤ A transformation is a change, such as a translation or a rotation, made to an object. *(p. 202)*

➤ To describe a rotation, you need to give the center of the turn, and the amount and direction of the turn. *(p. 204)*

STATISTICS & PROBABILITY ▸

➤ A fitted line on a scatter plot suggests the correlation between the sets of data. *(p. 212)*

➤ A correlation does not mean that there is a cause-and-effect relationship between two sets of data. *(p. 214)*

Key Terms

- **coordinate plane** (p. 184)
- **quadrant** (p. 184)
- **vertical axis** (p. 184)
- **translation** (p. 197)
- **center of rotation** (p. 202)
- **scatter plot** (p. 212)
- **dependent variable** (p. 218)
- **x-axis** (p. 226)
- **hyperbola** (p. 230)
- **absolute value function** (p. 230)

- **ordered pair** (p. 184)
- **coordinates** (p. 184)
- **coordinate geometry** (p. 190)
- **translational symmetry** (p. 199)
- **transformation** (p. 202)
- **correlation** (p. 212)
- **control variable** (p. 218)
- **y-axis** (p. 226)
- **identity function** (p. 230)
- **reciprocal function** (p. 230)

- **origin** (p. 184)
- **horizontal axis** (p. 184)
- **trapezoid** (p. 193)
- **rotation** (p. 202)
- **rotational symmetry** (p. 205)
- **fitted line** (p. 212)
- **function** (p. 220)
- **parabola** (p. 229)
- **squaring function** (p. 230)

Equations for Problem Solving

One person really can make a difference! In 1983, 11-year-old Trevor Ferrell watched a news report on homeless people and decided to try to help. He asked his parents to drive him into Philadelphia, where he gave his favorite pillow and a blanket to a homeless man. Since then, Trevor's Campaign for the Homeless has become a $1.4 million non-profit organization.

COMMUNITY SERVICE

Have you ever asked people to pledge a certain amount of money for every mile you walk for a cause ? Special events raise millions of dollars each year to fund organizations that fight homelessness, hunger, AIDS, and cancer, or promote community development.

One of the best ways to support a cause is to donate your time . People who are familiar with computer spreadsheets and databases can help groups keep accurate records of donors, donations, and expenses.

20 mi x pledge = total donation

About 100 students from the Chicago-area Niles West High School belong to the volunteer club West Helping Others. The students visit schools, hospitals, and shelters to help in any way they can. The group frequently organizes bake sales and car washes to finance its activities.

Planning a Car Wash

Your group project is to plan and organize a car wash. The money you raise will be used to help you provide a service to your school or community.

You will need to consider the conditions that will affect the success of your car wash and recommend a location, a time, and a price.

When your plan is complete, your group will present it to the class. Your plan should include the reasons for your recommendations and a prediction of the amount of money you will raise.

The class will decide on the best plan of action. The groups may want to work together to put the plan into action.

When disasters such as hurricanes, earthquakes, and floods strike, teenagers are among the first to reach out and help.

Students are often in the news, collecting food and clothing, filling sandbags, or even helping to rescue stranded people and pets.

239

Getting Started

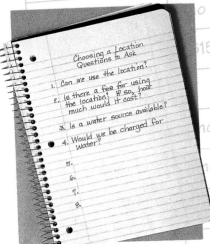

For this project, work in a group of four to six students. Here are some ideas to help you get started.

☞ As a class, consider which groups or organizations you may want to receive the funds you raise in your car wash.

☞ In your group discuss possible car wash locations.

Where will your car wash attract the most customers?

Where will your water supply come from? Will you pay for water?

Will you have room for several cars? If a line forms, how can you avoid blocking traffic?

Will there be a fee for the location?

☞ List some questions you might ask a property owner or business manager about holding a car wash at their place of business.

☞ Plan to contact the managers of several possible car wash locations and ask them your questions.

☞ In your group, decide on three locations that are most likely to meet your needs.

▰ Working on the Unit Project

Your work in Unit 5 will help you plan your car wash.

Related Exercises:

Section 5-1, Exercise 36

Section 5-2, Exercises 37, 38

Section 5-3, Exercises 34–36

Section 5-4, Exercises 42–45

Section 5-5, Exercises 32, 33

Section 5-6, Exercises 30, 31

Section 5-7, Exercises 28–30

Section 5-8, Exercise 28

Alternative Projects p. 294

Can We Talk   COMMUNITY SERVICE

➤ In his 1961 Inaugural Address, President John Kennedy inspired many people when he said,

"... ask not what your country can do for you— ask what you can do for your country."

What are some things that you can do to serve your community?

➤ How often do you think people your age volunteer?

➤ What ads or promotions catch your attention? Are any of them for volunteer or service groups?

➤ How often do you think people have their cars washed? Do you think car owners would rather have their cars washed at a professional car wash or by students? Why?

➤ How can you estimate the number of customers you will have?

Modeling Problem Situations

Focus

Use a table, graph, or equation to model situations and solve problems.

Would you pay $142 for a portable CD player? That was the cost in 1990, when 3,186,000 players were sold.

The graph shows the cost of portable CD players from 1990–1997. Graphs, tables, functions, equations, or inequalities that describe a situation are called **mathematical models.** Using mathematical models is called **modeling.**

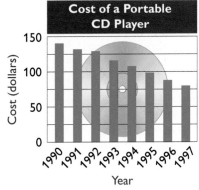

Cost of a Portable CD Player

Cost (dollars) / Year

Sample 1

Model and solve this situation. A portable CD player costs $85, including tax. You already have $11 and can save $5 per week. After how many weeks can you buy the player?

Sample Response

Method ❶ Model the situation using a table.

Number of weeks	Total saved ($) $11 + 5 \times$ (no. of weeks)
0	11
1	$11 + 5(1) = 16$
2	$11 + 5(2) = 21$
3	$11 + 5(3) = 26$
•	•
•	•
13	$11 + 5(16) = 76$
14	$11 + 5(17) = 81$
15	$11 + 5(18) = 86$

After 15 weeks, more than $85.

Method ❷ Model the situation using a spreadsheet.

Add $5 for each week.

	A	B
	Savings Table	
1	**Number of Weeks**	**Total saved <dollars>**
2	0	11
3	1	5 + B2
4	2	5 + B3
5	3	5 + B4
•	**•**	**•**
•	**•**	**•**
15	13	5 + B14
16	14	5 + B15
17	15	5 + B16

You can buy the player the week that the total saved is at least $85.
You can buy the player after 15 weeks.

Method ❸

Model the situation using a graph.

On graph paper, first label the number of weeks on the horizontal axis. Label the total amount saved on the vertical axis. Then follow steps 1 through 6.

3 Add $5 to each new total. Plot the points (2, 21), (3, 26), and so on. Draw a line through the points.

2 To find the next point, add $5 to $11. After one week the total saved is $16. Plot the point (1, 16).

1 You start with $11. Mark this point on the vertical axis as (0, 11).

4 Estimate 85 on the vertical axis. Read across to the line you drew.

5 Read down to the horizontal axis to find the number of weeks.

6 Read the estimate of the solution, 15 weeks, on the horizontal axis.

Method ❹

Model the situation using an equation.

The problem asks for the number of weeks until you will have $85.

Let w = the number of weeks.

Then $5w$ = the amount in dollars you can save in w weeks, and $11 + 5w$ = the total amount you will have saved in w weeks.

You will have enough money to buy the compact disc player when

the total amount saved = the amount you need.

$$11 + 5w = 85$$

Solve the equation using algebra:

$$11 + 5w = 85$$

$11 + 5w - 11 = 85 - 11$ ◄——— Subtract 11 from both sides.

$$5w = 74$$

$\dfrac{5w}{5} = \dfrac{74}{5}$ ◄——— Divide both sides by 5.

$$w \approx 14.8$$

You can buy the CD player after 15 weeks.

Model the situation using a graphics calculator.

First model the situation with an equation as in Method 4. Use y for the amount of money you need and x for the number of weeks.

Set an appropriate viewing window on a graphics calculator and graph the equation $y = 11 + 5x$.

$y = 11 + 5x$

$x = 14.968085 \quad y = 85.840426$

Trace along the graph until y is about 85. The x-value is about 14.8.

You can buy the CD player after 15 weeks.

Talk it Over

1. Which method do you like best? Why?

2. Suppose you could save $10 per week. What would the equation in Methods 4 and 5 be?

One Model for Different Situations

The same equation can be used to model different situations.

Sample 2

Writing Describe a situation that could be modeled by the equation $5 = 3 + 0.25x$.

Sample Response

Situation 1

There are many possible answers. For the expression $0.25x$, think of a situation that involves 25% or a quarter of something.

"I ran 3 miles. How many times (x) around a quarter-mile track must I run to complete a 5 mile run?"

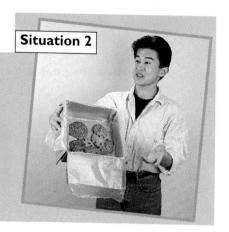

"I have sold three dollars worth of cookies at the neighborhood bake sale. How many 25-cent cookies (x) do I need to sell to bring my sales total up to five dollars?"

Talk it Over

Describe a situation that could be modeled by each equation.

3. $15 = 4p$

4. $100 = 50 + 2a$

Look Back

Model and solve this situation using two different methods. In chemistry class, Inez needs to estimate how long it will take for her mystery solution's temperature to reach the freezing point of water. She measures the starting temperature at 24°C and notices it drops about 4°C per hour. About how long will it take the temperature to reach 0°C?

5-1 Exercises and Problems

1. **Reading** In Method 4 of Sample 1, the expression $11 + 5w$ is used for the total amount saved. What expression is used for the total amount saved in Method 5?

For Exercises 2–7, model each situation using one of the five methods from Sample 1. Do not use the same method for all the exercises.

2. Denby High School has 278 students signed up to take a bus to the regional basketball finals. Each bus can hold 48 people. How many buses are needed to take the students to the game?

3. The expenses for a dance are $131. Tickets cost $6.75 each. How many tickets must be sold to cover the expenses?

4. Between 1998 and 2002, the population of Chile is expected to increase by about 177,450 people each year. In what year will the population be more than 15,200,000?

5. Between 1991 and 1998, the population of Argentina increased by about 430,600 people each year. What is the most recent year that the population was less than 35,000,000?

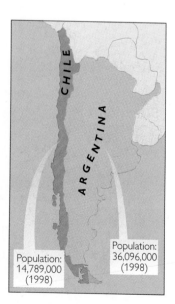

CHILE

ARGENTINA

Population: 14,789,000 (1998)

Population: 36,096,000 (1998)

6. The perimeter of an isosceles triangle is 47 in. The length of the longest side is 17 in. Find the length of each of the congruent sides.

7. A rectangular park has a perimeter of 1950 ft. One side is 800 ft long. What are the lengths of the other three sides?

Writing Describe a situation that could be modeled by each equation.

8. $x + 15 = 35$

9. $250 = 10d$

10. $100 = 20 + 5x$

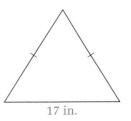

17 in.

The book *Rules of Thumb 2* by Tom Parker contains rules from common wisdom, including the ones in Exercises 11–15. Model each rule using an equation. Tell what each variable represents.

11. When microwaving solid vegetables, allow seven minutes per pound.

12. To estimate the age of a large lobster, multiply its weight in pounds by seven.

13.

One out of twenty words in everyday French is actually English.

14. On any day the high temperature in degrees Fahrenheit is 18 degrees higher than the temperature at 6 A.M.

15. The number of minutes you will wait in a line at the bank is equal to 2.75 times the number of people ahead of you, divided by the number of tellers.

Tell which rule or rules in Exercises 11–15 are modeled by each graph.

16.

17.

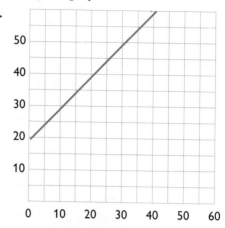

Ongoing **ASSESSMENT**

18. **Open-ended** Write a "rule of thumb" like the ones in Exercises 11–15 based on some experience in your life. Model the rule using an equation.

Review **PREVIEW**

Graph each equation. *(Section 4-7)*

19. $y = |x|$

20. $y = x^2 - 3$

21. $y = \dfrac{1}{x}$

Write the opposite of each number. *(Section 2-2)*

22. 7

23. -7

24. $\dfrac{3}{5}$

25. 0

26. -0.75

27. -6.3

Simplify. *(Sections 1-5, 2-2)*

28. $5 - 8$

29. $5 + (-8)$

30. $-4 - (-2)$

31. $-4 + 2$

32. $2(x + 4)$

33. $3(2k - 7) - 10k$

34. $\dfrac{2}{3}(t + 12) + 2$

35. $-6 + 5(3x - 8)$

 Working on the Unit Project

36. a. In your group, set a reasonable goal of how much money your class wants to raise at the car wash.

b. Make a table or spreadsheet to model your income if you charge $3 for each car you wash. Show the number of cars you need to wash to reach your goal.

c. What is the effect on the number of cars you need to wash to reach your goal if you raise the price by $2? lower the price by $2?

d. What do you think is the highest price you can charge and still attract customers?

Opposites and the Distributive Property

Focus
Simplify expressions and solve equations involving opposites, the distributive property, and combining like terms.

CHANGING + − SIGNS

Talk it Over

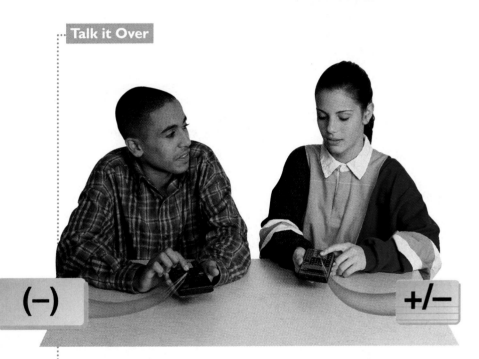

(−)   +/−

1. Read each expression aloud using the words "the opposite of" for the negative symbol.

   a. $-(-18)$ b. $-n$ c. $-(-n)$ d. $-(7 + 13)$

2. Keith thinks that it makes sense to use (−) to label the calculator key that gives the opposite of a number. Alison thinks +/− makes more sense. What do you think? Why?

3. Evaluate each pair of expressions. Are they equal?

   a. $-(7 + 13) \stackrel{?}{=} -7 - 13$ b. $-(11 - 6) \stackrel{?}{=} -11 + 6$

   c. $-(-2 - 5) \stackrel{?}{=} 2 + 5$ d. $-(-8 + 9) \stackrel{?}{=} 8 - 9$

4. Look at the expressions in question 3. How do you find the opposite of an expression in parentheses?

Simplify $-(a - 5)$.

Sample Response

Method ❶ Use the distributive property.

$-(a - 5) = -1(a - 5)$ ⟵ Use the fact that $-x = -1x$.

$= (-1)(a) - (-1)(5)$ ⟵ Use the distributive property.

$= -a - (-5)$

$= -a + 5$ ⟵ Subtracting a number is the same as adding its opposite.

Method ❷ Find the opposite of each term.

$-(a - 5) = -a - (-5)$ ⟵ To find the opposite of a difference, find the opposite of each term.

$= -a + 5$ ⟵ Subtracting a number is the same as adding its opposite.

Simplify each expression.

a. $5m - (3m - n)$ b. $19 - 2(x + 4)$

Sample Response

a. $5m - (3m - n) = 5m + (-3m + n)$

$= 5m - 3m + n$

$= 2m + n$

b. $19 - 2(x + 4) = 19 - (2x + 8)$

$= 19 - 2x - 8$

$= -2x + 11$

IDEAS ABOUT OPPOSITES

➤ Subtracting a number is the same as adding its opposite.

➤ $-(-n) = n$

➤ To find the opposite of a sum or difference, find the opposite of each term.

➤ Patterns: $-(a + b) = -a - b$

➤ $-(a - b) = -a + b$

······➤ Now you are ready for:
  Exs. 1–7 on p. 250

Multi-step Equations

Solving some equations may require many steps. The equation may involve finding the opposite of a number or an expression, combining like terms, or using the distributive property.

Sample 3

The temperature at noon today was 6°C. At 9 P.M., the temperature was −2°C. How many degrees did the temperature drop today?

Sample Response

Let x = the number of degrees the temperature dropped today.

$$6 - x = -2$$

$$6 + (-x) = -2 \quad \longleftarrow \text{ Subtracting } x \text{ is the same as adding the opposite of } x.$$

$$6 + (-x) - 6 = -2 - 6 \quad \longleftarrow \text{ Subtract 6 from both sides.}$$

$$-x = -8$$

$$-1x = -8 \quad \longleftarrow \text{ Use the fact that } -x = -1x.$$

$$\frac{-1x}{-1} = \frac{-8}{-1} \quad \longleftarrow \text{ Divide both sides by } -1.$$

$$x = 8$$

The temperature dropped 8 degrees today.

Sample 4

Solve the equation $12 + 6x - 8x = 20$.

Sample Response

$$12 + 6x - 8x = 20$$

$$12 - 2x = 20 \quad \longleftarrow \text{ Combine like terms.}$$

$$12 - 2x - 12 = 20 - 12 \quad \longleftarrow \text{ Subtract 12 from both sides.}$$

$$-2x = 8$$

$$\frac{-2x}{-2} = \frac{8}{-2} \quad \longleftarrow \text{ Divide both sides by } -2.$$

$$x = -4$$

The solution is −4.

$n = 3$ $n = 4$

The sum of the measures of the angles of a convex polygon with n sides is $(n - 2)180$. Can the sum of the measures of the angles of a convex polygon be $450°$?

Sample Response

Suppose there is such a polygon. Write an equation.

$(n - 2)180 = 450$ ← The sum of the measures of the angles is $450°$.

$180n - 360 = 450$ ← Use the distributive property.

$180n - 360 + 360 = 450 + 360$ ← Add 360 to both sides.

$180n = 810$

$\dfrac{180n}{180} = \dfrac{810}{180}$ ← Divide both sides by 180.

$n = 4.5$

Although 4.5 is the solution of the equation, a polygon cannot have 4.5 sides. The sum of the measures of the angles of a convex polygon *cannot* be $450°$.

Talk it Over

5. Another method for solving the equation $6 - x = -2$ in Sample 3 is to add the x term to both sides first. Show the steps of this method.

6. Another method for solving Sample 5 is to divide both sides of the equation $(n - 2)180 = 450$ by 180 first. Show the steps that follow when you divide by 180 first.

Look Back

Describe the steps you can use to solve the equation $3(x + 2) - 5x = 10$.

▶ Now you are ready for:
Exs. 8–38 on pp. 250–254

······· ● ●●●●●●●●●●●●●●●●●●●●● ●●●●●●●●●●●●●● ···········

5-2 Exercises and Problems

1. **Reading** Read "Ideas About Opposites" on page 248. Give an example of each idea.

Simplify.

2. $-(b - 8)$

3. $-(x + 6)$

4. $-(-3y + 4)$

5. $9 - (5k + 12)$

6. $5 - (-x + 2)$

7. $4x - (6x + 5)$

8. The temperature at 7 A.M. on a cold day was $-4°C$. At 3 P.M. the temperature was $1°C$. Write and solve an equation to find how many degrees the temperature rose between 7 A.M. and 3 P.M.

Solve.

9. $12 - x = -5$

10. $55 - 3n = 70$

11. $-23 = -13 - g$

12. $4x + 2 + 3x = 58$

13. $7 + 0.6y + 1.2y = 19.6$

14. $8n + 7 - 10n = 11$

15. $6(x - 3) = 48$

16. $-(3 + m) = 2$

17. $3(2 - x) = 12$

18. $4(x + 12) + 7x = 26$

19. $2(k + 5) - 3k = 4.3$

20. $9y - 4(y - 2) = 3$

For Exercises 21–23, use the fact that the sum of the measures of the angles of a convex polygon with n sides is $(n - 2)180$.

21. Writing Can the value of n be 3? less than 3? 3.5? 1000? Explain what kinds of numbers are reasonable in this situation.

22. Can the sum of the measures of the angles of a polygon be 800°?

23. Can the sum of the measures of the angles of a polygon be 1080°?

24. a. Write an equation that describes the relationship between the measures of $\angle ABD$ and $\angle DBC$.

b. Use your equation to find the measure of each angle.

25. Group Activity Work in a group of three students.

a. Open-ended Each student should create an equation that will take several steps to solve, as in Sample 4 or Sample 5.

b. Write your equation and single steps of the solution on separate strips of paper. Write "original equation" on the first strip.

c. Distribute one person's strips of paper among your group. Have students work together to put them in a correct order for solving the original equation. Repeat the process with the other equations.

26. To raise money for school activities, Central High School is collecting newspapers for recycling. A local business has promised to pledge enough money per pound to help the school reach its fundraising goal of $2000.

a. Students and parents have pledged a total of $32 per pound of newspapers collected. Let $x =$ the business's pledge per pound. Write an expression for the total amount pledged per pound.

b. The school collects 50 lb of newspapers. Write an expression for the amount of money collected.

c. Write and solve an equation to find the amount per pound that the business must pay to help the school reach its fundraising goal.

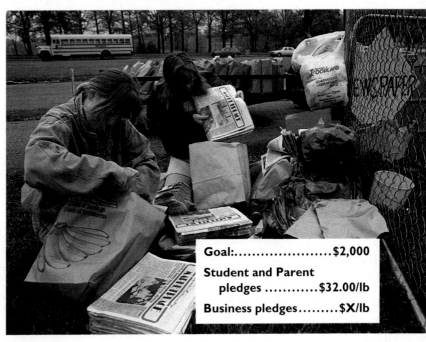

Goal:......................$2,000

Student and Parent
    pledges $32.00/lb

Business pledges........$X/lb

Sports For Exercises 27–30, use this information.

Shina, Aiyana, Terry, and Hanna are playing in a 9-hole golf tournament. They have completed 6 holes and their strokes for each hole so far are listed on the score card below.

Your score for the entire golf course is the sum of your strokes on all of the holes you played. Your score can be over par, under par, or equal to par.

Each hole on a golf course has a *par*, which is the number of strokes a very good golfer should take to get the ball from the tee to the hole.

These numbers tell how many yards from the red tee to the hole.

HOLE	1	2	3	4	5	6	7	8	9	OUT
RED	360	290	400	150	380	450	230	350	130	2740
PAR	4	4	5	3	4	5	4	4	3	36
Shina Nakeane	3	3	5	2	6	4				
Aiyana Draper	5	3	4	3	5	(4)				
Terry Maher	4	3	6	4	3	6				
Hanna Katz	6	(5)	4	2	4	6				

PLEASE REPLACE DIVOTS, REPAIR BALL MARKS, AND RAKE BUNKERS

Attested _____

Scorer _____

If you take fewer strokes, your score is under par.

If you take more strokes, your score for that hole is over par.

2 under par

Standings after 6 holes	
Shina Nakeane	−2
Aiyana Draper	+1
Terry Maher	?
Hanna Katz	?

27. a. What is par for the first six holes?

b. What is each golfer's score for the first six holes?

c. Complete the chart.

d. In golf, the player who takes the fewest strokes wins. Who is the leader of the four players on the chart?

28. Shina Nakeane's foursome is heading toward the seventh hole. Some teams have finished the course. They must wait until all the players finish nine holes to see who wins.

a. The current leader of the tournament has finished all nine holes and is 6 under par. What is her total score?

b. Suppose Shina scores par on the last three holes. What will her total score be?

c. How many strokes under par must Shina shoot on the next three holes to tie with the current leader?

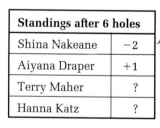

29. Two students are using equations to answer Exercise 28, part (c).

a. Solve Lindsay's equation.

Lindsay Hackstock
Let p = the number of strokes under par Shina must shoot on the next three holes.
−2 − p = −6

b. Solve Wei-Hwa's equations.

Wei-Hwa Chan
Let p = the number of strokes under par Shina must shoot on the next three holes.
Let t = the total score Shina must get to tie the current leader.
t = 30 − 23
p = 11 − t

c. **Writing** Choose either Lindsay's or Wei-Hwa's work and explain the meaning of his or her equation(s). Compare the student's work to your own method.

30. To even up the game when golfers of different abilities play against each other, each player may use a *handicap* to adjust his or her score. A handicap differential is used to find the player's handicap. Here is the formula for the handicap differential:

$$\frac{113(\text{player's score} - \text{course rating})}{\text{slope rating}} = \text{handicap differential}$$

a. Suppose that you submitted a score of 97 on a course with a 70.1 course rating and a slope rating of 116. What is the handicap differential for that score?

b. The handicap differential for the first score on Terry Maher's handicap card is 18.1. If the slope rating for the course is 123, find the course rating to the nearest tenth.

NAME **TERRY MAHER**
GOLF HANDICAP INFORMATION 477
CLUB Los Incas Golf Club
SCORES POSTED 20   USGA   HOME
HCP INDEX
14.1   16

SCORE HISTORY—MOST RECENT FIRST • IF USED

1	**92**	89		89*		
6	90*	88*	85*A	90*	85 A	
11	89 A	87*	86*A	100	85*	
16	99	88*A	92 A	96 A	88 A	
			91		95 A	

BY THE WAY...

Nancy Lopez is the only golfer, male or female, to be selected Rookie of the Year and Player of the Year in the same year.

31. a. **Group Activity** Work in a group of three students. Write a five-question quiz on Section 5-2. At least one question should involve geometry.

   b. Make enough copies of your group's quiz for students in another group. Have them take the quiz.

   c. Correct the quizzes. Did any answers surprise you? What was the average of the scores?

Review **PREVIEW**

32. Model and solve this situation. *(Section 5-1)*

Sharon Hall is an electrician. She charges a fee of $45 to come to a person's house and then $38 for each hour she works. How much would she charge for a job that took her 4 h to complete?

33. Two players have the same final golf score. The graph shows their strokes on each hole. Make two statements about the skill of each golfer. *(Section 1-1)*

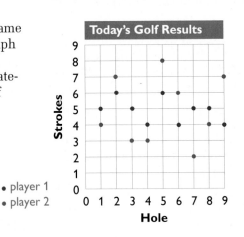

Today's Golf Results

• player 1
• player 2

Solve. *(Section 2-8)*

34. $x + (-4x) = 30$ **35.** $6t + 3t = 117$ **36.** $8x - 5x = -7 + 4$

Working on the Unit Project

37. a. In your group discuss ways you can advertise your car wash. Where are potential customers most likely to find out about the car wash?

   b. **Research** Find out the costs of your advertising options.

   c. Based on the costs and the number of potential customers you could reach, decide on two or three ways to advertise your car wash.

38. a. Make a list of supplies you will need for your car wash. Include advertising materials as well as cleaning supplies.

   b. **Research** Call or visit several stores to find the least expensive places to buy your supplies. Make a table to record the information.

Variables on Both Sides

Focus

Model situations and solve equations that have a variable on both sides of the equals sign.

Have you ever heard the expression "Slow but steady wins the race"? That is the moral of a classic fable about a race between a tortoise and a hare. The hare knows it is the faster runner and stops during the race to nap. The slower but steady tortoise wins the race.

$D = rt$

Distance = rate × time

Talk it Over

Suppose the tortoise averaged 0.2 mi/h and the hare averaged 35 mi/h. Use these rates and the formula $D = rt$ to answer questions 1–6.

1. How far would each animal go in 10 h?

2. If the hare stops for 9 h 30 min to take a nap, he will be running for only 30 min or $\frac{1}{2}$ h. How far will the hare go in 10 h if he takes a nap?

3. Suppose the race lasts for t hours and the tortoise runs continuously but the hare rests for 12 h during the t hours. Write an algebraic expression to represent each situation.

   a. the number of hours the hare actually runs

   b. the number of hours the tortoise runs

   c. the distance the hare runs in the race

   d. the distance the tortoise runs in the race

4. Suppose the race is a tie. What can you say about the distance each animal has traveled when they complete the race?

5. Using the expressions you wrote in questions 3(c) and 3(d), write an equation to show the relationship between the two animals' distances.

6. What information about the race can you find if you solve the equation in question 5?

Solving Equations with Variables on Both Sides

Many situations, like the tortoise and hare fable, are modeled by equations with variables on both sides of the equation. To solve these equations you first move the **variable terms** to one side of the equals sign and then solve.

Sample 1

Solve $4x = 2x + 6$.

Sample Response

You can model the equation with tiles.

Let represent x and ▢ represent 1.

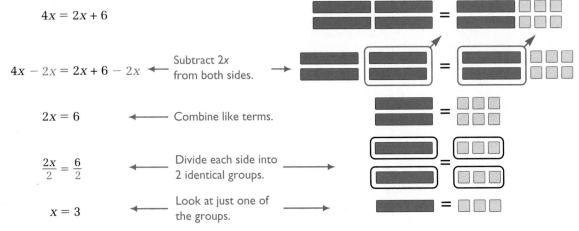

$$4x = 2x + 6$$

$$4x - 2x = 2x + 6 - 2x \quad \longleftarrow \begin{array}{l} \text{Subtract } 2x \\ \text{from both sides.} \end{array}$$

$$2x = 6 \quad \longleftarrow \text{Combine like terms.}$$

$$\frac{2x}{2} = \frac{6}{2} \quad \longleftarrow \begin{array}{l} \text{Divide each side into} \\ \text{2 identical groups.} \end{array}$$

$$x = 3 \quad \longleftarrow \begin{array}{l} \text{Look at just one of} \\ \text{the groups.} \end{array}$$

Check $\quad 4x = 2x + 6$

$$4(3) \stackrel{?}{=} 2(3) + 6 \quad \longleftarrow \begin{array}{l} \text{Substitute 3 for } x \text{ on both sides} \\ \text{of the original equation.} \end{array}$$

$$12 \stackrel{?}{=} 6 + 6$$

$$12 = 12 \ ✔$$

The solution is 3.

Use the tortoise and hare situation and *Talk it Over* questions
3–6 on pages 255 and 256. About how long did the race last?

Sample Response

Problem solving strategy: Use a formula

Use the formula $D = rt$ to write an expression for each animal's distance.
Let t = the number of hours the race lasts.

Distance in miles run by the tortoise = $0.2t$
Distance in miles run by the hare = $35(t - 12)$

Write an equation to find out how long the race lasts.

The animal's distances are equal. $\longrightarrow$	$0.2t = 35(t - 12)$
Use the distributive property. $\longrightarrow$	$0.2t = 35t - 420$
Subtract 35t from both sides. $\longrightarrow$	$0.2t - 35t = 35t - 420 - 35t$
Combine like terms. $\longrightarrow$	$-34.8t = -420$
Divide both sides by -34.8. $\longrightarrow$	$\dfrac{-34.8t}{-34.8} = \dfrac{-420}{-34.8}$
	$t \approx 12.1$

The race took about 12.1 h.

Talk it Over

7. How can you use the answer to Sample 2 to find the length
   of the race course?

8. In Sample 2 the race took 12.1 h. About how many minutes
   is 0.1 h?

Look Back

Compare the equations in Samples 1 and 2. How are they
alike? How are they different? What do the solutions have in
common?

5-3 Exercises and Problems

1. **Using Manipulatives** Suppose � ▬▬▬▬ represents x and ▢ represents 1.

   a. Use algebra tiles to make this model.

   b. What equation do your tiles model?

   c. Solve for ▬▬▬▬ using your model.
      Explain your steps.

   d. Write an equation for your result in part (c).

2. **Using Manipulatives** Model and solve the equation $3x + 6 = 5x$ using algebra tiles.

Tell whether the information shown is a *rate*, a *time*, or a *distance*.

3. 12 mi/h
4. 16 km
5. 64 h
6. $(x + 2)$ ft/s

7. **Reading** Which numbers in Sample 2 on page 257 are the rates at which the animals ran?

Solve.

8. $12x = 9x + 7$
9. $7x - 24 = 15x$
10. $x = 2x - 10$

11. $-c = 9(c + 40)$
12. $-4a + 6 = 2a - 36$
13. $5(t - 4) = 3t$

14. $-4(x - 4) = 6x + 36$
15. $0.5(4 - k) = 2.5k$
16. $3(6 + 3.2m) + 4 = 60.4$

17. Suppose the tortoise and the hare had another race. Again the tortoise averaged 0.2 mi/h and the hare averaged 35 mi/h. This time the hare rested 6 h and the race was still a tie. About how long did the race last?

18. The Quesadas and the Kemps leave a campsite at 10:00 A.M. and meet later at a rest stop that is 150 mi away. The Quesadas travel at 50 mi/h. Because of their trailer, the Kemps travel at only 30 mi/h.

    a. Copy the number lines below. Show each car's position at hourly intervals until the time the families meet.

    b. How long will the Quesadas need to wait at the rest stop for the Kemps?

    c. Use the formula $D = rt$ to find how long it will take each family to drive 150 mi. Use your solutions to tell if your answer to part (b) is correct.

19.

Salaries

Candace
Salary: $25,000/yr.
Annual raises of $1000.

Craig
Salary: $20,000/yr.
Annual raises of $1500.

    a. Write an expression to model Candace's salary in y years.

    b. Write an expression to model Craig's salary in y years.

    c. How long will it be before Candace and Craig earn the same salary?

Jack London's story "To Build a Fire" describes a man walking near the Yukon trail on a bitterly cold day. This is part of that story from the book *The Best Short Stories of Jack London.*

To Build a Fire

He was a newcomer in the land, a *chechaquo*, and this was his first winter. Undoubtedly it was colder than fifty below—how much colder he did not know. But the temperature did not matter. He was bound for the old claim on the left fork of Henderson Creek, where the boys were already. He held on through the level stretch of woods for several miles. . . and dropped down a bank to the frozen bed of a small stream. This was Henderson Creek, and he knew he was ten miles from the forks. He looked at his watch. It was ten o'clock. He was making four miles an hour, and he calculated that he would arrive at the forks at half-past twelve. He decided to celebrate that event by eating his lunch there.

20. a. Suppose the man used the formula $D = rt$ to find out how long it would take him to get to the forks. What information did he know?

b. Write and solve an equation to find the time it would take him to get to the forks.

c. According to the man's calculation, how long would it take him to reach the forks? Do you agree with his answer?

21. Suppose the man's rate slowed down when he reached a hilly, icy path. He did not arrive at the forks until three o'clock.

a. How many miles per hour did the man average for the ten miles?

b. Suppose the man spent 3.75 hours on the hilly, icy path. How slowly did he walk on that part of the path?

22. **Reading** Compare this story with the fable of the tortoise and the hare. What ideas do they share?

23. a. **Open-ended** Write your own story about a race or a walk. Include information like rates, times, and distances.

b. **Writing** Write a question that someone can answer using the information in your story.

c. **Group Activity** Give your story and question to another student to answer. Make changes to your story or question if necessary.

24. **Research** What do you think the word *chechaquo* means? Find a definition for the word. Were you right? What language does the word come from?

25. **a.** **Writing** Carmen modeled a situation with the equation $3x - 9 = 3(x - 3)$ and solved for x. She says that all numbers are solutions of this equation. Do you agree? Write a short paragraph explaining why you agree or disagree with Carmen.

   b. **Open-ended** Make up an equation that has many solutions.

Carmen

$$3x - 9 = 3(x - 3)$$
$$3x - 9 = 3x - 9$$
$$3x - 9 + 9 = 3x - 9 + 9$$
$$3x = 3x$$
$$\frac{3x}{3} = \frac{3x}{3}$$
$$x = x$$

Review **PREVIEW**

Solve. *(Section 5-2)*

26. $18 - 4n = 6$

27. $-3(2x + 5) = 9$

28. $8 - (3t + 7) = 19$

Write using exponents. *(Section 1-3)*

29. eight cubed   **30.** five to the second power   **31.** $3 \cdot 3 \cdot 3 \cdot 3$

32. Choose the statement represented by the graph. *(Section 3-3)*

   a. $x \geq 3$ **b.** $x = 3$

   c. $x < 3$ **d.** $x \leq 3$

$$\xleftarrow{\hspace{2em}} \underset{-5\ -4\ -3\ -2\ -1\ \ 0\ \ 1\ \ 2\ \ 3\ \ 4\ \ 5}{\rule{0pt}{0pt}} \xrightarrow{\hspace{2em}}$$

33. The average life of a one-dollar bill is at least 13 months but no more than 18 months. Write an inequality to represent the situation. *(Section 3-3)*

Working on the Unit Project

34. Write and solve an equation to find how many cars you have to wash to reach your goal if you charge:

   a. $3 per car

   b. $5 per car

   c. another price you are considering

35. **a.** Find the total cost for advertising and supplies based on your research.

   b. Write an equation to model your total income.

36. **a.** When your income equals your total expenses, you *break even*. Write and solve an equation to find out how many cars you need to wash at the price you are considering in order to break even.

   b. Is the number of cars you have to wash to break even a reasonable number? If you have to wash too many or too few cars, adjust your price and repeat part (a) until the number of cars you have to wash is reasonable.

Inequalities with One Variable

Focus
Understand how adding, subtracting, multiplying, and dividing affect an inequality and model situations with inequalities.

EXPLORATION

(How) *do adding, subtracting, multiplying, and dividing change an inequality?*

- **Materials: scientific calculators**
- **Work with a partner.**

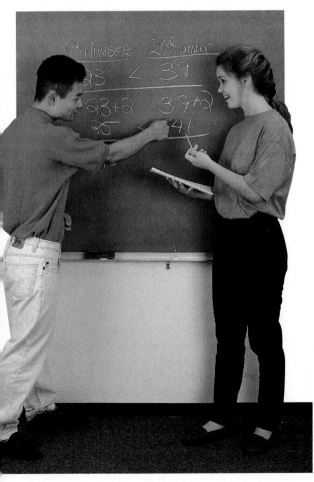

① Write down any two different numbers. Leave a space between them.

② Write the symbol < or > in the space between your numbers to make a correct statement about which is greater.

③ Apply each rule below to your original two numbers and simplify. Write the symbol < or > between the two new numbers.

a. Add 2.	**b.** Subtract 2.
c. Multiply by 2.	**d.** Multiply by −2.
e. Divide by 2.	**f.** Divide by −2.

④ Make a note about any changes in the direction of the inequality symbol in your results in parts (a)–(f) of step 3.

⑤ Repeat steps 1–4 at least two more times. Each time choose a different pair of numbers in step 1.

⑥ Repeat steps 1–4, but this time change the quantity 2 in parts (a)–(f) of step 3 to any number you wish.

⑦ Look for a pattern in the inequalities you wrote. Discuss how different operations affect inequalities. From your discussion, write a rule for inequalities that you and your partner agree on.

1. From your experience in the Exploration, which operation(s) change the direction of the inequality symbol in the sentence $25x > 50$?

   a. Multiply both sides by -4.

   b. Add -5 to both sides.

   c. Subtract -2 from both sides.

   d. Divide both sides by -5.

2. Why do you think you were not asked to add -2 or subtract -2 in step 3 of the Exploration?

Sample 1

Solve and graph the inequality $x + 2 < -1$.

Sample Response

$$x + 2 < -1$$
$$x + 2 - 2 < -1 - 2 \quad \longleftarrow \text{ Subtract 2 from both sides.}$$
$$x < -3$$

Check You cannot check every point on the graph, but you should check at least one. Choose a value for x that is less than -3. Try -7.

$$x + 2 < -1$$
$$-7 + 2 \overset{?}{<} -1 \quad \longleftarrow \begin{array}{l}\text{Substitute } -7 \text{ for } x \text{ in the} \\ \text{original inequality.}\end{array}$$
$$-5 < -1 \; \checkmark$$

The solution is all numbers less than -3.

Use an open circle. The graph does not include -3.

Draw a ray to the left to include all points less than -3.

Sample 2

Solve and graph the inequality $-8x \leq 40$.

Sample Response

$$-8x \leq 40$$
$$\frac{-8x}{-8} \geq \frac{40}{-8}$$
$$x \geq -5$$

← When you divide both sides by −8, reverse the inequality symbol.

Check Choose a value for x that is greater than or equal to −5. Try 0.

$$-8x \leq 40$$
$$-8(0) \overset{?}{\leq} 40$$
$$0 \leq 40 \; ✔$$

← Substitute 0 for x in the original inequality.

The solution is all numbers greater than or equal to −5.

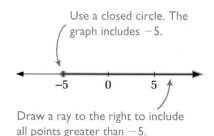

Use a closed circle. The graph includes −5.

Draw a ray to the right to include all points greater than −5.

Talk it Over

3. Is −3 a solution to Sample 1? Why or why not? Is −5 a solution to Sample 2? Why or why not?

4. Why is it impossible to check *every* point on the graph of an inequality?

5. The inequalities $7x > 35$ and $x > 5$ have the same solutions. They are **equivalent inequalities.** Write an inequality that is equivalent to $8x < 88$.

6. Write an inequality that is equivalent to $5 < -x$.

Sample 3

Solve and graph the inequality $4(x + 1.5) \leq 70$.

Sample Response

$$4(x + 1.5) \leq 70$$
$$4x + 4(1.5) \leq 70$$

← Use the distributive property.

$$4x + 6 \leq 70$$
$$4x + 6 - 6 \leq 70 - 6$$

← Subtract 6 from both sides.

$$4x \leq 64$$
$$\frac{4x}{4} \leq \frac{64}{4}$$

← Divide both sides by 4.

$$x \leq 16$$

The solution is all numbers less than or equal to 16.

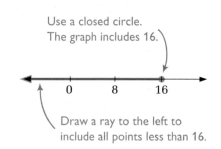

Use a closed circle. The graph includes 16.

Draw a ray to the left to include all points less than 16.

7. Explain how to check the solution in Sample 3.

8. Name the operation used to rewrite the first inequality to get the second one.

   a. $5x < 25$
      $x < 5$

   b. $10 \geq a - 4$
      $14 \geq a$

   c. $-3r > -3$
      $r < 1$

SOLVING INEQUALITIES

An inequality *stays the same* when you:

➤ add, subtract, multiply by, or divide by the same positive number on both sides of an inequality

➤ add or subtract the same negative number on both sides of an inequality

An inequality is *reversed* when you:

➤ multiply or divide by the same negative number on both sides of an inequality

➤ Now you are ready for:

Exs. 1–15 on p. 266

Modeling Situations with Inequalities

Sample 4

Jamal can afford to spend $50 to buy some concert tickets and pay for parking. Model this situation.

Sample Response

Let n = the number of tickets he can buy.

Then $18n$ is the total cost of the tickets.

The amount he can spend	is less than or equal to	$50
parking + ticket cost	$\leq$	50
$5 + 18n$	$\leq$	50

The inequality $5 + 18n \leq 50$ models the situation.

cost per ticket

TICKETS: $18.00

PARKING: $5.00

parking price

Jamal borrowed $50 from his mom for the concert. He repays the loan at the rate of $6 per week. When will his debt be under $20?

Sample Response

Model the situation using an inequality and solve.

Let w = the number of weeks Jamal has paid his mother.

Then $6w$ = the amount he has paid in w weeks and

$50 - 6w$ = the amount that Jamal still owes after w weeks.

Write an inequality to show when the amount Jamal owes is under $20.

$$50 - 6w < 20$$
$$50 - 6w - 50 < 20 - 50 \quad \longleftarrow \text{ Subtract 50 from both sides.}$$
$$-6w < -30$$
$$\frac{-6w}{-6} > \frac{-30}{-6} \quad \longleftarrow \begin{array}{l}\text{When you divide both sides by } -6, \\ \text{reverse the inequality symbol.}\end{array}$$
$$w > 5$$

Jamal's debt will be under $20 after the fifth week, or in 6 weeks.

Talk it Over

9. In Sample 5, why are the inequality symbols different in the inequality $50 - 6w < 20$ and the equivalent inequality $w > 5$?

10. Model each sentence with an inequality.

   a. The maximum number of tickets that can be sold for the concert is 12,000.

   b. The report is due in less than 2 weeks.

   c. Claire Rooney's hourly wage is at least $8 over the minimum wage.

   d. Kwai's test score is more than 10 points above the average.

11. The words *over, under, less than, more than, maximum,* and *minimum* can describe an inequality.

   a. Tell which one of the symbols $<, >, \leq,$ or $\geq$ is described by each word.

   b. Write three sentences that use words describing inequalities.

Look Back

How is solving an inequality like solving an equation? How is it different?

······▶ **Now you are ready for:**
Exs. 16–45 on pp. 266–269

Exercises and Problems

1. **Reading** Read the Solving Inequalities section on page 264. Give an example to support one of the ideas in the summary. Use $x > 0$ as the original inequality.

Solve each inequality and write the letter of its graph.

2. $3x \leq -15$

3. $-6x < 42$

4. $x - 4 \geq 1$

A.
B.
C.

Solve and graph each inequality.

5. $2q < -3$ 6. $-5x < 105$ 7. $8 \geq 5x + 10$

8. $7 - a < 25$ 9. $6(x - 4) \leq 3$ 10. $-2(x + 5) > 6$

11. $18 \leq 4(x + 2)$ 12. $12 - x \leq 7x$ 13. $3t \geq 8t - 75$

14. Which inequality is equivalent to $-5x > 10$?

   a. $x > -2$ **b.** $x < 2$ **c.** $x < -2$ **d.** $x = -2$

15. Which inequality is equivalent to $-3 > -p$?

   a. $p < -3$ **b.** $p < 3$ **c.** $p > 3$ **d.** $-3 = p$

For Exercises 16–19, choose the letter of the inequality that models each situation.

16. In 7 more years my car will be over 10 years old. Let y = my car's age in years.

   a. $y + 7 < 10$

   b. $y + 7 > 10$

   c. $y + 7 \geq 10$

17. The 237 tickets sold at tonight's game more than tripled the number sold at the last game. Let t = the number of tickets sold at the last game.

   a. $3t > 237$

   b. $3t < 237$

   c. $3t \geq 237$

18. If I buy one CD for $12, I won't have enough money left to buy another. Let m = the amount of money I have.

   a. $m - 12 \leq 12$

   b. $m - 12 \geq 12$

   c. $m - 12 < 12$

19. Five balcony seats for the concert cost over $20 more than three balcony seats. Let b = the cost of one balcony seat.

   a. $5b > 3b + 20$

   b. $5b + 20 > 3b$

   c. $5b \geq 3b + 20$

20. **Open-ended** Find a maximum or minimum number related to your school life and write an inequality to describe the number. (For example, is there a minimum number of credits for graduation? a maximum number of people allowed in a school bus?)

21. The temperature of lightning is about 50,000°F. This is more than 4.5 times the temperature of the sun's surface. Write and solve an inequality to find a maximum possible temperature for the sun's surface.

22. Cirrus clouds are found above 7 km. This is 3.5 times as high as cumulus clouds. Write and solve an inequality to determine the heights of cumulus clouds.

> **Weather Clouds**
>
> U.S. WEATHER SERVICE—Cumulus clouds that grow higher than 50,000 ft are called Cumulonimbus Towers. When these clouds reach a temperature between 32°F and 39°F, ice crystals start to form and fall to Earth as snow or rain. Cumulonimbus Towers are responsible for up to three-fourths of the world's rain and some of its most dangerous weather.

23. Reading Write two inequalities about the information in this article. Be sure to tell what your variables represent.

24. Career To study clouds, Joanne Simpson, a meteorologist and chief scientist at NASA, once flew directly into them in a single engine plane. Today she uses satellites, airplanes, and computers to study weather patterns. Simpson was the first person to write a paper about using math models to study cloud growth.

  a. Research Find the names and height ranges for two types of clouds other than cumulus, cirrus, or cumulonimbus towers. Write an inequality to show the relationship between their heights. Draw a picture of each type of cloud.

  b. Writing Joanne Simpson says that "science isn't just cold, hard facts. The crux is fitting unfitted things together and making them hang together. It's similar to composing music or art or poetry." Do you think this statement is true for mathematics? Explain why or why not.

Joanne Simpson, Meteorologist and NASA scientist.

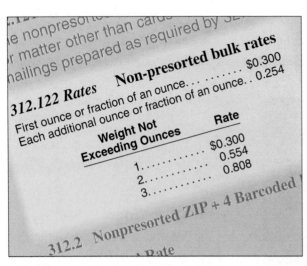

312.122 Rates   Non-presorted bulk rates

First ounce or fraction of an ounce. $0.300
Each additional ounce or fraction of an ounce. . 0.254

Weight Not Exceeding Ounces	Rate
1.	$0.300
2.	0.554
3.	0.808

312.2 Nonpresorted ZIP + 4 Barcoded

Use the postal chart for Exercises 25 and 26. Model each situation with an inequality and solve.

25. The Drum Corps club wants to send a newsletter to its members. If each newsletter weights 1.7 oz, how many newsletters can they afford to send if they can spend up to $150?

26. The admissions office at Arlington University wants to mail information packets to students. The budget allows them to spend a maximum of $1.75 to mail each packet. How heavy a packet can be sent to the students?

27. A town requires that a one-story house built on a standard lot be 2000 ft² or less in area. A builder plans to build a rectangular house on a standard lot. The width of the house is 20 ft. How long can the house be?

28. Fiona Wilson earns $8.50 an hour plus time-and-a-half for overtime as a pastry chef. Her normal work week is 37 h. How many full hours of overtime must she work to earn over $400 in a week?

29. Annette has $65 in her bank account. She can earn $9 for each lawn she mows. How many lawns must she mow in order to save at least $200?

Solve and graph each inequality.

30. $5x + 13 > 4(x + 3) + x$

31. $6x + 15 < 6(x + 1)$

BY THE WAY...

In 1851 it cost 25¢ to send a single page letter to someone 400 miles away! By 1885, the post office system grew and it only cost 2¢ to mail a first class letter. In 1974, the cost was once again in double digits — 10¢.

Ongoing **ASSESSMENT**

32. **Writing** Write an inequality like the ones in Samples 1–3. Write a paragraph to describe a situation that it models. Solve the inequality. Explain what the solution means.

Review **PREVIEW**

Solve. *(Sections 2-7, 2-8, 5-3)*

33. $4(5a + 1) = 104$

34. $7c + 5 = 68$

35. $-2y = 38$

36. $4x - 10 + 5x = -55$

37. $x = 3x + 16$

38. $3a + 4 = a - 8$

For each formula, tell what each variable represents. *(Sections 2-6, 5-3)*

39. $D = rt$

40. $P = 2l + 2w$

41. $V = lwh$

5 Working on the Unit Project

42. Write and solve an inequality to show how many cars you would have to wash at $5 per car to raise at least $300.

43. Write and solve an inequality to show how many cars you would have to wash at your price per car to at least reach your goal.

44. Write and solve an inequality to show how many cars you would have to wash at your price per car to raise more than you spend on supplies and advertising.

45. Decide on the price you will charge for each car you wash.

Unit 5   CHECKPOINT

1. Writing How would you teach someone to solve the equation $(x - 5)5 + 2x = 17$? Be sure to include the distributive property and combining like terms in your explanation.

```
PREMIUM ETR/CASSETTE
W/6 SPKERS   INC: EQUALIZER/
DIVERSITY ANT
6-DISC CHANGER. . . 1,200
```

2. Alma wants to save $1200 so that she can get a deluxe stereo system for her new car. She has already saved $500 and plans to save $22 each week. After how many weeks will she have saved at least $1200? Model the situation using a table or a graph and then solve.   **5-1**

3. Describe a situation that can be modeled by the equation $29 + 3x = 47$.

Write and solve an equation to find the measure of each angle shown.   **5-2**

4.

5.

Solve each equation.   **5-3**

6. $-(t + 5) = 8$ **7.** $6y - 4(y - 1) = 10$

8. $14x - 18 = 2x$ **9.** $2x = -4(x - 3)$

Solve and graph each inequality.   **5-4**

10. $9y \le 36$ **11.** $-15m > 45$ **12.** $3c + 10 < 4$

13. Chris earns $7 an hour plus $10 for each hour of overtime. If he normally works 40 h each week, how many full hours of overtime must he work to earn over $380?

5-5

Rewriting Equations and Formulas

ANOTHER VIEWPOINT

Focus

Learn to rewrite formulas to make them easier to use.

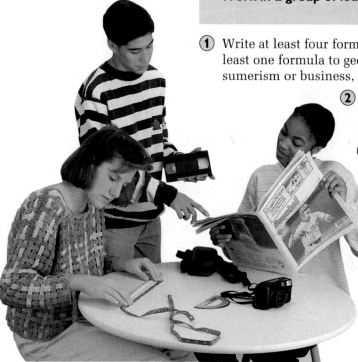

EXPLORATION

How *many formulas can you think of in two minutes?*

- **Work in a group of four students.**

(1) Write at least four formulas you know. Try to relate at least one formula to geometry, one to science, one to consumerism or business, and one to sports or hobbies.

(2) Choose one of your formulas and explain what the variables represent.

(3) Give an example of how each formula is used in everyday life.

Sometimes you need to rewrite a formula or an equation to use it more easily. You used the formula $D = rt$ to find the distances run by the tortoise and the hare. You can write this formula in other ways.

Sample 1

Solve $D = rt$ for t.

Sample Response

Problem Solving Strategy: Solve a simpler problem

Solve the formula $D = rt$ for t just as you would solve the equation $100 = 50t$. Undo any operations to get t alone on one side of the equals sign.

$100 = 50t$	← Divide both sides by the coefficient of t. →	$D = rt$
$\dfrac{100}{50} = \dfrac{50t}{50}$	← Divide by 50. Divide by r. →	$\dfrac{D}{r} = \dfrac{rt}{r}$
$2 = t$	← t is a number. t is an algebraic → expression.	$\dfrac{D}{r} = t$

Sample 2

Solve $2x + y = 180$ for y.

Sample Response

$$2x + y = 180 \qquad \leftarrow \text{To solve for } y, \text{ get } y \text{ alone on one side.}$$
$$2x + y - 2x = 180 - 2x \quad \leftarrow \text{Undo addition of } 2x. \text{ Subtract } 2x \text{ from both sides.}$$
$$y = 180 - 2x$$

Sample 3

Solve $P = 2l + 2w$ for w.

Sample Response

$$P = 2l + 2w \qquad \leftarrow \text{To solve for } w, \text{ get } w \text{ alone on one side.}$$
$$P - 2l = 2l + 2w - 2l \quad \leftarrow \text{Undo addition of } 2l. \text{ Subtract } 2l \text{ from both sides.}$$
$$P - 2l = 2w$$
$$\dfrac{P - 2l}{2} = \dfrac{2w}{2} \qquad \leftarrow \text{Undo multiplication by 2. Divide both sides by 2.}$$
$$\dfrac{P - 2l}{2} = w$$

Talk it Over

1. The formula $\dfrac{D}{r} = t$ is read, "distance divided by rate equals time." Solve the formula $D = rt$ for r. How would you read the rewritten formula?

2. Choose one of the formulas that your group wrote for the Exploration. Tell how you can solve the formula for a different variable.

Look Back

Compare solving the equation $158 = 18(x - 4)$ with solving the equation $y = 18(x - 4)$ for x.

Exercises and Problems

1. **Reading** Read Sample 1 on pages 270 and 271. Follow the format of the Sample Response and solve the equations $128 = r \cdot 32$ and $D = rt$ for r. Label the steps of each solution as in Sample 1.

Solve each equation for the variable shown in red.

2. The formula to convert a Celsius temperature to a Fahrenheit temperature:

$$F = \frac{9}{5}C + 32$$

3. The formula for the circumference of a circle: $C = \pi d$

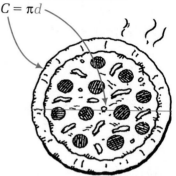

4. Lumber is sold by the board foot. The formula to find the board-foot measure for a piece of wood: $B = \dfrac{t \times w \times l}{12}$

5. Einstein's formula for the theory of relativity:

$$E = mc^2$$

6. The formula for finding the octane rating of a gasoline:

$$O = \frac{R + M}{2}$$

Research Method

Motor Method

Octane

7. The formula for optimum heart rate while exercising: $r = p(220 - a)$

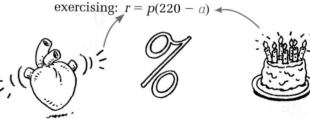

Solve each equation for the variable shown in red.

8. $E = IR$

9. $b = s - c$

10. $I = prt$

11. $x + y = 100$

12. $360 = 2y + x$

13. $5x + y = 75$

14. $c = ax - b$

15. $ax + by = c$

16. $s = 2\pi rh + 2\pi r^2$

17. Every Adventure Travel agent earns a base pay of $200 a week, plus 12% commission for each airline ticket the agent sells.

   a. Write a formula for an agent's weekly salary, s, when the agent sells d dollars worth of airline tickets.

   b. Rewrite your formula to show the amount, in dollars, of airline tickets an agent needs to sell in order to make a weekly salary of s dollars.

   c. How many dollars worth of airline tickets will Frances Medved have to sell each week in order to make a weekly salary of $600?

   d. The Tappan School band orders $8650 worth of airline tickets from Frances for their upcoming trip. What will her salary be if she does not sell any other tickets that week?

18. Saburo is traveling with the school band. He flies between two cities in Hawaii. A 10% tax is added to the base cost of a ticket for flights within Hawaii.

   a. Write a formula for finding the total cost of a plane ticket between cities within Hawaii. Let t = the total cost. Let b = the base cost.

   b. Solve the formula for b.

   c. Find the base cost for a ticket that costs $49.

19. Gus Uchida, the band's equipment manager, parked his car at the airport. Parking costs $12 the first day and $9 each additional day.

   a. Write a formula for the cost, c, to park d days at the airport.

   b. Gus paid $120 for parking. How many days was Gus' car parked at the airport?

   c. TECHNOLOGY Make a spreadsheet that shows the daily parking costs for 1 to 30 days.

20. Winona Birch, the director of the school band, took a taxicab from the airport to her home. She had to pay a flat fee of $1.50 plus $1.60 per mile.

   a. Write a formula for the cost, c, for a trip m miles long.

   b. The total cost of Winona's trip was $8.50. How many miles was her trip?

21. a. **Research** Find out what the minimum wage is.

   b. Write a formula for the amount earned for h hours worked at minimum wage.

   c. Solve the formula you wrote in part (b) for h.

22. **Writing** Josie says that $s = \dfrac{n}{n+1}$ and $\dfrac{s}{1-s} = n$ are two ways to write the same formula. Decide whether or not you agree with Josie. Explain how you made your decision.

23. Leo Hernandes told his mathematics class, "I am thinking of a rectangle. Its perimeter is 68 in. The measure of each side is a whole number of inches. I want you to write about such a rectangle."

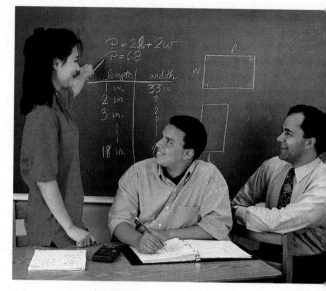

a. Solve the formula $P = 2l + 2w$ for l.

b. Use the formula you wrote for part (a) to complete the table in the photograph. How many different rectangles meet Leo Hernandes' conditions?

c. Sketch the rectangle with the largest area and the rectangle with the smallest area.

d. How could you use the problem solving strategy *Identify a pattern* to do part (b)?

e. **Writing** How could you describe the rectangles to Leo Hernandes?

Solve and graph each inequality. *(Section 5-4)*

24. $-6x > 12$

25. $15y \leq -60$

26. $6(x - 1.5) > -21$

27. Find the mean of 87%, 96%, 75%, 81%, and 64%. *(Section 3-2)*

Find the reciprocal of each number. *(Toolbox Skill 9)*

28. 3

29. $\frac{2}{5}$

30. $-\frac{11}{6}$

31. $\frac{9}{7}$

 Working on the Unit Project

32. Your *profit* from the car wash is your income minus your expenses. Your profit will depend on the number of customers you get.

    Write a formula for your profit after expenses. Let n = the number of cars you wash.

33. One way to estimate which location will have the most customers is to study traffic patterns. The number of cars on a certain street may depend on the day of the week or on the time of day.

    a. **Research** Design and carry out an experiment at your three location choices to estimate the number of customers you will have. Include different locations, days, and times.

    b. Summarize the results of your experiment. You may want to use a table or spreadsheet.

    c. Based only on the number of potential customers, which location is best? What are some reasons to choose another location?

    d. Choose one location to be the place for your car wash.

Using Reciprocals

THE **FLIP SIDE**

People who make quilts like to include interesting fabrics in their projects. To get patterns that they may not be able to find in their towns, quilters often exchange quarter-yard pieces of fabric with people around the world.

Some of the most desired fabrics are the uniquely-designed blue and white Japanese fabrics used to make *yukatas*, the traditional Japanese summer kimonos.

BY THE WAY...

When you cut 44 in. wide fabric into half-yard strips and then cut those strips in half, you get a "fat quarter." Quilt stores often sell fat quarters because the pieces are more practical to use than the 9 in. × 44 in. regular quarter-yard strips.

Talk it Over

1. Kimberly Quandt has three yards of fabric to share with the members of her quilt exchange group. How many quarter-yard pieces can she cut from the 3-yd piece of fabric?

   $3 \div \frac{1}{4} = \underline{\ ?\ }$.

2. You have learned that when the product of two numbers is 1, the numbers are called *reciprocals* of each other. Give an example of a number and its reciprocal.

3. What is the reciprocal of 1?

4. Give a reason why *zero* has no reciprocal.

5. In arithmetic, $\frac{5}{6} \div 2 = \frac{5}{6} \cdot \frac{1}{2}$ and $7 \div \frac{2}{3} = 7 \cdot \frac{3}{2}$. Complete the general statement: "Dividing by a number gives the same result as $\underline{\ ?\ }$ by the $\underline{\ ?\ }$ of the number."

6. Explain how you can rewrite the product $\frac{1}{6} \cdot 6h$ as h.

A goal in solving equations is to get the variable alone on one side of the equals sign. Sometimes the best way to do this is to use the fact that the product of a number and its reciprocal is 1.

Solve.

a. $15 = 6h$ b. $-\frac{2}{3}x = 97$ c. $12 = \frac{4}{5}x + 4$

Sample Response

a. **Method ❶** Use division.

Divide both sides by 6.

$$15 = 6h$$

$$\frac{15}{6} = \frac{6h}{6}$$

$$2.5 = h$$

The solution is 2.5.

Method ❷ Use multiplication.

Multiply both sides by the reciprocal of 6.

$$15 = 6h$$

$$\frac{1}{6} \cdot 15 = \frac{1}{6} \cdot 6h$$

$$2.5 = h$$

The solution is 2.5.

b. $-\frac{2}{3}x = 97$

$$-\frac{3}{2}\left(-\frac{2}{3}x\right) = -\frac{3}{2}(97) \quad \longleftarrow \text{ Multiply both sides by the reciprocal of } -\frac{2}{3}.$$

$$1 \cdot x = -145.5 \quad \longleftarrow \text{ The product of the reciprocals is 1.}$$

$$x = -145.5 \quad \longleftarrow 1 \cdot x = x.$$

The solution is −145.5.

c. $12 = \frac{4}{5}x + 4$

$$12 - 4 = \frac{4}{5}x + 4 - 4 \quad \longleftarrow \text{ Subtract 4 from both sides.}$$

$$8 = \frac{4}{5}x$$

$$\frac{5}{4} \cdot 8 = \frac{5}{4} \cdot \frac{4}{5}x \quad \longleftarrow \text{ Multiply both sides by the reciprocal of } \frac{4}{5}.$$

$$10 = 1 \cdot x \quad \longleftarrow \text{ The product of the reciprocals is 1.}$$

$$10 = x \quad \longleftarrow 1 \cdot x = x.$$

The solution is 10.

Student Resources Toolbox
p. 650 *Fractions*

Talk it Over

7. Are the numbers 4 and 0.25 reciprocals? Explain why or why not.

8. Are the numbers $\frac{1}{10}$ and −10 reciprocals? Explain why or why not.

9. Explain how you would solve the equation $-\frac{3}{4}x - 19 = -40$.

10. Describe two ways to solve the equation $0.4x + 12 = -34$. Which method do you like the best? Why?

Leela wants to use her new graphics calculator to see the graph of the equation $2x + 3y = 6$. She pressed the [Y=] key to enter the equation. Here is what she saw:

```
:Y1 =
:Y2 =
:Y3 =
:Y4 =
```

Rewrite the equation so that Leela can enter it on her calculator.

Sample Response

Solve $2x + 3y = 6$ for y.

$$2x + 3y = 6$$
$$2x + 3y - 2x = 6 - 2x \quad \longleftarrow \text{Subtract } 2x \text{ from both sides.}$$
$$3y = 6 - 2x$$
$$\tfrac{1}{3}(3y) = \tfrac{1}{3}(6 - 2x) \quad \longleftarrow \begin{array}{l}\text{Multiply both sides by the}\\ \text{reciprocal of 3. Then use the}\\ \text{distributive property.}\end{array}$$
$$y = 2 - \tfrac{2}{3}x$$

Leela entered the rewritten equation into her calculator and hit the [GRAPH] key. Here is what she saw:

Look Back ←

How are the equations $\frac{x}{3} = 7$ and $\frac{1}{3}x = 7$ alike? How are they different? Explain how to solve each equation.

5-6 Exercises and Problems

1. **Reading** In part (b) of Sample 1, what is the goal of multiplying both sides by the reciprocal of $-\frac{2}{3}$?

Solve.

2. $-80 = -32x$

3. $\frac{5}{8}y = 20$

4. $-\frac{3}{5}t = -9$

5. $\frac{1}{2}x + 7 = 15$

6. $10 = \frac{1}{5}m + 14$

7. $30 - \frac{2}{3}y = 10$

Solve each equation for the variable shown in red.

8. $5x + 6y = 30$

9. $-4y + 9x = 18$

10. $x - \frac{2}{3}y = 10$

11. $7x + 2y = 15$

12. $y = -\frac{1}{3}x - 8$

13. $y = \frac{5}{2}x + \frac{5}{2}$

14. Find a positive number that is equal to its reciprocal. Is there a negative number that is equal to its reciprocal? If so, which one?

15. Explain how you could use the division key on your calculator instead of the or key to find the reciprocal of 2.5.

16. **Writing** Kim tried to solve the equation $-3w = 12$ by adding 3 to both sides. She got $w = 15$. Explain what is wrong with her method. Show how you would solve the equation.

17. The formula $y = 12x$ converts x feet to y inches. Find a formula that converts y inches to x feet.

18. The formula $y = \frac{3}{5}x$ converts x kilometers to approximately y miles. Find a formula that converts y miles to approximately x kilometers.

connection to **MUSIC**

19. Sound waves vibrate at a certain frequency when instruments produce musical notes. Two notes are a "perfect fifth" apart when the frequency of the lower note (l) is $\frac{2}{3}$ the frequency of the higher note (h).

    a. Write a formula to describe this situation.

    b. Solve the formula for h.

    c. Find the frequency of the lower note when the higher note has a frequency of 440 vibrations per second.

    d. Find the frequency of the higher note when the lower note has a frequency of 440 vibrations per second.

20. The sound that you hear when a violin string is played is determined by the length of the string that is allowed to vibrate.

    a. Write a formula to describe this situation.

    b. Rewrite the formula to show the part of the E string that vibrates in relation to the length of the string that vibrates for an F note.

Length for an F note $= \frac{9}{10}$ of the length for an E note

G D A E

21. **Writing** Write all you know about using reciprocals. Include two examples of reciprocals and an example showing how to use reciprocals to solve equations and formulas.

Solve each equation for the variable shown in red. *(Section 5-5)*

22. $P = 2s + b$

23. $-6x + 5y = 46$

24. $4x - 2y = 28$

25. Describe the pattern in the table. *(Section 1-2)*

x	−5	−2	0	3	7	10
y	−10	−4	0	6	14	20

Evaluate each expression when $a = 5$, $b = 10$, and $c = \frac{1}{3}$. *(Section 2-2)*

26. a^2b

27. $\frac{1}{2}ab$

28. $\frac{1}{5}(a + b)$

29. $c(b + 32)$

 Working on the Unit Project

30. Suppose one student can wash a car in 20 min. In one minute the student can wash $\frac{1}{20}$ of the car.

    rate of washing $= \frac{1}{20}$ car per minute

    a. What part of a car can 10 students working together wash in one minute?

    b. Do you think 20 students working together can wash a whole car in one minute? Why or why not?

31. a. **Research** Suppose a group of students is washing a car together.

    group's rate of washing $= \dfrac{1}{\text{group's time to wash a car}}$

    Experiment with different numbers of students. Find the different group rates of car washing. Decide how many people are needed to wash a car quickly and efficiently.

    b. Using a group the size you choose in part (a), how long will it take you to wash enough cars to reach your goal?

    c. Will there be enough time in one day for your group to reach your fund-raising goal if only one group of students washes cars? Why or why not?

    d. If you do not have enough time, what are some things you could do to reach your goal?

Area Formulas

Focus

Use the formulas for the area of a parallelogram, a triangle, and a trapezoid to solve problem situations.

EXPLORATION

How can you cut a parallelogram to find its area?

- **Materials: rectangular sheets of paper, scissors**
- **Work with another student.**

(1) The length and width of a rectangle are also called the base (*b*) and height (*h*). Label your paper with *b* and *h* as shown. What is a formula for the area of your rectangle?

(2) Make a fold in your paper to form a triangle. Cut along the fold line.

(3) Slide or translate the triangle across your paper. What kind of quadrilateral is formed?

(4) What is a formula for the area of the quadrilateral you created in step 3? Explain how you arrived at your answer.

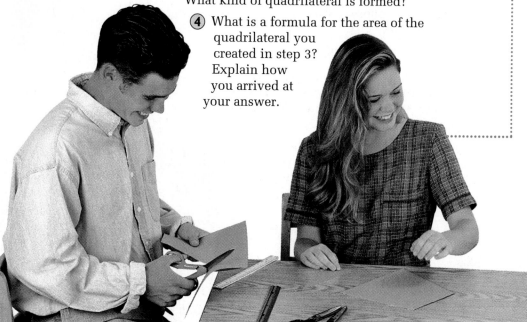

Any side of a parallelogram may be called a **base**. The **height** of a parallelogram is the distance to the base from a point on the opposite side.

The *distance from a point to a line* is the length of the perpendicular segment from the point to the line.

Sample 1

Find the area of the parallelogram.

6 in.

2 ft

Sample Response

Problem Solving Strategy: Use a formula

All the measures used must be in the same units, so write 2 ft as 24 in.

$A = bh$ ⟵ Area of a parallelogram = base × height.

$\quad = 24(6)$ ⟵ Substitute 24 for b and 6 for h.

$\quad = 144$

The area is 144 in.^{2}.

Sample 2

Find the height of a parallelogram with base 10 cm and area 25 cm^2.

Sample Response

Problem Solving Strategy: Use a formula

$A = bh$ ⟵ Area of a parallelogram = base × height.

$25 = 10h$ ⟵ Substitute 25 for A and 10 for b.

$\dfrac{25}{10} = \dfrac{10h}{10}$ ⟵ Divide both sides by 10.

$2.5 = h$

The height is 2.5 cm.

Talk it Over

1. a. Solve the formula $A = bh$ for h.

   b. Explain how to use the formula you wrote in part (a) to solve Sample 2.

2. After doing the Exploration, Brandon decides that the width of a rectangle is the same as the height of a parallelogram. Do you agree? Why or why not?

Area of a Triangle

You can think of a triangle as half of a parallelogram. The parallelogram and the yellow triangle have the same base and height.

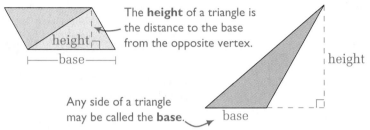

The **height** of a triangle is the distance to the base from the opposite vertex.

Any side of a triangle may be called the **base**.

Sometimes you need to extend the base to draw the height.

AREA OF A PARALLELOGRAM	AREA OF A TRIANGLE
Area of a parallelogram = base × height	**Area of a triangle = $\frac{1}{2}$ × base × height**
$A = bh$	$A = \frac{1}{2}bh$

Sample 3

A neighborhood committee wants to grow wildflowers on the traffic island shown. How many cans of wildflower seeds do they need to cover the traffic island?

Sample Response

Problem Solving Strategy: Use a formula

$A = \frac{1}{2}bh$ ← Area of a triangle $= \frac{1}{2}$ × base × height.

$= \frac{1}{2}(20)(30)$ ← Substitute 20 for b and 30 for h.

$= 300$

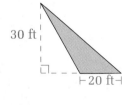

The area of the traffic island is 300 ft². Each can of wildflower seeds covers 80 ft².

$300 \div 80 = 3.75$

The committee needs 4 cans of wildflower seeds.

3. a. In Sample 3, why is the height drawn outside the triangle?

   b. The triangle in Sample 3 is obtuse. Can the height of an obtuse triangle lie inside the triangle?

······► Now you are ready for:
Exs.1–8 on p. 285

   c. Can the height of a right triangle or an acute triangle lie outside the triangle?

Area of a Trapezoid

Architect I. M. Pei was asked to design the new East Wing of the National Gallery of Art. The plot for the new building was in the shape of a trapezoid. This presented a design problem for the architect.

Pei came up with a solution when sketching a trapezoid on the back of an envelope. He drew a diagonal of the trapezoid. When he saw the two pieces, he had the idea to use the smaller triangle for the study center and the larger triangle for exhibits.

In Exercise 11, you will divide a trapezoid into two pieces to get the formula for the area.

X ⟋ab

AREA OF A TRAPEZOID

Area of a trapezoid $= \frac{1}{2} \times$ **the sum of the bases** $\times$ **height**

$$A = \frac{1}{2}(b_1 + b_2)h$$

b_1 means base 1.

b_2 means base 2.

550 ft
300 ft
700 ft

Sample 4

Find the approximate area of the plot of land where the East Wing of the National Gallery was built.

Sample Response

Problem Solving Strategy: Use a formula

$$A = \frac{1}{2}(b_1 + b_2)h \qquad \longleftarrow \text{ Area of a trapezoid} = \frac{1}{2} \times \text{sum of the bases} \times \text{height.}$$

$$A = \frac{1}{2}(550 + 300)(700) \quad \longleftarrow \text{ Substitute 550 for } b_1, 300 \text{ for } b_2, \text{ and 700 for } h.$$

$$A = \frac{1}{2}(850)(700)$$

$$A = 297{,}500$$

The area is about 297,500 ft².

Sample 5

street
Shotzke property
130 ft
Johns property
15,600 ft² area
water

Janelle Rose wants to buy the trapezoidal plot of land shown. She knows that the border along the water is twice as long as the border along the street. How long is the border along the water?

Sample Response

Problem Solving Strategy: Use a formula

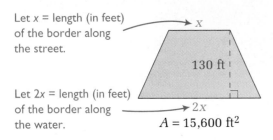

Let x = length (in feet) of the border along the street.

x

130 ft

Let 2x = length (in feet) of the border along the water.

2x

A = 15,600 ft²

$$A = \frac{1}{2}(b_1 + b_2)h \qquad \longleftarrow \text{ Area of a trapezoid}$$

$$15{,}600 = \frac{1}{2}(x + 2x)130 \quad \longleftarrow \begin{array}{l}\text{Substitute 15,600 for } A \\ \text{and 130 for } h. \text{ Substitute } x \\ \text{for } b_1 \text{ and } 2x \text{ for } b_2.\end{array}$$

$$15{,}600 = \frac{1}{2}(3x)130 \qquad \longleftarrow \begin{array}{l}\text{Combine like terms.} \\ \text{Since } x = 1x, x + 2x = 3x.\end{array}$$

$$15{,}600 = 195x \qquad \longleftarrow \text{ Simplify: } \frac{1}{2} \cdot 3 \cdot 130 = 195$$

$$\frac{15{,}600}{195} = \frac{195x}{195} \qquad \longleftarrow \text{ Divide both sides by 195.}$$

$$80 = x$$

The border along the street is 80 ft. The border along the water is twice as long as the border along the road, or 2 × 80. The border along the water is 160 ft.

Look Back ◄─────

Write all the area formulas you know. Draw diagrams to help someone else understand the formulas.

·····► **Now you are ready for:**
Exs. 9–30 on pp. 285–288

1. **Reading** On page 281, read about the distance from a point to a line. Describe the segment you would measure to find the distance from point P to segment $\overline{AB}$.

a.

A ————————————————— B

P •

b.

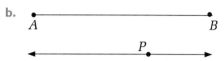

A ————————————————— B

←————————— P •————————→

Find the area of each parallelogram.

2.

12 m

8 m

3.

7 ft

4 ft

4. Find the area of a parallelogram with base 2.8 in. and height 6 in.

5. Find the base of a parallelogram with area 127.4 cm² and height 24.5 cm.

6. Find the area of a triangle with base 6.8 cm and height 3 cm.

7. Find the height of a triangle with area 28.5 cm² and base 6 cm.

8. Leela and Corey are finding the area of the same parallelogram. Leela calls the side closest to her the base. Corey calls the side closest to him the base. Both students use the formula $A = bh$.

   a. Are Leela's values for b and h the same as Corey's? Why or why not?

   b. Will they get the same area? Explain.

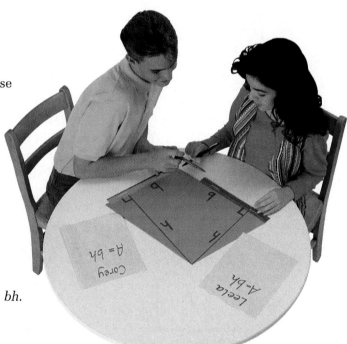

For Exercises 9 and 10, find the area of each trapezoid.

9.

4.56 m   2.28 m   157 cm

10.

61.6 in.

16.8 in.

22.4 in.

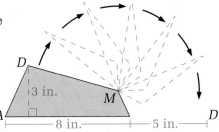

11. a. **Using Manipulatives** Draw any trapezoid *ABCD* on a piece of paper and label it as shown. Cut out the trapezoid.

   b. Find the midpoint of $\overline{BC}$ by folding and label it *M*. Then cut the trapezoid into two pieces by cutting along $\overline{DM}$. Rotate △*DCM*, as shown, to form a large triangle.

   c. Write an expression for the length of the base of the large triangle you made. Write an expression for the area of this triangle.

   d. **Writing** Explain how you can get the formula for the area of a trapezoid by using the formula for the area of a triangle.

12. A sign manufacturer needs to fill an order for 200 No Passing Zone signs. The diagram shows the dimensions required by the United States Department of Transportation.

   a. The signs are made from a sheet of metal. What is the maximum number of signs the manufacturer can cut from a 45 in. by 72 in. sheet? Make a sketch on graph paper to support your answer.

   b. How many 45 in. by 72 in. sheets are needed to make 200 signs?

   c. In part (b) how many square inches of metal will be left over after making the 200 signs?

13. **Open-ended** The United States Department of Transportation chooses the shape for a sign based on the danger of the traffic situation. Think of as many different traffic signs as you can. Give the shape and message of each sign. Describe any patterns you notice.

14. Kenisha and Joel are trying to find the area of a School Crossing sign. Each student started by drawing a diagram.

Kenisha's diagram

Joel's diagram

   a. Find the area of the School Crossing sign using Kenisha's method.

   b. Find the area of the School Crossing sign using Joel's method.

   c. **Writing** Describe how the methods are different. Which method do you think is easier? Why?

BY THE WAY...

Garrett Morgan invented the traffic signal in 1923 after seeing an accident between a car and a horse-drawn carriage.

15. The town council of Massapoag wants to build a bandstand. Architects were asked to submit plans. In the plan shown, the floor has the shape of a regular octagon.

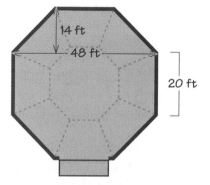

a. What is the area of the floor of the bandstand in this plan?

b. Compare the perimeter of the bandstand in this plan with the perimeter of a square bandstand with the same area.

c. **Writing** Suppose the cost of the bandstand depends on the length of the railing. Which shape costs the least? Write a proposal to the town council about the shape of the bandstand. Give reasons to support your proposal.

For Exercises 16–18, find the missing dimension(s).

16.

Area = 48

4

$2(x - 3)$

17.

16

$2y$

Area = $40(y - 3)$

18.

$x + 2$

$A = 28$

4

$4x - 1$

19. Explain how to solve $A = \frac{1}{2}(b_1 + b_2)h$ for h.

20. **Group Activity** Work with another student. Use the diagram to answer parts (a)–(e).

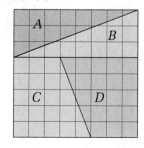

a. Find the areas of triangles A and B and trapezoids C and D.

b. What is the area of the big square?

c. **Using Manipulatives** Draw the triangles and trapezoids on graph paper. Carefully cut out each piece. Rearrange the pieces to form a rectangle 13 units long and 5 units wide. What is the area of the rectangle you formed?

d. Compare the area of the original square and the area of the rectangle. Are the areas the same or different? Did the areas of the triangle and trapezoid pieces change?

e. **Writing** Look up the word *paradox* in a dictionary. Do you think this type of problem is a paradox? Why?

Solve. *(Section 5-6)*

21. $\frac{2}{3}y = 50$

22. $-6 = \frac{1}{2}x + 2$

23. $14 = -\frac{3}{4}x + 2$

24. A quadrilateral has vertices at $(0, 4)$, $(-5, 1)$, $(-1, -6)$, and $(2, 4)$. If the quadrilateral is translated 3 units to the left, find the new vertices. *(Section 4-3)*

Solve each equation for y. *(Sections 5-5, 5-6)*

25. $2x + y = 20$

26. $x + 6y = -36$

27. $16 = \frac{4}{5}y - 4x$

Working on the Unit Project

28. Make a list of the number of students you need to work at the car wash. You may want to consider people for these jobs: advertisers, car washers, fee collectors, traffic controllers, and "runners" who bring dry towels and other supplies.

29. Make a diagram of the car wash area. Show where students will work. Also mark where you will have signs and the location of supplies (including the location of the water supply). Make sure each student has a big enough work area.

30. Decide on the hours of your car wash. Make a schedule listing the jobs and the time periods. Write in the number of students needed for each job during each time period.

Systems of Equations in Geometry

Focus
Model situations and solve
equations with two
variables using substitution.

THE ANGLE CONNECTION

Talk it Over

1. **a.** How are the measures
   of the acute angles of
   $\triangle ABC$ related?

   b. Write an equation that models this relationship.

   c. What is the measure of $\angle A$?

2. **a.** Write an equation that models the relationship between
   the measures of the acute angles of $\triangle PQR$.

   b. Can you use this equation to find the unknown angle
   measures? Why or why not?

   c. Suppose that the measures of the acute angles of $\triangle PQR$
   are equal. Write an equation that models this relationship. Find the measures of $\angle Q$ and $\angle R$.

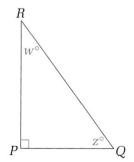

Some situations can be modeled by writing one equation that has
one variable. To model other situations you may need more than
one variable and write a *system* of two equations.

The measure of an acute angle of a right triangle is four times the measure of the other acute angle. Find the measure of each angle.

Sample Response

Problem Solving Strategy: Use a system of equations

Sketch and label a right triangle.

Let x and y be the measures of the two acute angles.

Think about what you know about the relationship between x and y. Write two equations to show these relationships.

$y = 4x$ ← The measure of one acute angle is four times the measure of the other acute angle.

$x + y = 90$ ← The sum of the measures of the acute angles of a right triangle is 90.

You can solve this system of equations with a method called *substitution*. Notice that the equation $y = 4x$ tells you that $4x$ is another name for y.

$$x + 4x = 90 \qquad \longleftarrow \text{Substitute } 4x \text{ for } y \text{ in the equation } x + y = 90.$$
$$5x = 90 \qquad \longleftarrow \text{Combine like terms.}$$
$$\frac{5x}{5} = \frac{90}{5} \qquad \longleftarrow \text{Divide both sides by 5.}$$
$$x = 18$$

To find y, substitute 18 for x in either of the original equations.

$$y = 4x \qquad \longleftarrow \text{Suppose you chose the equation } y = 4x.$$
$$y = 4(18) \qquad \longleftarrow \text{Substitute 18 for } x.$$
$$y = 72$$

Check Substitute the values of x and y in the other equation.

$$x + y = 90 \qquad \longleftarrow \text{Since you used } y = 4x \text{ to substitute 18 for } x, \text{ check the solution with } x + y = 90.$$
$$18 + 72 \stackrel{?}{=} 90 \qquad \longleftarrow \text{Substitute 18 for } x \text{ and 72 for } y.$$
$$90 = 90 \; \checkmark$$

Both equations are true when $x = 18$ and $y = 72$.

The measures of the two acute angles are 18° and 72°.

Solutions of Systems

Two or more equations that state relationships that must all be true at the same time are called a **system of equations.** The values of the variables that make both equations true at the same time are the **solution of a system.**

$$y = 4x$$
$$x + y = 90$$

a system of equations

$$x = 18, y = 72$$

the solution of the system

Talk it Over

3. Suppose the system of equations used to solve a problem has no solution. If the equations have been written correctly, what does this tell you about the conditions of the problem?

4. Cliff and Emma used different methods to solve the problem in the Sample.

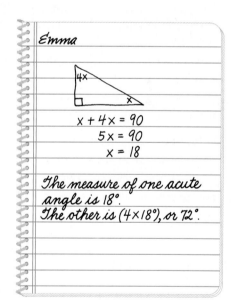

a. Describe Cliff's method.

b. Describe Emma's method.

c. Suppose you are showing a friend how to solve the Sample. Which method would you use? Why?

Look Back

Look back at the tortoise and hare problem in Sample 2 of Section 5-3. Explain how you can solve this problem using a system of two equations.

Exercises and Problems

1. **Reading** Read the Sample on page 290. What information is used to write the system of equations?

Check Matthew's, Zena's, and Corazon's work. If they solved incorrectly, find the correct solution.

2. $a = 3b$
   $4a + 2b = 28$

   Matthew's solution:
   $a = 2, b = 10$

3. $12r - 8t = -52$
   $5t = r$

   Zena's solution:
   $t = -1, r = -5$

4. $y = 13 - 2x$
   $y = 5x + 41$

   Corazon's solution:
   $y = 5, x = -4$

Solve each system of equations.

5. $y = 8x$
   $4x + y = -108$

6. $6a + 5c = 46$
   $a = 3c$

7. $m = 2p + 3$
   $3p - 2m = -12$

For Exercises 8–14, solve using a system of equations.

8. In $\triangle ABC$, the measures of $\angle B$ and $\angle C$ are equal, and $\angle B$ is twice as large as $\angle A$. Find the measure of each angle.

9. Two angles form a straight angle. The measure of one angle is five times the measure of the other angle. What are the measures of the angles?

10. Two angles are supplementary. One angle is 40° larger than the other. Find the measures of the angles.

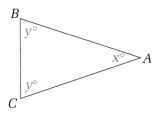

BY THE WAY...

In 1637 the French mathematician René Descartes showed that algebra equations could be used to solve problems in geometry.

11. In a triangle, the measure of the largest angle is twice the measure of the smallest. The measure of the third angle is 20° more than the measure of the smallest.

    a. Sketch the triangle and label the angles.

    b. Find the measures of the angles of the triangle.

12. The perimeter of a rectangle is 48 in. The width is 10 in. shorter than the length. What are the dimensions of the rectangle?

13. Solve this puzzle:

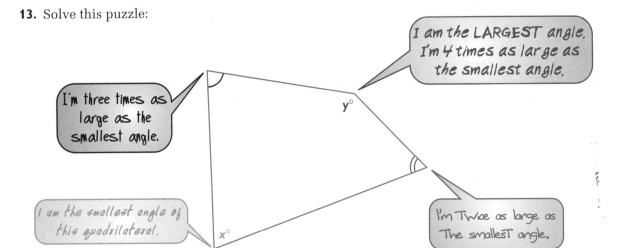

14. Delia and Gilberto are sharing the cost of a $99 camera. Delia paid $35 more than Gilberto. How much did each pay?

15. **Group Activity** Work in a group of three students.

    a. Each person should write a system of equations like the ones you have used in this section.

    b. Pass your paper to the person on your left. Solve the system you receive.

    c. Pass your paper to the left again and check the solution you receive. Help each other until everyone in your group can solve systems successfully.

In Exercises 16 and 17, rewrite one of the equations in each system to get one of the variables alone on one side of the equation. Then solve the system of equations.

16. $r + 2v = -5$
    $4r + v = 8$

17. $3a + b = 2$
    $2a - 5b = 7$

18. If you buy two hair clips and three head bands, you will get $3 change from your $10 bill. If you buy six hair clips and one head band, you will get $1 change. How much does each hair clip and head band cost?

Ongoing **ASSESSMENT**

19. **Writing** Write a set of directions for a student who was absent on the day of this lesson. The student should be able to use your directions to solve a system of equations by substitution and check the solution.

Review **PREVIEW**

20. Compare the areas of a rectangle, a parallelogram, and a triangle that each have $h = 3$ and $b = 8$. *(Section 5-7)*

Solve and graph each inequality. *(Section 5-4)*

21. $6q < 24$

22. $-5a \geq 25$

23. $m + 4 \geq 13$

Write each fraction or decimal as a percent. *(Toolbox Skill 11)*

24. 0.78

25. 1.56

26. $\frac{13}{30}$

27. $\frac{7}{8}$

Working on the Unit Project

28. **a.** The equation $P = I - E$ shows your profit after you subtract the expenses for the car wash from your income. Substitute your goal for P and your total expenses for E.

    b. Write an equation to represent your income after washing n cars at your price.

    c. Write a system of equations using your answers to parts (a) and (b).

    d. Solve the system you wrote in part (c) to find out how many cars you need to wash for your profit to equal your goal.

Completing the Unit Project

Now you are ready to present your plan of action. Your presentation should include reasons for your recommendations. Include these things in your presentation.

➤ a description of the best location for the car wash

➤ the price you have decided to charge for each car

➤ a list of the supplies you need and where you will purchase these items

➤ a discussion of how many cars you need to wash to break even

➤ a table showing your income and how many cars you need to wash to meet your fund-raising goal

➤ samples of advertisements and posters

➤ a diagram of your car wash area

➤ a list of the jobs and the number of people needed to run the car wash efficiently

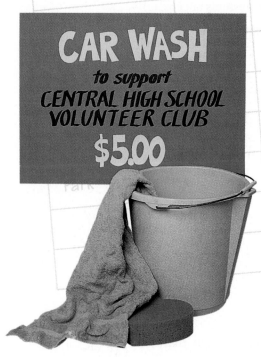

CAR WASH
to support
CENTRAL HIGH SCHOOL
VOLUNTEER CLUB
$5.00

Look Back ◄

What did you learn from this project that can help you plan for future fund-raising events?

Alternative Projects

Project 1: Working on Commission

Interview someone in a business to find out the salaries and commission rates for new salespeople and experienced salespeople.

Ask for some typical weekly or monthly sales figures. Make a table and a graph and write an equation for several different amounts of sales. Choose an income goal and figure out how many sales a new salesperson and an experienced salesperson need to earn that income.

Project 2: Researching Telephone Costs

Choose two locations you would like to call long distance. Decide on the time of day, the day of the week, and the length of each call. Contact two or three long-distance telephone services to find out the cost for each call. Make a table and graph the data. Use the results to choose a long-distance service for your calls. Explain your choice.

1. Karin types students' papers on a computer. She charges $6 for supplies and $2 per page.

   a. Model the situation using a table.

   b. Model the situation using a graph.

   c. Model the situation with an equation.

   d. How long a paper does Karin need to type to earn $30?

   5-1

   5-2

2. The sum of the measures of the angles of a convex polygon with n sides is $(n - 2)180$. Can the sum of the angles of a polygon be 1800°? Explain why or why not.

3. Evelyn and Kelsey have a bike race. Evelyn bikes at 18 ft/s and Kelsey bikes at 14 ft/s. Evelyn falls. She stops for 30 s before continuing the race. She and Kelsey tie. How many seconds long was the race?

   5-3

4. **Open-ended** Create a problem situation that you can model with a table, a graph, and an equation. Choose one of your models to solve the problem.

Solve.

   5-2, 5-3

5. $13 - y = 39$

6. $3x + 12 - x = 2$

7. $(n - 2)180 = 1080$

8. $x - 3(x - 5) = -9$

9. $2t = 5t + 6$

10. $10x - 2 = 20 - 34x$

11. **Writing** John and Dwayne each made a mistake in their work. Check their solutions. Explain each mistake and tell how to correct it.

   a. John's work:

   b. Dwayne's work:

Solve and graph each inequality.

   5-4

12. $-5x > 15$

13. $8 - a \le 12$

14. $4(x - 2) > 8$

15. Raoul has $82 in his bank account. He can earn $9 an hour working at the library. How many full hours must he work in order to have at least $250?

Solve for the variable in red. 5-5, 5-6

16. $I = prt$

17. $4x + y = 180$

18. $P = (n - 2)T$

19. $5 - \frac{4}{7}x = -3y$

20. $\frac{3}{8}x + 6 = y$

21. $\frac{5}{4}y + 5x = 1$

22. The formula $y = 4x$ converts x half-gallons to y pints. Write a formula that converts y pints to x half-gallons.

Identify the area formula represented by each diagram. 5-7

23.

24.

25. The shape of Nevada is nearly a trapezoid. Estimate the area of Nevada using the formula for the area of a trapezoid.

26. Solve the system. $\quad 3x + 2y = 10$
$\qquad\qquad\qquad\qquad\quad x = y + 5$

27. In an isosceles triangle, the measure of one angle is three times the measure of one of the congruent angles. Write and solve a system of equations to find the measure of each angle. 5-8

28. **Self-evaluation** Make a diagram that shows the types of equations that you can now solve. (See the concept map at the right for an idea.) Use a colored pencil or different shapes to show the types that you feel confident about and the types with which you need more experience.

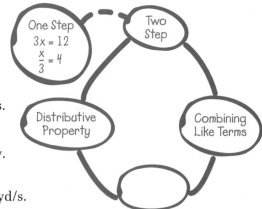

29. **a.** **Group Activity** Work in a group of four students. Write four different questions using the information below. At least one question should involve an equation and one should involve an inequality.

➤ The length of the football field is 100 yd.

➤ The fastest runner on the football team runs 6 yd/s.

➤ The time it takes to pass a football ranges from 0.5 s to 8 s.

➤ The slowest runner on the football team runs 3 yd/s.

b. Answer your questions on a separate sheet of paper.

c. Give another group your questions to answer. Compare answers and discuss any differences.

IDEAS AND (FORMULAS) $= X^2$

➤ **Problem Solving** Situations can be modeled with tables, graphs, and equations. The pattern in a table can help you write an equation for the situation. *(p. 241)*

➤ Different situations may have the same model. *(p. 243)*

➤ To solve multi-step equations, you may need to combine like terms, use the distributive property, or divide both sides by –1. *(pp. 256, 257)*

➤ **Problem Solving** Problem situations involving words such as *over*, *under*, *less than*, and *more than* may be solved using inequalities. *(pp. 264, 265)*

➤ You solve inequalities the same way as equations *except* that when you multiply or divide by a negative number, the inequality symbol is reversed. *(p. 264)*

➤ **Problem Solving** You can solve some problem situations by first writing a formula. *(p. 270)*

➤ To solve an equation or a formula for a variable, you rewrite the equation or formula so the variable is alone on one side. You use the same steps as in solving equations. *(p. 271)*

➤ You can use the fact that the product of reciprocals is 1 to get a variable alone on one side of an equals sign. *(p. 276)*

➤ **Problem Solving** You can solve problems by using more than one variable, then solving a system of equations. *(p. 289)*

➤ A system of equations may be solved using substitution. *(p. 290)*

➤ **Reasoning** The area formulas of several polygons can be derived from one another. *(pp. 280–283)*

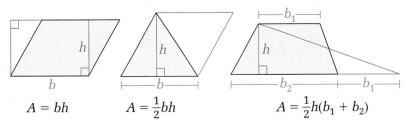

$A = bh$ $A = \frac{1}{2}bh$ $A = \frac{1}{2}h(b_1 + b_2)$

Key Terms

- **mathematical model** (p. 241)
- **equivalent inequalities** (p. 263)
- **height** (pp. 280–283)
- **modeling** (p. 241)
- **reciprocal** (p. 275)
- **system of equations** (p. 291)
- **variable terms** (p. 256)
- **base** (pp. 280–283)
- **solution of a system** (p. 291)

Ratios, Probability, and Similarity

Imagine you have invented some new product that you are sure students need, want, and can afford.

Locker Doctor
Find it fast between classes!

You wait and wait for customers. Nothing happens. Have you misunderstood students' needs? Probably not. Perhaps they have not heard about your product. As with most businesses, you have to advertise.

ADVERTISING
New and Improved!

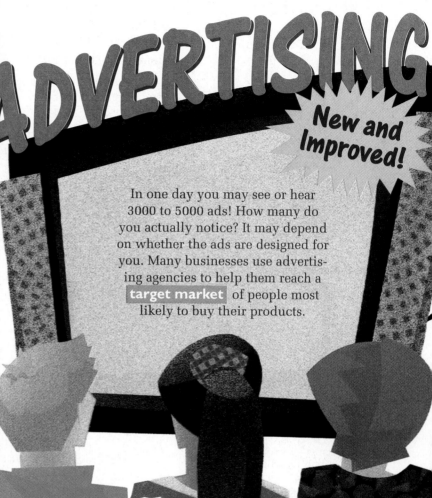

In one day you may see or hear 3000 to 5000 ads! How many do you actually notice? It may depend on whether the ads are designed for you. Many businesses use advertising agencies to help them reach a **target market** of people most likely to buy their products.

media selection

Ads appear in a variety of media—on TV and radio, in magazines and newspapers, at the movies and on videotapes, on T-shirts and hats, on billboards and scoreboards, on taxi cabs and blimps, at airports and bus terminals. Advertisers choose media that are most likely to reach their target market.

Plan an Advertising Campaign

Your project is to plan an advertising campaign for a product or service that you think will appeal to students in your school. You may use a product or service that already exists or invent a new one.

Your group's plan should explain how you decided whether to advertise on television or radio, or in newspapers or magazines. You will need to do research to determine the target markets and advertising costs for the different media. You will compare unit costs for different media and use probability to help you match up your target market with a media audience.

Your group's plan should also include a schedule of when and how often your ad will appear, as well as an estimate of costs.

If your group chooses to run its ad on radio or TV, you will write a script for the ad. If you choose a newspaper or magazine, you will make a sketch of the ad sized to fit the available space.

HOW MANY PEOPLE DOES IT TAKE TO PRODUCE AN AD?

Every ad is the result of the organized efforts of a creative team.

Account Executives

Plan and direct the ad campaign for a business.

Creative Directors

Photographers, Writers, and Artists

Media Planners and Buyers

Bring the ad to the consumer.
Media planners decide when and where ads run.
Media buyers purchase time or space for ads.

Unit Project 6

Getting Started

For this project you should work in a group of four students. Here are some ideas to help you get started.

☞ In your group, talk about the kinds of products and services students in your school may like.

☞ Decide whether to use an existing product or service or invent a new one.

☞ Discuss whether controlling costs or reaching your target audience is more important in deciding where to place your ad.

☞ Your group may wish to think about whether it is better to have a long ad that appears only a few times or a shorter ad that runs many times.

☞ You will be keeping a log of your TV viewing and newspaper and magazine reading. Think about how you can keep good records.

Can We Talk

➤ Where else have you seen ads? Which places do you think are the most effective? Which do you think are the most expensive?

➤ Think of a product that is popular at your school. Have you seen any advertisements for the product? Where did the ads appear?

➤ Have you ever bought a product because it was advertised on television or radio? in a magazine or a newspaper? If so, how did the ad convince you?

➤ How do you think advertising affects the costs of products?

➤ What kinds of knowledge and skills do you think media planners and media buyers need?

➤ A company proposed placing a giant billboard in orbit around Earth. The ads on the billboard would be clearly visible in the night sky. The proposal was very controversial. What do you think of this idea?

Working on the Unit Project

Your work in Unit 6 will help you plan your advertising campaign.

Related Exercises:

Section 6-1 Exercise 17
Section 6-2, Exercises 34–36
Section 6-3, Exercises 38–40
Section 6-4, Exercise 17
Section 6-5, Exercises 32, 33
Section 6-6, Exercise 24
Section 6-7, Exercise 29

Alternative Projects p. 351

6-1

Ratios and Rates

Focus

Write ratios in simplest form, solve problems involving ratios, and compare unit rates.

The Big Picture

Talk it Over

1. The size of a television screen is usually given by the length of the diagonal. What size is this TV screen?

2. A **ratio** is a quotient of two numbers or two quantities. You can write the ratio comparing quantity a to quantity b in three ways:

$$\frac{a}{b} \quad a{:}b \quad a \text{ to } b$$

What is the ratio of the length to the width of this TV screen?

16 in.

20 in.

12 in.

3. The ratio of length to width of a TV screen is called the *aspect ratio*. Standard TV screens have an aspect ratio of 4:3. Is this TV screen a standard screen? Why or why not?

Student Resources
p. 666 *Table of Measures*
p. 649 *Factors*

Sample 1

Find the aspect ratio of a movie screen that is 24 ft long and 13 ft 6 in. wide. Write the ratio in simplest form.

Sample Response

1 ft = 12 in.
24 ft = 24 · 12 in.

288 in.

162 in.

13 ft 6 in. = 13 · 12 in. + 6 in.

First write the ratio as a fraction.

$$\frac{\text{length}}{\text{width}} = \frac{288 \text{ in.}}{162 \text{ in.}}$$ ← Write each measure with the same unit.

Then simplify the ratio.

$$\frac{288}{162} = \frac{288 \div 18}{162 \div 18} = \frac{16}{9}$$ ← Divide the numerator and denominator by the greatest common factor.

The ratio is $\frac{16}{9}$ *or* 16:9 *or* 16 to 9.

The ratio of color TVs to black-and-white TVs sold at Electronics City is about 11:2. Of the next 100 TVs sold, how many do you estimate will be color sets?

Sample Response

The ratio 11:2 means that for every 13 sets sold, 11 are color and 2 are black and white.

Total sold	Color	BW
13	11	2
26	22	4
39	33	6
⋮	⋮	⋮
$13x$	$11x$	$2x$

Problem Solving Strategy: Use an equation

color TVs + BW TVs = total TVs

$$11x + 2x = 100$$
$$13x = 100 \quad \longleftarrow \text{Combine like terms.}$$
$$\frac{13x}{13} = \frac{100}{13} \quad \longleftarrow \text{Divide each side by 13.}$$
$$x \approx 7.7$$

Evaluate the expression $11x$ for $x = 7.7$.

$$11x = 11(7.7) \approx 85$$

About 85 of the next 100 TVs sold will be color sets.

Student Resources Toolbox
pp. 653–656 *Percent*

Talk it Over

4. Remember that a *percent* is a special ratio in which the second number is 100. In Sample 2, about what percent of the TVs sold will be black-and-white sets?

5. List at least three situations where percents are used.

Rates

A commercial shown during the Olympics may cost $575,000 for 30 seconds. The ratio 575,000 : 30 is an example of a *rate*. A **rate** is a ratio of two different types of measurements.

A **unit rate** is a rate for one unit of a given quantity. Some examples of unit rates are *55 miles per hour, 33 miles per gallon,* and *85 cents per pound.* A *unit price* is a unit rate that tells the price for one unit of measure.

During a regular prime-time TV program, 1.5 min of commercial time may cost $240,000. During the Olympics, a commercial may cost $575,000 for 30 seconds. Compare the unit prices for commercials during the Olympics and during a regular prime-time program.

Sample Response ....

Find the unit price for each commercial.

Olympics:

$$\frac{\text{cost}}{\text{seconds}} = \frac{\$575,000}{30 \text{ s}}$$

$$\approx \$19,170 \text{ per second}$$

Regular program:

$$\frac{\text{cost}}{\text{seconds}} = \frac{\$240,000}{90 \text{ s}} \longleftarrow 1.5 \text{ min} = 90 \text{ s}$$

$$\approx \$2670 \text{ per second}$$

A commercial during the Olympics costs about $16,500 more per second than a commercial during a regular prime-time program.

Look Back ◄─────────────────────────────

In what way is a rate a special kind of ratio? Give examples of rates that you have used.

6-1 **Exercises and Problems**

1. **Open-ended** Make a concept map for this section. Include the terms *ratio, percent, rate, unit rate*, and *unit price*, and examples of each.

2. **Movie Screens** One of the world's largest movie screens is in the Keong Emas Theater in Jakarta, Indonesia, and is 92.75 ft long and 70.5 ft wide.

   a. What is the aspect ratio of this screen?

   b. How does this aspect ratio compare with the standard TV screen ratio of 4:3?

3. What is the ratio of the length of a side of a square to its perimeter?

4. What is the ratio of the length of a side of an equilateral triangle to its perimeter?

5. What is the ratio of the length of the part of the telephone pole above the ground to the length of the part underground?

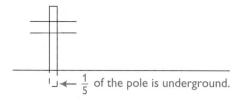

⌐ ← $\frac{1}{5}$ of the pole is underground.

6. A package of two 120-page notebooks sells for $2.29. A package of three 100-page notebooks sells for $2.49.

   a. What is the price per page for each package of notebooks? Which is the better buy? Why?

   b. Suppose the package of two notebooks goes on sale for 20% off. Which package will be the better buy? Why?

7. **Automobiles** Use the magazine article.

   a. What is the height in millimeters of the sidewall of a tire marked like this?

       P195/75R14 90H

   b. What is the total height in inches, including the rim, of the tire in part (a)? (*Hint:* Use the Table of Measures on page 666.)

   c. **Writing** Some drivers prefer a tire with a lower sidewall. Do you think that these drivers should buy tires with a larger or smaller aspect ratio? Explain.

   d. **Research** When you buy tires, you can choose the tire width and the aspect ratio. Look at an ad for tires. Choose one type of tire. Make a scatter plot comparing the tire width to the price. What conclusions can you draw?

8. Choose the letter of the rate of pay that gives you the highest yearly earnings. Assume you work 40 h per week.

   a. $20,000 per year

   b. $1600 per month

   c. $395 per week

   d. $9.85 per hour

9 TECHNOLOGY Use geometric drawing software.

   Open-ended Draw several triangles with the same ratio for the lengths of their sides. What is the ratio of the measures of the angles?

What Your Tires Can Tell You

The sidewall of a tire can make some interesting reading when your car needs new tires. A typical sidewall may contain the marking P205/60B15 85T.

tire width

sidewall height

rim diameter

"P" means the tire is for a passenger car.

"205" is the width of the tire in millimeters.

"60" is the aspect ratio, or the sidewall height as a percent of the tire width.

"B" stands for bias-belted. Other letters that indicate the type of construction include "R" for radial and "D" for diagonal bias.

"15" is the diameter of the rim in inches.

"85" is a code for the maximum weight the tire can carry.

"T" is the speed symbol. Other letters used are H, S, U, V, and Z.

10. **a.** Find the population per square mile for each country listed in the table.

   b. Which country has the largest number of people per square mile? the smallest number of people per square mile?

   c. Does the country with the highest rate have the most people? Does the country with the lowest rate have the least area?

11. **Research** Find the population per square mile for your city or town and for your state. How do these rates compare with the rate for your country?

Country	Population	Area (mi²)
Brazil	173,791,000	3,265,061
Canada	31,330,000	3,560,219
Egypt	68,495,000	384,344
India	1,017,645,000	1,147,950
Japan	126,434,000	152,411
Spain	39,208,000	192,819
United States	274,943,000	3,539,227

Ongoing **ASSESSMENT**

12. **Group Activity** Work in a group of three students.

   a. **Research** Find the population and the number of United States representatives for the United States and for each state.

   b. **Social Studies** For each state, calculate the ratio *people* : *representatives*. Describe the lowest and highest ratios.

   c. Make a scatter plot showing the relationship between population and number of representatives. What conclusions, if any, can you draw?

TECHNOLOGY NOTE

You can use spreadsheet software or a graphics calculator to analyze your data and to make a scatter plot.

Review **PREVIEW**

For Exercises 13–15, solve each system of equations. *(Section 5-8)*

13. $b = 3a$
    $34 = 25a + 3b$

14. $r = -s$
    $-5r + 18s = 115$

15. $d = 6e + 1$
    $2d - 14e = -2$

16. **Open-ended** Use a number anywhere along the scale to estimate the probability that on your way home from school today you will meet someone who speaks Spanish. Give a reason for your answer. *(Section 2-1)*

impossible	unlikely	possible	likely	certain
0%	25%	50%	75%	100%
0	0.25	0.5	0.75	1

Working on the Unit Project

17. **Research** Keep a daily record of the TV programs you watch and the magazines and newspapers you read.

   a. List the name of each TV program you watch, the day and time you watch it, and the products advertised during commercial breaks.

   b. List each magazine or newspaper you look at or read, and the products in the ads you look at or read.

Investigating Probability

Take a SPIN

EXPLORATION

Can you predict how often a spinner lands
on red?

- **Materials: paper clips, red and blue markers, protractors,
compasses**
  Optional: graphics calculator or spreadsheet software

- **Work in a group of three students.**

(1) To get ready for this experiment, assign each person in
your group one of these tasks:

Student 1:

Draw a large circle with eight equal
wedges numbered 1–8 and colored
as shown.

Student 2:

Straighten one end of a paper clip
as shown and use a pencil to hold
it at the center of
the circle.

	Number of spins	Number of landings on red	$\dfrac{\text{Number of landings on red}}{\text{Number of spins}}$
Student 1	10	?	$\dfrac{?}{10} = ?$
Students 1 and 2	20	?	$\dfrac{?}{20} = ?$
Students 1, 2, and 3	30	?	$\dfrac{?}{30} = ?$

Student 3:
Make a table like this one to record your results.

2. Have each person in your group spin the spinner 10 times. For each person, keep track of the number of times that the spinner lands on red.

 a. Record Student 1's results in the first row of the table.

 b. Add Student 2's results to Student 1's results. Then record the combined results in the second row.

 c. Add Student 3's results to the results of the other two students. Then record the combined results for your group in the third row.

3. a. Write the three ratios in the third column of the table as decimals. Round your answers to the nearest hundredth.

 b. Discuss how the three ratios compare.

4. Graph your group's results on a coordinate plane. Plot the points and connect them with segments.

landings on red to number of spins ⟶

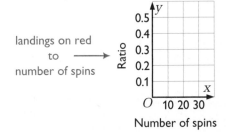

Ratio
Number of spins

5. Combine your group's results for the number of spins and the number of landings on red for Students 1, 2, and 3 with the results of the other groups. Plot the combined results on your graph.

6. Do you see any pattern in the points that were plotted? If so, describe it.

7. What conclusions, if any, can you draw about how the number of spins affects the ratio?

▸ **Now you are ready for:**
Exs. 1–6 on p. 311

Experimental Probability

Event: landing on red

some possible outcomes

Surveys used to collect data and activities like the one in the Exploration in which you observe and record data are *experiments*. There are one or more possible results or **outcomes** of an experiment that can make an **event** happen.

To describe how likely an event is, you use a number on a scale from 0 to 1. This number is called the **probability** of the event. Probability that is based on the result of an experiment is called **experimental probability**.

X·Lab

EXPERIMENTAL PROBABILITY

To find the experimental probability of an event *E*, you observe how often the event happens and calculate this ratio:

$$P(E) = \frac{\text{number of times an event } E \text{ happens}}{\text{number of times the experiment is done}}$$

You read $P(E)$ as, "the probability of event *E*."

Sample 1

A telemarketer types these requirements into a computer:

Age: 25 years or over

Last schooling: 4 years of high school

This means that everyone in the database has an equal chance of being selected.

The software selects a name *at random* from a database that contains the names and phone numbers of every person in the United States.

Use the table to estimate the probability that the person called is female. Round decimal answers to the nearest hundredth.

Last Schooling of U.S. Residents 25 Years or Older, 1998 (numbers in thousands)			
Last years of schooling	**Total**	**Male**	**Female**
Elementary: 0–8 years	17,180	9034	8146
High School: 1–3 years	25,104	12,952	12,152
High School: 4 years	95,966	46,381	49,585
College: 1–3 years	73,634	35,390	38,244
College: 4 or more years	75,391	40,069	35,322
TOTALS	287,275	143,826	143,449
Note: **Numbers may not add correctly due to rounding.**			

Sample Response

Problem Solving Strategy: Use a formula

Use the formula for experimental probability.

$$P(E) = \frac{49{,}585}{95{,}966}$$

← female residents at least 25 years old with 4 years of H.S.
← total residents at least 25 years old with 4 years of H.S.

$$\approx 0.517$$

The probability is about 0.52, or 52%.

Talk it Over

1. How likely is it that the person called in Sample 1 is a female? How did you get your answer?

2. Suppose the telemarketer in Sample 1 omits the "last schooling" requirement. Estimate the probability of selecting a male whose last schooling is 1–3 years of college.

····▶ **Now you are ready for:**
Exs. 7–13 on pp. 311–312

Theoretical Probability

Possible outcomes

tails
heads

Before a field hockey game, the referee tosses a coin to see which team has the ball first. For the team that chose heads, heads is a *favorable outcome*.

The coin that the referee uses must be *fair*. This means that the coin is equally likely to land with heads or tails on top. When all the possible outcomes are equally likely to happen, you can find the **theoretical probability** of an event without doing an experiment.

If you toss a fair coin over and over, the experimental probability of getting heads will get closer and closer to the theoretical probability, 0.5.

X(.△ab

THEORETICAL PROBABILITY

To find the theoretical probability of an event *E* when all outcomes are equally likely, you find this ratio:

$$P(E) = \frac{\text{number of favorable outcomes}}{\text{number of possible outcomes}}$$

Suppose you roll a fair die. Find each probability.

a. $P(\boxed{\cdot\cdot})$ b. $P(\boxed{\cdot}$ or $\boxed{\cdot\cdot})$ c. $P(\text{not } \boxed{\cdot\cdot})$

Sample Response

a roll of 5 on a die

There are six possible outcomes: $\boxed{\cdot}\ \boxed{\cdot}\ \boxed{\cdot\cdot}\ \boxed{\cdot\cdot}\ \boxed{\cdot\cdot}\ \boxed{\vdots}$

a. There is one favorable outcome: $\boxed{\cdot\cdot}$

$P(\boxed{\cdot\cdot}) = \dfrac{1}{6} \approx 0.17 \approx 17\%$

b. There are two favorable outcomes: $\boxed{\cdot}\ \boxed{\cdot\cdot}$

$P(\boxed{\cdot}$ or $\boxed{\cdot\cdot}) = \dfrac{2}{6} \approx 0.33 \approx 33\%$

c. There are five favorable outcomes: $\boxed{\cdot}\ \boxed{\cdot}\ \boxed{\cdot\cdot}\ \boxed{\cdot\cdot}\ \boxed{\vdots}$

$P(\text{not } \boxed{\cdot\cdot}) = \dfrac{5}{6} \approx 0.83 \approx 83\%$

Complementary Events

Sample 2(c) shows the event of not rolling a $\boxed{\cdot\cdot}$.

The events "not rolling a $\boxed{\cdot\cdot}$" and "rolling a $\boxed{\cdot\cdot}$" are **complementary events**.

←	All Possible Events	→
E	E does not happen	

COMPLEMENTARY EVENTS

You can find the probability of the *complement* of an event by using this formula:

$$P(\text{not } E) = 1 - P(E)$$

The probability that E does **not** happen.

BY THE WAY...

The numbers of dots on dominoes represent the outcomes of rolling two dice. Dominoes first appeared in China about 800 years ago.

Talk it Over

3. For the spinner used in the Exploration, an event may be defined as landing on a color or on a number. How many "color" events are there?

4. Sample 2(b) shows the probability of getting a $\boxed{\cdot}$ *or* a $\boxed{\cdot\cdot}$ when a die is rolled. What do you think the probability is of getting a $\boxed{\cdot}$ *and* a $\boxed{\cdot\cdot}$ when a die is rolled? Explain.

5. Why is there a "1" in the formula for the complement of an event?

6. How can the formula for the complement of an event be rewritten so it contains a sum rather than a difference?

⋯⋯▶ Now you are ready for:
Exs. 14–36 on pp. 312–313

Look Back ◀────

How are experimental probability and theoretical probability different? How are they alike?

6-2 Exercises and Problems

For Exercises 1–4, use the spinner in the Exploration.

Tell whether each event is impossible or certain to happen.

1. landing on green

2. landing on a number greater than 10

3. landing on a single-digit number

4. landing on red, white, or blue

Tosses	Heads	$\dfrac{\text{Heads}}{\text{Tosses}}$
10	?	?
20	?	?
⋮	⋮	⋮
100	?	?

5. **Using Manipulatives** Toss a coin 100 times.
   a. Keep track of your results. Complete a table like this for 10, 20, 30, 40, 50, 60, 70, 80, 90, and 100 tosses.
   b. Graph your results on a coordinate grid. Put the number of tosses on the horizontal axis and the ratio of heads to tosses on the vertical axis.
   c. **Writing** What conclusion can you draw about the chance of tossing a head? Explain your reasoning.

6. **Reading** When is the probability of an event 0? When is it 1?

7. Suppose there are 2000 students in your school and 1158 of them are female. A reporter for the school paper chooses a student at random to interview for the next issue.
   a. Is it more likely that a male or female is chosen? Why?
   b. What is the probability that the student chosen is male?

8. **Open-ended** Find a graph in a newspaper, a magazine, another textbook, or this book. Write two probability problems that can be answered by the data in the graph.

9. **Writing** Suppose you toss a coin and get 6 heads in a row. Do you think the probability is greater than 50% that you will get a tail in the next toss? Explain.

BY THE WAY...

The probability of winning a typical state lottery may be about 0.0000001. This is one tenth the probability of being hit by lightning.

For Exercises 10–13, use the graph.

The manager of Pizza Place kept a record of the types of crusts used for the last 1000 pizza orders. The manager uses the results to decide how much pizza dough to make.

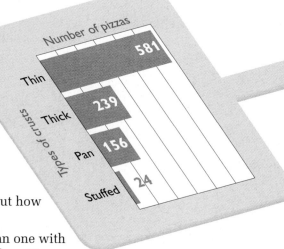

10. Which type of crust is a customer chosen at random most likely to order?

11. **a.** What is the probability that a customer chosen at random orders a thick crust?

    b. What is the probability that a customer chosen at random does not order a thick crust?

12. Of the next 500 pizzas ordered from Pizza Place, about how many will have thin crusts?

13. A cheese pizza with a stuffed crust costs $2 more than one with a thin crust. Of the next 500 cheese pizzas ordered, does Pizza Place expect to earn more money on stuffed crusts or thin crusts?

For Exercises 14–22, use the information about playing cards.

Games A standard deck of playing cards consists of 52 cards, with 13 cards in each of four *suits:* clubs, spades, diamonds, and hearts. *Face cards* are jacks, queens, and kings.

Clubs (♣):	ace, 2, 3, 4, 5, 6, 7, 8, 9, 10, jack, queen, king
Spades (♠):	ace, 2, 3, 4, 5, 6, 7, 8, 9, 10, jack, queen, king
Diamonds (♦):	ace, 2, 3, 4, 5, 6, 7, 8, 9, 10, jack, queen, king
Hearts (♥):	ace, 2, 3, 4, 5, 6, 7, 8, 9, 10, jack, queen, king

Find the probability of choosing each card at random.

14. P(diamond)

15. P(face card)

16. P(ace)

17. P(not a club)

18. P(not a 10 of diamonds)

19. P(club or spade)

20. P(red or black card)

21. P(5 of hearts)

22. P(numbered card and club)

23. A bag contains marbles of different colors. Use the clues below to find the probability of selecting each color. Complete the table.

Color	Probability
brown	0.3
red	?
yellow	?
green	?
orange	?
tan	?

Clue 1: Choosing brown is three times as likely as choosing tan.

Clue 2: Choosing green and choosing orange are each as likely as choosing tan.

Clue 3: Choosing red is as likely as choosing yellow.

24. **Group Activity** Work in a group of four students. Design an experiment. Choose an object to toss or roll, or choose a situation about which you can collect data. Some suggestions are tossing a paper cup or counting the colors of cars at an intersection.

   a. List the possible outcomes.

   b. Have each person in the group perform the experiment at least 30 times. Record all the results in a table.

   c. Choose one possible event for your experiment. What is its experimental probability?

   d. Suppose your group performed the experiment 200 more times. How many times do you expect the event in part (c) to happen?

   e. **Writing** Describe your experiment and summarize your results.

Review **PREVIEW**

Write each ratio as a fraction in simplest form. *(Section 6-1)*

25. 40 to 25   **26.** 37:3   **27.** 9 to 15

Find the square roots and the cube root of each number. *(Section 2-9)*

28. 25   **29.** 58   **30.** 72

Solve each equation. *(Section 5-6)*

31. $\frac{x}{19.5} = 37$ **32.** $27 = \frac{m}{-6}$ **33.** $\frac{n}{7} = -0.82$

Working on the Unit Project

Use the table.

34. a. Suppose a movie is showing on television. Find the probability that a movie viewer picked at random is an adult woman and the probability that the viewer is an adult man.

   b. Which event from part (a) has the greater probability? Are these complementary events? Why or why not?

35. Based on the data in the table, what kind of show do you think is most popular with teenagers? Give a reason for your answer.

36. Give two examples of how an advertiser could use the data shown.

Viewers (Thousands)

	Drama	Suspense/ Mystery	Comedy	News 6–7 P.M.	Movies
Women	9020	10,370	10,560	7270	10,730
Men	5890	7320	6530	5470	7230
Teens (12–17)	820	740	2070	380	1130
Children (2–11)	1400	1450	3400	790	1570
Total	17,130	19,880	22,560	13,910	20,660

Solving Proportions

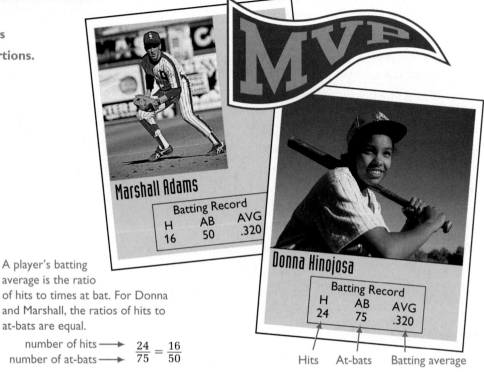

Marshall Adams

Batting Record		
H	AB	AVG
16	50	.320

Donna Hinojosa

Batting Record		
H	AB	AVG
24	75	.320

Hits   At-bats   Batting average

A player's batting average is the ratio of hits to times at bat. For Donna and Marshall, the ratios of hits to at-bats are equal.

number of hits ⟶ $\dfrac{24}{75} = \dfrac{16}{50}$
number of at-bats ⟶

A statement that two ratios are equal is a **proportion.** The batting averages proportion is read "24 is to 75 as 16 is to 50." The numbers 24, 75, 16, and 50 are the **terms of the proportion.**

Sometimes one of the terms of a proportion is not known. When you *solve* a proportion, you find the unknown term.

Sample 1

Solve the proportion $\dfrac{x}{15} = \dfrac{3}{4}$.

Sample Response

To get *x* alone on one side, undo the division.

$$\dfrac{x}{15} = \dfrac{3}{4}$$

$$\dfrac{x}{15} \cdot 15 = \dfrac{3}{4} \cdot 15 \quad \longleftarrow \text{ Multiply both sides by 15.}$$

$$x = 11.25$$

The solution is 11.25.

Check

$$\dfrac{x}{15} = \dfrac{3}{4}$$

$$\dfrac{11.25}{15} \stackrel{?}{=} \dfrac{3}{4} \quad \longleftarrow \text{ Substitute 11.25 for } x.$$

$$0.75 = 0.75 \ ✔$$

1. Describe a method for solving the proportion $\frac{x}{12} = \frac{3}{4}$ using mental math.

2. a. What is the lowest common denominator of the fractions in $\frac{x}{15} = \frac{3}{4}$?

   b. Multiply both sides of the proportion by the lowest common denominator of the fractions. Simplify the result. What is the new equation?

   c. Look at the expressions on both sides of the equation you wrote in part (b). How are the factors of these expressions related to the terms of the original proportion?

CROSS PRODUCTS OF A PROPORTION

For any proportion, the two **cross products** formed by multiplying the numerator of one fraction by the denominator of the other fraction are equal.

$$\frac{6}{2} \diagdown \frac{3}{1} \qquad\qquad \frac{a}{b} \diagdown \frac{c}{d}$$

$$6 \cdot 1 = 2 \cdot 3 \quad \longleftarrow \text{cross products} \longrightarrow \quad ad = bc$$

$$6 = 6$$

Sample 2

Solve the proportion $\frac{5}{6} = \frac{12}{y}$.

Sample Response

$$\frac{5}{6} = \frac{12}{y}$$

$$5 \cdot y = 6 \cdot 12 \quad \longleftarrow \text{Use cross products.}$$

$$5y = 72$$

$$\frac{5y}{5} = \frac{72}{5} \quad \longleftarrow \text{Divide both sides by 5.}$$

$$y = 14.4$$

The solution is 14.4.

3. Describe another way to solve the proportion in Sample 2.

4. Can you use cross products to solve $5 = \frac{12}{y}$? If so, how?

Latasha checks out a 145-page book from the library. She can read about 15 pages in 25 min. At this rate, about how long will it take Latasha to read the book?

Sample Response

Problem Solving Strategy: Use a proportion

The reading rates are the same for 15 pages and 145 pages. Therefore you can write a proportion.

Let t = the time it will take Latasha to read 145 pages.

number of pages $\longrightarrow$ $\dfrac{15}{25} = \dfrac{145}{t}$ $\longleftarrow$ time in minutes

Solve the proportion for t.

$$15 \cdot t = 25 \cdot 145 \qquad \longleftarrow \text{ Use cross products.}$$
$$15t = 3625$$
$$t \approx 242$$

60 min = 1 h
242 min = 4 h 2 min

Write 242 min as hours and minutes. It will take Latasha about 4 h to read the book.

Look Back

What is the difference between a ratio and a proportion? Describe three methods for solving a proportion.

6-3 Exercises and Problems

1. **Reading** What are the terms of the proportion $\frac{2}{3} = \frac{8}{12}$? Use cross products to rewrite the proportion.

2. **Writing** Describe how you could solve the proportion $\frac{37}{134} = \frac{23}{x}$ with a calculator.

Solve each proportion.

3. $\dfrac{x}{15} = \dfrac{60}{125}$

4. $\dfrac{2.59}{y} = \dfrac{5.92}{16}$

5. $\dfrac{18}{75} = \dfrac{300}{m}$

6. $\dfrac{1000}{18} = \dfrac{d}{0.036}$

7. $\dfrac{7}{18} = \dfrac{a}{6}$

8. $\dfrac{10}{t} = \dfrac{15}{32}$

For Exercises 9–12, use proportions A–D.

A. $\dfrac{6}{x} = \dfrac{84}{7}$ **B.** $\dfrac{x}{6} = \dfrac{84}{7}$

C. $\dfrac{6}{x} = \dfrac{7}{84}$ **D.** $\dfrac{x}{6} = \dfrac{7}{84}$

9. Which proportion has the same solution as proportion A?

10. Which proportion has the same solution as proportion B?

11. Write two other proportions that have the same solution and the same terms as proportion A.

12. Write two other proportions that have the same solution and the same terms as proportion B.

13. Write as many different proportions as you can that have a solution of 16 and whose terms are n, 36, 9, and 4.

Writing **Explain why proportional reasoning *is* or *is not* appropriate for each situation. If it is appropriate, write a proportion.**

14. If Cecilia walks 3 mi in 60 min, then Cecilia will walk 4.5 mi in 90 min.

15. If Tai is 86 cm tall when he is 3 years old, then Tai will be 430 cm tall when he is 15 years old.

16. If an 8 in. round pizza costs $6, then a 12 in. round pizza will cost $9.

17. If a car's gas mileage is 20 mi/gal at a speed of 30 mi/h, then it will be 40 mi/gal at a speed of 60 mi/h.

18. If a turkey weighs 25 lb standing on one leg, then it will weigh 50 lb standing on two legs.

19. If it takes 12 seconds to saw a log into 3 pieces, then it will take 16 seconds to saw a similar log into 4 pieces.

Solve using the problem solving strategy *Use a proportion.*

20. At the beginning of a basketball season, the Warriors won 11 games and lost 7. At this rate, how many games will they win in a normal 82-game season?

21. Running at a pace of 1 mi in 8 min, the average person burns 120 Cal/mi. How many minutes would a person have to run to burn off a 600 Cal meal?

22. Marla wanted to predict how many miles her car would travel on a full tank of gasoline. Her car's tank holds 14 gal of gasoline. She kept the record at the right and then averaged the amounts. How many miles did Marla predict her car would travel on a full tank?

gallons	miles
3.7	62.5
6.8	118.7
5.1	93.5

connection to **HEALTH**

To maintain good health it is important to eat properly and exercise regularly.

23. Nutritionists recommend that no more than 30% of total Calories consumed in a day come from fat. One gram of fat provides 9 Cal.

 a. A chicken sandwich that provides 427 Cal contains 19 g of fat. What percent of the Calories in the sandwich come from fat?

 b. Suppose that a person consumes 2000 Calories in one day. During lunch that day, the person eats two of the chicken sandwiches described in part (a). What percent of the total Calories for the day come from the fat in the chicken sandwiches?

 c. A different chicken sandwich has 40 g of fat and 55% of the Calories in the sandwich come from fat. How many Calories does the sandwich provide?

 d. Repeat part (b) for the chicken sandwich in part (c).

24. A single serving of Lite Recipe Fried Chicken that provides 199 Cal contains 13 g of fat. A single serving of Special Recipe Fried Chicken that provides 250 Cal contains 16 g of fat. Compare the percent of Calories from fat in a serving of Lite Recipe and a serving of Special Recipe.

 a. Complete this statement: The Lite Recipe is _?_ % lower in Calories than the Special Recipe.

 b. Complete this statement: The Lite Recipe is _?_ % lower in fat than the Special Recipe.

 c. What percent of the Calories in the Lite Recipe come from fat? in the Special Recipe?

25. Fitness Training The recommended maximum target heart rate for aerobic exercise is 80% of the maximum heart rate. To calculate the maximum heart rate, subtract age in years from 220.

 a. What is the maximum target heart rate for aerobic exercise for a person who is 22 years old?

 b. At what age is 140 the maximum target heart rate for aerobic exercise?

26. **Group Activity** Work in a group of four students. Translate the problem from Spanish into English. Then solve the problem. Try to answer the problem in both English and Spanish.

Resuelve usando una proporción.

Una máquina fotocopió 60 páginas en 1.5 min. A este ritmo, ¿cuánto tiempo tardará la máquina en fotocopiar 200 páginas?

27. **Open-ended** If someone in your group speaks a language other than English, write a proportion problem in that language. Work together to translate the problem into English. Answer the problem in both languages.

Ongoing ASSESSMENT

Open-ended Write a problem you could solve by using a proportion, the given information, and any additional information you want to include.

28. **Aviation** Aircraft carriers use 1 gal of fuel to travel 6 in.

29. **Access Standards** On signs indicating accessibility for the physically challenged, letters and numbers must have a width-to-height ratio between 3:5 and 1:1.

Review PREVIEW

A paper clip is chosen at random from a bag that contains 4 red paper clips, 3 green paper clips, 3 white paper clips, and 2 yellow paper clips. Find each probability. *(Section 6-2)*

30. P(yellow) 31. P(white or red) 32. P(not green)

Identify the control variable and the dependent variable for each function. *(Section 4-6)*

33. Sanjay is practicing for a race. He runs a mile in six minutes. The distance he runs on each practice run depends on how much time he runs.

34. Beryl charges $15 to mow a lawn. The more lawns she mows, the more money she earns.

Find each number. *(Toolbox Skill 14)*

35. 12% of 750 36. 25% of 4700 37. 5% of 1250

Working on the Unit Project

38. a. A typical cost for a 30-second commercial during prime time on network television is $100,000. At this rate, what would you expect the cost of a 45-second commercial to be?

b. Suppose a 30-second commercial will reach 300,000 teenage viewers. What is the cost per viewer?

39. **Research** Find the cost of a full-page ad in a local newspaper and how many copies of the newspaper are sold in a day. What is the cost per reader?

40. a. What do you think are some advantages of advertising on television? in a newspaper?

b. Why is it important for the advertiser to know the reading and viewing habits of the people who will buy the product?

Unit 6 CHECKPOINT

1. **Writing** Describe two types of ratios you have studied in this unit. In what ways are the types of ratios alike? How are they different?

2. The ratio of the measures of the acute angles of a right triangle is 13 : 5.

6-1

a. Find the measures of the two acute angles.

b. Find the ratio of the measure of the larger acute angle to the measure of the right angle.

Use the table from Sample 1 on page 308.

6-2

3. Suppose you pick a person at random from a database containing the names of all United States residents who are at least 25 years old. What is the probability that the person is male?

Find each probability.

The whole numbers from 10 through 49 are printed on separate slips of paper that are put into a box. Suppose you select one slip of paper at random from the box.

4. $P(\text{odd number})$ **5.** $P(\text{multiple of 5})$

6. $P(\text{not a multiple of 5})$

Solve each proportion.

6-3

7. $\dfrac{m}{3} = \dfrac{9}{30}$ **8.** $\dfrac{24}{15} = \dfrac{r}{2.5}$ **9.** $\dfrac{450}{800} = \dfrac{9}{z}$

10. In a 150-mile test drive, a new car model used 5.5 gal of gas. At this rate, how far can the new model travel on a full tank of 16.5 gal?

Section 6-4

Sampling and Making Predictions

Focus
Use sampling to make predictions.

Talk it Over

1. Describe some problems you might face if you tried to count all the whales in an ocean or all the squirrels in a city park.

2. **a.** What methods do you think you could use to estimate the size of a crowd?

   b. Could you use those methods to estimate the number of deer in a forest?

One way to estimate the number of deer in a forest is the *capture-recapture method.*

4. The biologists wait until the tagged deer have mixed with the other deer. Then they find a second group of deer and count how many in this group are tagged.

1. Suppose this diagram represents all the deer in a forest.

2. Wildlife biologists first find some deer and tag them.

3. Then the biologists release the tagged deer back into the forest.

Biologists use a proportion to estimate the total number of deer in the forest:

$$\frac{\text{tagged deer in second group}}{\text{total deer in second group}} = \frac{\text{tagged deer in forest}}{\text{total deer in forest}}$$

A whole group is called a **population.** A part of a group is a **sample.** When biologists study a group of deer, they are choosing a sample. The population is all the deer in the forest.

How can you estimate what you cannot see?

- **Materials: bags of dried beans, containers (bags or bowls that are not clear), nontoxic markers**
- **Work in a group of two to four students.**

(1) Pour a bag of beans into a container.

(2) Take out a handful of beans, mark them all, and record how many you marked.

(3) Put the beans back in the container. Mix the beans well.

(4) Take out another handful of beans. Record the total number of beans in the sample and how many are marked.

(5) Use this proportion to estimate the total number of beans (*x*) in the container.

$$\frac{\text{marked beans in handful}}{\text{total beans in handful}} = \frac{\text{marked beans in container}}{x}$$

Round your answer to the nearest whole number and record it.

(6) Repeat steps 3, 4, and 5 four times, to get five estimates in all.

(7) Find the mean of your five estimates.

(8) Count all the beans in the container. Compare your count with your estimates and the mean.

(9) What do you think would happen to the mean if you repeated steps 3, 4, and 5 one hundred times?

····► Now you are ready for:
Exs. 1–4 on p. 325

Sampling

Choosing a sample is called **sampling.** Data collected about a sample can be used to make predictions about a population. Samples are often used to take opinion polls, test the quality of a product, and find out what people buy.

Sample 1

A media rating service found that 860 of a sample of 4000 households with a TV watched a certain program one night. Estimate how many of the 93.1 million households in the United States with a TV watched this program that night.

Sample Response

Problem Solving Strategy: Use a proportion

Let n = millions of households with a TV that watched the program.

$$\frac{\text{households in sample that watched the program}}{\text{total households in sample}} = \frac{\text{households with a TV that watched the program (millions)}}{\text{total households with a TV (millions)}}$$

$$\frac{860}{4000} = \frac{n}{93.1}$$

$$\left(\frac{860}{4000}\right)(93.1) = \left(\frac{n}{93.1}\right)(93.1) \quad \longleftarrow \text{ Multiply both sides by 93.1.}$$

$$20.0 \approx n$$

About 20 million households watched the program.

Margin of Error

When polls are based on samples, the results are estimates. Estimates always contain some error. The **margin of error** estimates the interval that is most likely to include the exact result for the population.

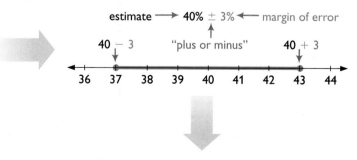

The interval is "about 37% to 43%."

Sample 2

A quality tester finds 3 faulty bulbs in a sample of 50 light bulbs. Suppose the margin of error is 2%. Estimate the interval that contains the number of faulty bulbs in the lot of 2000.

Sample Response

Method ❶

Problem Solving Strategy: Use a proportion

Let x = the number of faulty bulbs in the lot.

faulty bulbs in sample ⟶ $\dfrac{3}{50} = \dfrac{x}{2000}$ ⟵ faulty bulbs in lot
total bulbs in sample ⟶ ⟵ total bulbs in lot

$$\frac{3}{50} \cdot 2000 = \frac{x}{2000} \cdot 2000 \quad \longleftarrow \text{Multiply both sides by 2000.}$$

$$120 = x$$

Use the margin of error to estimate the interval.

$$2\% \text{ of } 2000 = (0.02)(2000) = 40$$

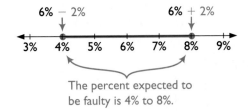

About 80 to 160 light bulbs are faulty.

Method ❷

Use percents.

First find what percent of the sample are faulty.

faulty bulbs in sample ⟶ $\dfrac{3}{50} = 0.06 = 6\%$
total bulbs in sample ⟶

Next use the 2% margin of error to estimate the interval.

The percent expected to be faulty is 4% to 8%.

Then estimate the number of faulty bulbs.

$$4\% \text{ of } 2000 = (0.04)(2000) = 80$$

$$8\% \text{ of } 2000 = (0.08)(2000) = 160$$

About 80 to 160 light bulbs are faulty.

Unit 6 Ratios, Probability, and Similarity

3. What would change in Method 1 if you used cross products?

4. If the margin of error in Sample 2 were 4%, would the estimate be more or less certain? Why?

······▶ Now you are ready for:
Exs. 5–17 on pp. 325–327

Look Back ◀

Suppose you are a member of Congress trying to decide whether to support a bill. How could you use a sample to estimate how many voters in your district favor the bill? Why would you want to know the margin of error?

6-4 Exercises and Problems

1. **a.** In the Exploration, what is the sample?

   b. In the Exploration, what is the population?

2. **Writing** Explain how the Exploration is like the method used by biologists to estimate the number of deer in a forest.

3. **Reading** Compare how the word *population* is used in this section with the way it is used in everyday language.

4. Biologists captured 400 penguins, tagged them, and released them back into the same region. Later, the penguin population of the region was sampled once a month for four months.

	Month 1	Month 2	Month 3	Month 4
Size of sample	200	100	150	100
Tagged animals in sample	50	30	45	24

   a. Estimate the size of the population of penguins in the region for each month.

   b. Find the mean of the four estimates you made in part (a).

   c. Suppose the biologists combine the four samples into one large sample. Estimate the size of the penguin population in the region.

   d. Compare your answers in parts (b) and (c).

5. A town's high school has 627 students. A sample of 200 people living in the town is picked at random. Of the 200, 40 are students at the high school.

   a. About how many people live in the town?

   b. Estimate an interval for the number of people living in the town. Assume a 4% margin of error.

6. **Writing** A bag contains 200 cubes of various colors. A person picked 15 cubes at random. The colors of the cubes are shown in the table. About how many green cubes do you think are in the bag? How did you get your answer?

red	⌁⌁⌁
green	IIII
blue	⌁⌁

connection to SOCIAL STUDIES

Exit polling is used to predict who will win an election. In an exit poll, people leaving a voting place are asked how they voted.

7. In one exit poll, a sample of 400 voters was polled out of about 483,000 people voting in the election. The table shows the results. The margin of error is 6%.

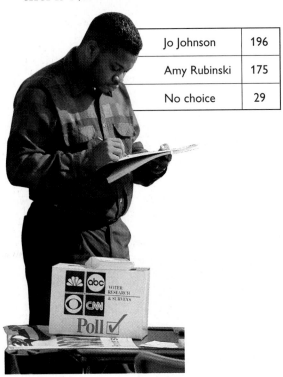

Jo Johnson	196
Amy Rubinski	175
No choice	29

a. Estimate the interval for the number of votes expected to go to Jo Johnson.

b. Whom do you expect to win the election? Explain your choice.

c. In a poll taken before the election, a sample of 400 out of about 1,295,000 registered voters were asked which candidate they supported. This poll predicted that Amy Rubinski would win by a wide margin. Give as many reasons as you can why the result does not agree with the exit poll.

8. **Research** Find out what percent of the people in your state who are eligible to vote are registered voters, and what percent of the registered voters voted in the last national election. Do the results surprise you?

9. **Career** A quality tester tests a random sample of 20 items. The graph shows the results. Item numbers are on the horizontal axis and item weights in grams are on the vertical axis. Each item should weigh 10 g, but any weight in the interval 10 ± 0.1 g is acceptable. There are 4000 items in the lot. Estimate the number of unacceptable items in the lot.

10. **Open-ended** Market researchers use samples to predict which products people will buy.

   a. **Research** Sample 30 students in your school. Ask which brand of sneaker or other product they prefer.

   b. Make a bar graph to show the results.

   c. Which brand did most students prefer?

   d. **Research** Find out how many students are in your school. Use the results shown in part (b) to predict the number of students in your school who prefer the brand in part (c).

········
Review **PREVIEW**

Solve each proportion. *(Section 6-3)*

11. $\frac{4}{5} = \frac{x}{45}$ **12.** $\frac{x}{34} = \frac{6}{13}$ **13.** $\frac{42}{70} = \frac{18}{x}$

14. List the pairs of corresponding vertices. *(Section 1-6)*

$\triangle RST \cong \triangle XYZ$

Find the perimeter of each rectangle. *(Toolbox Skill 17)*

15.   **16.**

 Working on the Unit Project

17. **Group Activity** Work with the whole class.

   a. Use the daily records of television and newspaper or magazine ads kept by you and your classmates. Which TV programs, magazines, and newspapers are the most popular? What types of products are advertised on or in them?

   b. **Research** Find out the total number of students in your school. Using your class as a sample, estimate the total number of students in the school who watch the most popular programs and read the most popular newspapers and magazines.

   c. Do you think the daily records kept by you and your classmates is a good sample for predicting the viewing and reading habits of teenagers throughout the country? Why or why not?

BY THE WAY...

Every time a song is played on the radio or TV, the songwriter receives a royalty payment. The royalties are estimated by sampling.

6-5

Similar Polygons

Focus

Apply proportions to problems using similar figures and scale drawings.

$2\frac{1}{2}$ in.

Photograph editors change the size of a photograph to fit in a column on a textbook, newspaper, or magazine page.

For a magazine article, this photograph of Ida B. Wells is enlarged to fill a $2\frac{1}{2}$ in. wide column.

To determine the new size, the editor may use a ruler to extend the diagonal of the photograph across the width of the column.

BY THE WAY...

Ida B. Wells lived from 1862 to 1931. She took part in the meeting that led to the founding of the NAACP. The Ida B. Wells apartment complex in Chicago is named for her.

EXPLORATION

What happens to a photograph when you enlarge it?

- **Work with another student.**
- **Materials: rulers, protractors**

	Height	Width
Enlarged Photo	?	?
Original Photo	?	?
$\dfrac{\text{Enlarged Photo}}{\text{Original Photo}}$	?	?

① Measure the widths and the heights of the original photo and the enlarged photo. Record your results in a table.

② Complete the third column. What do you notice about the ratios?

③ Measure the four angles of the original photo. Then measure the corresponding angles of the enlarged photo. What do you notice about the measures of the corresponding angles?

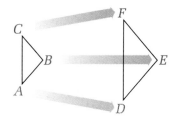

The original photo and the enlarged photo have the same shape. Two figures with the same shape are called **similar figures.** Similar figures may be the same size or different sizes.

You say, "triangle *ABC* is similar to triangle *DEF*."

You write △*ABC* ~ △*DEF*.

The symbol ~ means "is similar to."

Remember that the order of the vertices in the names of the triangles shows the corresponding parts.

PROPERTIES OF SIMILAR POLYGONS

➤ Corresponding angles are congruent.

➤ Corresponding sides are *in proportion.* Their lengths have the same ratio.

Sample 1

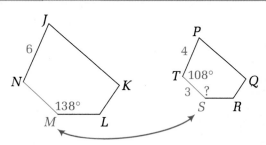

Polygon *JKLMN* ~ polygon *PQRST*. Find each measure.

a. ∠*S*   b. *NM*

Sample Response

a. ∠*S* corresponds to ∠*M*, so they have the same measure. ∠*M* = 138°, so ∠*S* = 138°.

b. **Problem Solving Strategy:** Use a proportion

Write a proportion using the lengths of $\overline{NM}$ and the corresponding sides whose lengths are given.

smaller polygon ⟶
larger polygon ⟶ $\dfrac{PT}{JN} = \dfrac{TS}{NM}$

Solve the proportion for *NM*.

$$\frac{4}{6} = \frac{3}{NM}$$ ⟵ Substitute the lengths you know.

$$4 \cdot NM = 18$$ ⟵ Use cross products.

$$NM = 4.5$$ ⟵ Divide both sides by 4.

6-5 Similar Polygons

1. What type of polygon is shown in Sample 1 on page 329?

2. List all the corresponding angles and corresponding sides of the similar polygons in Sample 1.

3. These triangles are congruent.

   a. What is the ratio of the lengths of the corresponding sides? What can you say about the measures of the corresponding angles?

   b. Are the triangles similar? Explain.

·······► Now you are ready for:
Exs. 1–9 on pp. 332–333

Scale Drawings

A **scale drawing** represents an actual object. A scale drawing of your classroom floor *is similar to* the floor of the room. The **scale** is the ratio of the size of the drawing to the actual size of the object. You might see scales written in several ways.

1 in.:40 ft   1 in. = 40 ft

├—— 40 ft ——┤

0   40 ft

Sample 2

What is the actual length of Store 10 in the Palm Court mall to the nearest foot?

scale: 1 in. = 40 ft

Problem Solving Strategy: Use a proportion

Write a proportion using the scale and the length of Store 10 in the drawing.

Use a ruler to measure Store 10. The scale shows that 1 in. on the drawing represents 40 ft in the actual mall.

Let a = the actual length of the store.

scale drawing measurements (in.) $\longrightarrow$ $\dfrac{1}{40} = \dfrac{1\frac{15}{16}}{a}$ $\longleftarrow$ In the scale drawing, the store is $1\frac{15}{16}$ in. long.
actual measurements (ft) $\longrightarrow$

Solve the proportion for a.

$$1 \cdot a = \left(1\frac{15}{16}\right)(40) \qquad \longleftarrow \text{ Use cross products.}$$
$$a = (1.9375)(40) \qquad \longleftarrow 1\frac{15}{16} = 1.9375$$
$$a = 77.5$$

Store 10 is about 78 ft long.

> **Talk it Over**
>
> **4.** Describe how to find the actual area of Store 18.
>
> **5.** Suppose the scale of the drawing in Sample 2 were $\frac{3}{4}$ in. = 40 ft. How would the proportion be different?

Indirect Measurement

Would you ever consider measuring the height of a tree or building using a ruler or tape measure? Probably not. Similar triangles give you a way to measure an object indirectly. To use indirect measurement, you need to know this important fact:

A TEST FOR SIMILAR TRIANGLES

Two triangles are similar whenever two angles of one triangle are congruent to two angles of the other triangle.

(Not drawn to scale)

├─0.3m

├── 4.5m ──┤

Karen, Lydia, and Dion are planning a mural for the side of a building. To estimate the height of the building, the students measured the length of a meter stick's shadow and the length of the building's shadow. Estimate the height of the building.

Sample Response

Problem Solving Strategy: Make a sketch

Your sketch will probably not be in the correct scale.

Write a proportion using the heights and the shadows.

Let h = the height of the building.

height of building ⟶ $\dfrac{h}{1} = \dfrac{4.5}{0.3}$ ⟵ building's shadow
height of stick ⟶ ⟵ stick's shadow

Solve the proportion for h.

$$h = 15$$

The building is about 15 m tall.

The sun's rays hit the ground at the same angle. The triangles formed are similar because two pairs of angles are congruent.

Look Back

Measure each side and each angle in the polygons at the right. Record the measurements and compare them. Which polygons are similar?

······▶ **Now you are ready for:**
Exs. 10–33 on pp. 333–336

················

6-5 # Exercises and Problems

1. a. **Reading** The symbol ≅ means "is congruent to." What is the symbol for "is similar to"?

   b. **Writing** Discuss how similarity and congruence are alike and how they are different. How do the symbols show this relationship?

2. Other proportions could have been used in part (b) of Sample 1 on page 329. Which of these could *not* have been used? Why?

   A. $\dfrac{JN}{PT} = \dfrac{MN}{TS}$ **B.** $\dfrac{PT}{TS} = \dfrac{JN}{NM}$ **C.** $\dfrac{PT}{TS} = \dfrac{NM}{JN}$ **D.** $\dfrac{TS}{PT} = \dfrac{NM}{JN}$

**Pentagon *JKLMN* ~ pentagon *PQRST*.
Find each measure.**

3. ∠*P*   4. ∠*L*

5. *PQ*   6. *KL*

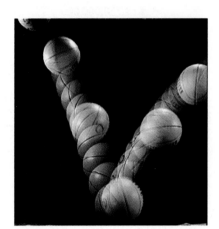

7. A basketball player "bounce passes" a ball to a player 6 m away as shown in the diagram. Can the other player easily catch the pass? Explain why or why not.

(*Hint:* From physics, the angles that the ball makes with the floor are congruent.)

1.5 m

2 m

6 m

8. **Using Manipulatives** Use a geoboard and rubber bands.

   Alternative Approach Use graph paper.

   How many rectangles similar to the one shown can be made on a 5 × 5 geoboard?

9. TECHNOLOGY Use geometric drawing software.

   Alternative Approach Work in groups using rulers and graph paper.

   Find the dimensions of a rectangle that can be cut into two congruent rectangles so that each is similar to the original rectangle.

---

connection to **BIOLOGY**

Use the drawing of a grasshopper.

10. Is the actual grasshopper larger or smaller than the scale drawing?

11. What does the scale 2:1 mean?

12. Describe how to find the actual length of the grasshopper.

13. About how long is one of the actual grasshopper's antennae?

14. **Research** Find a scale drawing in one of your textbooks. Explain what the scale means. Then use the scale to find an actual measurement.

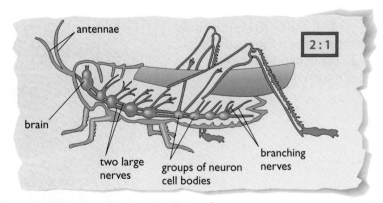

antennae

2:1

brain

two large nerves

groups of neuron cell bodies

branching nerves

Use the information below.

Miniature houses and furniture are usually built in one of three scales:

one-inch scale	half-inch scale	quarter-inch scale
1 in.:1 ft	$\frac{1}{2}$ in.:1 ft	$\frac{1}{4}$ in.:1 ft

These scales show the length of the miniature that represents 1 ft of the length of the full-size object.

15. Replace each _?_ with the correct number of feet.

    a. Half-inch scale is the same as 1 in.: _?_ ft.

    b. Quarter-inch scale is the same as 1 in.: _?_ ft.

16. How much longer is an object when it is built in one-inch scale than when it is built in half-inch scale?

17. The miniature Chinese table is being built in quarter-inch scale. A scale drawing of the miniature tabletop is shown.

    a. What are the length and width of the miniature table?

    b. How wide would the full-size table be?

    c. How long would the full-size table be?

$\frac{15}{32}$ in.   Miniature tabletop

$\frac{11}{32}$ in.

18. **Using Manipulatives** Measure a penny at its widest part. Then measure the penny in the photograph. Measure the length and width of the painting in the photograph. (Do not include the frame.) Estimate the length and width of the miniature painting.

Writing Explain why each pair of triangles is similar.
Then find the unknown length.

19.

25 m

d

6 m

12 m

20.

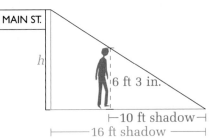

MAIN ST.

h

6 ft 3 in.

10 ft shadow

16 ft shadow

connection to **LITERATURE**

In *The Musgrave Ritual*, Sherlock Holmes uses mathematics to find some hidden objects. Here is his description of the process.

THE MUSGRAVE RITUAL

There were two guides given us to start with, an oak and an elm. Right in front of the house, ... stood a patriarch among oaks...

'Have you any old elms?' I asked.

'There used to be a very old one over yonder ... It was sixty-four feet.' [said Musgrave]

'How do you come to know it?' I asked in surprise.

'When my old tutor used to give me an exercise in trigonometry, it always took the shape of measuring heights.' [said Musgrave]

This was an unexpected piece of luck. ... I had, then, to find where the far end of the shadow would fall when the sun was just clear of the oak.

I ... whittled ... this peg, to which I tied this long string ... Then I took ... a fishing-rod, which came to just six feet, and I went back ... to where the elm had been. The sun was just grazing the top of the oak. I fastened the rod on end, marked out the direction of the shadow, and measured. It was nine feet in length.

Of course the calculation now was a simple one. If a rod of six feet threw a shadow of nine [feet], a tree of sixty-four feet would throw one of ninety-six [feet], and the line of the one [shadow] would of course be the line of the other. I measured out the distance ... and I thrust a peg into the spot.

21. Sherlock Holmes used shadows and indirect measurement to find an unknown length. Describe the objects and the method he used.

22. Make a sketch of the objects and the shadows in the story. Label all measurements. Be sure that the sketch is drawn to scale.

23. Show why Holmes's calculation of the unknown length is correct.

24. **Research** Read the entire story *The Musgrave Ritual*. What other measurements did Sherlock Holmes make? What were the objects that were hidden? What was their place in history?

Writing **Suppose you want to make a scale model of each object described. What scale would you use to make a model of reasonable size? Explain.**

25. a stadium that contains a rectangular field that is 110 yd by 80 yd

26. a car that is 13 ft 4 in. long and 5 ft high

27. the planet Jupiter, whose diameter is about 142,700 km

28. a red blood cell whose "thickness" is 9×10^{-6} m

Review **PREVIEW**

29. A marketing survey found that 525 people out of 2200 prefer clear dishwashing liquid. Estimate how many people out of a population of 2.5 million prefer clear dishwashing liquid. *(Section 6-4)*

30. Find the mean, median, and mode of these test scores. *(Section 3-2)*

76	84	65	87	84	58
92	74	76	84	94	70
68	80	84	76	82	90

31. Plot the points $(-3, 3)$, $(5, 3)$, $(0, -1)$, and $(-8, -1)$ on a coordinate plane. Connect the points in order and connect the last point to the first. Write the name of the polygon you formed. *(Section 4-2)*

 Working on the Unit Project

The cost of a newspaper ad is usually related to its size. The size is measured in *column inches*. One column inch is $2\frac{1}{16}$ in. wide (the width of one column of print in the newspaper) and 1 in. long.

32. a. An ad spreads across 2 columns and is 4 in. deep. Another ad spreads across 4 columns and is 2 in. deep. Are the ads similar? Explain.

   b. Which of the ads described in part (a) has a greater area?

33. In one newspaper, a full-page ad is 216 column inches. Is it similar to a quarter-page ad? to a half-page ad? Explain why or why not.

> # The Times
>
> Ida B. Wells, the daughter of a slave, began to write against lynchings in her newspaper, the *Memphis Free Speech.* Her outspoken attitude led to death threats and to the bombing of her newspaper's office while she was away speaking in the North. Wells did not return to the South. She set herself up in Chicago where she went on writing and speaking against lynching.
>
>   Lynching was not only a Southern crime, however. In Springfield, Illinois, the home of President Lincoln, in 1908

1 in.

1 column inch

$2\frac{1}{16}$ in.

Focus

Change the size of a figure without changing its shape.

Dilations

A drawing created on a computer is called a *graphic*. With most computer drawing software, you stretch or shrink a graphic by dragging a *handle* on a side or corner of its *bounding box*.

Lines drawn through corresponding points on the original figure and its image meet in a point called the **center of dilation.**

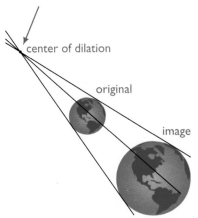

center of dilation

original

image

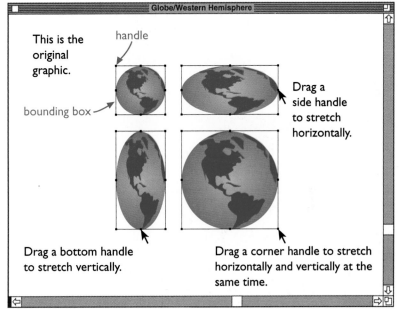

Globe/Western Hemisphere

This is the original graphic.

handle

bounding box

Drag a side handle to stretch horizontally.

Drag a bottom handle to stretch vertically.

Drag a corner handle to stretch horizontally and vertically at the same time.

Talk it Over

1. Compare the horizontal and vertical dimensions of the globe in the original graphic with its dimensions in each stretched graphic.

2. Are any of the stretched graphics congruent to the original? Are any of them similar to the original?

The result of a transformation is called an **image**. A **dilation** is a transformation in which the original figure and its image are similar.

The ratio of any length on the image to the corresponding length on the original figure is the **scale factor** of the dilation.

$$\text{scale factor for the globes} = \frac{\text{length on image}}{\text{length on original}}$$

$$= \frac{2}{1}$$

Enlargements and Reductions

When the image of a dilation is larger than the original figure, the dilation is an *enlargement*. The dilation on page 337 with scale factor $\frac{2}{1}$ is an enlargement. When the image is smaller than the original figure, the dilation is a *reduction*.

Sample 1

Draw a dilation of △ ABC with center P and scale factor 3.

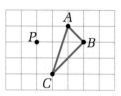

Sample Response

1 Copy the figure onto graph paper.

2 Draw rays from P through each vertex of △ABC.

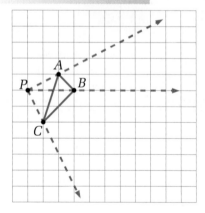

3 The scale factor is 3. Mark A' on $\overrightarrow{PA}$, B' on $\overrightarrow{PB}$, and C' on $\overrightarrow{PC}$.

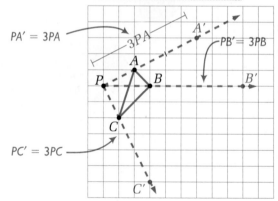

$PA' = 3PA$

$PB' = 3PB$

$PC' = 3PC$

4 Connect A', B', and C' to form the image, △A'B'C'.

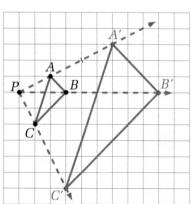

Draw a dilation of *JKLM* with center *J* and scale factor $\frac{1}{2}$.

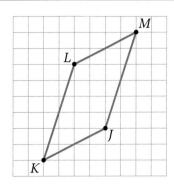

Sample Response

1 Copy the figure onto graph paper.

2 Draw rays from *J* through *K*, *L*, and *M*.

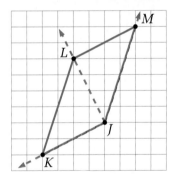

3 The scale factor is $\frac{1}{2}$.

Mark *K'* on $\overrightarrow{JK}$, *L'* on $\overrightarrow{JL}$, and *M'* on $\overrightarrow{JM}$.

$JL' = \frac{1}{2}JL$

$JM' = \frac{1}{2}JM$

$JK' = \frac{1}{2}JK$

4 Connect *J'*, *K'*, *L'*, and *M'* to form the image, quadrilateral *J'K'L'M'*.

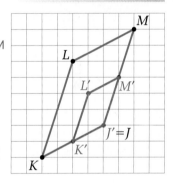

Talk it Over

Use Samples 1 and 2 to answer questions 3 and 4.

3. Check that $\triangle ABC$ and $\triangle A'B'C'$ are similar. Measure the sides and angles of the original figure and its image. Are the corresponding sides in proportion? Are the corresponding angles congruent? Also check *JKLM* and *J'K'L'M'*.

4. a. Which dilation is an enlargement?

   b. Which dilation is a reduction?

   c. Describe the scale factors that result in enlargements.

   d. Describe the scale factors that result in reductions.

5. In the dilations shown on page 337 and in Sample 1, the center of dilation is *outside* the original figure. In Sample 2, the center of dilation is *on* the original figure.

   Copy this figure onto graph paper. Draw a dilation where the center of dilation is *inside* the original figure.

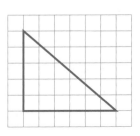

Look Back ◄

In Section 6-5 on page 328, a rectangular photograph was enlarged by drawing a diagonal through the rectangle. Where is the center of the dilation? What is the scale factor?

6-6 Exercises and Problems

1. **Reading** In the diagram at the top of page 337, which of the stretched graphics is an image of the original figure under a dilation?

Does each diagram show a *dilation*, a *rotation*, or a *translation*? There may be more than one answer.

2.

3.

4.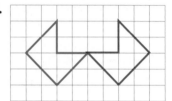

For Exercises 5–7, the blue figure is the original figure.

a. **State the coordinates of the center of the dilation.**

b. **Find the scale factor.**

5.

6.

7.

8. Use proportions to find the missing lengths in this dilation.

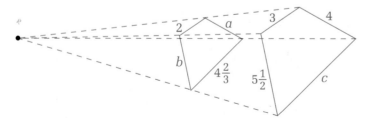

Draw a dilation of each polygon with the given center of dilation and scale factor.

9. center $R(2, 5)$; scale factor 2

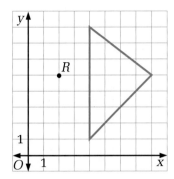

10. center $X(-4, -1)$; scale factor $\frac{1}{2}$

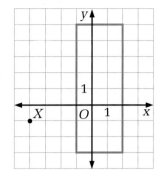

11. vertices $A(7, -1)$, $B(-1, 7)$, $C(-5, 3)$, $D(-1, -9)$; center $A(7, -1)$; scale factor $\frac{1}{4}$

12. vertices $A(3, 1)$, $B(2, 3)$, $C(0, 0)$; center $P(5, 5)$; scale factor 3

connection to **ART**

13. One way to create the illusion of a three-dimensional object is to draw it in *one-point perspective.*

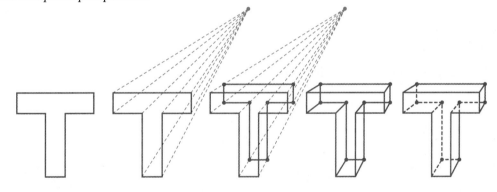

   a. On graph paper, draw your initials using block letters.

   b. Choose a center of dilation. This is called the *vanishing point.*

   c. Draw rays from the vanishing point through the vertices of the letters.

   d. Draw a reduction of the letter by locating image points on the rays. (*Hint:* Corresponding edges should be parallel.)

   e. Connect the original and image letters by joining corresponding vertices.

   f. Erase hidden lines.

   g. Color your three-dimensional initials in a creative way.

14. **Research** Measure the dimensions of a photographic negative and a photograph that has been made from it. Is the process a dilation? How can you tell?

BY THE WAY...

One of the first people to write about the geometric method of perspective drawing was Leon Battista Alberti, an Italian architect and artist.

15. **Using Manipulatives** Draw a diagonal across a rectangular sheet of paper. Mark any point on the diagonal. Make horizontal and vertical folds through the point. Unfold the paper.

   a. The two folds divide your paper into four rectangles. Which of the rectangles are similar to the original sheet of paper?

   b. Suppose that each rectangle you found in part (a) is the image of a dilation of the original sheet of paper. For each dilation, find the center of dilation and the scale factor.

16. **Open-ended** Draw a polygon on a coordinate plane. Mark a center of dilation.

   a. Draw two different dilations of your polygon. Use the same center of dilation but use two different scale factors. Label the new polygons with primes.

   b. Name some similar polygons in your diagram.

   c. Write some proportions that compare the lengths of sides in your diagram.

17. $\triangle ABC \sim \triangle DEF$. Find all the missing side and angle measures. *(Section 6-5)*

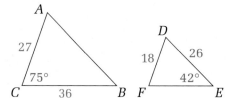

Solve. *(Section 5-3)*

18. $2x - 8 = x + 16$ 19. $e + 8 = 3e - 14$ 20. $3a + 7 = -2a - 38$

Write each ratio in simplest form. *(Section 6-1)*

21. $\frac{6}{36}$ 22. 14 to 21   23. $63:84$

Working on the Unit Project

24. a. Make a sketch of an ad for your product or trace a simple ad. Dilate the sketch with a scale factor of 2 and a center of dilation at one corner of the ad. Which size is more effective, the original or the enlargement?

   b. Suppose you want to put the ad on a billboard. What scale factor might you use?

6-7

Sine and Cosine Ratios

RIGHT ON

EXPLORATION

(What) relationships are there between the *sides of similar right triangles?*

- **Materials: graph paper, protractors**
- **Work with another student.**

1 Draw a right triangle ABC with $\angle C = 90°$, $AC = 3$, and $\angle A = 53°$. Draw straight lines. Call this triangle $\triangle 1$.

2 Draw three more right triangles similar to $\triangle 1$ using different lengths for side AC. Call the triangles $\triangle 2$, $\triangle 3$, and $\triangle 4$.

3 Use a strip of graph paper to measure the lengths of the sides of each triangle to the nearest half unit. Find the ratios $\frac{AC}{AB}$ and $\frac{BC}{AB}$ to the nearest hundredth. Make and complete a table like this one.

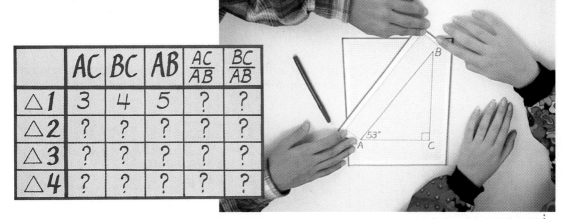

	AC	BC	AB	$\frac{AC}{AB}$	$\frac{BC}{AB}$
△1	3	4	5	?	?
△2	?	?	?	?	?
△3	?	?	?	?	?
△4	?	?	?	?	?

4 Do you see any pattern in the ratios $\frac{AC}{AB}$? in the ratios $\frac{BC}{AB}$?

5 Suppose you draw any size right triangle $\triangle ABC$ with $\angle A = 53°$. Predict the ratios $\frac{AC}{AB}$ and $\frac{BC}{AB}$ for the triangle.

For each right triangle in the Exploration, the measure of ∠A is 53°. In each triangle, $\overline{AB}$ is the **hypotenuse** because it is opposite the right angle. $\overline{AC}$ and $\overline{BC}$ are the **legs** of the right triangle.

The ratios $\frac{AC}{AB}$ and $\frac{BC}{AB}$ depend only on the measure of ∠A and not on the lengths of the sides of the triangle. These ratios have special names.

The **sine** of an acute angle of a right triangle is the ratio of the length of the opposite leg to the length of the hypotenuse. The **cosine** of an acute angle of a right triangle is the ratio of the length of the adjacent leg to the length of the hypotenuse.

SINE AND COSINE RATIOS

The sine of ∠A is written *sin A*.

$$\sin A = \frac{\text{leg opposite } \angle A}{\text{hypotenuse}} = \frac{BC}{AB}$$

The cosine of ∠A is written *cos A*.

$$\cos A = \frac{\text{leg adjacent to } \angle A}{\text{hypotenuse}} = \frac{AC}{AB}$$

hypotenuse

leg opposite ∠A

leg adjacent to ∠A

The sine and cosine ratios are called **trigonometric ratios.** They are programmed into your scientific calculator.

TECHNOLOGY NOTE

To find the value of sin 53° on most calculators, make sure the calculator is in degree mode, then press

53 [sin]

or

[SIN] 53 [ENTER]

Talk it Over

1. **a.** Use a calculator to find sin 53°. (Be sure your calculator is in degree mode.)

   b. Compare your answer in part (a) with the ratios $\frac{BC}{AB}$ in the Exploration. Why might the values be slightly different?

2. **a.** Use a calculator to find cos 53°.

   b. Compare your answer in part (a) with the ratios $\frac{AC}{AB}$ in the Exploration.

3. In △ABC above, which leg is opposite ∠B? Which leg is adjacent to ∠B?

Write each trigonometric ratio as a fraction and as a decimal rounded to the nearest hundredth.

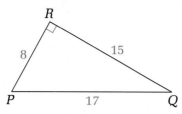

a. sin *P*

b. cos *P*

c. sin *Q*

d. cos *Q*

Sample Response

a. sin $P = \dfrac{\text{leg opposite } \angle P}{\text{hypotenuse}} = \dfrac{15}{17} \approx 0.88$

b. cos $P = \dfrac{\text{leg adjacent to } \angle P}{\text{hypotenuse}} = \dfrac{8}{17} \approx 0.47$

c. sin $Q = \dfrac{\text{leg opposite} \angle Q}{\text{hypotenuse}} = \dfrac{8}{17} \approx 0.47$

d. cos $Q = \dfrac{\text{leg adjacent to } \angle Q}{\text{hypotenuse}} = \dfrac{15}{17} \approx 0.88$

Talk it Over

4. Find the values of cos *K*, sin *K*, cos *L*, and sin *L* for this triangle. What do you notice about the ratios?

5. Suppose you know only the sine of an acute angle of a right triangle. How can you tell what the cosine of the other acute angle is?

6. In the Exploration, $\angle B = 37°$. Predict the values of sin 37° and cos 37°. Test your predictions on your calculator.

7. Do you think the values for the sine or the cosine of an angle in a right triangle can be greater than 1? Explain your reasoning.

▸ Now you are ready for:
Exs. 1–15 on pp. 348–349

To be used safely, a ladder should make an angle of about 75° with the ground. What is the maximum height that a 12-foot ladder can reach safely when it leans against a building?

Sample Response

Problem Solving Strategy: Make a sketch

maximum height

75°

Label the unknown height *h*.

12   *h*

75°

Use the sketch to decide which trigonometric ratio to use to solve the problem. In this problem, you know the measure of an acute angle and the length of the hypotenuse (the ladder). You need to find the height, *h*, which is the leg *opposite* the angle. The leg opposite the angle is part of the sine ratio.

$$\sin 75° = \frac{h}{12}$$ ◄——— Use the sine ratio: $\frac{\text{opposite}}{\text{hypotenuse}}$.

$$0.9659 \approx \frac{h}{12}$$ ◄——— Use the **SIN** key on your calculator.

$$(0.9659)(12) \approx (\frac{h}{12})(12)$$ ◄——— Multiply both sides by 12.

$$11.6 \approx h$$ ◄——— Round to the nearest tenth.

The maximum safe height is about 11.6 ft, or about 11 ft 7 in.

Talk it Over

8. Suppose the measure of the angle that the ladder in Sample 2 makes with the ground were greater than 75°. Would the foot of the ladder be farther from or closer to the base of the building?

9. How can you use the cosine ratio to find the distance between the foot of the ladder and the base of the building?

A wheelchair ramp makes a 4° angle with the ground. The beginning of the ramp is 366 cm away from the end of the ramp. What is the length of the ramp to the nearest centimeter?

Sample Response

Problem Solving Strategy: Make a sketch

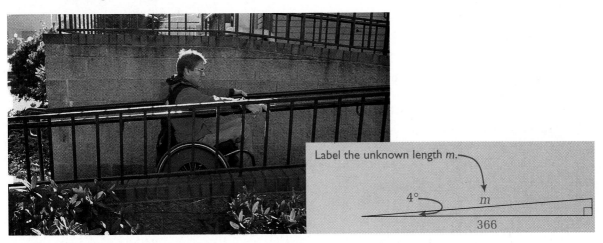

Label the unknown length m.

4° m

366

A right triangle is formed by the ramp and the ground. Use the sketch to decide which trigonometric ratio to use to solve the problem.

You want to find the ramp length, which is the hypotenuse of the triangle and is represented by m. You know the measure of the angle and the length of the leg adjacent to the angle. The leg adjacent to the angle is part of the cosine ratio.

$$\cos 4° = \frac{366}{m}$$ ◄—— Use the cosine ratio: $\frac{\text{adjacent}}{\text{hypotenuse}}$.

$$0.9976 \approx \frac{366}{m}$$ ◄—— Use the **COS** key on your calculator.

$$(0.9976)(m) \approx \left(\frac{366}{m}\right)(m)$$ ◄—— Multiply both sides by m to remove m from the denominator.

$$0.9976\,m \approx 366$$

$$\frac{0.9976\,m}{0.9976} \approx \frac{366}{0.9976}$$ ◄—— Divide both sides by 0.9976.

$$m \approx 367$$ ◄—— Round to the nearest centimeter.

The length of the ramp is about 367 cm.

Talk it Over

10. Suppose you know the length of a wheelchair ramp and the measure of the angle it makes with the ground. Which trigonometric ratio would you use to find the height of the ramp at its highest point? Explain your reasoning.

Now you are ready for
Exs. 16–29 on pp. 349–350

Look Back

Review the problem in Sample 2. What made it possible to solve the problem by using the sine ratio? What other measurements can you find from the given information?

6-7 Exercises and Problems

1. **Reading** Look back at the Sherlock Holmes story on page 335. How did Musgrave use trigonometry when he was a boy? What trigonometric ratios did you learn about in this section?

2. **Research** The Exploration with triangles led you to some special ratios. Use a dictionary to find the origin of the word "trigonometry." Why do you think sine and cosine are called trigonometric ratios?

Use a calculator to write each ratio as a decimal rounded to hundredths.

3. $\sin 32°$ 4. $\sin 85°$ 5. $\cos 10°$ 6. $\cos 63°$

Write each ratio as a fraction and as a decimal rounded to hundredths.

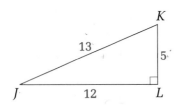

7. $\sin J$ 8. $\sin K$ 9. $\cos K$ 10. $\cos J$

11. **Open-ended** Use a ruler and protractor.

    a. Draw any right triangle. Label the right angle $\angle C$ and the other two angles $\angle A$ and $\angle B$. Measure the sides of your triangle.

    b. Use your measurements to find $\sin A$ and $\cos A$ to the nearest hundredth.

    c. Measure $\angle A$ with a protractor. Use a calculator to find $\sin A$ and $\cos A$ to the nearest hundredth.

    d. Compare your results for parts (b) and (c). Why might the values be slightly different?

For Exercises 12 and 13, draw and label a right triangle that fits each description.

12. $\triangle ABC$ with $\sin A = \dfrac{\text{leg opposite } \angle A}{\text{hypotenuse}} = \dfrac{6}{10}$ 13. $\triangle XYZ$ with $\cos X = \dfrac{\text{leg adjacent to } \angle X}{\text{hypotenuse}} = \dfrac{16}{34}$

14. **Writing** $\triangle P'Q'R'$ is a dilation of $\triangle PQR$. Describe the relationship between the sine and the cosine values of $\angle P'$ and $\angle P$.

15 TECHNOLOGY Use a graphics calculator or graphing software. Make sure you work in degree mode. Use the RANGE or WINDOW key to set the *x* values between 0° and 90°.

a. Graph $y = \sin x$. Do not clear the screen. Graph $y = \cos x$.

b. How can you use the graph to tell when $\sin x = \cos x$?

c. When $\sin x = \cos x$, what is the value of *x*? What is the value of *y*?

TECHNOLOGY NOTE

The Technology Handbook, p. 613, describes how to use the RANGE or WINDOW key.

Write two equations you could use to find the length *x*. Then find *x*.

16.

17.

18.

For Exercises 19–22, use the problem solving strategy *Make a sketch*.

19. What is the maximum height that a 15-foot ladder can reach safely when it leans against the side of a building? (*Note:* Use the safety information in Sample 2.)

20. Suppose an escalator makes a 30° angle with the ground floor. The part that people stand on is 15 m in length. How high is the top of the escalator from the ground floor?

21. A kite is on a 150-meter string that makes a 40° angle with the ground. Estimate how far the kite is above the ground.

22. **History** In a Chinese legend the famous general Han Xin flew a kite over his enemy's palace to calculate how far his troops were from the palace.

a. Suppose the general measured the length of the kite string and the angle the kite string made with the ground. Draw a sketch to model this situation. Label the information General Han Xin knew and what he was trying to find.

b. How do you think General Han Xin calculated the distance to the palace?

c. Suppose the string made a 28° angle with the ground and was 1800 ft long. About how far away were General Han Xin's forces from the palace?

BY THE WAY...

The best angle for flying a kite in mild wind is 45° to 60° from the ground. In this range, the forces on the kite are balanced.

23. Aviation An airplane is at an altitude of 33,000 ft when the pilot starts the descent to the airport. The pilot wants the plane to descend at an angle of 3°. How many miles away from the airport must the descent begin?

airport   (Not drawn to scale)

24. Find the lengths *a, b, c,* and *d.* (First decide in which order they can be found.)

Ongoing **ASSESSMENT**

25. **Writing** Describe how the sine and cosine ratios are alike and how they are different.

Review **PREVIEW**

26. Draw a dilation of △*RST* with center *A* and a scale factor of 2. *(Section 6-6)*

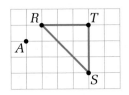

27. Is the graph misleading? Explain. *(Section 3-7)*

28. A grab bag contains 12 key rings. There are 6 silver-toned, 4 gold-toned, and 2 bronze-toned key rings. If you pick a key ring at random, what is the probability that it is gold-toned? *(Section 6-2)*

Working on the Unit Project

29. **Research** Find the costs of advertising in at least three of these media.

➤ your local newspaper   ➤ the magazines you read   ➤ a local TV station

➤ your school newspaper   ➤ a local radio station   ➤ some other source

Completing the Unit Project

Now you are ready to use the data you have collected to plan your advertising campaign. Your plan should include the following information.

➤ a description of the product or service you are advertising and the data that supports your choice of product

➤ your decision about where to advertise your product or service and the data that supports your choice of media

➤ a schedule of when and how often your ad will run

➤ an estimate of the cost of running your ad on the media you selected

➤ either a sketch of a print ad or a script for a TV or radio ad

Look Back ◄

Did your classmates all make the same decisions or were there many different results? Discuss why people may develop different plans even though they all target the same market segment.

Alternative Projects

Project 1: Changing the Rules

Use a game in which dice are thrown to determine the players' moves around a game board. Find the probabilities of several events in the game.

Change the rules of the game. How does this affect the probabilities? Present your conclusions in an oral report. Display the results on a poster.

Project 2: Finding Ratios

In a golden rectangle, the ratio $\frac{\text{length}}{\text{width}}$ is about 1.618. This is called the *golden ratio*.

➤ Research the history of the golden ratio. Find its exact value.

➤ Find examples of the golden ratio in art and architecture.

➤ Measure rooms, pictures, and furniture. Do any use the golden ratio?

➤ Summarize your results. Make a visual display.

1. What is the ratio of the perimeter of a regular hexagon to the length of a side?

6-1

2. A 15 oz box of cereal costs $2.39. What is the unit price?

3. From the people seated around you at a baseball game, you estimate the ratio of men to women is 3:2. If the attendance at the game is 48,000, about how many of the people at the game are women?

Estimate each probability of what will happen on Joan Laredo's next at-bat. The table shows her record against right-handed and left-handed pitchers.

6-2

	Right-handed pitchers	Left-handed pitchers
Hits	35	10
Outs	65	40
Total	100	50

4. P(gets a hit against a left-handed pitcher)

5. P(gets a hit)

6. P(does *not* get a hit against a right-handed pitcher)

7. Suppose Joan gets a hit the next time she is at bat. Estimate the probability that the pitcher is right-handed.

Suppose you spin this spinner.

8. How many possible number outcomes are there?

9. Is landing on each number equally likely?

10. How many possible color outcomes are there?

11. Is landing on each color equally likely?

Find each probability for a roll of a fair die.

12. $P(\because)$

13. P(even number)

14. $P(\text{not } \dddot{})$

15. P(a number less than 4)

16. **Writing** Write at least four ideas about probability. Be sure to include these points.

 ➤ the difference between experimental and theoretical probability

 ➤ how to use a data table or graph to find the probability of an event

Solve each proportion for y.

6-3

17. $\dfrac{5}{6.5} = \dfrac{y}{19.5}$

18. $\dfrac{30}{0.4} = \dfrac{100}{y}$

19. It takes 9 ft of twine to tie one stack of newspapers for recycling. How many stacks can be tied by a 60 yd ball of twine?

For Exercises 20–22, use this exit poll data.   6-4

A sample of 1500 voters took part in an exit poll during a recent election.
There were 3 million voters in this election. The poll has a 5% margin of
error. The table shows the results.

| ★ | Candidate A 690 | ★ | ★ | Candidate B 560 | ★ | ★ | Candidate C 250 | ★ |

20. About how many votes did each candidate expect to receive?

21. In this election, a candidate needed a majority (at least 50%)
    of the votes to win. Did any candidate expect to receive a majority?

22. Estimate an interval for the number of votes each candidate could
    expect.

Tell whether each statement is *True* or *False*. If it is false, give a   6-5
counterexample.

23. Two quadrilaterals that are similar must be congruent.

24. Corresponding sides of similar rectangles are in proportion.

25. **Open-ended** Write a problem about a situation in which indirect
    measurement can be used to find an unknown length or distance.

26. **a.** Explain why $\triangle ABC \sim \triangle DEC$.

    b. Find BC.

    c. Find AB.

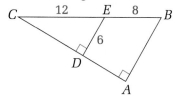

27. A scale model of a bridge was built to a scale of 1 in.: 240 ft.
    The actual bridge is 2000 ft long. How long is the scale model?

Draw a dilation of $\triangle ABC$ with $A(2, 4)$, $B(10, 4)$, and $C(7, 8)$, using each   6-6
center of dilation and scale factor.

28. center $P(0, 0)$; scale factor 3   **29.** center $A(2, 4)$; scale factor $\frac{1}{2}$

30. A length on an original figure is 15. The corresponding length on
    the image is 5. What is the scale factor of the dilation?

31. Solve $\frac{15}{x} = 0.25$ for x.   6-7

Express each trigonometric ratio as a fraction in simplest form.

32. $\cos Y$

33. $\sin X$

34. $\cos X$

35. $\sin Y$

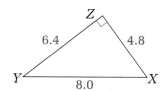

36. A TV tower is 1800 ft high and is supported by wires that make an angle of 63° with the ground.

   a. How long is each wire?

   b. How far from the base of the tower is each wire anchored in the ground?

37. **Self-evaluation** When you began this unit, which applications of ratios and proportions were you already familiar with? Now that you have completed this unit, do you know any more about these applications? Do you know any new uses for ratios and proportions?

38. **Group Activity** Work in a group of three students.

   a. Have each person in your group write about three different situations where ratios are used.

   b. For each situation, have each group member tell whether the ratio is a percent, a rate, a probability, a scale factor, or a trigonometric ratio.

   c. As a group, discuss each member's list. Make a combined group list and report back to the class.

IDEAS AND (FORMULAS)=X^2 $_5P_5$

ALGEBRA $)X^2$

➤ Three ways to write the ratio of a to b are: $\frac{a}{b}$, $a:b$, or a to b. *(p. 301)*

➤ When you solve a proportion, you find the value of the variable that represents the unknown quantity. *(p. 314)*

➤ For any proportion, the cross products are equal. *(p. 315)*

$$\text{If } \frac{a}{b} = \frac{c}{d}, \text{ then } ad = bc.$$

GEOMETRY

➤ For any similar polygons, the corresponding angles are congruent and the corresponding sides are in proportion. *(p. 329)*

$$\frac{AB}{DE} = \frac{BC}{EF} = \frac{CA}{FD}$$

➤ A scale drawing of an object is similar to the object. *(p. 330)*

➤ Two triangles are similar whenever two angles of one triangle are congruent to two angles of the other triangle. *(p. 331)*

➤ You can use similar triangles to estimate distances or heights that cannot be measured directly. *(p. 331)*

➤ A dilation image is similar to the original figure. *(p. 337)*

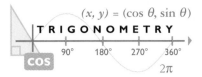

TRIGONOMETRY

$(x, y) = (\cos \theta, \sin \theta)$

➤ $\sin A = \dfrac{\text{length of the leg opposite } \angle A}{\text{length of the hypotenuse}}$

$\cos A = \dfrac{\text{length of the leg adjacent to } \angle A}{\text{length of the hypotenuse}}$

(p. 344)

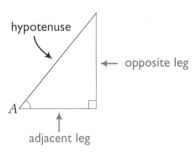

➤ You can use trigonometric ratios to solve problems involving right triangles. *(p. 346)*

STATISTICS & PROBABILITY

➤ The experimental probability that an event E will happen is

$P(E) = \dfrac{\text{number of times an event } E \text{ happens}}{\text{number of times the experiment is done}}$. *(p. 308)*

➤ The theoretical probability that an event E will happen is

$P(E) = \dfrac{\text{number of favorable outcomes}}{\text{number of possible outcomes}}$. *(p. 309)*

➤ The probability of the complement of an event E is

$P(\text{not } E) = 1 - P(E)$. *(p. 310)*

➤ By collecting data about a sample of a population, you can make predictions about the population. *(p. 323)*

Key Terms

- **ratio** (p. 301)
- **outcome** (p. 308)
- **experimental probability** (p. 308)
- **proportion** (p. 314)
- **population** (p. 321)
- **margin of error** (p. 323)
- **~** (p. 329)
- **image** (p. 337)
- **scale factor** (p. 337)
- **sine** (p. 344)

- **rate** (p. 302)
- **event** (p. 308)
- **theoretical probability** (p. 309)
- **terms of a proportion** (p. 314)
- **sample** (p. 321)
- **±** (p. 323)
- **scale drawing** (p. 330)
- **dilation** (p. 337)
- **hypotenuse** (p. 344)
- **cosine** (p. 344)

- **unit rate** (p. 302)
- **probability** (p. 308)
- **complementary events** (p. 310)
- **cross products** (p. 315)
- **sampling** (p. 323)
- **similar figures** (p. 329)
- **scale** (p. 330)
- **center of a dilation** (p. 337)
- **legs of a right triangle** (p. 344)
- **trigonometric ratios** (p. 344)

unit 7

Direct Variation

SPORTS DESIGN

Test your sports savvy with this trivia quiz!

① Why is a tennis ball fuzzy?

② How did home plate get its shape?

③ Why does a race car have wings?

④ Why is the rim of a basketball hoop ten feet high?

⑤ How did an airplane change the sport of diving?

⑥ Why is the surface of a soccer ball formed by a pattern of polygons?

⑦ How many dimples are on a golf ball?

See page 358 for answers.

aerodynamics

Cyclists, skiers, and speed skaters know that one of the biggest obstacles to winning a race is the **WIND**. Sports scientists use computers and wind tunnels to design equipment to decrease the wind's effect. In a 25-mi race, an aerodynamic handlebar can make a three-minute difference in a cyclist's time— the difference between finishing first or fifty-first!

The outer seams on a baseball may help a pitcher's curve ball, but the inside of the ball is on the batter's side. The light-weight materials found inside a baseball allow the ball to go farther when it is hit.

cowhide
blue-gray woolen yarn
white woolen yarn
blue-gray woolen yarn
cork
black rubber
red rubber

layers

Design a Sports Arena

Your project is to make a scale drawing or a model of an arena for skateboarding or in-line skating competitions.

Your group's design should include at least one ramp for launching jumps. The ramp may be straight or curved. You may want to create several "stations," each with a different kind of ramp.

Along with your design, you should include an estimate of the cost of building your arena.

Construction of the skateboard bowl arena at The Hanger in Charleston, N.C.

design

One arena can be the site of a concert on Friday, a basketball game Saturday afternoon, a hockey game Saturday night, and a trip to the circus on Sunday! With a good design, a multi-event arena can change from a floor of ice to hardwood within a few hours. The design of other arenas, like those for skateboarding events, affects the difficulty level of the competition.

quarter pipe

curved ramp

straight ramp

Unit Project 7

For this project you should work in a group of four students. Here are some ideas to help you get started.

☞ Consider the overall design of the arena. Do you want a shape that will include a track for long-distance in-line skating? Where will spectators watch the skaters?

☞ How many ramps will you include in your design?

☞ Books about skateboarding often include plans for ramps. You may want to refer to one for ideas.

☞ Think about what makes one skating arena more challenging than another. What level of difficulty do you want?

☞ You can build a model or make a scale drawing of your arena. Which one is most appealing to you?

Answers to trivia quiz from page 356.

(1) The fuzz on a tennis ball allows the racquet to grip the ball so that it can be hit more easily.

(2) These legs define the foul lines, but limit the pitcher's and umpire's ability to see the strike zone clearly.

This addition lets the pitcher and the umpire see when a pitch "hits the corner" of the strike zone.

(3) The wind hits the wings and then pushes the car to the ground, allowing it to go faster, especially around turns.

(4) When James Naismith created the game, peach baskets were hung from the gym's balcony, 10 feet from the floor.

(5) Surplus parts from a World War II airplane led to the design of a flexible diving springboard.

(6) The polygonal shapes control the distance that a soccer ball can be hit or kicked.

(7) There is an average of 400 dimples on a golf ball. Without dimples, a ball that would normally go 250 yards would go only 125 yards.

Working on the Unit Project

Your work in Unit 7 will help you create your model or scale drawing.

Related Exercises:

Section 7-1, Exercise 27
Section 7-2, Exercise 32
Section 7-3, Exercise 29
Section 7-4, Exercise 43
Section 7-5, Exercises 36, 37
Section 7-6, Exercises 34, 35

Alternative Projects p. 408

Can We Talk SPORTS DESIGN

➤ Why do you think skateboarding and in-line skating are popular?

➤ What protective equipment should skaters wear? Why?

➤ If you were building an arena in your neighborhood, where would you put it?

➤ Where else have you seen ramps? What other sports use ramps?

➤ What are some ways to measure the steepness of a straight ramp?

Direct Variation, Slope, and Tangent

Focus
Explore three relationships
that involve constant ratios.

RAISING
THE ROOF

Talk it Over

1. To build a roof a carpenter puts posts every 2 ft along a beam. Describe a pattern you see in the heights of the posts.

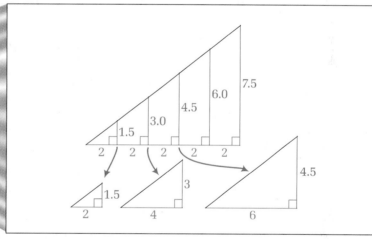

2. Copy and complete the table. For the last column, use a calculator to find the decimal ratio of height to horizontal distance. What do you notice about these ratios?

Post	Horizontal distance d of post from eaves (ft)	Height h of post (ft)	$\frac{h}{d}$
1	2	1.5	0.75
2	4	3	?
3	?	4.5	?
4	?	6	?
5	?	7.5	?

3. Use similar triangles to explain why all the ratios $\frac{h}{d}$ are the same.

Direct Variation

For the roof, the height of a post depends on its horizontal distance from the eaves. Although the height increases as the distance increases, the ratio of these two quantities is constant.

When two variable quantities have a constant ratio, their relationship is called **direct variation.** The constant ratio is called the **variation constant.** You can write an equation to show the relationship.

$$\frac{h}{d} = 0.75$$

ratio of quantities = variation constant

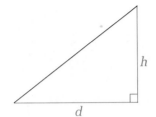

The equation $\frac{h}{d} = 0.75$ can also be written as $h = 0.75d$.

Both equations show that the height of the post varies directly with its horizontal distance from the eaves. You can use either equation to find the height of a post needed to support the roof at another point.

Sample 1

Suppose the carpenter of the roof shown on page 359 decides that a post should be 3 ft from the eaves. What should the height of the post be?

Sample Response

The equation $h = 0.75d$ describes the direct variation of the height h of a post and its distance d from the eaves.

Find the value of h when d is 3 ft.

$$h = 0.75d$$
$$h = 0.75(3) \quad \longleftarrow \quad \text{Substitute 3 for } d.$$
$$h = 2.25$$

The post should be 2.25 ft long.

BY THE WAY...

Carpenters sometimes use the word "pitch" to describe the slope of a roof.

Talk it Over

4. What step would you use to rewrite the equation $\frac{h}{d} = 0.75$ in the form $h = 0.75d$?

5. Suppose you know that $h = 5$ ft. Explain how can you find the value of d.

6. For a steeper roof, would the ratio $\frac{h}{d}$ be larger or smaller?

Marble Temple, Bangkok, Thailand

Slope

Some roofs are steeper than others. In mathematics, a number called *slope* is a measure of the steepness of a line. The **slope of a line** is the ratio of *rise* to *run* for any two points on the line.

Roofs of Rheinland Pfalz Freudenberg, Germany

rise = vertical change between two points

run = horizontal change between two points

$$\text{slope} = \frac{\text{rise}}{\text{run}}$$

Sample 2

Find the slope of the roof shown on page 359. Use the eaves and the peak as the two points.

Sample Response

Problem Solving Strategy: Make a sketch

The roof rises 7.5 ft across a distance of 10 ft.

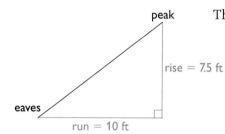

peak

rise = 7.5 ft

eaves

run = 10 ft

$$\text{slope} = \frac{\text{rise}}{\text{run}} = \frac{7.5}{10} = 0.75$$

The slope of the roof is 0.75.

> Now you are ready for:
> Exs. 1–12 on pp. 363–364

The Tangent Ratio

Remember the sine ratio and the cosine ratio of an acute angle in a right triangle? Each of these ratios compares a leg and the hypotenuse of a right triangle.

$$\sin A = \frac{\text{leg opposite } \angle A}{\text{hypotenuse}} = \frac{BC}{AB} \quad \cos A = \frac{\text{leg adjacent to } \angle A}{\text{hypotenuse}} = \frac{AC}{AB}$$

B

hypotenuse

leg opposite angle *A*

A

leg adjacent to angle *A*

C

The **tangent ratio** of an acute angle compares the two legs of a right triangle.

$$\tan A = \frac{\text{leg opposite } \angle A}{\text{leg adjacent to } \angle A} = \frac{BC}{AC}$$

7-1 Direct Variation, Slope, and Tangent

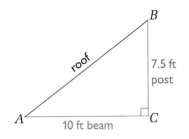

B

7.5 ft
post

A

10 ft beam

C

roof

Look again at the roof shown on page 359. What is the tangent ratio of the angle between the roof and the horizontal beam?

Sample Response

Use the right triangle formed by the roof, the beam, and the 7.5 ft post. The angle between the roof and the beam is $\angle A$.

$$\tan A = \frac{\text{leg opposite } \angle A}{\text{leg adjacent to } \angle A} = \frac{7.5}{10} = 0.75$$

The tangent ratio of the angle is 0.75.

Talk it Over

7. Use the triangle in Sample 3. What is the tangent ratio of $\angle B$? How is the tangent ratio of $\angle B$ related to the tangent ratio of $\angle A$?

8. Luisa made a scale drawing of the roof in Sample 3. Using a protractor, she measured $\angle A$ to be 37°.

   a. Use a scientific calculator to find the tangent ratio of a 37° angle.

   b. Explain why your answer in part (a) is not exactly 0.75.

9. Use the *inverse tangent* key of a scientific calculator to find the angle that has a tangent ratio of exactly 0.75. To the nearest tenth of a degree, what is the measure of $\angle A$? Compare this measure of $\angle A$ to the measure given in question 8.

10. Do you think the tangent ratio of a steeper roof is larger or smaller than the tangent ratio of this roof? Explain.

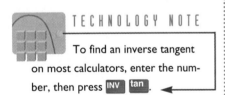

TECHNOLOGY NOTE

To find an inverse tangent on most calculators, enter the number, then press **INV** **tan**.

······▶ Now you are ready for:
Exs. 13–27 on pp. 365–366

Look Back

Explain how these three ideas are related: variation constant, slope, and tangent ratio.

Exercises and Problems

Use the direct variation equation $\frac{a}{b} = 1.25$.

1. What is the variation constant?

2. Rewrite the equation so that it does not have a fraction in it.

3. Find the value of a when $b = 8$.

4. Find the value of b when $a = 12$.

For Exercises 5 and 6, use the photograph at the right. The parasailor is 150 ft behind the boat and 200 ft above the water.

5. **a.** Write a direct variation equation relating height above the water and distance behind the boat.

   b. What is the variation constant?

6. If the parasailor is pulled in so he is 90 ft behind the boat, how far above the water will he be?

200 ft

150 ft

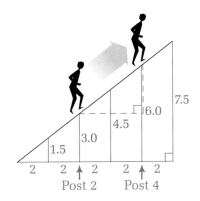

7.5
6.0
4.5
3.0
1.5

2   2 ↑ 2   2 ↑ 2
   Post 2   Post 4

original roof

9.0
7.5

2   2   2   2   2
       ?

7. The definition of slope on page 361 tells you that you can use any two points on a line to calculate the slope of the line.

   a. The roof shown is the same as the roof shown on page 359. Suppose the carpenter walks along the roof from post 2 to post 4. What is the rise and the run of the roof from post 2 to post 4?

   b. Use your answers in part (a) to find the slope of the roof. Is your answer the same as the slope of the roof calculated in Sample 2?

   c. Find the slope of the roof using the rise and run from post 1 to post 2.

   d. Find the slope of the roof using the rise and run from post 3 to post 5.

8. The roof shown is the same as the roof shown on page 359. Suppose the carpenter decides to extend the roof so it reaches a height of 9 ft instead of 7.5 ft. Find the length of the beam needed.

9. **Research** Estimate the slopes of roofs at your school or in the neighborhood. Discuss how slopes of roofs in areas that get a lot of snow in the winter might be different from slopes of roofs in areas that get very little snow.

10. **Research** Measure the slopes of wheel-chair access ramps at your school or in the neighborhood. What seems to be the steepest acceptable ramp? How does steepness affect the ease of using a ramp?

11. **Carpentry** A carpenter is asked to replace a staircase with one that is less steep. The steepness of a staircase depends upon the lengths of its *risers* and *treads*.

   a. A *carpenter's square* looks like two rulers joined at the 0 point to form a right angle. Use the carpenter's square shown in the diagram to read the riser height and tread length of the staircase.

   b. Find the ratio $\frac{\text{riser height}}{\text{tread length}}$. Explain why this ratio can be called the slope of the staircase.

   c. **Open-ended** Give three possible pairs of riser heights and tread lengths that the carpenter might use for a staircase that is less steep.

12. Each table shows a relationship between two quantities.

Table A		
units	seconds	$\frac{\text{seconds}}{\text{unit}}$
5	60	?
10	120	?
15	180	?

Table B		
numbers	price	$\frac{\text{price}}{\text{number}}$
10	1.50	?
12	1.80	?
16	2.40	?

Table C		
age	income	$\frac{\text{income}}{\text{age}}$
20	25,000	?
25	30,000	?
35	40,000	?

   a. Find the ratios.

   b. Which of the tables does not show direct variation? Explain.

For Exercises 13–15, use the diagram at the right.

13. What is the hypotenuse of $\triangle RST$?

14. Which leg is opposite the 63° angle? Which leg is adjacent to it?

15. a. Use $\triangle RST$ to find the value of tan 63°.

    b. Use your calculator to find the value of tan 63°.

    c. Do your answers in parts (a) and (b) agree exactly? Explain.

16. a. Express tan 25° as the ratio of the lengths of two sides of the triangle.

    b. Use a calculator to find tan 25°.

    c. Find the length of $\overline{XY}$ to the nearest 0.1 cm.

17. a. Use a calculator to complete a table of values for the tangent, sine, and cosine ratios of the following acute angles. Round values to four decimal places.

ANGLE	10°	20°	30°	40°	50°	60°	70°	80°
tangent	?	?	?	?	?	?	?	?
sine	?	?	?	?	?	?	?	?
cosine	?	?	?	?	?	?	?	?

    b. Describe any patterns you see in the table.

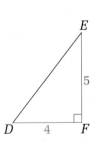

TECHNOLOGY NOTE

To find an inverse tangent on most calculators, enter the number, then press **INV** **tan**.

18. a. Which has the larger tangent ratio, $\angle A$ or $\angle D$? Explain.

    b. Use the inverse tangent key on a calculator to find the measures of $\angle A$ and $\angle D$.

    c. Which has the larger tangent ratio, $\angle B$ or $\angle E$? Explain.

    d. Use the inverse tangent key on a calculator to find the measures of $\angle B$ and $\angle E$.

19. A right triangle has a 20° angle and a leg of length 14 cm opposite it.

    a. Draw a picture of the triangle.

    b. **Writing** Explain how to use sine, cosine, or tangent ratios to find the lengths of the other leg and the hypotenuse.

    c. Find the lengths of the other leg and the hypotenuse to the nearest tenth of a centimeter.

20. A tourist is 150 ft from the base of the Leaning Tower of Pisa. From the tourist's position, the *angle of elevation* to the top of the tower is 50°. Find the height of the tower to the nearest tenth of a foot.

Ongoing **ASSESSMENT**

21. The height h of a post that supports the peak of a roof varies directly with the horizontal distance d from the peak to the eaves. The roof and the beam form a 30° angle.

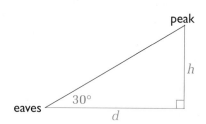

   a. Write a direct variation equation relating h and d. (*Hint:* Use the tangent ratio.)

   b. **Open-ended** Give three possible pairs of values for h and d.

   c. **Writing** Explain why the slope of the roof is tan 30°.

Review **PREVIEW**

22. Use $\triangle ABC$ to find sin A and cos A to four decimal places. (*Section 6-7*)

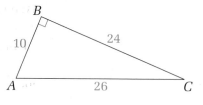

Solve. (*Sections 2-7, 2-8*)

23. $10x = 24$ **24.** $\frac{x}{24} = 10$ **25.** $10 = 24x$

26. Write an equation to model this statement: The length of an infant's arm is about one-third of the infant's height. (*Section 5-1*)

Working on the Unit Project

27. Suppose you decide to construct a straight skateboard ramp that makes an angle of 8° with the ground.

   a. How long would the base of the ramp have to be in order to reach a height of 3 ft above the ground?

   b. If you do not have enough space for a ramp that long, should you increase or decrease the angle? What is the disadvantage for the skater if you design the ramp this way?

   c. Explain why a curved ramp might be better than a straight ramp.

A Direct Variation Model

That's the Way The BALL Bounces

BALL

Focus

Model a direct variation situation and use the model to make predictions. Find the slope of a line in a coordinate plane.

EXPLORATION

How is the bounce of a ball related to the height of the drop?

- **Materials: tape measure or meter sticks, tape, five or six types of balls (such as a tennis ball, a rubber ball, a table tennis ball, a golf ball, a baseball, a soccer ball)**
- **Work in a group of three or four students.**

Measure from the bottom of the ball to the floor. Round to the nearest centimeter or half inch.

drop height

bounce height

Put the zero mark at the floor.

(1) Predict which ball has the most bounce and which has the least bounce. Discuss how you might measure this.

(2) Attach a tape measure or meter sticks to a wall. Put the zero mark at the floor. Choose one ball for your group to use.

(3) Choose a drop height. Drop the ball four times from that height. Each time, measure the height of the ball's first bounce.

(4) Record your results in one row of a table like the one shown.

Type of Ball:				
Drop height D	Bounce height		Mean bounce height B	Ratio $\frac{B}{D}$

    a. Record the drop height D and the four heights of the first bounce.

    b. Find the mean B of the bounce heights.

    c. Find the ratio of B to D.

(5) Repeat step 4 with four different drop heights. Complete the table.

(6) What patterns do you notice in your table?

(7) Make a scatter plot of your data. Use D as the control variable and B as the dependent variable.

(8) Compare your scatter plot with the scatter plots of other groups. Check your predictions in step 1.

A Mathematical Model: Direct Variation

To model the behavior of a bouncing ball with an equation, look for a relationship between the two variables, the drop height D and the mean bounce height B.

Sample 1

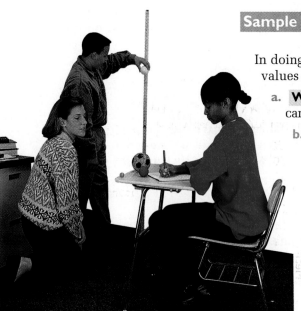

In doing the Exploration, Julio, Tara, and Linda recorded the values shown in the table.

a. **Writing** Julio thinks the relationship between D and B can be modeled by direct variation. Explain his reasoning.

b. Model the behavior of the ball with a direct variation equation relating D and B. What is the variation constant for the ball?

Drop height D (in.)	Mean bounce height B (in.)	Ratio $\frac{B}{D}$
20	15.0	0.75
30	24	0.8
40	32.5	0.8125
50	41	0.82
60	48.5	$0.808\overline{3}$

Sample Response

a. When two variables have a constant ratio, you can say that one variable varies directly with the other.

> State the meaning of direct variation.

Although the ratios $\frac{B}{D}$ are not all exactly the same, to the nearest tenth each ratio is 0.8. Direct variation is a good model for the relationship between D and B.

> Explain why the data fit a direct variation model.

b. The direct variation equation $\frac{B}{D} = 0.8$ models the behavior of the bouncing ball. The variation constant for the ball is about 0.8.

······▶ Now you are ready for:
Exs. 1–12 on pp. 370–372

Graphing Direct Variation

You can also model the direct variation relationship between D and B with a graph, and then use your graph to make predictions.

Because of errors in measurement, real-world results may not match exactly the predictions of a mathematical model. However, a good model should give reasonable approximations.

To model the data from the table in Sample 1, Tara made a scatter plot of the five data points (D, B). Then she drew a fitted line.

Use Tara's graph to predict how high the ball will bounce if she drops it from a height of 42 in.

Sample Response

1 From the 42 in. mark on the horizontal axis, draw a line up until it reaches the fitted line.

The drop height is the control variable.

2 Then draw a line to the left until it meets the vertical axis at about 34 in.

The bounce height depends on the drop height.

If Tara drops the ball from a height of 42 in., it will bounce to about 34 in.

Talk it Over

BY THE WAY...

The fuzzy felt on tennis balls slows them down and gives them a better "grip" on different surfaces. The dimples on a golf ball lift them farther through the air.

1. Use the equation in part (b) of Sample 1 to predict how high the ball will bounce if the group drops it from a height of 42 in. Compare your answer to the prediction in Sample 2.

2. Instead of using the equation $\frac{B}{D} = 0.8$ in question 1, Linda used the equation $B = 0.8D$. Do you think this equation is correct? Explain.

3. Julio wants the ball to bounce to a height of 12 in. How can Tara's graph help Julio estimate the drop height he should use?

4. What algebraic equation could Julio solve to find the drop height that will give a bounce height of 12 in.? Show how to solve it.

Finding Slope Using Coordinates

In Section 7-1, you learned about the slope of a line. You can use the coordinates of two points on a line to find the line's slope.

Use Tara's graph in Sample 2. Find the slope of the fitted line.

Sample Response

Choose any two points on the line. Compare the *x*-coordinates and the *y*-coordinates of the points.

The value of B changes from 24 to 48.5. The vertical change, or rise, is 48.5 − 24 = 24.5.

The value of D changes from 30 to 60. The horizontal change, or run, is 60 − 30, or 30.

Watch Out!
When finding the slope of a fitted line, be sure to use points that are near the fitted line.

The slope of the line $= \dfrac{\text{rise}}{\text{run}} = \dfrac{24.5}{30} = 0.81\overline{6}.$

Talk it Over

5. Compare the slope of the fitted line in Sample 3 to the variation constant found in part (b) of Sample 1.

6. Find the slope of the line that contains the points (2, 5) and (5, 9).

Look Back

Describe two ways to model data that have a direct variation relationship. Which type of model do you find easier to use to make a prediction?

Now you are ready for:
Exs. 13–32 on pp. 372–374

7-2 Exercises and Problems

1. **Reading** What are the two variables used in the Exploration? What does each represent?

2. **a.** In the Exploration, Kathryn gathers data using a lacrosse ball. Use her data to find the four ratios $\dfrac{B}{D}$ to the nearest hundredth.

   b. Estimate a variation constant for Kathryn's ball to the nearest tenth.

Lacrosse ball

Drop height D (in.)	Mean bounce height B (in.)	Ratio $\dfrac{B}{D}$
12	10	?
24	19	?
36	29	?
48	38	?

3. **Writing** Summarize the results of the Exploration for someone who missed the class. Use the data gathered by all the groups. Include these points.

   ➤ Did all groups use the same drop heights? Is this important?

   ➤ Did every ball display direct variation?

   ➤ Did each group have the same variation constant? What might cause any differences among groups' results?

   ➤ Which type of ball had the most bounce? the least bounce?

4. **Writing** In the Exploration, the variation constants are all less than 1. Write a story about an impossible ball for which $\frac{B}{D}$ is greater than 1. How would this ball act? How could people use the ball? Would it be hard to control?

Decide whether direct variation is a good model for the data in each table. Explain your reasoning.

5.

width	height
2	0.14
4	0.26
6	0.43
8	0.56
10	0.69

6.

age	weight
5	100
10	141
15	173
20	201
25	224

7.

errors	cost
3	63
6	127
9	188
12	251
15	314

For Exercises 8–10:

a. **Determine whether direct variation is a good model for each situation. Explain your reasoning.**

b. **Tell whether the data are discrete or continuous.**

Control variable	Dependent variable
8. number of batches of cookie dough	number of cookies
9. time	water level in a lake
10. gallons of gasoline bought	cost of the gasoline bought

11. **Driver Education** The faster you drive a car, the longer it takes to stop in an emergency.

   a. Which is the control variable and which is the dependent variable?

   b. Find the ratio $\frac{\text{dependent variable}}{\text{control variable}}$ for each pair of values.

   c. Is direct variation a good model for the data? Explain.

speed (mi/h)	10	20	30	40	50	60	70
stopping distance (ft)	15	40	75	120	175	240	315

12. Using a table tennis ball, Jennifer found that the ratio of bounce height to drop height is given by the equation $\frac{B}{D} = 0.7$.

   a. Suppose $D = 4$ ft. Find B.

   b. Suppose $B = 4$ ft. Find D.

   c. Suppose $D = 7.5$ ft. Find B.

   d. Suppose $B = 7.5$ ft. Find D.

   e. Which is easier, finding the bounce height when given the drop height, or finding the drop height when given the bounce height?

Scuba Diving For Exercises 13–16, use the graph.

13. A sea diver's pressure gauge shows how many atmospheres (atm) of pressure are caused by the weight of the water on the diver. The pressure varies directly with the depth below the surface. Estimate the variation constant.

14. Estimate the water pressure on a diver at a depth of 70 ft.

15. The recommended maximum depth for recreational diving is 130 ft. What is the approximate water pressure at that depth?

16. Sami's water pressure gauge reads 2 atm. About how many feet below sea level is she?

17. Veterinary Medicine A veterinarian uses a table to determine how many milligrams of medicine to give a dog to prevent heartworm.

Weight of dog, W (lb)	15	30	45	60
Dosage, D (180 mg tablets)	0.25	0.5	0.75	1.0

   a. Find the ratio $\frac{D}{W}$ for each weight in the table.

   b. Which quantity varies directly with the other? What is the variation constant? Write an equation relating D and W.

   c. What dosage should the veterinarian recommend for a 75 lb dog? Explain your answer.

   d. Plot the data for weight and dosage on a graph. Draw a fitted line through the four points.

   e. Find the slope of the fitted line.

Speed of bat swing (mi/h)	Distance ball travels (ft)
50	270
60	325
70	378
75	405

18. **Baseball** The table shows how far a baseball player can hit an 85 mi/h pitch.

   a. Do these data show direct variation? If so, write an equation to model the situation.

   b. Plot these data on a graph and draw a fitted line.

   c. Find the slope of the line you have drawn. Explain how you calculated the slope.

   d. Suppose the speed of a player's swing is 64 mi/h. Predict how far the ball will go.

19. A sky diver's speed varies directly with the amount of time spent falling. A sky diver's speed 2.5 s after jumping from a plane is 24.5 m/s.

   a. Draw a graph with time on the horizontal axis and speed on the vertical axis.

   b. Use your graph to predict the sky diver's speed after 3 s.

   c. Use your graph to predict the sky diver's speed after 4 s.

20. To solve Exercise 19 using an equation, you may write $\frac{v}{t} = k$, where v represents speed, t represents elapsed time, and k represents a constant.

   a. Use the data given in Exercise 19 to determine k.

   b. Find v when $t = 3$.

   c. Find v when $t = 4$.

   d. Compare the results of parts (b) and (c) with the results in Exercise 19.

2.5 s

21. **Group Activity** Work in a group of four students.

   a. Select a ball. Decide on a drop height. Predict how many bounces the ball will make and the height of each bounce.

   b. Drop the ball from the given drop height. Measure the height of the first three bounces.

   c. How are the drop height, the first bounce height, the second bounce height, and the third bounce height related to each other mathematically?

   d TECHNOLOGY Record your results in a spreadsheet. Use your spreadsheet to predict what might happen to the heights of the next five bounces, using various drop heights.

   e. Choose a drop height modeled in your spreadsheet. Drop the ball from this height. How closely does your model predict what actually happens?

7-2 A Direct Variation Model

22. What happens to the first bounce height of a ball if you double the drop height? if you triple the drop height? Explain your answers.

23. a. Find the slope of the line shown at the right.

   b. Use the tangent ratio to find the angle the line makes with the x-axis.

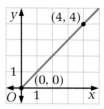

Ongoing **ASSESSMENT**

24. a. **Group Activity** Toss three coins 50 times. Count the number of times exactly two heads appear. Copy and complete the table.

Number of tosses	Number of times exactly two heads appear	Two heads appear / Number of tosses
10	?	?
20	?	?
30	?	?
40	?	?
50	?	?

   b. Graph the data from the table. Put the number of tosses on the horizontal axis and the number of times exactly two heads appear on the vertical axis.

   c. Is direct variation a useful model for predicting the number of times exactly two heads will appear when three coins are tossed 10 or 20 times? 50 times? Why or why not?

   d. Gather all the data from the groups in your class. What is the total number of tosses? What is the total number of times exactly two heads appeared? Is the ratio what you expect?

Review **PREVIEW**

25. Find the tangent ratio of $\angle A$. *(Section 7-1)*

Graph each equation. *(Section 4-7)*

26. $y = 3x$

27. $y = -5x$

28. $y = -|x|$

Give the formula for the perimeter of each figure. *(Toolbox Skill 17)*

29. rectangle

30. square

31. equilateral triangle

 Working on the Unit Project

32. **Research** Why is urethane used in making wheels for skateboards and in-line skates? How are the properties of urethane related to a bouncing ball?

Circumference and Arc Length

Focus

Find the circumference and the length of an arc of a circle.

How Far Around?

EXPLORATION

What is the relationship between the circumference and the diameter of a circle?

- **Materials: string or tape measures, metric rulers, scissors, circular shapes of different sizes (such as a coffee can, a jar lid, a round waste basket, a CD, a small wheel, or a plate)**
- **Work with another student.**

Use a ruler to find the diameter of the circular shape. The **diameter** of a circle is the distance across the circle at its widest part.

① Select five circular shapes of different sizes.

② Find and record the *diameter* and the *circumference* of each circular shape:

Wrap a string around the circular shape. When you unwrap it you can measure the circle's circumference. The **circumference** of a circle is the distance around the circle.

Record the diameters and circumferences in a table like the one shown below.

Circle	Diameter d (mm)	Circumference C (mm)	$\dfrac{C}{d}$
1	?	?	?
2	?	?	?
3	?	?	?
4	?	?	?
5	?	?	?

③ For each circle find the ratio $\dfrac{C}{d}$ to the nearest hundredth. Write it in the last column of the table.

④ What do you notice about the ratios in the last column? Does the relationship between diameter and circumference seem to be an example of direct variation?

For all circles, the ratio of circumference to diameter is a constant. This ratio is named by the Greek letter π (**pi**).

Common approximations for π are 3.14 and $\frac{22}{7}$. The exact value is a nonterminating and nonrepeating decimal between these two approximations.

$\frac{314}{100}$	π	$\frac{22}{7}$
3.140000000...	3.141592653...	3.142857142...
a terminating decimal	a nonterminating decimal	a repeating decimal

To see the value your calculator uses for π, press ▣. For calculations involving π, give your answers to the nearest tenth unless told otherwise.

You can use the equation $\frac{C}{d} = \pi$, or the form $C = \pi d$, to find the circumference of any circle when you know its diameter.

CIRCUMFERENCE OF A CIRCLE

$C = \pi d$ ⟵ diameter

⟵ circumference

$C = 2\pi r$ ⟵ radius

Sample 1

Find the circumference of the skateboard wheel to the nearest millimeter.

The diameter of the wheel is 60 mm.

Sample Response

Problem Solving Strategy: Use a formula

$C = \pi d$

$= \pi \cdot 60$ ⟵ Substitute 60 for d.

≈ 188 ⟵ ▣ ▣ 60 ENTER

The circumference of the wheel is about 188 mm.

▸ Now you are ready for:
Exs. 1–13 on pp. 378–379

Arc Length

When you cut a circle and straighten it to form a line segment, the length of the line segment is the circumference of the circle. An **arc** is a part of a circle. The length of an arc is a fraction of the circumference. This measurement is called **arc length.**

arc length

circumference

ARC LENGTH

The endpoints of an arc determine a central angle called the central angle of the arc.

You can use this proportion to find the length of an arc:

$$\frac{\text{arc length}}{\text{circumference}} = \frac{\text{measure of central angle of arc}}{360°}$$

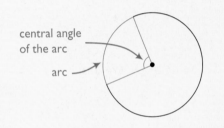

central angle of the arc

arc

Talk it Over

1. A circle graph with five central angles is "unwrapped" into a straight line of length 1. Complete the diagram to find the arc lengths.

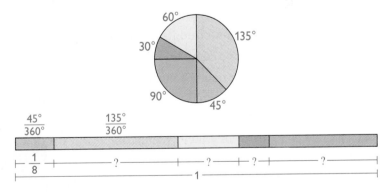

2. What is the measure of the central angle of an arc whose arc length is one fifth the circumference of a circle?

A launch ramp for skateboarders is formed by an arc with a central angle of 57° and a radius of 9 ft. Find the length of the arc to the nearest foot.

Sample Response

Problem Solving Strategy: Use a proportion

Let x = the unknown arc length. ⟶ $\dfrac{x}{56.5} \approx \dfrac{57}{360}$ ⟵ The measure of the central angle is 57°.

$d = 18$, so $C = \pi \cdot 18 \approx 56.5$ ⟶ ⟵ The measure of a complete circle is 360°.

$$\left(\frac{x}{56.5}\right)(56.5) \approx \left(\frac{57}{360}\right)(56.5)$$ ⟵ Multiply both sides by 56.5.

$$x \approx 8.9$$

The arc length is about 9 ft.

⋯⟶ **Now you are ready for:**
Exs. 14–29 on pp. 379–382

Look Back ⟵

For any circle, how are diameter, circumference, and arc length related?

7-3 Exercises and Problems

1. **Writing** Suppose Congress passed a law saying that the value of π is exactly 3. Would this law have any effect on the actual relationship between the circumference and the diameter of any circle? Use the results of the Exploration to help you explain why or why not.

2. Use the data you gathered in the Exploration.

   a. Plot your diameter and circumference data on a graph.

   b. Draw a fitted line and find its slope.

   c. How does the slope compare with π?

3. **Reading** Look at the number line on page 376 that shows π between the values 3.14 and $\frac{22}{7}$. How do you know that π is not exactly halfway between these values?

4. The five circles are congruent. Which of these segments is closest in length to the circumference of one of the circles: $\overline{AB}$, $\overline{AC}$, $\overline{AD}$, $\overline{AE}$, or $\overline{AF}$? Why?

Find the circumference of each circle.

5.

16 ft

6.

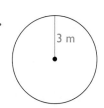
3 m

7. a. The Santa Maria del Tule tree in Oaxaca, Mexico, is a Montezuma cypress whose trunk is about 117 ft around. Suppose the trunk is circular. Estimate its diameter.

b. **Research** Measure the circumference of at least two tree trunks or columns. Estimate their diameters.

A gardener decides to plant tulip bulbs around the edge of a circular flower bed with a diameter of 12 ft.

8. About how many tulip bulbs can the gardener plant if the bulbs are spaced about 6 in. apart?

9. About how much space should the gardener leave between the bulbs if 50 bulbs are planted?

For Exercises 10–12, find the variation constant. Sketch and label a diagram to help you.

10. The perimeter of an equilateral triangle varies directly with the length of one side.

11. The perimeter of a square varies directly with the length of one side.

12. The circumference of a circle varies directly with the radius.

13. Choose the letter(s) of the equation(s) that correctly show the relationship between the circumference and diameter of a circle.

a. $C = \pi d$ **b.** $\dfrac{C}{d} = \pi$ **c.** $d = \dfrac{C}{\pi}$ **d.** $d = \pi C$

Find each arc length.

14.

45 in.

15.

2 ft

16. Six equilateral triangles form the regular hexagon drawn in the circle. The radius of the circle is 8 cm.

a. Find the perimeter of the hexagon.

b. Find the circumference of the circle.

c. How do your answers in parts (a) and (b) compare?

d. Find the length of one of the six arcs shown.

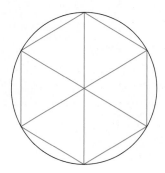

For Exercises 17 and 18, use the fact that the diameter of Earth is about 7900 mi.

17. a. Find the length of the equator. Round the answer to the nearest hundred miles.

b. Quito and Nairobi are two cities located very close to the equator. Quito is 79° west of the prime meridian, and Nairobi is 37° east of the prime meridian. Estimate the distance from Quito to Nairobi along the equator. Round the answer to the nearest 100 mi.

prime meridian

equator

Quito, Ecuador

Nairobi, Kenya

79° 37°

Quito, Ecuador

Nairobi, Kenya

18. **Using Manipulatives** On a globe, choose any two cities that have the same latitude but are not on the equator. (*Note:* For part (b) you will need to use your answer to part (a) of Exercise 17.)

a. Using the globe and a string, try to find the shortest path between the two cities. Is it along their line of latitude?

b. Use a proportion to find the length of the shortest path between the two cities. (*Hint:* You will need to measure the string length that represents the shortest path between the cities. What other distance on your globe will you need to measure?)

New York and Istanbul have about the same latitude.

19. Astronomy It takes Earth one year to travel around the sun. The distance from Earth to the sun is about 9.3×10^7 mi.

a. About how far does Earth travel in its orbit in one year? Assume the Earth's orbit is circular.

b. About how far does Earth travel in its orbit in one day? (Use 365.25 days for 1 year.)

c. Find the length of an arc of Earth's orbit with a central angle of 30°.

d. About how long does it take Earth to travel the length of the arc in part (c)?

20. A Chinese yin/yang symbol shows the relationship between two opposite forces. To make the symbol you draw circles and arcs. Is the blue curve longer than the red arc? Explain your answer.

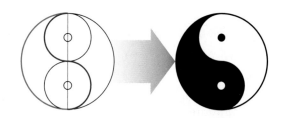

21. **Open-ended** A track has two straight portions of length *l* and two half-circle parts with a diameter *d*.

   a. Find values of *l* and *d* that result in a quarter-mile (1320 ft) track.

   b. Show that there is more than one possible answer.

   c. Which track do you think is best?

Ongoing **ASSESSMENT**

22. a. **Research** Gather data about the arm span of everyone in your class.

   b. What is the greatest length your class can cover if everyone joins hands in a line?

   c. Predict the diameter of the largest circle your class can make if everyone joins hands.

   d. **Group Activity** Test your prediction by making a circle with all your classmates and measuring its diameter.

Review **PREVIEW**

Draw a line through the points and find its slope. *(Section 7-2)*

23. (0, 0) and (5, 2)

24. (3, 2) and (7, 10)

25. Draw a box-and-whisker plot for the SAT scores. *(Section 3-5)*

SAT Scores (Math)				
553	602	407	346	701
778	475	530	427	307
621	602	575	525	522

Evaluate each expression for the given value of the variable. *(Section 2-2)*

26. $-3x$ when $x = -6$ **27.** $\frac{1}{2}x$ when $x = -2$ **28.** $0.75x$ when $x = 4$

Working on the Unit Project

29. A "half-pipe" skateboard ramp is formed by two quarter-circle ramps with flat space in between. The ramps reach a height of 11 ft and they are 16 ft apart. Find the distance a skateboarder travels from the top of one ramp to the top of the other ramp.

Unit 7 — CHECKPOINT

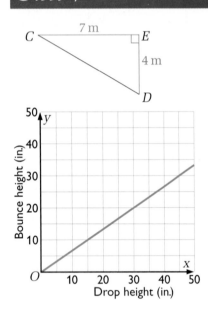

C —— 7 m —— □ *E*

4 m

D

1. **Writing** Suppose you have data involving two variables. How could you tell if one varies directly with the other? **7-1**

2. In right △*CDE*, find each tangent.

   a. tan *D* **b.** tan *C*

3. An escalator makes an angle of 30° with the horizontal. The horizontal length of the escalator is 24 ft. How high does the escalator rise?

4. The graph shows the relationship between the drop height and the bounce height of a rubber ball. Use the graph to estimate each height. **7-2**

   a. the bounce height when the drop height is 20 in.

   b. the drop height when the bounce height is 25 in.

5. Estimate the variation constant for the graph.

6. In a circle, the relationship between the circumference and the diameter can be written $\frac{C}{d} = \pi$. ($\pi \approx 3.14$) **7-3**

   a. Suppose $d = 400$ cm. Find *C*.

   b. Suppose $C = 60$ ft. Find *d*.

   c. Rewrite the equation in another form.

7. The Mather family orders a pizza. For toppings, they order $\frac{1}{3}$ vegetarian, $\frac{1}{2}$ ham and mushroom, and $\frac{1}{6}$ cheese.

   a. What is the circumference of the pizza?

   b. What is the length of the crust for the cheese section?

   c. What is the length of the crust for the vegetarian section?

cheese
60°

7 in.
radius

180°
ham and
mushroom

120°
vegetarian

382   **Unit 7** Direct Variation

Direct Variation with $y = kx$

BE ▶ DIRECT

·······Focus

Recognize general
characteristics of direct
variation equations and
graphs. Understand
negative slope.

Talk it Over

1. The table shows three examples of direct variation you have seen in this unit. How are the equations different? How are they alike?

$h = 0.75d$		height h of post varies directly with horizontal distance d
$B = 0.8D$		mean bounce height B varies directly with drop height D
$C = \pi d$		circumference C of a circle varies directly with diameter d

2. For each equation, identify the control variable, the dependent variable, and the variation constant.

You can model direct variation with an equation of the form $y = kx$.

one quantity **varies directly with** another quantity

$$y = k \cdot x$$

dependent variable   variation constant   control variable

The equation $y = kx$ is called the **general form for direct variation.**

The amount Cindy earns varies directly with the number of hours she works. She earns \$336 in a 40-hour work week. How much will Cindy earn in 130 h?

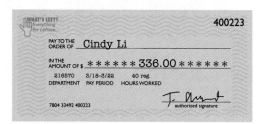

Sample Response

Method ❶

Model the situation with a direct variation equation in general form.

The amount earned varies directly with the number of hours worked.
Let y = the amount earned and x = the number of hours worked.

1. Solve $y = kx$ to find the variation constant k. ⟶ $y = k \cdot x$ ⟵ Substitute 336 for y and 40 for x.

$$336 = k(40)$$

$$\frac{336}{40} = \frac{k(40)}{40}$$ ⟵ Divide both sides by 40.

$$8.4 = k$$

2. Substitute the value k in the general form $y = kx$. ⟶ The equation is $y = 8.4x$.

3. Use the equation to find the amount earned in 130 h. ⟶ $y = 8.4(130)$ ⟵ Substitute 130 for x.

$$y = 1092$$

In 130 hours Cindy earns \$1092.

Method ❷

Problem Solving Strategy: Use a proportion

Let a = the amount earned in 130 h.

Use the fact that the ratio $\dfrac{\text{amount earned}}{\text{hours worked}}$ is always the same to write a proportion.

$$\frac{a}{130} = \frac{336}{40}$$

$$130 \cdot \frac{a}{130} = 130 \cdot \frac{336}{40}$$ ⟵ Multiply both sides by 130.

$$a = 1092$$

In 130 h Cindy earns \$1092.

Talk it Over

3. Suppose you want to find the amount Cindy earns in five different times, such as in 100 h, in 150 h, in 200 h, in 250 h and in 300 h. Which method in Sample 1 is easier to use? Explain your choice.

(2, 6.28318)

(6, 4.5)

(4, 3.2)

4. With a graphics calculator, Elia graphed the three equations shown in the table on page 383. She used TRACE to find coordinates of some points on the lines.

a. What is the y-intercept of each graph?

b. Find the slope of each line. (*Hint:* Use the y-intercept and the point Elia found with TRACE.)

c. Match each graph with its equation. What do you notice?

Direct variation graphs share some general characteristics.

DIRECT VARIATION GRAPHS

The graph of a direct variation equation $y = kx$ is a line that passes through the origin.

The variation constant k is the slope of the line.

Sample 2

Is direct variation a good model for the data shown in each graph? Explain why or why not.

a.

b.

c.

Sample Response

a.

No; the data points fit on a curve instead of a straight line.

b.
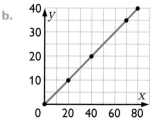

Yes; the data points fit on a line that goes through the origin.

c.
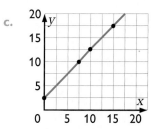

No; the data points fit on a line, but the line does not go through the origin.

······► Now you are ready for:
Exs. 1–7 on p. 388

7-4 Direct Variation with $y = kx$

The direct variation graph shown is a line with slope 3. Write an equation of the line.

$$\frac{\text{rise}}{\text{run}} = \frac{3}{1} = 3$$

Sample Response

The equation of a direct variation graph is in the form $y = kx$.

The variation constant k is the slope of the line.

The slope of the line is 3, so the equation of the line is $y = 3x$.

Negative Slope

Every direct variation graph you have seen in this unit so far is a line with positive slope. If the value of k is negative, then the graph of $y = kx$ is a line with negative slope.

Talk it Over

5. With a graphics calculator, Elia investigated the graph of $y = kx$ for three negative values of k.

   $y = -5x$
   $y = -1.5x$
   $y = -0.6x$

   Compare these three lines to the three lines in question 4.

   How are they alike?

   How are they different?

6. How do you think the sign of the slope affects the graph of a line?

7. Estimate the slope of the ground in the photograph of the biker.

Graph $y = -2x$.

Sample Response

$y = -2x$ is a direct variation equation in the form $y = kx$.

Make a table and plot points.

$y = -2x$	
x	y
-2	4
-1	2
0	0
1	-2
2	-4

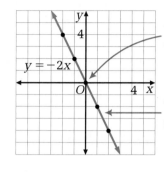

The graph is a line that goes through the origin.

$y = -2x$

The slope k is negative, so the graph falls from left to right.

Talk it Over

8. To check that the line $y = -2x$ has slope -2, two students find the ratio $\frac{\text{rise}}{\text{run}}$ between the points $(-1, 2)$ and $(2, -4)$.

   a. Explain why Regan says the run is positive and the rise is negative.

   b. Explain why Lianon says the run is negative and the rise is positive.

Regan moves from the upper point to the lower point.

Lianon moves from the lower point to the upper point.

   c. Show that both Regan and Lianon get -2 when they find the slope.

9. George looks at the table in Sample 4. He notices that as you go from row to row, the x-value increases by 1 and the y-value decreases by 2. He says that this also shows that the slope of the line is -2. Do you agree? Explain.

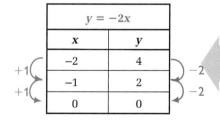

Look Back

Does an equation of the form $y = kx$ always represent a function? What special names are given to y, k, and x? What does the value of k tell you about the graph?

▶ Now you are ready for:
Exs. 8–43 on pp. 388–391

Exercises and Problems

1. **Reading** In Sample 1, what does the variation constant 8.4 represent in terms of the situation?

2. The cost of a soft drink varies directly with the number of ounces you buy. It costs 75 cents to buy a 12 oz bottle. How much does it cost to buy a 16 oz bottle?

3. The cost of gasoline varies directly with the number of gallons bought. It costs $10.29 to buy 7.4 gal of gasoline. How much does it cost to buy 9.3 gal of gasoline?

4. The mass of any substance varies directly with its volume. The mass of 5 cm³ of platinum is 107.5 g. Find the volume of 200 g of platinum.

Model each situation with a direct variation equation in general form.

5. Shelby can type 250 words in 4 minutes.

   a. How many words can Shelby type in half an hour?

   b. How long does it take Shelby to type 20,000 words?

6. A worker earns $490 in a 40-hour work week.

   a. How much does the worker earn after working 100 hours?

   b. How many hours does it take the worker to earn $5000?

7. An in-line skater covers 5 mi in 18 min.

   a. How many minutes does it take the skater to cover 16 mi?

   b. The skater skates for 10 min. Does the skater cover more than 2 mi? Explain.

Write an equation of the form $y = kx$ to describe each line.

8.

9.

10.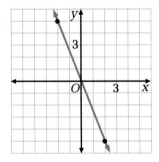

For Exercises 11–13:

   a. Does the graph show direct variation? Why or why not?

   b. If the graph shows direct variation, write an equation for the line.

11.

12.

13.

14. **Open-ended** Describe a situation that could be modeled by each of the graphs in Exercises 11–13.

15 TECHNOLOGY Use a graphics calculator or graphing software.
   a. Graph the line $y = \frac{2}{3}x$.
   b. Trace along your graph until y is about 5. What is x?
   c. Solve the equation $5 = \frac{2}{3}x$. How does your answer compare with part (b)? Which is more accurate?

The rise and run from (0, 0) to another point are given. Plot the other point using the directions below. Then draw the line.

16. rise = 6, run = 5   17. rise = −8, run = 3

18. rise = 5, run = −2   19. rise = −4, run = −8

20. a. For each rise and run in Exercises 16–19, find the slope of the line.
   b. **Writing** Look for a pattern in the signs of your results for part (a). Describe how the signs of the rise and run determine whether the slope is positive or negative.

21. **Writing** Describe the graphs of $y = x$ and $y = -x$. How are they alike? How are they different?

Match each equation with its graph.

22. $y = 0.5x$

23. $y = -0.5x$

24. $y = 2.5x$

25. $y = -2.5x$

A.

B.

C.

D.

Match each graph with its equation and explain how you arrived at your answer.

26. $y = 6x$
   $y = \frac{1}{6}x$

A.

B.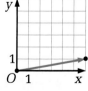

27. $y = -\frac{3}{5}x$
   $y = \frac{5}{3}x$

A.

B.

Graph each equation.

28. $y = -5x$ **29.** $y = 1.25x$ **30.** $y = -x$ **31.** $y = 0x$

32. In a direct variation equation of the form $y = kx$, the constant k is *multiplied* by the variable x. Now you will see what happens when k is added to x, subtracted from x, or divided by x.

  a. Choose a nonzero value of k. Create tables for the equations

     $y = x + k$, $y = x - k$, and $y = \dfrac{k}{x}$, using your value of k.
     List at least five ordered pairs in your tables.

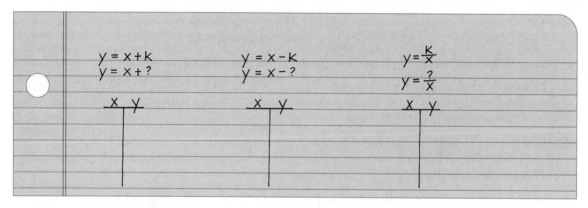

  b. Use your tables to graph the equations.

  c. Describe the graphs in words.

  d. Do any of the graphs represent direct variation? Explain.

33. On a cold day, a home furnace breaks down. For the first few hours, the drop in temperature varies directly with the time elapsed.

  a. Graph the data.

Time elapsed (h)	Temperature change (°F)
0.5	−1.5
0.75	−2.25
1	−3
1.5	−4.5

  b. Find the variation constant.

  c. Write an equation for the graph.

Ongoing **ASSESSMENT**

34. **Writing** Explain how changing the value of k affects the appearance of the graph of $y = kx$. Include both positive and negative values of k. Use diagrams to support your writing. Explain why the point $(0, 0)$ is found on all the graphs of equations of the form $y = kx$.

Find the circumference of each circle. *(Section 7-3)*

35. diameter = 14 in.

36. radius = 11 cm

Simplify. *(Section 5-2)*

37. $-2(3x + 2y)$ **38.** $-4(5a - 2b)$ **39.** $-7(-c + 5d)$ **40.** $-(-m - n)$

Multiply. *(Toolbox Skill 10)*

41. $\frac{2}{3} \times \frac{4}{5} \times \frac{1}{4} \times \frac{9}{10}$

42. $\frac{50}{63} \times \frac{7}{12} \times \frac{9}{11} \times \frac{33}{5}$

7 Working on the Unit Project

43. The frictional force on an in-line skater's wheels varies directly with the skater's weight.

   a. A 150 lb skater experiences 40.5 lb of friction when skating on a dry steel surface. Find the variation constant.

   b. Write a direct variation equation for this situation.

   c. Find the frictional force on a 130 lb skater.

   d. The variation constant for skating on a wet steel surface is 0.23. Is this greater or less than the variation constant you found in part (a)? Does this make sense?

   e. What kind of surfaces should you consider in your plans for a skateboard ramp?

Using Dimensional Analysis

Focus

Use dimensional analysis to work with the units in rates and conversion factors.

THE GOING RATE

At a gas station, self-serve unleaded gasoline sells for $1.369 per gallon. Here is what the gasoline pump might look like at various times as you fill your car's tank.

TOTAL SALE	TOTAL SALE	TOTAL SALE	TOTAL SALE
000.00	**004.11**	**006.85**	**011.44**
GALLONS	GALLONS	GALLONS	GALLONS
00.000	**03.000**	**05.000**	**08.350**
01.369	**01.369**	**01.369**	**01.369**
$Price Per Gallon	$Price Per Gallon	$Price Per Gallon	$Price Per Gallon

Here is how to calculate the amount you owe:

$$\text{cost} = \frac{1.369 \text{ dollars}}{1 \text{ gallon}} \cdot 8.35 \text{ gallons} \approx 11.44 \text{ dollars}$$

Notice that the gallons units cancel out. The result is measured in dollars. When you cancel units of measurement as if they are numbers, you are using a problem solving strategy called **dimensional analysis.**

1. Estimate to check that the dollar amounts shown for 3.00 gal and 5.00 gal are correct. Explain your method.

2. The amounts shown on the gas pump fit a direct variation model. What is the control variable? What is the dependent variable? What is the variation constant?

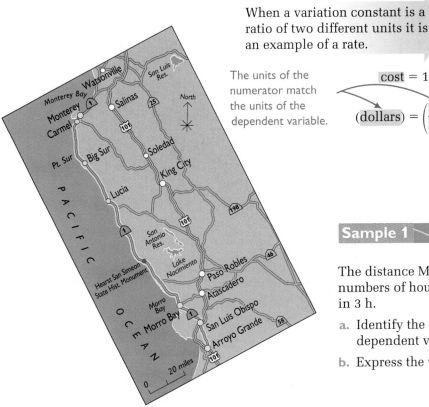

When a variation constant is a ratio of two different units it is an example of a rate.

$$\frac{1.369 \text{ dollars}}{1 \text{ gallon}}$$

$$\text{cost} = 1.369 \cdot \text{amount}$$

The units of the numerator match the units of the dependent variable.

$$(\text{dollars}) = \left(\frac{\text{dollars}}{\text{gallon}}\right) \cdot (\text{gallons})$$

The units of the denominator match the units of the control variable.

Sample 1

The distance Milo travels varies directly with the numbers of hours he drives. Milo drives 145 mi in 3 h.

a. Identify the control variable and the dependent variable.

b. Express the variation constant as a rate.

Sample Response

a. The control variable is the time traveled (h). The dependent variable is the distance traveled (mi).

b. The variation constant is $\frac{145 \text{ mi}}{3 \text{ h}} \approx 48.3$ mi/h.

Conversion Factors

A **conversion factor** is a ratio of two equal (or approximately equal) quantities that are measured in different units. For example, the ratio $\frac{2.54 \text{ cm}}{1 \text{ in.}}$ is a conversion factor, because 2.54 cm = 1 in. You use a conversion factor to convert a measurement from one unit to another.

Sample 2

a. How many centimeters are in 3 in.?

b. Write a direct variation equation that helps you convert inches to centimeters. What is the variation constant?

Sample Response

a. **Method ①** Use two rulers, one marked in inches, the other marked in centimeters. Place them so their zero marks line up.

```
0        5    ↓ 10 cm   15
|  |  |  |  |  |  |  |  |  |  |  |  |  |  |
0   1   2   3   4   5 in. 6
```

The 3 in. mark lines up with about 7.6 cm, so 3 in. ≈ 7.6 cm.

Method ② Use the conversion factor $\dfrac{2.54 \text{ cm}}{1 \text{ in.}}$.

Multiply the original amount by the conversion factor.

$$3 \cancel{\text{ in.}} \times \frac{2.54 \text{ cm}}{1 \cancel{\text{ in.}}} = 7.62 \text{ cm}$$

After the inches cancel, only centimeters are left.

Using the conversion factor gives a more accurate answer than the estimation from rulers in Method 1.

b. ➤ Let x = the number of inches.

➤ Let y = the number of centimeters.

The equation $y = 2.54x$ helps you convert inches to centimeters.

The variation constant is the conversion factor $\dfrac{2.54 \text{ cm}}{1 \text{ in.}}$, or 2.54 cm/in.

Talk it Over

3. Do you change the value of an expression when you multiply by a conversion factor? Why or why not?

4. What conversion factor would you use to convert centimeters to inches? Convert 12 cm to inches.

➤ **Now you are ready for:**
Exs. 1–8 on p. 396

5. Another well-known conversion factor is $\dfrac{365 \text{ days}}{1 \text{ year}}$. What other commonly-used conversion factors can you think of?

Converting the Units of a Rate

You can use conversion factors to convert the units of a rate.

Sample 3

In 1990 the French Train à Grande Vitesse (TGV) set a speed record of 515 km/h on the Atlantique line. Find its speed in miles per hour.

Sample Response

Problem Solving Strategy: Use dimensional analysis

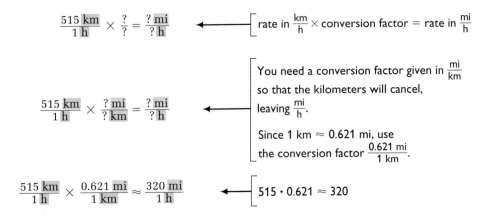

The TGV's speed was about 320 mi/h.

Sometimes you need many conversion factors to convert a rate to different units.

Sample 4

Convert 30 mi/h to ft/s.

Sample Response

Problem Solving Strategy: Use dimensional analysis

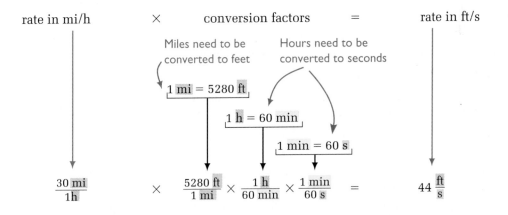

The rate 30 mi/h converts to the rate 44 ft/s.

6. In Sample 3, suppose you do not know that 1 km ≈ 0.621 mi. Instead you know that 1 mi ≈ 1.61 km. Explain how can you use the conversion factor $\frac{1 \text{ mi}}{1.61 \text{ km}}$ instead of the conversion factor $\frac{0.621 \text{ mi}}{1 \text{ km}}$.

7. Sam drives at a speed of 30 mi/h.

a. Write a direct variation equation that shows the relationship between the number of seconds Sam drives and the number of feet Sam drives. (*Hint:* Use the results of Sample 4.)

b. How many feet does Sam's car travel in 30 s?

Look Back

Now you are ready for: Exs. 9–37 on pp. 396–399

In what way is a rate a special kind of ratio? In what way is a conversion factor a special kind of rate?

7-5 Exercises and Problems

1. **Reading** What rates were used in the Samples of this section? What other rates can you think of?

For Exercises 2–5, each expression shows the units of a conversion problem. Use dimensional analysis to find the unit(s) of the answer.

2. $\frac{\text{yen}}{\text{dollars}} \times \text{dollars} = \underline{\ ?\ }$

3. $\frac{\text{h}}{\text{min}} \times \frac{\text{min}}{\text{s}} = \underline{\ ?\ }$

4. $\frac{\text{cups}}{\text{pt}} \times \frac{\text{pt}}{\text{qt}} = \underline{\ ?\ }$

5. $\frac{\text{mi}}{\text{h}} \times \frac{\text{h}}{\text{min}} \times \frac{\text{ft}}{\text{mi}} = \underline{\ ?\ }$

For Exercises 6–8:

a. Identify the control variable and the dependent variable.

b. Express the variation constant as a rate.

6. The cost paid for gasoline varies directly with the amount bought. Marshall pays $9.52 for 7 gal of gasoline.

7. The number of gallons of gasoline used varies directly with the distance traveled in miles. Mina's car uses 20 gal of gasoline when it travels 440 mi.

8. The cost of carpet varies directly with its area in square yards. Weston Carpets sells 9 yd² of a certain carpet for $324.

9. How many kilometers are in 50 mi? (1 mi ≈ 1.6 km)

10. How many gallons of juice are in a 2 L bottle? (1 gal ≈ 3.8 L)

11. How many feet are in 7.2 mi? (1 mi = 5280 ft)

12. On one day, one Japanese yen was equal to 0.009428 United States dollars. How many United States dollars equal 1,000,000 yen?

13. Before leaving for a vacation to Mexico, the Nguyen family exchanged $1250 for Mexican pesos. Each dollar was worth 3.10 pesos. How many pesos did they get?

14. Centavo coins are used in Mexico in amounts of 5, 10, 20, and 50 centavos. (100 centavos = 1 peso)

   a. How many centavos are in 53 pesos?

   b. **Research** What do you think the word *centavos* means? Look up the word in a Spanish-English dictionary. Why do you think it was chosen?

15. On their vacation, the Nguyens fill the tank of their rental car with gasoline *sin plomo*. They buy 32 L for 41.6 pesos.

   a. Find the cost per liter of the gasoline they bought.

   b. Write a direct variation equation that shows the relationship between the cost of gasoline and the amount bought.

   c. How much would it cost to buy 25 L of gasoline?

16. You can buy 9.8 gal of super unleaded gasoline for $13.23. You can buy 12 gal of regular unleaded at the same station for $12.60.

   a. What is the cost per gallon of super unleaded?

   b. Write a direct variation equation that shows the relationship between cost of super unleaded gasoline and number of gallons bought.

   c. Find the cost of 15 gal of super unleaded gasoline.

   d. How much will it cost to buy 10 gal of regular unleaded?

   e. Suppose you have $20 to spend on gasoline. How much super unleaded can you buy for this amount? How much regular unleaded?

17. In the graphs, one line represents super unleaded gasoline, and the other represents regular unleaded gasoline.

   a. Does the green line represent super unleaded or regular unleaded?

   b. Explain the comparison that the graph at the left shows.

   c. Explain the comparison that the graph at the right shows.

   d. What information does the length of the gray segment in each graph tell you?

18. Exchange rates on one day are shown at the right. Find out how many yen equaled one mark on that day. Use conversion factors.

COUNTRY	Foreign currency in U.S. dollars	U.S. dollar in foreign currency
Germany (Mark)	0.4834	2.0686
Japan (Yen)	0.009258	108.02

19. Regular unleaded gasoline costs 88 yen per liter in Japan. Find its cost in dollars per gallon. Assume that 108 yen equal one dollar and use the fact that there are 3.8 liters in one gallon.

20. Convert 4000 s to hours.

21. Convert 32,500 in. to miles.

22. How long is one million seconds? When will you be one billion seconds old?

23. Suppose you are driving at 76 km/h. How many miles per hour is this?

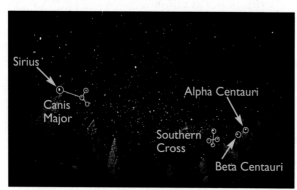

24. Aside from our own sun, the nearest star to Earth is Alpha Centauri. It takes light 4.3 years to reach Earth from that star. The speed of light is about 186,000 mi/s. Find the distance, in miles, from Earth to Alpha Centauri. Give your answer in scientific notation.

Alpha Centauri and the Southern Cross are visible in this photograph taken in Queenstown, New Zealand.

25. In a game against the Detroit Tigers, Nolan Ryan threw a pitch at a speed of 148 ft/s. Find the speed in miles per hour.

26. The scale you use for the vertical axis of a graph affects how steep a line looks. Here are three graphs of the equation $c = 1.5a$. Each has a different vertical scale.

a. Which line *looks as if* it has the steepest slope?

b. Which line *looks as if* it has the shallowest slope?

c. Are the variation constants the same or different for the three graphs?

d. Are the slopes the same or different for the three lines?

e. **Writing** Describe how the scale used for the vertical axis affects the way a graph of a line looks.

27. Open-ended Use the table at the right.

a. Find the exchange rates from United States dollars to the money of three countries of your choice.

b. List three consumer items whose price in United States dollars you know.

c. Use conversion factors to find the price of these items in the countries you have chosen. (Assume that the prices are equivalent.)

EXCHANGE RATES

SATURDAY, JUNE 3

	Fgn. currency in dollars	Dollar in fgn. currency
Australia (Dollar)	.5795	1.7256
Brazil (CruzeiroR)	.5556	1.800
Britain (Pound)	1.5127	.6611
Canada (Dollar)	.6778	1.4755
China (Yuan)	.1208	8.2771
Denmark (Krone)	.1266	7.8890
France (Franc)	.1442	6.9377
Germany (Mark)	.4834	2.0686
Hong Kong (Dollar)	.1283	7.7920
India (Rupee)	.0224	44.600
Israel (Shekel)	.2419	4.1350
Italy (Lira)	.000489	2047.88
Japan (Yen)	.009258	108.02
Mexico (Peso)	.1048	9.5420
N. Zealand (Dollar)	.4650	2.1506
Russia (Ruble)	.3553	28.150
Saudi Arabia (Riyal)	.2667	3.7505
Spain (Peseta)	.005683	175.977
Thailand (Baht)	.02563	39.020

Review PREVIEW

Graph. *(Section 7-4)*

28. $y = 5x$

29. $y = -3x$

Solve each proportion. *(Section 6-3)*

30. $\dfrac{x}{240} = \dfrac{120}{360}$

31. $\dfrac{x}{50} = \dfrac{40}{360}$

32. $\dfrac{20}{x} = \dfrac{40}{360}$

Find each value for x. *(Sections 2-5, 2-7)*

33.

34.

35.

7 Working on the Unit Project

Thickness of plywood	Cost per square foot
$\frac{3}{4}$ in.	$2.31
$\frac{1}{2}$ in.	$1.90
$\frac{1}{4}$ in.	$.99

36. One plan for building a skateboard launch ramp calls for four sheets of $\frac{3}{4}$ in. plywood, one sheet of $\frac{1}{2}$ in. plywood, and one sheet of $\frac{1}{4}$ in. plywood. All the sheets measure 4 ft by 8 ft. Find the total cost of purchasing the plywood needed for this ramp.

37. Research List the materials you would need to build the ramps for your skating arena. Check with a local lumber yard to find current prices. Estimate the cost of the materials you would need.

Areas of Circles and Sectors

Focus

Use the formula for the area of a circle and find the area of a sector.

Pieces Of Pi

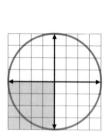

EXPLORATION

What *is the relationship between the area of a circle and its radius?*

- **Work in a group of three students. Have each person in your group use one of the diagrams on this page.**

① Estimate the area of the circle in your diagram by counting the squares inside the circle. Include parts of squares in your estimate.

② Find the area of the large shaded square in your diagram.

③ Find the ratio of the area you estimated in step 1 to the area you found in step 2:

$$\frac{\text{estimated area of circle}}{\text{area of shaded square}} = \frac{?}{}$$

④ Write your ratio as a decimal.

> ➤ Compare your ratio with the ratios found by the other students in your group.

>> ➤ What do you notice?

>>> ➤ Let A represent your estimate of the area of the circle in your diagram.

>>>> ➤ Discuss in your group why the ratio you wrote in step 3 can be represented by $\frac{A}{r^2}$.

⑤ Find the mean of the three ratios your group found in step 3. Use that number to complete this formula: $\frac{A}{r^2} = \frac{?}{}$

⑥ Compare your group's formula with the known formula for the area of a circle, $A = \pi r^2$. How close was your estimate to the value of π?

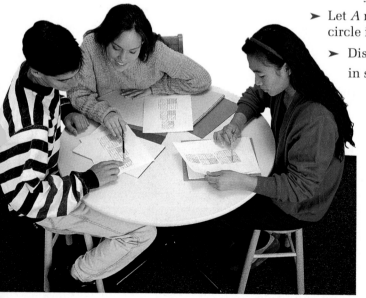

Find the area of a circle whose radius is 3 units. Round the answer to the nearest square unit.

Sample Response

Problem Solving Strategy: Use a formula

$$A = \pi r^2$$

$$= \pi \cdot 3^2 \quad \longleftarrow \text{ Substitute 3 for } r.$$

$$\approx 28.3 \quad \longleftarrow \quad \boxed{\pi} \quad \boxed{\times} \quad 3 \; \boxed{X^2} \quad \boxed{\text{ENTER}}$$

The area is about 28 square units.

In a center-pivot irrigation system, a moving arm sprinkles water over a circular region. How long must the arm be to water an area of 586,000 m²?

Round the answer to the nearest meter.

Sample Response

Problem Solving Strategy: Use a formula

The arm forms the radius of a circle with area 586,000 m².

$$A = \pi r^2$$

$$586{,}000 = \pi r^2 \quad \longleftarrow \text{ Substitute 586,000 for } A.$$

$$\frac{586{,}000}{\pi} = \frac{r^2}{\pi} \quad \longleftarrow \text{ Divide both sides by } \pi.$$

$$186{,}529.6 \approx r^2$$

$$\sqrt{186{,}529.6} \approx r \quad \longleftarrow \text{ Find the positive square root.}$$

$$431.9 \approx r$$

The arm must be about 432 m long.

Talk it Over

1. In Sample 2, why is only the positive square root considered as an answer to the problem?

······► **Now you are ready for:**
Exs. 1–11 on pp. 404–405

2. Explain why the equation $\frac{A}{\pi} = r^2$ is equivalent to $A = \pi r^2$.

Area of a Sector

The region of a circle formed by a central angle and its arc is called a **sector**. The area of a sector is a fraction of the area of the circle.

AREA OF A SECTOR

You can use this proportion to find the area of any sector:

$$\frac{\text{area of a sector}}{\text{area of the circle}} = \frac{\text{measure of the central angle}}{360°}$$

sector

central angle

r

Sample 3

A circular quilt pattern has a radius of 12 in. What is the area of the blue panel? Round the answer to the nearest square inch.

The wedge-shaped panel is a sector.

Sample Response

Problem Solving Strategy: Use a proportion

Let x = the area of the sector. ⟶ The measure of the central angle is 45°.

$$\frac{x}{452} = \frac{45}{360}$$

The area of the circle is $\pi \cdot 12^2$. ⟶ The measure of a complete circle is 360°.

$$\frac{x}{452} \cdot 452 = \frac{45}{360} \cdot 452 \quad \longleftarrow \text{Multiply both sides by 452.}$$

$$x = 56.5$$

The area of the blue panel is about 57 in.^{2}.

Expressing Areas in Terms of π

Sometimes you can solve problems without substituting a value for π.

About how many times more pizza do you get when you buy the large size instead of the small size?

The thickness of both pizzas is about the same.

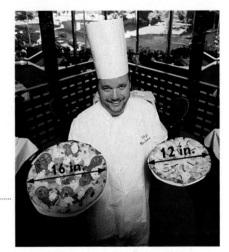

Sample Response

First find the area of each pizza in terms of π.

The radius of the large pizza is 8 in.

$$A = \pi r^2 = \pi \cdot 8^2 = 64\pi$$

$$A = \pi r^2 = \pi \cdot 6^2 = 36\pi$$

The radius of the small pizza is 6 in.

Then write an equation:

The area of large pizza is how many times the area of the small pizza?

$$64\pi = x(36\pi)$$

$$\frac{64\pi}{36\pi} = \frac{x(36\pi)}{36\pi}$$ ← Divide both sides by 36π.

$$1.8 \approx x$$

BY THE WAY...

The first restaurant specializing in pizza opened in New York City in 1895.

You get about 1.8 times more pizza when you buy the large size instead of the small size.

▶ Now you are ready for:
Exs. 12–35 on pp. 405–407

Look Back ◀

How is finding the area of a sector like finding its arc length? How is it different?

1. **Writing** How could you improve your estimate for π in the Exploration?

For Exercises 2–4, find the unknown measurement for each circle.

2. radius = 5 mm
   area = _?_

3. diameter = 12 ft
   area = _?_

4. area = 56 m²
   radius = _?_

5. Find the area of the circle at the right.

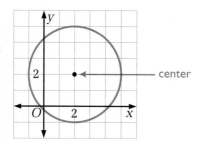

6. A circle on a coordinate plane has its center at $(1, -1)$. The circle goes through the point $(1, 7)$. What is the area of the circle?

7. Tanya says that when the radius of a circle is 2 units, the number of units in the circumference of the circle is equal to the number of square units in its area. Do you agree or disagree? Why?

Radius r (cm)	Area A (cm²)	$\frac{A}{r}$ (cm)
1	?	?
2	?	?
3	?	?
4	?	?
5	?	?
6	?	?

8. **a.** Complete the table of values for a circle of radius r.
   b. Is the ratio $\frac{A}{r}$ constant?
   c. Graph the data from the table with r on the horizontal axis and A on the vertical axis.
   d. Is the graph a straight line through the origin?
   e. Does the area of a circle vary directly with the radius? Why or why not?

9. **a.** Complete the table of values for a circle of radius r.
   b. What do you notice about the ratio column?
   c. Find the variation constant for the relationship between the area of a circle and the square of its radius.
   d. Suppose you make a graph with r^2 on the horizontal axis and A on the vertical axis. What do you think the graph will look like? Draw the graph. Was your prediction correct?

Radius r (cm)	r^2 (cm²)	Area A (cm²)	$\frac{A}{r^2}$
1	?	?	?
2	?	?	?
3	?	?	?
4	?	?	?
5	?	?	?
6	?	?	?

For Exercises 10 and 11, find the area of the circle in each figure.

10. Area of square = 64 cm²

11. Perimeter of rectangle = 28 in.

|← 9 in. →|

12. **Reading** In Sample 4, why is substituting a value for π not necessary?

For Exercises 13–15, find the area of each sector.

13.

65°
6 cm

14.

20°
14 in.

15.

The area of the circle is 25π ft².

80°

For Exercise 16, use the menu shown. Assume that large and small round pizzas have about the same thickness.

16. a. About how many times more pizza do you get when you order the large size instead of the small size?

b. Which size cheese pizza is the better buy? Why?

c. Do you think the prices of extra toppings are fair? Why or why not?

17. a. Tom cuts a 12 in. pizza into 6 slices of equal size. What is the area of one slice?

b. Vera cuts a 12 in. pizza into 8 slices of equal size. What is the area of one slice?

c. Compare the sizes of a slice of Vera's pizza and a slice of Tom's pizza.

18. a. Compare the areas of the sectors.

b. Compare the arc lengths of the sectors.

SLICES
House of Pizza

Small Cheese $8.65
(11 in. diameter)
$.95 per extra topping

Large Cheese $11.75
(14 in. diameter)
$1.80 per extra topping

120°
6 m

60°
12 m

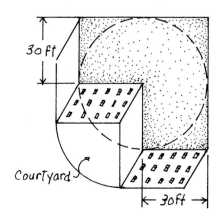

30 ft

Courtyard

← 30 ft →

19. The courtyard of an apartment building is shaped like one fourth of a circle. Cement that covers an area of one square foot costs $2.60. How much will it cost to repave the courtyard?

20. The end of a dog's leash is tied to a hook on the side of a shed.

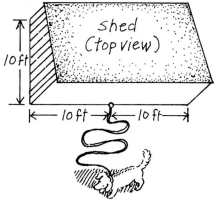

a. Over what area can the dog roam if the dog's leash is 10 ft long? 18 ft long? 25 ft long?

b. **Open-ended** Suppose the leash is 25 ft long. Will the dog have more room to roam if the hook is moved? If so, where do you think the hook should be placed?

21. A circular herb garden is divided into three equal sections. The radius of the garden is 4 ft.

a. Find the area of one sector.

b. A gardener decides to plant marigolds on the outside edge of two of the sectors. The marigolds should be planted 1 ft apart. How many marigold plants does the gardener need?

22. To estimate the area of a circle, the ancient Egyptians measured the diameter of a circle and drew a square with sides that are $\frac{8}{9}$ as long as the diameter.

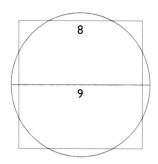

a. Compare the areas of a circle and a square with these dimensions:

circle: diameter = 9 in., *square:* side length = 8 in.

b. Compare the areas of a circle and a square with these dimensions:

circle: diameter = d, *square:* side length = $\frac{8}{9}d$

c. What value for π results from the Egyptian method? How close is this estimate to the value of π that you use?

23. **Writing** The area S of a sector can be found by using the formula $S = \frac{x}{360}(\pi r^2)$, where $x°$ is the measure of the central angle for the sector. Explain why this formula works.

Ongoing **ASSESSMENT**

Writing Tell whether each statement is *True* or *False*. Explain your choice.

24. The area of a circle varies directly with the diameter.

25. The area of a circle varies directly with the square of the diameter.

26. The area of a circle varies directly with the circumference.

27. The area of a sector varies directly with the arc length of the central angle for the sector.

Review **PREVIEW**

For Exercises 28 and 29, use conversion factors. *(Section 7-5)*

28. Convert 1100 ft/s to miles per hour.

29. Convert $22/ft² to dollars per square yard.

30. The graph shows a rotation around the origin. What is the direction of the rotation and the amount of turn? *(Section 4-4)*

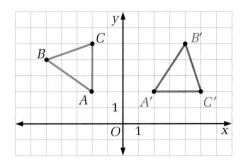

Solve. *(Sections 2-7, 2-8)*

31. $14 = 0.7x + 28$

32. $\frac{1}{3}y - 12 = 9$

33. $-4 = 12a + 8$

 Working on the Unit Project

34. To make the sides of a skateboard ramp, two corner-to-corner arcs are drawn from opposite corners of a plywood square. The wood where the sectors overlap is not used.

Center of first arc

Center of Second arc

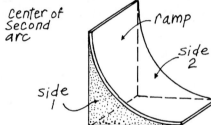

ramp

side 2

side 1

a. What is the area of each side of the ramp?

b. What is the area of the plywood that is not used?

c. What fraction of the plywood square is not used?

35. A circular arena for skaters includes a skating rink with a radius of 30 ft. There are benches in a circle 10 ft beyond the edge of the rink.

a. Find the total area of the arena, including the space between the rink and the benches.

b. Find the area of the space between the rink and the benches.

7-6 Areas of Circles and Sectors

Completing the Unit Project

Now you are ready to complete a scale drawing or a model of your skating competition arena. Label its parts and the dimensions.

Include answers to these questions on your drawing or in a description of your model.

➤ **What are the slopes of the ramps used in your arena?**

➤ **What are the arc lengths of any of the circular parts of your arena?**

➤ **What is the slope of the bleachers?**

➤ **What materials are needed to make your arena?**

➤ **What is the estimated cost of building your arena?**

Look Back ◄

Write an evaluation of each arena designed by your class. What features do many of the designs have in common? What features are unique? Which designs do you like the best? Why?

Alternative Projects

Project 1: A Trip to Another Country

Write a story about a trip to another country. Include how you might use direct variation during the trip. For example, show how the cost of a car rental varies with mileage, how to convert distances between cities from kilometers to miles, and how to change dollars into the currency of another country.

Project 2: The History of π

Research the number π. What are some of the approximations for π that have been used by different cultures? How many digits of π are known?

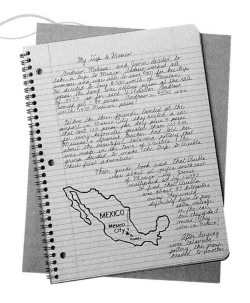

1. **Writing** Compare slope, tangent ratios, and direct variation ratios. How are they alike? How are they different? Give an example of a situation where you would use each.

2. **a.** Set up an equation to relate the height of a tree to its shadow when the sun is 35° above the horizon.

   b. Use a calculator to find tan 35° to the nearest thousandth.

   c. Find the height of a tree that casts a 20 ft shadow.

   d. Find the length of a shadow cast by a tree that is 42 ft tall.

   e. What is the variation constant in this situation?

7-1

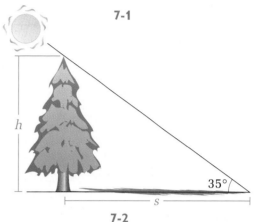

3. Arc lengths for a circle are related to the central angles as shown in the table

7-2

Central angle W (°)	180	240	300	360
Arc length M (m)	4.5	6.0	7.5	9.0

   a. Find the ratio $\frac{M}{W}$ for each central angle in the table.

   b. Write an equation relating M and W.

   c. What is the arc length for a 280° central angle?

4. Keisha and Kevin performed the bouncing ball exploration. Here are their data.

Drop height D (cm)	40	60	80	100	120	140
Bounce height B (cm)	17	24	31	47	48	57

   a. Make a graph of the data.

   b. Keisha and Kevin decide that one of their measurements is wrong. They cross it off their graph. Which one do they cross off?

   c. Is direct variation a good model for the set of data that remains? Explain.

   d. Estimate the variation constant from these data.

   e. Use your graph to predict the bounce height when the ball is dropped from a height of 70 cm.

5. The diameter of the sun is approximately 865,000 miles. Find its circumference.

7-3

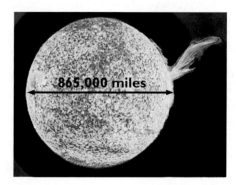

865,000 miles

6. A can with radius 2.5 in. rolls down a ramp a total distance of 96 in. How many complete turns will it make?

2.5 in.

96 in.

7. Four quarter-circles are attached to a 4 in. square to form a pinwheel design. Find the perimeter of the design.

4 in. 4 in.

8. The length (*L*) that a spring stretches varies directly with the force (*F*) that is applied. When a force of 3.5 lb is applied to a spring, it stretches 2.3 in.

7-4

2.3 in.

3.5 lbs

  a. Find the variation constant. What are its units?

  b. How far will the spring stretch when a 5 lb force is applied?

  c. How much force is needed to stretch the spring 3 in.?

9. a. Which line has negative slope? Explain.

  b. Which line has the smallest positive slope? Explain.

  c. Which line has the greatest variation constant? Explain.

10. a. Graph the equation $y = -1.5x$.

  b. What is the slope of this line?

  c. What quadrants does the line pass through?

  d. For what value of x does $y = -9$?

11. How many days are in 16 years?

7-5

12. Write a direct variation equation that helps you convert days to years. What is the variation constant?

13. A marathon is 26.2 mi. Convert this distance to meters.

14. It takes about 15,000 s for light to travel from the sun to the planet Neptune. Convert this amount to hours.

15. The speed limit on some highways is 65 mi/h. Convert to feet per second.

16. For Thanksgiving dinner, Grandpa makes his favorite recipe for apple pie. There are 7 people who want an equal share.

7-6

  a. Find the size of each slice of pie in degrees.

  b. If the pie has a diameter of 12 in., find the area of each slice.

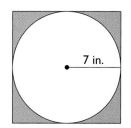

7 in.

17. A circle with a 7 in. radius just fits inside a square.

  a. Find the area of the shaded region.

  b. Find the ratio of the shaded area to the area of the circle.

  c. Do you think the ratio you found in part (b) would be different if the circle and square were each twice as large? Explain why or why not.

18. **Self-evaluation** What do you think are the important ideas of this unit? Make a concept map of these ideas and show how they relate to one another.

19. **Group Activity** Work in a group of four students. You will need a tape measure or meter stick scaled in both inches and centimeters.

  a. Measure the height of everyone in your group. For half the group, use centimeters. For the other half, use inches.

  b. Write an equation that relates height in centimeters (y) to height in inches (x). What is the variation constant? What are the units of the variation constant?

  c. Use the equation to find each group member's height in both inches and centimeters.

  d. Verify your results by measuring each member's height using the other unit of measurement.

IDEAS AND (FORMULAS) $= X^2$ $_5P_5$

➤ **Measurement** You can cancel units of measurement as if they are numbers when dividing. *(p. 392)*

➤ **Measurement** If two variables in direct variation have different units of measurement, then the variation constant will be a rate. *(p. 393)*

➤ **Measurement** You can use conversion factors to convert from one measurement or rate to another with different units. *(p. 393)*

➤ **Measurement** Sometimes you need to use more than one conversion factor. *(p. 395)*

➤ When two variables have a constant ratio, they are in direct variation. *(p. 360)*

➤ When two variables vary directly, you can find the value of one variable when given a value of the other variable. *(p. 360)*

➤ The slope of a line is the ratio of the rise to the run between any two points on the line. *(p. 361)*

➤ Direct variation can be used to model real-life behavior, like the bouncing of a ball. *(p. 368)*

➤ You can use a direct variation graph to make predictions. *(p. 368)*

➤ The letter k is sometimes used to represent a variation constant in the general form for direct variation: $y = kx$. *(p. 383)*

➤ The graph of direct variation is a straight line through the origin. *(p. 385)*

➤ The slope of a direct variation graph is the same as the variation constant. *(p. 386)*

➤ If the variation constant of a direct variation equation is negative, the slope of the line is negative. Lines with negative slope go down from left to right. *(p. 386)*

➤ The tangent ratio compares the legs of a right triangle.

$$\tan A = \frac{\text{length of the leg opposite } \angle A}{\text{length of the leg adjacent } \angle A} \quad (p.\ 361)$$

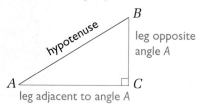

leg opposite angle A

leg adjacent to angle A

hypotenuse

➤ The circumference, C, of a circle varies directly with the diameter, d.
$$C = \pi d \ (p.\ 376)$$

➤ The value of π can be approximated by 3.14 or $\frac{22}{7}$. $(p.\ 376)$

➤ You can use the formula $C = \pi d$ to find the circumference of a circle when the diameter is known, or to find the diameter when the circumference is known. $(p.\ 376)$

➤ For any arc of a circle,
$$\frac{\text{arc length}}{\text{circumference}} = \frac{\text{central angle}}{360°} \ (p.\ 377)$$

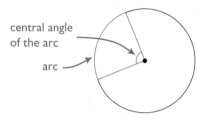

central angle of the arc

arc

➤ The area, A, of a circle varies directly with the *square* of the radius of the circle.
$$A = \pi r^2 \ (p.\ 400)$$

➤ You can use the formula $A = \pi r^2$ to find the area of a circle when the radius is known, or to find the radius when the area is known. $(p.\ 401)$

➤ For any sector,
$$\frac{\text{area of sector}}{\text{area of circle}} = \frac{\text{central angle}}{360°} \ (p.\ 402)$$

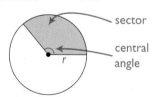

sector

central angle

r

➤ You can express areas of circles in terms of π. $(p.\ 403)$

GEOMETRY

Key Terms

- **direct variation** (p. 360)
- **rise** (p. 361)
- **diameter** (p. 375)
- **arc** (p. 377)

- **variation constant** (p. 360)
- **run** (p. 361)
- **circumference** (p. 375)
- **arc length** (p. 377)

- **slope** (p. 361)
- **tangent ratio** (p. 361)
- **pi (π)** (p. 376)
- **general form for direct variation** (p. 383)

- **dimensional analysis** (p. 392)

- **conversion factor** (p. 393)

- **sector** (p. 402)

8

unit

Linear Equations as Models

BREAKTHROUGHS

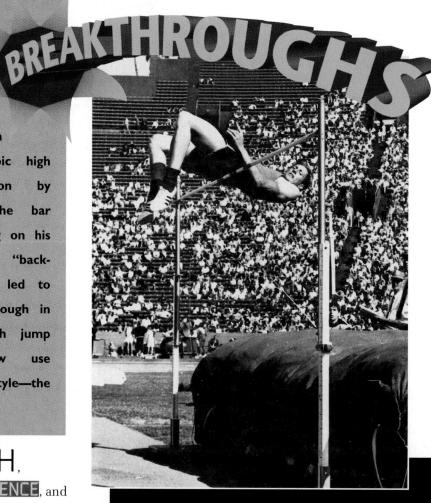

The secret to success may be to flop! Dick Fosbury won a gold medal in the 1968 Olympic high jump competition by flopping over the bar head first, landing on his back. Fosbury's "backwards" approach led to a major breakthrough in sports. Most high jump competitors now use his innovative style—the Fosbury flop!

What do **MATH**, **COMPUTER SCIENCE**, and **PHYSICS** have to do with coaching **SPORTS**?

Sports trainers use scientific breakthroughs to make athletes' training more efficient and productive. Gymnasts and ice skaters have their moves captured on film and analyzed by a computer. Mike Powell set an Olympic high jump record after initiating a scientific training plan that included pulling an open parachute behind him when he ran.

training

Predicting the Future

Your project is to write a news article predicting the new record-breaking time for the Olympic women's 400 m freestyle swimming event.

To write the article, you will use mathematical models to analyze past Olympic results and make your prediction. A completed project will include a data file you create to support the information you include in the article.

Have you ever seen a boat that FLIES?

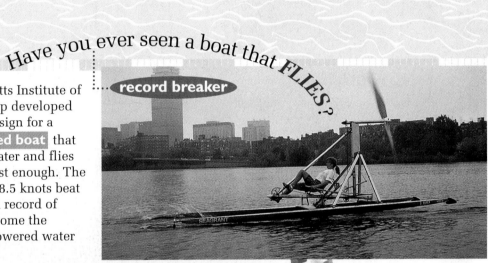

One Massachusetts Institute of Technology group developed an innovative design for a **human-powered boat** that lifts out of the water and flies when pedaled fast enough. The boat's speed of 18.5 knots beat the former world record of 14.4 knots to become the fastest human-powered water vehicle.

record breaker

A revolutionary **scientific** breakthrough occurred when James Watson, Francis Crick, and Rosalind Franklin discovered that DNA could be modeled by a double helix. Their work revealed the structure of genetic material and paved the way for modern medical research.

Getting Started

For this project you should work with a partner. Here are some ideas to help you get started on your project.

☞ Think about how you will organize the data you collect. Will you be able to use a computer database or spreadsheet?

☞ You should include graphs in your article. You may want to review the various types of data displays in Section 3-6.

☞ Think about a newspaper or magazine you may want to write for. Will you suit the style of your article to its readers?

Can We Talk BREAKTHROUGHS

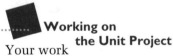

Working on the Unit Project

Your work in Unit 8 will help you make your predictions.

Related Exercises:

Section 8-1, Exercise 44

Section 8-2, Exercise 27

Section 8-3, Exercise 36

Section 8-4, Exercise 31

Section 8-5, Exercise 30

Section 8-6, Exercise 39

Section 8-7, Exercise 39

Alternative Projects p. 469

➤ What information can you learn about the 400 m freestyle winning times just by looking at the matrix?

➤ Suppose you want to predict the winning time for the men's 400 m freestyle in the year 2012. What information do you need to know?

➤ What factors do you think have caused Olympic records to improve?

➤ Records for Olympic sports have been improving ever since modern-day Olympics were first held in 1896. Do you think the records can continue to improve forever? Why or why not?

➤ Describe some of the advantages that modern Olympic athletes have over earlier Olympic athletes.

Winning Times Olympic 400 m Freestyle Swimming		
	Men	Women
Year	Time (seconds)	Time (seconds)
1960	258.3 AUS	290.6 USA
1964	252.2 USA	283.3 USA
1968	249.0 USA	271.8 USA
1972	240.27 USA	259.44 AUS
1976	231.93 USA	249.89 E.Ger
1980	231.31 USSR	248.76 E.Ger
1984	231.23 USA	247.10 USA
1988	226.95 E.Ger	243.85 USA
1992	225.00 UT	247.18 GER
1996	227.97 NZE	247.25 IRL

➤ Do you think events occurring now help you predict future events? Explain.

➤ What types of predictions have you made in your life? What information have you used to help you make a prediction?

Linear Growth and Decay

Focus
Recognize how the rate and
the initial value in a real-life
situation appear in an
equation and a graph
representing the situation.

RISING AND FALLING

Talk it Over

At a hot air balloon festival in Albuquerque,
New Mexico, a balloon takes off from a
spot 6000 ft above sea level. The
balloon rises 110 ft every minute.

? ft
t = 3 min

? ft
t = 2 min

6110 ft
t = 1 min

6000 ft
t = 0 min

6000 ft above sea level

Time in minutes (*t*)	Height of balloon in feet (*h*)
0	6000
1	6110
2	?
⋮	⋮

1. Model the situation with a table of values.

2. Write an equation for the height of the balloon after
   t minutes.

3. Which variable in the table is the control variable? Which is
   the dependent variable?

4. Plot the points. What pattern do you see? Connect the
   points.

5. Your graph is an example of *linear growth*. What does *linear*
   mean? What is *growing* in this situation?

6. What is the slope of the graph? How is the slope related to
   the situation?

7. Where does the graph meet the vertical axis? How is this
   point related to the height of the balloon?

Slope-Intercept Form

Another balloon takes off from 8200 ft above sea level and rises at a rate of 60 ft/min. The graph shows the height of this balloon over time. The equation below also shows the height (h) of the balloon after t minutes.

rise = vertical change
$= 8440 - 8260$
$= 180$

run = horizontal change
$= 4 - 1$
$= 3$

vertical intercept:
The line meets the vertical axis at (0, 8200). Its vertical intercept is 8200.

This is the height of the balloon when $t = 0$.

$$h = 60t + 8200$$

slope of the line:
$$\frac{\text{rise}}{\text{run}} = \frac{180}{3} = 60$$
This is the rate at which the balloon rises in feet per minute.

Often the variable m is used for the slope, b is used for the vertical intercept, x is the control variable, and y is the dependent variable. Below is the **slope-intercept form of an equation** for a line.

$$y = mx + b$$

slope ⌐ ⌐ vertical intercept

Watch Out!
The coefficient of the x-term is the slope, even if the equation is written in the form $y = b + mx$.

Talk it Over

8. Compare the equation you wrote in question 2 with the equation $h = 60t + 8200$. How are they alike? How are they different?

9. Suppose you redraw the graph of the balloon's height so that there is no gap in the scale. Would this change how the slope of the line looks? Would the slope still be 60? Explain.

10. Does the graph represent a function? How can you tell?

11. **a.** Does the graph represent direct variation? Why or why not?

   b. Explain how the equation $h = 60t + 8200$ is different from a direct variation equation.

BY THE WAY...

Since hot air is lighter than cold air, hot air balloons rise when the air inside the balloon is warmer than the air outside. The hottest air is at the top of a hot air balloon. The air ranges in temperature from 180°F to 225°F.

When you travel up from Earth's surface, the air temperature decreases by about 11°F for each mile you rise above the ground. Suppose the temperature of the air at ground level is 68°F.

a. Model the situation with a table of values.

b. Use your table to make a graph. Find the slope and the vertical intercept of the line that contains the points. Explain what they mean in terms of the situation.

c. Write an equation for the Fahrenheit temperature of the air (f) as a function of the height in miles above the ground (h).

Sample Response ....

a. The starting temperature is 68°F. Because the temperature is decreasing, subtract 11 for each mile above the ground.

Height above ground (mi)	Temperature (°F)
0	68
1	57
2	46
3	35
4	24

b. Plot the points and connect them.

rise = vertical change
= 24 − 46
= −22

The rise is negative because the line slants down from left to right.

(0, 68)
(2, 46)
(4, 24)

run = horizontal change
= 4 − 2
= 2

vertical intercept = 68
The vertical intercept is the temperature at ground level.

$$\text{slope} = \frac{\text{rise}}{\text{run}} = \frac{-22}{2} = -11$$

The slope is the rate at which the temperature changes in degrees per mile.

c. The equation is $f = -11h + 68$.

Watch Out!
Subtract in the same order to find the *run* as you do to find the *rise*.

second point   first point

$$\frac{\text{rise}}{\text{run}} = \frac{24 - 46}{4 - 2}$$

Talk it Over

12. Jena wrote the equation $f = 68 - 11h$ for the temperature in Sample 1. Compare Jena's equation and the equation $f = -11h + 68$. Do both equations have the same table of values? Do they have the same graph?

13. Suppose you want to graph $f = -11h + 68$ on a graphics calculator, using x and y as the control and dependent variables. Which variable represents f? Which represents h?

·······► Now you are ready for:
Exs. 1–18 on pp. 421–422

Linear Growth and Decay

The graphs modeling the height of a balloon and the temperature of the air are lines. They are examples of **linear growth** and **linear decay**. They are also *linear functions*.

	Linear Growth	Linear Decay
Characteristic	same value repeatedly added	same value repeatedly subtracted
Slope	positive	negative
Sketch		

Sample 2

Writing **Classify each situation as *linear growth*, *linear decay*, or *neither*. Explain your choice.**

a. Eleanor Basave put $5 in a piggy bank for her granddaughter when she was born. Every day after that Eleanor put a quarter in the bank.

b. During each year, the shortest distance between Earth and the sun is 9.14×10^7 mi and the greatest distance is 9.45×10^7 mi.

c. A teacher on a remote Arctic island buys 144 cans of fruit for the year. Each week the teacher eats 4 cans of fruit.

Sample Response

a. Linear growth. The value 0.25 is repeatedly added to the starting value, 5.

b. Neither. The distance increases and decreases during one year, then follows the same pattern the following year. There is not one number that is repeatedly added or subtracted.

c. Linear decay. The value 4 is repeatedly subtracted from the starting value, 144.

Look Back

What are two aspects of a linear growth or decay situation? How are they represented in the situation, on the graph, and in the equation?

······▶ **Now you are ready for:**
Exs. 19–44 on pp. 422–424

Exercises and Problems

For Exercises 1–4, match each equation with its graph.

1. $y = 3x + 2$

2. $y = 3x - 2$

3. $y = 2 - 3x$

4. $y = -3x$

A.

B.

C.

D.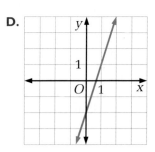

For Exercises 5–8, do these things.

a. Model each situation with a table and a graph.

b. Find the slope and the vertical intercept of each line. Explain how they are related to the original situation.

c. Model each situation with an equation.

5. Better Building Supplies sells sand for \$19/ton, plus \$25 for delivery.

6. For each kilometer beneath Earth's surface, the temperature increases by 25°C. Suppose the temperature at Earth's surface is 20°C.

7. The gas tank of a van contains 12 gal. The van uses $\frac{1}{15}$ gal/mi.

8. A truck rental company charges \$45 per day, plus \$.39 per mile.

9. Nancy noticed that in Exercises 5–8, the slope of the line is always the rate given in the situation, and the vertical intercept is always the starting value. Do you *agree* or *disagree* with her? Explain.

10. **Open-ended** Describe a situation that could be modeled by the equation $y = 0.25x + 1.75$.

Without graphing, find the slope and the vertical intercept of the line modeled by each equation.

11. $y = 3x - 5$

12. $y = 4.5 + 0.5x$

13. $y = -x - \frac{1}{2}$

14. $y = -1.2x + 6$

15. The table at the right shows the coordinates of points that lie on a line. Rupert says that the equation for the line is $y = 2x + 6$. Georgia says the equation is $y = 2(x + 3)$. Are they both right? Explain.

x	−6	−3	0	3	6
y	−6	0	6	12	18

16. The table at the right shows the coordinates of points that lie on a line. Write an equation for the line.

x	−4	−2	0	2	4
y	−11	−5	1	7	13

TECHNOLOGY **For Exercises 17 and 18, use a graphics calculator or software.**

Alternative Approach **Work in a group of two to four students.**

17. a. Use one set of axes to graph these four equations.

$y = 2x + 5$ $y = 5 + 0.75x$ $y = 5 - x$ $y = -\dfrac{1}{4}x + 5$

b. What property do the graphs share? Why? Write an equation for another line that has the same property and graph it with the others.

18. a. Use one set of axes to graph these four equations.

$y = 2x + 3$ $y = 2x - 1$ $y = 5 + 2x$ $y = -4 + 2x$

b. What property do the graphs share? Why? Write an equation for another line that has the same property and graph it with the others.

Writing **For Exercises 19–21, tell whether the amount spent on movies during a year is an example of linear growth. If it is, tell whether it is also an example of direct variation. Explain both answers.**

19.   **20.**   **21.**

22. **Reading** Linear growth and linear decay situations have a rate of change. What are three rates of change for the real-life situations on pages 417–419? How was each rate of change related to the slope of the line that modeled each situation?

23. **a.** Describe a situation that you think is a linear function. (For example, the cost of hiring a disc jockey for a school dance might be a function of the length of the dance.)

   b. **Research** Find some specific data related to the situation you described in part (a). Is it a linear function? Explain why or why not.

   c. If your situation is a linear function, is it *linear growth* or *linear decay*?

For Exercises 24–27, do these things.

a. Find the slope and the vertical intercept of each graph.

b. Write an equation for each line.

c. Tell whether each graph is an example of *linear growth* or *linear decay*.

d. Tell whether each graph is an example of direct variation. Write *Yes* or *No*. Explain why or why not.

24.

25.

26.

27.

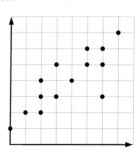

Decide whether each graph shows *linear growth*, *linear decay*, or *neither*. Explain your choice.

28.

29.

30.

31.

32. Which of the graphs in Exercises 28–31 are functions? Which are linear functions?

33. **Group Activity** Work with one or two other students.

    a. Complete the table.

    b. Graph the data in the second and fourth columns of the table.

    c. Use your graph to find the sum of the degrees of the angles in a decagon (10-sided polygon).

    d. The sum of the degrees of the angles of a polygon is 1800°. Find the number of sides of the polygon.

    e. Are the points of your graph on a line? If so, find the slope and the vertical intercept of the line and write its equation.

    f. Describe the relationship between the numbers in the middle two columns of the table. Is it linear? Is it direct variation? Explain.

You can draw *diagonals* to form triangles within a polygon. A **diagonal** is a segment other than a side that connects two vertices.

POLYGON	Number of sides	Number of triangles formed	Sum of degrees in all triangles
	?	?	?
	?	?	?
	?	?	?
	?	?	?
	?	?	?
	?	?	?

34. Regina cuts a circular 10-inch pizza into three slices of equal size. What is the area of one slice? *(Section 7-6)*

35. A line contains the origin and the point (6, −9). Find its slope. *(Section 7-2)*

Evaluate each expression when *x* = 5 and *y* = −2. *(Section 2-2)*

36. $x + 8y$ 37. $6x + 2y$ 38. $4x - 3y$ 39. $-x + \frac{1}{2}y$

Solve for y. *(Section 5-5)*

40. $by = c$ 41. $x + y = 60$ 42. $ax + y = b$ 43. $150 = 3y - x$

Working on the Unit Project

44. Use the data on page 416 for the Olympic 400 m freestyle swimming race.

    a. Find the slope of the line between 1972 and 1976 for the women.

    b. Find the slope of the line between 1972 and 1976 for the men.

    c. **Writing** Did the men or the women show more improvement in their times between 1972 and 1976? Describe two different ways you can justify your choice.

    d. **Writing** *True* or *False*? The rates of change in men's and women's times have been negative for the Olympic data. Describe how this is shown in a graph of data. How is it shown in the table?

Linear Combinations

The Right Mix

Focus

Use the standard form of an equation for a line to model real-life situations. Change standard form to slope-intercept form.

EXPLORATION

Is there a pattern in how you can spend the same amount of money to buy different combinations of two items?

- **Materials: graph paper**

- **Work in a group of at least four students. Each group has a different amount of money to "spend" at a music store: $72, $96, or $120. At this store tapes cost $8 and compact discs cost $12.**

1. How much does it cost to buy these combinations?

   a. 1 tape and no CDs

   b. no tapes and 1 CD

   c. 3 tapes and 2 CDs

   d. 1 tape and 3 CDs

2. **a.** Use the lattice to find the coordinates and the cost of each combination in step 1.

   b. Copy and fill out the lattice so that it contains all the combinations you can buy with the full amount of your group's spending money. (*Hint:* Look for patterns to help you fill the lattice faster.)

3. **a.** Circle all the numbers that equal the full amount of money your group can spend. What pattern do you see in the placement of these numbers?

   b. Draw a line through your group's numbers. What is the slope of your line? Write an equation for the line in slope-intercept form.

4. To compare your line with the other groups' lines, draw all the lines on one lattice. What do you notice about the lines?

5. **a.** Write a variable expression for the cost of *t* tapes and *d* compact discs.

   b. Use the variable expression to write an equation that relates *t*, *d*, and the full amount of money your group can spend.

This graph is a *lattice*. In this lattice, the cost of buying a given number of tapes and compact discs is written at points on the graph. A rule relates the cost to the number of items bought.

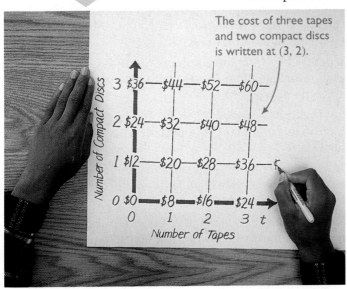

The cost of three tapes and two compact discs is written at (3, 2).

Graphs of Linear Combinations

An expression like $8t + 12d$ is an example of a *linear combination*. The combination of values of t and d that result in the same cost, say $48, lie on a line in the lattice.

Lattice for $8t + 12d$

Graph of $8t + 12d = 48$

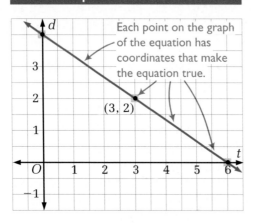

Each point on the graph of the equation has coordinates that make the equation true.

(3, 2)

A **solution of an equation with two variables** is an ordered pair of numbers that makes the equation true. For example, $(3, 2)$ is a solution of $8t + 12d = 48$ because $8(3) + 12(2) = 48$. All the points whose coordinates are solutions of an equation form the **graph of the equation.**

Talk it Over

1. In the Exploration, suppose your group has $48 and you buy only compact discs. How many can you buy? How is this shown on the lattice? on the graph?

2. Is the point (1.5, 3) on the graph of $8t + 12d = 48$? Can it represent numbers of tapes and compact discs you can buy? Explain why or why not.

3. Is (2, 3) a solution of $8t + 12d = 48$? Explain why the order of the coordinates of a point is important when testing them in an equation.

4. a. Compare the equations that all the groups wrote for step 3(b) of the Exploration. How are the equations alike? How are they different?

   b. Compare the equations that all the groups wrote for step 5(b) of the Exploration. How are the equations alike? How are they different? How are they different from the equations in step 3?

······➤ Now you are ready for:
Exs. 1–8 on pp. 429–430

Standard Form of an Equation for a Line

The equation $8t + 12d = 48$ is called a **linear equation** because it is an equation for a line. One form of a linear equation is slope-intercept form. The equation $8t + 12d = 48$ is written in *standard form*. Here is the **standard form of a linear equation.**

TECHNOLOGY NOTE

You need to use slope-intercept form, not standard form, to input an equation on most graphics calculators.

variable terms on one side ⎯⎯⎯⎯⎯⎯⎯⎯⎯ number on the other side

$$ax + by = c$$

a, b, and c depend on the situation

You can change an equation from standard form to slope-intercept form using algebra.

Sample 1

Several times a week, Dynah Colwin runs part of the way and walks part of the way on a trail that is 4 mi long. Her running speed is 6 mi/h and her walking speed is 4 mi/h.

a. Write an equation for this situation.

b. Rewrite the equation in slope-intercept form.

Sample Response

a. Let r = the time in hours Dynah Colwin spends running.
Let w = the time in hours she spends walking.

the distance she runs at 6 mi/h for r hours

$6r + 4w = 4$ ⟵ her total distance in miles

the distance she walks at 4 mi/h for w hours

b. The equation is in standard form. To rewrite it in slope-intercept form, solve the equation for the dependent variable. In this situation, either r or w can be the dependent variable. Suppose it is w.

$$6r + 4w = 4$$

$$6r + 4w - 6r = 4 - 6r \quad \longleftarrow \text{Subtract } 6r \text{ from both sides of the equation.}$$

$$4w = 4 - 6r$$

$$\tfrac{1}{4} \cdot 4w = \tfrac{1}{4}(4 - 6r) \quad \longleftarrow \text{Multiply both sides by the reciprocal of 4.}$$

$$w = \tfrac{1}{4} \cdot 4 - \tfrac{1}{4} \cdot 6r \quad \longleftarrow \text{Use the distributive property.}$$

$$w = 1 - \tfrac{3}{2}r$$

$$w = -\tfrac{3}{2}r + 1 \quad \longleftarrow \text{Rewrite the equation in slope-intercept form.}$$

For questions 5–7, use the situation in Sample 1.

5. What is the slope of the graph of $w = -\frac{3}{2}r + 1$? Does the graph show linear decay or linear growth?

6. Suppose $r = 0$. What is the value of w? How are these values related to the time Dynah Colwin spends running and walking?

7. a. Can r and w be negative numbers? Explain.

   b. Can r and w be fractions? Explain.

   c. Write an inequality to describe the possible values for r.

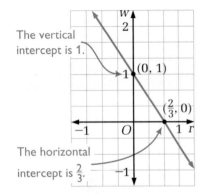

The vertical intercept is 1.

The horizontal intercept is $\frac{2}{3}$.

Intercepts of a Line

The graph of $w = -\frac{3}{2}r + 1$ crosses the vertical axis at $(0, 1)$. Its **vertical intercept** is 1. The graph crosses the horizontal axis at $(\frac{2}{3}, 0)$. Its **horizontal intercept** is $\frac{2}{3}$. One coordinate of each of these points is 0.

Sample 2

Find the intercepts of the graph of $2x - 5y = 15$. Use them to graph the equation.

Sample Response

To find the vertical intercept, substitute 0 for x.

$$2x - 5y = 15$$
$$2(0) - 5y = 15$$
$$-5y = 15$$
$$y = -3$$

The vertical intercept is -3.

The line crosses the vertical axis at $(0, -3)$.

To find the horizontal intercept, substitute 0 for y.

$$2x - 5y = 15$$
$$2x - 5(0) = 15$$
$$2x = 15$$
$$x = 7.5$$

The horizontal intercept is 7.5.

The line crosses the horizontal axis at $(7.5, 0)$.

Use what you found to make a graph.

Another point on the graph is $(5, -1)$.

Talk it Over

Use the equation $5x + 4y = 20$.

8. **a.** How can you find the vertical intercept of its graph?

   b. How can you find the horizontal intercept of its graph?

   c. How can you find another point on its graph?

······▶ **Now you are ready for:**
: **Exs. 9–27 on pp. 431–432**

Look Back ◀───────────────────

Describe two ways to graph the equation $5x + 3y = 2$.

8-2 Exercises and Problems

1. **Reading** Tell the meaning of each part of the expression $8t + 12d$ on page 426.

   a. 8   **b.** 12   **c.** d **d.** t **e.** $8t$ **f.** $12d$

2. An art department raises money by selling students' pottery work. Mugs cost $4 each and bowls cost $3 each. Write an expression for the cost of m mugs and b bowls.

3. On one section of the SAT (Scholastic Assessment Test), you receive 1 point for every right answer, lose one fourth of a point for every wrong answer, and receive no points for blank answers. You have r right answers, w wrong answers, and b blank answers.

   a. Write a variable expression for your score.

   b. Suppose your score is 32. Use the expression from part (a) to write an equation for your score.

4. $\angle A$ and $\angle B$ are supplementary angles. Write an equation relating their measures.

> **BY THE WAY...**
>
> The SAT was developed by Carl C. Brigham in the early 1920s. It was administered to high school students for the first time in 1926. By the end of the 1930s, the SAT was used as a scholarship test for all Ivy League schools. Today, the SAT is taken by over a million high school students each year.

5. The perimeter of a pool is 260 m.

   a. Make a table of possible widths (w) and lengths (l) for the rectangle.

   b. Write an equation relating w, l, and the perimeter, 260 m.

   c. Graph the equation you wrote in part (b). Put the widths on the horizontal axis.

   d. Explain why your graph should or should not cross either axis.

6. **Writing** After completing the Exploration on page 425, Erica decided that every time you buy two more compact discs, you can buy three fewer tapes. Erica's group had $72 to spend. Do you think her conjecture depends on the amount of spending money? Write a paragraph explaining why or why not.

Using Manipulatives For Exercises 7 and 8, use the information below about *tessellations.*

A *regular tessellation* is a pattern made of one regular polygon that covers the plane without gaps or overlaps.

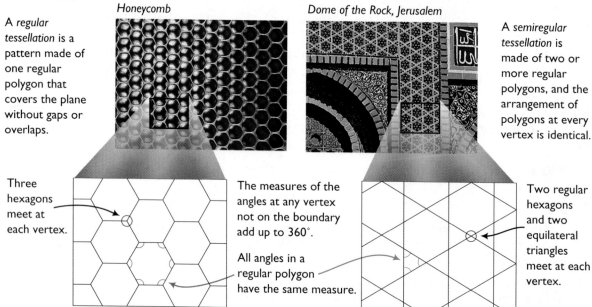

Honeycomb

Dome of the Rock, Jerusalem

A *semiregular tessellation* is made of two or more regular polygons, and the arrangement of polygons at every vertex is identical.

Three hexagons meet at each vertex.

The measures of the angles at any vertex not on the boundary add up to 360°.

All angles in a regular polygon have the same measure.

Two regular hexagons and two equilateral triangles meet at each vertex.

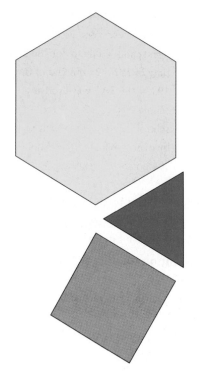

7. **a.** Trace and cut out several hexagons and triangles. Use them to make as many different regular and semiregular tessellations as you can. Make a sketch of each tessellation.

  b. Make a table showing the number of hexagons (h) and triangles (t) you used at one vertex in each tessellation.

  c. Write an equation for the sum of the measures of the angles of h hexagons and t triangles at a vertex.

  d. Find four solutions of the equation you wrote for part (c). Can all four solutions be included in the table for part (b)? Why or why not?

8. **a.** Write an equation for the sum of the measures of the angles of t equilateral triangles and s squares at each vertex of a tessellation.

  b. Find three solutions of your equation.

  c. Using cutouts, try to make the tessellations suggested by the solutions you found in part (b). Are all of them possible? Why or why not?

  d. One solution of the equation you found in part (b) leads to two different semiregular tessellations. Find the solution and sketch the tessellations.

Find three solutions of each equation.

9. $x + 3y = 11$

10. $x - \frac{1}{2}y = 3\frac{1}{2}$

11. $-5x - 2y = 2$

Rewrite each equation in slope-intercept form.

12. $5x + 8y = 48$

13. $\frac{2}{3}x + y = -2$

14. $6x - 2y = 11$

15. $9x - \frac{3}{4}y = 1$

Find the intercepts of the graph of each equation.

16. $-x - 8y = 16$

17. $0.2x + 0.3y = 3.6$

18. $-3x + \frac{3}{4}y = 21$

19. Banking A bank offers a savings account and a certificate of deposit that pay the annual interest rates shown in this promotional advertisement. Suppose you have s dollars in a savings account and a certificate of deposit for c dollars.

a. Suppose your total interest in one year is $18. Write an equation in standard form for your interest.

b. Find the intercepts of the graph of the equation. What do they represent in terms of the situation?

TECHNOLOGY **For Exercises 20 and 21, use a graphics calculator or software.**

Alternative Approach Work in a group of four students.

20. For parts (a)–(c), graph each group of four equations on its own set of axes.

a. $x + y = 6$ $x + y = 2$ $x + y = -2$ $x + y = -6$

b. $3x - y = 6$ $3x - y = -3$ $3x - y = 0$ $3x - y = -6$

c. $2x - y = 12$ $4x - 2y = 24$ $6x - 3y = 36$ $-2x + y = -12$

d. What do you observe about the equations in each of parts (a)–(c)? What do you observe about their graphs?

21. a. Graph these equations on the same set of axes.

$x + 4y = 0$ $6x - y = 0$ $2x + 3y = 0$

b. What property do the graphs share? Do they represent direct variation? Make a conjecture about the graph of an equation with the form $ax + by = 0$.

c. Test your conjecture by writing another equation with the form $ax + by = 0$ and graphing it.

22. **Sports** A basketball coach wants to encourage the players to make more assists (passes to a teammate who then scores a basket). The coach keeps track of the number of assists (*a*) and the number of baskets (*b*) each player makes per game.

a. The coach counts each assist as four points and each basket as two points. Write a linear combination for the total number of points the coach gives a player.

b. The coach rewards the players who earn a total of at least 32 points per game. Suppose a player earns exactly 32 points. Write an equation that relates *a*, *b*, and 32.

c. If Bonnie makes no baskets in a game, how many assists must she make in order to have a total of 32 points?

d. **Open-ended** The table shows Janine's record. Do you think that she has improved? Would the coach think so? Explain why or why not.

Game	Number of assists made	Number of baskets made
1	3	10
2	5	6
3	6	4

Ongoing **ASSESSMENT**

23. **Writing** Compare linear growth situations and linear combination situations. How are they alike? How are they different? How are they represented with equations?

Review **PREVIEW**

24. A tow truck driver charges $32 to hook up your car and $1.25 per *(Section 8-1)* mile towed.

a. Model the situation with a graph.

b. Find the slope and the vertical intercept of the line. Explain how they are related to the original situation.

25. a. Graph the points $A(7, 4)$, $B(-1, 4)$, $C(0, 4)$, $D(4, 4)$, and $E(-2, 4)$. *(Section 4-6)*

b. What pattern do you see in the graph? in the coordinates?

c. Is the graph a function? Explain why or why not.

26. Repeat Exercise 25 using the points $P(-3, 1)$, $Q(-3, -5)$, $R(-3, -2)$, $S(-3, 0)$, and $T(-3, 4)$.

 Working on the Unit Project

27. **Research** Find another set of winning times for the 400 m freestyle for the years shown in the table on page 416. You might look for world records, college records, or high school records. Find both men's and women's records.

Horizontal and Vertical Lines

Focus

Describe slopes of horizontal and vertical lines and write equations for horizontal and vertical lines.

What happens when one of the coefficients in an equation for a line in standard form is zero? Here are two ways that could happen.

1 **The coefficient of x could be zero.**

$$0x + 3y = 6$$
$$3y = 6$$
$$y = 2$$

All points with a y-coordinate of 2 are on the graph of the equation $y = 2$.

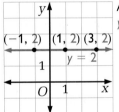

All points have y-coordinate 2.

When the coefficient of x is zero the graph is a horizontal line.

To find the slope, use any two points on the line, such as (1, 2) and (3, 2).

$$\frac{\text{change in } y}{\text{change in } x} = \frac{2 - 2}{3 - 1} = \frac{0}{2} = 0$$

The slope of a horizontal line is 0.

2 **The coefficient of y could be zero.**

$$2x + 0y = 6$$
$$2x = 6$$
$$x = 3$$

All points with an x-coordinate of 3 are on the graph of the equation $x = 3$.

All points have x-coordinate 3.

When the coefficient of y is zero the graph is a vertical line.

To find the slope, use any two points on the line, such as (3, 1), and (3, 5).

$$\frac{\text{change in } y}{\text{change in } x} = \frac{5 - 1}{3 - 3} = \frac{4}{0} \quad \text{undefined}$$

Because division by zero is undefined, the slope of a vertical line is undefined.

Find the slope of each line and write an equation for each line.

a.

b.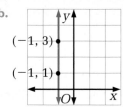

a. The graph is a horizontal line. The slope is 0.

Every point on the line has a y-coordinate of 2.5.

An equation for the line is $y = 2.5$.

b. The graph is a vertical line. The slope is undefined.

Every point on the line has an x-coordinate of -1.

An equation for the line is $x = -1$.

Write an equation for each line.

a. The points $(-2, 4)$ and $(-2, 0)$ are on the line.

b. The slope is zero, and the point $(2, 3)$ is on the line.

a. The x-coordinates are both -2. The graph is a vertical line 2 units left of the vertical axis. The slope is undefined.

Every point on the line has the same x-coordinate, -2.

An equation for the line is $x = -2$.

b. The slope is zero. The graph is a horizontal line.

Every point on the line has the same y-coordinate, 3.

An equation for the line is $y = 3$.

Talk it Over

Graph each equation and find the slope of each line.

1. $x = -4$ 2. $y = 2$ 3. $2y = -3$

4. Describe how the equation in question 3 is different from the other two. Does the difference affect the graph? Explain.

Look Back

On the same set of axes, graph the equations $x = 3$ and $y = 2$. Where do the lines intersect?

Exercises and Problems

Estimate the slope of the land in each picture.

1.

2.

3.

4. **Reading** Is the horizontal change equal to zero for a *horizontal* line or a *vertical* line? Why? Is the vertical change equal to zero for a *horizontal* line or a *vertical* line? Why?

Find the slope of each line and write an equation for each line.

5.

6.

7.
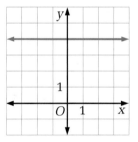

Graph each equation and find the slope of each line.

8. $y = 3$ 9. $x = -2.5$ 10. $6x = 12$ 11. $-4y = 10$

For Exercises 12–15, write an equation for each line.

12. The points $(3, 7)$ and $(-2, 7)$ are on the line.

13. The points $(4, -8)$ and $(4, 0)$ are on the line.

14. The slope is undefined, and the point $(5, 3)$ is on the line.

15. The slope is zero, and the point $(4, 6)$ is on the line.

16. List the coordinates of some points that lie on the *x*-axis. What do they have in common? Write an equation for the *x*-axis.

17. List the coordinates of some points that lie on the *y*-axis. What do they have in common? Write an equation for the *y*-axis.

For Exercises 18–21, tell whether each statement is *True* or *False*.

18. The graph of $x = 8$ is parallel to the *x*-axis.

19. The graph of $y = 12$ is parallel to the *x*-axis.

20. The graph of $x = -3$ is parallel to the *y*-axis.

21. The graph of $y = 1.1$ is parallel to the *y*-axis.

22. **Using Manipulatives** The *exterior angles* of a polygon are formed by extending the sides of the polygon.

   a. On four pieces of paper, draw a 3-gon, 4-gon, 5-gon, and 6-gon.

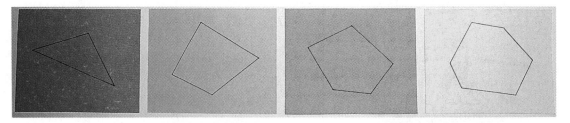

   b. Extend the sides to the edge of the paper. Shade the exterior angles.

   c. Cut along the lines and set aside the polygon.

   d. Estimate the sum of the measures of the exterior angles. (*Hint:* arrange the exterior angles around a point to see what part of a circle they fill.)

   e. Make a graph of your results in part (d). Put the *number of sides of the polygon* on the horizontal axis and the *sum of the measures of the exterior angles* on the vertical axis.

   f. Write an equation that describes your results from part (e).

23. **Government** The graph shows the number of senators for each state in the United States.

   a. What is the slope of the fitted line?

   b. Does the number of United States senators for a state vary directly as the population of the state?

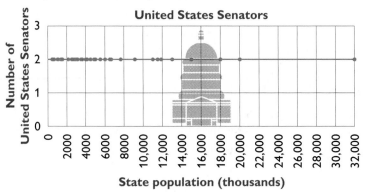

24. **Writing** Describe a situation that can be graphed with a horizontal line. Write an equation that describes the situation. Include the meaning of each variable that you use.

25. Writing The list below gives several different meanings of the word "slope." Which meanings can be used to describe the slopes of horizontal and vertical lines? Explain how.

Meanings of Slope

$$\frac{\text{rise}}{\text{run}} \qquad \frac{\text{vertical change}}{\text{horizontal change}} \qquad \frac{\text{change in } y}{\text{change in } x}$$

rate of change

variation constant

value repeatedly added or subtracted (linear growth and decay)

26 TECHNOLOGY Many graphics calculators graph only equations that represent functions. Which of these equations can *not* be input on these graphics calculators? Explain.

a. $y = 2x + 5$ **b.** $x = -5$ **c.** $y = 6$

Ongoing **ASSESSMENT**

27. Open-ended Rosa started making this list to help her remember the differences between equations that have only *x* and equations that have only *y*.

	equations with only x	equations with only y
example	X = 2	Y = 2
description	?	horizontal
slope	undefined	?
vertical intercept	doesn't have one	?
horizontal intercept	?	?
is parallel to	?	the x-axis
graph	?	?
other	can't be written in slope-intercept form	?

Copy and complete the list. What other ideas would you add?

Review **PREVIEW**

Rewrite each equation in slope-intercept form. If it is not possible to do so, explain why not. *(Section 8-2)*

28. $2x + 3y = 12$ **29.** $4x - 9y = 72$ **30.** $0x + 4y = 20$ **31.** $4x + 0y = 40$

Solve. *(Sections 2-7, 5-2, 5-3)*

32. $3(x - 8) = 14$ **33.** $5x + 9 = 2x - 15$ **34.** $415 = 37 + b$

35. Graph the line that contains the points $(-2, 1)$ and $(1, -5)$. Find the slope and the vertical intercept of the graph. Write an equation for the line. *(Section 8-1)*

36. The winning times in the 400 m swimming event at the Olympics have changed over the years. What numerical aspect of the event has *not* changed over time? Draw a graph that shows this.

Ethelda Bleibtrey, USA
1920   Time: 4:34.0

Debbie Meyer, USA
1968   Time: 4:31.8

Michelle Smith, Ireland
1996   Time: 4:07.4

Unit 8   CHECKPOINT 1

1. **Writing** How are linear growth and direct variation situations alike? How are they different?

Students can choose from three different weekly beverage plans.   8-1

> Plan A. Pay \$.75 per glass.
> Plan B. Pay \$2.50 and \$.50 per glass.
> Plan C. Pay \$10 and drink all you like.

2. Which plan(s) are examples of linear growth?

3. Which plan(s) are examples of direct variation?

4. Model Plan B with a graph and an equation.

5. Find the slope of the line that represents Plan C.

Mark's favorite store is having a sale. Suppose there is no sales tax.   8-2

6. Write an expression for how much it would cost to buy j pairs of jeans and s shirts on sale.

7. Mark spent \$60 on the items shown. Graph the possible numbers of jeans and shirts he bought.

8. Does your graph have a vertical intercept and a horizontal intercept? What do they represent?

9. **a.** Write an equation for the situation in Exercise 7.

   b. What is the slope of the line whose equation you wrote in part (a)? What does this slope mean in terms of the original situation?

Find the intercepts of the graph of each equation.

10. $2x - 3y = 12$ 11. $7x + 14y = 42$

12. Graph the equation $y = -4$. Find the slope of the line.   8-3

13. The slope of a line is undefined, and the point $(-3, 9)$ is on the line. Write an equation for the line.

Writing Equations for Lines

Focus

Use two points or the slope
and one point to write an
equation for a line. Use an
equation for a line to solve
problems.

THE LINE FORMS HERE

Olympic swimmers have generally been getting faster. In other
words, the winning time for the 400 m freestyle race is over
30 seconds shorter than it was in 1960.

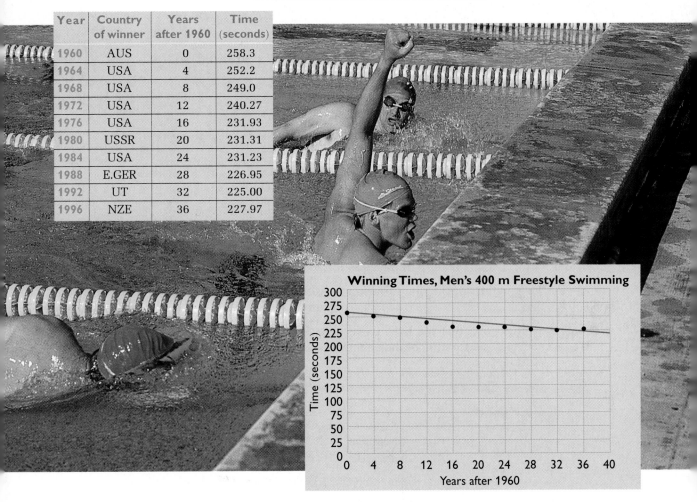

Year	Country of winner	Years after 1960	Time (seconds)
1960	AUS	0	258.3
1964	USA	4	252.2
1968	USA	8	249.0
1972	USA	12	240.27
1976	USA	16	231.93
1980	USSR	20	231.31
1984	USA	24	231.23
1988	E.GER	28	226.95
1992	UT	32	225.00
1996	NZE	36	227.97

Winning Times, Men's 400 m Freestyle Swimming

Time (seconds) vs. Years after 1960

Suppose you want to predict the winning time for the year 2008.
The points do not lie exactly on a line, but a line that passes
close to most of the points (a fitted line) is drawn. You can estimate an equation for a fitted line and use it to make predictions.

Estimate an equation for the fitted line for the Olympic data.

Sample Response

To write your equation, you can use slope-intercept form and the coordinates of two data points that are on or nearly on the fitted line. The closer the points are to the fitted line, the better your estimate will be.

1 Find the slope. Use the points (8, 249) and (32, 225).

$$\text{slope} = \frac{\text{rise}}{\text{run}}$$

$$= \frac{\text{change in winning times}}{\text{change in years}}$$

$$= \frac{225 - 249}{32 - 8} \longleftarrow \text{32 and 8 represent the number of years after 1960.}$$

$$= \frac{-24}{24}$$

$$= -1 \longleftarrow \text{The slope is } -1.$$

In the equation $y = mx + b$, you now know m: $y = -1x + b$.

2 Find the vertical intercept. Substitute the coordinates of either point for x and y in the equation and solve for b.

dependent variable = (slope · control variable) + vertical intercept

$$y = -1x + b$$

$$249 = (-1)(8) + b \longleftarrow \text{For the point (8, 249),}$$
$$249 = -8 + b \qquad\qquad x = 8 \text{ and } y = 249.$$

$$257 = b \longleftarrow \text{The vertical intercept is 257.}$$

3 Substitute -1 for m and 257 for b in the equation $y = mx + b$.

An estimate for the equation for the fitted line is $y = -1x + 257$, or $y = -x + 257$.

Check Check the other point that you used to find the slope, (32, 225). Are its coordinates a solution of the equation?

$$y = -x + 257$$

$$225 \overset{?}{=} -32 + 257 \longleftarrow \text{Substitute 32 for } x \text{ and 225 for } y.$$

$$225 = 225 \; ✔$$

Talk it Over

1. Does the fitted line on the graph on page 439 have a vertical intercept of about 257?

2. Cover up the scales on the graph on page 439. Does the fitted line look like it has a slope of -1? How do the scales affect the appearance of the graph?

3. Use the equation $y = -x + 257$ from Sample 1.

  a. Substitute 16 in the equation to find the predicted winning time for the race in 1976. How close is the prediction to the actual time?

  b. Predict the winning time for the race in the year 2008.

4. Suppose you use two different data points in Sample 1 to estimate the equation for the fitted line. Will the result be exactly the same?

Exact Equations from Two Points

You can estimate an equation for a fitted line using two points that are *close* to the fitted line. You can find an exact equation for any line if you know the coordinates of any two points *on* the line.

Sample 2

Two points on a line are (4, 3) and (−6, −2). Write an equation for the line.

Sample Response

First find the slope.

$$m = \frac{\text{change in } y}{\text{change in } x}$$

$$= \frac{-2 - 3}{-6 - 4}$$

$$= \frac{-5}{-10}$$

$$= \frac{1}{2}$$

Next find the vertical intercept. To do this, substitute $\frac{1}{2}$ for m and the coordinates of either point for x and y in the equation $y = mx + b$.

$$y = \frac{1}{2}x + b$$

$$3 = \frac{1}{2}(4) + b \longleftarrow \text{For the point (4, 3), } x = 4 \text{ and } y = 3.$$

$$3 = 2 + b$$

$$1 = b$$

You now know that $m = \frac{1}{2}$ and $b = 1$. The equation is $y = \frac{1}{2}x + 1$.

······▶ Now you are ready for:
Exs. 1–14 on pp. 443–445

Equations from Other Facts

You can use two points to find an equation for a line. You also know how to find an equation for a line from its graph. You can use other types of information to find an equation for a line.

Sample 3

The slope of a line is $\frac{3}{2}$. One point on the line is $(-4, 1)$. Write an equation for the line.

Sample Response

Method ❶ Use substitution to find the vertical intercept.

You know the slope and the coordinates of a point. First, substitute these numbers in the slope-intercept form of an equation for a line.

$$y = mx + b$$
$$1 = (\tfrac{3}{2})(-4) + b \quad \longleftarrow \text{ Substitute } (-4, 1) \text{ for } (x, y) \text{ and } \tfrac{3}{2} \text{ for } m.$$
$$1 = -6 + b$$
$$7 = b \quad \longleftarrow \text{ The vertical intercept is 7.}$$

Then substitute $\frac{3}{2}$ for m and 7 for b in the equation $y = mx + b$.

An equation for the line is $y = \frac{3}{2}x + 7$.

Method ❷ Graph the line to find the vertical intercept.

1 Graph the point $(-4, 1)$.

2 Use the slope: Move 3 units up and 2 units to the right.

3 Connect the points to graph the line.

4 The vertical intercept is 7.

5 Substitute $\frac{3}{2}$ for m and 7 for b in the equation $y = mx + b$.

An equation for the line is $y = \frac{3}{2}x + 7$.

Unit 8 Linear Equations as Models

5. Which step is the same for both methods in Sample 3?

6. The slope of a line is $-\frac{3}{5}$. One point on the line is $(15, -1)$. Find an equation for the line.

7. Kemitra is given some money for her birthday. She spends $7 every week. After 12 weeks she has $41 left.

   a. Is the amount of money she has left the *control variable* or the *dependent variable*?

   b. Write "after 12 weeks she has $41" as an ordered pair.

   c. What is the rate of change in this situation? Is it *positive* or *negative*? What does the rate of change represent in the equation $y = mx + b$? Explain your answer.

   d. Write an equation for the amount of money Kemitra has left after x weeks of spending. Graph your equation.

   e. In this situation, what is represented by the vertical intercept? by the horizontal intercept?

   f. Use the graph to find out how much money she had left three weeks after her birthday.

Look Back

Describe how to find an equation for a line if you have each type of information.

   a. a graph of the line

   b. two points on the line

   c. the slope and one point on the line

Now you are ready for:
Exs. 15–31 on pp. 445–446

8-4 Exercises and Problems

1. **Reading** How is estimating an equation of a fitted line different from finding an exact equation of a line?

For Exercises 2–7, write an equation for each line. If there is too little information, say so.

2. The slope is -3 and the vertical intercept is 1.

3. The points $(5, 2)$ and $(-1, 8)$ are on the line.

4. The point $(3, -8)$ is on the line.

5. The points $(-8, 2)$ and $(5, 2)$ are on the line.

6. The horizontal intercept is 6 and vertical intercept is -7.

7. The points $(3, 7)$ and $(-5, -9)$ are on the the line.

8. The Chu family is driving home. Because they are using cruise control, their speed is constant. After 3 h, they are 350 mi from home. After 6 h, they are 200 mi from home.

   a. What is the control variable? What is the dependent variable?

   b. Represent the given information as two points on a graph.

   c. Write an equation for the line through the two points.

   d. What do the slope and the vertical intercept of the equation mean in terms of the original situation?

9. **Science** Water freezes at 0°C, or 32°F. Water boils at 100°C, or 212°F.

   a. Use these two points to write an equation relating degrees Fahrenheit to degrees Celsius.

   b. Use the equation to convert 68°F to degrees Celsius.

10. **Economics** Use the median family income data.

    a. Model the data with an equation for the median family income in terms of the year.

    b. Use your model to predict the median family income in 2008.

Year	1993	1994	1995	1996	1997	1998
Median family income in the United States	$36,959	38,782	40,611	42,300	44,568	46,737

48906, 51075 53244, 55413,
56682, 58851, 61020, 63189,

11. **Geology** The length of time between eruptions of Old Faithful, a geyser in Yellowstone Park, can be predicted with a linear equation. The table below gives some data values (in minutes) for the geyser's eruptions.

65358 67577

BY THE WAY...

Old Faithful's eruption schedule is affected by earthquakes. In 1983, the average amount of time between eruptions increased from 69 min to 76 min because of an earthquake in Idaho.

Length of eruption (l)	3	4.5	4	2.5	3.5	5	2
Time until next eruption (t)	68	89	83	62	75	92	57

   a. Graph the data and draw a fitted line.

   b. Model the data with an equation for t in terms of l.

   c. Suppose an eruption lasts 4.2 min. Predict the number of minutes until the next eruption.

12 TECHNOLOGY Use the data from Exercise 10 or 11 and a graphics calculator or software.

    a. Enter the data points and make a scatter plot of the data.

    b. Use the calculator or software to find an equation for a fitted line for the data. (It may be called the line of best fit, or linear regression.) Graph the calculator's equation and the one that you found.

    c. Compare the graph of the equation that you found to the one from the calculator or software. How are they alike? How are they different?

13. In Exercise 18 on page 422, you saw that lines with the same slope are parallel. Use this fact and the diagram.

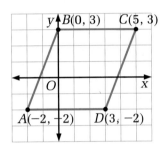

    a. Find the slopes of $\overline{AB}$, $\overline{BC}$, $\overline{CD}$, and $\overline{AD}$.

    b. Which pairs of segments are parallel?

    c. Write equations for $\overleftrightarrow{AB}$, $\overleftrightarrow{BC}$, $\overleftrightarrow{CD}$, and $\overleftrightarrow{AD}$.

14. a. How many lines contain the point $(-1, 3)$?

    b. How many lines contain the point $(6, 5)$?

    c. How many lines contain the point $(-1, 3)$ *and* the point $(6, 5)$?

For Exercises 15–22, write an equation for each line. If there is too little information, say so.

15. The slope is $\frac{4}{5}$ and the point $(-10, 3)$ is on the line.

16. The slope is -0.5.

17. The slope is $-\frac{3}{2}$ and the point $(6, -1)$ is on the line.

18. The slope is 4 and the point $(0, -3)$ is on the line.

19. The points $(-4, 0)$ and $(4, 6)$ are on the line.

20.

21.

22.
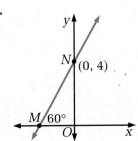

23. **Transportation** A taxi charges a base fee plus $.75 per mile. A 10 mi trip costs $8.70.

   a. Is the length of the trip the *control variable* or the *dependent variable*?

   b. Write "a 10 mi trip costs $8.70" as an ordered pair.

   c. What is the rate of change in this situation?

   d. Write an equation for the cost of hiring the taxi in terms of the length of the trip.

   e. Graph the equation.

   f. What is the cost of a 5 mi trip? a 17 mi trip? How are they shown on your graph?

   g. What does the vertical intercept represent in this situation?

24. The height of the water in a bathtub decreases at a constant rate of 3 cm per minute. After 11 min, the height of the water left in the tub is 2 cm. Write an equation for the height of the water left in the tub as a function of time.

Ongoing ASSESSMENT

25. **Writing** Suppose you are writing a "how to do math" guide for your friends. What would you include in the chapter called "How to Write Equations for Lines"? Write an outline and an introduction for the chapter.

Review PREVIEW

Write an equation for each line. *(Section 8-3)*

26. The points (3, 5) and (−2, 5) are on the line.

27. The slope is undefined, and the point (1, 8) is on the line.

Solve each system of equations. *(Section 5-8)*

28. $y = 5x$
    $3x + y = 44$

29. $y = 2x + 7$
    $-5x + y = -5$

30. $y = 2x - 4$
    $y = x - 6$

Working on the Unit Project

31. **Group Activity** Use the winning times for the women's 400 m freestyle swimming race in the Olympics on page 416. Use *Years after 1960* as the control variable. Have each person write an equation to model the data. Compare equations. Does one equation fit the data better than the other? Decide which equation you will use to model the data.

Graphing Systems of Linear Equations

Focus

Find the point where two lines intersect.

EXPLORATION

Can one triangle meet two conditions?

- **Materials: $8\frac{1}{2}$-by-11 inch paper (two different colors), protractors, rulers, scissors, tape**
- **Divide the class into two groups.**

(1) Assign Group I one color of paper and Group II the other color.

(2) Cut out a triangle that meets your group's rule. Make sure that no two triangles in your group are the same.

Group I rule:

Make angle *y* twice as big as angle *x*.

Use any value between 0 and 45 for *x*.

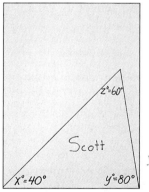

Scott

$x° = 40°$ $y° = 80°$ $z° = 60°$

$y = 2x$

Group II rule:

Make angle *y* and angle *x* complementary.

Use any value between 0 and 90 for *x*.

Tanya

$x° = 40°$ $y° = 50°$ $z° = 90°$

$y = 90 - x$

Both Groups:

➤ Use the $8\frac{1}{2}$ in. edge of your paper as the base of your triangle.

➤ Put angle *x* on the left and angle *y* on the right.

➤ Write your name and all three angle measures on your triangle.

Continued on next page.

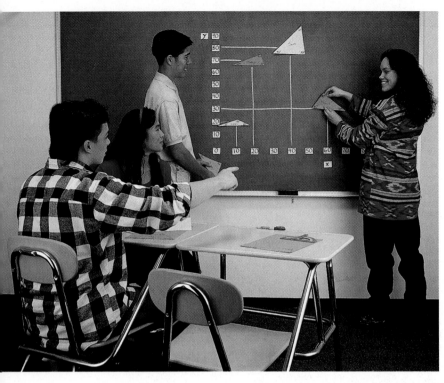

③ Tape all the triangles from both groups on a large graph in the front of the room.

④ Look for patterns in the graph. Describe any patterns you see.

⑤ Is there any triangle that both groups created? If so, what are the measures of its angles and where is it on the graph? If not, make a triangle that meets each group's rule. Tell its angle measures and its location on the graph.

⑥ What equation relates x and y for all the Group I triangles? What equation relates x and y for all the Group II triangles?

⑦ Solve the system of equations in step 6 by substitution.

⑧ How is the answer to step 7 related to the answer to step 5? Explain.

The graph of triangles you made in the Exploration illustrates a *system of equations.* You can estimate the solution of a system of equations by graphing the equations and looking for a point of intersection.

······▶ Now you are ready for:
: Exs. 1–5 on p. 451

Sample 1

TECHNOLOGY NOTE

You can zoom in on the point where the lines intersect with a graphics calculator. ◀

MoviesPlus rents videos for $2.50 each and has no membership fee. Videobusters rents videos for $2 each but has a $10 membership fee.

a. Write and solve a system of equations to model this situation.

b. What advice would you give to someone trying to decide which video store to use?

Sample Response

Problem Solving Strategy: Use a graph

a. Write an equation to describe the cost at each video store.

➤ Let c = the total cost of renting videos.

➤ Let n = the number of videos rented.

➤ MoviesPlus: $c = 2.50n$

➤ Videobusters: $c = 2.00n + 10$

Graph the system of equations.

b. Here is some advice you can give: "If you plan to rent fewer than 20 videos, then MoviesPlus is less expensive. If you plan to rent more than 20 videos, then Videobusters is less expensive."

The lines intersect at (20, 50). This means that if you rent exactly 20 videos, the cost is $50 at either video store.

Talk it Over

1. In Sample 1, how can you tell from the graph that Videobusters is less expensive if you rent more than 20 movies?

2. Check the solution in Sample 1 by substituting 20 for n and 50 for c in both equations.

Systems without Solutions

In Sample 1, the graph of the system of equations shows that the lines intersect. The coordinates of the point of intersection are the solution of the system.

Sometimes two lines do not intersect. In this case the system of equations has no solution.

Sample 2

Sandy and Rita are practicing for a 100 m dash competition. Sandy gives Rita a 10 m head start.

Write and graph a system of equations to model this situation.

Sandy's speed is 8 m/s.

Rita's speed is 8 m/s.

Sample Response

Write an equation for each runner's distance from the starting line.

➤ Let x = the time since the runner started.

➤ Let y = the runner's distance from the starting line.

➤ Sandy's distance from the starting line: $y = 8x$

➤ Rita's distance from the starting line: $y = 8x + 10$

The graph shows each runner's distance from the starting line as a function of time.

Because the lines are parallel, there is no point of intersection. The system of equations has *no solution*. The runners are never at the same point at the same time.

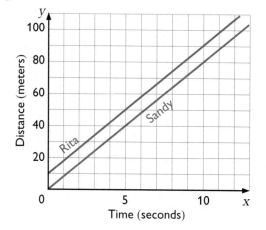

Check You can check the solution of a system of equations by using substitution.

$y = 8x$ and $y = 8x + 10$

$$8x = 8x + 10 \quad \longleftarrow \text{Substitute } 8x \text{ for } y \text{ in the second equation.}$$

$$8x - 8x = 8x + 10 - 8x \quad \longleftarrow \text{Subtract } 8x \text{ from both sides.}$$

$$0 = 10 \quad \longleftarrow \text{This statement is } \textit{false.}$$

Because $0 \neq 10$, there is no solution that makes the equation true. The system of equations has no solution.

Talk it Over

3. In Sample 2, the graph shows diagonal lines. Are Rita and Sandy running diagonally across the race track? Explain your answer.

4. Use the graph in Sample 2 to estimate the runners' race times. Who wins the race?

5. The graphs of two equations with the same slope are parallel. Use the equations $y = 8x$ and $y = 8x + 10$. Without graphing, how can you tell that the system of equations has no solution?

6. How can you tell from a graph that a system of equations has either a *solution* or has *no solution*?

Look Back ←

You can find the solution of a system of linear equations by graphing the equations or by using substitution. When is each method useful?

➤ Now you are ready for:
Exs. 6–30 on pp. 451–454

Exercises and Problems

1. Look back at the Exploration on pages 447 and 448.

   a. Does a 25°-50°-105° triangle meet the rule for *Group I* or *Group II?*

   b. Is there more than one triangle that meets the rule for both groups?

For Exercises 2–4, do these things.

a. Estimate the solution of each system of equations.

b. Use substitution to find the exact solution of each system.

2.

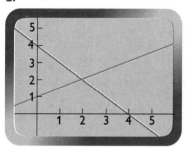

$y = \frac{1}{2}x + 1$

$y = -x + 4$

3.

$y = 3$

$y = 2x - 1$

4.

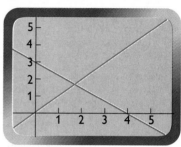

$y = -\frac{3}{4}x + 3$

$y = x$

5. **Open-ended** Write two different systems of equations that have the solution (5, 3).

6. **Reading** How can you tell just by looking at the equations whether a system of equations has a solution or no solution?

Graph each system of equations. Estimate the solution of the system, or write *no solution.*

7. $y = x - 2$

   $y = -2x + 5$

8. $y = 0.5x$

   $y = 0.5x + 3$

9. $y = x$

   $y = \frac{1}{2}x - 3$

A dog notices a squirrel 5 m away and starts chasing it.
Describe what happens in each case.

10.

11.

12.

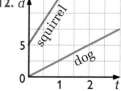

Without graphing, tell whether each system of equations has a *solution* or *no solution*.

13. $y = 3x + 4$
$y = 5x - 2$

14. $y = 2x - 5$
$y = 2x + 6$

15. $y = 100 - x$
$y = 50 - x$

16. Business The graph shows the income and expenses of a company. The company makes a profit if income is greater than expenses. It loses money if expenses are greater than income.

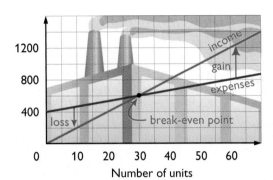
Number of units

a. What are the coordinates of the break-even point? What does this point represent?

b. When does the company make a profit? How can you tell this from the graph?

c. When does the company lose money? How can you tell this from the graph?

17. Entertainment A friend is trying to choose between cable TV and renting videos. Here is the information your friend gives you.

> "Cable TV costs $40 to install and then $20 each month. Adding a movie channel costs an extra $11 each month."
>
> "On the other hand, the cost of a video cassette player is $170. Renting a video costs $3, and I think I will rent 6 videos a month."

a. Write an equation for the cost of installing cable TV with a movie channel. Write an equation for the cost of buying a video cassette player and renting movies.

b. Graph the two equations on the same axes. Estimate the point of intersection of the graphs.

c. Solve the system of equations by substitution.

d. What advice would you give to your friend?

For Exercises 18–20, rewrite each equation in slope-intercept form. Then tell whether each system of equations has a *solution* or *no solution*.

18. $2x + 3y = 4$
$4x + 6y = 4$

19. $x - 3y = 2$
$x - 4y = 2$

20. $4x - 2y = 6$
$6x - 2y = 3$

21. TECHNOLOGY Use a graphics calculator or software.

You can solve an equation like $2(x + 4) = -3x - 7$ by making it into a system of equations and graphing the two equations.

a. Set the expression on each side of the equation equal to y. The equations are $y = 2(x + 4)$ and $y = -3x - 7$. Graph both equations.

b. Use the zoom and trace features to find the coordinates of the point of intersection. The value of x is the solution of the original equation.

c. Use this method to solve the equation $-\frac{1}{2}x + 11 = 4(-3 + x)$.

d. **Open-ended** Write another equation that has x on both sides and use this method to solve it.

In the book *Address Unknown,* James D. Wright writes about the causes of homelessness. He found that between 1977 and 1983, the population needing low-income housing in twelve United States cities increased from 2,522,000 to 3,425,000. During that time, the number of low-income housing units in those cities decreased from 1,607,000 to 1,128,000.

22. Suppose two people can be housed in each low-income housing unit. Then the number of available spaces would be 3,214,000 in 1977 and 2,256,000 in 1983.

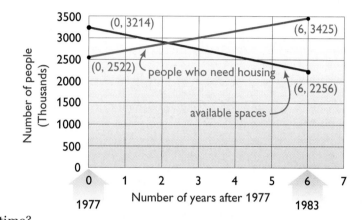

a. Interpret the information shown in the graph.

b. What does the point of intersection represent? What was the housing situation before this time? What was the housing situation after this time?

c. Write equations for each line. Use the coordinates of the points given on the graphs.

d. Solve the system of equations by substitution. Does your solution agree with the point of intersection on the graph?

A group of students help build a house as part of a Habitat for Humanity project in Coahoma, Mississippi.

23. Suppose three people can be housed in each available low-income housing unit. Then the number of available spaces would be 4,821,000 in 1977 and 3,384,000 in 1983.

a. Redraw the graph from Exercise 22 using the new data for the number of available spaces.

b. Estimate the point of intersection. Explain why it appears later in time than the point of intersection in Exercise 22.

c. Write a new system of equations and solve it by substitution to check your estimate.

d. What do the graphs in Exercise 22 and part (a) above suggest is one cause of homelessness?

24. **Writing** Graph this sytem of three equations. Explain why you think this system of three equations does or does not have a solution.

$$y = -0.5x + 4$$
$$y = 3$$
$$y = x - 2$$

Write an equation for each line. *(Section 8-4)*

25. The points (12, 7) and (6, 2) are on the line.

26. The slope is $\frac{5}{3}$ and the point (6, −1) is on the line.

Tell whether 5 is a solution of each inequality. Write *Yes* or *No*. Then solve and graph each inequality. *(Section 5-4)*

27. $-2x + 13 > 2$ 28. $4(x - 5) \geq 0$ 29. $-3 \leq x - 7$

8 Working on the Unit Project

30. The equations of the fitted lines for the graphs of some California high school record times are given. In the equations, *x* is the number of years since 1957 and *y* is the record time in seconds.

    a. Use a graph to estimate a solution of the system of equations.

    b. Use substitution to find a solution.

    c. What do the coordinates of the solution mean?

    > Girls' 400 m Individual Medley:
    > $y = -1.95x + 335.05$
    > Boys' 400 m Individual Medley:
    > $y = -1.68x + 299.1$

Unit 8   **CHECKPOINT 2**

1. **Writing** Describe two ways to tell that a system of equations has no solution.

Write an equation for each line.   8-4

2. The points (3, −4) and (4, 1) are on the line.

3. The horizontal intercept is 1 and the slope is $-\frac{1}{4}$.

Without graphing, tell whether each system has a solution or no solution.   8-5

4. $y = -2x + 5$
   $y = x + 5$

5. $y = 4 - 3x$
   $y = 8 - 3x$

6. $y = -2x$
   $y = x$

7. Natural Springs sells bottled water for $1.00 per gallon and charges $10 as a deposit. Water Fresh charges $1.50 per gallon, with no deposit. Write and solve a system of equations to model this situation.

Section 8-6

Graphing Linear Inequalities

WHICH SIDE ARE YOU ON?

Focus

Graph linear inequalities on a coordinate plane.

EXPLORATION

What does an inequality graphed on a coordinate plane look like?

• **Work with the whole class.**

Jeremy is (0, 4). He is standing because 4 is greater than or equal to 0.

(0, 4) (1, 4) (2, 4) (3, 4) (4, 4)

(0, 3) (1, 3) (2, 3) (3, 3) (4, 3)

(0, 2) (1, 2) (2, 2) (3, 2) (4, 2)

(0, 1) (1, 1) (2, 1) (3, 1) (4, 1)

(0, 0) (1, 0) (2, 0) (3, 0) (4, 0)

Origin

① Arrange the desks in rows. Make the number of desks in each row equal the number of rows. For example, there might be 5 rows of 5 desks each. When the desks are arranged, return to your seat.

② Choose a student at a corner desk to represent the origin so that your class forms the first quadrant of a coordinate plane. Who is (0, 0) in your class?

③ Each student represents an ordered pair. Have each student write down his or her coordinates.

Michelle is (3, 1). She is sitting because 1 is not greater than or equal to 3.

④ At a signal, stand up if your y-value is greater than or equal to your x-value. What inequality does this represent? Describe the shape formed by the people who are standing. Then sit down.

⑤ Repeat step 4 for a y-value that is less than twice your x-value.

⑥ Repeat step 4 for a y-value that is greater than 3.

⑦ Repeat step 4 for a y-value that is less than or equal to 2.

455

Linear Inequalities on a Coordinate Plane

You just modeled four *linear inequalities*. Another way to model a linear inequality is to draw its graph on the coordinate plane.

The graph of a **linear inequality** is a region on a coordinate plane whose edge is a line. This line is called a **boundary line.**

Sample 1

Graph each inequality.

a. $y \geq x$

b. $y < -\frac{1}{2}x + 4$

Sample Response

a. First graph the boundary line $y = x$. Draw it as a solid line.

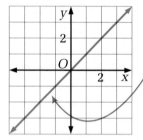

If the inequality has the symbol $\leq$ or $\geq$, use a solid line to show that the line is part of the shaded region.

Then shade the region above the line.

The shaded portion of the graph is the **solution region**.

All points in the shaded region have coordinates that make the inequality $y \geq x$ true.

b. First graph the boundary line $y = -\frac{1}{2}x + 4$. Draw it as a dashed line.

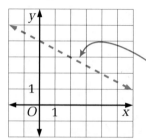

If the inequality has the symbol $>$ or $<$, use a *dashed* line to show that the line is *not* part of the shaded region.

Then shade the region below the line.

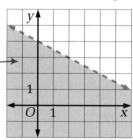

All points in the shaded region have coordinates that make the inequality $y < -\frac{1}{2}x + 4$ true.

Talk it Over

1. Which inequality in Sample 1 did you model in step 4 of the Exploration?

2. Describe how to graph $y \geq 3$.

3. **a.** Describe the graph of $x = 2$.

   b. Describe the graph of $x \le 2$.

Tell whether the boundary line for each inequality is *solid* or *dashed*. Then tell whether you would shade the region *above* or *below* the line.

4. $y \le 9x + 6$

5. $y > \dfrac{2}{3}x$

6. $y \ge -4x - 11$

7. $y < -x + \dfrac{1}{4}$

⋯⋯➤ **Now you are ready for:**
  Exs. 1–16 on pp. 459–460

The inequalities in Sample 1 have the dependent variable, y, alone on one side of the inequality symbol. Inequalities written this way are in *slope-intercept form*.

Sample 2

Derek has saved $48 by baby-sitting. He plans to use the money to buy tapes and compact discs at a music store. Tapes cost $8 and compact discs cost $12. The inequality $8x + 12y \le 48$ represents the amount Derek can spend at the store.

Graph the inequality $8x + 12y \le 48$.

Sample Response

First rewrite the inequality in slope-intercept form.

$$8x + 12y \le 48$$

$$8x + 12y - 8x \le 48 - 8x \quad \longleftarrow \text{Subtract } 8x \text{ from both sides.}$$

$$12y \le 48 - 8x$$

$$\frac{1}{12} \cdot 12y \le \frac{1}{12}(48 - 8x) \quad \longleftarrow \text{Multiply both sides by the reciprocal of 12.}$$

$$y \le 4 - \frac{2}{3}x$$

Next graph the boundary line $y = 4 - \dfrac{2}{3}x$.

Draw it as a solid line.

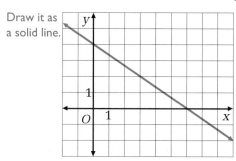

Then shade the region below the line.

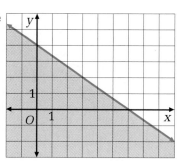

All points in the shaded region have coordinates that make the inequality $8x + 12y \le 48$ true.

8. In Sample 2, why are all the points in the shaded region solutions of the original inequality, $8x + 12y \leq 48$?

9. Which points in the shaded region in Sample 2 represent combinations of numbers of tapes and compact discs that Derek can afford?

BY THE WAY...

Thomas Harriot (1560–1621) was a British mathematician and astronomer. He may have been the first person to use the inequality symbols > and <.

Graphing Inequalities in Standard Form

In Sample 2, the inequality $8x + 12y \leq 48$ has both the dependent variable and the control variable on the same side of the inequality symbol. You can graph inequalities in this *standard form* without rewriting them in slope-intercept form.

Sample 3

Graph the inequality 8x − 12y < 48.

Sample Response

1 First use the intercepts to graph the boundary line $8x - 12y = 48$. Draw it as a dashed line.

2 Next evaluate the inequality at a point *not* on the line, such as (0, 0).

$$8x - 12y < 48$$
$$8(0) - 12(0) \overset{?}{<} 48 \quad \longleftarrow \text{ Substitute } x = 0 \text{ and } y = 0.$$
$$0 < 48 \; \checkmark \quad \longleftarrow \text{ The inequality is true.}$$

(0, 0) is part of the solution.

3 Then shade the region on the *same side* of the line as (0, 0).

10. Look back at the inequalities and graphs in Samples 2 and 3. Does the symbol < always mean you should shade below the boundary line? Explain.

11. Why do you need to pick only one point not on the line?

12. Why do you have to pick a point that is not on the line?

13. Rewrite the inequality in Sample 3 in slope-intercept form and then graph it. Is your graph the same as the one shown?

HOW TO GRAPH AN INEQUALITY

1. Graph the boundary line first. Decide whether to use a solid or a dashed line.

2. Pick a point that is not on the line. Evaluate the inequality for values of the coordinates of this point.

3. a. If the inequality is true for this point, shade the region on the same side of the line.

   b. If the inequality is false for this point, shade the region on the opposite side of the line.

········► **Now you are ready for:**
: **Exs. 17–39 on pp. 460–462**

Look Back ◄─────

In Samples 1 and 2 you graphed inequalities in slope-intercept form. Write a general method for doing this.

···

Exercises and Problems

1. Look back at the Exploration on page 455. Which ordered pairs in the diagram have *y*-values less than their *x*-values? What inequality does this represent?

2. **Reading** How can you tell when to use a solid boundary line and when to use a dashed boundary line?

Match each inequality with its graph.

3. $y \leq 2.5x + 1$

4. $y < 2.5x + 1$

5. $y > 2.5x + 1$

6. $y \geq 2.5x + 1$

A.

B.

C.

D.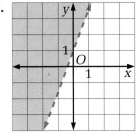

Graph each inequality.

7. $y \geq 5$ **8.** $x < 8$ **9.** $y \geq 2x$ **10.** $y > -x$

11. $y < \frac{1}{3}x + 2$ **12.** $y \leq -3x + 4$ **13.** $y > -\frac{2}{3}x - 5$ **14.** $y \leq \frac{1}{2}x - 1$

15. Four different brands of wheat flakes are sold at Super Shop.

a. Find the unit price for each brand.

b. Which brand is the best buy?

c. Graph the data in the table. Put the weight on the horizontal axis and the price on the vertical axis.

d. Draw a line from the origin through the point for Treat-O-Wheat.

Brand	Weight	Price
Flakies	12 oz	$2.39
Nutri-Flakes	14 oz	$3.29
Wheat Delight	15 oz	$3.49
Treat-O-Wheat	20 oz	$4.29

e. Which data points lie above the line drawn? Which lie below the line?

f. Interpret the results of part (e).

16. a. **Research** At a supermarket, find a single product that is packaged in several different sizes by the manufacturer. Make a table of size and cost data.

b. Make a scatter plot that shows the cost and size data. Is the unit price constant?

c. Describe any patterns you observe in your scatter plot.

d. Why is unit price usually less for larger sizes?

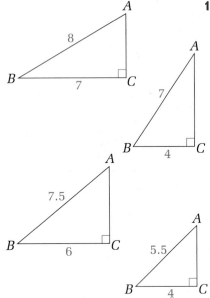

17. Use these right triangles.

a. Write each triangle's given measurements as an ordered pair (AB, BC).

b. Graph the ordered pairs. Put the length of the hypotenuse (AB) on the horizontal axis.

c. Graph the line $y = x$ on the same set of axes. What is the slope of this line?

d. Do the points you found in part (a) lie *above* or *below* the line?

e. Complete each $\underline{\ ?\ }$ with >, <, or =.

In all four triangles, $AB \underline{\ ?\ } BC$.

In all four triangles, $\frac{BC}{AB} \underline{\ ?\ } 1$.

f. The ratio $\frac{BC}{AB}$ represents cos B. In part (e), you showed that cos $B < 1$. Explain how your graph supports this.

Graph each inequality.

18. $2x - 5y \leq 10$ **19.** $3x + 3y > -6$ **20.** $4y - 3x < 12$

21. $-y + 2x \geq 8$ **22.** $y - 2x < 1$ **23.** $y + 3x \geq -2$

Lattice for x + 2y

			y			
3	4	5	6	7	8	9
1	2	3	4	5	6	7
−1	0	1	2	3	4	5
−3	−2	−1	0	1	2	3
−5	−4	−3	−2	−1	0	1
−7	−6	−5	−4	−3	−2	−1
−9	−8	−7	−6	−5	−4	−3

Use the lattice to help you graph the inequalities in Exercises 24–26.

24. $x + 2y > 2$

25. $x + 2y \le 6$

26. $x + 2y \ge 0$

BY THE WAY...

Gold that is 100% pure is 24-carat gold. 18-carat gold is 75% pure. It is 18 parts gold and 6 parts another metal. 14-carat gold is 58.3% pure. It is 14 parts gold and 10 parts another metal.

connection to **SCIENCE**

27. According to legend a king asked the Greek mathematician Archimedes (287?–212 B.C.) for help. The king worried that his crown might not be pure gold. Archimedes weighed the crown and measured its volume. He then found the density of the crown.

a. The *density* $\left(\dfrac{\text{mass}}{\text{volume}}\right)$ of gold is 19.3 g/cm³. The volume of the king's crown was 300 cm³. If the crown were made of pure gold, how many grams would it weigh?

b. Suppose Archimedes measured three objects that he knew were made of pure gold and plotted their data points on the graph at the right. Why do the three points lie on a line through the origin?

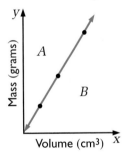

c. Archimedes found that the king's crown had a lower density than gold. Would a data point for the king's crown lie in region *A* or region *B* of this graph? Explain.

Archimedes is pictured in this mosaic found at Pompeii, a Roman city near Naples, Italy, that was destroyed by the eruption of Mt. Vesuvius.

28. The density of silver is 10.5 g/cm³.

a. Draw a graph that models the situation in which the ratio $\dfrac{\text{mass}}{\text{volume}}$ is *less* than the density of silver. Put the mass on the vertical axis.

b. Draw a graph that models the situation in which the ratio $\dfrac{\text{mass}}{\text{volume}}$ is *greater* than the density of silver. Put the mass on the vertical axis.

29. Banking A bank offers a savings account with an annual interest rate of 2.10%. The bank also offers a 12-month certificate of deposit (CD) with an annual interest rate of 6.31%.

a. Write an expression for the interest you receive in one year if you invest x dollars in the savings account and y dollars in the CD.

b. You want to receive $80 or more interest each year. Write an inequality that expresses this and graph the inequality.

c. Choose a point in the solution region and check that the interest you would receive each year is greater than or equal to $80.

d. What is the smallest amount of money you could invest to earn $80 in interest? How would you have to invest it?

30. Research Find annual interest rates for a savings account and a 12-month CD in a newspaper or at a bank. Using the rates you found, repeat Exercise 29.

Ongoing **ASSESSMENT**

31. Writing Write a quiz on graphing linear inequalities. Include at least six questions. Explain why you think your questions are good.

Review **PREVIEW**

Without graphing, tell whether each system has a *solution* or *no solution*. *(Section 8-5)*

32. $y = 2x - 7$
$y = -2x + 3$

33. $y = 0.5x + 9$
$y = 0.5x + 10$

34. $y = x + 1$
$3x - 3y = 2$

35. An inspector checked 40 books at random from a group of 1500 books that had just been printed. The inspector found errors in 5 books. About how many of the printed books had errors? *(Section 6-2)*

36. There are 36 nuts in a bag. Six of the nuts are almonds, twelve are cashews, and the rest are peanuts. Find the probability of not getting an almond.

Graph each inequality on a number line. *(Section 3-3)*

37. $-3 \leq x < 1$

38. $5 < x < 20$

Working on the Unit Project

39. Look at the graph of the winning times for men's 400 freestyle swimming on page 439. Which points clearly lie below the fitted line? Which years do they represent? Write an inequality to describe the region below the fitted line.

Systems of Linear Inequalities

Focus
Solve problems by writing
and graphing systems of
inequalities.

COMMON GROUND

Sue Hansen uses a mid-year test score and a year-end test score to calculate the testing component of her students' final grades. To reward improvement, she uses this formula.

x is a student's mid-year test score.

y is a student's year-end test score.

$$0.4x + 0.6y$$

The mid-year test score is 40% of the final grade.

The year-end test score is 60% of the final grade.

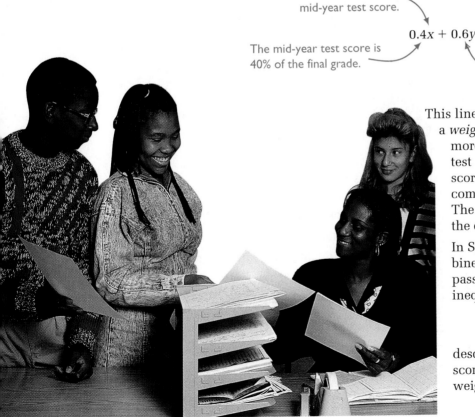

This linear combination is called a *weighted average.* It gives more weight to the year-end test score. The year-end test score is 60% of the testing component of the final grade. The mid-year test score adds the other 40%.

In Sue Hansen's class a combined score of 60 or higher is a passing score. The linear inequality

$$0.4x + 0.6y \geq 60$$

describes the pairs of test scores that give a passing weighted average.

Is it possible for a student in Sue Hansen's class to fail the mid-year test and still have a passing weighted average? Only if both of these inequalities are true at the same time.

$$x < 60 \quad \longleftarrow \text{failing mid-year test score}$$
$$0.4x + 0.6y \geq 60 \quad \longleftarrow \text{passing weighted average}$$

Graph the **system of inequalities** to find out.

Sample Response

Problem Solving Strategy: Use a graph

Graph both inequalities on the same set of axes. The shaded regions may overlap. If they do, darken the region of overlap.

The coordinates of the points in the doubly shaded region are **solutions of the system of inequalities.**

failing mid-year test score

passing weighted average

failed mid-year test but still has a passing weighted average

There is a region on the graph where the shading overlaps. This doubly shaded region contains the possible test scores for students who fail the mid-year test but still have a passing weighted average. This shows that it is possible to fail the mid-year test and still have a passing weighted average.

Talk it Over

BY THE WAY...

Weighted averages are used to score diving competitions. An average of the judges' scores is weighted by a dive's degree of difficulty, which ranges from 1.3 to 3.5.

Use Sample 1 for questions 1–4.

1. Why is the boundary line of the graph of $x < 60$ dashed?

2. Is the point (60, 60) part of the solution of the system of inequalities?

3. Suppose one of Sue Hansen's students scores 50 on the mid-year test. What grade does he or she have to get on the year-end test in order to have a passing weighted average?

4. Pick a point outside the doubly shaded region on the graph for the weighted average. Tell whether its coordinates make *none*, *one*, or *both* of the inequalities true and what the coordinates mean in terms of the situation.

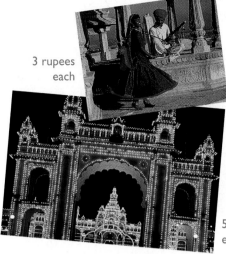

3 rupees
each

5 rupees
each

Raj is visiting relatives in India. He wants to send postcards to at least 8 friends. He has 30 rupees to spend. Large postcards cost 5 rupees each, and small postcards cost 3 rupees each.

a. Write and graph a system of inequalities to model the situation.

b. Suppose Raj wants to buy at least one large postcard. What combination of small and large postcards should he buy?

Sample Response

a. Write two inequalities.

➤ Let x = the number of small postcards Raj buys.

➤ Let y = the number of large postcards Raj buys.

➤ Total number of items: $x + y \geq 8$

➤ Total cost: $3x + 5y \leq 30$

Graph the system of inequalities.

b. Raj can only buy whole numbers of postcards. The combinations in the doubly shaded region that include at least one large postcard are (5, 3), (6, 2), (7, 1), and (8, 1). To get the most for his money, he should buy 8 small postcards and 1 large postcard.

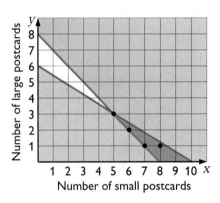

Look Back

How is graphing a system of linear inequalities different from graphing a system of linear equations? How is it similar?

8-7 Exercises and Problems

1. **Reading** In Sample 2, why isn't the combination (10, 1) a possible solution?

For Exercises 2–7, use the graph to tell whether each ordered pair is a solution of this system. Write *Yes* or *No*.

$$y \geq -3$$
$$x < 3$$

2. (0, 0)   3. (3, 1)   4. (3, −3)

5. (5, −5)   6. (2, −4)   7. (−4, 4)

8. The graph of this system is shown.

$$y \geq 1 - 2x$$
$$y \leq 2 + x$$

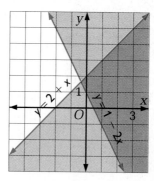

a. Choose a point in the solution region and show that it makes both inequalities true.

b. Choose a point that is *not* in the solution region and show that it does *not* make both inequalities true.

For Exercises 9–14, graph each system of inequalities.

9. $x + y \leq 10$
$y \leq 2x$

10. $y < -3$
$x > 3$

11. $2x + 3y > 18$
$y > x$

12. $y < 2x + 6$
$y > 5$

13. $x > -1$
$y > 5$

14. $3x + y \geq 15$
$3x - y < 15$

15. a. Graph the inequality $x + y < 8$.

b. On the same set of axes, graph $y > -x + 10$.

c. What is special about the lines?

d. **Writing** Where do the two regions overlap? Explain.

16. a. Graph this system: $\quad x + y > 8$
$\qquad\qquad\qquad\qquad y < -x + 10$

b. Describe the shape of the solution region.

c. **Writing** Compare this system with the system in Exercise 15. How are the systems alike? How are they different?

17. Suppose the teacher mentioned on page 463, Sue Hansen, uses the mean of the mid-year and end-year test grades to determine the testing component of her students' scores. She uses the linear combination $0.5x + 0.5y$.

a. To find the mean of x and y, she could also use the formula $\frac{x + y}{2}$. Explain why this is the same as $0.5x + 0.5y$.

b. What percent of the testing component of the score comes from the mid-year test now? What percent comes from the year-end test?

c. Graph the inequality $0.5x + 0.5y \geq 60$.

d. **Writing** Describe the differences between your graph and the graph on page 464.

18. This system has one equation and one inequality.

$$y = 2x + 4$$
$$x + y \leq 10$$

a. Draw a graph to show the points that make both sentences true.

b. What is the geometric name for the solution?

19. Budgeting Nadine has two part-time jobs. A neighbor hires her to do odd jobs for no more than 4 h per week and pays her $6 per hour. Nadine also works with a photographer in a darkroom for $5 per hour. Nadine wants to earn enough money in a week to buy a new flash for her camera. The flash will cost more than $90.

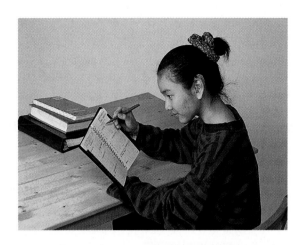

a. Write and graph a system of inequalities to model this situation.

b. How can Nadine divide her time so that she works the minimum number of hours needed to buy the flash for her camera?

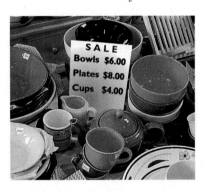

20. Budgeting Cheryl and Jim Sherman got a $50 gift certificate to a department store as a wedding gift. They decided to use it to buy at least 4 bowls and some plates to add to the dishes that Cheryl already had.

a. Write and graph a system of inequalities to model this situation.

b. How many of each item should they buy to minimize the amount of change they get back?

21. Career Suppose you are a customer service representative at the bank described in Exercise 29 on page 462. A customer has $1500 to invest and wants to decide how much to invest in a CD, how much to invest in a savings account, and how much to keep as cash.

a. Copy the graph for part (b) of Exercise 29 on page 462.

b. On the same set of axes, graph the inequality $x + y \leq 1500$. The solution region for this inequality shows the possible ways to invest $1500 or less in the two accounts.

c. Describe the region that is doubly shaded. What are its vertices?

d. List the vertices of the solution region in a table like this. Complete the table.

Vertex	Amount in savings account	Amount in CD	Amount in cash	Interest
(0, 1500)	$0	$1500	$0	$94.65
?	?	?	?	?
?	?	?	?	?

e. Customers must pay a penalty if they withdraw money from a 12-month CD before the year is over. The money is "locked up" for a 12-month period. Money kept in a savings account is always available. How should your customer split the $1500 if he or she wants to earn at least $80 in interest, but wants to minimize the amount locked up in a CD?

Graph each system of three or more inequalities. Describe the shape of the region where the shading for *all* the inequalities overlaps.

22. $y \geq -3$
$x \leq 4$
$y \leq 2x - 5$

23. $x + y \leq 7$
$x + y \geq 4$
$x \geq 0$
$y \geq 0$

24. $y > 2x - 5$
$y > -2x - 5$
$2x + 2y < 5$
$-2x + 2y < 5$

Ongoing **ASSESSMENT**

25. **Open-ended** Create a system of inequalities whose solution region is a polygon.

Review **PREVIEW**

Graph each inequality. *(Section 8-6)*

26. $x < 4$

27. $y \leq -2$

28. $y \geq \frac{1}{4}x + 3$

29. $4x - 8y > 24$

Find each unknown measure. *(Sections 2-5, 6-7, 7-1)*

30.

31.

32.

30. 5 mm, 40°, x

31. y, 20°, 6 cm

32. a, b, 55°, 10 m

33. Which angles in Exercise 32 are complementary? Why? *(Section 2-5)*

Estimate each square root within a range of two integers. *(Section 2-9)*

34. $\sqrt{50}$

35. $\sqrt{58}$

36. $\sqrt{193}$

37. $\sqrt{0.18}$

38. $\sqrt{0.0136}$

 Working on the Unit Project

39. **Group Activity** Use the data you researched in Section 8-2.

  a. Compare the data you found to the Olympic data on page 416. Which values are greater? Which are less? Which are equal?

  b. Have one person graph the men's winning times and the other graph the women's. Put *Years after 1960* on the horizontal axis.

  c. For each graph, decide whether there is a negative correlation between the winning times and the number of years since 1960. If so, draw a fitted line and write an equation to model your data.

Completing the Unit Project

Now you can analyze the trends in the Olympic swimming data. Make each of these predictions.

> **In what year will the men's and women's winning times for the 400 m freestyle event be equal?**

> **How will the men's and women's times compare in the years after their times are equal?**

> **In what year will the women's 400 m freestyle record be broken? What do you think the new record will be?**

Write your news article predicting the new record-breaking time for the women's 400 m freestyle swimming event. Use graphs to present some of the information in your article.

OLYMPIC UPDATE
New World Record Set!

Look Back

How accurate do you think your predictions are? List some reasons why the model you used may not be suitable for making long-term predictions. Keep your news article and data file. Watch the news to see whether your predictions come true!

Alternative Projects

Project 1: Playing the Market

Use a stock market report from a newspaper and "invest" $1000 in a stock of your choice. Check the paper every day and record the value of your stock. At the end of a week, graph the data and find an equation for a fitted line.

Find out what the interest rate is for a savings account at a bank and calculate how much interest $1000 will earn in one week.

Write a report to present your findings. Include answers to these questions: Do you think investing money in stock is better than leaving it in a bank? Why or why not? Is this a good way to decide how to invest?

Project 2: Projected Savings

Research a long-term payment plan for a car or another item. Find out the initial payment, the monthly payments, and the number of months in the plan.

Model the plan with a graph and an equation. Write a report that describes your model. Include answers to these questions: Suppose you saved the amount of money needed to pay the total cost all at once. When could you buy the item? How much money would you save by not paying interest with monthly payments? Which payment plan is the best? Why?

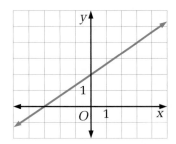

1. Use the graph at the left. **8-1**

   a. Find the slope and the vertical intercept.

   b. Write an equation for the line.

   c. Tell whether the graph is an example of *linear growth* or *linear decay*.

   d. Tell whether the graph is an example of *direct variation*. Explain.

2. The Levy family keeps their cement fish pond filled to a height of 20 in. At the end of the summer, they drain the pond. The height of the water drops at a rate of 1.5 in. per minute.

   a. Model the situation with a graph.

   b. Find the slope and the vertical intercept of the line and explain how they are related to the original situation.

   c. Model the situation with an equation.

   d. How long will it take to empty the pond? Where does this information appear on your graph?

3. When triathlete Jim MacLaren prepares for an event, **8-2** his biking speed might be 20 mi/h and his running speed might be 7.5 mi/h. After swimming for a while, he might ride his bicycle part of the way and run the rest of the way on a 30 mi trail.

   a. Write an equation for this situation.

   b. Rewrite the equation in slope-intercept form.

   c. Graph the equation.

   d. Find the intercepts of the graph and explain what each means in terms of the situation.

Graph each equation and find the slope of each line. **8-3**

4. $x = -3$ 5. $y = 4$

6. A line has a slope of zero and includes the point $(-5, 7)$.

   a. Graph the line.   b. Write an equation for the line.

7. **Writing** Suppose you plan to graph $y = 2x - 3$ and $5x - 4y = 12$ on graph paper. For each equation, describe a method you could use and explain your choice. If you have a graphics calculator, also describe how you can use it to graph each line.

For Exercises 8 and 9, write an equation for each line.

8. The horizontal intercept is 4 and the vertical intercept is -2.

9. The slope is 2 and the point $(-3, 5)$ is on the line. **8-4**

10. **Open-ended** Write an equation for a line that goes through quadrants two, three, and four on a coordinate plane.

11. Monthly dues for a union are a fixed amount plus a fraction of a member's hourly pay. A member who earns $10 per hour pays $23.75 in union dues each month. A member who earns $12 per hour pays $25.25.

   a. Model the situation with an equation.

   b. What are the values of the slope and the vertical intercept? What does each mean in terms of the original situation?

   c. A union member earns $14.50/h. How much does this person pay in monthly dues?

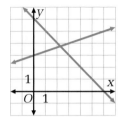

12. a. Use the graph to estimate the solution to the system of equations.   8-5

   b. Use substitution to find the exact solution.

   $$y = \frac{1}{3}x + 3$$
   $$y = -x + 6$$

Without graphing, tell whether each system has a *solution* or *no solution*.

13. $y = 3x - 8$
   $y = 3x + 8$

14. $y = x$
   $y = 2x$

15. $y = 5 - x$
   $y = 5 + x$

16. OverKnight Xpress charges $5.00 plus $1.00 per ounce for sending a package to another state. NextDay Express charges $3.50 plus $1.25 per ounce.

   a. Write a system of equations to model this situation.

   b. Graph both equations on the same set of axes.

   c. For what weight package is the cost the same?

   d. When is OverKnight Xpress less expensive than NextDay Express?

For Exercises 17–20, graph each system of inequalities.   8-6, 8-7

17. $y \geq -2$
   $x < 1$

18. $y > x$
   $x + y < 20$

19. $\frac{1}{2}x - y > 10$
   $y > -x$

20. $y \geq 2x - 3$
   $x + 2y < 6$

21. An interior designer plans to put plants in an office building. Ferns cost $20 each. Palms cost $25 each. The designer may need as many as 65 plants and can spend no more than $1200 for the plants.

   a. Let x = the number of ferns. Let y = the number of palms. Write an inequality for the total number of plants.

   b. Write an inequality for the cost of the project in terms of x and y.

   c. Graph the system of inequalities.

   d. What is the largest number of palms that the designer can buy? How is this shown on the graph?

22. **Self-evaluation** Without graphing, describe as much as you can about this system of inequalities.
   $y > 4$
   $y < -3x + 4$

23. **Group Activity** The table shows the winning times for the men's and women's 100 m dash in the Olympics. Work with another student. Have one student use the women's data and the other use the men's data.

a. Make a scatter plot for the data and draw a fitted line. Put years after 1896 on the horizontal axis.

b. Estimate an equation for your fitted line.

c. Does your graph show *linear growth* or *linear decay*? Explain.

d. Exchange papers with your partner and check each other's work.

e. Have one student find the solution of the system of equations by substitution. Have the other student find the solution by graphing. Compare solutions.

f. Tell what the solution of the system means in terms of the situation.

Year	Men's 100 m Dash (seconds)	Women's 100 m Dash (seconds)	Year	Men's 100 m Dash (seconds)	Women's 100 m Dash (seconds)
1896	12.0	—	1952	10.4	11.5
1900	11.0	—	1956	10.5	11.5
1904	11.0	—	1960	10.2	11.0
1906	11.2	—	1964	10.0	11.4
1908	10.8	—	1968	9.95	11.0
1912	10.8	—	1972	10.14	11.07
1920	10.8	—	1976	10.06	11.08
1924	10.6	—	1980	10.25	11.06
1928	10.8	12.2	1984	9.99	10.97
1932	10.3	11.9	1988	9.92	10.54
1936	10.3	11.5	1992	9.96	10.82
1948	10.3	11.9	1996	9.84	10.94

IDEAS AND (FORMULAS) $= X^2_{sP_s}$

STATISTICS & PROBABILITY

➤ The equation of a fitted line can be estimated using two points close to or on the fitted line. The equation can be used to analyze a set of data points and make predictions. *(p. 440)*

ALGEBRA $)X^2$

$(X$

➤ The slope-intercept form of an equation is $y = mx + b$. The variable m represents the slope and the variable b represents the vertical intercept. *(p. 418)*

➤ Graphs of linear functions model linear growth if the slope is positive. If the slope is negative, the graph of a linear function models linear decay. *(p. 420)*

➤ The standard form of a linear equation is $ax + by = c$. *(p. 427)*

➤ The horizontal and vertical intercepts can be used to graph a line. To find the horizontal intercept, substitute 0 for y. To find the vertical intercept, substitute 0 for x. *(p. 428)*

➤ All points on a horizontal line have the same y-coordinate. All points on a vertical line have the same x-coordinate. *(p. 433)*

➤ When the control variable is x and the dependent variable is y, you can express slope this way: *(p. 440)*

$$\frac{\text{change in } y}{\text{change in } x}$$

➤ The equation of a line can be found in different ways: from the coordinates of any two points on the line, from the slope and the coordinates of one point on the line, and from the graph. *(p. 441)*

➤ You can graph a line using one point on the line and the slope. *(p. 442)*

➤ To estimate the solution to a system of linear equations, find the point of intersection on the graph of the lines. *(p. 448)*

➤ A system of linear equations has no solution when the lines do not intersect. *(p. 449)*

➤ When you graph a linear inequality, use a solid boundary line for ≥ and ≤, and use a dashed boundary line for > and <. *(p. 456)*

➤ To graph a linear inequality in slope-intercept form, shade the region above the boundary line if the inequality symbol is > or ≥. Shade below the boundary line if it is < or ≤. *(p. 456)*

➤ To graph a linear inequality in standard form, find a point whose coordinates make the inequality true. Then shade the region on that side of the boundary line. *(p. 458)*

➤ To solve a system of inequalities, you graph each inequality to find out what solutions they have in common. *(p. 464)*

GEOMETRY

➤ The slope of a horizontal line is 0. The slope of a vertical line is undefined. *(p. 433)*

➤ Lines that have the same slope are parallel. *(p. 450)*

Key Terms

- **slope** (p. 418)

- **linear growth** (p. 420)

- **graph of an equation** (p. 426)

- **horizontal intercept** (p. 428)
- **solution region** (p. 456)

- **vertical intercept** (p. 418)

- **linear decay** (p. 420)

- **linear equation** (p. 427)

- **linear inequality** (p. 456)
- **system of inequalities** (p. 464)

- **slope-intercept form of an equation** (p. 418)
- **solution of an equation with two variables** (p. 426)
- **standard form of a linear equation** (p. 427)
- **boundary line** (p. 456)
- **solution of a system of inequalities** (p. 464)

Reasoning and Measurement

Can a concrete boat float? University students from around the world participate in national concrete canoe competitions to answer this question. The contestants are judged on their canoe's design and racing ability, as well as on the team's oral and written reports. To qualify for the competition, the canoe must float when filled with water!

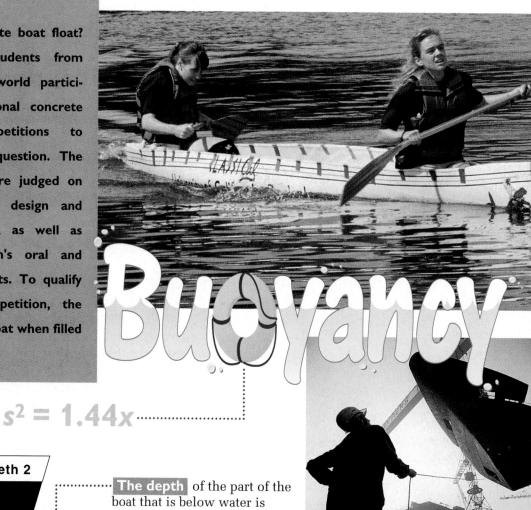

Buoyancy

$$s^2 = 1.44x$$

Queen Elizabeth 2

The depth of the part of the boat that is below water is called the *draft* of the boat. Knowing the draft of a boat allows sailors of freighters and pleasure boats to pass over sandbars and reefs safely.

The speed of a boat affects the draft. In 1992, the Queen Elizabeth II hit a ridge of rock when the ship's speed caused its draft to change from 32 ft to 39 ft.

Ship designers use a boat's planned weight and volume to determine how much cargo the boat will be able to carry safely. The weight of the boat's cargo affects the ship's draft. The temperature and the amount of salt in the water also determine how low in the water a boat will float.

draft

474

32 ft

39 ft

Build Your Own Boat

Your project is to build a cardboard boat using a milk or juice carton.

Before you float your boat, you will use the math skills you learn in this unit to predict the draft of your boat. You will also predict the amount of cargo your boat will hold before it sinks.

You will launch your boat on water to test your calculations. Keep a folder of your sketches, notes, and observations for a group discussion at the end of the unit.

It may seem odd to make a boat out of concrete, but many other **materials** have been used to make boats—reeds, tree trunks, and even caribou skins!

The Inuit peoples of the Arctic built the first *kayaks* thousands of years ago by stretching seal or caribou skins over a wooden frame.

In about A.D. 700, the Vikings made ships with overlapping planks, like siding on a house.

Clipper ships often brought tea to America in the mid-1800s.

The Chinese developed *junks*, which are still used today.

The Carib Indians of the Caribbean Islands used the term *kanu* for these boats dug out of large tree trunks.

The ancient Egyptians made riverboats by tying bundles of reeds together.

Dhows originated in Arabia. Today, adaptations are common in ports of India.

Getting Started

For this project you should work with another student. Here are some ideas to help you get started on your project.

☞ You will need to collect an empty milk or juice carton to make your boat. It may be a good idea to have each partner bring a carton to school.

☞ You will be testing your boat's ability to carry cargo. Think about what objects you can use as cargo and where you can get them. Here are some suggestions: marbles, table tennis balls, beads, coins, lipstick tubes, dried beans.

☞ Label a folder in which you will keep your project notes.

Can We Talk

Buoyancy

▸ Oil tankers, garbage barges, icebergs, and surfboards all have something in common with you—they float in water. Have you ever tried to float in fresh water? in salt water? What happened?

▸ If a fish did not have a gas-filled swim bladder, it would sink instead of swim! Sharks do not have them and need to swim constantly to stay afloat. What do you have in your chest cavity that is similar to a swim bladder?

▸ An inflatable raft weighs about the same whether or not it is inflated. Does inflating it affect its ability to float? Why do you think so?

▸ Why will a boat with a hole in the bottom start to sink when you put it into a pond?

▸ Do you think a glass marble will float? What about a sealed glass bottle with a message inside it?

▸ About 70% of Earth is covered with water. How might history have been different if everything put into water sank to the bottom?

■ **Working on the Unit Project**

Your work in Unit 9 will help you build and test your boat.

Related Exercises:

Section 9-1, Exercise 36
Section 9-2, Exercises 36, 37
Section 9-3, Exercises 47–51
Section 9-4, Exercises 19, 20
Section 9-5, Exercises 31, 32
Section 9-6, Exercise 29
Section 9-7, Exercises 23–25
Section 9-8, Exercises 32, 33

Alternative Projects p. 539

The Pythagorean Theorem and Reasoning

THE RIGHT REASON

EXPLORATION

How are the lengths of the sides of a right triangle related?

- **Work with another student.**

(1) Measure the horizontal and vertical sides of △A by counting the number of grid units in their lengths.

(2) Make a unit ruler by marking off the distance between grid lines along the edge of a piece of paper. Use this ruler to measure the remaining side of △A.

Triangle	Lengths of sides			Squares of lengths of sides		
	x	y	z	x^2	y^2	z^2
△A	3	4	5	9	16	25
△B	?	?	?	?	?	?
△C	?	?	?	?	?	?
△D	?	?	?	?	?	?

(3) Do your measurements in steps 1 and 2 agree with the numbers recorded for △A in the columns labeled x, y, and z?

(4) For each of the other right triangles on the grid, measure and record the lengths of the sides in a table like the one shown. For each triangle, find the square of the length of each side. Enter your results in columns x^2, y^2, and z^2.

(5) What do you observe from your results? Make a conjecture about how the lengths of the sides of a right triangle are related.

Writings from China, Babylonia, India, and Greece show that the relationship among the lengths of the sides of a right triangle was known and used by many civilizations thousands of years ago. One of the earliest *proofs* of the relationship may have been given about 2500 years ago by the Greek mathematician Pythagoras. Today the Pythagorean theorem continues to be one of the best-known and most useful theorems in mathematics.

THE PYTHAGOREAN THEOREM

In any right triangle, the square of the length of the hypotenuse is equal to the sum of the squares of the lengths of the legs.

$$c^2 = a^2 + b^2$$

·····► Now you are ready for:
Exs. 1–4 on p. 481

Sample 1

The size of a rectangular TV screen is given by the length of its diagonal. What is the size of this screen?

16.2 in.

21.6 in.

Sample Response

16.2 in.

21.6 in.

Problem Solving Strategy:
Make a sketch

The diagonal divides the screen into two congruent right triangles with legs of 21.6 in. and 16.2 in. The diagonal forms the hypotenuse of both triangles.

Watch Out!
$a^2 + b^2 \neq (a + b)^2$

$c^2 = a^2 + b^2$ ◄———————— Use the Pythagorean theorem.

$c^2 = (21.6)^2 + (16.2)^2$ ◄— Substitute 21.6 for a and 16.2 for b.

$c^2 = 466.56 + 262.44$

$c^2 = 729$

$c = \sqrt{729}$ ◄——————— Find the positive square root.

$c = 27$

The length of the diagonal is 27 in. The TV has a 27-inch screen.

12 in. | 20 in.

Sample 2

An appliance store advertises a sale on 20 in. TVs. The ad says that the screen is 12 in. tall but does not mention the width. Find the width.

Sample Response

Problem Solving Strategy: Make a sketch

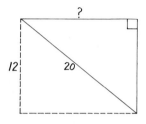

The 20 in. diagonal is the hypotenuse of a right triangle with a 12 in. leg. The length of the other leg is the width of the screen.

$$c^2 = a^2 + b^2 \quad \longleftarrow \text{Use the Pythagorean theorem.}$$
$$20^2 = a^2 + 12^2 \quad \longleftarrow \text{Substitute 20 for } c \text{ and 12 for } a \text{ or } b.$$
$$400 = a^2 + 144$$
$$400 - 144 = a^2 + 144 - 144 \quad \longleftarrow \text{Subtract 144 from both sides.}$$
$$256 = a^2$$
$$\sqrt{256} = a \quad \longleftarrow \text{Find the positive square root.}$$
$$16 = a$$

The width of the screen is 16 in.

:·····▶ **Now you are ready for:**
: **Exs. 5–21 on pp. 481–483**

Inductive and Deductive Reasoning

In the Exploration you made a conjecture that the relationship you saw for *four* right triangles would hold true for *all* right triangles. When you make a conjecture based on several observations, you are using **inductive reasoning.** It would be impossible to test all right triangles to prove your conjecture.

Next year you will prove the Pythagorean theorem. When mathematicians want to show that a statement is always true, they use *deductive reasoning*. **Deductive reasoning** uses facts, definitions, and accepted principles and properties to prove general statements.

> **BY THE WAY...**
>
> James A. Garfield (1831–1881) wrote a deductive proof of the Pythagorean theorem 5 years before he was elected the 20th President of the United States.

Writing Do you think the acute angles of a right triangle are complementary? Explain your reasoning.

Sample Response

Method ❶ Use inductive reasoning.

TECHNOLOGY NOTE
For Sample 3, Charles could have used geometric drawing software to draw triangles and measure angles.

Charles

I drew several right triangles and measured the acute angles with a protractor.

I recorded the angle measures and their sum in a table. I noticed a pattern: the measures of ∠A and ∠B add up to 90° for the triangles I tested. So I think that the acute angles of a right triangle are complementary.

Triangle	∠A	∠B	∠A + ∠B
I	53°	37°	90°
II	14°	76°	90°
III	45°	45°	90°
IV	37.5°	52.5°	90°

Barbara

I thought about what is true for any right triangle with acute angles at A and B and a right angle at C.

$$\angle A + \angle B + \angle C = 180$$
$$\angle C = 90°$$
$$\angle A + \angle B + 90 = 180$$
$$\underset{90}{\underline{\angle A + \angle B}} + 90 = 180$$

The measures of ∠A and ∠B add up to 90°, so I conclude that the acute angles of a right triangle are complementary.

Method ❷ Use deductive reasoning.

Talk it Over

1. What definition do you need to know for Sample 3?

2. Does Method 1 prove that the acute angles of a right triangle are complementary? Does Method 2? Explain.

Look Back

How is inductive reasoning different from deductive reasoning? Describe situations in which you have used inductive or deductive reasoning.

▸ **Now you are ready for:**
Exs. 22–36 on pp. 483–485

1. **a.** On graph paper, draw three right triangles of different sizes.

   b. Make a table like the one you used in the Exploration on page 477. Measure the lengths of the sides of each triangle you drew in part (a). Record your results in the table.

   c. Find the square of the length of each side. Enter your results in the table. Do your results support the conjecture you made in the Exploration?

2. The Pythagorean theorem states that in a right triangle $c^2 = a^2 + b^2$. What does the Pythagorean theorem tell you about this triangle?

3. Which statements are true for this triangle?

   a. $y^2 = x^2 + z^2$ **b.** $x^2 = y^2 + z^2$

   c. $y^2 = x^2 - z^2$ **d.** $z^2 = x^2 + y^2$

4. **Research** As a young man, the Greek mathematician and philosopher Pythagoras studied in Egypt and Babylonia. Around 530 B.C. he settled in southern Italy, where he founded a group known as the Pythagoreans. Pythagoras and his followers developed a theory of harmony when they studied the relationship between the length of a musical instrument's string and the pitch of its tone. Write a short report on the Pythagorean theory of harmony.

5. **Reading** What problem solving strategy is used in Samples 1 and 2? Why is this strategy helpful?

The portrait on this Greek vase from about 490 B.C. shows a man singing and playing a kithara, a stringed instrument similar to a lyre.

Find the missing length in each right triangle.

6.
24 cm
10 cm
x

7. 15 in.
x
9 in.

8. x
8 m
15 m

9. x
10 mi
24 mi

Find the area of each triangle by first finding the height _h_.

10.
50 ft
h
30 ft

11.
13 m
h
⊢10 m⊣

12. 17 cm
h
⊢15 cm⊢18 cm⊣

13. **Baseball** A major league baseball diamond is a square that is 90 ft on each side. When a runner on first base tries to steal second base, the catcher has to throw from home to second. How far is that throw?

14. **Writing** Suppose the shortstop is standing right on the line between second and third. Describe how the Pythagorean theorem could be used to find the distance from the shortstop to home plate.

2nd base

3rd base

1st base

90 ft   90 ft

Home

John is planning what furniture to move up to his new room in the attic of his family's home. The only entrance to the attic is a pull-down stairway in the ceiling of the second floor hallway. The opening in the ceiling is a rectangle that is 54 in. long and $25\frac{1}{2}$ in. wide.

15. John wants to move his stereo cabinet up to his new room. The cabinet is 26 in. wide, 48 in. tall, and 20 in. deep. Will the cabinet fit through the opening in the ceiling? Explain.

16. The top of John's desk can be removed from the legs of the desk. The top of the desk is 56 in. long, 36 in. deep, and 1 in. thick. Will John be able to fit the top of his desk through the opening in the ceiling? Explain.

The lengths of two sides of a right triangle are given. The length of the missing side is an integer. Find the length of the missing side and tell whether the missing side is a leg or a hypotenuse.

17. 9, 15, __?__

18. 15, 36, __?__

19. 21, 72, __?__

20. 75, 85, __?__

21. Find the length of the diagonal d of this rectangular box. (*Hint:* You will need to use two different right triangles.)

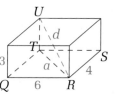

For Exercises 22–26, tell whether each person is using *inductive* or *deductive* reasoning.

22. Kim thinks that the product of two even numbers is always even. Here is her evidence:

$$2 \cdot 4 = 8 \qquad 12 \cdot 20 = 240 \qquad 32 \cdot 16 = 512 \qquad 100 \cdot 200 = 20{,}000$$

23. Sheila agrees that the product of two even numbers is always even. Here is her argument: Let the two even numbers be $2m$ and $2n$, where m and n are integers. Then their product is $4mn$, which equals $2(2mn)$. Since $4mn$ is the product of 2 and an integer, it is always even.

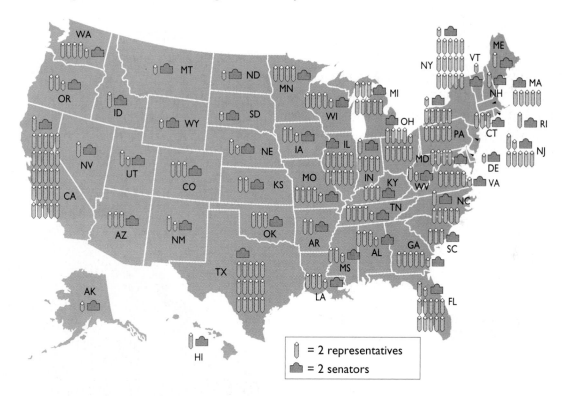

= 2 representatives
= 2 senators

24. Government Sara's history class is studying the presidential election. In the Electoral College, the number of electors from each state equals the number of representatives it has in the House plus the number of senators it has in the Senate. The Constitution requires each state to have two senators. Sara says, "If n is the number of representatives from a state, then $n + 2$ is the number of presidential electors from that state."

25. Javier draws several pairs of parallel lines and draws a third line across each pair. He conjectures that the angles inside the letter Z are always equal in measure.

26. Kira claims that the sum of two odd numbers is even. Here is her argument:

Kira Y.

Suppose m and n are any integers.
Then $2m$ is even.
$2n$ is even.
$2m + 1$ is odd.
$2n + 1$ is odd.
Add two odd numbers:
$(2m+1) + (2n+1) = 2m + 2n + 2$
$= 2(m+n+1)$
This number is evenly divisible by 2. It's even!
So the sum of any two odd numbers is even.

27. **Writing** Nilu claims that the sum of the measures of the angles of any quadrilateral is 360°.

   a. Use inductive reasoning to support Nilu's claim.

   b. Use deductive reasoning to support Nilu's claim. (*Hint:* Draw a diagonal.)

BY THE WAY...

The integers 3, 4, and 5 are called a *Pythagorean triple* because they can be the lengths of the sides of a right triangle. A clay tablet from the second century B.C. shows that the Babylonians knew of at least fifteen Pythagorean triples, including 119, 120, 169, and 2291, 2700, 3541.

Ongoing **ASSESSMENT**

28. **Writing** Use deductive reasoning to show that $(\sin A)^2 + (\cos A)^2 = 1$ for the triangle at the right. (*Hint:* Use the sine and cosine ratios.)

Review **PREVIEW**

Graph each system. (*Section 8-5, 8-7*)

29. $y = 5x$
    $y = -x + 6$

30. $2x + y \leq 1$
    $y > 2$

Find the square roots of each number. (*Section 2-9*)

31. 0.04   **32.** $\frac{1}{9}$ **33.** 64   **34.** 196

35. The area of a square is 400 ft². Find the length of a side of the square. (*Section 2-9*)

Working on the Unit Project

36. **Group Activity** Work with another student.

You will need a ruler, scissors, and a protractor. You will use your results in Exercise 37 on page 491.

a. Draw any isosceles triangle.

b. **Using Manipulatives** Cut out the isosceles triangle. Fold the triangle to line up the sides of equal length.

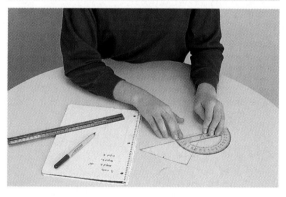

c. Open up your triangle. Measure all the angles and segments. You may want to record the measurements in a table.

d. Draw at least three other isosceles triangles. Repeat parts (a)–(c) for each new triangle.

e. **Writing** Describe what you have learned about isosceles triangles from parts (a)–(d). Did you use inductive or deductive reasoning?

f. Write a formula for finding h if you know a and b. Write any fraction in the formula in decimal form for easy use on a calculator.

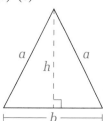

Investigating Properties of Square Roots

Focus
Simplify and multiply square roots and solve equations like $2x^2 = 36$.

A √Radical Idea

Talk it Over

1. Give a convincing argument that the value of x in the larger triangle is $\sqrt{18}$.

2. The two triangles are similar. What do you know about the sides of similar triangles? Give a convincing argument that the value of x in the larger triangle is $3\sqrt{2}$. ($3\sqrt{2}$ means $3 \cdot \sqrt{2}$.)

3. a. From questions 1 and 2, what can you conclude about the expressions $\sqrt{18}$ and $3\sqrt{2}$?

   b. Do you think that $\sqrt{9 \cdot 2}$ equals $\sqrt{9} \cdot \sqrt{2}$? Why or why not?

   c. On your calculator, compare the results of these two key sequences:

   9 ☒ 2 ＝ INV x^2

   9 INV x^2 ☒ 2 INV x^2 ＝

4. Choose any positive number for a. On your calculator, find the results of this key sequence:

   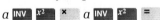
   a INV x^2 ☒ a INV x^2 ＝

PRODUCT PROPERTIES OF SQUARE ROOTS

For nonnegative numbers a and b:

$\sqrt{ab} = \sqrt{a} \cdot \sqrt{b}$

$\sqrt{a} \cdot \sqrt{b} = \sqrt{ab}$

$\sqrt{a} \cdot \sqrt{a} = a$

Example:

$\sqrt{39} = \sqrt{13} \cdot \sqrt{3}$

$\sqrt{13} \cdot \sqrt{3} = \sqrt{39}$

$\sqrt{3} \cdot \sqrt{3} = 3$

When you use your calculator to evaluate a square root like $\sqrt{18}$, your calculator gives you a decimal approximation. When you write an answer using the $\sqrt{}$ symbol, you are writing the answer in **radical form.**

You can simplify an expression in radical form when the number under the $\sqrt{}$ symbol has a perfect square factor.

> **Watch Out!**
> "Simplify" means to find an expression with the same value, not to find a decimal approximation.

Sample 1

▶ **Simplify $\sqrt{50}$.**

Sample Response

Identify any perfect square factors of the number under the $\sqrt{}$ symbol.

$$\sqrt{50} = \sqrt{25 \cdot 2} \quad \longleftarrow \quad \begin{array}{l} \text{25 is a perfect square factor of 50.} \\ \text{Write 50 as the product of 25 and 2.} \end{array}$$

$$= \sqrt{25} \cdot \sqrt{2} \quad \longleftarrow \quad \text{Use the property } \sqrt{ab} = \sqrt{a} \cdot \sqrt{b}.$$

$$= 5\sqrt{2} \quad \longleftarrow \quad \text{Write } \sqrt{25} \text{ as 5.}$$

Sample 2

Simplify $3\sqrt{2} \cdot 5\sqrt{10}$.

Sample Response

$$3\sqrt{2} \cdot 5\sqrt{10} = 3 \cdot 5 \cdot \sqrt{2} \cdot \sqrt{10} \quad \longleftarrow \quad \text{Group radical factors.}$$

$$= 15\sqrt{20} \quad \longleftarrow \quad \text{Use the property } \sqrt{a} \cdot \sqrt{b} = \sqrt{ab}.$$

$$= 15\sqrt{4 \cdot 5} \quad \longleftarrow \quad \begin{array}{l} \text{4 is a perfect square factor of 20.} \\ \text{Write 20 as the product of 4 and 5.} \end{array}$$

$$= 15 \cdot \sqrt{4} \cdot \sqrt{5} \quad \longleftarrow \quad \text{Use the property } \sqrt{ab} = \sqrt{a} \cdot \sqrt{b}.$$

$$= 15 \cdot 2\sqrt{5} \quad \longleftarrow \quad \text{Write } \sqrt{4} \text{ as 2.}$$

$$= 30\sqrt{5}$$

Talk it Over

5. Explain why it is not efficient to rewrite $\sqrt{50}$ as $\sqrt{5} \cdot \sqrt{10}$ when you want to simplify $\sqrt{50}$.

6. To simplify $\sqrt{72}$, Jeremy writes:

$$\sqrt{72} = \sqrt{9 \cdot 8}$$
$$= \sqrt{9} \cdot \sqrt{8}$$
$$= \sqrt{9} \cdot \sqrt{4 \cdot 2}$$
$$= \sqrt{9} \cdot \sqrt{4} \cdot \sqrt{2}$$
$$= 3 \cdot 2\sqrt{2}$$
$$= 6\sqrt{2}$$

Martha writes:

$$\sqrt{72} = \sqrt{36 \cdot 2}$$
$$= \sqrt{36} \cdot \sqrt{2}$$
$$= 6\sqrt{2}$$

Which method do you think is easier to use? Explain.

7. a. Simplify $-\sqrt{40}$.

   b. What are the solutions of $x = \pm\sqrt{40}$?

   c. What are the solutions of $x^2 = 40$?

Sample 3

Solve $5x^2 = 315$.

Sample Response

$$5x^2 = 315$$
$$\frac{5x^2}{5} = \frac{315}{5} \longleftarrow \text{Divide both sides by 5 to get } x^2 \text{ by itself.}$$
$$x^2 = 63$$
$$x = \pm\sqrt{63} \longleftarrow \text{Undo the squaring.}$$
$$x = \pm\sqrt{9 \cdot 7} \longleftarrow \text{Write 63 as the product of 9 and 7.}$$
$$x = \pm\sqrt{9} \cdot \sqrt{7} \longleftarrow \text{Use the property } \sqrt{ab} = \sqrt{a} \cdot \sqrt{b}.$$
$$x = \pm 3\sqrt{7} \longleftarrow \text{Write } \sqrt{9} \text{ as 3.}$$

The solutions are $3\sqrt{7}$ and $-3\sqrt{7}$.

In some situations, only a positive answer to an equation like the one in Sample 3 makes sense. If the variable is the length of a segment, use only the positive solution.

2 in.

The perimeter of a rectangle is 32 in. Find the length of a diagonal of the rectangle. Write the answer in simplified radical form.

Sample Response

Problem Solving Strategy: Break the problem into parts

Step 1 Find the length of the rectangle.

Let x = the length of the rectangle.

2 in.   2 in.

x

y

x

Perimeter = 32 in.

$2x + 4 = 32$	Use the formula $P = 2l + 2w$.
$2x = 28$	Subtract 4 from both sides.
$x = 14$	Divide both sides by 2.

Step 2 Find the length of the diagonal.

$14^2 + 2^2 = y^2$	Use the Pythagorean theorem.
$196 + 4 = y^2$	
$200 = y^2$	
$\sqrt{200} = y$	Find the positive square root.
$\sqrt{100 \cdot 2} = y$	Write 200 as the product of 100 and 2.
$\sqrt{100} \cdot \sqrt{2} = y$	Use the property $\sqrt{ab} = \sqrt{a} \cdot \sqrt{b}$.
$10\sqrt{2} = y$	Write $\sqrt{100}$ as 10.

The length of the diagonal of the rectangle is $10\sqrt{2}$ in.

Look Back

Explain how the product properties of square roots can be used to simplify $\sqrt{24}$ and to multiply $\sqrt{3}$ and $\sqrt{11}$.

9-2   Exercises and Problems

1. a. Reading Put one of the properties that you learned in this lesson in your own words.

  b. Give a numerical example of the property.

Simplify.

2. $\sqrt{90}$ **3.** $\sqrt{68}$ **4.** $\sqrt{125}$ **5.** $3\sqrt{8}$

6. $\sqrt{25\pi}$ **7.** $\sqrt{3} \cdot \sqrt{7}$ **8.** $\sqrt{6} \cdot \sqrt{8}$ **9.** $\sqrt{15} \cdot \sqrt{24}$

10. $\sqrt{7} \cdot \sqrt{7}$ **11.** $\left(\sqrt{11}\right)^2$ **12.** $2\sqrt{3} \cdot 4\sqrt{6}$ **13.** $5\sqrt{12} \cdot 3\sqrt{20}$

Solve for x.

14. $x^2 = 8$ **15.** $x^2 = 48$ **16.** $2x^2 = 36$

17. $15x^2 = 180$ **18.** $y^2 + y^2 = x^2$ **19.** $(2a)^2 + (5a)^2 = x^2$

20. a. On the map at the right, what is the distance from point A to point B?

    b. What is the distance from point B to point C?

    c. What is the distance from point C to point A? Give your answer in simplified radical form.

    d. If each unit on the grid represents five miles, what is the actual distance from point C to point A, to the nearest mile?

21. A square $ABCD$ has vertices with coordinates $A(4, -4)$, $B(4, 4)$, $C(-4, 4)$, and $D(-4, -4)$. Find the length of the diagonal $\overline{AC}$ in simplified radical form.

22. Find the length of the hypotenuse of this triangle in terms of x. Simplify the answer.

23. The maximum speed that some types of boats can travel can be estimated using the formula $s^2 = 1.44x$, where s is the speed in nautical miles per hour (or "knots") and x is the length of the boat's water line in feet.

    a. Solve the formula for s.

    b. Estimate the maximum speed of a boat with a water line of 25 ft.

24. a. The triangle shown is an isosceles right triangle with legs of length a. Write a formula in simplified radical form for the length of the hypotenuse, c, in terms of a.

    b. Use the formula you wrote in part (a). Find the length of the hypotenuse of an isosceles right triangle that has legs of length 6 cm.

25 TECHNOLOGY Enter the key sequences on your calculator to find each answer.

    a. $\dfrac{\sqrt{45}}{\sqrt{5}}$ ⟶ 45 [INV] [x^2] ÷ 5 [INV] [x^2] = _?_

    b. $\dfrac{\sqrt{32}}{\sqrt{2}}$ ⟶ 32 [INV] [x^2] ÷ 2 [INV] [x^2] = _?_

    c. Use your answers to parts (a) and (b) to simplify $\dfrac{\sqrt{75}}{\sqrt{3}}$ without using your calculator. Describe a shortcut.

26. Writing Kristin wonders whether the statement $\sqrt{a+b} = \sqrt{a} + \sqrt{b}$ is true for all values of a and b. Can you find a counterexample? Write a note to Kristin to help her decide.

TECHNOLOGY NOTE

To find $\sqrt{a+b}$ on a calculator:

a `+` b `=` `INV` `x²`

Review **PREVIEW**

For Exercises 27–30, find the missing length in each right triangle. *(Section 9-1)*

27.

16 m x 12 m

28.

x 2 in.   5 in.

29.

8 ft   17 ft x

30.

x 9 cm   15 cm

31. The vertices of a triangle are $A(3, 2)$, $B(5, 4)$, and $C(4, -1)$. Draw a dilation of $\triangle ABC$ with center $A(3, 2)$ and scale factor 2. *(Section 6-6)*

Solve. *(Sections 5-2, 5-6)*

32. $\frac{2}{3}x = 0$

33. $3x + 34.5 = 0$

34. $0 = -5x$

35. $39 - 13x = 0$

Working on the Unit Project

Use the empty milk carton or other container you collected.

36. Construct a boat using these steps.

1 Open the top of the carton completely.

2 Cut through two opposite side edges and along a diagonal of the base of the carton.

3 Use either half of the carton to construct a boat with triangular ends.

You will need to use tape or a stapler to keep the walls of the boat in place.

37. a. Measure the sides and height of a triangular end of the boat you built.

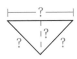

b. Explain why you can use the formula you found in Exercise 36 on page 485 to approximate the height of a triangular end of your boat.

c. Test the formula you wrote in Exercise 36 on page 485. How close is the height from the formula to the measured height you found in part (a)?

If-Then Statements and Converses

IS IT RIGHT?

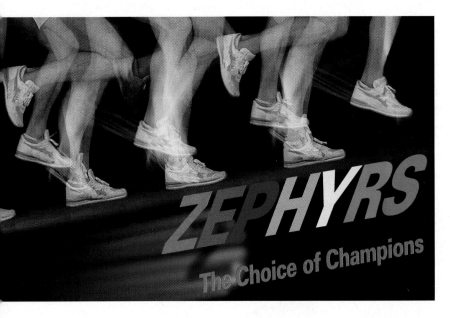

The Choice of Champions

What does this ad say to you? Does it lead you to believe the following statements?

1) If you are a champion, then you choose Zephyrs.

2) You are a champion if you choose Zephyrs.

Statements like these are called **if-then statements** or *conditional statements*. The *if* part is called the **hypothesis** and the *then* part is called the **conclusion.**

hypothesis   conclusion

If you are a champion, then you choose Zephyrs.

conclusion   hypothesis

You are a champion if you choose Zephyrs.

Notice that the words "if" and "then" are not parts of the hypothesis and conclusion.

If-then statements are either true or false. One way to show that an if-then statement is false is to find a counterexample.

Watch Out!
The hypothesis does not always come first. Also, the word *then* does not always appear in an if-then statement.

∘∘∘∘∘ ►

| **Sample 1** |

Tell whether each if-then statement is *True* or *False*.

a. If it is 11 P.M., the sun has set.

b. If a triangle is equilateral, then it is isosceles.

This time-lapse photo shows the sun in the sky over Kavtovic, Alaska from 9 P.M. to 4 A.M. on June 24.

Sample Response

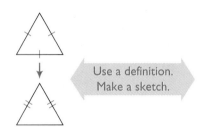

Use a definition. Make a sketch.

a. There is a counterexample. In parts of Alaska, the sun never sets during some summer nights.

Apply what you know about geography.

The statement is false.

b. By definition, an isosceles triangle has *at least two* sides of equal length. Since every equilateral triangle has *three* sides of equal length, every equilateral triangle is also an isosceles triangle. There is no counterexample.

The statement is true.

Sample 2

Identify the hypothesis and the conclusion of each statement.

a. If concert tickets cost less than $10, I will buy one.

b. We will go to the park if it is sunny.

Sample Response

a. hypothesis: Concert tickets cost less than $10.
conclusion: I will buy one.

b. hypothesis: It is sunny.
conclusion: We will go to the park.

Talk it Over

1. Suppose there really is a brand of shoes called Zephyrs. Are statements (1) and (2) on page 492 *True* or *False*? Explain.

2. Discuss whether you think each statement is *True* or *False*.

   a. If the sun is shining, then there are no clouds in the sky.

   b. If a figure is a square, it is a rectangle.

3. Write at least one if-then statement about the Zephyr advertisement or about another subject. Identify the hypothesis and the conclusion of your statement. Tell whether your statement is *True* or *False*. Explain why.

Converse of an If-Then Statement

The **converse** of an if-then statement is formed by interchanging the "if" and "then" parts.

if-then statement: If you are an 18 year old U.S. citizen, then you can vote.

converse: If you can vote, then you are an 18 year old U.S. citizen.

The converse of a true if-then statement is not necessarily true. In the example above, the converse is false because voters may be older than 18.

Sample 3

Write the converse of each if-then statement and tell whether the converse is *True or False*.

a. If you are in the kitchen, then you are in the house.

b. If an integer is divisible by 2, then it is even.

Sample Response

a. converse: If you are in the house, then you are in the kitchen.

Make a sketch.

There is a counterexample. You could be in the house, but in a room that is not the kitchen.

The converse is false.

b. converse: If an integer is even, then it is divisible by 2.

Use a definition.

The definition of an even integer is that it is an integer that is divisible by 2. There is no counterexample.

The converse is true.

▶ Now you are ready for:
Exs. 1–20 on pp. 496–497

An Important Converse

Sometimes a statement and its converse are both true. You know from arithmetic that if you multiply any number by zero, the result is zero. This property can be stated as an if-then statement.

If $a = 0$ or $b = 0$, then $ab = 0$.

The *zero-product property* is the converse of this statement.

ZERO-PRODUCT PROPERTY

If a product of factors is zero, one or more of the factors must be zero.

If $ab = 0$, then $a = 0$ or $b = 0$.

Sample 4

Solve $x(x + 1) = 0$.

Sample Response

Use the zero-product property.

At least one factor must be 0. $\longrightarrow$ $x(x + 1) = 0$

$$x = 0 \quad \text{or} \quad x + 1 = 0.$$
$$x + 1 - 1 = 0 - 1$$

The equation has *two* solutions. $\longrightarrow x = -1$

The solutions are 0 and -1.

Talk it Over

4. Do both $x = 0$ and $x = -1$ make the equation $x(x + 1) = 0$ true? Explain.

5. a. Use the zero-product property to solve $-1.3x = 0$.

   b. Describe another method of solving $-1.3x = 0$.

6. Can you use the zero-product property to solve $x(x + 1) = -1$? Explain why or why not.

The Converse of the Pythagorean Theorem

Theorem:
If a triangle is a right triangle, then $c^2 = a^2 + b^2$.

Converse:
If $c^2 = a^2 + b^2$, then the triangle is a right triangle.

The Pythagorean theorem can be written as an if-then statement.

You already know that the Pythagorean theorem is a true statement. The converse of the Pythagorean theorem is also true.

You can use the converse of the Pythagorean theorem to decide whether or not a triangle is a right triangle.

The lengths of the sides of a triangle are given. Is the triangle a right triangle? How do you know?

a. 15 ft, 20 ft, 25 ft

b. 8 cm, 10 cm, 13 cm

Sample Response

If a triangle is a right triangle, the longest side will be the hypotenuse.

a.

$a^2 + b^2 \overset{?}{=} c^2$

$15^2 + 20^2 \overset{?}{=} 25^2$

$225 + 400 \overset{?}{=} 625$

$625 = 625$

The triangle is a right triangle because $a^2 + b^2 = c^2$.

> Let the two shorter sides be a and b. Let the longest side be c.

> Compare $a^2 + b^2$ and c^2.

b.

$a^2 + b^2 \overset{?}{=} c^2$

$8^2 + 10^2 \overset{?}{=} 13^2$

$64 + 100 \overset{?}{=} 169$

$164 \neq 169$

The triangle is *not* a right triangle because $a^2 + b^2 \neq c^2$.

Look Back

State the hypothesis and the conclusion of the Pythagorean theorem. Explain how to form the converse of the Pythagorean theorem.

▶ **Now you are ready for:**
Exs. 21–51 on pp. 497–499

9-3 Exercises and Problems

1. **Reading** What is one way to show that an if-then statement is false?

For Exercises 2–9, do these things.

a. **Identify the hypothesis and the conclusion of each statement.**

b. **Tell whether the statement is *True* or *False*. If it is false, give a counterexample.**

2. If you visit the State Aquarium, then you will see some fish.

3. If you see an advertisement for a product, you will buy the product.

4. If the measure of an angle is less than 90°, the angle is acute.

5. If $x^2 = 25$, then $x = \pm\sqrt{25}$.

6. If a figure is a rectangle, then the area of the figure is the product of the length and width of the figure.

7. If a and b are nonnegative integers, then $\sqrt{ab} = \sqrt{a} \cdot \sqrt{b}$.

8. If $\angle A = 30°$, then $\sin A = 0.5$.

9. If $2y = 0$, then $y = 0$.

BY THE WAY...

The Maya of Mexico and Central America were among the first peoples to use a symbol to represent zero. The symbol looked somewhat like a shell, as shown in this section of a Mayan manuscript.

For Exercises 10–18, do these things.

a. Write the converse of the statement.

b. Tell whether the converse is *True* or *False*.
If it is false, give a counterexample.

10. If you are in Africa, then you are south of the equator.

11. If you are in Zimbabwe, then you are south of the equator.

12. If you are at Lake Tanganyika, then you are in Africa.

13. If m and n are even numbers, then $(m + n)$ is an even number.

14. A number is divisible by 3 if the number is divisible by 6.

15. If a figure is a triangle, then the area of the figure is half the area of some parallelogram with the same base and height.

16. If the coordinates of a point are $(0, -3)$, then the point is on the y-axis.

17. If the probability of an event is 1, then the event is certain to happen.

18. If $(x + 3)(x - 4) = 0$, then $x + 3 = 0$.

19. **Group Activity** Work in a group of three or four students.

   a. Write if-then statements suggested by your day at school or by an advertisement on TV or in a magazine.

   b. **Writing** Write a paragraph explaining why your statements and their converses are true or false.

20. **Open-ended** Write a true if-then statement whose converse is also true.

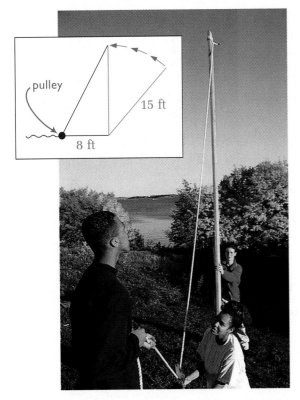

pulley

15 ft

8 ft

Solve.

21. $\frac{3}{5}t = 0$

22. $y(y - 4) = 0$

23. $m(m + 1) = 0$

24. $q(5q + 4) = 0$

25. $3j(j - 2) = 0$

26. $12z(3 - z) = 0$

The lengths of the sides of a triangle are given. Is it a right triangle? How do you know?

27. 7 yd, 24 yd, 25 yd   **28.** 8 in., 11 in., 15 in.

29. 4 in., 5 in., 6 in.   **30.** 24 mm, 26 mm, 10 mm

31. 2 ft, 8 ft, 7 ft   **32.** 34 mm, 16 mm, 30 mm

33. Use the photo and diagram at the left. A science class is doing an experiment using pulleys to raise a pole. Some students say that the pole will stand at a right angle to the ground when the length of rope between the pulley and the top of the pole is 17 ft. Are they correct?

34. Suppose the pole in Exercise 33 is 12 ft long. Let d be the distance between the pulley and the base of the pole, and let l be the length of the rope between the pulley and the top of the pole. Find two pairs of integers d and l for which the pole will stand at a right angle to the ground.

Surveyors in ancient Egypt may have used knotted ropes to build walls at right angles.

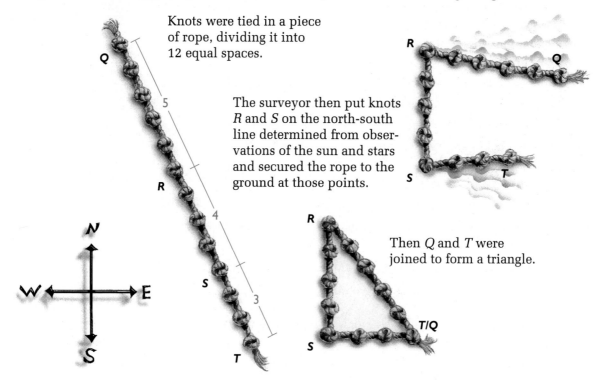

Knots were tied in a piece of rope, dividing it into 12 equal spaces.

The surveyor then put knots *R* and *S* on the north-south line determined from observations of the sun and stars and secured the rope to the ground at those points.

Then *Q* and *T* were joined to form a triangle.

35. The knots at *R* and *S* divide the rope into what lengths?

36. How do you know that $\angle RST = 90°$?

37. Egyptian pyramids were built so that their four sides faced directly north, south, east, and west. Does $\overline{ST}$ lie on an east-west line? How do you know?

Ongoing **ASSESSMENT**

38. **Open-ended** Write a problem situation about school or home that can be solved using the Pythagorean theorem. Write another problem situation that can be solved using the converse of the Pythagorean theorem.

Review **PREVIEW**

Simplify. *(Section 9-2)*

39. $\sqrt{72}$ **40.** $\sqrt{8} \cdot \sqrt{6}$ **41.** $5\sqrt{3} \cdot \sqrt{12}$ **42.** $10\sqrt{15} \cdot 8\sqrt{6}$

A die is rolled. Find each probability. *(Section 6-2)*

43. $P(\boxed{\vdots})$ **44.** $P(\boxed{\cdot\cdot} \text{ or } \boxed{\because})$ **45.** $P(\text{number} > 6)$ **46.** $P(\text{not } \boxed{\vdots})$

Working on the Unit Project

For Exercises 47–49, tell whether you think each statement is *True* or *False*. Give a reason for your choice.

47. If a boat has a hole in it, the boat sinks.

48. If an object can float in fresh water, the object can float in salt water.

49. If an object is made of steel, the object cannot float in water.

50. Write the converse of each statement in Exercises 47–49. Tell whether you think the converse is *True* or *False*. Give a reason for your choice.

51. Gather some small objects (for example, a coin, a pencil, a toothpick, a paper clip, a piece of paper, cardboard, wood, or string). Tell whether you think the probability is 0 or 1 that each object will float in a pan of water. Then test your predictions.

Unit 9 — CHECKPOINT 1

1. **Writing** How would you teach a friend to multiply square roots? Start with $\sqrt{10} \cdot \sqrt{15}$ and write an explanation of how to get a result of $5\sqrt{6}$.

Find the missing length in each right triangle. 9-1

2.   36 in.   15 in.
         x

3.   25 cm   15 cm
         x

even number: 2n
odd number: 2p+1
even × odd = 2n(2p+1)
= 4np + 2n
= 2(2np+n)
2(2np+n) is even, because it is a multiple of 2.

4. Jonah claims that the product of an odd number and an even number is an even number. He writes the steps shown at the left. What kind of reasoning is he using?

Simplify. 9-2

5. $\sqrt{300}$

6. $\sqrt{6} \cdot \sqrt{42}$

7. Solve $6x^2 = 300$.

8. Use the statement "If a number is odd, then it is a multiple of 3." 9-3

   a. Identify the hypothesis and the conclusion of the statement.

   b. Tell whether the statement is *True* or *False*. If it is false, give a counterexample.

   c. Write the converse of the statement.

9. Solve $x(2x + 3) = 0$.

10. The lengths of the sides of a triangle are 45 m, 50 m, and 14 m. Is it a right triangle? How do you know?

Geometric Probability

A Likely Spot

Focus

Use lengths and areas to
determine theoretical
geometric probabilities.

EXPLORATION

*(How) can you use geometry to find the
probability that an event will happen?*

- **Materials:** $8\frac{1}{2} \times 11$ paper; several $\frac{1}{4}$ in. diameter
disks of paper (use a paper punch)

- **Work with another student.**

(1) Divide your sheet of paper into four regions by drawing
diagonals. Shade one region, as shown in the photograph.

(2) In this experiment, you are going to drop a paper disk
from a point above the center of your sheet of paper.
Before you begin, predict the probability that the disk
will land in the shaded
region. Discuss your
reasoning.

(3) Hold a disk about 4 in. above the center of the paper and then drop the disk. If the disk lands in the shaded region, record it as a *win* in a table like the one shown in the photograph on page 500. If it does not land in the shaded region, record it as a *loss*. (If the disk lands on a line or off the paper, do not count it. Drop the disk again.)

(4) Drop the disk 20 times and record your results.

(5) Calculate the experimental probability: $\dfrac{\text{number of wins}}{20 \text{ trials}}$.

Do your results support the prediction you made in step 2?

(6) Collect the experimental probabilities calculated by all the groups in your class. Find the mean of these values. Do the results support the prediction you made in step 2?

(7) Find the ratio of the shaded area of your paper to the area of the whole sheet of paper. Compare this ratio to the experimental probability you found in step 6.

······▶ **Now you are ready for:**
: **Exs. 1–5 on p. 504**

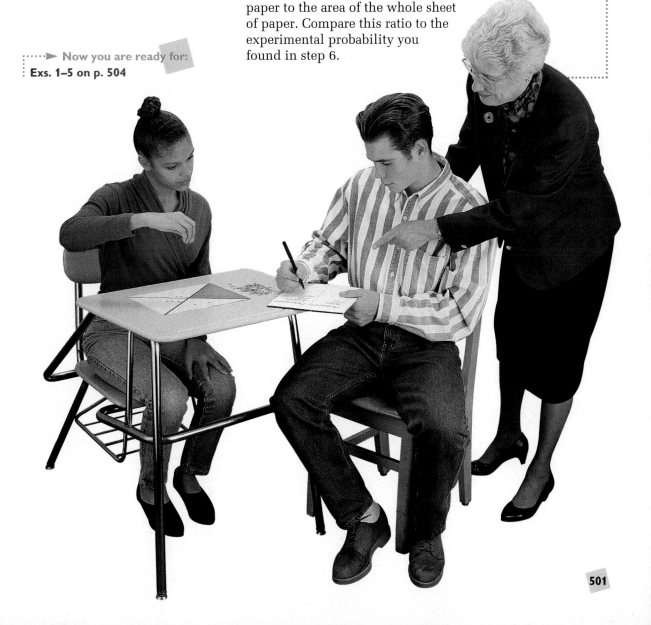

Theoretical Geometric Probability

Geometric probability is probability based on areas and lengths.

Suppose a point on the landing strip at the left is picked at random. The probability that the point is in the glider's shadow is

$$\frac{\text{area of the glider's shadow}}{\text{area of the landing strip}}.$$

Suppose a point on the landing strip's yellow line $\overline{AC}$ is picked at random. The probability that the point is on $\overline{AB}$ is

$$\frac{\text{length of }\overline{AB}}{\text{length of }\overline{AC}}.$$

Sample 1

In competition, parachutists may aim for a small target placed on a foam pad with a diameter of 20 ft. Suppose that when jumping for recreation, this parachutist controls her flight only enough to be sure that she lands in the field. What is the probability that she will land on the foam pad?

20 ft. diameter foam pad

150 ft

300 ft

Sample Response

Problem Solving Strategy: Use a formula

Use the formula $A = \pi r^2$ to find the area of the foam pad.

$$\text{probability} = \frac{\text{area of foam pad}}{\text{area of field}} = \frac{(3.14)(10)^2}{(150)(300)} \approx 0.007$$

Use the formula $A = bh$ to find the area of the field.

The probability that the parachutist will land inside the target is about 0.007.

A delivery person will deliver a package to your home sometime between 4:00 P.M. and 6:00 P.M. What is the probability that you will miss the delivery person if you get home at 4:15 P.M.?

Sample Response

Method **❶**

Problem Solving Strategy: Draw a diagram

Draw a time line divided into 15-minute intervals.

interval of time
before you get home

You get home at 4:15.

⊢1 unit⊣

4:00   4:15   4:30   5:00   5:30   6:00

8 units

interval of time when delivery person may arrive

Find the ratio of the length of the segment for the interval of time before you get home to the length of the segment for the interval of time when the delivery person may arrive.

$$\text{probability} = \frac{\text{length of segment for 4:00–4:15}}{\text{length of segment for 4:00–6:00}} = \frac{1}{8}$$

The probability that you will miss the delivery person is $\frac{1}{8}$.

Method **❷**

Find the probability that the delivery person arrives before you get home.

Find the probability that a time chosen at random from 4:00 P.M. to 6:00 P.M. is between 4:00 P.M. and 4:15 P.M.

$$\text{probability} = \frac{\text{minutes from 4:00 to 4:15}}{\text{minutes from 4:00 to 6:00}} = \frac{15}{(2)(60)} = \frac{15}{120} = \frac{1}{8}$$

The probability that you will miss the delivery person is $\frac{1}{8}$.

Talk it Over

1. Would you use a ratio of *lengths* or a ratio of *areas* to find each probability?

   a. the probability that a point is in a particular region

   b. the probability that a point is on a particular segment

2. In Sample 2, which method do you prefer, drawing a time line or counting the number of minutes? Why?

9-4 Geometric Probability

Look Back

What facts do you need to know to find the theoretical probability that this spinner will land on the green sector? Describe how you could find the theoretical probability if these facts were given. Do you need these facts to find the experimental probability? Explain.

┈┈► **Now you are ready for:**
┊ **Exs. 6–20 on pp. 504–506**

9-4 Exercises and Problems

1. Suppose you perform a probability experiment like the one in the Exploration using the piece of paper shown at the right. Do you think the probability that a disk will land in the shaded region of this piece of paper is *greater than* or *less than* the probability that a disk will land in the shaded region of the paper used in the Exploration? Why?

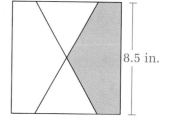

2. Would the results of the Exploration be different if the sheet of paper you used was a *circle* divided into four equal parts?

3. **a.** In step 5 of the Exploration, you found the ratio $\frac{\text{number of wins}}{20 \text{ trials}}$.

   Use the table you made in step 3 to find the ratio $\frac{\text{number of losses}}{20 \text{ trials}}$.

   b. What is the sum of the two ratios in part (a)?

Find the probability that a point chosen at random from each figure is in the shaded region. Then tell which probability is greater.

4. **A.**   **B.**

5. **A.**   **B.**

6. **Reading** Read the paragraph on theoretical geometric probability on page 502. Suppose you pick a point at random on $\overline{AC}$. How can you find the probability that the point is on $\overline{BC}$?

7. Which would be greater, the probability that a point chosen at random from *circle A* or from *circle B* is in the shaded region?

   A.   **B.**

8. A 44 ft × 165 ft rectangular barge has sunk in a river. A salvage boat anchors at a random spot in the shaded section of river so that a diver can search for the barge.

   a. What is the approximate shape of the shaded section of river?

   b. What is the area of the shaded section of river?

   c. What is the area of the barge?

   d. What is the probability that the boat will anchor over the sunken barge?

9. Jerome is expecting a call from his grandmother sometime between 12:00 noon and 6:00 P.M. During this time, he goes outside to shoot baskets for 45 min. What is the probability that his grandmother will call while he is outside?

10. Every 10 minutes, a bus drives up to an airline terminal and waits 2 minutes while passengers get on and off. If a passenger walks out of the terminal at a random time, what is the probability that the bus will be there?

11. **Writing** In a game of darts, the players aim for the bull's-eye at the center of the dart board.

   a. Does the skill of the player affect the probability that a player will hit the bull's-eye? Explain.

   b. Would you use *experimental* or *theoretical* probability to find the probability that a particular player will hit the bull's-eye? Explain why and how.

12. a. Find the area of the calculator screen at the left in the units marked on the axes.

   b. Find the area of the triangle whose sides are the x-axis, the y-axis, and the line $y = -x + 6$.

   c. Suppose a point of the calculator screen is chosen at random. What is the probability that the point lies on or below the line $y = -x + 6$?

13. Suppose a point of this calculator screen is chosen at random. Find the probability that each statement is true.

   a. The point lies on or above the line $y = x + 3$.

   b. The point lies on or below the line $y = x$.

   c. The coordinates of the point are a solution of the inequality $y \leq x + 3$.

   d. The coordinates of the point are a solution of this system of inequalities: $y \leq x + 3$
   $y \geq x$

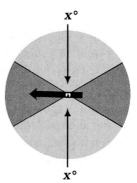

14 a. What must the value of x be so that the probability of the spinner landing on a yellow sector is $\frac{1}{4}$? $\frac{1}{3}$? $\frac{1}{6}$?

b. Let P = the probability that the spinner will land on a yellow sector. Write an equation for P in terms of x.

c. Graph your equation from part (b). What values of x make sense?

d. Does your graph represent a function? a direct variation situation? Explain why or why not.

Ongoing **ASSESSMENT**

15. a. **Open-ended** Design a dart board with three possible scores: 100, 200, and 300. Use these guidelines.

➤ The probability of getting 100 should be 50%.

➤ The probability of getting 200 should be 30%.

➤ The probability of getting 300 should be 20%.

(Assume that a dart will always land on the dart board and has an equal chance of landing anywhere on the board.)

b. **Writing** Describe your design. How did you make sure that the probabilities of getting each score met the guidelines?

Review **PREVIEW**

16. a. Write the converse of the statement "If Raymond lives in Toronto, then he lives in Canada."

b. Tell whether the converse is *True* or *False*. If it is false, find a counterexample. *(Section 9-3)*

17. Suppose a figure is a rectangle. What are three things you know about the figure? *(Section 1-7)*

18. Write each formula. *(Sections 5-7, 7-3)*

a. area of a triangle   **b.** circumference of a circle

 Working on the Unit Project

19. **Research** Read the entry on *water* in an encyclopedia or a science book.

a. What is the weight in grams of 1 cubic centimeter of water?

b. What is the weight in pounds of 1 cubic foot of water?

c. What does H_2O stand for?

d. Is ice heavier than water?

20. **Research** Read the entry on *buoyancy* in an encyclopedia or a science book. Describe what determines the buoyancy of an object.

Surface Area of Space Figures

It All Adds Up

Talk it Over

Suppose you cut open this popcorn box and lay it flat.

16 cm

4.5 cm

10 cm

1. What is the shape of each side of the box? What are the dimensions of each side?

2. What formula can you use to find the area of each side?

3. Find the total area of all the sides of the box.

4. Explain why your answer to question 3 is called the *surface area* of the popcorn box.

A **prism** is a space figure with two sides that are congruent, parallel polygons. These sides are called the **bases** of the prism. The other sides of the prism are called **faces**. In this book, the faces of prisms are rectangles.

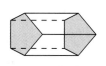
pentagonal prism

triangular prism

A prism is named by the shape of its bases. The popcorn box is a *rectangular prism* because the bases are rectangles.

FORMULA: SURFACE AREA OF A PRISM

Surface area (S.A.) = areas of two bases + areas of faces

Surface area is measured in square units.

Find the surface area of this triangular prism.

6.8 cm
4 cm
5.5 cm
2.5 cm

Sample Response

> Surface area (S.A.) is the sum of the areas of the bases and the faces.

Problem Solving Strategy: Make a sketch

Make sketches of each base and each face of the prism.

The bases are triangles.

4 cm
5.5 cm
4 cm
5.5 cm

The faces are rectangles.

2.5 cm
6.8 cm
4 cm
2.5 cm
2.5 cm
5.5 cm

Use $A = \frac{1}{2}bh$.

area of two bases

Use $A = lw$.

area of three faces

$$\text{S.A.} = 2(\tfrac{1}{2})(5.5)(4) \quad + \quad (4)(2.5) + (6.8)(2.5) + (5.5)(2.5)$$
$$= 22 \quad + \quad 10 + 17 + 13.75$$
$$\approx 62.8$$

The surface area is about 62.8 cm².

Surface Area of a Cylinder

The shape of a tin can is an example of a *cylinder*. A **cylinder** is a space figure with a curved surface and two congruent parallel bases that are circles. You have to look straight at one end to see a circle.

cylinder

Talk it Over

5. Imagine cutting up a cylinder as shown below. Explain what is happening in each step.

6. In the last step, what does $2\pi r$ represent?

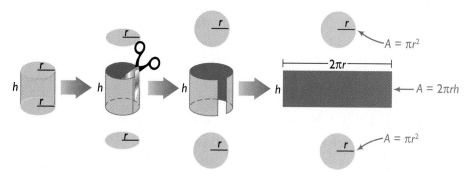

r
h
r
$A = \pi r^2$
$2\pi r$
$A = 2\pi rh$
$A = \pi r^2$

FORMULA: SURFACE AREA OF A CYLINDER

Surface area = areas of two circular bases + area of curved surface

$$S.A. = 2\pi r^2 + 2\pi rh$$

radius r

height h

Sample 2

A company packages vegetables in this can. How much material is needed to make the can? Give your answer to the nearest square inch.

Sample Response

Problem Solving Strategy: Break the problem into parts

The can is a cylinder. Use the formula $S.A. = 2\pi r^2 + 2\pi rh$.

Step 1 Find the radius of the can.

The radius of the can is half the diameter.

$$r = \frac{1}{2}(3.5) = 1.75$$

4.25 in.

3.5 in.

Step 2 Use the radius to find the surface area of the can.

$S.A. = 2\pi r^2 + 2\pi rh$ ⟵ Write the formula for the surface area of a cylinder.

$\quad = 2\pi(1.75)^2 + 2\pi(1.75)(4.25)$ ⟵ Substitute 1.75 for r and 4.25 for h.

$\quad \approx 19.24 + 46.73$

$\quad \approx 65.97$

The company will need about 66 in.² of material.

⋯⋯► Now you are ready for:
Exs. 1–16 on pp. 512–513

Surface Area of a Pyramid

A **pyramid** is a space figure with only one base. A pyramid is identified by the shape of its base. Its faces are triangles.

In this book, you will work only with *regular pyramids*. A **regular pyramid** has these properties.

➤ The base is a regular polygon.

➤ All faces are congruent isosceles triangles.

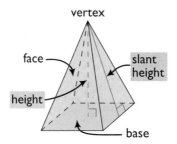

vertex

The **height** of a regular pyramid is the length of the perpendicular segment from the vertex to the center of the base.

face

slant height

height

base

The **slant height** of a regular pyramid is the height of one of the congruent triangular faces.

FORMULA: SURFACE AREA OF A PYRAMID

Surface Area = area of base + areas of faces

Talk it Over

7. These diagrams show a regular square pyramid being unfolded into a flat figure. Which dimension is given in the first figure, the *height* of the pyramid or the *slant height*?

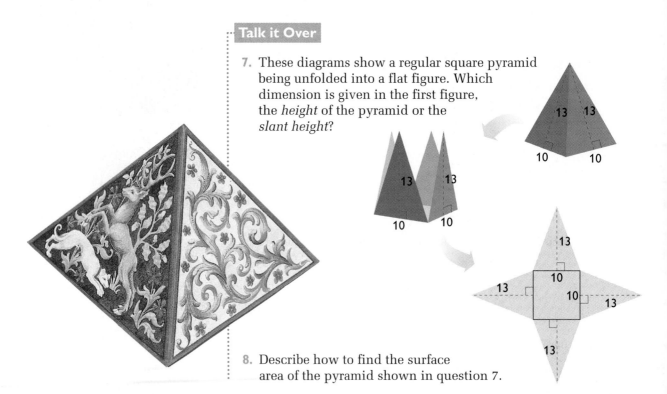

8. Describe how to find the surface area of the pyramid shown in question 7.

Sample 3

Find the surface area of this regular square pyramid.

24 ft

16 ft

Problem Solving Strategy: Break the problem into parts

To find the surface area, you need to know the slant height. The slant height is not given, but you can find it using the other dimensions.

24 ft

The slant height is the hypotenuse.

16 ft

The length of the shorter leg of the triangle is 8 ft, half the length of the square base.

Step 1 Find the slant height.

Sketch the pyramid. Draw a right triangle inside the pyramid using the 24 ft height as one of the legs.

Use the Pythagorean theorem to find the slant height.

$c^2 = a^2 + b^2$

$c^2 = 24^2 + 8^2$ ◄—— Substitute 24 for a and 8 for b.

$c^2 = 640$

$c = \sqrt{640}$ ◄—— Find the positive square root.

$c \approx 25.30$

The slant height is about 25.30 ft.

Step 2 Find the surface area of the pyramid.

S.A. = area of square base + area of four triangular faces

= □ + 4 × △

S.A. = $s^2 + 4(\frac{1}{2}bh)$

   = $16^2 + 4(\frac{1}{2})(16)(25.30)$ ◄—— Substitute 16 for s and for b and 25.30 for h.

   ≈ 1065.6

The surface area of the regular square pyramid is about 1065.6 ft^2.

Look Back ◄

What space figures are these? Tell how you would find the surface area of each figure.

········► **Now you are ready for:**
Exs. 17–32 on pp. 513–514

Exercises and Problems

1. **Reading** What are two strategies for solving problems about surface area?

Identify each type of prism and find its surface area.

2.

5 cm
5 cm
5 cm

3.

10 cm
6 cm
16 cm
8 cm

4.

2 in.
6 in.
4 in.

5.

12 cm
5 cm
4 cm
6 cm
10 cm

connection to ART

6. Follow the steps to draw a pentagonal prism.

| Draw two congruent pentagons. | Connect the corresponding vertices. | Dash the lines that cannot be seen. |

7. **a.** Follow the steps in Exercise 6 but draw two congruent triangles in the first step.

   b. Name the space figure you have drawn.

8. Follow the steps to draw a cylinder.

| Draw two congruent ovals. | Join the ovals. | Dash the lines that cannot be seen. |

9. **a.** **Open-ended** Draw a building or a scene that includes at least one prism and one cylinder.

   b. Give the space figures in your drawing dimensions. Find their surface areas.

10. Dana is painting the walls and ceiling of a rectangular classroom with dimensions 35 ft × 25 ft × 12 ft. Each can of paint covers 400 ft². About how many cans of paint will she need to paint the room?

11. Writing Describe how the two figures at the right are alike and how they are different.

3 cm

6 cm   6 cm

Find the surface area of each cylinder or half cylinder.

12.

3 in.

6 in.

13. 2 m

6 m

14.

5 yd

4 yd

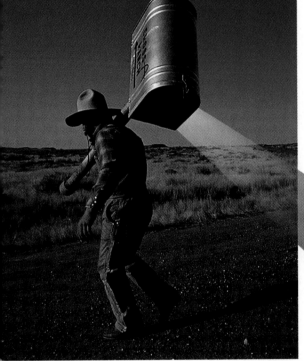

15. a. Draw two cylinders with the same radius. Make the height of one cylinder twice the height of the other cylinder.

b. Do you think the surface area of the taller cylinder will be twice the surface area of the shorter cylinder? Check your conjecture by finding the surface area of each cylinder.

16. Jeremy Szabo wants to paint the sides and top of this mailbox. He has enough paint to cover about 2600 in.². Does he have enough paint for two coats?

half cylinder

CROSS RANCH

30 in.

11 in.

14 in.

Identify each space figure and find its surface area.

17.

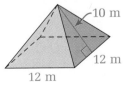

10 m

12 m

12 m

18.

8 cm

12 cm   6 cm

19.

8 in.

10 in.

10 in.

20. A *tetrahedron* is a regular pyramid whose base is a triangle. The base and faces of this tetrahedron are congruent equilateral triangles. Find its surface area.

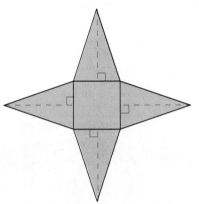

21. **Writing** Jody draws a regular square pyramid and labels the edges of the base 6 in., the height 8 in., and the slant height 8 in. Pat claims that Jody's pyramid cannot really exist. Do you agree or disagree? Explain why.

22. The surface area of a regular square pyramid is 168 cm². The area of the base is 36 cm².

  a. Sketch the pyramid. Label the slant height x.

  b. What is the length of one edge of the base of the pyramid?

  c. Write and solve an equation to find the value of x.

23. **Using Manipulatives** This diagram is a pattern for a pyramid. Create a pattern for a regular square pyramid whose base has an area of 4 in.² and whose slant height is 3 in.

Ongoing **ASSESSMENT**

24. **Writing** Describe how the methods for finding the surface areas of prisms, cylinders, and pyramids are alike and how they are different.

Review **PREVIEW**

For Exercises 25–27, suppose a point on $\overline{XZ}$ is picked at random. Find the probability that the point is on each segment. *(Section 9-4)*

25. $\overline{XY}$ **26.** $\overline{YZ}$ **27.** $\overline{XZ}$

28. Sketch a trapezoid. What dimensions would you need to know to find the area of your trapezoid? *(Section 5-7)*

Find the volume of each box. *(Toolbox Skill 19)*

29. a box with length 5 in., width 7 in., and height 2 in.

30. a box with length 6 in., width 3 in., and height 3 in.

Working on the Unit Project

31. What type of space figure is your boat?

32. **a.** Make a sketch of your boat. Record its measurements in centimeters. (Use the conversion factor 1 in. = 2.54 cm if necessary.)

  b. Find the area of a triangular base of your boat.

Volumes of Prisms and Cylinders

Focus

Find the volumes of prisms and cylinders.

When these Japanese yen are stacked, they form a rectangular prism. To find the volume of the prism, notice that its base is a piece of paper whose area is length × width. Rewrite the formula $V = lwh$.

Volume = (length × width) × height

= area of a base × height

You can think of the volume of any prism as the volume of layers of paper with the same shape as the base. For all prisms, the formula for finding the volume is the same.

FORMULA: VOLUME OF A PRISM

Volume of a prism = area of a base × height of the prism

$$V = Bh$$

Volume is measured in cubic units.

height h

base area B

Find the volume of this prism.

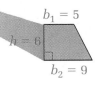

5 in.

6 in.

8 in.

9 in.

Sample Response

Problem Solving Strategy:
Break the problem into parts

$b_1 = 5$

$h = 6$

$b_2 = 9$

Step 1 Find the area of a base of the prism.

A base of a prism is one of the two congruent, parallel polygons. A base of this prism is a trapezoid.

$B = \frac{1}{2}(b_1 + b_2)h$ ⟵ Write the formula for the area of a trapezoid.

$= \frac{1}{2}(5 + 9)(6)$ ⟵ Substitute 5 for b_1, 9 for b_2, and 6 for h.

$= \frac{1}{2}(14)(6)$

$= 42$

The area of a base of the prism is 42 in.²

Step 2 Find the volume of the prism.

$V = Bh$ ⟵ Write the formula.

$= (42)(8)$ ⟵ Substitute 42 for B, the area of a base. Substitute 8 for h, the height of the prism.

$= 336$

The volume of the prism is 336 in.³

THE CLASSIC "A"
Capacity: 2
Floor size: 7 ft x 6 ft
Peak height: 4 ft
Weight: 8 lbs 2 oz

Unbeatable value! Our classic "A-Frame" style tent features mosquito-proof mesh doors on either end; reinforced seams; full-coverage fly for maximum storm protection. Easy assembly with five shock-corded aluminum poles. Fully waterproof. Color: loden.

Talk it Over

1. In Sample 1, the values substituted for h in the formulas $B = \frac{1}{2}(b_1 + b_2)h$ and $V = Bh$ are not the same. Explain.

2. Before Will buys the tent shown in this ad, he wants to make sure that it is as roomy as his old tent.

   a. The tent and its floor form a prism. What kind of prism?

   b. Explain how Will can find the volume of the tent.

Sample 2

The volume of this rectangular prism is 12.5 ft³. Find the missing dimension h.

5 ft

h

5 ft

Sample Response

Use what you know:
the length, the width, and
the volume of the prism.

$V = Bh$ ⟵ Write the formula for the volume of a prism.

$V = 25h$ ⟵ The base is a square. $B = 5 \cdot 5$.

$12.5 = 25h$ ⟵ Substitute 12.5 for V.

$\dfrac{12.5}{25} = \dfrac{25h}{25}$ ⟵ Divide both sides by 25.

$0.5 = h$

The height of the rectangular prism is 0.5 ft.

▶ Now you are ready for:
Exs. 1–10 on p. 519

Volume of a Cylinder

The pictures show a prism changing
into a cylinder. As the number of
faces increases, the prism looks
more and more like a cylinder.

The formula $V = Bh$ can be used
to find the volume of a cylinder.

FORMULA: VOLUME OF A CYLINDER

Volume of a cylinder = area of a base × height of the cylinder

$V = \mathbf{B}h$

$V = \pi r^2 h$

base area $B = \pi r^2$ ⟶

height h

Sample 3

**Find the volume of this
penny. Give your answer
to the nearest hundredth.**

$r = 0.374$ in.

$h = 0.062$ in.

Sample Response

Write the formula for the
volume of a cylinder.

A penny is a cylinder.

$V = Bh$

$= \pi r^2 h$ ⟵ The base is a circle with area πr^2.

$= (\pi)(0.374)^2(0.062)$ ⟵ Substitute 0.374 for r and 0.062 for h.

≈ 0.03 ⟵ $\boxed{\pi}$ $\boxed{\times}$ 0.374 $\boxed{x^2}$ $\boxed{\times}$ 0.062 $\boxed{=}$

The volume of a penny is about 0.03 in.^{3}.

half
cylinder

44 in.

25 in.

32 in.

······► Now you are ready for:
Exs. 11–29 on pp. 520–522

Sample 4

The dimensions of this jukebox are shown below. Find the volume of the jukebox.

Sample Response

Problem Solving Strategy: Break the problem into parts

Step 1 Find the area of the base of the jukebox.

⊖ + ▯ ◄ The front of the jukebox is the base. It is made of a half circle and a rectangle.

$B = \frac{1}{2}$(area of the circle) + area of the rectangle

$= \frac{1}{2}\pi r^2 + lw$

$= \frac{1}{2}(\pi)(16)^2 + (44)(32)$ ◄ Substitute 16 for r, 44 for l, and 32 for w.

$\approx 402.1 + 1408$ ◄ 0.5 × π × 16 x^2 + 44 × 32 =

≈ 1810.1

The area of the base is about 1810.1 in.^{2}.

Step 2 Find the volume of the space figure.

$V = Bh$

$\approx (1810.1)(25)$ ◄ Substitute 1810.1 for B and 25 for h.

$\approx 45,252.5$ in.^{3}

The volume of the jukebox is about 45,253 in.^{3}.

Talk it Over

3. In Sample 4, how do you know that the 25 in. label gives the height of the space figure?

4. Figures like the one in Sample 4 are often called *composite space figures*. Why do you think this name is used?

Look Back ◄

The formula $V = Bh$ can be used to find the volume of many kinds of space figures. The shapes at the right are designs for notepads. All the pieces of paper in a pad will have the same shape. How can you decide which side of each pad to use as the base in the formula $V = Bh$?

Unit 9 Reasoning and Measurement

1. **Reading** Is the prism in Sample 1 sitting on one of its two *bases*? How can you tell?

Find the volume of each prism.

2.

3 in.
2 in.
5 in.

3.

26 ft
13 ft
26 ft

4.

48 cm
24 cm
36 cm
72 cm

Find the missing dimension h.

5.

6.5 yd
14.2 yd
h
Volume = 350.74 yd³

6.

20 cm
10 cm
h
30 cm
Volume = 5400 cm³

7.

3.6 m
5.2 m
h
Volume = 37.44 m³

8. **Open-ended** Describe a situation in which a person would need to find surface area. Describe a situation in which a person would need to find volume.

9. Liz is buying fish for her aquarium. To avoid overcrowding the tank, she should buy one fish for every gallon of water. (There are 231 in.³ of water in one gallon.) How many fish can Liz have in her new aquarium if she fills it to a depth of 11 in.?

10 in.
12 in.
20 in.

10. **a.** Make a table to record the volume of water in Liz's aquarium when the water is 1 in. deep, 2 in. deep, and 3 in. deep. Graph the volume of water as a function of depth.

    b. What is the slope of the line you graphed in part (a)? How is the slope related to the dimensions of the aquarium?

    c. Sam's aquarium has a 12 in. × 24 in. base. He is going to graph the volume of water as a function of depth for his aquarium. Predict whether the slope of the line he graphs will be *greater than* or *less than* the slope of the line you graphed in part (a).

Find the volume of each space figure.

11.
5 cm

8 cm

12.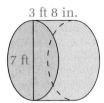
3 ft 8 in.

7 ft

13.
4 m   4 m

6 m

2 m

Find the missing dimension *h*.

14.
2.5 cm

h

Volume ≈ 58.9 cm³

15.
h

40 yd

Volume ≈ 18,840 yd³

16.
8 in.

h

4.3 in.

Volume ≈ 628.9 in.³

17. **Writing** Which will increase the volume of a cylinder more, doubling its *height* or doubling its *radius*? Explain.

18. A cake recipe calls for a 9 in. × 13 in. × 2 in. rectangular pan. A chef wants to use two identical cylindrical pans instead. Which of the sets shown would you recommend the chef use? Give a reason for your choice.

diameter: 9 in.
height: 1.75 in.

diameter: 8 in.
height: 2.5 in.

19. These two mugs have the same volume.

8 cm

9.25 cm

11.7 cm

a. Find the volume of the taller mug.

b. Use your answer to part (a) to help you write an equation about the volume of the shorter mug.

c. Solve the equation you wrote in part (b).

d. What is the diameter of the shorter mug?

20. The thickness of a new penny can be as small as 0.059 in. or as large as 0.067 in. Find the smallest and the largest possible volume of a new penny. Give your answers to the nearest thousandth.

21. Packaging A food manufacturer needs to package 56 crackers in a box. Each cracker is about $\frac{1}{4}$ in. thick and has a diameter of about $2\frac{1}{4}$ in.

a. If the crackers are packed in two cylindrical rows as shown, what are the approximate dimensions of the box? (Assume the crackers touch the top, bottom, and sides of the box.)

b. Find the ratio of the surface area to the volume for the box.

c. How else could the crackers be packaged? Experiment with other shapes and sizes of boxes. Can you design a box that has a smaller surface area to volume ratio?

Ongoing **ASSESSMENT**

22. Group Activity Work with another student.

a. Collect data on the dimensions of different sizes and shapes of cans. Record your data in the first three rows of a table like the one shown.

b. Complete the table by finding each can's surface area (S.A.), volume, and the $\frac{\text{surface area}}{\text{volume}}$ ratio.

c. For which can is the surface area to volume ratio the smallest? the largest? Sketch these cans and label their dimensions.

d. Compare your results with those of your classmates. How do size and shape affect the $\frac{\text{surface area}}{\text{volume}}$ ratio?

e. What recommendations would you make to the manufacturers of the cans you measured?

TYPE OF CAN	?	?	?
Height	?	?	?
Diameter	?	?	?
S.A.	?	?	?
Volume	?	?	?
$\frac{\text{S.A.}}{\text{Volume}}$	?	?	?

Review **PREVIEW**

Identify each space figure and find its surface area. *(Section 9-5)*

23.

4 in.
4 in.
3 in.

24.

7.6 m
8.4 m

25.

3.1 ft
6.8 ft
4.6 ft

26. Convert 72 km/h to m/s. *(Section 7-5)*

27. Find the height of this pyramid. *(Sections 9-1, 9-5)*

28. Two points on a line are (2, −3) and (−1, 5). Write an equation for the line. *(Section 8-4)*

20 m
h
12 m
12 m

Working on the Unit Project

Imagine your boat floating in water. Part of the boat will be below the water level. Here are two scientific facts that you may have learned in your research on buoyancy and water.

➤ When an object floats in water, the object sinks until the weight of the water it displaces equals the weight of the object.

➤ Since 1 cm³ of water weighs 1 g, the volume of any amount of water (in cubic centimeters) equals the weight of the water (in grams).

29. The weight of your milk-carton boat is about 35 g. Later, you will add 300 cm³ of water to your boat to make it stable.

B = area of part of base that is under water

a. What is the weight of 300 cm³ of water?

b. What will be the total weight of your boat with the added water?

c. What will be the weight of the water your boat will displace when it floats?

d. What volume of water will your boat displace?

e. When you float your boat, the part under water will be shaped like a triangular prism as shown above. Complete this equation: $Bh = \underline{\ ?\ }$.

f. Find B for your boat.

Unit 9   CHECKPOINT 2

1. Writing Describe how to find the surface area of this space figure.

14 yd   14 yd
12 yd   7.5 yd

9-4

2. Suppose a point in the rectangle at the left is picked at random. What is the probability that the point is in the shaded region?

4 · 4 · 6 · 4 · 12

Find the surface area and volume of each space figure.   **9-5, 9-6**

3. a regular square pyramid with base edge length 20 mm and height 18 mm (Find surface area only.)

4. a cylinder with diameter 3.25 in. and height 1.5 in.

Volumes of Pyramids and Cones

Fill 'er Up

Focus
Find the volumes of pyramids and cones.

Talk it Over

Does it surprise you to know that the total volume of three identical pyramids equals the volume of one prism with the same base area and height? You will test this idea in the exercises.

1. What is the formula for the volume of a prism?

2. Suppose you know the volume of the green prism. How can you find the volume of one of the red pyramids?

FORMULA: VOLUME OF A PYRAMID

height h

base area B

Volume of a pyramid $= \frac{1}{3} \times$ area of base $\times$ height of the pyramid

$$V = \frac{1}{3}Bh$$

Sample 1

The Great Pyramid was built by pharaoh Khufu of Egypt about 4500 years ago. The base of the pyramid was a square about 756 ft long on each side. The original height of the pyramid was about 481 ft. Find the volume of the Great Pyramid to the nearest cubic foot.

Sample Response

$$V = \frac{1}{3}Bh \quad \longleftarrow \text{Write the formula for volume of a pyramid.}$$

$$\approx \frac{1}{3}(756^2)(481) \quad \longleftarrow \begin{array}{l}\text{The area of the square base is } 756 \cdot 756.\\ \text{Substitute } 756^2 \text{ for } B \text{ and } 481 \text{ for } h.\end{array}$$

$$\approx 91{,}636{,}272$$

The volume of the pyramid was about 91,636,272 ft^3.

Volume of a Cone

A **cone** is a space figure with one circular base and a vertex that is directly above the center of the base. The pictures show a pyramid changing into a cone. Notice that as the number of faces increases, the base of the pyramid looks more like a circle.

The formula $V = \frac{1}{3}Bh$ can be used to find the volume of a cone.

FORMULA: VOLUME OF A CONE

Volume of a cone $= \frac{1}{3} \times$ area of base $\times$ height of the cone

$$V = \frac{1}{3}Bh$$

$$V = \frac{1}{3}\pi r^2 h$$

height h

vertex

base area $B = \pi r^2$

radius r

Sample 2

Aquaculture is the science of raising marine fish and shellfish for food. Some farmers raise salmon in large cone-shaped pens that are under water. Find the volume of the pen shown.

11 yd

12 yd

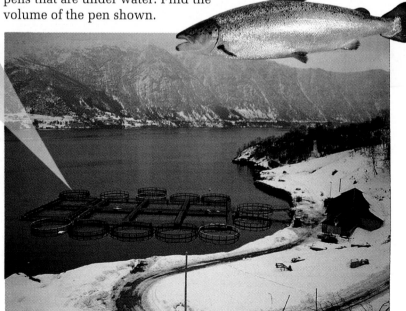

Use the formula for the volume of a cone.

$V = \frac{1}{3}Bh$

$= \frac{1}{3}\pi r^2 h$ ⟵ The base is a circle with area πr^2.

$= (\frac{1}{3})(\pi)(5.5)^2(12)$ ⟵ The radius is half of 11. Substitute 5.5 for r and 12 for h.

≈ 380.1 ⟵ 1 ÷ 3 × π × 5.5 x^2 × 12 =

The volume of the cone-shaped pen is about 380.1 yd³.

Talk it Over

The cylinder and cone at the right have the same base and height.

3. How are the volumes of the cylinder and cone related?

4. What is the volume of the cone?

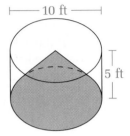
├—— 10 ft ——┤
5 ft

Look Back ⟵

Describe how the methods for finding the volume of a pyramid and the volume of a cone are alike and how they are different.

9-7 Exercises and Problems

1. **Using Manipulatives** You will need stiff paper, a ruler, scissors, masking tape, and sand or uncooked rice.

   a. Cut out four identical isosceles triangles. Tape the edges of the four triangles together to build a pyramid with an open base.

   b. Make a paper pattern for an open box that is a rectangular prism. Your prism should have the same base area and height as your pyramid. Cut out your prism and tape it together.

   c. Fill your pyramid with sand or rice. Pour the contents of the pyramid into the prism. How many times do you need to fill the pyramid to fill the prism completely?

   d. What formula does your experiment support?

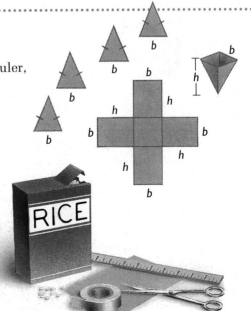

2. **Reading** What does B stand for in the formula for the volume of a pyramid, $V = \frac{1}{3}Bh$?

Find the volume of each space figure.

3.

12 mm
12 mm
7.5 mm

4.

12 cm
40 mm

5.

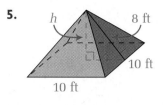

h
8 ft
10 ft
10 ft

6. **a.** Predict which of these two cone-shaped paper cups will hold the most water.

b. Find the volume of each cone to test your prediction.

3 in.
4 in.

2.75 in.
4.25 in.

7. **Drawing** Follow the steps to draw a cone.

Draw an oval and a point over the center.

Join the point to the oval.

Dash the lines that cannot be seen.

8. **a.** Draw two cones that have the same base, but one cone is twice as tall as the other. Record the diameter and height of each cone. Make a prediction about the relationship between the volumes of the cones. Then check your prediction.

b. Draw two cones that have the same height, but the diameter of one cone is twice the diameter of the other cone. Record the diameter and height of each cone. Make a prediction about the relationship between the volumes of the cones. Then check your prediction.

c. **Writing** Which has a greater effect on the volume of a cone, changing the *height* or changing the *diameter*? Explain your answer.

9. The Great Pyramid is the largest of the Pyramids of Giza. The second largest pyramid was built for pharoah Khafre. The base of Khafre's pyramid was a square about 708 ft long on each side. The height was about 471 ft. Find the volume of Khafre's pyramid.

BY THE WAY...

Ancient Egyptians made their homes out of mud but used stones to build their tombs. The pyramids were made to last forever.

For hundreds of years Native American groups of the Great Plains made their tipis from buffalo hides sewn together and stretched over wooden frames.

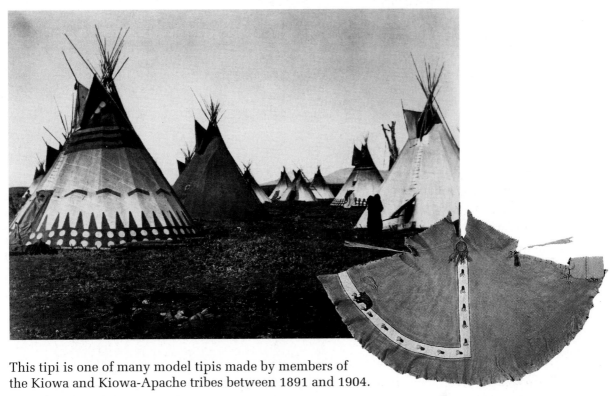

This tipi is one of many model tipis made by members of the Kiowa and Kiowa-Apache tribes between 1891 and 1904.

10. Although tipis are not always true cones, you can use a cone to approximate the shape of a tipi.

   a. Find the approximate volume of the model tipi.

   b. When the tipi is spread flat, it almost forms a half circle. Use this fact to estimate the surface area of the model tipi. (*Hint:* First find the tipi's slant height.)

   c. The surface area you found in part (b) does not include the floor. Find the approximate area of the floor of the model tipi.

   d. Suppose the artist who made the model tipi used a scale of 1 in.:0.7 ft. Find the approximate height and diameter of the full-size tipi. Then find its volume, its surface area, and the area of its floor.

26 in.

30 in.

11. a. Find the volume, the surface area, and the area of the floor of each of these tents.

   b. Compare your answers from part (a) to your answers from part (d) of Exercise 10. What advantage does the tipi have over the tents?

18.2 ft

18.6 ft

18.6 ft

12.15 ft

18.6 ft

18.6 ft

12. Research Find out how the Kiowa and Kiowa-Apache peoples, or another group who used the tipi, lived during the 1800s and earlier. Describe some of the advantages that the tipi had for their way of life.

13. a. What trigonometric ratio can you use to find the height of this cone?

b. Find the height of the cone.

c. Find the volume of the cone.

14. For a math project, a student cuts pyramid-shaped and cone-shaped blocks from cube-shaped wooden blocks.

a. How much wood will *not* be used to make the pyramid-shaped block?

b. How much wood will *not* be used to make the cone-shaped block?

15. a. Find the volume of the regular square pyramid at the right.

b. Suppose a cone is put inside the pyramid as shown. Find the volume of the cone.

c. The cone's volume is what percent of the pyramid's volume?

Ongoing **ASSESSMENT**

16. **Group Activity** Work in a group of four people. Design and carry out a demonstration to show that the volume of a cone is one third of the volume of a cylinder with the same base area and height. Describe the work done by your group.

BY THE WAY...

Ice cream was first served on a cone at the St. Louis World's Fair in 1904. A waffle maker assisted an ice cream vendor who had run out of paper dishes. A waffle was rolled into a cone and ice cream was put on top.

Identify each space figure and find its volume. *(Section 9-6)*

17.

10 ft

6 ft

18.

5.4 m

4 m   1.7 m

Polygon *JKLMN* ~ polygon *PQRST*. Find each measure. *(Section 6-5)*

19. *KL*

20. *SR*

21. Polygon *PQRST* is a dilation of polygon *JKLMN*. What is the scale factor? *(Section 6-6)*

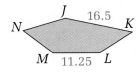
N   J 16.5 K

M 11.25 L

P   22
T   Q

S   R   10

22. Solve the proportion $\frac{x^2}{4} = \frac{25}{16}$. *(Sections 6-5, 9-2)*

 Working on the Unit Project

23. a. Draw two parallel lines and a third line that crosses them. Label the angles as shown. Measure ∠1 and ∠2. What do you notice?

b. Draw another pair of parallel lines with a third line that crosses them. Draw the third line at a different angle than you used above. Find and measure two angles that are in corresponding positions the way ∠1 and ∠2 are in this diagram. What do you notice?

2

1

∠1 and ∠2 are *below* the parallel lines and to the *right* of the blue line. They are in *corresponding positions.*

c. Repeat part (b) several more times.

d. Make a conjecture about the measures of angles in corresponding positions when a line crosses two parallel lines.

24. The diagram below shows one triangular base of your boat. When your boat is in the water, a portion of the base (△*XYT*) will be under water. As long as the boat is level, $\overline{XY}$ will be parallel to $\overline{RS}$.

a. How is $\overline{RT}$ like the blue line in the diagram in Exercise 23?

b. Using the conjecture that you made in part (d) of Exercise 23, what can you say about ∠*TXY* and ∠*R*?

c. What can you say about ∠*XTY* and ∠*RTS*? Why?

d. What two triangles in the diagram are similar? How do you know?

R   S

X   Y

T

25. Use a ruler to mark a centimeter scale along the height of one triangular base of your boat. Include a scale mark at least every 5 mm. Describe how you can use the scale to find the *draft* of your boat (see page 474) when it is in the water.

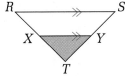
4 cm

Put 0 at the bottom.

Similar Figures: Area and Volume

Mountains

AND MOLEHILLS

Focus

Use ratios of corresponding lengths, areas, and volumes in similar figures.

Talk it Over

Do you remember this misleading graph from Unit 3? The ratio of the *number* of cable systems in 1995 to the *number* of cable systems in 1975 is about 3 to 1.

Cable Systems in the United States, 1975–1995

1995
1985
1975

0 1
3.51   6.6   11.13
Number of systems (millions)

1. The fronts of the TV sets are similar rectangles. Do the *areas* of the fronts of the TV sets for 1995 and 1975 look as if they are in the ratio 3 to 1? Why or why not?

2. The TV sets are space figures with the same shape. Does it look as if the *volumes* of the TV sets for 1995 and 1975 are in the ratio 3 to 1? Why or why not?

3. Which part of this graph gives you the correct impression of the growth in the number of cable systems from 1975 to 1995?

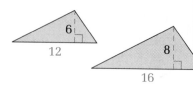

6
12
8
16

The triangles at the left are similar.

4. What is the ratio of corresponding lengths of the figures?

5. What is the ratio of the areas of the figures?

6. Is the ratio you found for question 5 equivalent to $3^2 : 4^2$?

The ratio of corresponding lengths of two similar figures is always the same. The ratio of the areas of the similar figures is not the same as the ratio of corresponding lengths. If you look at several pairs of similar figures, you will see a pattern.

$X_c \triangle ab$

AREAS OF SIMILAR FIGURES

If the ratio of corresponding lengths of two similar figures is $a:b$, then the ratio of their areas is $a^2:b^2$.

The ratio of the lengths of the corresponding sides of two similar pentagons is 8:5. What is the ratio of their areas?

Sample Response ....

The ratio of their areas is

$(8^2):(5^2)$, or $64:25$, or $\frac{64}{25}$. ◄∘∘∘∘∘○

> **Watch Out!**
> The pentagons do not necessarily have areas of 64 and 25. Their areas might be 128 and 50.

Trapezoid *ABCD* ∼ trapezoid *JKLM*. The area of trapezoid *ABCD* is 150 cm². What is the area of trapezoid *JKLM*?

Sample Response ....

Problem Solving Strategy: Break the problem into parts

Step 1 Find the ratio of the lengths of corresponding sides $\overline{AB}$ and $\overline{JK}$.

$$\frac{AB}{JK} = \frac{20}{24} = \frac{5}{6} \longleftarrow \text{Write the ratio in its simplest form.}$$

Step 2 Set up a proportion.

Let x = the area of trapezoid *JKLM*.

$$\frac{\text{area of trapezoid } ABCD}{\text{area of trapezoid } JKLM} \longrightarrow \frac{150}{x} = \frac{25}{36} \longleftarrow \substack{\text{The ratio of areas is} \\ (5^2):(6^2), \text{ or } 25:36.}$$

Step 3 Solve the proportion.

$$\frac{150}{x} = \frac{25}{36}$$

$$(150)(36) = 25x \longleftarrow \text{Use cross products.}$$

$$5400 = 25x$$

$$\frac{5400}{25} = \frac{25x}{25} \longleftarrow \text{Divide both sides by 25.}$$

$$216 = x$$

The area of trapezoid *JKLM* is 216 cm².

Talk it Over

7. Suppose you know the scale factor of two similar figures. How can you find the ratio of their areas?

8. The ratio of the areas of two similar triangles is 49:36. What is the ratio of the lengths of their corresponding sides?

······► Now you are ready for:
Exs. 1–11 on pp. 533–534

Volumes of Similar Space Figures

Similar space figures have the same shape but not necessarily the same size. To decide whether two space figures are similar, first check whether their bases are similar. Then check whether all their corresponding lengths are in proportion.

Talk it Over

The bases are similar rectangles.

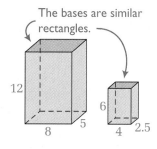

9. How can you tell that these two prisms are similar?

10. What is the ratio of corresponding lengths of the prisms?

11. What is the ratio of the volumes of the prisms?

12. Is the ratio you found for question 11 equivalent to $2^3 : 1^3$?

If you look at several pairs of similar space figures, you will see a pattern.

VOLUMES OF SIMILAR SPACE FIGURES

If the ratio of corresponding lengths of two similar space figures is $a:b$, then the ratio of their volumes is $a^3:b^3$.

BY THE WAY...

To understand how a dinosaur ran, paleontologists need to know the dinosaur's body mass. The scientists use the volume of a plastic model to estimate the volume of the actual dinosaur. Then they multiply this value by 1000 kg/m³ to approximate the dinosaur's mass.

Talk it Over

13. Paleontologists and other scientists use plastic replicas of dinosaurs. The scientist in the photo is measuring the water a model displaces to find the volume of the model.

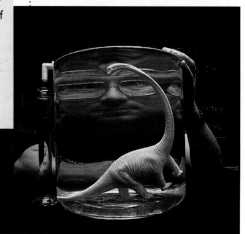

a. Suppose the model is made to a scale of 1:40. What is the ratio of corresponding lengths of the model and the actual dinosaur?

b. What value would the scientist multiply the volume of the model by to estimate the volume of the dinosaur?

Two cylinders are similar if their diameters are in the same ratio as their heights. What is the ratio of the volumes of these two similar cylinders?

Sample Response

The ratio of their corresponding lengths is 3:4, so the ratio of their volumes is $(3^3):(4^3)$, or 27:64.

Two similar regular square pyramids have base edges with lengths 8.5 in. and 12 in. The volume of the larger pyramid is 54 in.³. What is the volume of the smaller pyramid?

Sample Response

Problem Solving Strategy: Use a proportion

Let x = the volume of the smaller pyramid.

$\dfrac{\text{volume of smaller pyramid}}{\text{volume of larger pyramid}} \longrightarrow \quad \dfrac{x}{54} = \dfrac{(8.5)^3}{12^3} \longleftarrow$ The ratio of corresponding lengths is 8.5:12, so the ratio of the volumes is $(8.5)^3 : 12^3$.

$$\frac{x}{54} = \frac{614.125}{1728}$$

$$54 \cdot \frac{x}{54} = 54 \cdot \frac{614.125}{1728} \longleftarrow \text{Multiply both sides by 54.}$$

$$x \approx 19.2$$

The volume of the smaller pyramid is about 19.2 in.³.

⋯⋯▶ **Now you are ready for:**
⋮ **Exs. 12–33 on pp. 534–538**

Look Back ◀

Describe three ideas you have learned about similar space figures.

9-8 Exercises and Problems

1. The ratio of the lengths of the corresponding sides of two similar triangles is 3:4. What is the ratio of their areas?

2. The ratio of the lengths of the corresponding sides of two similar rectangles is 6:5. What is the ratio of their areas?

3. The scale factor of two similar figures is 7:10. What is the ratio of their areas?

4. All circles are similar figures. Suppose the diameter of one circle is 12 cm and the diameter of a second circle is 8 cm. What is the ratio of their areas?

Find the ratio of the areas of each pair of similar figures. Then find the missing area.

5.
5 mm
Area = 30 mm²
8 mm
Area = ?

6.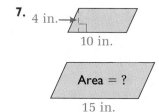
20 m Area = 600 m²
25 m Area = ?

7. 4 in.→
10 in.
Area = ?
15 in.

8. **Writing** Suppose you work at a store that develops film. A customer wants a photograph enlarged to "twice its original size." What questions would you ask the customer?

9. △*ABC* has vertices with coordinates *A*(0, 0), *B*(1, 2), and *C*(3, 0).

   a. Sketch △*ABC* on a coordinate plane. Find its area.

   b. Draw a dilation of △*ABC* with center (0, 0) and scale factor 3.

   c. What is the area of the image of △*ABC*, △*A′B′C′*?

   d. Suppose you enlarged △*ABC* by a scale factor of 20. Find the area of △*A′B′C′* without sketching the triangle. Describe your method.

10. a. How do you know that these two triangles are similar?

    b. Use sin 30° to find the value of *x*.

    c. Find the ratio of corresponding lengths of the triangles.

    d. Find the ratio of the area of the small triangle to the area of the large triangle.

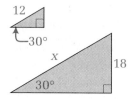
12
30°
x
18
30°

11. **Photocopying** Copy machines often have percent settings for making enlarged or reduced copies. Suppose you set a copy machine to reduce this page to 50% of its original size. The copy will be half as long and half as wide as this page.

    a. To what percent of its original area will the area of this page be reduced if the copy machine is set to reduce to 50%? 75%? 60%?

    b. Suppose the copy machine is set to enlarge to 120%. To what percent of its original area will the area of the page be enlarged?

12. **Reading** How can you decide whether two space figures are similar?

13. **Career** Exploding houses and terrifying monsters add thrills to movies. Special-effects designers often use scale models to create these scenes. Suppose a special-effects designer plans a model of a *pteranodon*, using a scale of 1 in.:3 ft.

    a. Some pteranodons had wingspans of about 25 ft. What should the wingspan of the model be?

    b. Find the ratio of the volume of the original pteranodon to the volume of the scale model.

In *Gulliver's Travels* by Jonathan Swift, Captain Lemuel Gulliver travels to several fictional nations of the world. At one point in his travels he is held captive in Lilliput, the land of the Lilliputians, "human creature[s] not six inches high." He tells this story.

A VOYAGE TO LILLIPUT

The reader may please to observe, that in the last article for the recovery of my liberty, the Emperor stipulates to allow me a quantity of meat and drink sufficient for the support of 1728 Lilliputians. Some time after, asking a friend at Court how they came to fix on that determinate number, he told me, that his Majesty's mathematicians, having taken the height of my body by the help of a quadrant, and finding it to exceed theirs in the proportion of twelve to one, they concluded from the similarity of their bodies, that mine must contain at least 1728 of theirs, and consequently would require as much food as was necessary to support that number of Lilliputians. By which, the reader may conceive an idea of the ingenuity of that people, as well as the prudent and exact economy of so great a prince.

14. Explain why the Lilliputians might think that Gulliver is a giant.

15. What is the ratio of Gulliver's height to the height of a Lilliputian?

16. What is the ratio of the amount of food needed to support Gulliver to the amount of food needed to support one Lilliputian?

17. If you were one of the Emperor's mathematicians, how would you explain why the number 1728 is used to find the amount of food Gulliver needs?

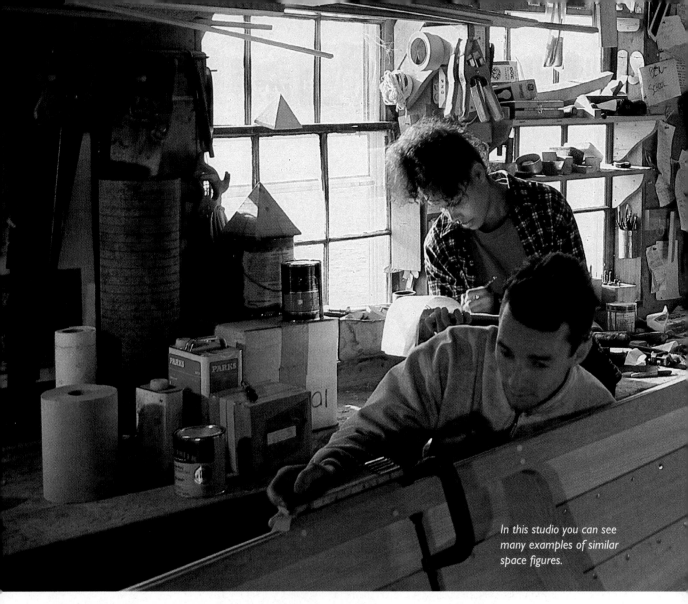

In this studio you can see many examples of similar space figures.

Decide whether the space figures in each pair are similar. Give reasons for your answers.

18. 30 cm, 30 cm, 30 cm, 21 cm, 21 cm, 21 cm, 21 cm

19. 5 in., 3 in., 3 in., 2.5 in.

20. 1.5 in., 4 in., 6 in., 7.5 in., 11.25 in., 2 in.

21. The bases are squares. 12 cm, 10 cm, 18 cm, 15 cm

22. The ratio of corresponding lengths of two similar prisms is 6:5. What is the ratio of their volumes?

23. The ratio of corresponding lengths of two similar cylinders is 4:15. What is the ratio of their volumes?

Find the ratio of the volumes of each pair of similar space figures. Then find the missing volume. In Exercises 25 and 26, leave your answers in terms of π.

24.
10 in.

$V = 255$ in.^{3}

6 in.

$V = ?$

25.
6 in.

$V = ?$

8 in.

$V = 32\pi$ in.^{3}

26. ⊢11 cm⊣
4 cm

$V = ?$

$V = 552\pi$ cm^3

27. The bases are squares.
10 cm

$V = 400$ cm^3

$V = ?$

12 cm

28. **Group Activity** Work with another student. Make a conjecture about how the ratio of the surface areas of two similar space figures is related to the ratio of their corresponding lengths. Design and carry out a test of your conjecture.

29. a. **Writing** Which of the three graphs below gives the most accurate picture of the increase in whole milk sales? Write a paragraph explaining your reasons.

Whole Milk Sales in the United States

1975

1996

🥛 = 1 billion gallons

Whole Milk Sales in the United States

Whole Milk Sales in the United States (Billions of Gallons)

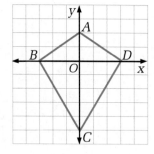

b. **Open-ended** In 1975, 1.3 billion gallons of low-fat milk were sold in the United States. In 1996, 8.2 billion gallons were sold. Draw a graph that accurately represents this increase in sales.

30. Find the volume of a cone with radius 8 yd and height 20 yd. *(Section 9-7)*

31. a. What are the coordinates of the vertices of quadrilateral *ABCD*? *(Section 4-1)*

b. What is the line of symmetry? *(Section 1-7)*

c. Translate quadrilateral *ABCD* 4 units to the right. What are the coordinates of the vertices of the image *A'B'C'D'*? *(Section 4-3)*

d. Rotate quadrilateral *ABCD* 180°. What are the coordinates of the vertices of the image *A"B"C"D"*? *(Section 4-5)*

Working on the Unit Project

32. Label a sketch of one base of your boat as shown. △*XYT* is the part of the base that will be under water when you float your boat. Use the results of earlier *Working on the Unit Project* exercises to complete each statement.

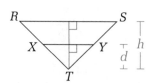

a. From part (b) of Exercise 32 on page 514, area of △*RST* = _?_.

b. From part (f) of Exercise 29 on page 522, area of △*XYT* = _?_.

c. From part (a) of Exercise 37 on page 491, height of △*RST*, *h* = _?_.

33. In Exercise 24 on page 529 you discovered that △*RST* ~ △*XYT*.

a. Use the values from Exercise 32 to write a proportion to find *d*, the height of △*XYT*.

b. Solve your proportion for *d*.

c. Explain why your answer to part (b) is the *draft* of your boat.

Completing the Unit Project

Now you are ready to find the actual draft of the boat you built.

➤ Fill your boat with 300 cm^3 of water and float the boat in a large sink or container.

➤ Read the boat's draft from the scale that you marked on your boat. Record your results.

Now you can determine how much cargo your boat can carry.

➤ Select one object for the first test and predict how many of these objects will cause your boat to sink.

➤ Record your predictions and then test your guesses by filling your boat with these objects.

➤ Count how many items your boat can hold until it sinks and record these results.

When you have gathered data from at least three cargo tests, describe your observations in a report. Include the effect of the size of the object, the relative heaviness of the object, and the number of each object it took to sink your boat.

Look Back

Get together with a small group of students. Share your results. Discuss these questions: How close is the actual draft to your prediction? Why might the actual draft and the predicted draft be different? What have you learned about buoyancy?

Alternative Projects

Project 1: Boating in Various Seas

Water takes up less space as it starts to cool but more space as it freezes. Write a story describing how this affects the draft of a boat passing through the Arctic, through the North Atlantic, through the Panama Canal, and across the Equator.

Project 2: Design a Container

Create a design for a container to keep things hot or cold. First decide what objects you want to carry in your container and then plan a shape to fit those objects. Keep in mind that a container with a large surface area relative to its volume will generally lose heat faster than one with a smaller surface area.

1. Find the length of the diagonal of this rectangle.

9-1

2. Cary notices that Joelle has driven to school for the last six Fridays. Cary decides that Joelle will drive to school this Friday. Is Cary using *inductive* or *deductive* reasoning?

Simplify.

3. $\sqrt{96}$

4. $2\sqrt{3} \cdot 4\sqrt{8}$

9-2

5. Solve $3y^2 = 81$.

6. Use the statement "If you have a fever, then you should stay home from school."

9-3

   a. Identify the hypothesis and conclusion of the statement.

   b. Write the converse of the statement.

   c. Tell whether the converse in part (b) is *True* or *False*. If it is false, give a counterexample.

7. **Open-ended** Write a statement from mathematics or from your life at school or at home that is false, but whose converse is true.

Solve for x.

8. $x(x + 4) = 0$ 9. $6x(x - 2) = 0$

10. The lengths of the sides of a deck are 12 ft and 16 ft. A carpenter measures the diagonal from one corner to the other, as shown. The diagonal is 20 ft. Is the corner of the deck a right angle? How do you know?

16 ft   20 ft

12 ft

11. a. A paper bag has a rectangular base that is 6 in. wide and 13 in. long. A circular hole with diameter 4 in. has been cut out of the base. If you drop a small bead into the bag without aiming, what is the probability that it will fall through the hole?

9-4

   b. What would the probability that you found in part (a) be if the hole was a 4 in. by 4 in. square?

12. The side of a cube is 5 in. long. What is the surface area of the cube?

9-5

13. Find the surface area of a regular square pyramid with base edge length 8 in. and slant height 3 in.

4 in.

13 in.

6 in.

14. The wall of a downtown office building lobby contains a floor-to-ceiling aquarium. The aquarium is a rectangular prism with length 3 ft and width 2 ft. Its walls are 12 ft high. How much water does the aquarium hold?

9-6

15. **Writing** A manufacturer has a choice of two different cans to use in packaging a new product. Which of these two cans would you recommend the manufacturer use? Explain your choice. Consider the amount of material needed to produce the can. What other factors might influence the manufacturer's decision?

Can 1   Can 2

16. Find the volume of the space figure at the left.

9-7

17. The ratio of the sides of two similar polygons is 2:3 and the area of the smaller polygon is 24 square units. Find the area of the larger polygon.

9-8

18. The height of one cylinder is 5 times the height of a similar cylinder. How many times greater is the volume of the larger cylinder than the volume of the smaller cylinder?

19. **Self-evaluation** What did you learn about geometry and about space figures in this unit that you did not know before?

20. **Group Activity** Work with another student.

The two right triangles shown below are similar. Find the area of the smaller triangle using the two methods described below.

a. One student should use the Pythagorean theorem to find x. Then find the area of the smaller triangle.

b. Another student should use the fact that the two triangles are similar. Write and solve a proportion to find the area of the smaller triangle.

c. Show that your two answers are the same. Which method do you think is easier to use? Why?

IDEAS AND (FORMULAS)=X^2

➤ **Reasoning** If-then statements are either true or false. For an if-then statement to be true, it must be true in all cases. *(p. 492)*

➤ **Reasoning** One way to show that an if-then statement is false is to find a counterexample. *(p. 492)*

➤ **Reasoning** The converse of a true if-then statement is not necessarily true. *(p. 494)*

➤ To multiply and simplify square roots of nonnegative numbers, use these properties. *(p. 486)*

$$\sqrt{ab} = \sqrt{a} \cdot \sqrt{b} \qquad \sqrt{a} \cdot \sqrt{b} = \sqrt{ab} \qquad \sqrt{a} \cdot \sqrt{a} = a$$

➤ To simplify an expression in radical form, look for perfect square factors of the number under the $\sqrt{}$ symbol. *(p. 487)*

➤ If a product of factors is zero, one or more of the factors must be zero. (zero-product property) *(p. 495)*

$$\text{If } ab = 0, \text{ then } a = 0 \text{ or } b = 0.$$

➤ You can use the zero-product property to solve equations. These equations may have more than one solution. *(p. 495)*

➤ In any right triangle, the square of the length of the hypotenuse is equal to the sum of the squares of the lengths of the legs. (Pythagorean theorem) *(p. 478)*

➤ The acute angles of a right triangle are complementary. *(p. 480)*

➤ If the square of the length of one side of a triangle is equal to the sum of the squares of the lengths of the other two sides, then the triangle is a right triangle. (converse of the Pythagorean theorem) *(p. 495)*

➤ You can use the converse of the Pythagorean theorem to decide whether or not a triangle is a right triangle. *(p. 495)*

➤ Prisms and pyramids are named by the shapes of their bases. *(pp. 507, 509)*

➤ You can use formulas to find the surface areas and volumes of different space figures. *(pp. 507, 509, 510, 515, 517, 523, 524)*

Cylinder

Prism

S.A. = areas of bases + areas of faces

S.A. = $2\pi r^2 + 2\pi rh$

V = area of base $\times$ height = Bh

V = area of base $\times$ height = $\pi r^2 h$

Pyramid

Cone

S.A. = area of base + area of faces $\qquad$ $V = \frac{1}{3} \times$ area of base $\times$ height

$V = \frac{1}{3} \times$ area of base $\times$ height $= \frac{1}{3}Bh$ $\qquad$ $= \frac{1}{3}\pi r^2 h$

➤ If the ratio of corresponding lengths of two similar figures is $a{:}b$, then the ratio of their areas is $a^2{:}b^2$. *(p. 530)*

➤ If the ratio of corresponding lengths of two similar space figures is $a{:}b$, then the ratio of their volumes is $a^3{:}b^3$. *(p. 532)*

STATISTICS
& PROBABILITY

➤ Suppose a point in the rectangle below is picked at random. Then the probability that the point is in the shaded region is $\dfrac{\text{area of shaded region}}{\text{area of rectangle}}$. *(p. 502)*

➤ Suppose a point on $\overline{AC}$ is picked at random. Then the probability that the point is on $\overline{AB}$ is $\dfrac{\text{length of } \overline{AB}}{\text{length of } \overline{AC}}$. *(p. 502)*

$A \qquad B \qquad\qquad C$

········ **Key Terms**

- **inductive reasoning** (p. 479)
- **if-then statements** (p. 492)
- **converse** (p. 494)
- **bases of a prism** (p. 507)
- **pyramid** (p. 509)

- **deductive reasoning** (p. 479)
- **hypothesis** (p. 492)
- **geometric probability** (p. 502)
- **faces of a prism** (p. 507)
- **regular pyramid** (p. 509)

- **radical form** (p. 487)
- **conclusion** (p. 492)
- **prism** (p. 507)
- **cylinder** (p. 508)
- **height of a regular pyramid** (p. 510)

- **slant height of a regular pyramid** (p. 510)

- **cone** (p. 524)

- **similar space figures** (p. 532)

10

Quadratic Equations as Models

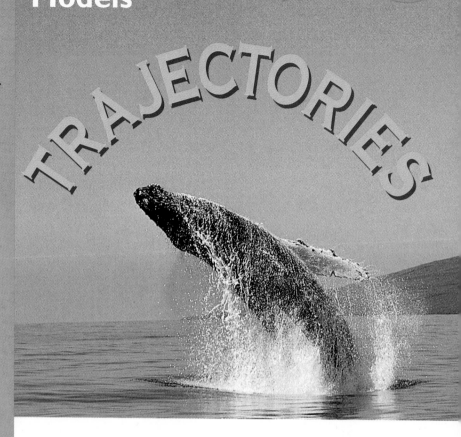

TRAJECTORIES

"Thar she blows!" — On the dark, choppy surface of the ocean, the first sign of a whale is often its spout. When a whale breathes out, air and water mix to form a spout that arcs out of the whale's blowhole. Water droplets in the spout follow a ⌒-shaped *trajectory*, or path, that is a parabola. The spout often rises as high as 25 ft before being pulled back down by gravity. When a whale or dolphin leaps, its center of gravity also traces a parabolic path.

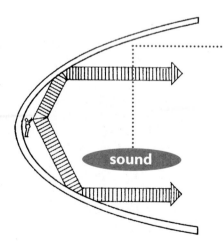

sound

Acoustical engineers use parabolas to direct sound waves. The parabolic curve of a band shell directs the music to the audience at an outdoor concert. During a TV reporter's interview, small parabolic reflectors direct the speakers' words to the microphone. Car headlights and some telescopes contain parabolic surfaces that direct light rather than sound waves.

Ballplayers and many other athletes know a lot more about parabolas than they may think. The outfielder running to catch a fly ball is actually predicting the parabolic trajectory of the batted ball. The pitcher who throws a knuckle ball or curve ball is trying to outwit the batter by making the ball change course from the expected parabola.

Write a Math Story

Your group's project is to write a story that reveals the mathematics in the world around you.

Include at least three situations modeled by equations or formulas from earlier units.

Include a situation in which the trajectory of a batted ball is modeled by one of the equations from this unit.

By the end of the unit, you can figure out whether each of the equations below applies to a ball kicked or hit off a player's head, and how far and how high the ball travels. Include one of these trajectories in your story, too.

Equations for the Paths of Some Soccer Balls		
(x = horizontal distance in feet and y = vertical distance in feet)		
Strike angle	Starting speed	Equation
20°	93 ft/s	$y = x(0.364 - 0.002x)$
45°	30 ft/s	$y = -0.036x^2 + x + 6$
45°	103 ft/s	$y = -0.003x^2 + x$
60°	30 ft/s	$y = -0.071(x + 3)(x - 27.5)$

WELCOME TO PARABOLIC PARK

How could we resist the fireworks and fountains of Parabolic Park, only two miles away! Thirty minutes was all it took our group to cover the uphill distance at a pace of 15 min per mile (d=rt). The slope was an easy tan 10°—no problem. When we arrived, we found that the ads told a true story: "If you come to Parabolic Park, then the parabolas will dazzle you."

Getting Started

WHAT TYPE OF STORY?
humor, science fiction, mystery, adventure, sports

WHO are your characters?

WHAT are they doing?

WHEN and WHERE does the story take place?

WHERE'S THE MATH? equations, formulas

WHAT KIND OF PICTURES? drawings, photos, cutouts

For this project you should work in a group of four students. Here are some ideas to help you get started.

☞ Think of a setting for your story.

☞ Outline your story.

☞ Review the equations and formulas you studied in this course. Discuss which ones you could use in your group's story.

☞ Think about where you can find reasonable values for the variables in the equations and formulas your group has decided to use in its story.

☞ Plan to meet later to discuss the baseball equations in the "Working on the Unit Project" exercises and the soccer equations in the table on page 545. For each equation, figure out all you can about the trajectory of the ball and how it was struck.

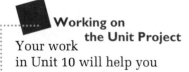

Working on the Unit Project

Your work in Unit 10 will help you write your math story.

Related Exercises:

Section 10-1, Exercise 31
Section 10-2, Exercises 53, 54
Section 10-3, Exercise 25
Section 10-4, Exercise 43
Section 10-5, Exercises 41–43
Section 10-6, Exercises 41, 42
Section 10-7, Exercise 43
Section 10-8, Exercises 34, 35

Alternative Projects p. 606

Can We Talk

TRAJECTORIES

➤ Where else have you seen parabolas in nature?

➤ Do you think you can kick a soccer ball as far as you can hit a baseball? a volleyball? Why or why not?

➤ Suppose two balls are hit at the same speed, but at different angles. Which ball do you think will land farther away? Why?

➤ Why would someone who designs baseball stadiums want to know about the trajectory of a baseball after it has been hit?

➤ How do you think wind affects the path of a kicked, thrown, batted, headed, or punched ball?

Reflections

Draw with
a ruler.

Draw dashed
lines for your
tracing.

Draw the
fold line.

Left Right Left Right

EXPLORATION

What *happens when you flip a shape over a line?*

• **Materials: paper, rulers, protractors**
• **Work with another student.**

(1) Fold a sheet of paper in half. Without unfolding your paper, draw any polygon you want. Be sure to use a dark pencil or pen.

(2) Turn over your folded paper and trace your drawing.

(3) Unfold your paper and draw a line along the crease. It should look as if you have flipped your original drawing over the fold line.

(4) Connect all corresponding vertices.

(5) The fold line divides each segment you drew in step 4 into two parts. Measure the length of each part. Write the measurements on your drawing.

(6) The fold line crosses each segment you drew in step 4. Measure each angle formed. Write the measurements on your drawing.

(7) Look at the measurements you have written. What is the relationship between the fold line and the segments you drew?

(8) Hold your paper so that the fold line is vertical. Pick any point on the right side of your original drawing. Is the corresponding point on the tracing located on its right side? Try other points. What do you find?

(9) Compare your results. What do you find?

Another name for a flip over a line is a **reflection.** The line is called the **line of reflection.** In the Exploration the fold line is the line of reflection.

A reflection is a kind of transformation that produces a mirror image. You see reflections in:

line of reflection

A reflection does *not* change size or shape.

Orientation is reversed.

Equal distance

In a mirror, right and left are switched because a reflection reverses *orientation.* **Orientation** is the direction in which the points on a figure are ordered.

PROPERTIES OF A REFLECTION

➤ The image is congruent to the original figure.

➤ The orientation of the image is reversed.

➤ The line of reflection is perpendicular to and cuts in half any segment connecting corresponding points on the image and the original figure.

➤ Now you are ready for:
Exs. 1–12 on pp. 551–552

Writing Tell whether each transformation is a reflection. If it is, trace the diagram and draw the line of reflection. If it is not, tell why not.

a.　　　　　　b.　　　　　　c.

Sample Response

a. This is *not* a reflection. The image is congruent to the original figure but the orientation is not reversed.

b. This is a reflection. The image is congruent to the original and its orientation is reversed.

The line of reflection is halfway between the original and the image.

c. This is *not* a reflection. The orientation of the image is reversed, but the image is not congruent to the original figure.

Check You can check that the diagram shows a reflection by tracing and folding or with a MIRA® transparent mirror.

BY THE WAY...

Watch water swirling down a drain. It spins clockwise above the Equator and counter-clockwise below it—and so do tornadoes and hurricanes.

The cause of this reversal of orientation, called the *Coriolis effect*, is the spin of Earth on its axis.

The orientation of a polygon may be *clockwise* or *counterclockwise*.

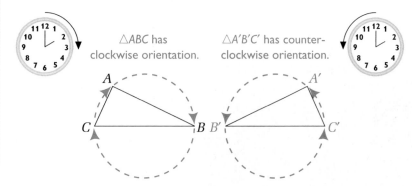

△*ABC* has clockwise orientation.

△*A'B'C'* has counter-clockwise orientation.

Reflections on a Coordinate Plane

When a polygon is drawn on a coordinate plane, you can reflect it over the horizontal or the vertical axis. These axes are also called the **x-axis** and the **y-axis.**

TECHNOLOGY NOTE

With geometric drawing software, you can reflect any figure you draw over any line you draw.

Copy △ABC and reflect it over the x-axis. Describe the orientation of △ABC and its image.

Sample Response

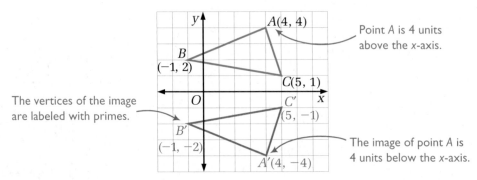

Point A is 4 units above the x-axis.

The vertices of the image are labeled with primes.

The image of point A is 4 units below the x-axis.

△ABC has counterclockwise orientation.

△A′B′C′ has clockwise orientation.

Talk it Over

1. What is the line of reflection in Sample 2? What is its equation?

2. In Sample 2, a point on △ABC is 3 units above the line of reflection. Is the corresponding point on △A′B′C′ above or below the line of reflection? How many units above or below?

3. Suppose a polygon is reflected over a vertical line. One point on the polygon is 2 units to the right of the line of reflection. Where is the image of this point located?

4. a. Discuss the symmetric shape in the photo at the left in terms of a reflection. Identify the line of reflection, the original, and the image.

   b. Can a figure be its own reflection image? Explain.

····▶ Now you are ready for:
Exs. 13–31 on pp. 553–554

Look Back ◀─────────

How is a reflection like the other transformations you have learned about—translations, rotations, and dilations? How is it different?

10-1 Exercises and Problems

1. **Reading** To decide whether a transformation is a reflection, what three properties should you look for?

2. **a.** Repeat the Exploration using your printed first name instead of a polygon.

   b. What property of reflections makes your name hard to read?

   c. Describe what happens to your original printed name and its reflection when you look at them in a mirror.

3. Imagine you are looking at yourself in a mirror.

   a. When you raise your right arm, what does your mirror image do?

   b. When you walk toward the mirror, what does your mirror image do?

   c. Suppose you are wearing a T-shirt that says "Plant a Tree." When you look in a mirror, can you read the words on your T-shirt?

4. **a.** Print the word AMBULANCE so that someone can read it in a mirror.

   b. When is it important to be able read this word in a mirror?

5. **Writing** Which of these photos do you think show a reflection? Explain your choice.

6. You have now worked with four different kinds of transformations: rotations, translations, dilations, and reflections. Make a concept map that shows how they are alike and how they are different. You might want to include a sketch of each type of transformation.

7. Point P' is the image of point P after a reflection over $\overleftrightarrow{AB}$. How is $\overleftrightarrow{AB}$ related to segment PP'?

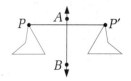

8. Open-ended The words MOM, COOKBOOK, and HAT HUT are unchanged when they are reflected over the dashed line shown. Write three other words that are unchanged when reflected over a vertical or horizontal line through the word, and draw each line of reflection.

connection to **LANGUAGE ARTS**

Braille signs are read with the fingertips. Each sign is a pattern of raised dots on a 3 × 2 matrix. In the alphabet shown, the large black circles represent raised dots. The tiny circles represent positions in the matrix that do *not* contain raised dots.

Use the Braille alphabet shown.

9. Some pairs of Braille letters are reflections of each other. Draw each pair with the line of reflection between the letters.

10. Some pairs of Braille letters are rotations of each other. Draw each pair with a curved arrow to show the rotation.

11. There are *no* pairs of Braille signs that are translations of each other. Why do you think this is so?

12. **Research** There are also Braille signs for words, parts of words, and punctuation. Do some research about Braille. What other signs can you find that are reflections of each other?

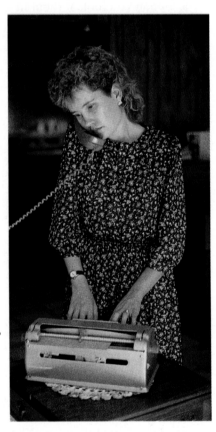

▶ **BY THE WAY...**

The Braille alphabet was invented almost 175 years ago by a fifteen-year-old French student named Louis Braille. Braille himself was visually impaired.

Writing Tell whether each transformation is a reflection. If it is, trace the flags and draw the line of reflection. If it is not, tell why not.

13.

Nepal

14.

Olympics

15.

Republic of Korea

Each diagram shows a figure and its image. What is the line of reflection?

16.

17.

18.

19.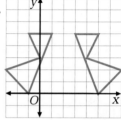

Copy each figure and reflect it over the indicated line. Describe the orientation of the original figure and its image.

20. a. x-axis
    b. y-axis

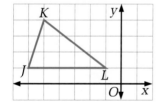

21. a. x-axis
    b. y-axis

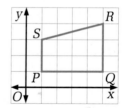

22. a. x-axis
    b. y-axis

23. The x-axis is the line of symmetry for the figure shown. Suppose you reflect the figure over the x-axis.

  a. Describe the image after this transformation.

  b. What are the coordinates of the point of the figure that lies on the x-axis? What are the coordinates of its image?

  c. What are the coordinates of the image of point A? Explain how you arrived at your answer.

  d. What are the coordinates of the image of point B? Explain how you arrived at your answer.

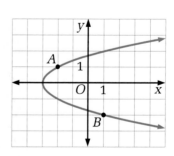

24. **Writing** Draw any picture you wish. For example, you could draw a flower, a geometric shape, a combination of the two, or something else. Then create a design by reflecting, translating, and rotating your picture. Describe how you made your design.

25. Find the ratio of the surface areas of a cylinder with radius 6 in. and a similar cylinder with radius 15 in. *(Section 9-8)*

26. The ratio of the heights of two similar prisms is 3:2. The volume of the smaller prism is 720 cm^3. What is the volume of the larger prism? *(Section 9-8)*

Graph each equation. *(Section 8-3)*

27. $x = 2$

28. $x = -1$

29. $y = 4$

30. $y = -3$

> **BY THE WAY...**
>
> To make a right-handed actor appear to be playing baseball left-handed in the movie *The Pride of the Yankees*, the numbers on his uniform were printed as a mirror image, he ran to third base instead of first, and the film was processed in reverse.

Working on the Unit Project

31. **Group Activity** Work in a group of three students. Two of you should toss a ball back and forth in front of a wall while the third observes the path of the ball (you can use a crumpled piece of paper for a ball). Toss the ball a few different ways, and take turns until each student has had a chance to be the observer.

a. Each of you should make a sketch of one path that he or she observed.

b. Does the path you drew have symmetry? If so, sketch the line of symmetry.

c. Compare every-one's drawings. How are they alike? How are they different?

Transforming Parabolas

A strobe photo shows that the path of a thrown ball looks like an upside-down U.

A thown or batted ball, water rising from a fountain, a whale's spout, and the light trails of fireworks all follow a curve called a **parabola.** This curve has the same general shape as the graph of the *squaring function* $y = x^2$.

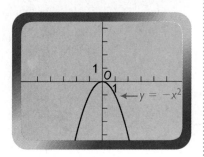

Talk it Over

1. Look at the graph of $y = x^2$.

   a. What is the line of symmetry of the graph?

   b. The point of a parabola that lies on the line of symmetry is called the **vertex** of the parabola. What are the coordinates of the vertex of the graph?

2. Look at the graph of $y = -x^2$ (read $-x^2$ as "the opposite of x^2").

   a. What is the line of symmetry of the graph?

   b. What are the coordinates of the vertex of the graph?

   c. Suppose you want to find the value of y when $x = 2$. Which do you write, $(-2)^2$ or -2^2? Does it matter?

3. How do the values of y compare for $y = -x^2$ and $y = x^2$ when $x = 1$? when $x = 0$? when $x = -2$? in general?

4. The graph of $y = -x^2$ is a reflection of the graph of $y = x^2$. What is the line of reflection?

(How) *can you find other functions whose graphs are parabolas?*

- **Materials: graphics calculators or graphing software**
- Alternative approach: **Make a table of values for each function and sketch the parabola on graph paper.**
- **Work in a group of four students.**

① Using a standard viewing window, graph the function $y = x^2$.

② On the same axes, graph the function $y = x^2 + 4$. Describe the relationship between the graphs of the two functions.

③ Repeat step 2 comparing the graph of $y = x^2$ with the graph of $y = x^2 - 4$.

④ Repeat step 2 comparing the graph of $y = x^2$ with the graph of $y = (x + 4)^2$.

⑤ Repeat step 2 comparing the graph of $y = x^2$ with the graph of $y = (x - 4)^2$.

⑥ Summarize your findings by answering these questions.

 a. How is the graph of $y = x^2$ translated when a number is added to or subtracted from x^2?

 b. How is the graph of $y = x^2$ translated when a number is added to or subtracted from x *before* it is squared?

····▶ Now you are ready for:
Exs. 1–16 on pp. 558–560

Tell how to translate the graph of $y = x^2$ in order to produce the graph of each equation.

a. $y = x^2 + 2$

b. $y = x^2 - 2$

c. $y = (x + 2)^2$

d. $y = (x - 2)^2$

Sample Response

a. $y = x^2 + 2$

2 is added to x^2

Translate the graph of $y = x^2$ 2 units up.

b. $y = x^2 - 2$

2 is subtracted from x^2

Translate the graph of $y = x^2$ 2 units down.

c. $y = (x + 2)^2$

2 is added to x

Translate the graph of $y = x^2$ 2 units to the left.

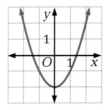

d. $y = (x - 2)^2$

2 is subtracted from x

Translate the graph of $y = x^2$ 2 units to the right.

BY THE WAY...

A water jet from a fountain forms a parabola. If there are many jets, their outlines also form a parabola.

Talk it Over

5. Which of the parabolas in Sample 1 have the y-axis as their line of symmetry?

6. Which of the parabolas in Sample 1 have their vertex on the x-axis?

7. In which quadrants does each parabola in Sample 1 appear?

8. Can the value of y be a negative number for any of the parabolas in Sample 1? How do you know?

For the graph of each equation, write the equation of the line of symmetry and the coordinates of the vertex.

a. $y = x^2 - 5$

b. $y = (x + 6)^2$

Sample Response

a. $y = x^2 - 5$

Translate $y = x^2$ down 5 units.

↓

The vertex moves down 5 units.

↓

The line of symmetry stays the same.

The equation of the line of symmetry is $x = 0$.

↓

Substitute 0 for x in the equation $y = x^2 - 5$ to find the value of y.

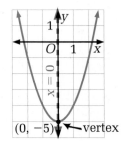

$(0, -5)$ ← vertex

The vertex is at the point $(0, -5)$.

b. $y = (x + 6)^2$

Translate $y = x^2$ to the left 6 units.

↓

The vertex moves to the left 6 units.

↓

The line of symmetry moves to the left 6 units.

vertex
$(-6, 0)$

The equation of the line of symmetry is $x = -6$.

↓

Substitute -6 for x in the equation $y = (x + 6)^2$ to find the value of y.

The vertex is at the point $(-6, 0)$.

Look Back

Explain how you would change the equation $y = x^2$ to produce a graph translated up, down, left, or right.

······▶ **Now you are ready for:**
: **Exs. 17–54 on pp. 560–561**

10-2 Exercises and Problems

1. **Reading** How are the graphs of $y = x^2$ and $y = -x^2$ shown on page 555 alike? How are they different?

Use the diagram showing the path of a beach ball in the air.

2. What does the vertex mean in terms of this situation?

3. What horizontal distance does the ball travel from the moment it is thrown in the air until it falls back down?

4. What horizontal distance has the ball traveled when it first begins to fall back down?

← Line of symmetry

Distance (ft)

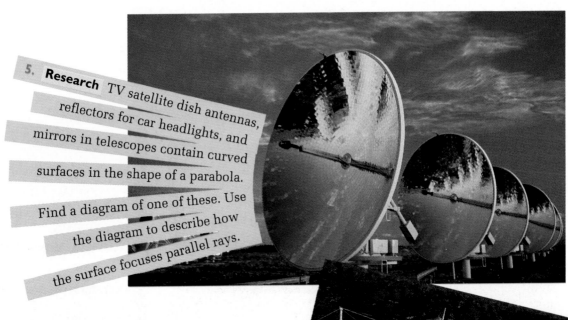

5. Research TV satellite dish antennas, reflectors for car headlights, and mirrors in telescopes contain curved surfaces in the shape of a parabola.

Find a diagram of one of these. Use the diagram to describe how the surface focuses parallel rays.

For Exercises 6–16, use the summary you made in the Exploration.

Match each equation with the translation of $y = x^2$ that produces it.

6. $y = x^2 - 9$ **A.** to the left 9 units

7. $y = x^2 + 9$ **B.** up 9 units

8. $y = (x - 9)^2$ **C.** down 9 units

9. $y = (x + 9)^2$ **D.** to the right 9 units

Match each equation with its graph.

10. $y = (x + 3)^2$ 11. $y = x^2 + 3$ 12. $y = (x - 3)^2$

13. $y = -x^2$ 14. $y = x^2 - 3$

BY THE WAY...

Are ETs on other worlds calling to us from across the universe? In Arecibo, Puerto Rico, a telescope with a 1000 foot wide parabola-shaped disk is waiting to pick up their signals.

A.

B.

C.

D.

E.

15. Writing Ariel says that $y = x^2 + 7$ *cannot* be the equation of the path of water from a fountain. Do you agree with her? Why or why not?

16. a. What translation of $y = -x^2$ produces each graph?

A.

B.

C.

D.

(left graph, labeled $y = -x^2$)

b. Using a graphics calculator or a table of values for each equation, match each graph in part (a) with one of these equations.

I. $y = -x^2 + 2$ **II.** $y = -x^2 - 2$ **III.** $y = -(x - 2)^2$ **IV.** $y = -(x + 2)^2$

Tell how to translate the graph of $y = x^2$ or $y = -x^2$ to produce the graph of each equation.

17. $y = x^2 + 10$ **18.** $y = x^2 - 7$ **19.** $y = (x + 11)^2$

20. $y = (x - 7)^2$ **21.** $y = -x^2 + 10$ **22.** $y = -x^2 - 6$

23. $y = -(x + 6)^2$ **24.** $y = (x + 3)^2 - 4$ **25.** $y = (x - 1)^2 + 2$

Which equations in Exercises 17–25 have graphs with each characteristic?

26. The line of symmetry is the y-axis. **27.** The line of symmetry is the x-axis.

28. The vertex is on the x-axis. **29.** The vertex is on the y-axis.

30. There is only one point on the x-axis. **31.** There is no point on the x-axis.

For the graph of each equation, do these things.

a. Write the equation of the line of symmetry.

b. Write the coordinates of the vertex.

32. $y = (x + 12)^2$ **33.** $y = x^2 + 8$ **34.** $y = x^2 - 12$ **35.** $y = (x - 11)^2$

For Exercises 36–41, write an equation whose graph fits each description and has the same shape as the graph of $y = x^2$.

36. translation of $y = x^2$ to the right 1 unit **37.** translation of $y = x^2$ down 9 units

38. vertex at the point $(0, 5)$

39. vertex at the point $(-10, 0)$

40. translation of $y = -x^2$ up 4 units

41. translation of $y = -x^2$ to the left 5 units

Ongoing ASSESSMENT

42. **Group Activity** Work in a group of three students.

   a. Have one group member describe a translation of the parabola $y = x^2$. Have another member draw a graph of the translated parabola. Have the third member of the group write an equation for the translated parabola.

   b. Exchange roles and repeat the process until each group member has given a description, drawn a graph, and written an equation. Work together to check that the graphs and equations match the translations. Correct any errors that you find.

Review PREVIEW

$\triangle A'B'C'$ is the reflection image of $\triangle ABC$. **Tell whether each statement is *True* or *False*. If it is false, rewrite the statement so that it is true.** *(Section 10-1)*

43. The y-axis is the line of reflection.

44. $\triangle A'B'C'$ is congruent to $\triangle ABC$.

45. $\triangle A'B'C'$ has the same orientation as $\triangle ABC$.

46. The midpoint of $\overline{CC'}$ is on the x-axis.

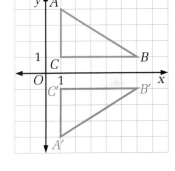

Solve. *(Section 2-7)*

47. $3x + 9 = 0$ **48.** $15 - 4x = 15$ **49.** $12x - 24 = 0$

Use the zero-product property to solve each equation. *(Section 9-3)*

50. $-5k = 0$ **51.** $2(t + 4) = 0$ **52.** $3x(x - 1) = 0$

Working on the Unit Project

53. Suppose the origin on a coordinate plane represents the point where a baseball is hit. Which equation has a graph that might be the path of the baseball? Explain how you made your choice.

   A. $y = x^2$ **B.** $y = (x - 10)^2 + 100$

   C. $y = -x^2$ **D.** $y = -(x - 10)^2 + 100$

54. For the graph you chose in Exercise 53, write the equation of the line of symmetry and the coordinates of the vertex.

Factors and Intercepts

WHAT PRICE IS RIGHT?

Use a table of values to sketch a parabola, and use algebra to find the coordinates of the points where a parabola crosses the axes.

The survey showed that for every $1 drop in price, the class will sell 5 more sweatshirts.

Predicting Income from Sweatshirt Sales

Drop in price	Price	Number of sweatshirts sold	Income (price × shirts sold)
0	$20	30	$20 × 30 = $600
$1	$20 − $1 = $19	30 + 5(1) = 35	$19 × 35 = $665
$2	$20 − $2 = $18	30 + 5(2) = 40	$18 × 40 = $720
$3	$20 − $3 = $17	30 + 5(3) = 45	$17 × 45 = $765
$4	$20 − $4 = $16	30 + 5(4) = 50	$16 × 50 = $800
$5	$20 − $5 = $15	30 + 5(5) = 55	$15 × 55 = $825
$6	$20 − $6 = $14	30 + 5(6) = 60	$14 × 60 = $840
$7	$20 − $7 = $13	30 + 5(7) = 65	$13 × 65 = $845
$8	$20 − $8 = $12	30 + 5(8) = 70	$12 × 70 = $840
$9	$20 − ? = ?	30 + ? = ?	? × ? = ?
$10	?	?	?
⋮	⋮	⋮	⋮
x	$20 − x$	$30 + 5x$	$(20 − x)(30 + 5x)$

I think that we can earn a lot of money for our class trip by selling sweatshirts. Last year the class sold 30 shirts at $20 each. Now that we've done this survey, what do *you* think? Can we raise even more money if we lower the price?

Talk it Over

1. What do you notice about the income from sweatshirt sales as the price drops from $20 to $13?

2. a. Complete the table for drops in price of $9 and $10.

   b. How is income affected when the price is below $13?

3. a. What will the income be if the drop in price is $20?

   b. What will the income be if no shirts are sold?

4. The table shows information about two variables: the drop in price and the income.

   a. Which is the control variable? Which is the dependent variable?

   b. Does the table represent a function? How can you tell?

Suppose you let y represent the income from selling sweatshirts. Then the table and the equation

$$y = (20 - x)(30 + 5x)$$

model the same situation. A third way to model the situation is to draw a graph.

Sample 1

Graph $y = (20 - x)(30 + 5x)$.

Sample Response

1 Make a table of values for x and y. Choose both positive and negative values for x.

TECHNOLOGY NOTE

With a graphics calculator or graphing software, use the table of values to help you set an appropriate viewing window.

Watch Out!
Plot enough points to see the shape of the graph. Include the vertex and make sure that your graph is symmetric.

2 Plot the points and draw a smooth curve.

$y = (20 - x)(30 + 5x)$

x	y	(x, y)
-6	0	$(-6, 0)$
-3	345	$(-3, 345)$
0	600	$(0, 600)$
7	845	$(7, 845)$
10	800	$(10, 800)$
15	525	$(15, 525)$
20	0	$(20, 0)$

At the point $(0, 600)$, $y = 600$.

At the point $(-6, 0)$, $x = -6$.

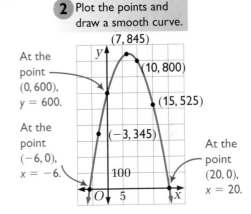

At the point $(20, 0)$, $x = 20$.

The graph of the function $y = (20 - x)(30 + 5x)$ is a parabola.

Talk it Over

Use the graph in Sample 1.

5. For which values of x does the graph model the income from sweatshirt sales? Explain.

6. The class president predicts that the class will raise the most money by reducing the price to $13. Explain how the graph shows this.

7. Horizontal and vertical intercepts are also called **x-intercepts** and **y-intercepts**. What is the y-intercept of the graph?

8. **a.** An x-intercept of the graph occurs when $x = 20$. Substitute 20 for x in the factor $(20 - x)$. What do you notice?

   b. What do you think will happen when you substitute -6 for x in the factor $(30 + 5x)$? Test your guess.

10-3 Factors and Intercepts

Finding the x-Intercepts of a Graph

You can use the zero-product property and algebra to find the x-intercepts of the graph of an equation written in the form

$$y = \text{factor} \times \text{factor}.$$

Sample 2

Without graphing, find the x-intercepts and the y-intercept for the graph of $y = (20 - x)(30 + 5x)$.

Sample Response

Step 1. Find the x-intercepts. The graph crosses the x-axis where $y = 0$.

$$y = (20 - x)(30 + 5x)$$
$$0 = (20 - x)(30 + 5x) \quad \longleftarrow \quad \text{Substitute 0 for } y.$$

By the zero-product property, when a product is zero at least one of the factors is zero. Set both factors equal to zero.

$20 - x = 0$	*or*	$30 + 5x = 0$
$20 - x + x = 0 + x$		$30 + 5x - 30 = 0 - 30$
$20 = x$		$5x = -30$
		$\dfrac{5x}{5} = \dfrac{-30}{5}$
		$x = -6$

The x-intercepts are 20 and -6.

Step 2. Find the y-intercept.

The graph crosses the y-axis where $x = 0$.

$$y = (20 - x)(30 + 5x)$$
$$y = (20 - 0)(30 + 5 \cdot 0) \quad \longleftarrow \quad \text{Substitute 0 for } x.$$
$$y = (20)(30)$$
$$y = 600$$

The y-intercept is 600.

Look Back

The graph of $y = (x + 3)(x - 2)$ is a parabola. What does its equation tell you about its intercepts?

BY THE WAY...

Any freely hanging cable forms a curve that looks like a parabola but is really a curve called a *catenary*.

Suspending weights from the cable turns the catenary into a parabola! This happens when a suspension bridge like the Golden Gate in San Francisco is built.

Exercises and Problems

1. **Reading** Read the statement of the zero-product property on page 495. How does this statement help you solve the equation $(20 - x)(30 + 5x) = 0$ in Sample 2 on page 564?

2. **a.** Complete the table of values.

   b. Plot the ordered pairs on a coordinate plane and draw a smooth curve through the points.

   c. Does your graph look more like the graph of $y = x^2$ or of $y = -x^2$?

   d. What are the x-intercepts of your graph?

   e. What is the y-intercept of your graph?

$y = x(x - 4)$	
x	y
-1	?
0	?
1	?
2	?
3	?
4	?
5	?

3. **Writing** Colby is graphing a parabola. He is having trouble deciding which points to pick for his table of values. What would you suggest to help Colby?

Graph each parabola.

4. $y = (x - 2)x$

5. $y = (x - 3)(3 - x)$

6. $y = (x - 4)(x + 4)$

Without graphing, find the x-intercepts and the y-intercept of the graph of each equation.

7. $y = x(x + 7)$

8. $y = (x + 12)(x - 1)$

9. $y = (x + 7)(4 - x)$

10. $y = (x + 4)(x + 13)$

11. $y = (x - 4)(3x + 13)$

12. $y = (4x - 1)(3x + 4)$

13. **a.** Suppose you translate the graph of $y = (x + 4)(x + 13)$ to the right 4 units. What are the x-intercepts of the new graph?

   b. Suppose you translate the graph of $y = (x + 4)(x + 13)$ down 5 units. What is the y-intercept of the new graph?

14. During a golf tournament, Chet Washington hits a ball that lands 200 yd from the tee. The path of the ball is a parabola.

   a. Sketch a possible path for the ball, using the x-axis as the ground and the origin as the tee.

   b. What are the x-intercepts of the graph?

   c. What do the x-intercepts mean in terms of the situation?

   d. **Writing** Amalia wrote the equation $y = -2x(4x - 800)$ for a possible path of the ball. Elizabeth wrote the equation $y = -2x(2x - 100)$. Which student's equation *cannot* be correct? Why?

Use Sara Ortiz's presentation.

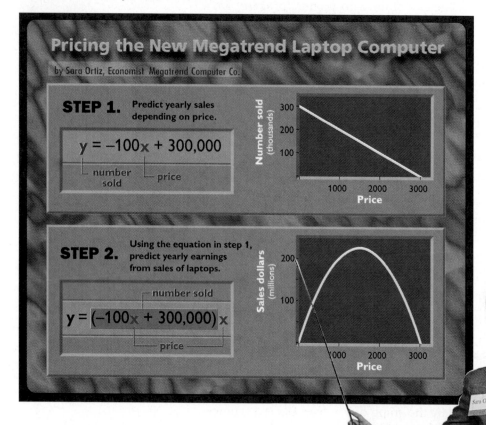

15. Look at the equation and graph in Step 1 of Sara Ortiz's presentation.

   a. Is this function an example of *linear growth* or *linear decay*?

   b. Which is the control variable? Which is the dependent variable?

   c. As the price goes up, what happens to the number sold? Why do you think this happens?

   d. What is the *x*-intercept? What does it mean in terms of the situation?

   e. When Sara Ortiz wrote the equation, she assumed that Megatrend will never sell more than 300,000 laptops in any given year. How can you tell?

16. Look at the equation and graph in Step 2 of Sara Ortiz's presentation. The graph is a parabola.

   a. Which is the control variable in the equation above? Which is the dependent variable?

   b. What are the *x*-intercepts? What do they mean in terms of the situation?

   c. What is the *y*-intercept? What does it mean in terms of the situation?

   d. What price should Megatrend set for the laptop computer? Why?

17. **Writing** Write a summary of what you can tell about a parabola from its equation. Give at least one example for each property.

Review **PREVIEW**

Tell how to translate the graph of $y = x^2$ in order to produce the graph of each equation. *(Section 10-2)*

18. $y = x^2 - 7$ **19.** $y = x^2 + 3$ **20.** $y = (x - 1)^2$

Write each expression as a power of ten. *(Section 1-3)*

21. $10^5 \times 10^2$ **22.** $10^{10} \times 10^{-8}$ **23.** $\dfrac{10^9}{10^5}$ **24.** $\dfrac{10^4}{10^8}$

Working on the Unit Project

25. Suppose a batter hits a ball that is very low to the ground. The ball lands at a spot 100 ft away.

   a. Suppose the ball is hit from the ground. Sketch a graph of a possible path of the ball. Use the x-axis as the ground and the origin as the point where the ball was hit.

   b. What are the x-intercepts of your path?

   c. Is there more than one possible path with these intercepts? Explain.

   d. Could the graph of the equation $y = -x(x - 100)$ represent the ball's path? Describe your reasoning.

Unit 10 **CHECKPOINT 1**

1. **Writing** Find a picture of a parabola. Sketch it on graph paper. Tell at least three things you know about it.

2. Copy the figure and reflect it over each axis. Write the   **10-1**
   coordinates of the vertices of its image. Describe the orientation of the original figure and its image.

   a. x-axis   **b.** y-axis

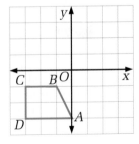

Tell how to transform the graph of $y = x^2$ in order to   **10-2**
produce the graph of each equation.

   3. $y = x^2 + 8$ **4.** $y = (x - 1)^2$ **5.** $y = -x^2$

   6. Graph the parabola $y = (x + 2)(x - 3)$. Plot enough   **10-3**
   points to show the shape of the curve.

Without graphing, find the x-intercepts and the
y-intercept of the graph of each equation.

   7. $y = (x + 5)(x + 11)$ **8.** $y = x(x - 12)$

10-3 Factors and Intercepts

Section 10-4

Focus
Use shortcuts for
simplifying powers.

Working with Powers

The **POWER** OF SHORTCUTS

Talk it Over

1. Write each product as a power of 4.
   a. $4 \cdot 4 \cdot 4 = 4^?$
   b. $4 \cdot 4 = 4^?$
   c. $(4 \cdot 4 \cdot 4) \cdot (4 \cdot 4) = 4^? \cdot 4^?$
   d. $(4 \cdot 4 \cdot 4) \cdot (4 \cdot 4) = 4^?$

2. Write each product as a power of x.
   a. $x \cdot x \cdot x = x^?$
   b. $x \cdot x = x^?$
   c. $(x \cdot x \cdot x) \cdot (x \cdot x) = x^? \cdot x^?$
   d. $(x \cdot x \cdot x) \cdot (x \cdot x) = x^?$

3. Use your calculator to complete parts (a) and (b) below to see if $4^3 \cdot 4^2 = 4^5$.

   a. ?

   b. **4** **yˣ** **5** **=** ?

4. Use your answers to questions 1–3. Do you see a way to write $3^6 \cdot 3^4$ as a power of 3 without writing out the factors? Describe a shortcut.

5. Marissa drew a diagram to show how she came up with a shortcut for multiplying $5^{12} \cdot 5^9$. Explain her reasoning.

6. Draw a diagram like Marissa's to show that $(-3)^2 \cdot (-3)^3 = (-3)^{2 + 3}$.

Marissa

$5^{12} \cdot 5^9 = 5^?$

$\overbrace{12 \text{ factors}}\quad \overbrace{9 \text{ factors}}$
$5^{12} \cdot 5^9 = \underbrace{(5 \cdot 5 \cdot 5 \cdots 5) \cdot (5 \cdot 5 \cdots 5)}_{12 + 9 \text{ factors}} = 5^{12+9}$

so $5^{12} \cdot 5^9 = 5^{12+9} = 5^{21}$

The shortcut is- you can add the exponents!

568

Unit 10 Quadratic Equations as Models

Marissa's diagram can be used to model a general rule:

$$a^m \cdot a^n = \underbrace{\overbrace{(a \cdot a \cdot \ldots \cdot a)}^{m \text{ factors}} \cdot \overbrace{(a \cdot a \cdot \ldots \cdot a)}^{n \text{ factors}}}_{m + n \text{ factors}} = a^{m+n}$$

PRODUCT OF POWERS RULE

$$a^m \cdot a^n = a^{m+n}$$

same base

Example:

$$2^3 \cdot 2^7 = 2^{3+7}$$
$$= 2^{10}$$

To multiply powers that have the same base, you add the exponents.

Sample 1

Simplify.

a. $a^6 \cdot a^5$

b. $x \cdot x^2$

c. $y^2 \cdot y^3 \cdot y^4$

Sample Response

a. $a^6 \cdot a^5 = a^{6+5}$ ← The powers have the same base. Use the product of powers rule.

$\quad = a^{11}$

b. $x \cdot x^2 = x^1 \cdot x^2$ ← Rewrite x as x^1.

$\quad = x^{1+2}$ ← Use the product of powers rule.

$\quad = x^3$

c. $y^2 \cdot y^3 \cdot y^4 = (y^2 \cdot y^3) \cdot y^4$ ← Group two of the factors.

$\quad = y^{2+3} \cdot y^4$ ← Use the product of powers rule.

$\quad = y^5 \cdot y^4$

$\quad = y^{5+4}$ ← Use the product of powers rule.

$\quad = y^9$

Talk it Over

7. Which property of multiplication allows you to group two factors in part (c) of Sample 1?

8. In part (c) of Sample 1, can you use the shortcut $y^2 \cdot y^3 \cdot y^4 = y^{2+3+4}$? Why or why not?

To simplify some products you begin by regrouping the factors.

Simplify.

a. $2a^2 \cdot 9a^3$

b. $-x^2y \cdot 3xy^3$

Sample Response

a. $2a^2 \cdot 9a^3 = (2 \cdot 9) \cdot (a^2 \cdot a^3)$ ← Group numbers and group powers with the same base.

$= 18 \cdot a^{2+3}$ ← The powers have the same base. Use the product of powers rule.

$= 18a^5$

b. $-x^2y \cdot 3xy^3 = (-1x^2y) \cdot (3xy^3)$ ← Rewrite $-x^2y$ as $-1x^2y$.

$= (-1 \cdot 3) \cdot (x^2 \cdot x) \cdot (y \cdot y^3)$ ← Group numbers, group powers of x, and group powers of y.

$= -3 \cdot (x^2 \cdot x^1) \cdot (y^1 \cdot y^3)$ ← Rewrite x as x^1 and y as y^1.

$= -3 \cdot (x^{2+1}) \cdot (y^{1+3})$ ← Use the product of powers rule for powers with the same base.

$= -3x^3y^4$

▶ **Now you are ready for:**
Exs. 1–19 on pp. 572–574

Talk it Over

9. Use the product of powers rule to complete each statement.

   a. $(3^4)^2 = 3^4 \cdot 3^4 = 3^?$

   b. $(a^2)^3 = a^2 \cdot a^2 \cdot a^2 = a^?$

10. Look at your answers to question 9. Describe a shortcut for simplifying $(a^2)^3$ without writing out the factors.

11. Dan made this diagram for his shortcut.

a^m is a factor n times ⏞ n terms ⏞

$$(a^m)^n = a^m \cdot a^m \cdot \ldots \cdot a^m = a^{m+m+\ldots+m} = a^{m \cdot n}$$

Explain his reasoning.

Dan's diagram models this general rule:

POWER OF A POWER RULE

$$(a^m)^n = a^{m \cdot n}$$

To find a power of a power, you multiply the exponents.

Example:

$(x^3)^4 = x^{3 \cdot 4}$

$= x^{12}$

Simplify.

a. $(x^5)^2$

b. $(y^4)^5 \cdot y^4$

Sample Response

a. $(x^5)^2 = x^{5 \cdot 2}$ ⟵ Use the power of a power rule.

$= x^{10}$

b. $(y^4)^5 \cdot y^4 = (y^{4 \cdot 5}) \cdot y^4$ ⟵ Use the power of a power rule.

$= y^{20} \cdot y^4$

$= y^{20 + 4}$ ⟵ Use the product of powers rule.

$= y^{24}$

Talk it Over

BY THE WAY...

The number 10^{100} is called a *googol*. The number 10 raised to the googol power is called a *googolplex*.

12. Simplify.

 a. $(2x)^3 = 2x \cdot 2x \cdot 2x = \underline{\,?\,}$

 b. $(xy)^3 = \underline{\,?\,} \cdot \underline{\,?\,} \cdot \underline{\,?\,} = \underline{\,?\,}$

 c. $(xy^2)^3 = \underline{\,?\,} \cdot \underline{\,?\,} \cdot \underline{\,?\,} = \underline{\,?\,}$

13. Look at your answers to question 12. Describe a shortcut for simplifying $(2x)^3$ without writing out the factors. Explain your reasoning.

14. Meghan made this diagram for her shortcut. Explain her reasoning.

$$\underbrace{ab \text{ is a factor } n \text{ times}}_{} \qquad \underbrace{n \text{ factors}}_{} \qquad \underbrace{n \text{ factors}}_{}$$

$$(ab)^n = \overbrace{(ab) \cdot (ab) \cdot \ldots \cdot (ab)} = \overbrace{(a \cdot a \cdot \ldots \cdot a)} \cdot \overbrace{(b \cdot b \cdot \ldots \cdot b)} = a^n \cdot b^n$$

Meghan's diagram models this general rule:

POWER OF A PRODUCT RULE

$$(ab)^n = a^n \cdot b^n$$

To find a power of a product, you find that power of each factor and then multiply.

Example:

$(2x)^4 = 2^4 \cdot x^4$

$= 16x^4$

Simplify.

a. $(4n)^3$ b. $(-k^2)^3$ c. $(2a^5b^2)^4$

Sample Response

a. $(4n)^3 = 4^3 \cdot n^3$ ⟵ Use the power of a product rule.

$= 64n^3$

b. $(-k^2)^3 = (-1k^2)^3$ ⟵ Rewrite $-k^2$ as $-1k^2$.

$= (-1)^3 \cdot (k^2)^3$ ⟵ Use the power of a product rule.

$= -1k^6$ ⟵ Use the power of a power rule.

$= -k^6$

c. $(2a^5b^2)^4 = 2^4 \cdot (a^5)^4 \cdot (b^2)^4$ ⟵ Use the power of a product rule.

$= 16a^{20}b^8$ ⟵ Use the power of a power rule.

Look Back ⟵

There are three rules about powers in this section. Which rule would you use to simplify each expression?

$$(2x)^5, \quad x^{12} \cdot x^5, \quad \text{and} \quad (x^{12})^5$$

Explain how to decide which rule to use.

⋯▶ **Now you are ready for:**
Exs. 20–43 on pp. 574–575

10-4 Exercises and Problems

1. **Reading** Why can you use the product of powers rule to simplify $x^4 \cdot x^3$ but not to simplify $x^4 \cdot y^3$?

Simplify.

2. $x^4 \cdot x^3$ 3. $t^2 \cdot t^8$ 4. $y^5 \cdot y$ 5. $k^3 \cdot k^2 \cdot k^5$

6. $x^2 \cdot x \cdot x^3$ 7. $6a^3 \cdot 9a^3$ 8. $y \cdot 5y^2$ 9. $(-4z^2)(7z^3)$

10. $(-b^2)(3b^3)$ 11. $ab \cdot a^3b$ 12. $(-8x^3y^3)(x^2y^2)$ 13. $(4m^5)(-2mn^2)$

14. **Writing** Suppose your friend missed today's class. Write a note to convince your friend that $x^5 \cdot x^3 = x^{5+3}$. What would you show? What would you say?

This mylar and fabric wall hanging was designed and created by artist Patricia Malarcher. She uses a basic geometric grid design and explores ways of breaking up geometric shapes such as squares. A twelve-inch square is her basic design element.

In Exercises 15 and 16, write the area of each square and compare it to the area of the original square.

Original:

x

 x

Area $= x^2$

15. $\frac{1}{2}x$

$\frac{1}{2}x$

16. $2x$

$2x$

17. a. Complete each equation.

$$\frac{4^5}{4^3} = \frac{4 \cdot 4 \cdot 4 \cdot 4 \cdot 4}{4 \cdot 4 \cdot 4}$$

$$= \underline{\ ?\ } \cdot \underline{\ ?\ }$$

$$= 4^?$$

b. Complete each equation.

$$\frac{x^7}{x^2} = \frac{x \cdot x \cdot x \cdot x \cdot x \cdot x \cdot x}{x \cdot x}$$

$$= \underline{\ ?\ } \cdot \underline{\ ?\ } \cdot \underline{\ ?\ } \cdot \underline{\ ?\ } \cdot \underline{\ ?\ }$$

$$= x^?$$

c. From your answers to parts (a) and (b), do you see a way to write $\frac{5^{12}}{5^9}$ as a power of 5 without writing out the factors? Describe a shortcut.

18. a. Use the shortcut you wrote in part (c) of Exercise 17 to complete the equation $\frac{6^2}{6^2} = 6^?$.

b. Look at the equation in part (a). What do you think is the value of 6^0? Explain your reasoning.

19. Use the product of powers rule to simplify $x^0 \cdot x^b = x^{? + ?} = x^?$. What do you conclude about the value of x^0?

Simplify.

20. $(k^5)^3$ **21.** $(y^3)^8$ **22.** $(2x)^3$ **23.** $(-d^5)^2$

24. $(2x^3)^4$ **25.** $(-3h^3)^5$ **26.** $(-4m^2n)^2$ **27.** $(5y^6z^3)^4$

28 TECHNOLOGY Which calculator key sequence is *not* a way to calculate $(2^5)^2$?

a. 2 y^x 5 = x^2
b. 2 y^x 5 y^x 2 =
c. 2 y^x 1 0 =
d. 2 y^x 7 =

29. **Writing** Use the area models to write a convincing argument that $(2x)^2$ is greater than $2x^2$ for any positive value of x.

30. The calculator shows the graphs of $y = 2x^2$ and $y = (2x)^2$ on the same axes. For what values of x is $2x^2$ less than $(2x)^2$?

$y = (2x)^2$ $y = 2x^2$

31. Terry and Alec disagree on an answer.

Who is right?

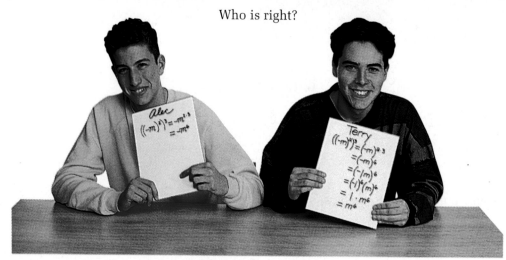

Alec
$((-m)^2)^3 = -m^{2 \cdot 3}$
$= -m^6$

Terry
$((-m)^2)^3 = (-m)^{2 \cdot 3}$
$= (-m)^6$
$= (-1/m)^6$
$= (-1)^6(m)^6$
$= 1 \cdot m^6$
$= m^6$

32. Insert parentheses in the expression on the left side of each equation to make a true statement.

a. $2a^2b^3 = 2a^6b^3$
b. $2a^2b^3 = 4a^2b^3$
c. $2a^2b^3 = 8a^6b^3$

33 TECHNOLOGY Use a graphics calculator or graphing software. Graph $y = x^2$ and $y = x^3$ on the same screen.

a. In which quadrants does each graph lie?

b. For which graph is the y-axis a line of symmetry?

c. **Writing** Write about how the graphs of $y = x^2$ and $y = x^3$ are alike and how they are different.

34 TECHNOLOGY Functions of the form $y = x^n$ are called *power functions.* Use a graphics calculator or graphing software to graph $y = x^4$, $y = x^5$, $y = x^6$, and $y = x^7$ on the same axes.

a. In which quadrants does each graph lie?

b. Describe the similarities and differences of the graphs. Are some more alike than others? Which?

c. Predict what the graphs of $y = x^8$ and $y = x^9$ will look like. Graph the equations to check your predictions.

Ongoing ASSESSMENT

35. **Writing** Fred wonders whether $2^4 \cdot 2^3 = 2^{12}$ is true. Write him a note describing two or three ways he can find out.

Review PREVIEW

Find the x- and y-intercepts of the graph of each equation. *(Section 10-3)*

36. $y = (x - 5)(x - 2)$

37. $y = x(x + 3)$

38. a. Write a statement represented by the figure formed by x-tiles and 1-tiles. *(Section 1-5)*

b. Draw a diagram similar to the one in part (a) to represent the statement $2(x + 3) = 2x + 2 \cdot 3$.

Use the distributive property to rewrite each expression. *(Section 1-5)*

39. $2(n - 5)$ **40.** $6(4r + 3)$ **41.** $-3(x + 12)$ **42.** $(m + n)8$

Working on the Unit Project

43. **Research** The pull of gravity is not the same on every planet. Do some research to find out how this affects a ball thrown or dropped on other planets.

Factored Form and x-Intercepts

Focus
Factor and expand algebraic expressions, and use factoring to find the x-intercepts of parabolas.

EXPLORATION

How can you picture an algebraic expression?

- **Materials: algebra tiles**
- **Work with another student.**

1
x

Area = _?_   Area = _?_

x 1
x

Area = _?_

① Suppose your algebra tiles have the dimensions shown. What is the area of each kind of tile? What is the area of a rectangle made with the two tiles?

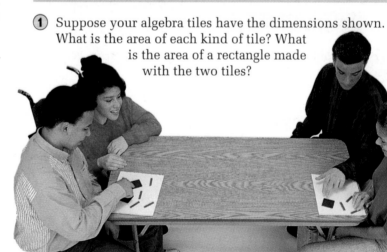

② **a.** Build a rectangle with these tiles. The tiles should touch but not overlap.

b. Complete: Length of your rectangle = _?_
Width of your rectangle = _?_

c. Complete:
Area of your rectangle = length × width
= _?_

d. Complete:
Area of your rectangle = sum of the areas of the tiles
= _?_

e. Write a mathematical statement that relates the expressions you wrote in parts (c) and (d).

3 **a.** Build a rectangle with these tiles.

    b. Repeat parts (b)–(e) of step 2 for the rectangle you build with these tiles.

4 **a.** Build a different rectangle with the same tiles you used in step 3.

    b. How does the area of this rectangle compare to the area of the rectangle you built in step 3?

5 Complete each equation by writing two expressions for the area of the rectangle. If a tile is red, subtract the area of that tile from the others.

Example:

x -1 -1

a.

Area = $\underline{?} \times \underline{?} = \underline{?} + \underline{?}$

b.

Area = $\underline{?} \times \underline{?} = \underline{?} - \underline{?}$

······➤ **Now you are ready for:**

Exs. 1–7 on p. 580

Expanding and Factoring Expressions

In the Exploration you wrote pairs of equal expressions for the area of a rectangle.

product of length and width ↘ ⌒factoring⌒ ↙ sum or difference of the tile areas

$x(x + 3) = x^2 + 3x$

factored form   **expanded form**

⌣ expanding ↗

Sample 1

Expand $x(x - 3)$.

Sample Response

⊢——x——⊢—3—⊣

x

$x(x - 3) = x \cdot x - x \cdot 3$ ◄——Use the distributive property.

$ = x^2 - 3x$

Factor $x^2 + x$.

Sample Response

$x^2 + x = x \cdot x + x \cdot 1$ ← Rewrite each term as a product.

$= x \cdot x + x \cdot 1$ ← Look for a common factor in each term.

$= x(x + 1)$ ← Use the distributive property in reverse.

In the Exploration you built two rectangles with an area of $2x^2 + 6x$.

An expression like $2x^2 + 6x$ is called a *binomial*. A **binomial** is the sum of two *monomials*. A **monomial** can be any of these.

➤ a number, like 8 or -8,

➤ a variable raised to any power, like x^2,

➤ the product of numbers and variables raised to any power, like $2x^2$, $6x$, or $-8x$.

By building two rectangles with the same area, you showed that there is sometimes more than one way to factor an expression.

Area: $x(2x + 6) = 2x^2 + 6x$ Area: $2x(x + 3) = 2x^2 + 6x$

Look at the two different factored forms of $2x^2 + 6x$.

greatest common factor

$x(2x + 6) = 2x(x + 3)$

The expression $2x(x + 3)$ has been **factored completely** since x and 3 have no common factors other than 1.

Finding x-Intercepts

You can find the x-intercepts of some parabolas without graphing if you begin by factoring completely one side of the equation for the parabola.

The graph of $y = 3x^2 - 6x$ is a parabola. Find the x-intercepts of the graph.

Sample Response

Student Resources Toolbox
p. 648 *Factors*

Step 1. Factor the binomial $3x^2 - 6x$ completely.

$3x^2 - 6x$

$3 \cdot x \cdot x - 6 \cdot x$ ◄——— Rewrite each power as a product.

$3 \cdot x \cdot x - 2 \cdot 3 \cdot x$ ◄——— Write each number as a product of primes.

$3 \cdot x \cdot x - 2 \cdot 3 \cdot x$ ◄——— Look for the common factors.

$3x(x - 2)$ ◄——— Factor out 3x, the greatest common factor.

Step 2. Write the original equation in its factored form.

$y = 3x(x - 2)$

$0 = 3x(x - 2)$ ◄——— The x-intercepts occur when $y = 0$. Substitute 0 for y and solve.

$3x = 0 \quad or \quad x - 2 = 0$ ◄——— Use the zero-product property. Set each factor equal to zero.

$x = 0 \qquad x - 2 + 2 = 0 + 2$

$x = 2$

The x-intercepts of the parabola are 0 and 2.

BY THE WAY...

Secret codes can be made by multiplying two 100-digit numbers. To break the code, you must factor the 200-digit expanded product. Not even a computer can factor a number this big!

·······► Now you are ready for:
Exs. 8–43 on pp. 580–582

Talk it Over

1. **a.** Describe how to find the greatest common factor of 12 and 15.

   b. Find the greatest common factor of the two terms of $12x^2 - 15x$.

2. Explain how to solve $0 = 5x(x + 1)$.

Look Back ◄

The expression $4x^2 - 16x$ has the form $ax^2 + bx$. Explain how to factor completely an expression of this form.
The expression $4x(x - 4)$ has the form $ax(x + b)$. Explain how to expand an expression of this form.

10-5 Exercises and Problems

Express the area of each rectangle built from algebra tiles as the product of its length and width.

1.

2.

3.

Using Manipulatives For Exercises 4–6, use algebra tiles or paper models.

4. **a.** Build a rectangle using the tiles at the right.

   b. Sketch your rectangle and label the length and width.

   c. Express the area of your rectangle in two ways, as a sum and as a product.

5. Repeat Exercise 4 using two x^2-tiles and three x-tiles.

6. **a.** **Open-ended** Use at least one x^2-tile and at least one x-tile to build any rectangle you want.

   b. Express the area of the rectangle you built in part (a) as a product.

   c. Express the area of the rectangle you built in part (a) as a sum.

7. **Writing** Do you think it is possible to build a rectangle using any number of x^2-tiles and any number of x-tiles? Give a reason for your answer.

Expand each product.

8. $x(x + 9)$

9. $-x(x - 15)$

10. $(x + 11)x$

11. $6x(x - 7)$

12. $3x(2x + 4)$

13. $-4x(5x - 9)$

14. **Reading** Give two examples of binomials and monomials that appear on page 578.

The graph of each equation is a parabola. For each equation, do these things.

a. Factor one side completely.

b. Find the x-intercepts and the y-intercept of the graph.

15. $y = x^2 - 5x$

16. $y = x^2 + 10x$

17. $y = 12x + x^2$

18. $y = -x^2 - 5x$

19. $y = -x^2 + 10x$

20. $6x - x^2 = y$

21. $y = 8x^2 - 40x$

22. $-4x^2 + 12x = y$

23. $y = 12x - 6x^2$

24. **a.** **Open-ended** Write an expression in the form $ax^2 + bx$ that can be factored.

   b. Write an expression in the form $ax^2 + bx$ that can be factored in two ways.

Tell whether each expression is a *monomial* or a *binomial*.

25. $x - 2$

26. $3x^2 + 8$

27. $-7a^2b^3$

28. $6y^3 + 4xy$

29. Urban Planning A town is planning to put a concrete walkway around a Japanese garden. The walkway should be the same width on each side. It must be at least 5 ft wide to allow two wheelchairs to pass.

a. Let x represent the width of the walkway. Write an expression in expanded form to represent the area of the walkway. (*Hint:* Divide the walkway into squares and rectangles. Add up the areas of the pieces.)

b. Factor your expression.

c. Let y represent the area of the walkway. Write an equation for the area.

d. Find the x-intercepts of the graph of your equation.

e. Complete the table of values for your equation.

x	y
-70	?
-35	?
-25	?
-15	?
20	?

f. Use the x-intercepts and the table of values to sketch the parabola on graph paper. Mark the horizontal axis with units of 5 and the vertical axis with units of 500.

g. **Writing** In which quadrants does the graph contain ordered pairs that are not realistic solutions for the situation? Explain.

h. Suppose there is only enough concrete to cover an area of 1500 ft². Use the graph to estimate the largest possible width for the walkway. Round your answer to the nearest foot.

30. **Group Activity** Work in a group of three students. Take turns until each student has been first, second, and third. Have the first student write an equation in the form $y = ax^2 + bx$. Have the second student factor completely the right side of the equation. Have the third student name the x-intercepts of the graph of the equation.

Review **PREVIEW**

Simplify. *(Sections 10-4, 10-5)*

31. $m^3 \cdot 2m^5$
32. $(-5x^2)(-2x^3)$
33. $(3ac)^3$
34. $(3n^2)^2$

35. $x^2 + x + 7x + 7$
36. $x^2 - 2x - 10x - 8$
37. $x^2 + 4x - 5x + 14$

For the graph of each equation, write the equation of the line of symmetry and the coordinates of the vertex. *(Section 10-2)*

38. $y = x^2 - 13$
39. $y = x^2 + 42$
40. $y = (x - 11)^2$

10 Working on the Unit Project

41. One equation for the path of a ball hit at a 45° angle is $y = x(1 - 0.005x)$.

    a. Find the x-intercepts of the graph of the equation.

    b. What do the x-intercepts represent in this situation?

    c. Write the expanded form of the equation.

42. Another equation for the path of a ball hit at a 45° angle is $y = -0.003x^2 + x$.

    a. Write the factored form of the equation.

    b. Find the x-intercepts of the graph of the equation.

    c. In this situation, what is represented by the x-intercepts?

43. Which of the equations in Exercises 41 and 42 represents the path of the ball that lands farther away? What do you think made it land farther away?

10-6

Expanded Form and Line of Symmetry

THE LONG AND THE SHORT OF IT

Focus

Multiply two binomials and use a formula to find the line of symmetry of a parabola.

Talk it Over

1. Can you build a rectangle with the dimensions

   length = $x + 1$

   width = $x + 1$

   using only x^2-tiles and x-tiles?

2. a. In the rectangle shown, what is the area of the piece shown with dashed lines?

   b. How many 1-tiles do you need to fill in the dashed area?

   c. Express the area of the rectangle as the product of its length and width.

   d. Express the area of the rectangle as the sum of the areas of the tiles.

3. a. Express the area of this rectangle as the product of its length and width.

   b. Express the area of this rectangle as the sum of the areas of the tiles.

   c. Are the expressions you wrote in parts (a) and (b) equal?

One way to find the product of two binomials is to build a rectangle from algebra tiles. Another way is to use the distributive property.

Expand $(x + 2)(x + 3)$.

Sample Response

$$(x + 2)(x + 3) = (x + 2)x + (x + 2)3 \quad \longleftarrow \text{Use the distributive property.}$$
$$= x^2 + 2x + 3x + 6 \quad \longleftarrow \text{Use the distributive property again.}$$
$$= x^2 + 5x + 6 \quad \longleftarrow \text{Combine like terms.}$$

BY THE WAY...

Biologists use trinomials to track the changes in DNA as it breaks apart and recombines. The long strands of DNA form complicated loop patterns.

Each pattern is represented by a different trinomial.

Talk it Over

4. For the first step of Sample 1, Sonia wrote
$$(x + 2)(x + 3) = x(x + 3) + 2(x + 3).$$
Will she get the same answer?

In Sample 1 you multiplied two binomials. The product is the sum of three monomials and has the form $ax^2 + bx + c$.

$$x^2 \qquad + \qquad 5x \qquad + \qquad 6$$
$$\uparrow \qquad\qquad\qquad \uparrow \qquad\qquad\qquad \uparrow$$
$$a = 1 \qquad\qquad b = 5 \qquad\qquad c = 6$$

An expression with three monomial terms is called a **trinomial**.

Expand $(x - 3)(2x + 1)$.

Sample Response

$$(x - 3)(2x + 1) = (x - 3)2x + (x - 3)1 \quad \longleftarrow \text{Use the distributive property.}$$
$$= 2x^2 - 6x + x - 3 \quad \longleftarrow \text{Use the distributive property again.}$$
$$= 2x^2 - 5x - 3 \quad \longleftarrow \text{Combine like terms.}$$

······► **Now you are ready for:**
Exs. 1–13 on p. 587

5. What is the equation of the line of symmetry of the three parabolas shown?

$y = (x + 2)(x + 2)$

$y = (x + 3)(x + 1)$

$y = x(x + 4)$

6. Angela says she can find the equation of the line of symmetry from the equation $y = (x + 3)(x + 1)$ without drawing the graph. Here is her thinking.

"The x-intercepts are −3 and −1."   **a.** How does she know?

"The line of symmetry crosses the x-axis halfway between the x-intercepts."   **b.** Which point is halfway between $(−3, 0)$ and $(−1, 0)$?

"So, the line of symmetry is x = −2."   **c.** Do you agree?

7. Celine found this formula in an algebra book.

> For the graph of $y = ax^2 + bx + c$, the equation of the line of symmetry is $x = -\dfrac{b}{2a}$.

She wanted to see how this works for the graphs of the equations in question 5. Here is what she did.

"I rewrote each equation in the form $y = ax^2 + bx + c$."   **a.** What did she write for each equation?

"I found that the coefficients a and b are the same in each equation."   **b.** Does this surprise you?

"I substituted the values of a and b in $x = -\dfrac{b}{2a}$."   **c.** Did she get the same answer as Angela did in question 6?

8. Why do you think the coefficient c does not appear in Celine's formula?

Without graphing, find each feature of the graph of the equation $y = x^2 + 6x - 17$.

a. the equation of the line of symmetry

b. the coordinates of the vertex

c. the y-intercept

Sample Response

a. Use the formula for the line of symmetry.

$$x = -\frac{b}{2a}$$

$$= -\frac{6}{2 \cdot 1} \qquad \longleftarrow \text{Substitute 6 for } b \text{ and 1 for } a.$$

$$= -3$$

The equation of the line of symmetry is $x = -3$.

b. The vertex is on the line of symmetry. The equation of the line of symmetry tells the x-coordinate of the vertex.

$$y = x^2 + 6x - 17$$

$$= (-3)^2 + 6(-3) - 17 \qquad \longleftarrow \text{Substitute } -3 \text{ for } x.$$

$$= -26$$

The coordinates of the vertex are $(-3, -26)$.

c. The value of x is 0 where the graph crosses the y-axis.

$$y = x^2 + 6x - 17$$

$$= 0^2 + 6(0) - 17 \qquad \longleftarrow \text{Substitute 0 for } x.$$

$$= -17$$

The y-intercept is -17.

BY THE WAY...

To record a concert in stereo, sound engineers use a parabolic disk to direct the sound to two microphones placed on opposite sides of the line of symmetry.

Look Back

Describe as many different methods as you can for finding the equation of the line of symmetry of a parabola without graphing. If a method can be used with only certain kinds of equations, be sure to include this information.

······▶ **Now you are ready for:**
Exs. 14–42 on pp. 588–590

Exercises and Problems

Using Manipulatives **For Exercises 1–3, do these things.**

a. **Write each product in expanded form.**

b. **Check your answer to part (a) by using algebra tiles to build a rectangle. Sketch your rectangle.**

1. $(x + 1)(x + 2)$ **2.** $(x + 2)(x + 3)$ **3.** $(x + 4)(x + 1)$

4. A shortcut for expanding the product of two binomials is called *FOIL*. "FOIL" is made up of the first letters of the words First, Outer, Inner, and Last.

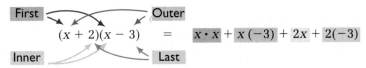

First   Outer

$(x + 2)(x - 3) = x \cdot x + x(-3) + 2x + 2(-3)$

Inner   Last

Use the distributive property to show that FOIL works.

Expand each product.

5. $(x + 2)(x + 3)$ **6.** $(x + 5)(x + 4)$ **7.** $(x - 4)(x + 4)$ **8.** $(x - 7)(x + 7)$

9. $(x - 2)(x - 2)$ **10.** $(x + 4)(x + 4)$ **11.** $(x + 2)(2x - 5)$ **12.** $(4x - 6)(2x + 7)$

connection to **HISTORY**

13. Five years before he was elected president of the United States, James A. Garfield proved the Pythagorean theorem this way.

① Draw a rectangle and cut along the diagonal to form two triangles.

② Put the two triangles next to each other and draw a dashed line to make a third triangle.

③ Draw dashed lines to extend each side to make a square.

a. What is the sum of the measures of angles 1, 2, and 3?

b. Why is the sum of the measures of angles 1 and 3 equal to 90°?

c. What is the measure of angle 2?

d. What is the area of the square formed by extending the sides as shown? Write the product in expanded form.

e. Find the sum of the areas of the three triangles.

f. Study the diagram. Write an equation that shows how the total area of the three triangles is related to the area of the square.

g. Combine like terms to simplify the equation you wrote in part (f). Rewrite the equation so c^2 is alone on one side.

14. What is the equation of the line of symmetry of these three parabolas?

$$y = -x(x + 4)$$

$$y = (-x - 3)(x + 1)$$

$$y = (-x - 2)(x + 2)$$

15. **Reading** Questions 6 and 7 on page 585 describe two methods for finding the line of symmetry from an equation without drawing the graph. Describe how to use Abe's and Celine's methods on one of the equations in Exercise 14.

Writing **Match each equation with its graph. Then explain how you decided which graph matches each equation.**

16. $y = x^2 + 5x - 6$

17. $y = x^2 + 5x + 6$

18. $y = x^2 - 5x + 6$

19. $y = x^2 - 5x - 6$

A.

B.

C.

D.

Without graphing, find each feature of the graph of each equation.

a. the equation of the line of symmetry

b. the coordinates of the vertex

c. the y-intercept

20. $y = x^2 + 4x - 11$ **21.** $y = x^2 + 8x + 12$ **22.** $y = x^2 - 4x - 15$

23. $y = x^2 + 16x + 15$ **24.** $y = x^2 + 6x + 18$ **25.** $y = x^2 - 6x + 7$

26. **a.** **Writing** Describe how you can use the factored form of an equation for a parabola to find some features of its graph.

     b. **Writing** Describe how you can use the expanded form of an equation for a parabola to find some features of its graph.

Use equations (a)–(h). The graphs of these equations are parabolas.

     a. $y = x^2 - 4$ **b.** $y = x(x - 8)$ **c.** $y = (x + 4)^2$ **d.** $y = -x^2 + 8x$

     e. $y = -x^2 + 8x - 1$ **f.** $y = x^2 - 8x + 8$ **g.** $y = x^2 + 4$ **h.** $y = (x - 4)^2$

27. Which parabolas have the same line of symmetry?

28. Which parabolas have the same vertex?

29. Roxanne found 72 ft of leftover fencing in the garage. She decided to use it to make a rectangular pen for her dog Wolf. She wants to make the area of the pen as large as possible. Her mother allows her to use their house as one side of the pen.

a. Draw a diagram to represent this situation.

b. Let x be the width of the pen. Write an expression for the length of the pen in terms of x.

c. Let y be the area of the pen. Use your answer to part (b) to write an equation for the area of the pen.

d. Find the x-intercepts of the graph of the equation you wrote in part (c). What do the x-intercepts mean in this situation?

e. Find the coordinates of the vertex of the graph. What does the vertex mean in this situation?

f. What length and width should Roxanne use to build the pen?

30. **Group Activity** Work with another student.

For each translation (a)–(d) of the graph of $y = x^2$, find the equation of the line of symmetry and the coordinates of the vertex. Take turns using these methods.

Method ❶

Sketch a graph of the translated parabola.

Method ❷

Write an equation in expanded form for the translated parabola. Use the formula $x = -\dfrac{b}{2a}$.

Compare your answers. If they are different, find any errors and correct them together.

a. 6 units left   **b.** 7 units right   **c.** 4 units left   **d.** 2 units right

Expand each product. *(Section 10-5)*

31. $(x + 3)x$ **32.** $x(2x - 3)$ **33.** $3x(4x + 5)$ **34.** $-2x(x - 8)$

35. Factor the right side of the equation $y = -2x^2 - 6x$. Then find the x-intercept(s) and y-intercept of the graph of the equation.

36. Find the x-intercepts of the graph of $y = (x + 11)(x - 20)$. *(Section 10-3)*

Write all the pairs of factors for each number. *(Toolbox Skill 7)*

37. 15   **38.** 17   **39.** 24   **40.** 21

Working on the Unit Project

41. An equation for the path of a ball hit at a 45° angle with an initial speed of 80 ft/s is $y = -0.005x^2 + x$. Find each feature of the graph of this equation.

   a. the y-intercept

   b. the equation of the line of symmetry

   c. the coordinates of the vertex

   d. the maximum height reached by the ball

42. Suppose you repeated Exercise 41 with the equation $y = -0.005x^2 + x + 4$. Predict how the results would be different. Then repeat Exercise 41 with this equation to check your prediction.

Unit 10   CHECKPOINT 2

1. **Writing** Factor the expression $6x^2 + 18x$. Explain your method.

Simplify.   10-4

   2. $m \cdot m^2 \cdot m^4$ **3.** $(-a^2b)(3a^3b^5)$

   4. $(y^2)^5$ **5.** $(-3m^2n)^4$

Expand each product.   10-5

   6. $x(x + 5)$ **7.** $x(x - 10)$ **8.** $-2x(x + 6)$

The graph of each equation is a parabola. For each equation, do these things.

   a. Factor one side completely.

   b. Find the x-intercepts and the y-intercept of the graph.

   9. $y = x^2 + 3x$ **10.** $y = -5x^2 + 10x$

11. Expand the product $(x + 3)(x - 4)$.   10-6

12. Without graphing, find each feature of the graph of the equation $y = x^2 - 8x + 6$.

   a. the equation of the line of symmetry

   b. the coordinates of the vertex

   c. the y-intercept

Using Factors to Sketch $y = x^2 + bx + c$

Focus
Factor trinomials and
sketch the graph of a
parabola.

TTRiple play

$x^2 + 5x + 6$

$x^2 + 3x + 2$

$x^2 + 6x + 9$

Talk it Over

1. Zoe and Sandy built rectangles to model some trinomials.

a. What do you notice about the number of ▮ tiles and the number of ▢ tiles in each model?

b. Build a rectangle for $x^2 + 8x + 15$. Repeat part (a) for your rectangle.

2. Try to build a rectangle for $x^2 + 2x + 3$. What do you notice?

3. Expand each product.

a. $(x + 5)(x + 3)$ b. $(x - 2)(x + 6)$ c. $(x - 3)(x - 8)$

4. For each product in question 3, look at the numbers in your expanded form and the numbers in the factored form. How are these numbers related?

5. Make a conjecture about the relationship between the integers b and c in any trinomial of the form $x^2 + bx + c$ and the numbers in the factored form.

Factor $x^2 + 7x + 12$.

Sample Response

Problem Solving Strategy: Work backward

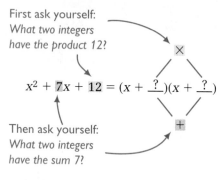

First ask yourself:
*What two integers
have the product 12?*

$$x^2 + 7x + 12 = (x + \underline{\;?\;})(x + \underline{\;?\;})$$

Then ask yourself:
*What two integers
have the sum 7?*

$$x^2 + 7x + 12 = (x + 3)(x + 4)$$

1 List pairs of integers whose product is 12.

1, 12   2, 6   3, 4

2 Add the integers in each pair.

$1 + 12 = 13$ $2 + 6 = 8$ $3 + 4 = 7$

3 Substitute the pair of integers that add up to the coefficient of x in the expanded form. Since $3 + 4 = 7$, use 3 and 4.

Check

Method ❶

Multiply using the distributive property.

$$x^2 + 7x + 12 \stackrel{?}{=} (x + 3)(x + 4)$$
$$x^2 + 7x + 12 \stackrel{?}{=} (x + 3)x + (x + 3)4$$
$$x^2 + 7x + 12 \stackrel{?}{=} x^2 + 3x + 4x + 12$$
$$x^2 + 7x + 12 = x^2 + 7x + 12 ✔$$

Method ❷

Use algebra tiles to make a rectangle.

$$(x + 3)(x + 4) = x^2 + 7x + 12 ✔$$

├─── $x + 3$ ───┤

$x + 4$

Talk it Over

6. Suppose you want to factor $x^2 - 7x + 12$.

   a. How is this trinomial different from the one factored in Sample 1?

   b. What questions would you ask yourself to find the factors?

   c. What are the factors of $x^2 - 7x + 12$?

7. In Sample 1, why are pairs of integers like -1 and -12 *not* listed?

Factor $x^2 + 4x - 12$.

Sample Response

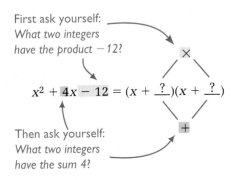

First ask yourself:
What two integers have the product -12?

$x^2 + 4x - 12 = (x + \underline{?})(x + \underline{?})$

Then ask yourself:
What two integers have the sum 4?

$x^2 + 4x - 12 = (x - 2)(x + 6)$

1 List pairs of integers whose product is -12.

1, −12	2, −6	3, −4
−1, 12	−2, 6	−3, 4

2 Add the integers in each pair.
$1 + (-12) = -11$ $2 + (-6) = -4$ $3 + (-4) = -1$

3 Substitute the pair of integers that add up to the coefficient of x in the expanded form. Since $(-2) + 6 = 4$, use -2 and 6.

··· **Talk it Over**

Explain how to factor each expression.

8. $x^2 - 4x - 12$ 9. $x^2 - 4x + 4$

Factor $x^2 + 3x + 10$.

Sample Response

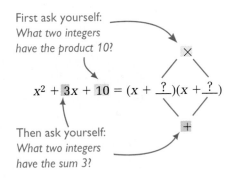

First ask yourself:
What two integers have the product 10?

$x^2 + 3x + 10 = (x + \underline{?})(x + \underline{?})$

Then ask yourself:
What two integers have the sum 3?

1 List pairs of integers whose product is 10.
1, 10   2, 5

2 Add the integers in each pair.
$1 + 10 = 11$ $2 + 5 = 7$

3 There is no pair of integers that have a product of 10 and that add up to 3.

The expression $x^2 + 3x + 10$ cannot be factored.

······▶ **Now you are ready for:**
Exs. 1–23 on pp. 595–596

10-7 Using Factors to Sketch $y = x^2 + bx + c$

Sketching the Graph of $y = x^2 + bx + c$

You can graph a parabola from its equation by using a table of values or by using a graphics calculator or graphing software. You can also use the line of symmetry, the vertex, and the intercepts to sketch a parabola.

Sample 4

Use the line of symmetry, the vertex, and the intercepts to sketch the graph of $y = x^2 + 4x - 12$.

Sample Response

Step 1. Find the line of symmetry and the vertex.

The vertex is on the line of symmetry of the parabola. First find the equation of the line of symmetry.

$x = -\dfrac{b}{2a}$ ⟵ Use the formula for the line of symmetry.

$x = -\dfrac{4}{2 \cdot 1}$ ⟵ Substitute 1 for a and 4 for b.

$x = -2$

The equation of the line of symmetry is $x = -2$.

The equation of the line of symmetry gives the x-coordinate of the vertex. Use this value to find the y-coordinate of the vertex.

$y = (-2)^2 + 4(-2) - 12$ ⟵ Substitute -2 for x.

$y = -16$

The coordinates of the vertex are $(-2, -16)$.

Step 2. Find the y-intercept.

The y-intercept is found where $x = 0$.

$y = 0^2 + 4 \cdot 0 - 12$ ⟵ Substitute 0 for x.

$y = -12$

The y-intercept is -12.

Step 3. Find the x-intercepts.

Use the factored form of the equation from Sample 2:

$y = (x - 2)(x + 6)$

By the zero-product property,

$0 = x - 2$ *or* $0 = x + 6$

$2 = x$ $-6 = x$

The x-intercepts are 2 and -6.

BY THE WAY...

Switch on a flashlight and hold it sideways against a wall in a darkened room.

The light from the flashlight forms a parabola.

Step 4. Sketch the graph.

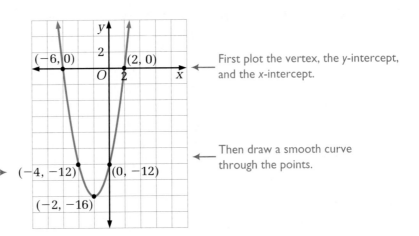

First plot the vertex, the y-intercept, and the x-intercept.

Then draw a smooth curve through the points.

The line of symmetry is $x = -2$. Plot the point opposite $(0, -12)$.

······▶ Now you are ready for:
Exs. 24–43 on pp. 596–597

Look Back ◀

Explain how to use algebra to find the x-intercepts of the graph of $y = x^2 + 3x + 2$.

Exercises and Problems

Express the area of each rectangle in expanded form and in factored form.

1.

2.

Using Manipulatives **Use algebra tiles.**

a. **Build a rectangle for each trinomial.**

b. **Use your rectangles to help you factor each trinomial.**

c. **Check your answers to part (b) by multiplying the factors.**

3. $x^2 + 8x + 16$ **4.** $x^2 + 9x + 20$ **5.** $x^2 + 9x + 14$

Factor each trinomial.

6. $x^2 + 6x + 5$ **7.** $x^2 + 9x + 18$ **8.** $x^2 - 11x + 18$

9. $x^2 - 5x + 6$ **10.** $x^2 + 8x + 12$ **11.** $x^2 - 13x + 12$

Writing **Factor each trinomial that can be factored using integers. For each trinomial that cannot be factored, explain why not.**

12. $x^2 - 12x + 20$ **13.** $x^2 + 9x + 10$ **14.** $x^2 - 5x + 24$

Find an expression for the height of each figure with the given base(s) and area.

15. Area $= x^2 + 7x + 10$

16. Area $= x^2 + 13x + 42$

17. Area $= x^2 - 11x + 30$

$x + 5$

$2x + 12$

$x - 7$

$x - 3$

Factor each trinomial.

18. $x^2 + 3x - 10$

19. $x^2 - 2x - 8$

20. $x^2 - 3x - 10$

21. $x^2 - 8x + 12$

22. $x^2 - 7x + 10$

23. $x^2 + 6x - 16$

24. **Reading** Sample 4 shows how to sketch the graph of a parabola. List the steps. How do these steps help you make an accurate sketch?

Use the line of symmetry, the vertex, and the intercepts to sketch the graph of each equation.

25. $y = x^2 + 4x + 4$

26. $y = x^2 - x - 12$

27. $y = x^2 - 6x - 7$

28. Alissa is throwing her bridal bouquet from a balcony that is 14 ft high. The path of the bouquet as it flies through the air is a parabola. An equation for this parabola is $y = -x^2 + x + 20$, where y represents the height in feet of the bouquet and x represents its distance in feet from the edge of the balcony.

a. Can the equation $y = -x^2 + x + 20$ also be written $y = -(x^2 - x - 20)$? Explain.

b. Suppose Alissa's mother is standing 12 ft from the balcony, her brother is standing 8 ft from the balcony, and her best friend is standing 5 ft from the balcony. Which of them is in the best position to catch the bouquet? Explain your reasoning.

29. a. Copy and complete the table.

b. Describe at least two patterns that you see in your table.

c. Use the patterns in the table to help you write this product in expanded form: $(x - a)(x + a) = \underline{\ ?\ }$

Factored Form	Expanded Form
$(x - 2)(x + 2)$	?
$(x - 3)(x + 3)$	?
$(x - 5)(x + 5)$	?

Describe how these trinomials are different from the other trinomials in this section. Then factor each trinomial.

30. $2x^2 - x - 6$ **31.** $3x^2 - 9x + 6$ **32.** $2x^2 + 6x + 6$

33. **Group Activity** Work with another student.

$x^2 + 4x + 4$
$x^2 + 6x + 9$
$x^2 + 8x + 16$
$x^2 + 10x + 25$

  a. Discuss any patterns you see in the four trinomials shown at the right. Describe the patterns using mathematical terms such as *coefficient* and *constant*.

  b. Use algebra tiles to build a rectangle for each of the four trinomials.

  c. Describe anything special you notice about the rectangles you built.

  d. Express the area of each rectangle as a product.

  e. Why do you think the trinomials are called *perfect square trinomials*?

  f. Write two more perfect square trinomials and factor them.

Expand each product. *(Section 10-6)*

34. $(x + 2)(x + 6)$ **35.** $(x - 7)(x + 4)$ **36.** $(x + 8)(x - 5)$

Solve. *(Sections 2-7, 2-9)*

37. $9x + 12 = 4$ **38.** $x^2 = 144$ **39.** $x^2 = 28$

Evaluate each expression when $a = 3$, $b = 2$, $c = -5$, and $d = 9$.
(Section 1-2)

40. $b^2 - 4ac$ **41.** $-\dfrac{24}{2a}$ **42.** $-b + \sqrt{d}$

 Working on the Unit Project

43. **Baseball** An equation for the path of a baseball hit at a 45° angle with an initial speed of about 103 ft/s is $y = -0.003x^2 + x + 4$. In factored form, this equation can be approximated by $y = -0.003(x + 4)(x - 337)$.

  a. At what height off the ground is the ball hit? Which form of the equation helps you answer this question most easily?

  b. How far from home plate will the ball hit the ground? Which form of the equation helps you answer this question most easily?

  c. Suppose the left field fence is 325 ft from home plate and stands 10 ft high. Will a ball hit down the left field line go over the fence? Why or why not?

Section 10-8

Solving Quadratic Equations

FORMULA
For $\sqrt{\text{Success}}$

Focus

Solve problems about situations modeled by parabolas.

Talk it Over

1. **a.** Model the student-driver's rule of thumb with an equation. One car length is about 15 ft. Use d and s for the variables.

    b. Is your equation for this rule of thumb a linear function? How do you know?

    c. What is the control variable?

    d. What is the dependent variable?

2. **a.** Is the formula $d = 0.05s^2 + s$ a linear function? How do you know?

    b. What is the control variable?

    c. What is the dependent variable?

"My driver's education textbook contains this formula for the distance a car travels once the driver has decided to stop the car."

d = stopping distance in feet
s = speed in miles per hour
$d = 0.05s^2 + s$

"I use this rule of thumb for keeping far enough in back of the car ahead:

"Leave one car length between your car and the car in front for every 10 miles per hour of speed."

Driving School

TECHNOLOGY NOTE

When you graph a quadratic equation on a graphics calculator, you enter the equation in the form $y = ax^2 + bx + c$. Use the TRACE feature to find the coordinates of points on the graph. ◄

Suppose the stopping distance of a car is 60 ft. When you substitute 60 for d in the textbook formula $d = 0.05s^2 + s$, you produce the equation

$$60 = 0.05s^2 + s.$$

This new equation is a *quadratic equation*. A **quadratic equation** is an equation that can be written in the form

$$0 = ax^2 + bx + c$$

where a, b, and c are numbers and a is not equal to zero. A function that leads to a quadratic equation is called a *quadratic function*. The graph of a quadratic function is a parabola.

Talk it Over

3. **a.** Change $60 = 0.05s^2 + s$ to the form $0 = ax^2 + bx + c$.

 b. What are the values of a, b, and c in the equation you wrote?

4. How is a quadratic equation different from a linear equation?

Finding the Solutions of $0 = ax^2 + bx + c$

The solutions of a quadratic equation of the form $0 = ax^2 + bx + c$ are found where the graph of $y = ax^2 + bx + c$ crosses the x-axis.

X $\cdot$ *ab*

SOLVING A QUADRATIC EQUATION

➤ First rewrite the equation in the form $0 = ax^2 + bx + c$.

➤ Then find the x-intercepts of the graph of $y = ax^2 + bx + c$.

The x-intercepts are the solutions.

Section 10-3 includes a way to use the zero-product property to find the x-intercepts of a parabola without graphing. To use this method, you must first write the equation in factored form. Many equations cannot be factored. To find the solutions of equations like these, you can draw the graph of the equation.

Use the textbook formula $d = 0.05s^2 + s$. What is the fastest speed at which four car lengths is a safe following distance? One car length is 15 ft.

car in front   my car

Sample Response

Problem Solving Strategy: Use a formula

Step 1. Write an equation in the form $0 = ax^2 + bx + c$.

$$d = 0.05s^2 + s \qquad \longleftarrow \text{Use the textbook formula.}$$

$$4 \cdot 15 = 0.05s^2 + s \qquad \longleftarrow \text{Substitute four car lengths for } d.$$

$$60 = 0.05s^2 + s$$

$$60 - 60 = 0.05s^2 + s - 60 \qquad \longleftarrow \text{Subtract 60 from both sides.}$$

$$0 = 0.05s^2 + s - 60$$

Step 2. Replace s, the control variable, with x. Graph the function $y = 0.05x^2 + x - 60$. You might want to use a graphics calculator.

1 Make a table of values. Use enough values to show where the graph crosses the x-axis.

The sign of y changes when the graph crosses the x-axis.

2 Then plot the points and draw a smooth curve.

3 Look at the graph or zoom in. The x-intercepts are about 25 and −45.

$y = 0.05x^2 + x - 60$	
x	(x, y)
−50	(−50, 15)
−40	(−40, −20)
−30	(−30, −45)
−20	(−20, −60)
−10	(−10, −65)
0	(0, −60)
10	(10, −45)
20	(20, −20)
30	(30, 15)
40	(40, 60)

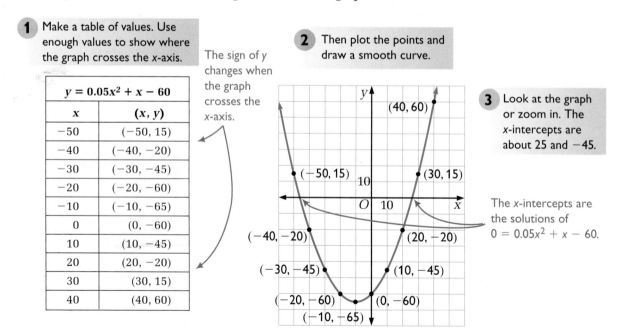

The x-intercepts are the solutions of $0 = 0.05x^2 + x - 60$.

The x-intercepts are about 25 and −45, but you cannot drive −45 mi/h. The fastest speed at which it is safe to drive four car lengths behind another car is about 25 mi/h.

BY THE WAY...

Carefully spinning any liquid in a pan forms a parabola-shaped surface. Try it yourself with water!

⟶ Now you are ready for:
Exs. 1–15 on pp. 603–604

Talk it Over

5. Is it safe to use the student-driver's rule of thumb at the speed found in the response to Sample 1? Why or why not?

6. Answer these questions about the equation and graph in Sample 1.

   a. Use the formula $x = -\dfrac{b}{2a}$ to write the equation of the line of symmetry of the graph.

   b. About how far is each of the x-intercepts from the point where the line of symmetry crosses the x-axis?

   c. Express each x-intercept in terms of the answers to parts (a) and (b).

Using the Quadratic Formula

Unless you have a graphics calculator or graphing software, solving a quadratic equation by graphing may take a long time. Also, it is often difficult to read the solutions from a hand-drawn graph accurately.

Another way to solve any quadratic equation is to use the *quadratic formula*. The **quadratic formula** uses the values a, b, and c in the equation $0 = ax^2 + bx + c$ to find the values of x that are solutions of the equation.

QUADRATIC FORMULA

For an equation in the form $0 = ax^2 + bx + c$, there are two solutions.

x-coordinate of the vertex, which is on the line of symmetry ⟶

⟵ distance from each x-intercept to the line of symmetry

$$x = -\frac{b}{2a} \pm \frac{\sqrt{b^2 - 4ac}}{2a}$$

"$\pm$" means there are two solutions.

The solutions are:

$$x = -\frac{b}{2a} + \frac{\sqrt{b^2 - 4ac}}{2a} \quad \text{and} \quad x = -\frac{b}{2a} - \frac{\sqrt{b^2 - 4ac}}{2a}$$

Use the quadratic formula to solve $0 = 0.05x^2 + x - 60$. Round decimal answers to the nearest tenth.

Sample Response

Step 1. Decide what values to use for a, b, and c.

$$0 = 0.05x^2 + x - 60$$

$$0 = 0.05x^2 + 1x + (-60)$$

$$a = 0.05, \ b = 1, \text{ and } c = -60$$

Step 2. Write the quadratic formula.

$$x = -\frac{b}{2a} \pm \frac{\sqrt{b^2 - 4ac}}{2a}$$

$$x = -\frac{1}{2(0.05)} \pm \frac{\sqrt{1^2 - 4(0.05)(-60)}}{2(0.05)}$$

←── Substitute 0.05 for a, 1 for b, and −60 for c.

$$x = -10 \pm \frac{\sqrt{13}}{0.10}$$

$$x \approx -10 \pm \frac{3.61}{0.10}$$ ←── Use a calculator to find $\sqrt{13}$.

$$x \approx -10 \pm 36.1$$

$$x \approx -10 + 36.1 \qquad or \qquad x \approx -10 - 36.1$$

$$x \approx 26.1 \qquad\qquad or \qquad x \approx -46.1$$

The solutions are about 26.1 and about −46.1

BY THE WAY...

The solution of a quadratic equation appears in the ninth and final chapter of the ancient Chinese book *The Nine Chapters on the Mathematical Art.*

This 2000-year-old book covers 600 years of mathematics in China.

九章算術

Check

$$60 = 0.05x^2 + x$$ ←── Use the *original* equation. ──→ $$60 = 0.05x^2 + x$$

$$60 \overset{?}{=} 0.05(26.1)^2 + 26.1$$ ←── Substitute for x. ──→ $$60 \overset{?}{=} 0.05(-46.1)^2 + (-46.1)$$

$$60 \approx 60.16 \ ✔$$ $$\qquad\qquad 60 \approx 60.16 \ ✔$$

Talk it Over

7. Why is the expression $0.05x^2 + x$ not exactly equal to 60 when 26.1 and −46.1 are substituted for x?

8. Which answer in Sample 2 is a solution to the problem situation in Sample 1? Did the graph in Sample 1 produce a good enough estimate for the problem situation? Why or why not?

THREE METHODS FOR SOLVING QUADRATIC EQUATIONS

➤ **Factoring**
Fastest method for equations that are easy to factor.

➤ **Graphing**
Works well if you are using a graphics calculator or graphing software.

➤ **Quadratic Formula**
Useful when factoring and graphing are not practical.
You will need a scientific calculator.

Look Back ◄───────────────────

Which method would you use to solve each of these quadratic equations? Why?

$$0 = x^2 + 5x - 36 \qquad 0 = 3.4x^2 - 2.3x - 8.6$$

➤ Now you are ready for:
Exs. 16–35 on pp. 604–605

10-8 Exercises and Problems

BY THE WAY...

NASA uses a plane flying in a parabolic path to create a weightless environment for astronaut training and some scientific experiments.

1. **Open-ended** Different cars and road conditions may produce different stopping distance formulas. Describe how each of these conditions could affect the stopping distance.

   a. how quickly the driver begins to brake (reaction time)

   b. the condition of the road

   c. the weight of the car

Use the stopping distance formula $d = 0.05s^2 + s$.

2. What is the stopping distance for a speed of 15 mi/h?

3. What is the stopping distance for a speed of 55 mi/h?

4. What is the fastest speed at which 175 ft is a safe following distance?

5. What is the fastest speed at which five car lengths is a safe following distance? (A car length is about 15 ft.)

Use the graph of $y = x^2 + 6x + 8$ at the right.

6. a. What are the x-intercepts of the graph?

   b. What are the solutions of the equation $0 = x^2 + 6x + 8$?

7. a. Where does the graph cross the line $y = 3$?

   b. What are the solutions of the equation $3 = x^2 + 6x + 8$?

Make a graph to solve each quadratic equation.

8. $0 = x^2 + 4x + 4$

9. $-4 = -4.8x^2 - 6x$

10. $10 = 3x^2 - 4x + 8$

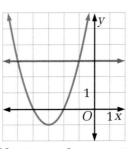

11. **Marine Biology** When dolphins are traveling very fast, they use less energy if they leap. The length and height of a dolphin's leap are related to the dolphin's speed. The formula for the height of one dolphin's leap was found to be $y = -0.4x^2 + x$.

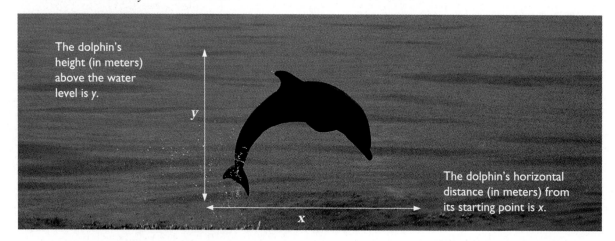

The dolphin's height (in meters) above the water level is y.

The dolphin's horizontal distance (in meters) from its starting point is x.

   a. How high above the water is this dolphin when $x = 2$?

   b. How far is this dolphin from its starting point when it is 0.6 m high?

For Exercises 12–14, use the graph.

12. What are the x-intercepts of the graph?

13. What is the equation of the line of symmetry?

14. Which equation matches the graph?

   A. $y = (x + 1)(x + 5)$ **B.** $y = (x - 1)(x + 5)$ **C.** $y = (x - 1)(x - 5)$

15. **a.** Rewrite the equation $12 = x^2 + x - 8$ in the form $0 = ax^2 + bx + c$.

   b. Factor the equation you wrote in part (a).

   c. Use your answer to part (b) to find the solutions of the equation.

16. **Reading** In the quadratic formula, what does the $\pm$ symbol mean?

17. **a.** Solve the equation $0 = x^2 - 2x - 8$ by factoring.

   b. Solve the equation $0 = x^2 - 2x - 8$ using the quadratic formula.

   c. **Writing** Compare your answers to part (a) and part (b). Which method do you think is better for this equation?

Solve each quadratic equation. Tell which method you used.

18. $0 = x^2 - 4$

19. $0 = -5x^2 + 3x + 2$

20. $8 = x^2 + 6x$

21. $x^2 - 10x = -21$

22. $2 = -0.036x^2 + x + 9$

23. $0.5x^2 - 0.5x - 4 = 6$

24. The height of a square prism is 6 in.

   a. Write an expression for the surface area of the prism.

   b. The surface area of the prism is 176 in.^{2}. Write an equation in terms of x for the surface area.

   c. Solve the equation you wrote in part (b). What does your solution represent in terms of the prism?

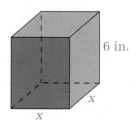

6 in.

25. **Group Activity** Work in a group of six students. Divide the group into two teams.

   ➤ Students on Team 1 solve equations (a)–(c) by graphing.

   ➤ Students on Team 2 solve the equations with the quadratic formula.

   ➤ When both teams are finished, compare solutions. Look for any errors and correct them.

Quadratic Equations
a. $6 = 5x^2 + 8x + 2$
b. $15 = 3x^2 - 4x + 10$
c. $-3 = 4x^2 + 4x - 2$

Ongoing **ASSESSMENT**

26. **Open-ended** The equation $y = -4.9x^2 + 3.03x + 0.22$ gives the height in meters of a table tennis ball above the table. The height is represented by y and the number of seconds the ball is in the air is represented by x.

   a. Suppose you want to know how long it takes for the ball to reach a height of 0.3 m. Do you think that factoring, graphing, or the quadratic formula is the best method for finding the answer? Explain your choice.

   b. Use the method you chose to find the answer.

Review **PREVIEW**

Factor each trinomial. *(Section 10-7)*

27. $x^2 - 8x + 7$ 28. $x^2 + x - 20$ 29. $x^2 - 2x - 24$

30. Use the vertex and the intercepts to sketch the graph of the equation $y = x^2 + 7x - 18$.

Find the x-intercepts and the y-intercept of the graph of each equation. *(Sections 8-1, 10-5)*

31. $y = -2x + 1$ 32. $y = 3x$ 33. $y = x^2 - 3x$

 Working on the Unit Project

34. An equation for the path of a baseball hit at a 50° angle with an initial speed of 80 ft/s is $y = -0.006x^2 + 1.192x + 4$. How far from home plate will the ball first hit the ground?

35. When a baseball is hit at a 45° angle, the equation $r = \dfrac{v^2}{32}$ gives the *range*, how far away the ball hits the ground. In the equation, v represents the initial speed of the ball in feet per second. Suppose the range is 300 ft. What is the initial speed?

Completing the Unit Project

Now you are ready to write your math story. It should include these things.

➤ a setting, characters, and a plot

➤ at least three situations modeled by equations or formulas you studied earlier in this course

➤ at least one situation modeled by a baseball equation given in the "Working on the Unit Project" exercises

➤ at least one situation modeled by a soccer equation in the table on page 545

Look Back ←

Which form of the baseball and soccer path equations was most helpful in finding how far the ball traveled or how high it traveled? What difference did you find between the soccer equations when the ball was kicked and when it was struck with the head?

Alternative Projects

Project 1: Mickey Mantle's Record Home Run

On May 22, 1963, Mickey Mantle hit a home run in Yankee Stadium that nearly went out of the park. This is reportedly the closest anyone has ever come to hitting an out-of-the-park home run in this stadium.

Find out the details about this home run. Model the path of the ball with an equation and a graph. About how far from home plate would the ball have landed if it had not hit anything before it reached the ground?

Project 2: Making Parabolas from Straight Lines

Parabolas can be formed by straight lines. Research how this is done—with paper folding, paper and pencil, or string. Then create a design that contains at least three parabolas formed by straight lines.

1. The diagram shows a figure in blue and its image in red. **10-1**

   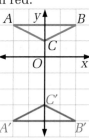

   a. What is the line of reflection?

   b. What is the relationship between $\overline{BB'}$ and the line of reflection?

   c. How far from the line of reflection is point C? point C'?

   d. How does the orientation of $\triangle ABC$ compare with the orientation of its image?

Tell whether each transformation is a reflection. If it is, trace the figure and draw the line of reflection. If it is not, tell why not.

2.   3.

4. Copy $\triangle ABC$ from Exercise 1. Reflect it over the x-axis. Write the coordinates of the vertices of its image.

5. Tell how to transform the graph of $y = x^2$ in order to produce the graph of $y = x^2 - 15$. **10-2**

6. Find the equation of the line of symmetry and the coordinates of the vertex for the graph of $y = (x + 8)^2$.

7. Graph the parabola $y = (x + 3)(2x - 1)$. Plot enough points to show the shape of the curve. **10-3**

8. Without graphing, find the x-intercepts and the y-intercept of the graph of $y = (x - 2)(x + 6)$.

Simplify. **10-4**

9. $b^2 \cdot b \cdot b^7$ 10. $-6x^2 \cdot 5x^2y^3$ 11. $(m^4)^7$ 12. $(-5ab^2)^3$

13. Expand the expression $2x(3x - 5)$. **10-5**

14. Factor the right side of the equation $y = 7x^2 + 21x$ completely. Then find the x-intercepts and y-intercept of the graph of the equation.

15. **Open-ended** Write the equation of a parabola that has x-intercepts at -3 and 0.

16. Expand the product $(x - 3)(x - 6)$. **10-6**

17. Without graphing, find each feature of the graph of the equation $y = x^2 - 10x - 4$.

   a. the equation of the line of symmetry

   b. the coordinates of the vertex

   c. the y-intercept

Factor each trinomial that can be factored using integers. For each trinomial that cannot be factored, explain why not. 10-7

18. $x^2 - 10x + 16$ **19.** $x^2 - 3x - 18$ **20.** $x^2 + 6x - 8$

21. Use the vertex, the x-intercepts, and the y-intercept to sketch the graph of the equation $y = x^2 + 2x - 15$.

22. Writing Write about the similarities and differences between solving quadratic equations and solving linear equations. 10-8

23. Solve the quadratic equation $0.4 = 2.4x^2 - 0.06x - 1$. Tell which method you used.

24. Self-evaluation You have learned several methods for solving a quadratic equation.

  a. Describe the method you like the most. What do you like about it?

  b. Describe the method you like the least. Why is it your least favorite?

25. Group Activity Work in a group of three students. Sit in a circle.

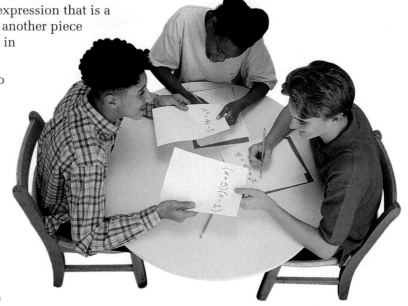

  a. Each person should write an expression that is a product of two binomials. On another piece of paper, write the expression in expanded form.

  b. Pass your expanded version to the person on your left, and the factored version to the person on your right. You will receive two pieces of paper yourself.

  c. Factor the expanded expression you receive. Write the factored version below the expanded expression.

  d. Expand the factored expression you receive. Write the expanded version above the factored expression.

  e. As a group, look at all your pieces of paper and compare them to see if your work is correct. There should be three pairs of matching papers.

  f. Choose one of the expressions. Suppose it is the rule for a function. Draw a graph of the function. On your graph, label the coordinates of the x-intercepts, the y-intercept, and the vertex.

IDEAS AND (FORMULAS) $=x^2$

ALGEBRA

> You can use the zero-product property and algebra to find the x- and y-intercepts of a parabola from its equation. *(p. 564)*

> The product of powers rule says that to multiply powers that have the same base, you add the exponents *(p. 569)*:
> $$a^m \cdot a^n = a^{m+n}$$

> The power of a power rule says that to find a power of a power, you multiply the exponents *(p. 570)*:
> $$(a^m)^n = a^{m \cdot n}$$

> The power of a product rule says that to find a power of a product, you find that power of each factor and then multiply *(p. 571)*:
> $$(ab)^n = a^n \cdot b^n$$

GEOMETRY

> You can use the quadratic formula
> $$x = -\frac{b}{2a} \pm \frac{\sqrt{b^2 - 4ac}}{2a}$$
> to solve a quadratic equation of the form $0 = ax^2 + bx + c$. *(p. 601)*

> A reflection produces an image that is congruent to the original, but reversed in orientation. Any segment that connects corresponding points on the original figure and its image is perpendicular to the line of reflection and is intersected at its midpoint by the line of reflection. *(p. 548)*

> The graph of $y = -x^2$ is a reflection of the graph of $y = x^2$ over the x-axis. *(p. 555)*

> You can draw some parabolas by translating the graph of $y = x^2$ up, down, left, or right. The numbers in the equation tell you the length and the direction of the translation. *(p. 556)*

> The line of symmetry of the graph of $y = ax^2 + bx + c$ is the line $x = -\frac{b}{2a}$. *(p. 585)*

> You can use the line of symmetry, the vertex, and the x- and y-intercepts to sketch the graph of $y = ax^2 + bx + c$. *(p. 594)*

Key Terms

- **reflection** (p. 548)
- **x-axis** (p. 550)
- **vertex** (p. 555)
- **factored form** (p. 577)
- **monomial** (p. 578)
- **quadratic equation** (p. 599)

- **line of reflection** (p. 548)
- **y-axis** (p. 550)
- **x-intercept** (p. 563)
- **expanded form** (p. 577)
- **factored completely** (p. 578)
- **quadratic formula** (p. 601)

- **orientation** (p. 548)
- **parabola** (p. 555)
- **y-intercept** (p. 563)
- **binomial** (p. 578)
- **trinomial** (p. 584)

Contents of Student Resources

611-619   Technology Handbook

- Using a Graphics Calculator 611
- Performing Calculations 611
- Displaying Graphs 613
- Reading a Graph 615
- Taking a Closer Look at a Graph 616
- Displaying Statistical Graphs 618
- Using a Spreadsheet 619

620-639   Extra Practice for Units 1-10

640-665   Toolbox

- **Numbers and Operations**
  - 640 Integers • Skills 1-4
  - 645 One-Step Equations • Skills 5 and 6
  - 648 Factors • Skills 7 and 8
  - 650 Fractions • Skills 9 and 10
  - 653 Percent • Skills 11-15
- **Measurement**
  - 657 Angles • Skill 16
  - 658 Perimeter • Skill 17
  - 658 Area • Skill 18
  - 659 Volume • Skill 19
- **Graphing**
  - 660 A Coordinate System • Skills 20 and 21
  - 661 Data Displays • Skills 22-25
- **Problem Solving**
  - 664 Skills 26 and 27

666-669   Tables

- Measures 666
- Symbols 667
- Squares and Square Roots 668
- Trigonometric Ratios 669

670-673   Appendices

- Domain and Range 670
- Slope and y-Intercept 672

674-691   Glossary and Index

Technology Handbook

Using a Graphics Calculator

This handbook introduces you to the basic features of most graphics calculators. Because there are so many different kinds of calculators, this handbook does not always give specific keystrokes. Check your calculator's instruction manual for any details not provided here.

Performing Calculations

➤ ### The Keyboard

Look closely at your calculator's keyboard. Notice that most keys serve more than one purpose. Each key is labeled with its primary purpose, and labels for any secondary purposes appear somewhere near the key. You may need to press **2nd**, **SHIFT**, or **ALPHA** to use a key for a secondary purpose.

Number	Square of the Number
X	X^2
-3	9
-2.5	6.25
-2	4
-1.7	
-1.3	
-1	
-0.5	
0	
0.5	
1	
1.3	
1.7	
2	
2.5	
3	

Examples of using the **x^2** key:

Press **x^2** to square a number.

Press **2nd** and then **x^2** to take a square root.

Press **ALPHA** and then **x^2** to get the letter I.

➤ **The Home Screen**

Your calculator has a "home screen" where you can do calculations. You can usually enter a calculation on a graphics calculator just as you would write it on a piece of paper. This is unlike a scientific calculator, where you often must work backwards. For example, compare the steps for calculating $\sqrt{2}$:

Graphics Calculator

$\sqrt{2}$ 1.414213562

1. Enter $\sqrt{}$.

2. Enter 2.

3. Press ENTER or EXE .

Scientific Calculator

1. Enter 2.

2

2. Enter $\sqrt{}$.

1.414213562

Shown below are other things to remember as you enter calculations on your graphics calculator.

2(3)

3 − ⁻2   6

$\sqrt[3]{8}$ 5

          2

The calculator may recognize implied multiplication.

The calculator has a subtraction key, [−] , and a negation key, [(−)] . If you use these incorrectly, you will get an error message.

You may need to get a cube root (or other operation that is not often used) from a MATH menu.

Try This

1. Use your calculator to find the value of each expression.

a. $(-1.5)^2$ **b.** $-2(33 - 47)$ **c.** $\tan 45°$

2. a. Which calculation, $-15 + 29 \div 2$ or $(-15 + 29) \div 2$, gives the correct value for the average of –15 and 29?

b. Find the average of -15, 29, and 43.

3. Find $\sqrt{ab}$ when $a = 32$ and $b = 128$.

Displaying Graphs

➤ **The Viewing Window**

When you use a graphics calculator to display graphs, think of the screen as a "viewing window" that lets you look at a portion of the coordinate plane.

On many calculators, the standard viewing window uses values from −10 to 10 on both the x- and y-axes. You can adjust the viewing window by pressing the RANGE or WINDOW key and entering new values for the window variables.

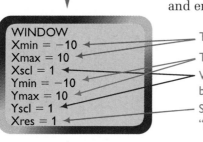

WINDOW
Xmin = −10
Xmax = 10
Xscl = 1
Ymin = −10
Ymax = 10
Yscl = 1
Xres = 1

The x-axis will be shown for $-10 \le x \le 10$.

The y-axis will be shown for $-10 \le y \le 10$.

With scale variables set to equal 1, tick marks will be 1 unit apart on both axes.

Some calculators have a resolution variable. This controls how "smooth" the graph will look.

➤ **Entering and Graphing a Function**

To graph a function, enter its equation and set the variables for an appropriate viewing window. (You may need to experiment to find a good viewing window.) The graph of $y = \frac{1}{2}x + 3$ is shown using the standard viewing window.

$Y_1 = (1/2)X + 3$
$Y_2 =$
$Y_3 =$
$Y_4 =$
$Y_5 =$
$Y_6 =$
$Y_7 =$
$Y_8 =$

Use parentheses when entering the function. If you enter $y = 1/2x + 3$ instead, the calculator may interpret the equation as $y = \frac{1}{2x} + 3$.

➤ **Function Form**

To graph an equation, you must enter it in the form $y = \ldots$, which is called *function form* because y is expressed as a function of x. For example, before graphing $3x - 4y = 8$, first solve the equation for y. Since $y = \frac{3}{4}x - 2$, enter either $y = (3/4)x - 2$ or $y = 0.75x - 2$.

Try This

4. Enter and graph each equation separately. Use the standard viewing window. You may need to put the equation in function form first.

   a. $y = 3x + 1$ **b.** $x + 2y = 4$ **c.** $y = |x|$ **d.** $y = \frac{5}{x}$

5. Find a good viewing window for the graph of $y = 65 - 3x$. Be sure your window shows where the graph crosses both axes.

➤ **Squaring the Screen**

A "square screen" is a viewing window with equal unit spacing on the two axes. For example, the graph of $y = x$ is shown for two different windows.

Standard Viewing Window

Square Screen Window

On a square screen, the line $y = x$ makes a 45° angle with the x-axis.

On many graphics calculators, the ratio of the screen's height to its width is about 2 to 3. Your calculator may have a feature that gives you a square screen. If not, choose values for the window variables that make the "length" of the y-axis about two-thirds the "length" of the x-axis:

$$(\text{Ymax} - \text{Ymin}) \approx \tfrac{2}{3}(\text{Xmax} - \text{Xmin})$$

Reading a Graph

➤ **The TRACE Feature**

After a graph is displayed, you can use the calculator's TRACE feature. When you press [TRACE], a flashing cursor appears on the graph. The *x*- and *y*-coordinates of the cursor's location are shown at the bottom of the screen. Press the left- and right-arrow keys to move the TRACE cursor along the graph.

The TRACE cursor is at the point (2.3684211, 2.3684211) on the graph of $y = x$.

X = 2.3684211 Y = 2.3684211

➤ **Friendly Windows**

As you press the right-arrow key while tracing a graph, you may notice that the *x*-coordinate increases by "unfriendly" increments. Your calculator may allow you to control the *x*-increment, Δx, directly. If not, you can control it indirectly by choosing an appropriate Xmax for a given Xmin. For example, on a TI-82 or TI-83 graphics calculator, choose Xmax so that

$$\text{Xmax} = \text{Xmin} + 94\Delta x.$$

This number depends upon the calculator you are using.

Suppose you want Δx to equal 0.1. If Xmin $= -5$, then set Xmax equal to $-5 + 94(0.1)$, or 4.4. This gives a "friendly window" where the TRACE cursor's *x*-coordinate will increase by 0.1 each time you press the right-arrow key.

WINDOW
Xmin $= -5$ ⟵
Xmax $= 4.4$ ⟵
Xscl $= 1$
Ymin $= -10$
Ymax $= 10$
Yscl $= 1$
Xres $= 1$

6. Graph the equation $y = x^2 + 2x - 1$. Choose a friendly window where $\Delta x = 0.1$. Use the TRACE feature to determine, to the nearest tenth, the x-coordinate of each of the two points where the graph crosses the x-axis.

➤ **The TABLE Feature**

Instead of tracing the graph of an equation, you may wish to examine a table of values. Not all calculators have a TABLE feature. Check to see if yours does.

The screen shows a table of values for $y = x^2 + 2x - 1$.

Notice that the y-values change sign between $x = 0.4$ and $x = 0.5$

Taking a Closer Look at a Graph
➤ **The ZOOM Feature**

Suppose you are interested in the point where the graph of the equation $y = x^2 + 2x - 1$ crosses the positive x-axis. Tracing the graph shows that the x-coordinate of the point is between 0.4 and 0.5.

Move the TRACE cursor to a point just below the x-axis. The y-coordinate of this point is negative but close to 0.

Move the TRACE cursor to a point just above the x-axis. The y-coordinate of this point is positive but close to 0.

To get a closer look at the point of interest, you can use the ZOOM feature. Your calculator may have more than one way to zoom. A common way is to put a "zoom box" around the point. The calculator will then draw what's inside the box at full-screen size.

Define a "zoom box" . . .

X = 1   Y = −1.746032

and then zoom.

X = .41578947 Y = .00445983

You create a "zoom box" by fixing first one corner and then the opposite corner of the box. (See your calculator's instruction manual for details.)

Tracing the new graph reveals that the graph crosses the x-axis between $x = 0.41$ and $x = 0.42$. Repeated zooming and tracing give better estimates.

Try This

7. Try zooming in on the point where the graph of $y = x^2 + 2x - 1$ crosses the negative x-axis. Between what two values, to the nearest hundredth, does the x-coordinate of the point lie?

➤ **Solving Problems with a Graphics Calculator**

Suppose a school's student council sponsors a dance that costs $248 for a band, decorations, and so on. The council plans to charge $3.50 per couple attending the dance. How many couples must attend the dance for the student council to recover its costs?

One way to solve this problem is to graph the equation $y = 3.5x - 248$, since the council's profit or loss, y, is equal to its income ($3.50 per couple times x couples) minus its costs ($248). Where the graph crosses the x-axis tells you how many couples must attend for the council to *break even*.

X = 71   Y = .5

Tracing the graph shows that 71 couples must attend for the council to break even.

Try This

8. Suppose the student council wants the dance to make a profit of $100. Use your calculator to find how many couples must attend.

Displaying Statistical Graphs

➤ ## Histograms, Line Graphs, and Box-and-Whisker Plots

Many graphics calculators can display histograms, line graphs, and sometimes even box-and-whisker plots of data that you enter. For example, the histogram below displays the data about the readers of *Galaxy*, a science magazine (see pages 150–151).

Readers of
galaxy
Magazine

Age group	Frequency
10–14	1110
15–19	3398
20–24	4344
25–29	3215
30–34	332
35–39	112

➤ ## Scatter Plots and Curve Fitting

Curve fitting is the process of finding an equation that describes a set of ordered pairs. Often, the first step is to graph the paired data in a scatter plot. For example, the scatter plot below displays the data for an Olympic event (see page 416). It also shows a *regression line* that the calculator fit to the data.

Men's Winning Times in Olympic 400 m Freestyle Swimming

Year	Country of winner	Years after 1960	Time (seconds)
1960	AUS	0	258.3
1964	USA	4	252.2
1968	USA	8	249.0
1972	USA	12	240.27
1976	USA	16	231.93
1980	USSR	20	231.31
1984	USA	24	231.23
1988	E.GER	28	226.95
1992	UT	32	225.00
1996	NZE	36	227.97

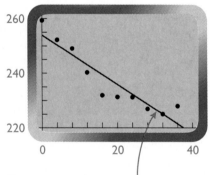

The equation of the regression line is $y = 254 - 0.911x$ where x is the years after 1960 and y is the winning time.

➤ Using a Spreadsheet

In addition to using a graphics calculator, you may want to use a computer with a spreadsheet program. A spreadsheet can help you solve a problem like this one: Suppose you want to buy a portable CD player that costs $85, including tax. You already have $11 and can save $5 per week. After how many weeks can you buy the player? (See Sample 1 in Section 5-1.)

A spreadsheet is made up of cells named by a column letter and a row number, like A3 or B4. You can enter a label, a number, or a formula into a cell.

	A	B
1	Week number	Total saved
2	0	11
3	= + A2 + 1	= + B2 + 5
4	= + A3 + 1	= + B3 + 5
5	= + A4 + 1	= + B4 + 5
6	= + A5 + 1	= + B5 + 5
7	= + A6 + 1	= + B6 + 5
8	= + A7 + 1	= + B7 + 5
9	= + A8 + 1	= + B8 + 5
10	= + A9 + 1	= + B9 + 5
11	= + A10 + 1	= + B10 + 5
12	= + A11 + 1	= + B11 + 5
13	= + A12 + 1	= + B12 + 5
14	= + A13 + 1	= + B13 + 5
15	= + A14 + 1	= + B14 + 5
16	= + A15 + 1	= + B15 + 5
17	= + A16 + 1	= + B16 + 5

CD Savings

Cell B1 contains the label "Total saved."

Cell B2 contains the number 11.

Cell B3 contains the formula "=+B2+5." This formula tells the computer to take the number in cell B2, add 5 to it, and put the result in cell B3. (Likewise, the formula in cell A3 tells the computer to take the number in cell A2, add 1 to it, and put the result in cell A3.)

Instead of typing a formula into each cell individually, you can use the spreadsheet's copy and fill commands.

	A	B
1	Week number	Total saved
2	0	11
3	1	16
4	2	21
5	3	26
6	4	31
7	5	36
8	6	41
9	7	46
10	8	51
11	9	56
12	10	61
13	11	66
14	12	71
15	13	76
16	14	81
17	15	86

CD Savings

In this spreadsheet, the computer has replaced all the formulas with calculated values. You can have the computer draw a scatter plot with a line connecting the plotted points. As you can see, you will have enough money to buy the portableCD player after 15 weeks.

CD Savings

Extra Practice

Unit 1

Evaluate each variable expression for $a = 5$, $b = 2$, and $c = 15$. **1-2**

1. $9 - a$
2. $7b$
3. $\frac{1}{3}c$
4. $8 \div b$
5. bc
6. $a + c$
7. $\frac{c}{a}$
8. $c - b$
9. $2c - a$
10. $3a - c$
11. $4a + 3b$
12. $ab + c$

Write as a power of ten. **1-3**

13. $10 \cdot 10 \cdot 10$
14. $10 \cdot 10$
15. $10 \cdot 10 \cdot 10 \cdot 10$
16. $10^8 \cdot 10^5$
17. $10^7 \cdot 10$
18. $10^3 \cdot 10^3$
19. $\frac{10^{12}}{10^9}$
20. $\frac{10^{50}}{10}$
21. $\frac{10^4}{10^4}$
22. $10^2 \cdot 10^3 \cdot 10^4$
23. $10^8 \cdot 10^{15} \cdot 10^{11}$
24. $\frac{10^{14}}{10^{10}} \cdot 10^5$

Evaluate each variable expression for $x = 4$, $y = 8$, and $z = 3$. **1-4**

25. $x + yz$
26. $(x + y)z$
27. $9y - xz$
28. $xy - z^2$
29. $(xy - z)^2$
30. $z + 10y \div x$
31. $x^2 + 4x + 3$
32. $z^2 + z + 7$
33. $3y^2 + 9y + 5$
34. $2z^3 + 5z + 6$
35. $y^3 + 5y^2$
36. $x^3 - 3x + 8$

Rewrite each expression without parentheses. **1-5**

37. $4(a - b)$
38. $9(x + 3)$
39. $2(2r + s)$
40. $3(5x - y)$
41. $\frac{1}{2}(4x^2 - 8)$
42. $\frac{1}{6}(12b^2 + 36b)$

Combine like terms if possible. If not, explain why. **1-5**

43. $7a + 5a$
44. $k + 3k$
45. $9d - d$
46. $x^2 + 8x$
47. $5x + 3y$
48. $3k^2 + 2k + 1$
49. $3r + r^3 + 4r + 6$
50. $m + 2m^2 + 7m + 3$
51. $x^3 + 5x^2 + 7x + 1$
52. $2b + 4(b + 5) + 7$
53. $8x + 6(x + 3) - 9$
54. $2(a + 1) + 5(a + 2)$

Name the congruent polygons. Then list the pairs of congruent sides. 1-6

55.

56.

57.

58.

59.

60.

What name best describes the quadrilateral? 1-7

61.

62.

63.

64.

65.

66.

67.

68.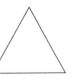

Draw all lines of symmetry for each figure or write *no symmetry*. 1-7

69.

70.

71.

72.

73.

74.

Unit 2

Evaluate each expression for the given values of the variables. `2-2`

1. a. $7 - x$ when $x = -8$ **b.** $7x$ when $x = -8$

2. a. $y^2 + 3y$ when $y = 5$ **b.** $y^2 + 3y$ when $y = -5$

3. a. $-k$ when $k = -\dfrac{7}{8}$ **b.** $|k|$ when $k = -\dfrac{7}{8}$

4. a. $rs - s$ when $r = -4$ and $s = 6$ **b.** $rs - s$ when $r = -4$ and $s = -6$

5. a. $m^2 \div n$ when $m = -8$ and $n = -2$ **b.** $m^2 + n$ when $m = -8$ and $n = -2$

6. a. $at - 16t^2$ when $a = 10$ and $t = 5$ **b.** $-4.9t^2 + at$ when $a = 10$ and $t = 5$

Write each number in scientific notation. `2-3`

7. 0.057 **8.** $2{,}350{,}000$

9. $64{,}970$ **10.** 0.000091

11. 48 billion **12.** 8 ten thousandths

Simplify. Write each number in decimal notation. `2-3`

13. $(9 \times 10^5)(4 \times 10^2)$ **14.** $10^{-6} \cdot 10^6$

15. 10^{-3} **16.** $\dfrac{1.8 \times 10^7}{3.0 \times 10^5}$

17. $\dfrac{1.2 \times 10^4}{2.5 \times 10^8}$ **18.** $\dfrac{3 \times 10^4}{6 \times 10^4}$

In the diagram, $\angle COD$ is a right angle, $\overrightarrow{OB}$ bisects $\angle GOC$, and $\angle AOG = 60°$. Use angle relationships to find the measure of each angle. `2-5`

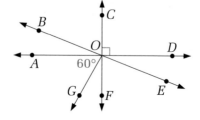

19. $\angle FOG$ **20.** $\angle GOC$

21. $\angle BOG$ **22.** $\angle DOE$

23. $\angle EOF$ **24.** $\angle AOB$

25. $\angle COE$ **26.** $\angle BOF$

Find the unknown angle measures. `2-5`

27.

28.

29.

Simplify if possible. If not, write *not possible.* 2-6

30. $(7a)(-2b)$ **31.** $\frac{1}{2}(8r^2)$ **32.** $x \cdot 2x \cdot 3x$

33. $3s - 4st - 2t + 7s$ **34.** $2a^2 + 4ab + b^2 - 7a$

35. $4x^3 - x^2 + 7x + x^2 - 3x - 1$ **36.** $y^2 + 2y - y^3 + 7y^2$

37. $-4w + 5k - 7k + w + 3wk$ **38.** $s^2t^2 - 8st + 7 + 7s$

Solve. 2-7

39. $d + 3 = 10$ **40.** $-2x = -2$

41. $m - 8 = 0$ **42.** $7n = -21$

43. $8 = r + 18$ **44.** $3 - y = 5$

45. $2k + 19 = 19$ **46.** $5a - 9 = 11$

47. $1 + 8t = 57$ **48.** $x + x + 9 = 17$

49. $35 + 90 + b = 180$ **50.** $v + v + 70 = 180$

Solve. 2-8

51. $\frac{x}{3} - 1 = 5$ **52.** $3 = 0.04j + 1$

53. $-7 = 2 - \frac{y}{5}$ **54.** $2.5 - 7.5m = 3.1$

55. $\frac{z}{8} + 7 = 2$ **56.** $24 = 18 + 15r$

57. In a recent season, the Houston Astros had as many wins as losses. They played 162 games in all. How many wins did they have?

58. Rory bought a 9-volt battery for $2.79 and a three-pack of video tapes on sale. The total cost excluding tax was $8.76. Find the cost of each tape.

Estimate each number within a range of two integers. Then use a calculator to find each number to the nearest hundredth. 2-9

59. $\sqrt{30}$ **60.** $\sqrt{105}$

61. $\sqrt[3]{70}$ **62.** $\sqrt[3]{200}$

Find the square roots of each number. 2-9

63. $\frac{64}{49}$ **64.** 0.81

65. 625 **66.** 0.09

67. Write the numbers in order from least to greatest:
$\sqrt{87}$, 9.4, and $\sqrt[3]{800}$.

Unit 3

For each data set, find the range, the mean, the median, the mode(s), and the outlier(s) when they exist. 3-2

1. Number of touchdowns in a season by leading football scorers:
   11, 11, 11, 11, 13, 14, 15, 19

2. Per season points scored by Smythe Division NHL teams:
   39, 74, 81, 82, 84, 96

3. Number of football passes caught in a season by leading receivers:
   64, 67, 68, 68, 69, 77, 78, 84, 93, 108

4. Wins in a season by National League baseball teams
   (consider the data as a single set):
   Eastern Division—73, 75, 76, 76, 89, 92, 96
   Western Division—64, 72, 72, 77, 86, 90, 96

Solve. 3-2

5. $\frac{x - 8}{6} = 9$

6. $\frac{x + 93}{2} = 96$

7. $\frac{275 + x}{4} = 89$

8. $\frac{x + 25 + 56}{3} = 30$

9. $\frac{2x + 1}{4} = 1.5$

10. $\frac{3x - 7}{5} = 4$

Graph each inequality on a number line. 3-3

11. $x \geq -2$

12. $x < 5$

13. $-3.5 < x \leq -2$

14. $x \neq -1$

15. $x \leq 1\frac{1}{2}$

16. $-3 < x < 3$

Write an inequality for the graph. 3-3

17.

18.

19.

Make a stem-and-leaf plot for the data in the specified exercise (above). 3-4

20. Exercise 2

21. Exercise 3

22. Exercise 4

Make a box-and-whisker plot to compare the two sets of data. 3-5

23. Number of touchdowns in a season by leading football scorers
    American Conference: 8, 8, 8, 8, 9, 9, 10, 11, 12
    National Conference: 11, 11, 11, 11, 13, 14, 15, 19

24. Wins in a season by Campbell Conference NHL teams
    Norris Division: 30, 32, 36, 36, 43
    Smythe Division: 17, 31, 33, 35, 36, 42

25. Wins in a season by National League baseball teams:
    Eastern Division—73, 75, 76, 76, 89, 92, 96
    Western Division—64, 72, 72, 77, 86, 90, 96

Choose an appropriate type of graph to display the data and draw the graph. Explain your choice. 3-6

26. Total number of medals earned by the top ten countries in the 1998 Winter Olympics: 10, 10, 11, 12, 13, 15, 17, 18, 25, 29

27. 1996 world gemstone sales by value

Japan, 33%
United States, 35%
Europe, 17%
Southeast Asia, 3%
Others, 12%

28. U.S. factory sales (in millions of dollars) for pagers

Year	1993	1994	1995	1996	1997
Sales	198	230	300	370	460

Unit 4

For Exercises 1–4, plot the points and connect them in order. Then write the specific name of the polygon formed and find its area. 4-2

1. $R(3, 3)$, $S(-2, 3)$, $T(-3, -2)$

2. $W(-2, 0)$, $X(0, 4)$, $Y(2, 0)$, $Z(0, -3)$

3. $J(1, 3)$, $K(1, -2)$, $L(5, -1)$, $M(5, 1)$

4. $A(-4, -1)$, $B(1, -1)$, $C(1, -4)$, $D(-2, -6)$, $E(-4, -4)$

Find the coordinates of the vertices of the polygon in the specified exercise above after the given translation. 4-3

5. Exercise 1; 2 units up

6. Exercise 2; 7 units left

7. Exercise 3; 3 units right and 4 units down

8. Exercise 4; 5 units left and 1 unit down

Write the coordinates of P' after each translation of $P(-3, 2)$. 4-3

9. $(x, y) \rightarrow (x + 3, y - 1)$

10. $(x, y) \rightarrow (x - 1, y - 4)$

The following graphs show rotations around the origin. Describe the direction and amount of the rotation of each graph. 4-4

11.

12.

13.

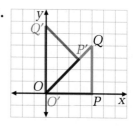

Copy the figure on polar graph paper. Draw each indicated rotation of the figure around the origin. 4-4

14. 70° clockwise

15. 140° counterclockwise

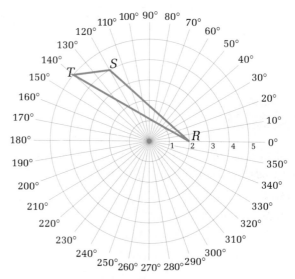

Make a scatter plot for each relationship. State whether the scatter plot shows a *positive correlation*, a *negative correlation*, or *no correlation*. 4-5

16.

Amount financed at 8% for a 25-year mortgage	Monthly payment
$70,000	$540.27
$80,000	$617.45
$90,000	$694.63
$100,000	$771.82

17.

New England States	Area (mi²)	1999 population
Connecticut	4,845	3,282,000
Maine	30,865	1,253,000
Massachusetts	7,838	6,175,200
New Hampshire	8,969	1,201,100
Rhode Island	1,045	1,990,800
Vermont	9,249	593,700

Tell whether each graph represents a function. Explain your answer. `4-6`

18.

19.

20.
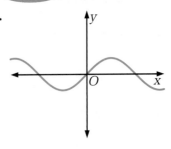

Choose the most reasonable graph for each situation. `4-6`

21. The amount of gas in the tank of Felicia's car is a function of the length of time Felicia has been driving.

a.

b.

c.

22. The cost of a mushroom pizza is a function of its diameter.

a.

b.

c.

Write an equation to represent each function. `4-7`

23.

x	y
−6	2
−3	1
0	0
3	−1
6	−2

24.

x	y
−2	−5
−1	−4
0	−3
1	−2
2	−1

25.

x	y
−2	3
−1	2
0	1
1	0
2	−1

Write each function as an equation. Then graph the function. `4-7`

26. The area of a square depends on the length of each side.

27. The Fashion Shoppe is offering 20% off on all its merchandise during its spring sale. The sale price of an item depends on the original price of the item.

28. To find a Fahrenheit temperature if you know the Celsius temperature, multiply the Celsius temperature by 1.8 and then add 32.

Unit 5

Simplify. 5-2

1. $-(2x - 3)$
2. $-3(-2a + 5)$
3. $-(-x - 3y)$
4. $-2t - 4(2t - t^2)$
5. $8 - (-9 - 7m)$
6. $7y - (8y + z)$

Solve. 5-2

7. $7 - x = 15$
8. $-2d - 3 = 9$
9. $-(r + 2) = 5$
10. $-5(1 - 2b) = 20$
11. $8 = 7y - 4(y - 1)$
12. $3a + 2 + a = 34$
13. $5(x + 3) - 6x = -12$
14. $1.9k - 3 - 7.5k = 4$
15. $-2 = -6(n - 1) + 4$

Solve. 5-3

16. $3x = 12 - x$
17. $5c - 3 = 6c$
18. $2r + 15 = -r$
19. $0.6(b - 5) = b$
20. $4j = 6(j - 9)$
21. $-8(1 - b) = 6b$
22. $9 - 4(1 - w) = -w$
23. $3k + 8(k + 6) = 4$
24. $2(3x - 1) + 7 = x$
25. $-6(4d + 5) + 7d = -2d$

Solve and graph each inequality.

26. $-3x > -9$
27. $8 - y \le 15$
28. $15 > 7z - 6$
29. $-4(a + 1) \ge 2$
30. $8 > 5 - 9b$
31. $3(8 - j) < -12$
32. $-(5 - 2p) \le -1$
33. $2k < 8k - 24$
34. $-m \ge 3(m - 16)$

Solve each equation for the variable indicated. 5-5

35. $P = 4s$, for s
36. $2k = x - 3y$, for x
37. $I = Ed^2$, for E
38. $2x + y = 4$, for y
39. $h = at - 16t^2$, for a
40. $s = \pi r^2 + \pi rl$, for l

Solve. 5-6

41. $35 = -14k$
42. $-\frac{2}{3}b = -6$
43. $\frac{3}{4}c = 18$
44. $\frac{1}{6}z - 7 = -1$
45. $2 - \frac{3}{2}t = 11$
46. $-\frac{1}{3}r + 5 = 1$
47. $\frac{5}{8}x + 3 = -2$
48. $11 - \frac{1}{7}v = 18$
49. $\frac{5}{6}s + 1 = -9$

Solve each equation for y. 5-6

50. $3x - 2y = 6$
51. $ax - by = c$
52. $c = ay + b$
53. $x - \frac{3}{4}y = 12$
54. $2x - \frac{1}{2}y = -4$
55. $\frac{1}{2}x + \frac{1}{3}y = 6$

Find the area of each parallelogram, triangle, and trapezoid. 5-7

56.

9m

5m | 4m

57.

58.

4.0 cm

12.8 cm — 10.4 cm

59. A right triangle with perpendicular sides of lengths 9 m and 10 m

60. A parallelogram with base 7.5 cm and height 4 cm

61. A trapezoid with bases 7 ft and 10 ft, and with height 8 ft

Find the specified dimension. 5-7

62. The height of a parallelogram with area 9.5 in.^{2} and base 2.5 in.

63. The base of a triangle with area $12(y - 3)$, base $6y$, and height 2

64. The height of a trapezoid with bases 7 and 15, height $(x - 4)$, and area 55

Solve each system of equations. 5-8

65. $y = 3x$
$2x + y = 20$

66. $b = 7a$
$a + 2b = 21$

67. $2r + 3s = -5$
$6s = 2r$

68. $d = 5c$
$3c - d = 6$

69. $7a + b = 28$
$b = 2a + 1$

70. $y = x - 2$
$5x - y = 10$

71. $b = a + 2$
$4a + 5b = 16$

72. $t = s + 5$
$6s - t = 30$

73. $y = 3x - 6$
$7x + 2y = 66$

Unit 6

A survey of 500 registered voters from Carverville found that 257 favored increased funding for schools, 185 oppposed it, and the rest were undecided. 6-2

1. Suppose more than 50% of the voters must vote in favor of increased funding for schools for the funding to be increased. Is it likely that the funding will be increased? Explain.

2. a. Find the probability that a voter is undecided about the funding issue.

   b. Is the probability in part (a) theoretical or experimental probability? Explain.

A card is drawn at random from a deck of ten cards numbered from 1 to 10.
Find the probability of getting the indicated card. 6-2

3. an even or an odd number

4. a multiple of 3

5. a factor of 20

6. a number that is greater than 20

7. not a 7

8. a number that is less than 8

Solve each proportion. 6-3

9. $\dfrac{x}{18} = \dfrac{15}{27}$

10. $\dfrac{32}{m} = \dfrac{48}{36}$

11. $\dfrac{35}{64} = \dfrac{5.6}{t}$

12. $\dfrac{250}{12} = \dfrac{k}{15}$

13. $\dfrac{2.5}{a} = \dfrac{8}{28}$

14. $\dfrac{2.4}{2} = \dfrac{3}{y}$

15. $\dfrac{9}{0.02} = \dfrac{b}{5}$

16. $\dfrac{r}{1.5} = \dfrac{1.28}{4}$

17. $\dfrac{0.4}{8} = \dfrac{x}{6}$

18. $\dfrac{0.4}{0.14} = \dfrac{z}{7}$

19. $\dfrac{3}{k} = \dfrac{25}{7}$

20. $\dfrac{40}{g} = \dfrac{48}{105}$

Quadrilateral *ABCD* ~ quadrilateral *WXYZ*.

Complete each statement. 6-5

21. $\angle X = \underline{\ ?\ }°$

22. $\angle W \cong \angle \underline{\ ?\ }$

23. $YZ = \underline{\ ?\ }$ units

24. $AB = \underline{\ ?\ }$ units

25. perimeter of *ABCD* = $\underline{\ ?\ }$ units

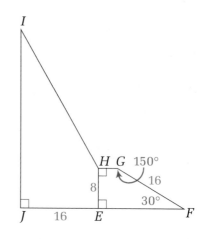

Quadrilateral *EFGH* ~ quadrilateral *JIHE*.

Complete each statement. 6-5

26. $\angle HEF$ corresponds to $\angle \underline{\ ?\ }$.

27. $\angle EHI = \underline{\ ?\ }°$

28. $\angle I = \underline{\ ?\ }°$

29. $HI = \underline{\ ?\ }$ units

30. $GH = \underline{\ ?\ }$ units

31. Name two similar triangles in the diagram. Explain why they must be similar. 6-5

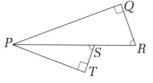

32. $\triangle A'B'C'$ is the image of $\triangle ABC$ under a dilation. Find the coordinates of the center of the dilation and the scale factor. 6-6

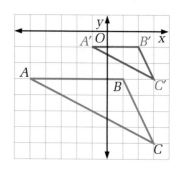

Draw a dilation of △DEF with vertices D(−6, 0), E(0, 3), and F(3, −6) using the specified center of dilation and scale factor. 6-6

33. center D, scale factor 2

34. center (0, 0), scale factor $\frac{1}{3}$

35. center (6, 0), scale factor $\frac{4}{3}$

Use a calculator to write each ratio as a decimal rounded to hundredths. 6-7

36. sin 7°   **37.** sin 75°

38. cos 58°   **39.** cos 60°

Write each ratio as a fraction and as a decimal rounded to hundredths. 6-7

40. sin A   **41.** cos A

42. sin C   **43.** cos C

44. Use your answer to Exercise 40 and a calculator to find the measure of ∠A the nearest degree. 6-7

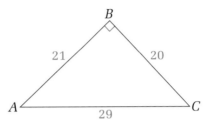

Unit 7

Use a calculator to write each ratio as a decimal rounded to hundredths. 7-1

1. tan 58°   **2.** tan 9°

3. tan 81°   **4.** tan 45°

Refer to right △ABC. 7-1

5. Find tan A and tan B.

6. Use the inverse tangent key on a calculator to find the measure of ∠A to the nearest degree.

7. Use right △DEF. Find the length of EF to the nearest 0.1 cm.
7-1

Find the circumference of each circle. 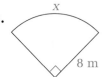 7-3

8. The diameter is 50 ft.

9. The radius is 1.5 mm.

10. The radius is $\frac{3}{4}$ in.

11. The diameter is 85 m.

Find each arc length. 7-3

12.

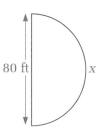

60°

3 in.   3 in.

x

13.

x

8 m

14.

80 ft

x

15.

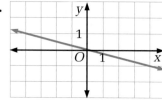

10 cm

50°

x

Graph each equation. 7-4

16. $y = -3x$

17. $y = -\frac{1}{2}x$

18. $y = -1.25x$

19. $y = -\frac{2}{3}x$

20. $y = -5x$

21. $y = -\frac{3}{4}x$

22. $y = -0.3x$

23. $y = -2.4x$

Write an equation of the form $y = kx$ to describe each line. 7-4

24.

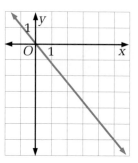

25.

26.

Each expression shows the units of a conversion problem. Use dimensional analysis to find the unit(s) of the answer. 7-5

27. $\dfrac{\text{km}}{\text{mi}} \times \text{mi} = \underline{\ ?\ }$

28. $\dfrac{\text{dollars}}{\text{h}} \times \dfrac{\text{h}}{\text{day}} = \underline{\ ?\ }$

29. $\dfrac{\text{cycles}}{\text{min}} \times \dfrac{\text{min}}{\text{s}} = \underline{\ ?\ }$

30. $\dfrac{\text{cents}}{\text{kWh}} \times \text{kWh} = \underline{\ ?\ }$

31. $\dfrac{\text{min}}{\text{page}} \times \text{pages} \times \dfrac{\text{h}}{\text{min}} = \underline{\ ?\ }$

32. $\dfrac{\text{dollars}}{\text{lb}} \times \dfrac{\text{lb}}{\text{oz}} \times \text{oz} = \underline{\ ?\ }$

Find the area of the circle described. 7-6

33. The radius is 7 in.

34. The diameter is 20 m.

35. The diameter is 1.8 mm.

36. The radius is $\frac{3}{8}$ in.

Find the area of each sector. In Exercise 39, the area of the entire circle is 9π cm². 7-6

37.

38.

39.

Unit 8

Without graphing, find the slope and the vertical intercept of the line modeled by each equation. 8-1

1. $y = 2x + 7$

2. $y = \frac{1}{3} - \frac{2}{3}x$

3. $y = 0.7x - 3.5$

4. $y = 7x$

5. $y = 5 - x$

6. $y = -\frac{1}{8}x + \frac{7}{8}$

Find the slope and vertical intercept of each graph. Then write an equation for the line. 8-1

7.

8.

9.

10.

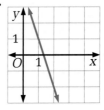

Rewrite each equation in slope-intercept form. 8-2

11. $5x - y = 7$

12. $2x + 5y = -10$

13. $\frac{1}{2}x + y = -4$

14. $8x - 5y = -15$

15. $2x + \frac{1}{3}y = 6$

16. $8x - \frac{2}{3}y = 2$

Find the intercepts of the graph of each equation. Then use the intercepts to graph the equation. 8-2

17. $x + 4y = -8$

18. $4x - 9y = -18$

19. $\frac{3}{2}x - 5y = 15$

20. $-0.6x + 0.5y = 3$

21. $2.5x + 2y = -5$

22. $\frac{3}{4}x - \frac{4}{3}y = 6$

Find the slope of each line and write an equation for the line.

23.   **24.**   **25.**   **26.**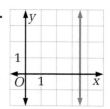

Graph each equation and find the slope of the line. 8-3

27. $x = 5$

28. $y = 0$

29. $5x = -20$

30. $-\frac{1}{2}y = -4$

31. $1.2x = -1.2$

32. $-3y = -18$

33. $\frac{3}{4}x = 0$

34. $-2x = 7$

Write an equation for the line. If there is too little information, state this. 8-4

35. The slope is $\frac{3}{5}$ and the vertical intercept is -2.

36. The slope is 3 and the origin is on the line.

37. The points $(7, 5)$ and $(5, 9)$ are on the line.

38. The slope is undefined.

39. The horizontal intercept is -6 and the vertical intercept is 4.

40. The slope is $-\frac{1}{4}$ and the point $(4, 3)$ is on the line.

41. The slope is -5 and the horizontal intercept is 1.

42. The vertical intercept is -8.

43. The points $(8, -1)$ and $(3, -1)$ are on the line.

44. The points $(2, 3)$ and $(3, 2)$ are on the line.

Graph the system of equations. Estimate the solution of the system or write *no solution* if there is none. 8-5

45. $y = 3x + 4$
  $y = -3x - 6$

46. $y = 2x + 3$
  $y = 2x - 3$

47. $y = -\frac{1}{2}x + 2$
  $y = -2x - 2$

48. $y = \frac{2}{3}x$
  $y = \frac{2}{3}x + 3$

49. $y = 0.4x$
  $y = 4x - 2$

50. $y = -2.5x + 1$
  $y = 0.5x + 5$

Graph each inequality. 8-6

51. $x \le 0$

52. $y > -3$

53. $y \le \frac{1}{2}x$

54. $y > -3x$

55. $y < 2x + 3$

56. $y \ge -x - 1$

57. $\frac{1}{3}x + 2 > y$

58. $-\frac{2}{5}x - 4 \le y$

59. $3x + 2y \le -10$

60. $5y - x > -5$

61. $4x - 3y > 6$

62. $3x + 4y \ge 12$

Graph each system of inequalities. `8-7`

63. $y \le 4$
$x > -2$

64. $y < 2x + 5$
$y > -3x + 2$

65. $y \le -2x + 4$
$y \le 3x + 4$

66. $y > -x$
$x \le 3$

67. $2x - y > 4$
$3x + 5y \ge -15$

68. $x + 3y > -3$
$4x - 5y < -10$

Unit 9

Find the missing length in each triangle. `9-1`

1.

2.

3.

4.

5.

6.

7.

8.

Simplify. `9-2`

9. $\sqrt{48}$

10. $2\sqrt{27}$

11. $\sqrt{90}$

12. $5\sqrt{175}$

13. $\sqrt{7} \cdot \sqrt{7}$

14. $\sqrt{6} \cdot \sqrt{14}$

15. $\sqrt{24} \cdot \sqrt{3}$

16. $\sqrt{28} \cdot 3\sqrt{45}$

17. $(-\sqrt{6})^2$

18. $(-7\sqrt{2})^2$

19. $3\sqrt{5} \cdot 2\sqrt{15}$

20. $6\sqrt{18} \cdot \frac{1}{3}\sqrt{6}$

Solve for x. `9-2`

21. $x^2 = 56$

22. $5x^2 = 140$

23. $x^2 + (2x)^2 = 100$

24. $4x^2 = 25$

25. $\frac{1}{2}x^2 = 81$

26. $x^2 + 3x^2 = y^2$

Write the converse of the statement and tell whether the converse is *true* or *false*. If it is false, give a counterexample. `9-3`

27. If m and n are even numbers, then $m \times n$ is an even number.

28. If $x > -2$, then $-2x > 4$.

29. A pair of angles are congruent if they are vertical angles.

30. If $k = 6$, then $|k| = 6$.

Solve. 9-3

31. $-1.6r = 0$

32. $z(z - 4) = 0$

33. $2m(m + 3) = 0$

34. $4j^2 = 0$

35. $x(9 + x) = 0$

36. $5y(1 - 4y) = 0$

The lengths of the sides of a triangle are given. Is the triangle a right triangle? How do you know? 9-3

37. 8 cm, 10cm, 12cm

38. 15 in., 8 in., 17 in.

39. 29 m, 20 m, 21 m

40. 6 yd, 8 yd, 7 yd

41. 40 ft, 9 ft, 41 ft

42. 16 mm, 12 mm, 8 mm

A point P on $\overline{AG}$ is chosen at random. Find the probability that P is on the specified segment. 9-4

$$
\begin{array}{ccccccc}
A & B & C & D & E & F & G \\
0 & 1 & 2 & 3 & 4 & 5 & 6
\end{array}
$$

43. $\overline{AC}$ **44.** $\overline{BE}$ **45.** $\overline{EF}$ **46.** $\overline{BF}$ **47.** $\overline{GA}$ **48.** $\overline{BG}$

Find the probability that a point chosen at random from the region shown is in the shaded region. 9-4

49.

50.

51.

52.

Identify each space figure and find its surface area. 9-5

53.
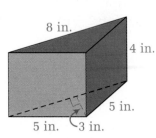

8 in.   4 in.   5 in.   5 in.   3 in.

54.

3 m   5 m

55.

20 cm   24 cm   24 cm

Identify each space figure and find its surface area. `9-5`

56.

1.5 cm 6 cm 4 cm

57.

6 ft 16 ft 16 ft

58.

1 ft 3 in.

59.

6 m 8 m

60.

8 ft 20 ft 17 ft

61.

4 in. 5 in. 3 in. 9 in. 8 in.

Find the volume of the space figure above. `9-6`

62. The figure in Exercise 53

63. The figure in Exercise 54

64. The figure in Exercise 56

65. The figure in Exercise 58

66. The figure in Exercise 59

67. The figure in Exercise 60

68. The figure in Exercise 61

Find the volume of the space figure. `9-7`

69. The figure in Exercise 55

70. The figure in Exercise 57

71. A cone with radius 12 mm and height 15 mm

72.

2 m
├─8 m─┼─8 m─┼─8 m─┤

Find the ratio of the areas of each pair of similar figures. Then find the unknown area. `9-8`

73.

8 m 4 m
6 m
area = ?

74.
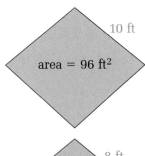
10 ft
area = 96 ft²
8 ft
area = ?

75.

60 m² 10 m
area = ? 12 m

Extra Practice

Find the ratio of the volumes of each pair of similar space figures. Then find the unknown volume. 〈9-8〉

76. Two rectangular prisms with heights 9 cm and 12 cm, if the volume of the smaller one is 180 cm^3

77. Two cylinders with diameters 12 m and 8 m, if the volume of the larger one is 180 πm^3 (Give the volume of the smaller cylinder in terms of π.)

Unit 10

Copy each figure and reflect it over (a) the x-axis and then (b) the y-axis. Describe the orientation of the original figure and its image. 〈10-1〉

1.

2.

3.

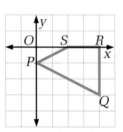

Match each function with its graph. 〈10-2〉

4. $y = -(x + 2)^2$ **5.** $y = (x - 2)^2$ **6.** $y = -x^2 + 2$ **7.** $y = x^2 - 2$

A.

B.

C.

D.

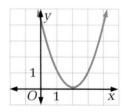

Graph each parabola. 〈10-3〉

8. $y = -x(x + 4)$ **9.** $y = (x + 4)(x - 2)$ **10.** $y = (2x - 6)(x - 1)$

Without graphing, find the x-intercepts and the y-intercept of the graph of each equation. 〈10-3〉

11. $y = x(x - 4)$ **12.** $y = -x(x + 2)$ **13.** $y = (x + 8)(x - 3)$

14. $y = (2x - 1)(x + 7)$ **15.** $y = (3x - 2)(4x + 1)$

Simplify. `10-4`

16. $x^6 \cdot x$

17. $2b^2 \cdot 3b^4$

18. $(-3m^3)(2m^5)$

19. $5xy^2 \cdot 7x^3y$

20. $-a^5b^2 \cdot 2a^7 b^3$

21. $(t^4)^3$

22. $(-j^7)^2$

23. $(5a^3)^5$

24. $(-2a)^4$

25. $(-4ab^3)^3$

26. $(3x^2y^4)^4$

27. $(-2r^5 s^2)^6$

Expand each expression. `10-5`

28. $x(x - 6)$

29. $-a(a + 4)$

30. $2x(x - 2)$

31. $3x(2x - 5)$

32. $-4x(1 - 3x)$

33. $7x(4x + 9)$

Factor the binomial side of the equation. Then find the x-intercepts and the y-intercept of the graph of each equation. `10-5`

34. $y = x^2 + 8x$

35. $y = 3x - x^2$

36. $y = -x^2 - 7x$

37. $x^2 - 4x = y$

38. $-x^2 + 9x = y$

39. $y = 2x^2 - 6x$

Expand each product. `10-6`

40. $(x - 5)(x - 2)$

41. $(x - 5)(x + 2)$

42. $(x + 5)(x - 2)$

43. $(x - 6)(x - 6)$

44. $(x - 6)(x + 6)$

45. $(x + 6)(x + 6)$

46. $(3x + 1)(x - 2)$

47. $(4x - 3)(x - 4)$

48. $(5x - 2)(x + 2)$

49. $(2x + 7)(5x + 4)$

50. $(8x + 3)(3x - 2)$

51. $(7x - 1)(3x + 4)$

Without graphing, find (a) the equation of the line of symmetry, (b) the coordinates of the vertex, and (c) the y-intercept of the graph of each equation. `10-6`

52. $y = x^2 - 2x - 3$

53. $y = x^2 + 2x + 1$

54. $y = x^2 - 2x + 3$

55. $y = x^2 - 10x - 5$

Factor each trinomial that can be factored using integers. If a trinomial cannot be factored, write *not possible*. `10-7`

56. $x^2 - 11x + 28$

57. $x^2 + 12x - 28$

58. $x^2 + 27x - 28$

59. $x^2 - 13x + 30$

60. $x^2 - 17x - 30$

61. $x^2 - x - 30$

Use the line of symmetry, the vertex, and the intercepts to sketch the graph of each equation. `10-7`

62. $y = x^2 - 6x + 9$

63. $y = x^2 - 6x + 5$

64. $y = x^2 + 3x - 10$

65. $y = x^2 - 2x - 3$

66. $y = x^2 + 8x + 15$

67. $y = x^2 - x - 6$

Solve each quadratic equation. Tell which method you used. `10-8`

68. $0 = 0.5x^2 - 8$

69. $x^2 - 14x = -45$

70. $7x - x^2 = 3.75$

71. $0 = x^2 - 6x + 8$

72. $x^2 - 3x + 1 = 0$

73. $1 = 2x^2 - 4x - 5$

74. $0.2x^2 - 1.5x = 4$

75. $3x^2 - x = 14$

76. $5 = 2x^2 - 6x + 3$

77. $2x^2 - x = 1$

Student Resources

➤Numbers and Operations

Integers

Skill 1	Using Properties of Addition and Multiplication

➤ **Commutative Property** You can add or multiply numbers in any order.

$$7 + 5 = 5 + 7 \qquad 7(5) = 5(7)$$

➤ **Associative Property** When you add or multiply three or more numbers, you can group the numbers as you like, without changing the sum or product.

$$(8 + 3) + 2 = 8 + (3 + 2) \qquad 8 \times (3 \times 2) = (8 \times 3) \times 2$$

➤ **Identity Property of Addition** Adding 0 to a number does not change the number.

$$46 + 0 = 46$$

➤ **Identity Property of Multiplication** Multiplying a number by 1 does not change the number.

$$46 \times 1 = 46$$

You can use these properties to help you compute in your head. Just change the order of the numbers and regroup.

Example
$$27 + 18 + 13 = (27 + 13) + 18 \longleftarrow \text{Reorder and regroup.}$$
$$= \quad 40 \quad + 18 \longleftarrow \text{Add within parentheses first.}$$
$$= 58$$

Example
$$50 \times 7 \times 2 = (50 \times 2) \times 7 \longleftarrow \text{Reorder and regroup.}$$
$$= \quad 100 \quad \times 7 \longleftarrow \text{Multiply within parentheses first.}$$
$$= 700$$

Use the properties of addition and multiplication to find each answer mentally.

1. $36 + 15 + 25$ **2.** $27 + 0 + 9$ **3.** $12 + 19 + 18$

4. $7 \times 1 \times 7$ **5.** $25 \times 3 \times 4$ **6.** $9 \times 2 \times 5$

7. $17 + 9 + 21 + 13$ **8.** $34 + 0 + 16 + 51$ **9.** $2 \times 1 \times 50 \times 11$

10. $9 \times 5 \times 7 \times 20$ **11.** $11 + 15 + 29$ **12.** $4 \times 6 \times 50$

The **integers** are the numbers

$$..., -3, -2, -1, 0, 1, 2, 3, ...$$

3 dots mean *and so on.*

To compare two integers on a *number line,* remember that the *greater* number is to the *right* of the lesser number on a horizontal number line.

$-3 < 3$

-3 is less than 3.

$3 > -3$

3 is greater than -3.

The arrowheads show that the numbers continue in both directions.

Example To write the numbers $-3, 3,$ and -1 in order from least to greatest, first locate them on a number line.

Look at the number line above. Write the numbers in order as they appear from left to right: $-3, -1, 3.$ Using symbols, write the *inequality*

$-3 < -1 < 3.$

You read this inequality as "-1 is between -3 and 3."

Show each pair of integers on a number line. Then compare the integers using $>$ or $<$.

1. $7, 10$ **2.** $-4, 0$ **3.** $5, -7$ **4.** $-5, -7$

Write each set of numbers in order from least to greatest. Then complete the inequality $\underline{?} < \underline{?} < \underline{?}$.

5. $0, 2, -1$ **6.** $-3, 0, -5$ **7.** $3, -7, 1$ **8.** $-2, -4, -6$

9. $12, -9, -19$ **10.** $-17, -27, -7$ **11.** $56, -100, 0$ **12.** $-1, -10, 10, 1$

Think of positive integers as arrows pointing to the right and negative integers as arrows pointing to the left.

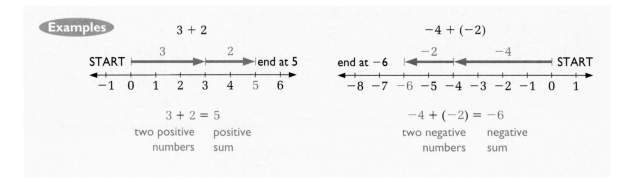

Think of 0 as a point without direction.

Begin each sum at zero on a number line.

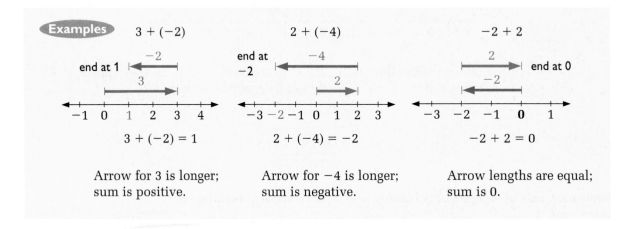

Examples $3 + 2$

$3 + 2 = 5$

two positive   positive
numbers   sum

$-4 + (-2)$

$-4 + (-2) = -6$

two negative   negative
numbers   sum

The sum of a positive and a negative integer can be positive, negative, or zero. The direction of the longer arrow gives the sign of the sum.

Examples $3 + (-2)$ $2 + (-4)$ $-2 + 2$

$3 + (-2) = 1$ $2 + (-4) = -2$ $-2 + 2 = 0$

Arrow for 3 is longer;   Arrow for -4 is longer;   Arrow lengths are equal;
sum is positive.   sum is negative.   sum is 0.

When the integers to be added have *opposite* signs, subtract and choose the appropriate sign if the result is not 0.

Find each sum. Think of a number line.

1. $7 + 2$ **2.** $-7 + (-2)$ **3.** $7 + (-2)$ **4.** $-7 + 2$

5. $3 + (-3)$ **6.** $0 + (-8)$ **7.** $-4 + 9$ **8.** $3 + (-9)$

9. $-8 + (-10)$ **10.** $6 + (-5)$ **11.** $-5 + 5$ **12.** $-5 + (-5)$

13. $-50 + 40$ **14.** $15 + (-6)$ **15.** $-30 + (-3)$ **16.** $-50 + 50$

You can use integer chips to model integers.

+1, or 1   −1   0   −2   0 + 2, or 2

Since $1 + (-1) = 0$, the plus and minus chips form a *zero pair,* with the value 0.

Examples To add with integer chips, you model the first number. Add chips for the second number. Count the chips.

$$3 + 2 = 5 \qquad\qquad -3 + (-2) = -5$$

Examples Find each difference.   **a.** $-2 - (-1)$ **b.** $-2 - 1$ **c.** $-2 - (-5)$

Method ❶ Use integer chips.

a.   Subtract 1 negative chip.

1 negative chip remains.

$$-2 - (-1) = -1$$

b. Add a zero pair to give you a positive chip to subtract.

  Subtract 1 positive chip. 3 negative chips remain.

$$-2 - 1 = -3$$

c. Add zero pairs until you have 5 negative chips to subtract.

  Subtract 5 negative chips. 3 positive chips remain.

$$-2 - (-5) = 3$$

Method ❷ To *subtract* an integer, *add its opposite.*

a. $-2 - (-1) = -2 + 1$ **b.** $-2 - 1 = -2 + (-1)$ **c.** $-2 - (-5) = -2 + 5$
$\qquad\qquad = -1 \qquad\qquad\qquad\qquad = -3 \qquad\qquad\qquad\qquad = 3$

Subtract using integer chips. Then subtract by adding an opposite.

1. $7 - 5$ **2.** $3 - 4$ **3.** $6 - (-2)$

Subtract.

4. $-3 - 2$ **5.** $-2 - (-3)$ **6.** $0 - 6$ **7.** $0 - (-1)$ **8.** $5 - (-5)$

9. $9 - 0$ **10.** $-4 - 4$ **11.** $-4 - (-4)$ **12.** $25 - 35$ **13.** $10 - (-30)$

Example Multiply $2 \times (-4)$.

Method ❶ Two groups of -4 is the same as 1 group of -8.

 $2 \times (-4) = -8$

Method ❷ Multiplying by a negative number changes the sign.

$$2 \times (-4) = 2 \times (-1 \times 4)$$
$$= -1 \times (2 \times 4) \longleftarrow \text{Reorder and regroup}$$
$$= -1 \times 8$$
$$= -8$$

When you multiply or divide nonzero integers, be careful to choose the correct sign (positive or negative) for the product or quotient. (See the table.)

× or ÷	+	−
+	+	−
−	−	+

Examples Multiply or divide.

a. $-7 \times (-4) = 28$ **b.** $\dfrac{-15}{3} = -5$ **c.** $-18 \div (-6) = 3$

Remember: When you multiply any number by 0, the result is 0. When you divide 0 by a nonzero number, the result is 0, but you cannot divide by 0.

Examples Multiply or divide.

a. $0 \times 9 = 0$ **b.** $0 \times (-12) = 0$ **c.** $0 \div 7 = 0$

Multiply or divide.

14. $8 \times (-1)$ **15.** $-8 \times (-1)$ **16.** -8×0

17. $20 \div (-5)$ **18.** $-72 \div 8$ **19.** $-27 \div (-9)$

20. -5×5 **21.** 5×5 **22.** $-5 \times (-5)$

23. $18 \div 6$ **24.** $0 \div (-4)$ **25.** $30 \div (-3)$

26. $-1 \div (-1)$ **27.** $6 \times (-8)$ **28.** $-1 \times (-2) \times (-3)$

29. $-3 \times 2 \times (-5)$ **30.** $9 \times (-4) \div 2$ **31.** $(6 \div 2) \times (-7)$

One-Step Equations

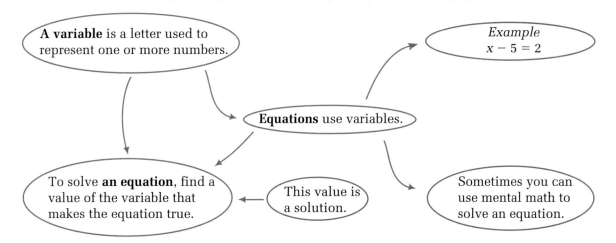

A **variable** is a letter used to represent one or more numbers.

Equations use variables.

Example
$x - 5 = 2$

To solve **an equation**, find a value of the variable that makes the equation true.

This value is a solution.

Sometimes you can use mental math to solve an equation.

To use mental math to solve an equation, think about what the equation says.

Example Solve each equation using mental math.

a. $3x = -12$

3 times a number is -12.

$3(-4) = -12$, so $x = -4$.

b. $n - 5 = 2$

When 5 is subtracted from a number, the result is 2.

$7 - 5 = 2$, so $n = 7$.

Is the given number a solution of the equation? Write *Yes* or *No*.

1. $9 - x = 2$; 7
2. $y + 5 = 8$; -13
3. $-5n = 45$; -9

4. $z - 2 = 12$; -10
5. $6m = 3$; 18
6. $6 + x = 15$; 9

Solve each equation using mental math.

7. $x + 2 = 8$
8. $y - 4 = 0$
9. $-4z = 20$

10. $\frac{n}{5} = 2$
11. $-5 + t = -1$
12. $5 - a = 6$

13. $-k = 9$
14. $d \div 6 = -4$
15. $b + 7 = 3$

16. $m - 6 = -1$
17. $-3x = -3$
18. $\frac{y}{-4} = -8$

19. $8r = 56$
20. $8 + r = 56$
21. $m - 2 = -4$

22. $\frac{m}{3} = -4$
23. $m + 2 = -4$
24. $2m = -4$

You can use algebra tiles to model and solve equations. Make the same changes to both sides of the equation until there is one x-tile ( ) left on one side.

Example Solve $x + (-4) = -1$.

First, model the equation.

$$x + (-4) = -1$$

Then add 4 "plus" chips to *both* sides.

$$x + (-4) + 4 = -1 + 4$$

$$x + 0 = 3$$

These represent 0.

$$x = 3$$

Notice: Since $x + (-4) = x - 4$, you can model and solve

$$x - 4 = -1$$

the same way as

$$x + (-4) = -1.$$

Use algebra tiles or sketch the model.

1. a. What equation does the model represent?

b. Solve the equation you wrote in part (a) by making the same change to both sides of the model.

Solve.

2. $x - 3 = 2$

3. $1 + x = 5$

4. $-2 + x = -5$

5. $x - 1 = 1$

6. $x + 6 = 2$

7. $-3 + x = -3$

Example Solve $3x = -6$.

Method ❶ Use a model.

To find what x equals (modeled by one x-tile), divide each side into three identical groups.

$$3x \quad = \quad -6$$

Each x-tile represents -2, so $x = -2$.

Method ❷ Use algebra to solve $3x = -6$.

$$3x = -6$$

$$\frac{3x}{3} = \frac{-6}{3} \longleftarrow \text{Divide both sides by 3.}$$

$$x = -2$$

Use algebra tiles or sketch the model.

8. a. What equation does the model below represent?

b. Use two methods to solve the equation. Include a sketch of what you did with the tiles to solve the equation.

Solve.

9. $5x = 20$

10. $2x = -8$

11. $-3x = 18$

12. $-4x = -16$

13. $7x = 42$

14. $6x = -6$

15. $\frac{x}{2} = 4$

(*Hint:* Multiply both sides by 2.)

Factors

Since 7 · 5 = 35, 7 and 5 are **factors** of 35.

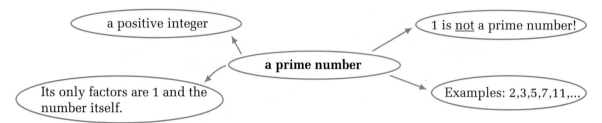

a positive integer

1 is <u>not</u> a prime number!

a prime number

Its only factors are 1 and the number itself.

Examples: 2,3,5,7,11,...

To find the **prime factorization** of a whole number, write it as a product of prime numbers.

Example Write the prime factorization of 135.

Method ❶ See if you can identify a factor at sight. Here, since 135 has 5 as the ones' digit, 135 is divisible by 5.

$$135 = 5 \cdot 27$$
$$3 \cdot 3 \cdot 3$$

$135 = 3 \cdot 3 \cdot 3 \cdot 5$ ⟵ Write the primes in increasing order.

Method ❷ Test the prime numbers in order as divisors to see which are factors. *Remember:* A prime number can be a factor more than once.

135 ÷ 2 is not a whole number; 2 is *not* a factor.

135 ÷ 3 = 45; make a *factor tree* as shown.

Using the factor tree, 135 = 3 · 3 · 3 · 5.

Write the prime factorization of each number that is not a prime number. If the number is prime, write *prime*.

1. 40	**2.** 39	**3.** 41	**4.** 84	**5.** 104
6. 102	**7.** 110	**8.** 125	**9.** 97	**10.** 147
11. 252	**12.** 144	**13.** 133	**14.** 58	**15.** 176

A **common factor** of two numbers is a number that is a factor of both. For example:

$$3 \cdot 8 = 24 \text{ and } 3 \cdot 12 = 36$$

3 is a common factor of **24** and **36**.

The **greatest common factor** (**GCF**) of two numbers is the *largest* number that is a common factor of both.

Example Find the GCF of 24 and 36.

First write the prime factorization of each number.

$24 = 2 \cdot 2 \cdot 2 \cdot 3 \longleftarrow$ prime factorization

$36 = 2 \cdot 2 \cdot 3 \cdot 3 \longleftarrow$ prime factorization

Circle each number that is in *both* lists to find the common factors:

$24 = ② \cdot ② \cdot 2 \cdot ③$

$36 = ② \cdot ② \cdot ③ \cdot 3$

$②\cdot②\cdot③= 12$ is the GCF.

A **common multiple** of two numbers is a number that is a multiple of both. For example:

$$8 \cdot 10 = 80 \text{ and } 20 \cdot 4 = 80$$

80 is a common multiple of 8 and 20.

The **least common multiple** (**LCM**) of two numbers is the *smallest* number that is a common multiple of both.

Example Find the LCM of 8 and 20.

First find the greatest common factor of the two numbers.

$8 = ② \cdot ② \cdot 2$

$20 = ② \cdot ② \cdot 5$

$GCF = ② \cdot ② = 4$

To find the LCM, multiply the GCF by the factors that are not circled:
$LCM = 4 \cdot 2 \cdot 5 = 40$.

Find the GCF and the LCM of each pair of numbers.

1. 6, 9   **2.** 10, 55   **3.** 35, 42   **4.** 30, 45

5. 9, 27   **6.** 18, 48   **7.** 25, 50   **8.** 12, 20

9. 21, 30   **10.** 4, 32   **11.** 22, 55   **12.** 60, 100

Fractions

Reciprocals are two numbers whose product is 1. Every number except 0 has exactly one reciprocal. Zero has no reciprocal.

$$2 \text{ and } \frac{1}{2} \text{ are reciprocals: } 2 \times \frac{1}{2} = 1$$

$$\frac{3}{4} \text{ and } \frac{4}{3} \text{ are reciprocals: } \frac{3}{4} \times \frac{4}{3} = 1$$

$$-\frac{3}{4} \text{ and } -\frac{4}{3} \text{ are reciprocals: } \left(-\frac{3}{4}\right) \times \left(-\frac{4}{3}\right) = 1$$

Notice that a positive number has a positive reciprocal, and a negative number has a negative reciprocal.

Example Find the reciprocal of $\frac{2}{7}$.

Find the reciprocal of a fraction by exchanging the *numerator* and the *denominator* .

$\frac{2}{7}$ ← numerator
$\phantom{\frac{2}{7}}$ ← denominator

The reciprocal of $\frac{2}{7}$ is $\frac{7}{2}$.

Example Find the reciprocal of -3.

First write -3 as a fraction whose denominator is 1: $-\frac{3}{1}$.
Then find the reciprocal.

The reciprocal of -3 is $-\frac{1}{3}$.

Example Find the reciprocal of $1\frac{1}{3}$.

First write the mixed number $1\frac{1}{3}$ as a fraction: $\frac{4}{3}$.
Then find the reciprocal.

The reciprocal of $1\frac{1}{3}$ is $\frac{3}{4}$.

Find the reciprocal of each number.

1. $\frac{3}{5}$

2. $-\frac{7}{4}$

3. -6

4. 1

5. 6

6. $-2\frac{1}{4}$

7. $1\frac{5}{6}$

8. $-\frac{1}{9}$

9. $-4\frac{2}{3}$

10. 0.7

Student Resources

To add (or subtract) fractions with the same denominator, you add (or subtract) the numerators.

Example $\dfrac{7}{8} + \dfrac{5}{8} = \dfrac{7+5}{8}$ ←——— Add the numerators.

$= \dfrac{12}{8}$

$= \dfrac{3}{2}$, or $1\dfrac{1}{2}$ ←——— Write the answer in simplest form.

Example $\dfrac{5}{6} - \dfrac{1}{6} = \dfrac{5-1}{6}$ ←——— Subtract the numerators.

$= \dfrac{4}{6}$

$= \dfrac{2}{3}$ ←——— Write the answer in simplest form.

To add or subtract fractions with *different* denominators, you rewrite them as equivalent fractions with the same denominator. Use the LCM of the denominators as the new denominator. Then add or subtract.

Example $\dfrac{11}{12} + \dfrac{1}{18} = \dfrac{33}{36} + \dfrac{2}{36}$ ←——— 36 is the LCM of 12 and 18.

$\times \dfrac{2}{2}$ $\times \dfrac{3}{3}$

$= \dfrac{33+2}{36}$ ←——— Add the numerators.

$= \dfrac{35}{36}$

Add or subtract. Write the answer in lowest terms.

1. $\dfrac{11}{18} + \dfrac{3}{18}$ **2.** $\dfrac{7}{12} - \dfrac{1}{12}$ **3.** $\dfrac{8}{9} - \dfrac{1}{9}$ **4.** $\dfrac{3}{4} + \dfrac{1}{4}$

5. $\dfrac{5}{6} + \dfrac{13}{18}$ **6.** $\dfrac{1}{6} + \dfrac{3}{10}$ **7.** $\dfrac{1}{3} - \dfrac{1}{12}$ **8.** $\dfrac{5}{6} - \dfrac{4}{9}$

9. $-\dfrac{3}{5} + \dfrac{1}{3}$ **10.** $-\dfrac{2}{7} - \dfrac{3}{8}$ **11.** $\dfrac{5}{18} - \dfrac{11}{22}$ **12.** $\dfrac{47}{50} + \left(-\dfrac{3}{10}\right)$

13. $-\dfrac{2}{3} + \left(-\dfrac{1}{9}\right)$ **14.** $-\dfrac{2}{11} - \left(-\dfrac{3}{11}\right)$ **15.** $\dfrac{7}{8} - \left(-\dfrac{1}{6}\right)$ **16.** $\dfrac{3}{5} + \dfrac{5}{7}$

To multiply two fractions, you multiply the numerators and the denominators. Remember to simplify before you multiply if possible.

Example

$$7 \times \frac{3}{4} = \frac{7}{1} \times \frac{3}{4}$$ ◄——— Write 7 as $\frac{7}{1}$.

$$= \frac{7 \times 3}{1 \times 4}$$ ◄——— Multiply numerators.
◄——— Multiply denominators.

$$= \frac{21}{4}, \text{ or } 5\frac{1}{4}$$

Example

$$\frac{5}{6} \times \frac{9}{10} = \frac{5 \times 9}{6 \times 10}$$ ◄——— Multiply numerators.
◄——— Multiply denominators.

$$= \frac{\overset{1}{\cancel{5}} \times \overset{3}{\cancel{9}}}{\underset{2}{\cancel{6}} \times \underset{2}{\cancel{10}}}$$ ◄——— Simplify.

$$= \frac{3}{4}$$

To divide by a number, multiply by its reciprocal.

Example

$$\frac{3}{4} \div \frac{2}{3} = \frac{3}{4} \times \frac{3}{2}$$ ◄——— The reciprocal of $\frac{2}{3}$ is $\frac{3}{2}$.

$$= \frac{3 \times 3}{4 \times 2}$$

$$= \frac{9}{8}, \text{ or } 1\frac{1}{8}$$

Example

$$\frac{4}{9} \div 6 = \frac{4}{9} \times \frac{1}{6}$$ ◄——— The reciprocal of 6 is $\frac{1}{6}$.

$$= \frac{4 \times 1}{9 \times 6}$$

$$= \frac{2}{27}$$

Multiply or divide. Write the answer in lowest terms.

17. $\frac{3}{4} \times \frac{2}{7}$

18. $\frac{2}{3}\left(-\frac{3}{5}\right)$

19. $\left(-\frac{1}{3}\right)\left(-\frac{5}{6}\right)$

20. $\frac{4}{15} \times \frac{9}{20}$

21. $\frac{3}{5} \div 9$

22. $4 \div \frac{1}{2}$

23. $-\frac{15}{16} \div \frac{3}{8}$

24. $-\frac{1}{2} \div \left(-\frac{2}{3}\right)$

25. $\left(-\frac{9}{10}\right)\left(-\frac{3}{5}\right)$

26. $\frac{7}{12} \times \frac{10}{21}$

27. $\frac{11}{18}\left(-\frac{27}{44}\right)$

28. $\frac{5}{7}\left(-\frac{7}{5}\right)$

29. $-\frac{9}{10} \div \left(-\frac{3}{5}\right)$

30. $\frac{3}{8} \div \frac{5}{6}$

31. $\frac{5}{9} \div \frac{3}{4}$

32. $\frac{5}{7} \div \left(-\frac{7}{5}\right)$

Student Resources

Percent

Skill 11   Writing Percents

Percent means *divided by 100.*

Example To write a percent as a decimal, move the decimal point two places to the *left* and remove the percent symbol.

$$24\% = 0.24 \longleftarrow \text{percent to decimal}$$

$$24\% = \frac{24}{100} = \frac{6}{25} \longleftarrow \text{percent to fraction in lowest terms}$$

$$24\% = \frac{24}{100}$$

Example To write a decimal as a percent, move the decimal point two places to the *right* and write the percent symbol.

$$0.75 = 75\% \longleftarrow \text{decimal to percent}$$

$$0.75 = \frac{75}{100} = \frac{3}{4} \longleftarrow \text{decimal to fraction in lowest terms.}$$

To write a fraction as a percent, write the fraction as a decimal and then write the decimal as a percent.

Example $\dfrac{6}{5} = \dfrac{6 \cdot 20}{5 \cdot 20} = \dfrac{120}{100} = 1.20 = 120\%$

Example $\dfrac{2}{3} = 2 \div 3 = 0.6666\ldots = 66.\overline{6}\% \approx 66.7\%$

You should memorize the chart below.

Equivalent Percents, Decimals, and Fractions

$1\% = 0.01 = \frac{1}{100}$	$33\frac{1}{3}\% = 0.\overline{3} = \frac{1}{3}$	$66\frac{2}{3}\% = 0.\overline{6} = \frac{2}{3}$
$10\% = 0.1 = \frac{10}{100}$	$40\% = 0.4 = \frac{2}{5}$	$75\% = 0.75 = \frac{3}{4}$
$20\% = 0.2 = \frac{1}{5}$	$50\% = 0.5 = \frac{1}{2}$	$80\% = 0.8 = \frac{4}{5}$
$25\% = 0.25 = \frac{1}{4}$	$60\% = 0.6 = \frac{3}{5}$	$100\% = 1$

Toolbox

Write each percent as a decimal and as a fraction in lowest terms.

1. 70%   **2.** 32%   **3.** 125%   **4.** $\frac{3}{4}$%   **5.** 7.5%

Write as a percent and as a fraction in lowest terms.

6. 0.66   **7.** 0.333...   **8.** 0.009   **9.** 0.375   **10.** 1.6

Write as a decimal and as a percent.

11. $\frac{18}{25}$ **12.** $\frac{29}{1000}$ **13.** $\frac{72}{125}$ **14.** $\frac{27}{20}$ **15.** $\frac{1}{6}$

Skill 12	The Percent One Number is of Another

To find the percent one number is of another, begin by writing an equation. Then solve and write your answer as a percent.

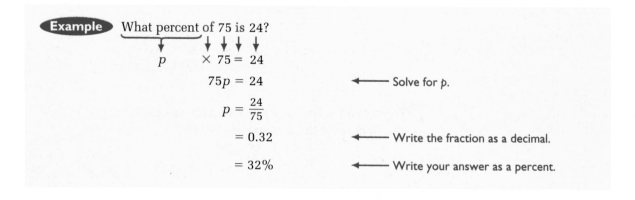

Example What percent of 75 is 24?

$$p \times 75 = 24$$

$$75p = 24 \qquad \longleftarrow \text{Solve for } p.$$

$$p = \frac{24}{75}$$

$$= 0.32 \qquad \longleftarrow \text{Write the fraction as a decimal.}$$

$$= 32\% \qquad \longleftarrow \text{Write your answer as a percent.}$$

Remember: The word *of* implies *multiply*.

Find each answer.

1. What percent of 60 is 24?

2. What percent of 24 is 60?

3. What percent of 125 is 5?

4. What percent of 96 is 36?

5. 6 is what percent of 80?

6. 20 is what percent of 16?

7. 7.5 is what percent of 25?

8. 13.5 is what percent of 72?

9. 2 is what percent of 400?

10. What percent of 57 is 19?

To find a percent of increase or decrease, use these equations:

$$\text{percent of increase} = \frac{\text{amount of increase}}{\text{original amount}}$$

$$\text{percent of decrease} = \frac{\text{amount of decrease}}{\text{original amount}}$$

Example   A price increased from $120 to $135. Find the percent of increase.

$$\text{percent of increase} = \frac{\text{amount of increase}}{\text{original amount}}$$

$$= \frac{135 - 120}{120} \longleftarrow \text{Amount of increase equals new amount minus original amount.}$$

$$= \frac{15}{120} = 0.125 = 12.5\%$$

Find the percent of increase or decrease.

1. original price, $25   new price, $23

2. original price, $.50   new price, $.55

3. original price, $6.25 new price, $6.40

4. original price, $12.50   new price, $9.25

To find a percent of a number, first rewrite the percent as a decimal or as a fraction. Then multiply by the given number.

Example   Find: **a.** 25.6% of 375   **b.** $5\frac{1}{2}\%$ of $40   **c.** $33\frac{1}{3}\%$ of 60

a. Rewrite 25.6% as a decimal: 0.256

Multiply by the given number: 0.256(375) = 96

25.6% of 375 is 96.

b. Rewrite $5\frac{1}{2}\%$ as a fraction: $\frac{5.5}{100}$

Multiply by the given number: $\frac{5.5}{100}(40) = \frac{220}{100} = 2.2$

$5\frac{1}{2}\%$ of $40 is $2.20

c. $33\frac{1}{3}\%$ of $60 = \frac{1}{3} \cdot 60 = 20$

Find each number.

1. 6% of 30

2. 75% of 28

3. $66\frac{2}{3}$% of 39

4. 2.5% of 148

5. 105% of 94

6. $9\frac{1}{4}$% of 80

7. 40% of 275

8. 0.4% of 20

9. $62\frac{1}{2}$% of 72

10. A blouse that sells for $26.50 is on sale at a 30% discount. Find the amount of discount and the new price.

11. Estimate 79% of $50.

12. If $\frac{1}{2}$% of 500 manufactured items are defective, is it reasonable to say that about 250 items are defective? Explain.

| Skill 15 | When a Percent of a Number is Known |

To find a number when a percent of it is known, write an equation where n is the number you want to find. Write the percent as a decimal or fraction and solve the equation.

Example 8% of what number is 30?

$$8\% \cdot n = 30$$
$$0.08 \cdot n = 30$$
$$n = \frac{30}{0.08} = 375$$

The number is 375.

Example 9 is $33\frac{1}{3}$% of what number?

$$9 = 33\frac{1}{3}\% \cdot n$$
$$9 = \frac{1}{3} \cdot n$$
$$27 = n$$

The number is 27.

---

1. 40% of what number is 32?

2. 32% of what number is 40?

3. 6% of what number is 57?

4. 25% of what number is 162?

5. 14 is $66\frac{2}{3}$% of what number?

6. 9 is 2.4% of what number?

7. 2 is $\frac{1}{4}$% of what number?

8. 12 is 160% of what number?

9. 0.7% of what number is 3.5?

10. 62.5% of what number is 8?

11. 80 is 128% of what number?

12. 128 is 80% of what number?

13. Kim earned a score of 92% on a math final and got 12 questions wrong. How many questions were on the final?

➤Measurement

Angles

Angle S is formed by two rays
(called *sides*) with the same endpoint
(called the *vertex*).

side

S

side

An angle is measured
in *degrees*.

Example **Use a protractor to draw an angle that measures 132°.**

1 Draw a ray.

A

2 Line up the ray with 0.

3 Draw a dot at 132.

4 Draw a ray from the
vertex through the dot.

132°

A

∠A = 132°

When you measure or draw an angle, be careful to choose the
scale on the protractor that has 0 on one side of the angle.

Use a protractor to find the measure of each angle.

1.

O

2.

E

3. P

4.

T

Draw an angle with the specified measure.

5. 60°   **6.** 25°   **7.** 108°   **8.** 180°

9. The sum of the measures of ∠1, ∠2, and ∠3 is 180°.

   a. If ∠1 = 55° and ∠3 = 37°, find the measure of ∠2.

   b. If ∠1 = 55° and ∠2 = x°, write the measure of ∠3 in terms of x.

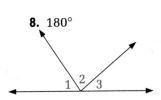

Toolbox

Perimeter

The **perimeter** (P) of a figure is the distance around it.

Examples

$$P = 4 + 4 + 4$$
$$= 3(4)$$

$$P = x + x + x$$
$$= 3x$$

$$P = 3 + 4 + 3 + 4$$
$$= (2 \times 3) + (2 \times 4)$$

$$P = l + w + l + w$$
$$= 2l + 2w$$

Find the perimeter.

1.

10, 6, 3, 8

2.

1.2 cm, 1.2 cm, 1.2 cm, 1.2 cm

3.

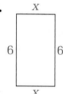

x, 6, 6, x

Area

The **area** (A) of a figure is the number of square units enclosed.

Examples

$$A = 6 \times 2$$
$$= 12 \text{ square units}$$

$$A = \text{length} \times \text{width}$$
$$= l \times w$$

$$A = \text{side} \times \text{side}$$
$$= s \times s$$

Example   Find the area of a rectangle with length 10 m and width 3.5 m.

$$A = l \times w = 10(3.5) = 35 \text{ m}^2 \longleftarrow \text{meters} \times \textit{meters} = \text{square meters (m}^2)$$

Find the area of each figure.

1. a square with sides of length 8 cm

2. a rectangle with length 11 ft and width 9 ft

3. a square with sides of length 1.5 mm

4. a rectangle with length 8 yd and width t yd

5. a rectangle with length 2.4 in. and width 1.2 in.

Volume

Skill 19   Finding Volume

The **volume** (V) of a space figure is the amount of space it encloses. An amount of space is measured in *cubic units,* such as cubic inches (in.³), cubic centimeters (cm³), and so on.

one cubic centimeter, written 1 cm³

Example   The box below has two layers. Each layer encloses $4 \times 3 = 12$ cubic units, so the entire box encloses $12 \times 2 = 24$ cubic units.

$$V = 4 \times 3 \times 2$$
$$= 24 \text{ cubic units}$$

$$V = \text{length} \times \text{width} \times \text{height}$$
$$= l \times w \times h$$

Example   Find the volume of a box with length 8.6 mm, width 4 mm, and height 3 mm.

$$l \times w \times h = (8.6)(4)(3) = 103.2 \text{ mm}^2$$

Find the volume of each box.

1. a box with length 20 cm, width 15 cm, and height 8 cm

2. a box with length 12 in., width 2.5 in., and height 0.75 in.

3. a box with length 4 ft, width $\frac{1}{2}$ ft, and height 2 ft

4. A cube is a box whose length and width and height are all the same length. Find the volume of each cube.

    a. a cube with sides of length 7 yd

    b. a cube with sides of length 0.5 ft

➤Graphing

A Coordinate System

Skill 20   Locating Points on a Coordinate Plane

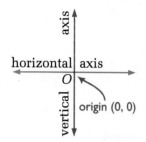

A **coordinate system** is a grid of horizontal and vertical lines.

A horizontal line and a vertical line are chosen as *axes*. The **origin** is the point where the axes cross.

The positive direction is to the right of the origin on the horizontal axis and upward on the vertical axis.

The **coordinates** of a point in a coordinate plane are an **ordered pair** of numbers in the form (**horizontal coordinate**, **vertical coordinate**) or (**x, y**).

Example   Point *A* on the graph at the right is 4 units to the left of the origin and 1 unit up in a vertical direction. The coordinates of *A* are (−4, 1).

Example   Point *B* is 4 units to the right of the origin and 0 units in a vertical direction. The coordinates of *B* are (4, 0).

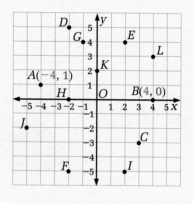

Use the graph. Name the coordinates of each point.

1. *C*   2. *D*   3. *E*   4. *F*   5. *G*

6. *H*   7. *I*   8. *J*   9. *K*   10. *L*

Skill 21   Graphing Points on a Coordinate Plane

To **graph** or **plot** a point, you start at the origin.

Example   Graph $M(-2, -3)$.

The horizontal coordinate −2 tells you to move left 2 units from the origin. The vertical coordinate −3 tells you to move **down 3** units from there.

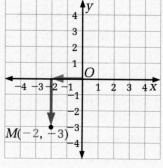

Graph each point on a coordinate plane.

1. $P(3, 2)$ 2. $Q(5, -1)$ 3. $R(-4, 0)$

4. $S(0, 2)$ 5. $T(-5, -3)$ 6. $U(-2, 2)$

Data Displays

Nutritional Information about One Brand of Turkey Meats			
	Percent Fat	Calories per slice	Fat per slice in grams
Turkey bologna	21	70	5
Turkey ham	4	40	2
Turkey salami	12	50	3

A bar graph is a visual display of data that fall into distinct categories, such as the data in this table.

Example   You can use a bar graph to display the percent of fat in the turkey meats.

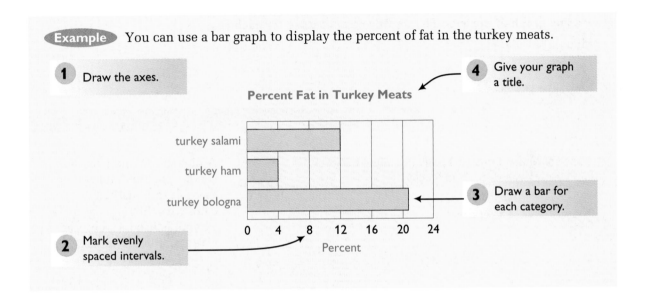

Draw a bar graph for each set of data from the table.

1. grams of fat per slice of turkey meats

2. calories per slice of turkey meats

Average Monthly Temperatures (°F)				
	Jan.	Apr.	Jul.	Oct.
Juneau, Alaska	24.2	39.7	56.0	42.2
Miami, Florida	67.2	75.2	82.6	78.3
Peoria, Illinois	21.6	51.4	75.5	54.0

The table shows the average temperature in each of four months for three cities. You can use a line graph to show how data change over time.

Example Use the temperature table at the bottom of page 661. Display the average monthly temperature in Juneau, Alaska, on a line graph.

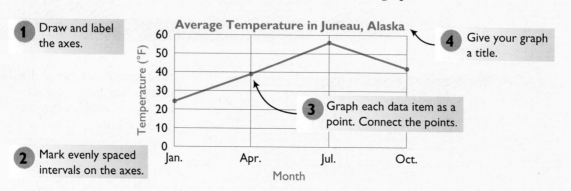

1 Draw and label the axes.

4 Give your graph a title.

3 Graph each data item as a point. Connect the points.

2 Mark evenly spaced intervals on the axes.

Draw a line graph of the average monthly temperature for each city.

1. Miami, Florida

2. Peoria, Illinois

| Skill 24 | Making a Pictograph |

National Football League Leading Punters 1999–2000			
	Number of punts	Longest in yards	Total yards
Rouen	84	65	3908
Berger	61	75	2769
Miller	84	75	3795
Tupa	81	69	3659

A pictograph and a bar graph can be used to display data that fall into distinct categories. In a pictograph a symbol is used to represent a given number of items.

Example Draw a pictograph to show the number of punts kicked by each player.

Let a football represent 10 punts. Rouen's 84 punts are about $8\frac{1}{2}$ symbols.

National Football League Leading Punters, 1999–2000

Rouen — $\frac{84}{10} = 8.4 \approx 8\frac{1}{2}$ symbols

Berger — $\frac{61}{10} = 6.1 \approx 6$ symbols

Miller — $\frac{84}{10} = 8.4 \approx 8\frac{1}{2}$ symbols

Tupa — $\frac{81}{10} = 8.1 \approx 8$ symbols

Remember to include a title and a key. → = 10 punts

Draw a pictograph for each set of data from the table on page 662.

1. the longest punt for each player

2. the total number of yards kicked by each player

Skill 25	Making a Circle Graph

A circle graph shows how parts relate to a whole and to each other.

Example Draw a circle graph to show the wins, losses, and ties for the Canadiens.

Standings of Three Teams in the National Hockey League, 1999-2000			
Team	Wins	Losses	Ties
Canadiens	35	38	9
Bruins	24	39	19
Sabres	35	36	11

Follow these steps to figure out how big to make the "wins" sector of the circle. Do the same for the other two sectors.

Write the wins as a fraction of the whole.

$$\frac{35}{82} \cdot 360° = 153.7°$$

Find the total number of games:
$35 + 38 + 9 = 82$

Multiply by 360° to find the number of degrees for the sector.

Follow these steps to draw the circle graph.

1. Draw a circle.

2. Use a protractor to draw the angle for each sector.

3. Label each sector and give your graph a title.

Canadiens' Record 1999–2000

$\frac{9}{82} \cdot 360° = 39.5°$ ⟶ Ties

$\frac{38}{82} \cdot 360° = 166.8°$ ⟶ Losses

Wins

Use the table above. Draw a circle graph to show the wins, losses, and ties for each team.

1. Bruins

2. Sabres

➤Problem Solving

One step toward being a good problem solver is to use an organized plan for approaching a problem. Here is a four-step plan.

Understand	• Read the problem. • Decide what facts are given and what you need to find. • There may be more information than you need or not enough. (The Table of Measures on page 666 can supply a missing fact.)
Plan	• Choose one or more strategies for solving the problem. (Get ideas from the list of strategies on page 665.) • Choose the correct operations for calculations.
Work	• Use the strategies you have chosen. • Estimate before you calculate, if you can. • Do any necessary calculations. (For tips on using a graphics calculator or a spreadsheet, see the Technology Handbook.)
Answer	• Check whether your answer is reasonable. • Read the problem again and give your answer using the words of the problem.

Example Students at the Booster Club Car Wash earned $41 between 7:30 A.M. and 9:30 A.M. They charged $7 per truck and $4 per car. How many of each kind of vehicle did they wash in those two hours?

Understand Facts given: prices charged, $7 per truck and $4 per car

total earned, $41

time period, 2 hours ← Unnecessary information

Facts to find: the number of trucks and of cars washed

Plan If you knew the number of trucks, ← It seems as if there is not
you could calculate the number   enough information.
of cars, and vice versa.

Guess an equal number of trucks ← Try the strategy of "guess
and cars. Check the total earned   and check."
using multiplication and addition.
Continue to guess and check until
you find a correct total of $41.

Work Guess 5 trucks and 5 cars: $(5 \times \$7) + (5 \times \$4) = \$55$ ← Too high
Guess 3 trucks: $(3 \times \$7) + (5 \times \$4) = \$41$ ← The correct total

Answer The students washed 3 trucks and 5 cars.

Use the four-step plan to solve each problem.

1. The Computer Club has saved $520 to buy graphics calculators. Each calculator costs $72 including tax. How many calculators can the club buy?

2. Anika Miller participates in a frequent flyer plan. She needs 20,000 mi to earn a free airline ticket. Her January statement showed that she had earned 12,102 frequent flyer miles. Trips in February and April earned her 3534 mi and 1802 mi. How many more miles does Anika need to get a free ticket?

3. Student tickets for the basketball playoffs cost $2 each. All other tickets cost $5 each. Suppose 347 tickets worth $1108 were sold. How many of them were student tickets?

Skill 27   Choosing Strategies

Good problem solvers have a checklist of strategies in their toolbox of skills. Here are examples of some strategies you may have used.

Examples
- Make a table ⟵ When you have data to organize
- Draw a diagram ⟵ When words describe a picture
- Guess and check ⟵ When you do not seem to have enough information
- Use an equation ⟵ When you know a relationship between quantities
- Use a formula ⟵ When you recognize a known relationship
- Identify a pattern ⟵ When you can examine several cases
- Solve a simpler problem ⟵ When easier numbers help you understand the problem
- Work backward ⟵ When you are looking for a fact leading to a known result
- Use a proportion ⟵ When you know that two ratios are equal

Solve each problem.

1. One week Winona Jones earned $306.25 for 35 hours of work at the library. The next week she worked 28 hours. How much did she earn that week?

2. The seniors sold 287 boxes of stationery to earn money for their gift to the school. Each box of stationery included 18 sheets of paper and 12 envelopes. The students collected $1363.25 in sales. What did each box cost?

3. A machine manufactures an item every 12 seconds. Three people are needed to operate the machine. How many items are manufactured in an 8 h work day?

4. A rectangular vegetable garden has a perimeter of 46 ft and a length of 10 ft. What is its area?

Table of Measures

Student Resources

Time

60 seconds (s) = 1 minute (min)
60 minutes = 1 hour (h)
24 hours = 1 day
7 days = 1 week
4 weeks (approx.) = 1 month

365 days
52 weeks (approx.) } = 1 year
12 months

10 years = 1 decade
100 years = 1 century

Metric

Length

10 millimeters (mm) = 1 centimeter (cm)

100 cm
1000 mm } = 1 meter (m)

1000 m = 1 kilometer (km)

Area

100 square millimeters = 1 square centimeter
(mm^2)   (cm^2)
10,000 cm^2 = 1 square meter (m^2)
10,000 m^2 = 1 hectare (ha)

Volume

1000 cubic millimeters = 1 cubic centimeter
(mm^3)   (cm^3)
1,000,000 cm^3 = 1 cubic meter (m^3)

Liquid Capacity

1000 milliliters (mL) = 1 liter (L)
1000 L = 1 kiloliter (kL)

Mass

1000 milligrams (mg) = 1 gram (g)
1000 g = 1 kilogram (kg)
1000 kg = 1 metric ton (t)

Temperature — Degrees Celsius (°C)

0°C = freezing point
of water
37°C = normal body
temperature
100°C = boiling point
of water

United States Customary

Length

12 inches (in.) = 1 foot (ft)

36 in.
3 ft } = 1 yard (yd)

5280 ft
1760 yd } = 1 mile (mi)

Area

144 square inches (in.^{2}) = 1 square foot (ft^2)
9 ft^2 = 1 square yard (yd^2)

43,560 ft^2
4840 yd^2 } = 1 acre (A)

Volume

1728 cubic inches (in.^{3}) = 1 cubic foot (ft^3)
27 ft^3 = 1 cubic yard (yd^3)

Liquid Capacity

8 fluid ounces (fl oz) = 1 cup (c)
2 c = 1 pint (pt)
2 pt = 1 quart (qt)
4 qt = 1 gallon (gal)

Weight

16 ounces (oz) = 1 pound (lb)
2000 lb = 1 ton (t)

Temperature — Degrees Fahrenheit (°F)

32°F = freezing point
of water
98.6°F = normal body
temperature
212°F = boiling point
of water

Table of Symbols

Symbol		Page	Symbol		Page
$\cdot$	$\times$ (times)	10	$\pm$	plus-or-minus sign	112
a^n	nth power of a	19	$\sqrt[3]{a}$	cube root of a	114
( )	parentheses—a grouping symbol	27	$>$	is greater than	144
[ ]	brackets—a grouping symbol	28	$<$	is less than	144
			$\geq$	is greater than or equal to	144
$\cong$	congruent, is congruent to	40	$\leq$	is less than or equal to	144
-3	negative 3	64	(x, y)	ordered pair of numbers	184
$-a$	opposite of a	64	$\triangle ABC$	triangle ABC	191
$|a|$	absolute value of a	64	$A \rightarrow A'$	point A goes to point A' after a transformation	198
$\approx$	is approximately equal to	73	$\dfrac{1}{a}$	reciprocal of a	230
$\overleftrightarrow{AB}$	line AB	82	$a : b$	ratio of a to b	301
$\overline{AB}$	segment AB	82	$P(E)$	probability of event E	308
AB	the length of AB	82	$\sim$	similar, is similar to	329
$\overrightarrow{AB}$	ray AB	85	$\sin A$	sine of A	344
$\angle A$	angle A	85	$\cos A$	cosine of A	344
$\circ$	degree(s)	86	$\tan A$	tangent of A	361
$=$	equals, is equal to	99	π	pi, a number approximately equal to 3.14	376
$\stackrel{?}{=}$	is this statement true?	100			
$\sqrt{a}$	nonnegative square root of a	112	m	slope	418

Table of Squares and Square Roots

No.	Square	Sq. Root	No.	Square	Sq. Root	No.	Square	Sq. Root
1	1	1.000	51	2,601	7.141	101	10,201	10.050
2	4	1.414	52	2,704	7.211	102	10,404	10.100
3	9	1.732	53	2,809	7.280	103	10,609	10.149
4	16	2.000	54	2,916	7.348	104	10,816	10.198
5	25	2.236	55	3,025	7.416	105	11,025	10.247
6	36	2.449	56	3,136	7.483	106	11,236	10.296
7	49	2.646	57	3,249	7.550	107	11,449	10.344
8	64	2.828	58	3,364	7.616	108	11,664	10.392
9	81	3.000	59	3,481	7.681	109	11,881	10.440
10	100	3.162	60	3,600	7.746	110	12,100	10.488
11	121	3.317	61	3,721	7.810	111	12,321	10.536
12	144	3.464	62	3,844	7.874	112	12,544	10.583
13	169	3.606	63	3,969	7.937	113	12,769	10.630
14	196	3.742	64	4,096	8.000	114	12,996	10.677
15	225	3.873	65	4,225	8.062	115	13,225	10.724
16	256	4.000	66	4,356	8.124	116	13,456	10.770
17	289	4.123	67	4,489	8.185	117	13,689	10.817
18	324	4.243	68	4,624	8.246	118	13,924	10.863
19	361	4.359	69	4,761	8.307	119	14,161	10.909
20	400	4.472	70	4,900	8.367	120	14,400	10.954
21	441	4.583	71	5,041	8.426	121	14,641	11.000
22	484	4.690	72	5,184	8.485	122	14,884	11.045
23	529	4.796	73	5,329	8.544	123	15,129	11.091
24	576	4.899	74	5,476	8.602	124	15,376	11.136
25	625	5.000	75	5,625	8.660	125	15,625	11.180
26	676	5.099	76	5,776	8.718	126	15,876	11.225
27	729	5.196	77	5,929	8.775	127	16,129	11.269
28	784	5.292	78	6,084	8.832	128	16,384	11.314
29	841	5.385	79	6,241	8.888	129	16,641	11.358
30	900	5.477	80	6,400	8.944	130	16,900	11.402
31	961	5.568	81	6,561	9.000	131	17,161	11.446
32	1,024	5.657	82	6,724	9.055	132	17,424	11.489
33	1,089	5.745	83	6,889	9.110	133	17,689	11.533
34	1,156	5.831	84	7,056	9.165	134	17,956	11.576
35	1,225	5.916	85	7,225	9.220	135	18,225	11.619
36	1,296	6.000	86	7,396	9.274	136	18,496	11.662
37	1,369	6.083	87	7,569	9.327	137	18,769	11.705
38	1,444	6.164	88	7,744	9.381	138	19,044	11.747
39	1,521	6.245	89	7,921	9.434	139	19,321	11.790
40	1,600	6.325	90	8,100	9.487	140	19,600	11.832
41	1,681	6.403	91	8,281	9.539	141	19,881	11.874
42	1,764	6.481	92	8,464	9.592	142	20,164	11.916
43	1,849	6.557	93	8,649	9.644	143	20,449	11.958
44	1,936	6.633	94	8,836	9.695	144	20,736	12.000
45	2,025	6.708	95	9,025	9.747	145	21,025	12.042
46	2,116	6.782	96	9,216	9.798	146	21,316	12.083
47	2,209	6.856	97	9,409	9.849	147	21,609	12.124
48	2,304	6.928	98	9,604	9.899	148	21,904	12.166
49	2,401	7.000	99	9,801	9.950	149	22,201	12.207
50	2,500	7.071	100	10,000	10.000	150	22,500	12.247

Student Resources

Table of Trigonometric Ratios

Angle	Sine	Cosine	Tangent	Angle	Sine	Cosine	Tangent
1°	.0175	.9998	.0175	46°	.7193	.6947	1.0355
2°	.0349	.9994	.0349	47°	.7314	.6820	1.0724
3°	.0523	.9986	.0524	48°	.7431	.6691	1.1106
4°	.0698	.9976	.0699	49°	.7547	.6561	1.1504
5°	.0872	.9962	.0875	50°	.7660	.6428	1.1918
6°	.1045	.9945	.1051	51°	.7771	.6293	1.2349
7°	.1219	.9925	.1228	52°	.7880	.6157	1.2799
8°	.1392	.9903	.1405	53°	.7986	.6018	1.3270
9°	.1564	.9877	.1584	54°	.8090	.5878	1.3764
10°	.1736	.9848	.1763	55°	.8192	.5736	1.4281
11°	.1908	.9816	.1944	56°	.8290	.5592	1.4826
12°	.2079	.9781	.2126	57°	.8387	.5446	1.5399
13°	.2250	.9744	.2309	58°	.8480	.5299	1.6003
14°	.2419	.9703	.2493	59°	.8572	.5150	1.6643
15°	.2588	.9659	.2679	60°	.8660	.5000	1.7321
16°	.2756	.9613	.2867	61°	.8746	.4848	1.8040
17°	.2924	.9563	.3057	62°	.8829	.4695	1.8807
18°	.3090	.9511	.3249	63°	.8910	.4540	1.9626
19°	.3256	.9455	.3443	64°	.8988	.4384	2.0503
20°	.3420	.9397	.3640	65°	.9063	.4226	2.1445
21°	.3584	.9336	.3839	66°	.9135	.4067	2.2460
22°	.3746	.9272	.4040	67°	.9205	.3907	2.3559
23°	.3907	.9205	.4245	68°	.9272	.3746	2.4751
24°	.4067	.9135	.4452	69°	.9336	.3584	2.6051
25°	.4226	.9063	.4663	70°	.9397	.3420	2.7475
26°	.4384	.8988	.4877	71°	.9455	.3256	2.9042
27°	.4540	.8910	.5095	72°	.9511	.3090	3.0777
28°	.4695	.8829	.5317	73°	.9563	.2924	3.2709
29°	.4848	.8746	.5543	74°	.9613	.2756	3.4874
30°	.5000	.8660	.5774	75°	.9659	.2588	3.7321
31°	.5150	.8572	.6009	76°	.9703	.2419	4.0108
32°	.5299	.8480	.6249	77°	.9744	.2250	4.3315
33°	.5446	.8387	.6494	78°	.9781	.2079	4.7046
34°	.5592	.8290	.6745	79°	.9816	.1908	5.1446
35°	.5736	.8192	.7002	80°	.9848	.1736	5.6713
36°	.5878	.8090	.7265	81°	.9877	.1564	6.3138
37°	.6018	.7986	.7536	82°	.9903	.1392	7.1154
38°	.6157	.7880	.7813	83°	.9925	.1219	8.1443
39°	.6293	.7771	.8098	84°	.9945	.1045	9.5144
40°	.6428	.7660	.8391	85°	.9962	.0872	11.4301
41°	.6561	.7547	.8693	86°	.9976	.0698	14.3007
42°	.6691	.7431	.9004	87°	.9986	.0523	19.0811
43°	.6820	.7314	.9325	88°	.9994	.0349	28.6363
44°	.6947	.7193	.9657	89°	.9998	.0175	57.2900
45°	.7071	.7071	1.0000				

A-1 Domain and Range

For use after Section 4-7

Talk it Over

Height of Water in a Fish Pond

Height (cm): 0, 3, 6, 9, 12, 15, 18

Minutes after tap is turned on: 0, 1, 2, 3, 4, 5

1. The graph above represents a function. Identify the control variable and the dependent variable.

2. Describe all possible values of the control variable. Then describe all possible values of the dependent variable.

3. Did your descriptions include the values between the numbers shown on the scales of the axes? Why or why not?

In Question 2, you described the *domain* and the *range* of the water height function. For any function, the **domain** is all the values of the control variable. The **range** is all the values of the dependent variable. The range depends on the domain.

Sample

Describe the domain and the range of the function represented by the graph.

Sample Response

The control variable is the number of days. The domain is the numbers 0, 1, 2, 3, 4, ...

The dependent variable is the amounts earned. The range is the dollar amounts 0, 50, 100, 150, ...

The points on the graph are not connected. The domain and range values are discrete.

Earnings of a Camp Counselor

Earnings (dollars): 0, 100, 200, 300

Number of days: 0, 1, 2, 3, 4, 5, 6, 7

Choosing Reasonable Values

Various conditions can limit or restrict the domain and range values of a function. Thinking about such restrictions can help you choose domain and range values that make sense for a particular function.

> **Talk it Over**
>
> **4.** A library charges $.10 for each day a book is overdue. Your total fine depends on the number of days a book is overdue. Describe a reasonable domain and range for the function. Explain your thinking.

Exercises and Problems

Describe the domain and the range of the function represented by each graph.

1.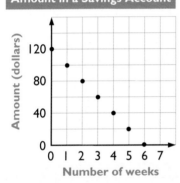

Amount in a Savings Account

2.

Wool Yarn Production

For Exercises 3–7, describe a reasonable domain and range for each function. Explain your thinking.

3. John Ramos is buying gasoline for his car. The price per gallon is $1.69. His total cost depends on the amount of gasoline he buys.

4. The height of a burning candle depends on how long it burns. Lisa found that the height of one candle decreased by about 1 in. per hour. The original height of the candle was 10 in.

5. Tariq has 12 tickets to sell to a play. The tickets cost $3.50 each. The amount of money he collects depends on the number of tickets he sells.

6. Jan Amdahl pays for some groceries with a $50 bill. The amount of change she receives depends on the cost of the groceries.

7. Customers at a music store can use a coupon for $1.50 off any purchase costing at least $15. The store allows only one coupon per customer. The amount that a customer using a coupon pays depends on the amount of his or her purchase.

A-2 Slope and y-Intercept

For use after Section 8-1

Ilona Rostov wants to sell some hand-made pins. She first draws a line to predict how much money she can make if she charges $25 for each pin. Then she realizes that it is going to cost her $300 to buy materials for the pins. She draws a second line to show her expected profit minus her start-up costs.

Focus

Analyze and interpret the effects of changing the slope and the y-intercept of a graph.

Talk it Over

1. What do you notice about the slopes of the two lines? What real-world information do the slopes give you?

2. Give the vertical intercept of each graph. What real-world information do the vertical intercepts give you?

You can use what you know about the slope-intercept form of an equation to predict how the graph of one equation will compare with another.

Sample

Describe how the graphs of y = 2x and y = 0.5x will compare with the graph of y = x. Then graph all three equations.

Sample Response

Each equation is in slope-intercept form, $y = mx + b$, where m = slope and b = y-intercept.

$y = x$	$y = 2x$	$y = 0.5x$
slope = 1	slope = 2	slope = 0.5
y-intercept = 0	y-intercept = 0	y-intercept = 0

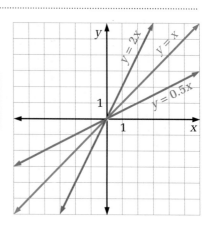

The graph of y = 2x will be steeper than the graph of y = x because its slope is greater. The graph of y = 0.5x will be less steep because its slope is less. All three graphs will pass through the origin.

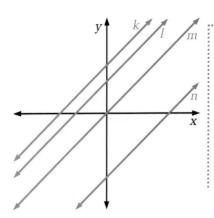

Talk it Over

3. Match each line at the left with one of the equations below. Explain your thinking.

    A. $y = x$ **B.** $y = x + 3$

    C. $y = x - 4$ **D.** $y = x + 2$

4. Describe how changing the values of m and b in an equation in the form $y = mx + b$ changes the graph of the equation. Be sure to talk about both positive and negative values of m and b.

A-2 Exercises and Problems

1. Describe how the graphs of $y = -3x$ and $y = 3x$ compare with the graph of $y = x$. Then graph all three equations.

2. Describe how the graphs of $y = x - 20$ and $y = x + 20$ compare with the graph of $y = x$. Then graph all three equations.

3. In Section 8-1, you used the equation $h = 110t + 6000$ to model the height h above sea level of a balloon t minutes after it takes off from a location that is 6000 ft above sea level. Height is measured in feet.

    a. Suppose a balloon takes off from Leadville, Colorado (elevation 10,152 ft above sea level), and rises at a rate of 55 ft/min. Write an equation to describe the height above sea level of this balloon t minutes after it takes off.

    b. Describe how the graph of the equation you wrote in part (a) will compare with the graph of the equation $h = 110t + 6000$. Then graph both equations on the same set of axes.

4. Does doubling the value of m in an equation of the form $y = mx$ double the angle between the graph and the x-axis? Explain your reasoning.

5. Look back at the jewelry-sales graph on page 672. Suppose Ilona decides to lower her start-up costs by using cheaper materials. She also decides to charge less for each pin.

    a. Write an equation to model this new situation.

    b. Describe how the graph of your equation will compare with the lines on the jewelry-sales graph on page 672. Then graph your equation.

6. One way to graph an equation is to make a table of values, plot points, and draw a line through the points. Based on what you know about slope-intercept form, describe another method for graphing an equation.

absolute value (p. 64) The distance that a number is from zero on a number line.

absolute value function (p. 230) The function $y = |x|$.

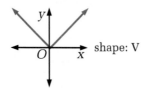

shape: V

acute angle (p. 86) An angle that measures between 0° and 90°.

acute triangle (p. 88) A triangle with three acute angles.

angle (p. 85) A figure formed by two rays that have the same endpoint, called the *vertex*.

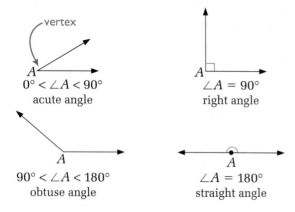

vertex

A
$0° < \angle A < 90°$
acute angle

A
$\angle A = 90°$
right angle

A
$90° < \angle A < 180°$
obtuse angle

A
$\angle A = 180°$
straight angle

arc (p. 377) Part of a circle. Any angle with its vertex at the center of a circle is a *central angle of the circle*. The region formed by a central angle and its arc is a *sector*.

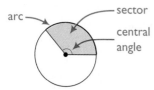

arc

sector

central angle

arc length (p. 377) The measurement of an arc.

at random (p. 308) *See* sampling.

base (pp. 281, 282, 283) *See* parallelogram, trapezoid, triangle.

base of a power (p. 19) *See* power.

bases of a prism (p. 507) *See* prism.

binomial (p. 578) The sum of two monomials.

boundary line (p. 456) *See* linear inequality.

box–and–whisker plot (p. 158) A method for displaying the median, quartiles, and extremes of a data set.

Test Scores

lower extreme

lower quartile

median

upper quartile

upper extreme

cell (p. 129) *See* spreadsheet.

center of dilation (p. 337) *See* dilation.

center of rotation (p. 202) *See* rotation.

central angle of a circle (p. 85) An angle with its vertex at the center of a circle. *See also* arc.

circumference (p. 375) The perimeter of a circle. A segment that joins two points of the circumference with the center of the circle is a *diameter*.

diameter

$C = \pi d$

circumference

coefficient (p. 33) A number multiplied by a variable in a term of an expression. *See also* term.

combined inequality (p. 144) An inequality with two inequality signs such that a value of a variable is between two quantities. A combined inequality like $-3 < x \le 5$ is graphed on a number line as a segment or *interval*.

complementary angles (p. 86) Two angles whose measures have the sum 90°.

complementary events (p. 310) Two events such that only one or the other is possible. For example, the event "E happens" is the complement of the event "E does not happen."

concept map (p. 5) A visual summary that helps you remember the connections between ideas.

conclusion (p. 492) *See* if-then statement.

conditional statements (p. 492) *See* if-then statement.

cone (p. 524) A space figure with one circular base and a vertex.

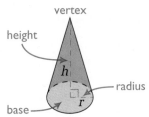

congruent (p. 38) Having the same size and shape.

congruent angles (p. 87) Angles with equal measures.

congruent segments (p. 82) Segments with equal measures.

conjecture (p. 21) A statement, opinion, or conclusion based on observation.

constant term (p. 33) Any term of an expression which contains only a number. *See also* term.

continuous (p. 60) Quantities that are measured.

control variable (p. 218) *See* function.

converse (p. 494) A statement in "if-then" form obtained by interchanging the "if" and "then" parts of an original if-then statement.

converse of the Pythagorean theorem (p. 495) If the square of the length of one side of a triangle is equal to the sum of the squares of the lengths of the other two sides, then the triangle is a right triangle.

conversion factor (p. 393) A conversion factor is a ratio of two equal (or approximately equal) quantities that are measured in different units.

coordinate geometry (p. 190) Geometry involving the drawing, analyzing, finding area, and comparison of figures on a coordinate plane.

coordinate plane (p. 184) A grid formed by two perpendicular number lines or *axes* intersecting at the *origin*. The axes split the plane into four *quadrants*.

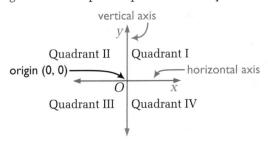

coordinates (p. 184) The unique *ordered pair* of real numbers associated with each point in a coordinate plane. The first number of the ordered pair is the *x-coordinate*, the second number is the *y-coordinate*.

correlation (p. 212) The relationship between two data sets. Two data sets can have positive correlation if they increase or decrease together, negative correlation if one set increases as the other set decreases, or no correlation.

corresponding vertices and sides (p. 40) In congruent polygons, matching vertices are corresponding vertices and matching sides are corresponding sides.

cosine (p. 344) *See* trigonometric ratios.

counterexample (p. 22) An example that shows that a statement is false.

cross products (p. 315) Equal products formed by multiplying the numerator of each of a pair of equal fractions by the denominator of the other.

cube root (p. 114) One of three equal factors of a number.

cylinder (p. 508) A space figure with a curved surface and two parallel, congruent circular bases.

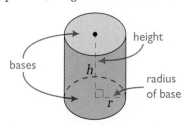

deductive reasoning (p. 479) Using facts, definitions, and accepted principles and properties to prove general statements.

dependent variable (p. 218) *See* function.

diagonal (p. 424) A segment joining two nonconsecutive vertices of a polygon.

diameter (p. 375) *See* circumference.

dilation (p. 337) A transformation in which the original figure and its image are similar. Lines drawn through the corresponding points on the original figure and its image meet in a point called the *center of dilation*.

dimensional analysis (p. 392) A problem solving strategy where you cancel units of measurement as if they are numbers.

dimensions (p. 128) *See* matrix.

direct variation (p. 360) A linear function defined by an equation of the form $y = kx$, $k \neq 0$. You say that y is directly proportional to x.

discrete (p. 60) Quantities that are counted.

distance from a point to a line (p. 281) The length of the perpendicular segment from a point to a line.

distributive property (p. 32) Each term inside a set of parentheses can be multiplied by a factor outside the parentheses. For example, $3(x + 2) = 3x + 6$.

endpoint (p. 82) A point that marks the first point or the last point of a line segment. *See also* ray.

equation (p. 99) A statement formed by placing an equals sign between two numerical or variable expressions.

equilateral triangle (p. 44) A triangle with all three sides congruent.

equivalent equations (p. 100) Equations that have the same solution set.

equivalent inequalities (p. 263) Inequalities that have the same solution set.

evaluate (p. 12) To find the value of a variable expression when a number is substituted for the variable.

event (p. 308) *See* outcome.

expanded form (p. 577) The form an expression is in when it has no parenthesis.

$$x(x + 3) = x^2 + 3x$$
factored form   expanded form

experimental probability (p. 308) In an experiment, the ratio of the number of times an event occurs to the number of times the experiment is run.

exponent (p. 19) *See* power.

extremes (p. 158) The lowest and highest numbers of a data set.

faces of a prism (p. 507) *See* prism.

factor (p. 19) When two or more numbers or variables are multiplied, each of the numbers or variables is a factor of the product.

factored completely (p. 578) When the greatest common factor of all the terms in an expression is 1.

factored form (p. 577) The form an expression has when it is factored completely.

$$x^2 + 3x = x(x + 3)$$
expanded form   factored form

fitted line (p. 212) *See* scatter plot.

frequency (p. 150) The number of times an event or data item occurs within an interval.

frequency table (p. 151) A table that displays the exact number of data items in an interval.

function (p. 220) A relationship between two variables in which the value of the *dependent variable* is dependent on the value of the *control variable*. There can only be one value of the dependent variable for each value of the control variable.

geometric probability (p. 502) Probability based on areas and lengths.

graph of an equation (p. 426) The points whose coordinates are the solutions of the equation.

height (pp. 281, 282) *See* parallelogram, triangle.

height of a regular pyramid (p. 510) *See* regular pyramid.

heptagon (p. 39) A polygon with seven sides.

hexagon (p. 39) A polygon with six sides.

histogram (p. 150) A type of bar graph that displays frequencies.

horizontal axis (p. 184) *See* coordinate plane.

horizontal intercept (p. 428) *See* x-intercept.

hyperbola (p. 230) The graph of $xy = k$, $k \neq 0$. *See also* reciprocal function.

hypotenuse (p. 344) *See* right triangle.

hypothesis (p. 492) *See* if-then statement.

identity function (p. 230) The function $y = x$.

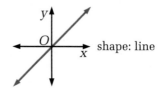
shape: line

if-then statement (p. 492) A statement with an *if* part and a *then* part. The *if* part is the *hypothesis* and the *then* part is the *conclusion*. Also called a *conditional statement*.

image (p. 337) The result of a transformation.

inductive reasoning (p. 479) A method of reasoning in which a conjecture is made based on several observations.

inequality (p. 144) A statement formed by placing an inequality sign between two numerical or variable expressions.

integer (p. 113) Any number that is a positive or negative whole number or zero.

interval (p. 145) *See* combined inequality.

irrational number (p. 113) A real number that cannot be written as the quotient of two integers.

isosceles triangle (p. 44) A triangle with at least two sides congruent.

kite (p. 45) A quadrilateral with two pairs of consecutive sides equal in measure. These pairs do not have a side in common.

legs of a right triangle (p. 344) *See* right triangle.

length of a segment (p. 82) The measure of the distance between and including the two endpoints of a segment.

like terms (p. 33) Terms with the same variables or variable powers.

line (p. 82) A straight arrangement of points that extends forever in opposite directions.

line plot (p. 137) A method of displaying a data set on a number line. It is helpful in showing the outliers and the range of a data set.

line of reflection (p. 548) *See* reflection.

line of symmetry (p. 45) *See* symmetry.

linear combination (p. 426) The result of adding two or more linear expressions.

linear decay (p. 420) A decreasing linear function that can be defined by $y = mx + b$, $m < 0$.

linear equation (p. 427) An equation of a line.

linear function (p. 420) A function that can be defined by $y = mx + b$.

linear growth (p. 420) An increasing linear function that can be defined by $y = mx + b$, $m > 0$.

linear inequality (p. 456) An inequality whose graph on a coordinate plane is a region bounded by a line, called the *boundary line*.

lower quartile (p. 158) The median of the data in the lower half of a data set.

margin of error (p. 323) In an experiment or poll, the interval most likely to include the exact result.

mathematical model (p. 241) An equation or graph that represents a real-life problem. Using such equations or graphs is *modeling*.

matrix (p. 128) An arrangement of numbers in rows and columns. The number of rows by the number of columns gives you the *dimensions* of the matrix.

mean (p. 136) The sum of the data in a data set divided by the number of items.

median (p. 136) In a data set, the middle number or the average of the two middle numbers when the data are arranged in numerical order.

midpoint (p. 82) The point that divides a segment into two congruent parts.

mode (p. 136) The most frequently occurring item, or items, in a data set.

modeling (p. 241) *See* mathematical model.

monomial (p. 578) A number, a variable, or the product of a number and one or more variables.

obtuse angle (p. 86) An angle that measures between 90° and 180°.

obtuse triangle (p. 88) A triangle with one obtuse angle.

octagon (p. 39) A polygon with eight sides.

opposites (p. 64) A number and its opposite are the same distance from 0 on the number line but on opposite sides. The opposite of 3 is -3.

order of operations (p. 26) A set of rules that orders the way you simplify an expression: simplify inside parentheses, calculate any powers, multiply or divide left to right, and finally add or subtract left to right.

ordered pair (p. 184) *See* coordinates.

orientation (p. 548) The direction, clockwise or counterclockwise, in which the points on a figure are ordered.

origin (p. 184) *See* coordinate plane.

outcome (p. 308) One possible result in an experiment in a probability problem. A set of outcomes is an *event*.

outliers (p. 137) Data values that are much larger or much smaller than the other values in a data set, and therefore not typical of the data set.

parabola (pp. 229, 555) The graph of $y = ax^2 + bx + c$, $a \neq 0$. The point where the curve turns is either the maximum or the minimum and is called the *vertex*. *See also* squaring function.

parallel lines (p. 44) Two lines in the same plane that do not intersect.

parallelogram (p. 45) A quadrilateral with both pairs of opposite sides parallel.

pentagon (p. 39) A polygon with five sides.

perfect cube (p. 114) A number whose cube root is an integer.

perfect square (p. 114) A number whose square root is an integer.

perpendicular (p. 44) Two lines, segments, or rays that intersect to form right angles.

polygon (p. 39) A plane figure formed by line segments, called *sides*. Each side intersects exactly two other sides, one at each endpoint or *vertex*. No two sides with a common vertex are on the same line.

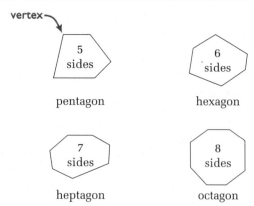

pentagon   hexagon

heptagon   octagon

population (p. 321) The entire set of objects being studied.

power (p. 19) A number that is used as a factor a given number of times. In the power 5^2, 5 is the *base* and 2 is the *exponent*.

prism (p. 507) A space figure with two parallel congruent *bases*. The other sides of the prism are *faces*.

rectangular prism

probability (p. 308) The ratio of the number of favorable outcomes to the total number of outcomes.

proportion (p. 314) An equation that shows two equal ratios.

pyramid (p. 509) A space figure with one base and triangular faces.

Pythagorean theorem (p. 478) If the length of the hypotenuse of a right triangle is c and the lengths of the legs are a and b, then $c^2 = a^2 + b^2$.

quadrant (p. 184) *See* coordinate plane.

quadratic equation (p. 599) Any equation that can be written in the form $ax^2 + bx + c = 0$, $a \neq 0$.

quadratic formula (p. 601) The formula

$$x = -\frac{b}{2a} \pm \frac{\sqrt{b^2 - 4ac}}{2a},$$

given $0 = ax^2 + bx + c$, $a \neq 0$.

quadratic function (p. 599) Any function of the form $y = ax^2 + bx + c$, $a \neq 0$.

quadrilateral (p. 39) A polygon with four sides.

radical form (p. 487) An expression that uses the radical symbol ($\sqrt{}$). For example, $\sqrt{11}$.

radius (p. 376) One half of a diameter of a circle.

range (p. 137) The difference between the extremes in a data set.

rate (p. 302) A ratio that compares the amounts of two different kinds of measurements, for example, meters per second.

ratio (p. 301) The quotient you get when one number is divided by a second number not equal to zero.

rational number (p. 113) A real number that can be written as a quotient of two integers $\frac{a}{b}$, $b \neq 0$.

ray (p. 85) A part of a line that starts at a point, the *endpoint,* and extends forever in one direction.

real number (p. 113) Any number that is either rational or irrational.

reciprocals (p. 275) Two numbers whose product is 1.

reciprocal function (p. 230) The function $y = \frac{1}{x}$.

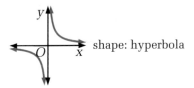

shape: hyperbola

rectangle (p. 45) A quadrilateral with four right angles.

rectangular prism (p. 507) *See* prism.

reflection (p. 548) The image you get when you flip a figure over a line. This line is the *line of reflection*.

regular pyramid (p. 509) A pyramid in which the base is a regular polygon, and all other faces are congruent isosceles triangles. The *height* is the perpendicular length from the vertex to the center of the base. The height of a face is the *slant height*.

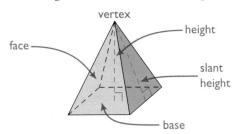

vertex

face

height

slant height

base

rhombus (p. 45) A quadrilateral with four congruent sides.

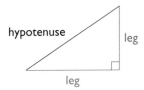

right angle (p. 86) An angle that measures 90°.

right triangle (p. 44) A triangle with one right angle. The side opposite the right angle is the *hypotenuse*, the other sides are the *legs*.

hypotenuse

leg

leg

rise (p. 361) The vertical change between two points on a line.

rotation (p. 202) A turn around a point called the *center of rotation*. A figure that looks the same after a rotation of less than 360° has *rotational symmetry*.

rotational symmetry (p. 205) *See* rotation.

run (p. 361) The horizontal change between two points on a line.

sample (p. 321) A subset of the population on which a study or an experiment is being done.

sampling (p. 323) Choosing a sample from a population for an experiment or study. The sample is chosen *at random*, meaning each member of the population has an equal chance to be chosen.

scale (p. 330) The ratio of the size of a representation of an object to the actual object.

scale drawing (p. 330) A drawing representing and similar to an actual object.

scale factor (p. 337) The ratio of a length on an image to the corresponding length on the original figure of a dilation.

scalene triangle (p. 44) A triangle with no sides congruent.

scatter plot (p. 212) A graph that shows the relationship between two sets of data. A line that passes close to most of the data points is called a *fitted line*.

scientific notation (p. 72) A number written as a number that is at least one but less than ten, multiplied by a power of ten.

sector (p. 402) *See* arc.

segment (p. 82) Two points on a line and all points between them.

side (p. 40) *See* polygon.

similar figures (p. 329) Two figures with the same shape, but not necessarily the same size.

similar space figures (p. 532) Space figures that have the same shape, but not necessarily the same size.

sine (p. 344) *See* trigonometric ratios.

slant height of a regular pyramid (p. 510) *See* regular pyramid.

slope (p. 361) The measure of the steepness of a line given by the ratio of rise to run for any two points on the line.

slope-intercept form of an equation (p. 418) An equation of the form $y = mx + b$, where m represents the slope and b represents the y-intercept of a line.

solution (p. 99) Values for variables that make an equation true.

solution of an equation with two variables (p. 426) An ordered pair of values that makes an equation with two variables true.

solution of a system (p. 291) Values for variables that make a system of equations true.

solution of a system of inequalities (p. 464) Values for variables that make a system of inequalities true.

solution region (p. 456) *See* linear inequality.

solving an equation (p. 99) Finding all values of a variable that make an equation true.

spreadsheet (p. 129) A computerized version of a matrix. Each position in a spreadsheet is a *cell*.

square (p. 45) A quadrilateral with four right angles and four congruent sides.

square root (p. 112) One of two equal factors of a number.

squaring function (p. 230) The function $y = x^2$.

shape: parabola

standard form of a linear equation (p. 427) An equation in the form $ax + by = c$, where a, b, and c are integers and a and b are not both zero.

stem-and-leaf plot (p. 152) A display of data where each number is represented by a *stem* and a *leaf*.

straight angle (p. 86) An angle that measures 180°.

substitute (p. 12) To replace variables with given values.

supplementary angles (p. 86) Two angles whose measures have the sum 180°.

symmetry (p. 45) When a polygon can be folded so that one half fits exactly over the other half, the polygon has symmetry. The fold line is called the *line of symmetry*.

system of equations (p. 291) Two or more equations in the same variables.

system of inequalities (p. 464) Two or more inequalities in the same variables.

tangent ratio (p. 361) *See* trigonometric ratios.

term (p. 33) Each expression in a sum.

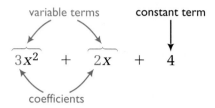

terms of a proportion (p. 314) The numbers or variables in a proportion.

theoretical probability (p. 309) When all outcomes of an experiment are equally likely, the probability of an event is the ratio of favorable outcomes to the number of possible outcomes.

transformation (p. 202) A change made to an object or its position.

translation (p. 197) Sliding a figure without changing its size or shape and without turning or flipping it over. When a figure can translate within a pattern, the pattern has *translational symmetry*.

translational symmetry (p. 199) *See* translation.

trapezoid (p. 193) A quadrilateral with one pair of parallel sides, called bases. The other sides are legs.

triangle (p. 39) A polygon with three sides.

trigonometric ratios (p. 344) The *cosine*, *sine*, and *tangent ratios*.

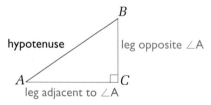

$$\cos A = \frac{\text{adjacent}}{\text{hypotenuse}} = \frac{AC}{AB}$$

$$\sin A = \frac{\text{opposite}}{\text{hypotenuse}} = \frac{BC}{AB}$$

$$\tan A = \frac{\text{opposite}}{\text{adjacent}} = \frac{BC}{AC}$$

trinomial (p. 584) The sum of three monomials.

unit rate (p. 302) A rate for one unit of a given quantity.

upper quartile (p. 158) The median of the data in the upper half of a data set.

variable (p. 10) A symbol, usually a letter, that represents a number.

variable expression (p. 10) An expression that contains a variable.

variable terms (p. 256) Terms of an expression that contain a variable. *See also* term.

variation constant (p. 360) The nonzero constant k in a direct variation defined by $y = kx$.

vertex of an angle (p. 85) *See* angle.

vertex of a parabola (p. 555) *See* parabola.

vertex of a polygon (p. 40) *See* polygon.

vertical angles (p. 87) Two congruent angles formed by intersecting lines and facing in opposite directions.

vertical axis (p. 184) *See* coordinate plane.

vertical intercept (p. 418) *See* y-intercept.

vertical-line test (p. 221) When two or more points of a graph lie in the same vertical line, the graph is not a function.

x-axis (pp. 226, 550) The horizontal axis in the coordinate plane.

x-intercept (p. 563) The x-coordinate of a point where a graph intersects the x-axis (where $y = 0$). Also called a *horizontal intercept*.

y-axis (pp. 226, 550) The vertical axis in the coordinate plane.

y-intercept (p. 563) The y-coordinate of a point where a graph intersects the y-axis (where $x = 0$). Also called a *vertical intercept*.

zero-product property (p. 495) When a product of factors is zero, one or more of the factors must be zero. If $ab = 0$, then $a = 0$ or $b = 0$.

Absolute value, 64

Absolute value function, 230

Acute angle, 86

Acute triangle, 88

Algebra, 53, 123, 179, 237, 297, 354, 412, 472-473, 542, 609
  binomials, 578, 583-584
  coordinate graphing, 184, 220, 225-230, 243, 369-370, 385-387, 418-420, 426, 428, 433-434, 442, 448-450, 456-459, 464-465, 555-558, 563, 585, 594-595, 600, 660-661
  direct variation, 360, 368-369, 383-387
  equation solving, 99-102, 105-107, 115, 138, 242, 249-250, 255-257, 270-271, 276-277, 599-603, 645-647
  exponents, 19-22, 71-75, 568-572
  expressions, 10-13, 20-21, 26-28, 32-33, 66, 93-95, 247-248, 577
  factors, 19-20, 562-564, 568-571, 576-579, 592-593, 648-649
  functions, 218-221
  inequality, 143-146, 261-265, 455-459, 463-465
  linear functions, 229, 230, 385, 417-420, 426-428, 433-434, 440-443
  monomial, 578
  quadratic equation, 599-603
  quadratic formula, 601-603
  quadratic functions, 225, 229, 230, 555-558, 562-564, 585-586, 594-595
  radicals, 112-115, 478-479, 486-489
  ratio and proportion, 301-303, 314-316
  systems of equations, 289-291, 448-450
  systems of inequalities, 463-465

  tiles, 13, 16, 21, 28, 29, 32, 100-101, 256, 257, 258, 576-578, 580, 583, 591-592, 646-647
  transforming formulas, 270-271
  trinomial, 584, 591-593
  variable, 10, 20, 95, 99, 218-220
  See also Formulas, Integers, *and* Properties.

Algorithmic thinking, 25 (Ex. 41), 26-27, 29 (Ex. 35), 31, 34 (Ex. 20), 35 (Ex. 31), 36 (Ex. 32), 49 (Exs. 24, 26), 78 (Ex. 1), 92 (Ex. 31), 105, 138, 293 (Ex. 19), 316 (Ex. 2), 446 (Ex. 25), 499 (Ex. 1), 522 (Ex. 1), 572 (Ex. 14), 588 (Ex. 26), 592, 593
  See other exercises under Writing.

Alternative assessment
  See Assessment, Explorations, Group Activities, Open-ended exercises, Projects, *and* Writing.

Angle(s), 85-86, 657
  acute, 86
  central, 85
  complementary, 86
  congruent, 87
  exterior, 92
  measure of, 85-89, 657
  obtuse, 86
  remote interior, 92
  right, 86
  special relationships, 89
  straight, 86
  sum of measures in a triangle, 89
  supplementary, 86
  vertex of, 85
  vertical, 87, 89

Applications
  access standards, 319, 364
  archeology, 188
  art, 200, 210, 235
  astronomy, 120, 140, 210, 380, 398
  aerodynamics, 356
  American Sign Language, 6
  automobiles, 304
  aviation, 319, 350
  banking, 431, 462

  baseball, 482, 597
  budgeting, 467
  business, 133, 452
  carpentry, 359-364
  census, 18
  chemistry, 77
  commissions, 231
  consumerism, 232
  drawing, 526
  driving, 147
  driver education, 371, 603
  economics, 131, 397, 399, 444, 538, 541
  education, 149, 175
  exit polling, 326
  furniture moving, 482
  geography, 98, 120, 168, 169, 244, 296, 380, 497
  geology, 444
  government, 436, 483
  graphic design, 42
  health, 231, 318
  languages, 7, 51, 319
  maps, 83, 98
  marine biology, 222, 604
  meteorology, 173, 231, 267
  nutrition, 318
  packaging, 521
  photocopying, 534
  photography, 341
  scuba diving, 372
  social studies, 305
  sports, 222, 252, 373, 432
  science, 15, 131, 231, 444
  technology, 445
  theater, 303
  transportation, 446
  urban planning, 581
  veterinary medicine, 372
  See also By the way, Career, Connections, Projects, *and* Research.

Approximation symbol, 73

Arc of a circle, 377

Arc length, 377

Area, 280-284, 658-659
  estimating, 79

of a circle, 400-401, 403
of a parallelogram, 194 (Ex. 12), 280-282
of a rectangle, 81, 192-193, 280, 658
of a right triangle, 191-192
of similar figures, 530
of a square, 20, 111, 658
surface, 507-511
of a trapezoid, 193, 283
of a triangle, 195 (Ex. 13, 14), 282

Assessment
Checkpoints, 30, 78, 98, 149, 210, 269, 320, 382, 438, 454, 522, 567, 590
Ongoing Assessment problems, 8, 17, 25, 29, 36, 43, 49, 63, 70, 77, 84, 92, 97, 104, 110, 118, 134, 142, 148, 157, 163, 169, 174, 188, 196, 201, 209, 217, 224, 233, 246, 254, 260, 268, 274, 279, 287, 293, 305, 313, 319, 327, 336, 342, 350, 366, 374, 381, 390, 399, 406, 424, 432, 437, 446, 454, 462, 468, 484, 491, 498, 506, 514, 521, 528, 538, 554, 561, 567, 575, 582, 589, 597, 605
Review and Assessment, 51-52, 120-122, 177-178, 235-236, 295-296, 352-354, 409-411, 470-472, 540-541, 607-608
Self-evaluation questions, 52, 122, 178, 236, 296, 354, 411, 471, 541, 608.
See also Alternative assessment.

Astronomical unit, 140

Authentic assessment
See Alternative assessment.

Average, 136

Bar graph, 164, 661
histogram, 150, 164

Base(s)
of cone, 524
of cylinder, 508
of parallelogram, 281
of prism, 507
of pyramid, 509, 510
repeated factor, 19
of trapezoid, 283
of triangle, 282

Binomial, 578

Biographical note
Surendra Apharya, 77
Louis Braille, 552
René Descartes, 292
Petra Felke, 147
Martin Luther King, Jr., 61
Florence Nightingale, 132
Ida B. Wells, 328, 336

Boundary line of a linear inequality, 456

Box-and-whisker plot, 158

By the way
calories, 137
frog jumping contest, 172
googol, 21
hurricanes, 173
long jump record, 143
pitch, 360
secret codes, 579
solar system, 334
vibrating violin strings, 278
Other interesting facts appear in other "By the Way" notes in the text margins.

Calculator
graphics
in discussion, 227, 243, 277, 385, 386, 419, 603
in exercises, 157, 175, 214, 232, 349, 389, 422, 431, 437, 445, 452, 505, 575
in Explorations, 225, 556
scientific or graphics
in discussion, 20, 26, 64, 73, 74, 106, 112, 113, 115, 344, 346, 347, 362, 376, 401, 517, 518, 525, 603
in exercises, 29, 76, 348, 365, 490, 574
in Explorations, 65, 71
See also Technology Handbook *and* Technology Notes.

Capture-recapture method, 321

Career
acoustical engineer, 544
artist, 187
ball player, 544
biologist, 325
computer programmer, 181, 196
customer service representative, 467
engineer, 180
graphic artist, xxvi
market researcher, 124
medical technician, 60
medicine (doctor), 117
meteorologist, 267
ship designer, 474
special effects designer, 534
sports statistician, 147
sports trainer, 414

Cell in a spreadsheet, 129

Center of dilation, 337

Center of rotation, 202

Central angle of a circle, 85

Checkpoints
Unit 1, 30
Unit 2, 78, 98
Unit 3, 149
Unit 4, 210
Unit 5, 269
Unit 6, 320
Unit 7, 382
Unit 8, 438, 454
Unit 9, 522
Unit 10, 567, 590

Circle
arc of, 377
area of, 400-401
area of sector of, 402
circumference of, 375-376
relationship to pi, 376

Circle graph, 164, 663

Circumference, 375-376

Coefficient, 33

Collaborative learning
See Explorations, Group Activities, *and* Projects.
"Talk It Over" questions for group discussion occur in each section of each unit.

Column
of a matrix, 128
of a spreadsheet, 129

Combined inequality, 144

Communication, 3-6, 46
See also Discussion, Group Activities, Reading, *and* Writing.

Complementary angles, 86

Complementary events, 310

Computer
animation, 180-181, 189
background patterns, 198
in business, 62
database, 308
drawing software, 337

geometric drawing software, 91, 104, 223, 304, 333, 480, 550

graphing software, 170, 175, 214, 227, 228, 232, 349, 389, 422, 431, 445, 452, 556, 563, 575, 603

spreadsheets, 129-130, 141, 168, 220, 241, 273, 305, 619

statistical analysis, 136

statistical graphs, 130, 157, 168, 172, 212, 214

See also Technology Handbook and Technology Notes.

Concept map, 5

Conclusion, 492

Conditional statement, 492

Cone, 524

Congruent, 38, 44
angles, 87
figures, 38
polygons, 37-38
segments, 82

Conjecture, 21
See also Inductive reasoning and Patterns.

Connections
art, 187, 208, 512, 573
biology, 333
business education, 62-63, 566
earth science, 156, 216
geography, 61, 68, 83, 154, 305, 380
health, 318
history, 109, 132, 498, 527, 587
language arts, 15, 552
literature, 17, 69, 188, 259, 335, 535
music, 278
physics, 116
science, 70, 109, 148, 267, 461
social studies, 97, 186, 326, 453
See also Applications, Careers, Multicultural connections, Projects, and Research.

Continuous quantities, 60, 145

Control variable, 218

Converse, 494-495

Conversion factors, 393

Cooperative learning
See Explorations, Group Activities, and Projects.
"Talk It Over" questions for group discussion occur in each section of each unit.

Coordinates, 184, 660

Coordinate geometry, 190-193

Coordinate graphing, 184, 220, 225-230, 243, 369-370, 385-387, 418-420, 426, 428, 433-434, 442, 448-450, 456-459, 463-464, 555-558, 563, 585, 594-595, 600, 660-661

Coordinate plane, 184, 660

Coordinate systems, 183-185, 660
axes, 184, 660
coordinates, 184, 660
quadrant, 184

Correlation, 212, 214

Corresponding sides, 40

Corresponding vertices, 40

Cosine of an angle, 344

Counterexample, 22
See also Inductive Reasoning.

Critical thinking. See Reasoning.

Cross-curriculum connections
See Connections.

Cross products, 315

Cube root, 114, 115

Cylinder, 508
surface area, 508
volume, 517

Data analysis. See Statistics.

Data display
bar graph, 130, 164, 661
box-and-whisker plot, 158, 164
circle graph, 164, 663
correlation, 212, 214
frequency, 150
frequency table, 151
fitted lines, 212-213
histogram, 150, 153, 164
line graph, 128, 661-662
line plot, 137
matrix, 128
mean, 136
median, 136
mode, 136
outliers, 137
pictograph, 133, 662
range, 137
scatter plots, 212-214, 367
spreadsheets, 129
stem-and-leaf plots, 152-153

Decimals and percents, 653

Deductive reasoning, 479-480, 486, 492-494

Dependent variable, 218

Diagonal, 424

Diameter of a circle, 375

Dilation, 337-339

Dimensions of a matrix, 128

Dimensional analysis, 392-395

Direct variation, 360-362, 367-369, 375-376, 383-387
graphs, 385
model, 367-370
with $y = kx$, 383-387

Discrete mathematics
algorithms, 26-27, 31, 35 (Ex. 31), 592, 593
counting procedures, 8 (Ex. 29), 19, 321-325, 333 (Ex. 8)
decision-making, 462 (Ex. 29), 465, 562, 566
discrete vs. continuous, 60, 145, 371 (Exs. 8-10)
functions with discrete domains, 220, 241-242, 326 (Ex. 9), 562
lattices, 425, 426, 455
matrices, 128, 141 (Ex. 17)
patterns in discrete data sets, 11-12, 14 (Exs. 5, 6)
recursion, 129, 133 (Ex. 16), 134 (Ex. 22) , 241
See also Data displays, Probability, and Statistics.

Discrete quantities, 60

Discussion
Can We Talk? 2, 56, 126, 182, 240, 300, 358, 416, 476, 546
Look Back and Talk It Over discussion questions occur in each section.

Distance from a point to a line, 281

Distributive property, 31, 32, 247-248
in equation solving, 250

Domain of a function, 670-671

Endpoint, 82
of an angle, 85
of a segment, 82
of a ray, 85

Enlargement, 338

Equation(s)
cubic, 115
definition, 99
equivalent, 100
factored form, 579

for a function, 225-230
graphing, 227-230, 243, 385-387, 426, 428, 433, 449-450, 555-558, 563, 594-595, 600
linear, 427
modeling with algebra tiles, 100-101, 256, 646-647
multi-step, 102, 249-250
in problem solving, 102, 107, 138, 141
quadratic, 115, 599
rewriting, 270-271
slope-intercept form of, 418
solution of, 99, 426
standard form of, 427
two-step, 100-101, 106-107, 138
variables on both sides, 256-257
write, given slope and a point, 442
write, given two points, 441
See also Solution(s).

Equilateral triangle, 44

Equivalent equations, 100

Equivalent inequalities, 263

Estimation
by comparison, 58-59
of length and area measures, 79
on a map, 80
of numbers, 57
of probability, 59
of a square root, 114

Evaluating expressions, 12, 26-28
involving negative numbers, 66
involving powers of variables, 20

Event, 308

Expanded form, 577

Experimental probability, 308, 500-501

Explorations
area of a circle, 400
area of a parallelogram, 280
circumference of a circle, 375
congruent polygons, 37, 39
coordinate geometry, 190
direct variation between bounce of ball and height of drop, 367
estimating a number of beans by sampling, 322
expanded and factored form modeled with algebra tiles, 576
exploring quadrilaterals, 44
formulas, 270
geometric probability, 500
graphing linear inequalities, 455

inequalities, 261
linear combinations, 425
negative numbers, 65
negative powers of ten, 71
probability experiment, 306
Pythagorean theorem, 477
reflections, 547
using a scatterplot for height and lower-arm length, 211
similar polygons in a photo enlargement, 328
similar triangles, 343
squaring function, 225
sum of angles of a triangle, 88
system of linear equations, 447
translating parabolas, 556
variable expression for perimeter, 13
See also Group Activities.

Exponent(s), 19-22, 71-75, 568-572
order of operations, 27
rules of, 75, 568-572

Expression(s), 10-13, 20-21, 26-28, 32-33, 66, 93-95, 247-248, 577
binomial, 578
evaluating, 12, 20, 66
factoring, 577
monomial, 578
trinomial, 584

Exterior angle, 92, 436

Extra Practice
Unit 1, 620-621
Unit 2, 622-623
Unit 3, 624-625
Unit 4, 625-627
Unit 5, 628-629
Unit 6, 629-631
Unit 7, 631-633
Unit 8, 633-635
Unit 9, 635-638
Unit 10, 638-639

Extremes of a data set, 158

Faces of a prism, 507

Factors, 19-20, 568-571, 648-649

Factoring, 576-579, 591-593

Factored completely, 578

Factored form, 577

Fitted line, 212-213, 369, 439-440

Formula(s)
in applications, 67, 70, 272, 278, 490, 598
arc length, 377

area, 94, 192, 281, 282, 283, 401, 402, 658
circumference, 376
direct variation, 383
distance, 255, 257, 270-271
perimeter, 658
probability, 308, 309, 310, 502
in problem solving, 94, 281, 282, 284, 309, 401, 502
Pythagorean theorem, 478
quadratic, 601
scale factor, 337
slope, 361
stopping distance, 598
surface area, 507, 509, 510, 543
transforming, 270-271
trigonometric, 344, 361
volume, 94, 515, 517, 523, 524, 543, 659

Fractions, 650-652
in equations, 106, 138
and percents, 653-654
See also Reciprocals.

Frequency, 150

Frequency table, 151

Function(s), 220-221
absolute value, 230
domain and range, 670-671
graph of, 220-221
identity, 230
reciprocal, 230
squaring, 225-226, 230, 555
vertical-line test, 220-221

Geometric probability, 500-504

Geometry, 53, 123, 237, 297, 354, 413, 473, 542-543, 609
angles, 85, 89, 657
area, 280-284, 507, 510, 658-659
circumference, 375-378
congruence, 38, 44, 82, 87
coordinate, 190-193
parallel and perpendicular lines, 44
perimeter, 12-13, 44, 46, 93
pi, 376
polygon, 39, 329-332, 430
Pythagorean theorem, 477-480, 495
similarity, 328-332, 530-533
volume, 515-518, 523-525, 659
See also Geometric probability, Reasoning, Tessellation, *and* Transformations.

Graph(s), 218-219, 227-230, 242, 369-370, 660-663
bar, 130, 164, 661
box-and-whisker plot, 158, 164
circle, 164, 663
on a coordinate plane, 184, 220, 225-230, 243, 369-370, 385-387, 418-420, 426, 428, 433-434, 442, 448-450, 456-459, 464-465, 555-558, 563, 585, 594, 600, 660
of an equation, 227, 426, 563
histogram, 150, 153, 164
hyperbola, 230
lattice, 425
line graph, 662
of a linear combination, 426
of a linear equation, 447-450
of linear inequalities, 455-459
parabola, 229, 555, 563
pictograph, 133, 662
on polar graph paper, 204-205
scatter plots, 212-214
shapes of, 229-230
of spreadsheet, 129
stem-and-leaf plot, 152-153
vertical intercept of, 428
x-axis of, 226
y-axis of, 226
of $y = x^2 + bx + c$, 594-595
Greatest common factor, 578, 649
Group Activities
area, 287, 541
congruent shapes, 41
coordinate geometry, 195
data display, 178
equation, 251, 296
graphing, 118, 174, 236, 422, 424, 431
If-then statements, 497
inequalities, 296
numerical facts, 98
patterns, 35
perfect square trinomial, 597
polygons, 43
probability, 313
problem solving, 109, 110
product of two binomials, 608
quadratic equation, 582, 605
rates and ratios, 354
rates, times, distances, 259
rectangles, 52, 195
rotational symmetry, 209
sampling and making predictions, 327
scatterplot, 217, 305, 472

scientific notation, 78
solving quadratic equation, 605
Spanish, 319
spreadsheet (height of bounce), 373
stem-and-leaf plot, 156
surface area, 521, 537
system of equations, 293
temperature, 70
translating parabolas, 561, 589
triangles, 92, 122
variation (direct)
    and height, 411
    and probability, 374
volume, 521, 528
writing a quiz, 254
See also Projects *and* Explorations.

Height
of a parallelogram, 281, 282
of a regular pyramid, 510
slant height, 510
of a trapezoid, 283
of a triangle, 282
Heptagon, 39
Hexagon, 39
Histogram, 150, 153, 164
History. *See* Biographical note *and under* Connections.
Horizontal axis, 184, 660
Horizontal intercept, 428
Horizontal line, 433
Hyperbola, 230
Hypotenuse, 344
Hypothesis, 492

Ideas and Formulas
Unit 1, 53
Unit 2, 123
Unit 3, 179
Unit 4, 237
Unit 5, 297
Unit 6, 354-355
Unit 7, 412-413
Unit 8, 472-473
Unit 9, 542-543
Unit 10, 609
Identity function, 230
If-then statements, 492-494
conclusion of, 492
conditional, 492
converse of, 494

hypothesis of, 492
Image, 337
Independent variable, 218
Indirect measurement, 331
Inductive reasoning, 11-12, 14 (Exs. 5, 6), 21-22, 71, 88, 92 (Ex. 30), 424 (Ex. 33), 431 (Ex. 21), 477, 479-480
Inequalities
combined, 144-145
equivalent, 263
graphing, 145, 455-459
and intervals, 143-146
linear, 455-459
modeling situations, 264-265
on a number line, 145, 641
solutions of systems of, 464
solving, 264
systems of, 463-465
with one variable, 261-265
Integer(s), 113, 641
absolute value of, 64
adding, 65, 642, 643
comparing, 641
dividing, 65, 644
modeling with integer chips, 643-644
multiplying, 65, 644
on a number line, 641-642
operations, 65, 640-644
properties, 640
subtracting, 65, 643
Interval, 145-146
frequency, 150
frequency table, 151
stem-and-leaf plot, 152
Investigations
See Explorations *and* Group activities.
Irrational number, 113
Isosceles triangle, 44

Key terms, 53, 123, 179, 237, 297, 355, 413, 473, 543, 609
Kite, 45

Latitude line, 186
Lattice, 425, 426, 455
Least common multiple, 649
Legs of a right triangle, 344
Length of a segment, 82
Like terms, 33
with two variables, 95

Line(s), 82
horizontal, 433-434
line plot, 137
vertical, 433-434
writing equation for, 439-443

Line of reflection, 548

Line segment(s), 82

Line of symmetry, 45, 585
of a parabola, 555, 558, 585-586
for polygons, 45

Linear combination, 425-426, 463

Linear decay, 420

Linear equation(s), 427

Linear function, 420

Linear growth, 420

Linear inequality, 456
boundary line for, 456

Linear regression, 214, 445

Logical reasoning
See Reasoning.

Longitude line, 186

Manipulatives
algebra tiles, 13, 16, 17, 21, 28, 29, 32, 100-102, 256, 257, 258, 576-578, 580, 583, 587, 592, 595, 646-647
balls, 367, 373, 554
beans, 322
coins, 311, 334, 374
flip book, 181
geoboard, 333
globe, 380
index cards or self stick notes, 155
integer chips, 643-644
milk carton, 475
MIRA®, 549
paper cutting or folding, 44, 84, 88, 91, 97, 209, 280, 286, 287, 342, 430, 436, 447, 514, 525, 547, 587
rice, 525
sand, 525
spaghetti, 142, 216
spinner, 306
string, 195, 375, 380
toothpicks 11, 48

Margin of error, 323

Mathematical argumentation, 83 (Ex. 10), 149 (Ex. 1), 161 (Ex. 7), 174 (Ex. 21), 215 (Ex. 11), 311 (Ex. 5), 326 (Ex. 6), 378 (Ex. 1), 406 (Exs.

24-27), 424 (Ex. 44), 430 (Ex. 6), 484 (Ex. 28)
See also Reasoning, *other exercises under* Writing, *and Talk it Over discussion questions in all sections.*

Mathematical modeling. *See* Modeling.

Matrix, 128, 141

Mean, 136

Measure(s), 57, 60
of an angle, 86, 657
dimensional analysis, 392-395
estimating, 79-81, 87
of the sum of the angles of a triangle, 87
Table of, 666

Median, 136, 158

Midpoint of a line segment, 82

Mode, 136

Modeling, 241-246, 295, 368-369, 383, 417-420, 430, 508, 515, 570, 643-644
with inequalities, 264-265
to solve problems, 241-246, 266, 268
with system of equations, 289-290
with an equation, 242-244
with a graph, 242-243, 418-420
with a spreadsheet, 241
with a table, 241, 417, 596
See also Manipulatives *and* Multiple representations.

Monomial, 578

Multicultural connections, xxvi, 1, 3, 4, 5, 6, 7, 8, 9, 10, 15 (Exs. 12–15), 18, 19, 30 (Exs. 1, 2), 51 (Exs. 1–3), 56, 61 (Exs. 8, 9, 11, 14, 15), 77 (Exs. 43–46), 78 (Exs. 3, 4), 83 (Exs. 6–8, 9–13), 97 (Exs. 26–31), 98 (Exs. 2–4), 99, 109 (Exs. 20–23), 120 (Exs. 2, 15–18), 125, 131 (Exs. 2–5), 132 (Exs. 9, 10), 135, 139 (Exs. 6–8), 141, 143, 144, 147 (Exs. 14, 15), 148 (Ex. 25), 149 (Ex. 5), 165, 167 (Exs. 9, 10), 168 (Ex. 13), 169 (Exs. 20, 21), 184, 185 (Exs. 6, 8), 186 (Exs. 14–16), 187 (Exs. 17–23), 188 (Ex. 32), 190, 200 (Exs. 11–14), 205, 208 (Exs. 12–18), 210 (Exs. 7, 8), 233, 234, 235 (Exs. 2, 8, 9), 244 (Exs. 4, 5), 245 (Ex. 15), 253, 259, 275, 278, 283, 286, 292, 298, 299, 303 (Ex. 2),

305 (Exs. 10, 11, 16), 310, 319 (Exs. 26, 27), 328, 334 (Ex. 17), 341, 349 (Ex. 22), 366 (Ex. 20), 379 (Ex. 7), 380 (Exs. 17, 18), 381 (Ex. 20), 394, 397 (Exs. 12–15), 398 (Exs. 18, 19), 399 (Ex. 27), 406 (Ex. 22), 408, 416, 430, 438, 439, 458, 461 (Ex. 27), 462, 465, 478, 481 (Ex. 4), 484, 488, 496, 497 (Exs. 10–12), 498 (Exs. 35–37), 523, 526 (Ex. 9), 527 (Exs. 10–12), 552, 553 (Exs. 13–15), 559, 573, 602

Multiple Representations, 11-12, 20, 32, 99-100, 129-130, 152-153, 225-230, 241-243, 359-362, 368-369, 377, 426, 439-440, 447-448, 455-456, 503, 562-563, 576-577, 585, 592
See also Manipulatives *and* Modeling.

Negative slope, 386

Number(s)
absolute value of, 64
continuous, 60
counting, 57
cube root of, 114
decimal, 57
discrete, 60
estimate of, 57
exact, 57
identifying, 57, 113
integers, 64-65, 113, 640-644
irrational, 113
measuring, 57
negative, 57, 64-67
opposites of, 64
ordering, 57
perfect cube, 114
perfect square, 114
positive, 64-67
rational, 113
real, 113
square root of, 112

Number line, 145, 641, 642

Obtuse angle, 86

Obtuse triangle, 88

Octagon, 39

Open circle on a number line, 145

Open-ended exercises, 7, 8, 17, 28, 29, 41, 48, 49, 51, 52, 62, 63, 70, 77, 84, 97, 108, 116, 121, 134, 140, 142,

162, 169, 173, 177, 187, 188, 195, 196, 200, 201, 208, 210, 215, 224, 233, 235, 246, 251, 259, 260, 266, 286, 295, 303, 304, 305, 311, 319, 327, 342, 348, 353, 366, 381, 389, 399, 406, 421, 432, 437, 451, 452, 468, 470, 497, 498, 506, 512, 519, 538, 540, 552, 580, 603, 605, 607

Opposite, 64

Order of operations, 26-28

Ordered pair, 184, 660

Orientation, 548

Origin, 184

Outcomes, 308

Outliers, 137

Parabola, 229, 555, 563
  line of symmetry of, 585
  vertex of, 555, 558

Parallel, 44

Parallelogram, 45, 281
  area of, 280-282
  base of, 282

Patterns
  algebraic expressions for, 17, 248, 486, 530, 532, 569, 570, 571, 596 (Ex. 29)
  describing, 11-12, 21-22, 46, 65, 71, 183, 211, 261, 385, 400, 417, 425, 477, 530, 532, 547, 568, 571, 591
  in exercises, 14 (Exs. 5, 6), 23 (Ex. 20), 24 (Ex. 27), 91 (Ex. 29), 134 (Ex. 31), 431 (Ex. 20)
  in shapes of basic functions, 225, 230, 420
  for space figures, 96, 507, 514, 525
  in tables, 10, 12, 131 (Ex. 7), 279 (Ex. 25), 359, 365 (Ex. 17), 367, 375, 387, 404 (Exs. 8, 9), 562, 596 (Ex. 29)
  in tessellations, 104, 430
  See also Correlation *and* Transformation.

Pentagon, 39

Percent, 302, 653-656
  and probability, 59, 309-310

Perfect cube, 114

Perfect square, 114

Perimeter, 12-13, 44, 46, 93, 658

Perpendicular, 44

Perspective drawing, 341, 512, 526

Pi, 376

Pictograph, 133, 662

Pixel, 189

Polar graph paper, 204-205

Polygon, 39, 430

Population, 321

Power(s)
  of a number, 19
  rules for, 75, 568-572
  in scientific notation, 72-74
  of ten, 21, 71, 75
  of variables, 20

Practice. *See* Extra Practice *and* Review.

Prediction(s), 321-325
  margin of error, 323-325
  sampling, 321-323
  of swimming record (Unit 8 project), 415
  See also Probability, Scatter plots, *and* Fitted line.

Prime factorization, 648

Prime meridian, 186

Prism, 507
  base of, 507
  faces of, 507
  pentagonal, 507
  rectangular, 507
  surface area for, 507
  triangular, 507
  volume of, 515

Probability, 59, 306-311, 500-504
  complementary events, 310
  experimental, 308
  geometric, 500-504
  theoretical, 309

Problem solving, 664
  See also Applications *and* Problem solving strategies.

Problem solving strategies, 665
  Break the problem into parts, 193, 489, 509, 511, 516, 518
  Guess and check, 27, 138, 141, 664
  Identify a pattern, 11, 226, 274
  Make a sketch, 332, 346-347, 361, 478, 479, 508
  Solve a simper problem, 270
  Use a diagram, 192, 503
  Use dimensional analysis, 395
  Use an equation, 102, 107, 138, 141
  Use a formula, 94, 281, 282, 284, 309, 401, 502
  Use a graph, 449

  Use a proportion, 316, 323, 324, 331, 378, 384, 402, 533
  Use a system of equations, 290
  Work backward, 141, 592, 665

Projects
  Alternative Projects
    Analyzing a Process, 176
    Boating in Various Seas, 539
    Changing the Rules, 351
    Collecting and Graphing Data, 234
    Collecting Data Displays, 176
    Conducting an Interview, 119
    Create a Polygon Pattern, 50
    Designing a Container, 539
    The Fibonacci Sequence, 50
    Finding Ratios, 351
    The History of π, 408
    Making a Map, 234
    Making Parabolas from Straight Lines, 606
    Mickey Mantle's Record Home Run, 606
    Playing the Market, 469
    Projected Savings, 469
    Recognizing Functions in Science, 234
    Redesigning a Room, 119
    Researching Telephone Costs, 294
    Supporting an Opinion, 176
    A Trip to Another Country, 408
    Working on Commission, 294
  Unit Projects
    Build Your Own Boat (Unit 9), 475, 476, 485, 491, 499, 506, 514, 522, 529, 538, 539
    Design a Logo (Unit 1), 1, 2, 9, 18, 25, 30, 36, 43, 49, 50
    Design a Sports Arena (Unit 7), 357, 358, 366, 374, 382, 391, 399, 407, 408
    Make a Flip Book (Unit 4), 181, 182, 189, 196, 201, 210, 217, 224, 233, 234
    Plan an Advertising Campaign (Unit 6), 299, 300, 305, 313, 320, 327, 336, 342, 350, 351
    Plan a Car Wash (Unit 5), 239, 240, 246, 254, 260, 269, 274, 279, 288, 293, 294
    Predict the Future (Unit 8), 415, 416, 424, 432, 438, 446, 454, 462, 468, 469

Stock a Music Store (Unit 3), 125, 126, 134, 142, 149, 157, 163, 169, 175, 176
Theme Poster Contest (Unit 2), 55, 56, 63, 70, 78, 84, 92, 98, 104, 110, 118, 119
Write a Math Story (Unit 10), 545, 546, 554, 561, 567, 575, 582, 590, 597, 605, 606
See also Group Activities.

Property(ies)
associative, 640
commutative, 640
distributive, 32, 53
of equality, 99-100
of exponents, 75, 568-572
identity, 640
of inequality, 264
of opposites, 248
of a proportion, 315
of square roots, 486, 542
of transformations, 197, 202, 237, 337, 354, 547, 548, 609
zero-product, 495, 542, 564

Proportion(s), 314-316
a problem solving strategy, 316, 323, 324, 331, 378, 384, 402, 533
cross products, 315
direct variation, 384
terms of, 314

Pyramid
height of, 510
regular, 509
slant height of, 510
surface area, 509
volume of, 523

Pythagorean theorem, 477-479
converse of, 495

Quadrant, 184
Quadratic equation, 599
solution of, 599, 603
Quadratic formula, 601
Quadratic function, 599
Quadrilateral, 39, 44-45
Quartiles, 158

Radical form, 487
Radicals, 112-115, 478-479, 486-489
Radius, 376
Random, 308
Range, 137
line plot, 137

Range of a function, 670-671
Rate, 302-303
converting units of, 394-396
unit price, 302
unit rate, 302
Ratio, 301-303, 530-533
Rational number, 113
Ray, 85
Reading, in exercises, 6, 7, 14, 23, 28, 42, 61, 75, 82, 89, 96, 103, 108, 116, 131, 139, 147, 154, 160, 166, 172, 185, 194, 199, 206, 215, 222, 231, 244, 250, 258, 259, 266, 267, 272, 277, 285, 292, 311, 316, 325, 332, 340, 348, 370, 378, 388, 396, 405, 423, 429, 435, 443, 451, 459, 465, 481, 489, 496, 504, 512, 519, 526, 534, 551, 558, 565, 572, 580, 588, 596, 604
Real number, 113
Reasoning, 542
conclusion, 492
conditional statement, 492
conjecture, 21
counterexample, 22
deductive, 479-480, 486, 492-494
hypothesis, 492
if-then statement, 492
inductive, 11-12, 14 (Exs. 5, 6), 21-22, 71, 92 (Ex. 30), 424 (Ex. 33), 477, 479-480
interpreting data and graphs, 4-5, 130, 135, 170, 212, 214, 367, 420, 530
visual thinking. *See* Manipulatives, Modeling, *and* Multiple representations.
See also Algorithmic thinking, Patterns, *and* Writing. *Also, Talk it Over discussion questions in each section promote critical thinking skills.*
Reciprocal(s), 275-277, 650
Reciprocal function, 230
Rectangle, 45
area of, 192, 193, 658
perimeter of, 13, 658
Reduction, 338
Remote interior angle, 92
Reflection, 547-550
line of, 548
orientation of, 548
properties of, 548

Regular pyramid, 509
Research (out of textbook), in exercises, 8, 17, 63, 78, 82, 97,109, 131, 140, 142, 155, 157, 169, 187, 201, 209, 217, 254, 259, 267, 274, 279, 304, 305, 320, 326, 327, 333, 335, 348, 350, 363, 364, 374, 379, 381, 397, 399, 423, 432, 460, 462, 481, 506, 527, 552, 575
Review
Checkpoints, 30, 78, 98, 149, 210, 269, 320, 382, 438, 454, 522, 567, 590
Extra Practice, 620-639
Review and Assessment, 51-53, 120-123, 177-179, 235-237, 295-297, 352-354, 409-413, 470-473, 540-543, 607-609
Review/Preview. *The exercise set in each section of each unit contains Review/Preview exercises.*
Toolbox (examples and practice of prealgebra skills), 640-665
Rhombus, 45
Right angle, 44-45, 86
Right triangle, 44, 88
area of, 191-192
hypotenuse of, 344
Rise, 361
Rotation(s), 202-206
amount of turn, 203
center of, 202
drawing, 204-205
symmetry, 205
Rotational symmetry, 205, 206
Row
of a matrix, 128
of a spreadsheet, 129
Rules
of exponents, 75
of powers, 569-572
Run, 361

Sample, 321
Sampling, 321-325
Scale, 330, 334
Scale drawings, 330-331
Scale factor, 337
Scalene triangle, 44
Scatter plot(s), 212-214, 460, 472
fitted line of, 212, 369, 439-440

Scientific notation, 71-75
  on a calculator, 73-75
Sector
  area of, 402
  of a circle graph, 663
Segment, 82
Side of polygon, 40
Similar polygons, 328-332
  areas of, 530-532
  figures, 329
  properties of, 329
  triangles, 331
Similar space figures, 532
  volume of, 532
Sine of acute angle, 344
Slant height, 510
Slope, 361, 418-419, 672-673
  of horizontal line, 433
  negative, 386-387
  rise, 361
  run, 361
  using coordinates, 369, 370
  of vertical line, 433
Slope-intercept form
  of an equation, 418, 672-673
  inequalities, 457
Solutions
  using algebra tiles, 100-101, 256,
    646-647
  of cubic equations, 115
  using the distributive property,
    250, 263
  of equations, 99
  of equations involving fractions,
    106, 138
  of equations with two variables,
    426
  of equations with variables on
    both sides, 256-257
  of inequalities, 262-263, 456
  using mental math, 645
  of multi-step equations, 100-102,
    105-107, 138, 249-250
  of systems of equations, 291
  of systems of inequalities, 464
  of quadratic equations, 115, 599-
    603
  using quadratic formula, 601-602
  of trigonometric equations, 346-
    347
  using zero-product property, 495,
    564, 579

See also Graph(s), on a coordinate plane.
Space figure(s)
  cone, 524
  cylinder, 508
  prism, 507
  pyramid, 509
  similar, 532
Spatial reasoning. *See*
  Manipulatives.
Spreadsheets, 129-130, 141, 168,
  220, 241, 273, 305, 619
  cells of, 129
Square, 45
  area of, 20, 111, 658
  perimeter of, 658
Square of a number, 20, 225-226,
  668
Squaring function, 225-226, 230,
  555
Square root(s), 112
  on a calculator, 612
  equations, solving, 115, 488-489
  estimating, 114
  Table of, 668
**Standard form of a linear equa-
  tion,** 427
Statistics, 127-130, 135-138, 143-146,
  150-153, 158-160, 164-166, 170-171,
  179, 211-214, 241, 321-325
  in exercises, 78, 83, 118, 120, 131-
    134, 139-142, 146-149, 154-157,
    160-163, 166-169, 172-175, 177-
    178, 214-217, 236, 246, 311-313,
    319-320, 325-327, 336, 444, 452,
    453
  See also Data display, Graph(s),
    Predictions, Probability,
    Sampling, Scatterplots, *and*
    Spreadsheets.
Stem-and-leaf plot, 152
  making a histogram, 153
Straight angle, 86
Substitution, 12
Supplementary angles, 86
Surface area, 507-511
  of cylinder, 508-509
  of prism, 507-508
  of pyramid, 510-511
Symbols, 82
  Table of, 667

Symmetry, 45
  line of, 45
  rotational, 205-206
  translational, 198-199
System of equations, 289-291, 447-
  450
System of inequalities, 463-465

Tangent ratio, 361-362
Technology exercises
  See under Calculator *and*
    Computer.
Technology Handbook, 611-619
Technology Notes
  on calculator use
    analyzing data, 136
    exponents, 20, 66, 74
    fitted lines, 212, 215
    graphing, 170, 175, 228, 349, 427,
      448, 563, 599
    negative numbers, 65, 66
    square roots, 112, 491
    trigonometric ratios, 344, 362,
      365
  on computer use, 220, 305, 480,
    550
  See also Calculator *and*
    Computer.
Term(s), 33
  combining like, 33
  constant, 33
  variable, 33
Terms of a proportion, 314
Tessellation, 50, 104, 430
Testing. *See* Assessment.
Theoretical probability, 309-310
Toolbox (examples and practice of
  prealgebra skills), 640-665
Transformation(s), 202
  and congruence, 38
  dilation, 337-339
  of a formula, 270-271
  reflection, 547-550
  rotation, 202-206
  slides, flips, turns, 38
  translation, 197-199
Translation, 197-199
Translational symmetry, 198-199
Trapezoid, 47, 193, 283
  area of, 283
  base of, 283

Triangle, 39
  acute, 88
  area of, 282
  base of, 282
  equilateral, 44
  isosceles, 44
  obtuse, 88
  right, 44, 88
  scalene, 44
  sum of angle measures, 89
Trigonometric ratios
  cosine, 344
  sine, 344
  Table of, 669
  tangent, 361-362
Trinomial, 584

Unit price, 302
Unit rate, 302

Vanishing point, 341
Variable(s), 10
  and the distributive property, 32-33
  control, 218, 226
  dependent, 218, 226
  evaluating powers of, 20
  independent, 218
  opposites of, 66, 247-248
Variable expression(s), 10-13
  adding like terms, 95

  evaluating, 12
  expanding and factoring, 577-578
Variable terms in an equation, 256
Variation. *See* Direct variation.
Variation constant, 360
Vertex
  of an angle, 85
  of a parabola, 555
  of a polygon, 40
Vertical angles, 87, 89
Vertical axis, 184, 186, 660
  y-axis, 226, 550
Vertical intercept, 418, 428
Vertical line, 433
Vertical line test for function, 220-221
Volume, 515-518, 523-525, 659
  cone, 524
  cube, 20, 94, 115
  cylinder, 517
  prism, 515
  pyramid, 523
  of similar figures, 532, 533

Weighted average, 463
Writing, 46
  in exercises, 7, 15, 16, 17, 25, 29, 34, 35, 36, 48, 49, 52, 61, 62, 68, 76, 78, 83, 92, 97, 98, 104, 109, 132, 133, 134, 139, 148, 149, 155, 156, 157, 161, 162, 163, 167, 169, 172, 174, 175, 178, 187, 188, 189, 194, 201, 207, 210, 215, 223, 231, 233, 236, 245, 251, 253, 259, 260, 267, 268, 287, 293, 295, 304, 311, 316, 317, 320, 325, 326, 332, 335, 336, 348, 350, 365, 366, 371, 378, 382, 389, 390, 398, 404, 406, 409, 422, 424, 430, 432, 436, 437, 438, 446, 454, 462, 466, 470, 482, 484, 485, 497, 499, 505, 513, 514, 520, 522, 526, 534, 538, 541, 551, 553, 554, 560, 565, 567, 572, 574, 575, 580, 581, 588, 590, 595, 604, 608
  in Samples, 59, 165, 171, 368, 549

x-axis, 226, 550
x-intercept, 428, 563, 564

y-axis, 226, 550
y-intercept, 418, 428, 563, 564, 672-673

Zero-product property, 495, 564, 579

Credits
. . . .

DESIGN

Book Design: Two Twelve Associates, Inc.
Cover Design: McDougal Littell Design Department
Electronic Technical Art: American Composition & Graphics, Inc.

ACKNOWLEDGMENTS

17 From "Animalimericks" in *Jamboree: Rhymes for All Times,* by Eve Merriam. Copyright © 1962, 1964, 1966, 1973, 1984 by Eve Merriam. Reprinted by permission of Marian Reiner.

69, 259 From "To Build a Fire," by Jack London. First appeared in *The Century Magazine,* by The Century Company, August, 1908. Subsequently published in *Lost Face,* by Jack London. Copyright © 1910 by Macmillan Publishing Company.

132 Data for Exercises 11–14 from The Recording Industry Association of America's 1999 Year-end Statistics.

188 From *The Hunt for Red October,* by Tom Clancy. Annapolis, Maryland: United States Naval Institute, 1984.

245 From *Rules of Thumb 2,* by Tom Parker. Boston: Houghton Mifflin Company, 1987.

335 From "The Adventure of the Musgrave Ritual," by Arthur Conan Doyle. Originally appeared in Arthur Conan Doyle's *The Memoirs of Sherlock Holmes,* published in 1893 by George Newnes, Limited. First U.S. edition, Copyright © 1894 by Harper & Brothers.

336 From *A More Perfect Union* in Houghton Mifflin Social Studies, by Armento et al. Copyright © 1991 by Houghton Mifflin Company. Reprinted by permission of Houghton Mifflin Company.

535 From *Gulliver's Travels,* by Jonathan Swift. Originally published in London by B. Motte, Publishers, 1726.

STOCK PHOTOGRAPHY

v Michael Newman/Photo Edit (t); **viii** © Allsport USA/ Michael Hans; **ix** P.L.I./Westlight; **xi** Photo Tal Streeter, *The Art of the Japanese Kite*, Weatherhill Inc. (t); **xi** Superstock (c); **xi** Dr. Jeremy Burgess/Science Photo Library/Photo Researchers (inset); **xiii** © 1993 Mark Zemnick (t); **xiii** Dan Paul (b); **xxvi** © James Hart (r); Kevin Morris/Allstock (l); (logo sketches) Courtesy Larry DesJarlais, (finished logo) The Smithsonian Institution National Museum of the American Indian National Campaign Office; **1** (Seattle, Colorado, Florida, Milwaukee, Toronto, New York) The Major League logos pictured in this book are reproduced with the permission of Major League Properties, Inc. and are the exclusive property of Major League Baseball Clubs. The logos may not be reproduced without the consent of Major League Properties, Inc. or the appropriate individual Club.; (Utah) Courtesy NBA Properties, Inc.; **3** (Vietnam) Scribner/The Picture Cube; (USA) Frank Siteman/The Picture Cube; (Alaska) Soames Summerhays/Photo Researchers, Inc.; (Africa) Owen Franken/Stock Boston; (S. America) Juan Pablo Lira/The Image Bank; (India) Porterfield/Chickering/Photo Researchers, Inc.; **9** Travelpix 1991/FPG International (l); Dave Wilhelm/The Stock Market (tr); Robert Frerck/ Tony Stone Images/Chicago Inc. (br); **10-11** John Elk, III/ Stock Boston; **11** © Bob Daemmrich; **12** John Colwell/ Grant Heilman Photography; **15** Thomas Del Brase/ The Stock Market; **17** Photo by Bachrach; **19** Fred Conrad/© 1985 *Discover* Magazine; **30** Betsy Pillsbury; **37** Michael Newman/Photo Edit; **48** Blair Seitz/Photo Researchers, Inc.; **54** Curt Teich Postcard Archives, Lake County Museum; **55** Stephen Derr/The Image Bank (b); Chuck Carter/© National Geographic Society (t); **57** © Allsport USA/Darrell Ingham (t); © Bob Daemmrich (b); **58** Tom Van Sant, Geosphere Project, Santa Monica/Photo Researchers, Inc.; **60** Richard Megna/Fundamental Photo (tl & r); © 1990 Bruce Iverson (b); **61** Fred Ward/Black Star; **62** Nantucket Nectars Wood Pressed Apple Juice Label; **64** Sonya Hagopian/Woods Hole Oceanographic Institution (t); Rod Catanagh/ Woods Hole Oceanographic Institution (b); **67** © Kindra Clineff (t); Terence Turner/ FPG International (b); **70** National Baseball Hall of Fame; **73** Dr. Jeremy Burgess/Science Photo Library/Photo Researchers (inset); Superstock; **76** © Bruce Iverson (tl); Photo Researchers, Inc. (bl); © David Liebman (bc); Doc White/Images Unlimited, Inc. (tc); © Allsport USA/ Vandystadt (br); Warren Morgan/Westlight (tr); **78** Tony Stone Images/Chicago Inc.; **81** EROS Data Center/USGS; **83** Courtesy Belize Tourist Board (r); Courtesy Indonesian Consulate (l); **85** Tom Croke/ Lightwave; **91** Vince Streano/Tony Stone Images/Chicago Inc. (l); Alex MacLean/Landslides (c); Guido Alberto/The Image Bank (r); **92** István Bodóczky; **93** Chris Mooney/ FPG International; **94** L. Hafencher/H. Armstrong Roberts; **96** Alex MacLean/Landslides (l); © Kindra Clineff (r); **97** Theodores Wores (1859-1939), Dai Nichi Do Garden, Nikko, Japan, 1887. Oil on canvas. Courtesy Jim Lyons.; **99** Photo Tal Streeter, *The Art of the Japanese Kite*, Weatherhill Inc.; **103** Courtesy of Jose Sainz (l); Alex MacLean/Landslides (c); Jonathan L . Barkin/The Picture Cube (r); **104** Excavations of the Metropolitan Museum of Art, 1936, and Rogers Fund, 1937. (37.40. 26) (t); America Hurrah, New York, NY (l); Myron/Tony Stone Images/ Chicago Inc. (br); **110** © 1992 Jack Vartoogian; **115** © 1993 Terry Wild Studio; **116** © Jerry Sinkovec (t); Philip & Karen Smith/Tony Stone Images/Chicago Inc. (b); **124** (1900) Northwind Picture Archives; (1910) Courtesy Antique Automobile Club of America ; (1920 & 1930) Collection Lester Glassner; (1940) FPG International; **124-125** (1950) Courtesy Antique Automobile Club of America; (1960) FPG International; (1970) From the Collection of the Museum at F.I.T., NY; (1980) Rob Lang/FPG International; (1990) General Motors;

Al Tielemans (t); **484** George A. Plimpton Collection, Rare Book & Manuscript Library, Columbia University; **490** Leo Mason/The Image Bank; **492** Globus Brothers/The Stock Market; **493** Wiancko Braasch/Allstock; **496** Barbara & Justin Kerr; **498** Nancy Dudley/Stock Boston; **502** © Allsport USA/Vandystadt/Didier Klein; **505** David Blum/Pixel Studios/The Stock Market; **510** Copyright © 1992 Dorling Kindersley Limited, London. From *Press-out Romantic Gift Boxes*, published in the United States by Dorling Kindersley Publishing Inc., NY (l); **512** Donovan Reese/Tony Stone Images/Chicago Inc.; **513** Richard Olsenius/© National Geographic Society; **514** Courtesy Sony Electronics Inc.; **517** Sam Gray (bl); **518** Wurlitzer Jukeboxes; **519** Morris Lane/The Stock Market (fish); **520** Grant Heilman Photography (br); **524** Courtesy T. Skretting AS; **527** Catalogue No. 245023, Department of Anthropology, Smithsonian Institution (r); Photography by Edward S. Curtis, courtesy San Diego Museum of Man (l); **528** Missouri Historical Society; **532** © 1993 Louis Psihoyos/Matrix; **534** John Sibbick © National Geographic Society; **535** From Great Ocean Publishers Edition of *Gulliver's Travels* by Jonathan Swift with illustrations by J.J. Grandville. (t); **539** Richard Megna/Fundamental Photo; **544** Doug Perrine/Innerspace Vision (t); **544-545** Sportschrome East/West (b); **545** Tim Murphy/The Image Bank (r); **548** Bill Stanton/International Stock Photo (r); Suzanne & Nick Geary/Tony Stone Images/Chicago Inc. (l); **550** Flip Nicklin/Minden Pictures; **551** © Stan Osolinski (b); Mitch Reardon/Tony Stone Images/Chicago Inc. (br); Darrell Gulin/ Allstock; **552** Willie L. Hill, Jr./Stock Boston; **555** © Doranne Jacobson (r); Bert Blokhuis/Tony Stone Images/Chicago Inc. (l); Dick Luria/FPG International (t); **559** Philippe Psaila/Gamma-Liaison (r); Nadia Mackenzie/Tony Stone Images/Chicago Inc.; **561** Ralph Cowan/Tony Stone Images/Chicago Inc.; **565** © Duomo (b); © Kindra Clineff; **573** © Rhoda Sidney; Courtesy Patricia Malarcher; **582** © Duomo/David Madison; **587** The Bettmann Archive; **590** © Henry Horenstein; **597** Chuck Rydlewski/*Sports Illustrated*; **598** © Bob Daemmrich; **600** © 1993 Ron Kimball; **604** Stuart West-Moreland/Allstock; **605** © Henry Horenstein; **607** Robert Caputo/Stock Boston

ASSIGNMENT PHOTOGRAPHERS

Kindra Clineff **v** (b), **14, 31, 39** (r), **42** (l), **45, 50, 56, 60, 79** (c), **79** (b), **108, 119, 125** (t), **134, 135, 137, 140, 142, 155** (tr), **179, 240, 282, 294, 299** (tl), **299** (tr), **299** (bc), **299** (bl), **300, 351, 374, 382** (b), **408, 436, 447, 455, 469, 476, 491, 494, 504, 506, 507, 509, 510, 511, 515, 517, 520, 521, 545** (c), **556** (t), **606**

David Conover **102, 314** (r), **478, 482** (b), **497, 522, 536-537, 537**

Steven Greenberg **227** (r)

Richard Haynes/RM International **vi, x, xiv, xv, 1, 3** (b), **13, 16, 23, 35, 39** (t), **39** (c), **39** (l), **42** (r), **44, 65, 71, 88, 122, 155** (b), **160-161, 190** (b), **193, 199** (c), **199** (r), **211, 214, 219, 225, 227** (c), **261, 264, 269, 270, 274, 277, 279, 280-281, 285, 288, 299** (br), **306, 307, 308, 322, 343, 367, 368, 375, 380** (r), **400, 411** (b), **416, 425, 448, 475** (t), **485, 491, 500, 501, 547, 549, 554, 556** (b), **562, 562-563** (b), **576, 577, 591, 608**

Ken Karp **22, 26, 27, 28, 36, 48, 63, 79** (t), **181** (t), **189, 192, 247, 433, 467** (t), **487, 519, 566, 574, 585,** Ken O'Donoghue **611** (r)

David Shopper **vii, 185**

ILLUSTRATIONS

Mary Azarian **69, 255, 256, 259**
Annie Bissett **77, 90, 118, 148** (b), **167, 169** (b), **313, 325, 350** (b)
Roger Boehm **298-299**
Jana Brenning **74, 121, 188** (l)
John Carrozza **490, 505**
Chris Costello **183, 356** (t)
Christine Czernota **200, 202, 208, 224, 235, 298** (l), **545**
Dartmouth Publishing, Inc. **59**
DECODE, Inc. **211, 333** (b)
DLF Group **7, 18, 83, 98, 120, 139, 169** (t), **184, 185, 186, 188** (r), **234** (b), **303, 393, 483, 497**
Bob Doucet **523**(t&b), **527**
Nancy Chandler Edwards **5, 25** (b)**, 126** (c), **165** (b), **178** (b), **370, 390, 437, 480, 484, 499**
Arn Franzen **581** (t)
Walt Fournier **6, 20, 23**
George Guzzi **349**
Piotr Kaczmarek **68, 148** (c), **154, 156, 164, 177** (t), **178** (br), **189** (b), **198, 216-217, 273, 502, 549** (t), **558** (b), **566**
Joe Klim **249, 267, 312** (b), **415, 477, 498, 518, 522, 525**
Jason P. Lee **258**
Andrew Meyer **54, 317, 435, 575** (b), **597**
Morgan Cain & Associates **132** (b), **133** (b), **143, 150, 151, 152, 163, 172, 174, 201, 321, 332, 397** (tl), **409, 410** (br), **452, 453, 455, 538, 564, 586, 594, 601**
Linda Phinney-Crehan **25** (t)
Neil Pinchin **125** (l&r), **126** (tl), **126** (r)
Lisa Rahon **xii, 516**
Photo manipulations by Lisa Rahon **xxvi, 10, 11, 183, 189, 195, 197, 199, 206, 214, 219, 228, 252-253** (b), **356, 357, 364** (cl), **372, 418, 419, 475, 482, 492, 513, 515, 519, 544, 600**
Patrice Rossi **8, 15**
Fred Schrier **272**
George Ulrich **358** (t), **378** (tr), **382** (tl), **405** (bl), **406** (tr), **407** (c), **544**

TYPOGRAPHIC TITLES

Frank Loose Design **3, 10, 19, 26, 31, 37, 44, 301, 306, 314, 321, 328, 337, 343, 359, 367, 375, 383, 392, 400, 417, 425, 433, 439, 447, 455, 463, 477, 486, 492, 500, 507, 515, 523, 530, 555, 562, 568, 583, 591, 598**

Midnight Oil Studios **57, 64, 71, 79, 85, 93, 99, 105, 111, 127, 135, 143, 150, 158, 164, 170, 183, 190, 218, 225, 241, 247, 255, 261, 270, 275, 280, 289**

DECODE, Inc. **211**

Scott Kim **547**

Selected Answers

· ·

Unit 1

Pages 3 and 5 Talk it Over

1–2. Answers may vary. Examples are given. **1. a.** slippery when wet **b.** steep hill **c.** merge left **d.** railroad crossing
2. a. food/restaurant **b.** boarding area **c.** waiting area **d.** emergency phone/security **3.** Answers may vary. An example is given. The person has learned about issues involved with the subject of communication. **4.** Answers may vary. An example is given. One might include ideas about shapes of signs, colors of signs, messages, proper placement, and so on.

Pages 6–9 Exercises and Problems

9, 11, 13, 15. Answers may vary. Examples are given.
9. restrooms **11.** elevators **13.** two-way traffic
15. intersection **17.** Answers may vary. An example is given. Immigration is resulting in an increase in the number (and percentage) of American homes where a language other than English is used for conversation; article **19.** Wyoming; table **21.** Georgia; table **23.** Answers may vary. An example is given. The number of people speaking a language other than English at home in 1990, and the percent of change in this category for each state from 1980 to 1990
27. Answers may vary. An example is given. Native and Total People Who Speak Each Language **32.** 16
33. 16 **34.** 16 **35, 36.** Answers may vary.

Pages 11–12 Talk it Over

1. The variable expressions are alike because they both multiply a variable by 12. They are different because the first expression has a d for days and the second one has an h for hours. **2.** Answers may vary. An example is given. How many quarters are in x dollars? **3.** 2,000,001 toothpicks **4. a.** 15 **b.** $\frac{1}{2}$ **c.** 21 **d.** 25

Pages 14–16, 18 Exercises and Problems

1. A variable is a letter used to represent one or more numbers. **3. a.** 168; 8760 **b.** $24d$

5. Shape 4 Shape 5

shape	perimeter
1	16
2	32
3	48
4	64
5	80

perimeter = $16n$

7. $p + t$ **9.** $p + t$ **11.** Answers may vary. An example is given. They use the same variables. The variables represent different things. **13.** D **15.** A
27. $x = \frac{1}{2}$

Perimeter

Number of x-tiles	Long rectangles	Tall rectangles
1	3	3
2	4	5
3	5	7
4	6	9
5	7	11

31. $2x + 6$ **42.** B **43.** Choices may vary. **44.** 2401
45. 59,049 **46.** 0.125

Pages 20–22 Talk it Over

1. $2^8 = 256$ **2.** $2^{12} = 4096$ **3.** Answers may vary. An example is given. I prefer the exponent key because it is faster. **4.** about 3.9 mi **5. a.** 9 zeros
b. $10^9 = 1,000,000,000$ **6. a.** n zeros **b.** 100 zeros
7. Answers may vary. An example is given. The sum of the exponents of the two powers of 10 on the left is equal to the power of ten on the right. **8. a.** 10^8
b. 10^8 **c.** 10^9 **9.** Answers may vary. An example is given. To multiply powers of ten, add the exponents.
10. a. 10^2 **b.** 10^4 **c.** 10^7 **11.** Answers may vary. An example is given. To divide powers of ten, subtract the exponents.

Pages 23–25 Exercises and Problems

1. Answers may vary. An example is given.
$2 \cdot 2 \cdot 2 \cdot 2 \cdot 2$; $2^3 \cdot 2^2$; $2^4 \cdot 2^1$ **3.** 4^3; four cubed
5. x^3; x cubed **7.** z^6; z to the sixth power **9.** 5^2
11. 7^3 **13.** x^6 **15, 17, 19.** Explanations may vary. An example is given. **15.** $4^3, 4^4, 4^5, 4^6$; Four is used as a factor an increasing number of times. Since four is a

positive number greater than one, the larger the exponent, the larger the number. **17.** $\left(\frac{1}{2}\right)^5, \left(\frac{1}{2}\right)^4, \left(\frac{1}{2}\right)^3, \left(\frac{1}{2}\right)^2$;

Since $\frac{1}{2} < 1$, multiplying it by itself makes it smaller (the numerator stays the same, but the denominator gets larger). The larger the exponent, the smaller the number. **19.** $(0.1)^2, (0.3)^2, (0.4)^2, (0.8)^2$; Each base is multiplied by itself the same number of times (2). Since the bases are all positive, the larger the base, the larger the number. **21.** $x^2 + 1$; 50 **23.** $x^2 + x + 1$; 57 **25.** $x^2 + 4x + 4$ **29.** 10^{12} **31.** 10^{500} **33.** 10^0 **35.** 10^{446} **37.** 10^{a-b} **39. a.** 10^{15} **b.** 10^{15} **c.** 10^{15} **d.** 10^{a+b+c} **42. a.** 6.59s **b.** 16.99l **c.** \$32.95; \$50.97 **43.** Answers may vary. Examples are given. The word polygon means many angles. A triangle is a 3-gon. A quadrilateral is a 4-gon. **44.** about 88

Page 26 Talk it Over
1. Answers may vary, but should be near 78. **2.** The calculator added 84 and 2, multiplied this result by 75, and then divided by 3. **3.** The graphics calculator did the multiplication first, then the division, and did the addition last. **4.** Enter $(\boxed{84}\boxed{+}\boxed{2}\boxed{\times}\boxed{75}\boxed{)}$ $\boxed{\div}\boxed{3}\boxed{\text{ENTER}}$; 78 **5.** Enter $\boxed{2}\boxed{\times}\boxed{75}\boxed{+}\boxed{84}\boxed{=}\boxed{\div}\boxed{3}$ $\boxed{=}$

Pages 28–29 Exercises and Problems
3. 23 **5.** 13 **7.** 3 **9.** 12 **11.** 1009 **13.** 43 **15.** 9 **17.** 77 **19.** 70 **23.** $48 \div 4 + 8 - (4 + 2) = 14$ **25.** $48 \div (4 + 8) - 4 + 2 = 2$ **36–37.** Counterexamples may vary. Examples are given. **36.** When $x = 2$, $2^2 + 2 \neq 2^3 (4 + 2 \neq 8)$. **37.** When $x = 2$, $2^2 \cdot 2^4 \neq 2^8$ ($4 \cdot 16 \neq 256$). **38.** Yes. **39.** No. **40.** Yes. **41. a.** Answers may vary. Examples are given: $x = 4$: $2x + 3 = 11$, $2(x + 3) = 14$; $x = 3$: $2x + 3 = 9$, $2(x + 3) = 12$; $x = 2$: $2x + 3 = 7$, $2(x + 3) = 10$ **b.** addition and multiplication; For $2x + 3$, multiply first, then add. For $2(x + 3)$, add first, then multiply. **c.** $2(x + 3)$; The expression $2(x + 3)$ is equivalent to $2x + 6$, which is 3 more than $2x + 3$.

Page 30 Checkpoint
1. Answers may vary. Examples are given. The biggest increase from 1980 to 1990 is in the number of people speaking Vietnamese at home. The number of people speaking Thai at home has more than doubled from 1980 to 1990. Among languages listed, the fewest number of people still speak Mon-Khmer. **2.** The languages are listed in order of highest percent change to lowest percent change from 1980 to 1990. **3.** 12 **4.** 24 **5.** 31 **6.** 10^8 **7.** 10^{18} **8.** 10^7 **9.** 82 **10.** 90 **11.** 6571 **12.** 40

Pages 31, 33 Talk it Over
1. Alicia adds the cost of the sandwich and the drink first and then multiplies by 4. Ben multiplies the cost of the sandwich by 4 and the cost of the drinks by 4,

and then adds these totals together. **2.** \$15.36; They are the same. **3.** Answers may vary. An example is given. Alicia's; \$2.25 + \$.75 = \$3.00, and 4(3) is easier to solve than (4 · 2.25) + (4 · 0.75). **4.** $12 - 0.2 = 11.80$ **5.** Answers may vary. An example is given. Think of \$.89 as \$.90 − \$.01: $4(0.9 - 0.01) = 4(0.9) - 4(0.01) = 3.56$. **6.** Answers may vary. An example is given. When combining like terms, use the distributive property in reverse to group the coefficients of the like terms. Add the coefficients to get the new coefficient of the variable. **7.** unlike terms

Pages 34–36 Exercises and Problems
1. 600 + 100 **3.** 200 + 40 **5.** 1025 **7.** 34 **9.** 4790 **11.** 2500 **13. a.** Answers may vary. Examples are given. Add together the area of each wall, or find the perimeter of the floor and multiply by the height. **b.** $ab + ac + ad + ae$ **15.** $x(x + 3)$; $x^2 + 3x$ **17.** $6a - 3b$ **19.** $4t^2 + 1$ **25.** They cannot be combined because there are no like terms. **27.** $9y + 19$ **29.** $9y + 54$ **33.** 100 **34.** 361 **35.** 841 **36.** 10^2 **37.** 10^{10} **38.** 10^4 **39.** $2(v + u)$; $2v + 2u$ **40.** $3(s + t)$; $3s + 3t$

Pages 38–39 Talk it Over
1–2. Answers may vary. **3.** Answers may vary. An example is given. I think they should be considered the same because if either one is flipped over, it will match the other one exactly. Also, the pieces are the same shape and size. **4. a.** turn **b.** flip **c.** slide **5.** Yes. **6–8.** Answers may vary.

Pages 41–43 Exercises and Problems
1. slide **3.** turn **5.** No. **7.** Answers may vary. An example is given. Someone in a group may suggest an idea, a method, or a solution that you would not have suggested. Someone in a group might correct a mistaken idea of yours and set you back on a correct solution path. Working in a group allows you to get more answers to a problem situation. **9.** Answers may vary. **13.** Answers may vary. **17.**

19, 21. Choices of variables may vary. Examples are given.
19. ; $4s$ **21.** ; $2a + 2b + c$

23. pentagon $HIJKL \cong$ pentagon $ONMLK$; side HI corresponds to side ON, side IJ corresponds to side NM, side JK corresponds to side ML **26.** $10x + 15$ **27.** $6y^2 - 18y + 24$ **28.** 0 **29.** 0 **30.** $4a$ **31.** $2b + 2c$

1. Answers may vary. An example is given. Parallelograms have opposite sides that are parallel and congruent. **2.** Answers may vary. An example is given. Kites have two pairs of adjacent sides that are congruent. **3.** Yes. Yes. **4.** parallelograms that are not rhombuses **5.** kite, isosceles triangle **6.** rhombus, rectangle; The square has four lines of symmetry. **7–10.** Answers may vary Examples are given. **7.** Several words ("triangel," "inchs," and "perimters") are misspelled, and "maybe 'cause" is not standard grammar. **8.** The writer uses the terms "quadrilateral," "congruent," "parallelogram," "kites," "perimeters," "triangles," and "rectangles" correctly. **9.** The first report mentions the fact that when working with the triangle that had side lengths which were consecutive numbers (3, 4, 5), the perimeters of the figures made were consecutive even numbers (14, 16, 18). This idea could be developed inductively by testing other triangles with consecutive numbers as side lengths. It could be developed deductively by testing a general triangle with consecutive sides a, $a + 1$, and $a + 2$. **10.** The first report simply shows the two different triangles with no pictures of the shapes formed from these triangles. In the second report, the writer shows the triangles forming quadrilaterals, and labels the sides to show which congruent sides were joined. This gives the reader a visual summary of the shapes formed in the triangle exercise.

1. Jeanine: equilateral (also isosceles); Alain: isosceles; Helen: scalene; Duane: right, scalene **3.** 22, 24, 26
5. perimeter = $4b$ perimeter = $2a + 2b$

7. Trapezoids and perimeters may vary. Examples are given. **a.**   **b.** 20; 18

9. rhombus **11.** parallelogram

13.   **15.** no symmetry

19. Quadrilateral *EFGH* has two pairs of opposite sides that are congruent, so it is a parallelogram.
27. Explanations may vary. An example is given. From Exercise 6, we know that for congruent scalene triangles with sides a, b, and c, the perimeters of all possible quadrilaterals are $2a + 2b$, $2a + 2c$, and $2b + 2c$. These perimeters will hold true for any type of

triangle, for if the triangles are not scalene then we know that if the triangles are isosceles then $a = b$ or $a = c$ or $b = c$ or if the triangles are equilateral we know $a = b = c$. **29.** Answers may vary.
30. $a + b + 3c$ **31.** $2a + 2b$ **32.** 100; ten squared or one hundred **33.** 1000; ten cubed or one thousand **35.** 1,000,000,000; ten to the ninth power or one billion

1. German, Italian, Polish **2.** Explanations may vary. An example is given. A bar graph might be hard to read because the numbers are close. **3.** Answers may vary. An example is given. Spanish is the language spoken most at home by United States residents 5 years old and over who speak a language other than English; Portuguese is spoken the least; speaking Polish has declined from 1980 to 1990. **4.** $n + 4$
5. $x \div 4$ **6.** $4x$ **7. a.** 252 mi **b.** $21x$

8.

Rectangle	Perimeter
1	$2x + 4$
2	$4x + 4$
3	$6x + 4$
4	$8x + 4$
5	$10x + 4$

9. 10^{11} **10.** 10^3 **11.** 10^{12} **12. a.** Answers may vary. An example is given. $10^2 + 10^3 \neq 10^{2+3}$, because $100 + 1000 \neq 100,000$. **b.** No. **c.** $10^a \cdot 10^b = 10^{a+b}$
13. 1041 **14.** 6 **15.** 3740 **16.** 1386 **17.** $12x^2 + 3x$
18. There are no like terms. **19.** $5x^2 + 10x$
20. Amy's mistake is that she added the 4 and 6 together and then used the distributive property: $10(3x + 12) = 30x + 120$. She should have used the distributive property first, $6(3x + 12) = 18x + 72$, and then combined like terms: $4 + 18x + 72 = 18x + 76$.
21. Answers may vary. Examples are given. *ABGK* ≅ *JEDH*; *ABGK* ≅ *SNMQ*; *JEDH* ≅ *SNMQ*
22. A *flip* across the line that passes through *D* and *H* will show that *ABGK* ≅ *SNMQ*. A *slide* up two units and to the right one unit will show that *SNMQ* ≅ *JEDH*. A *slide* up two units and to the right one unit and a *flip* will show that *ABGK* ≅ *JEDH*.
23. Answers may vary. An example is given. Using *ABGK* and *JEDH*, side *AB* ≅ side *JE*, side *BG* ≅ side *ED*, side *GK* ≅ side *DH*.
24. hexagon

25. Choices of variables may vary. An example is given. $a + b + c + 2d + e$

26. a. no perpendicular sides   **b.** sides *AC* and *MO*; sides *AM* and *CO*   **c.** parallelogram   **27. a.** sides *LR* and *RJ*; sides *RJ* and *JD*; sides *JD* and *DL*; sides *DL* and *LR*   **b.** sides *LR* and *DJ*; sides *LD* and *RJ*   **c.** rectangle   **28. a.** sides *KW* and *WO*; sides *WO* and *OC*; sides *OC* and *CK*; sides *CK* and *KW*   **b.** sides *KC* and *WO*; sides *KW* and *CO*   **c.** square   **29. a.** no perpendicular sides   **b.** sides *LC* and *WN*; sides *LW* and *CN*   **c.** rhombus

Unit 2

Pages 57–60 Talk it Over

1. Answers may vary. An example is given. thousands   **2.** Answers may vary. An example is given. Split the crowd into equal-size smaller sections. Count or estimate the number of people in one of these smaller sections, then multiply by the number of sections.   **3.** Answers may vary.   **4.** Answers may vary.   **5.** Answers may vary. Examples are given. Yes, hair could be separated into equal parts and a smaller group counted. Yes, you could choose a section of the movie theater and count the number of people seated in that section. No, you cannot see the entire population of a city in order to divide it into equal groups. You would have to conduct a survey.
6. Answers may vary. Examples are given. A fraction might be used to indicate yardage of fabric; a decimal might be used to indicate a price; a negative number might be used to indicate a business loss.
7–9. Answers may vary. Examples are given.
7. exact; Each student has only one school identification number, and each school identification number identifies only one student.   **8.** estimated; The population of a state capital is constantly changing. People move in and out of the city and there are births and deaths. Generally, it is not possible to determine an exact population count and an estimate is used instead.   **9.** estimated; People often read books over several days and experience many interruptions.
10. Answers may vary. An example is given. about 1 million groups   **11.** Answers and methods may vary. Examples are given. thousands; Count the number of math books laid flat, end to end, that will fit along a longer wall of the classroom; then count the number of math books, laid flat, side by side, that will fit along a shorter wall of the classroom. Count or estimate the number of books that would fit in a pile from the floor to the ceiling of the classroom. Multiply these three counts to estimate the number of books that could be stacked in the classroom.   **12.** the population of the United States in 1998 and the population of the world in 1998; Yes.   **13.** Estimates may vary. An example is given. thousands   **14.** Answers may vary.   **15.** 0.8   **16.** continuous   **17.** continuous   **18.** discrete   **19.** (16) measure; (17) measure; (18) count

Pages 60–63 Exercises and Problems

1. a–d. Answers may vary. Examples are given.
a. hundreds   **b.** Split the dish into 4 parts, count the bacteria in one part and multiply by 4.   **c.** about 220   **d.** My guess was right.   **3.** Guesses, estimates, and methods may vary. An example is given. hundreds; about 130 photographs; Suppose there are 13 photographs in Unit 2 of your textbook and there are 10 units in the textbook; 13 · 10 = 130 photographs.
5. Answers may vary. Examples are given. identify: school ID number; order: periods of the day; count: number of students in each class; measure: length of playing field   **7, 9.** Estimates may vary. Examples are given.   **7.** thousands   **9.** thousands   **11.** more than   **13.** unreasonable; Los Angeles has fewer residents than New York City, which had only about 7.4 million residents in 1998.   **15.** about 1.2 billion
17. No, the average weight of an adult is much less than 400 lb, so it is very unlikely that the combined weight of the 10 adults is near the capacity weight of the elevator.   **19, 21.** Answers may vary.   **23.** 1
25. discrete   **27.** continuous
36.

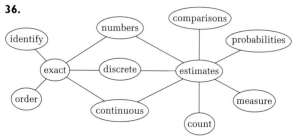

37. 2 · 3 · 7   **38.** 2 · 2 · 3 · 3   **39.** 2 · 7 · 7   **40.** 5 · 5 · 5
41.

$$\xleftarrow{\quad\bullet\;\mid\;\bullet\;\mid\;\mid\;\mid\;\bullet\;\mid\;\mid\;\bullet\;\bullet\;\mid\;\bullet\;\quad}\rightarrow$$
$$\;-7\;-5\qquad 0\qquad 3\;4\qquad 7$$

7 and −7 are the same distance from 0.

Pages 64–66 Talk it Over

1. They are used to show measurement below sea level. Answers may vary. Examples are given: temperature below zero, overdrawn bank balance
2. between −6 and −9, closer to −9   **3. a.** the absolute value of twelve; 12   **b.** the absolute value of negative four; 4   **4.** 10 and −10   **5.** −7; 2; 0   **6.** *negative 12* or *the opposite of 12*   **7.** −15; 27   **8.** 0   **9.** 0   **10.** 0   **11.** 0
12. −1.3, 5, 0; The results are the same as those in Sample 1. The opposite of a number is equal to the product of −1 and the number: $-x = -1 \cdot x$.   **13.** 88
14. Answers may vary. An example is given. I can do Sample 1 by mental math. I prefer to use a calculator for Sample 2 because it involves more than one calculation at a time.

1. absolute value: 17; opposite: 17 **3.** absolute value: $\frac{1}{2}$; opposite: $\frac{1}{2}$ **5.** absolute value: 3,785,200; opposite: 3,785,200 **7.** False. When $x = -2$, $-x = -(-2) = 2$, which is positive. **9.** True. **11.** False. For example, when $x = -3$, $|-3| \neq -3$. **13.** -53 **15.** 18 **17.** 24 **19.** -19 **21.** -180 **23.** -30 **25.** -4.5 **27.** Answers may vary. An example is given. Exercises 18, 20, 21, and 26 can be easily done by mental math. In Exercise 21, just add 120 and 60 together in your head and keep the negative sign; you get -180. In Exercise 26, multiplying 21 by 100 is easy and you know that the product of two negatives is a positive; the product is 2100. **31.** $300
33. $3 + 18 \div 2 \cdot (-3) = 3 + 9 \cdot (-3) = 3 + (-27) = -24$
35. $-9 \div 2 \cdot 10 \div 3 = (-4.5) \cdot 10 \div 3 = -45 \div 3 = -15$
37. $\frac{-20-5}{2} = \frac{-25}{2} = -12.5$ **39.** -12.5 **41.** -16 **43.** -3
49. $37°C$ **51.** $-243.4°F$ **55–57.** Estimates may vary. Examples are given. **55.** millions **56.** thousands **57.** thousands **58.** base, exponent or power; factor **59.** 10^{14} **60.** 10^{40} **61.** 10^{15} **62.** 10^{27}

1. a. 6 **b.** 5 **c.** 6 **2.** $\frac{1}{10^{12}}$, $\frac{1}{1,000,000,000,000}$
3, 4. Descriptions may vary. Examples are given.
3. 3.4×10^4; You can think of 34,000 as 3.4 ten thousands. Since ten thousand is the fourth power of ten, 34,000 is the same as 3.4×10^4. **4.** 2.19×10^{-6}; The first digit not equal to zero, 2, is in the millionths' place. Since millionths is the sixth decimal place, 0.00000219 is the same as 2.19×10^{-6}. **5.** 9,300,000; nine million, three hundred thousand **6.** 0.00048; forty-eight hundred-thousandths **7.** No, it should be 4×10^{14}. **8.** No, it should be 1.27×10^{-5}.
9. You need to know how long the recording time is.
10. 10^5 **11.** 10^{-1}; 10^{-2} **12.** 10,000; 100,000; 10 EXP 4 means $10 \cdot 10^4$ or 10^5.

1. Scientific notation writes a number as the product of a number greater than or equal to one and less than 10, and a power of 10. **3. a.** Descriptions may vary. Examples are given. Use a calculator, rewrite 10^{-7} as $\frac{1}{10^7}$ and find its decimal form, or use the rule that 10^{-7} has seven decimal places (six zeros to the right of the decimal point, followed by a one).
b. 0.0000001 **5.** = **7.** > **9.** < **11.** 10^{10} **13.** 10^0
17. 2.39×10^{-8} Cal **19.** 5.036×10^5 kg **21.** 0.04 m
23. 2.2 m **25.** 26 m **27.** C **29.** G **31.** 1.44×10^{10}
33. 3.78×10^{-7} **35.** 2×10^3 **37.** Explanations may vary. An example is given. Rewrite the product as $(3.4)(1.2)(10^{15} \cdot 10^{23})$. This can be simplified to give the answer 4.08×10^{38}; [3.4 EE 15 × 1.2 EE 23 =] **43.** Estimates may vary. Examples are given. United

States: about $9.5 \times 10^8 = 950,000,000$; United Kingdom: about $1.8 \times 10^8 = 180,000,000$; Japan: about $2.5 \times 10^8 = 250,000,000$ **45.** about $7 \times 10^8 = 700,000,000$ **48.** 1.8 **49.** -48 **50.** -3.2 **51.** 4 **52.** 24 **53.** 0.8 **54.** 600

1. Answers may vary. An example is given. You could estimate how many kernels fit in a handful or a measuring cup and then estimate how many of these handfuls or cupfuls would fit in a shoebox.
2. Estimates may vary. An example is given. hundreds **3.** millions **4.** discrete **5.** Answer may vary with location of city. **6.** 7 **7.** 14 **8.** 3.45×10^{-4} **9.** 2.671×10^7 **10.** 800,000,000,000

1. 1 in. **2.** 1 in. **3.** 1 m **4.** 1 mi **5.** 1 m; Answers may vary. An example is given. Look in a dictionary or encyclopedia under *measurement* or *metric system*. **6. a.** one hundredth; 10^{-2} **b.** one thousand; 10^3 **7–8.** Estimates may vary. Examples are given. **7.** about 90 ft or about 30 m **8.** about 7 ft or about 2 m **9.** Answers may vary. An example is given. A hairdresser is likely to be good at estimating inches or centimeters; a carpenter, inches, feet, and yards, or millimeters, centimeters, and meters; and a runner, yards and miles, or meters and kilometers.
10. Estimates may vary. An example is given: about 1700 mi north to south; about 2800 mi east to west **11.** Answers may vary. An example is given. Find the total area of the large rectangle that contains both A and B and subtract the area of the small rectangle in the upper right-hand corner. **12. a.** about 7 squares **b.** 2800 mi^2 **13.** $\overleftrightarrow{AB}$ represents the line shown. $\overline{AB}$ is the segment with endpoints A and B. AB is the distance from A to B, which is 6 units. **14.** Estimates may vary. An example is given. about 1.5 in.

3. QR is about 1 in. or 2.5 cm; QT is about 0.5 in. or 1.5 cm; TS is about 0.5 in. or 1.5 cm; SR is about $\frac{3}{8}$ in. or 1 cm **7.** No. The distance is approximately 1425 km. **9.** about 7,600,000 km^2 **15.** True. **17.** False. **19.** True. **24.** 2.5×10^{-7}; 0.00000025 **25.** parallelogram **26.** rectangle **27.** kite **28.** Definitions may vary. Examples are given. An acute angle is an angle that measures between 0° and 90°. A right angle is an angle that measures 90°. An obtuse angle is an angle that measures between 90° and 180°.

1. Answers may vary but should include three of the following: $\overrightarrow{OW}$, $\overrightarrow{OX}$, $\overrightarrow{OY}$, $\overrightarrow{OZ}$. **2.** Answers may vary but should include three different angles from among the following: $\angle 1$, $\angle 2$, $\angle 3$, $\angle WOX$, $\angle WOY$, $\angle WOZ$,

$\angle XOW$, $\angle XOY$, $\angle XOZ$, $\angle YOW$, $\angle YOX$, $\angle YOZ$, $\angle ZOW$, $\angle ZOX$, $\angle ZOY$. **3.** $\angle WOX$, $\angle XOW$ **4.** vertex **5.** No. Explanations may vary. An example is given. There are many angles with vertex O, so it isn't clear which angle "$\angle O$" would identify. **6.** Answers may vary but should include two different angles from among the following: $\angle 1$, $\angle 2$, $\angle 3$, $\angle WOX$, $\angle WOY$, $\angle WOZ$, $\angle XOW$, $\angle XOY$, $\angle XOZ$, $\angle YOW$, $\angle YOX$, $\angle ZOW$, $\angle ZOX$, $\angle ZOY$. **7.** "under 15" and "15" **8. a.** "15" and "15.5" **b.** 90° **c.** They are complementary. **9–11.** Answers may vary. Examples are given. **9.** Method 1: Draw a straight angle. Sketch two rays to divide the angle into three equal parts. Each part is close to a 60° angle. Method 2: Divide a 90° angle into thirds. Two thirds that are side by side are close to a 60° angle. **10.** Sketch a 45° angle as described in Sample 1, part (b). Sketch a 30° angle adjacent to the 45° angle using Method 2 of question 9. The result is close to a 75° angle. **11.** Draw a straight angle. From its vertex, draw a ray not perpendicular to the sides of the straight angle. The larger angle will be an obtuse angle.

Pages 89–92 Exercises and Problems

1. Answers may vary. An example is given. An angle can be named one way by a number or two ways by three letters. The middle letter must always be the vertex, but the other two letters, which represent a point on each side of the angle, can be either first or last. **3.** $\overrightarrow{OP}$, $\overrightarrow{OL}$, $\overrightarrow{OM}$, $\overrightarrow{ON}$ **5.** $\angle LOM$ ($\angle MOL$), $\angle PON$ ($\angle NOP$) **7.** $\angle LON$ **9. a.** supplementary **b.** Yes. $\angle AOB = 90°$ and $\angle LOP = 90°$ **11.** 60°
13. a. Answers may vary. **b.** Answers may vary. An example is given. $\angle 4 = \angle 2 \approx 70°$; $\angle 1 = \angle 3 \approx 110°$ **c.** Answers may vary. **15, 17.** Sketches, methods, and descriptions may vary. Examples are given. **15.** Sketch a 90° angle and divide it in half to estimate a 45° angle. Then divide in half one of the 45° angles to estimate a 22° angle.

17. Sketch a straight angle. Sketch two rays to divide the angle into three angles of equal measure. Combine two of the angles, as shown, to estimate a 120° angle.

19. $\angle AKB$, $\angle GKD$ **21.** 45° **23.** 22.5° **25.** $y + 102 + 32 = 180$; 46° **27.** $c + 6 + 14 = 90$; 70° **32.** segment AB **33.** length of segment JK **34.** line RS **35.** length of segment PQ **36.** commutative property of multiplication **37.** associative property of addition **38.** $4x + 8$ **39.** $8a + 6$

Pages 93, 95 Talk it Over

1. $90 + 90 + 3x + 2x + 3x = 180 + 8x$ **2.** $y + 12 + 12 + y + 2y = 24 + 4y$ **3.** $18y^2$ **4.** $x^3 + 8x^3 + x^3 + 3x^3 = 13x^3$ **5.** No. **6.** Yes. **7.** No. **8.** No. It cannot be simplified, because there are no like terms.

Pages 96–98 Exercises and Problems

3. $2(3a + 3b) + 2(7a + 7b - 1) = 20a + 20b - 2$ **5.** $2(x \cdot z) + 2(y \cdot z) + 2(x \cdot y) = 2xz + 2yz + 2xy$ **7.** $30m^2$ **9.** $40ac$ **11.** $14h + 7hk + 11k$ **13.** $11m^3 + 4n$ **15.** $2xy$ **17.** $8cf - 6f + 3$ **19.** $9y \cdot 5z = 45yz$ **21.** $10c \cdot 5c \cdot 3c = 150c^3$ **23.** C **25.** D
35. 40° is a little less than half of 90°.

36. ▭ **37.** ▭ **38.** ▭

Page 98 Checkpoint

1. Explanations may vary. An example is given. To estimate distances on a map, you use the given scale as a ruler to determine lengths by finding out how many of these scale units are in a given distance and then multiply the value of the scale by the number of units. To estimate areas on a map, you determine the dimensions of a given area using the method described above and then use the appropriate area formula. To estimate angle measures, you compare a given angle to an angle of known measure, usually a 90° or 180° angle, and estimate depending on whether the given angle is smaller or larger than the angle it is being compared to. **2.** about 500 km **3.** No, it measures approximately 800 km. **4.** about 720,000 km^2 **5.** $AB \approx \frac{3}{4}$ in. ≈ 2 cm; $AC \approx 1\frac{3}{4}$ in. ≈ 4.5 cm; $BC \approx 1$ in. ≈ 2.5 cm **6.** False. $AX = XC$ if X is the midpoint of $\overline{AC}$. **7.** $22 + 19 + x = 180$, $x = 139°$

8. 15° is $\frac{1}{6}$ of a 90° angle. **9.** $14y^3$ **10.** $9c^3 - 9c^2 - 7c$ **11.** $-3mn + 5m - 4n$ **12.** $7a + 8b$

Page 101 Talk it Over
1. No. Reasons may vary. An example is given. $46 + 18 = 64$, not 28, so 23 is not a solution. **2.** Yes. Reasons may vary. An example is given. Both equations have the solution 2. Equations with the same solution are equivalent. **3.** Subtract 9 from both sides. 45 **4.** Divide each side by 6. 6.5 **5.** Add 10 to both sides, then divide both sides by 6. 37

Pages 103–104 Exercises and Problems
5. 7 **7.** 3 **9.** 5 **11.** 4 **13.** The correct solution is 11. The other solver added 6 to both sides instead of subtracting 6 from both sides. **15.** The correct solution is 6. The other solver divided by 5 first instead of adding 10 first to both sides of the equation. In doing so, the solver forgot to divide 10 by 5. **19.** B **21.** D **23.** $n + 69 + 98 + 54 = 360$; 139° **25.** $x + x + 40 = 180$; 70°; $y + y + 30 = 116$; 43 cm **30.** $-32x^3$ **31.** The expression cannot be simplified because there are no like terms. **32.** $-5a^3 + 3ab + 4a$ **33.** -1 **34.** -16 **35.** 4.8 **36.** -50

Page 106 Talk it Over
1. a. $-49 = 4n + 7$
Undo addition of 7. Subtract 7 from both sides.
$-49 - 7 = 4n + 7 - 7$
$\quad -56 = 4n$
Undo multiplication by 4. Divide by 4.
$-\dfrac{56}{4} = \dfrac{4n}{4}$
$-14 = n$
b. You would add 7 to both sides instead of subtracting 7. **2.** $\boxed{4}\,\boxed{9}\,\boxed{+/-}\,\boxed{-}\,\boxed{7}\,\boxed{=}\,\boxed{\div}\,\boxed{4}\,\boxed{=}$; -14

Page 108, 110 Exercises and Problems
3. 16 **5.** -2 **7.** 10.5 **9.** 1540 **11.** -108 **13.** $-0.08\overline{3}$
15. $255.50 = 150.50 + 35x$; 3 h
17. $11.97 = 1.29 + 12x$; $.89
19. $33.88 = 3.99x + 4.48x$; 4 yd
27. a. $3x + 2 = 11$ **b.**

Subtract two unit tiles from each side.

Divide each side into three identical groups.

Look at one of the groups.

$x = 3$

28. 63,000,000 **29.** 0.000018 **30.** 11, 11, 121
31. 7, 7, 7, 343

Pages 111, 112, 114 Talk it Over
1. 3; 4; 5 **2.** 6 units; 7 units; 8 units; 10 units; 20 units **3.** greater than; The diagonal of a square with side 1 is greater than 1. **4.** less than; One way is to measure two units on the grid and compare this to the length of the diagonal. **5.** BD is greater than AB and BC; BD is greater than 3; BD is less than 4. **6.** PQ is greater than AB and BC; PQ is less than BD; PQ is greater than 2; PQ is less than 3. **7.** Answers may vary. Examples are given: 1.5; 2.25; 2.75; 3.25; 3.5 **8.** $\sqrt{2} \approx 1.41$; $\sqrt{5} \approx 2.24$; $\sqrt{8} \approx 2.83$; $\sqrt{10} \approx 3.16$; $\sqrt{13} \approx 3.61$ **9.** Yes, the results should be about the same. Yes, the square roots and the estimated lengths of the sides are about the same. Explanations may vary. An example is given. In the formula for the area of a square, $A = s^2$, the side, s, is the positive square root of the area, A. **10.** 27 cm³
11. 2 cm

Pages 116–118 Exercises and Problems
3. $\dfrac{1}{9}$ and $-\dfrac{1}{9}$ (or $0.\overline{1}$ and $-0.\overline{1}$) **5.** $\dfrac{10}{3}$ and $-\dfrac{10}{3}$ (or $3.\overline{3}$ and $-3.\overline{3}$) **7.** rational **9.** rational **11.** rational **13.** $\sqrt{21}$ is a number between 4 and 5. 4.58 **15.** $\sqrt{38}$ is a number between 6 and 7. 6.16 **19.** $\sqrt[3]{90}$ is a number between 4 and 5. 4.48 **21.** $10 < \sqrt[3]{1300} < 11$; $\sqrt[3]{1300} \approx 10.91$ **23.** F **25.** C **27.** E **29.** $\sqrt[3]{14}$, 3, $\sqrt[3]{48}$, $\sqrt{48}$, $\sqrt[3]{1100}$, $\sqrt{169}$, 18, $\sqrt{700}$ **33.** 15 cm **35.** about 10.86 ft **37.** 4 cm **39.** about 7.05 in. **41.** 8 units, 9 units **48.** 0.9 **49.** 64 **50.** -2 **51.** 25% **52.** 36 **53.** 420
54.

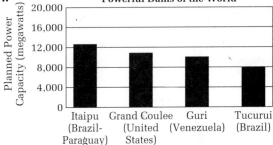

Powerful Dams of the World

Pages 120–122 Unit 2 Review and Assessment
1. Answers may vary. hundreds; 340; Count the number of spaces between the words in the first line (10) and multiply by the number of lines (34). **2.** millions **3.** Answers may vary. **4.** continuous **5.** 4 **6.** 7 **7.** 1 **8.** 28 **9.** 0.00000001 **10.** 1 **11.** 7.151×10^8 **12.** 9.06×10^{-3} **13.** 3.065×10^{-3}; 0.003065; 3065 millionths **14. a.** 4.8×10^{12} m (rounding 5.79 to 6 and 78 to 80) **b.** 4,516,200,000,000 m **15.** about 1250 km **16.** No. It is closer to 750 km. **17.** about 562,500 km² **18.** about 5,625,000 km² **19.** True. **20.** True. **21.** False. **22.** Answers may vary. Examples are given. $\angle DCE$ and $\angle DCA$, $\angle ECB$ and $\angle BCA$ **23.** $\angle ACB$ **24.** Answers may vary.

Examples are given. $\angle DCE$ and $\angle ACB$, $\angle DCA$ and $\angle ECB$ **25. a.** 52° **b.** 128° **26.** 100° is slightly larger than a right angle.

100°

27. Paragraphs may vary. An example is given. Measurements can be estimated or exact. You need to estimate when the number of objects to be counted is very large or if you do not have precise measuring instruments. You can estimate a number of objects by estimating a small portion of the whole and then multiplying this estimate by the number of portions of that size in the whole. Also, you can estimate an unknown quantity by relating it to a known quantity, such as the population of a large city. You can estimate distances by using a map scale or by using a familiar object, like a foot, whose estimated length is known. When the measurement that you need is limited in some way, such as the dimensions of a door through which you must carry a piece of furniture or the width of a shade that you have to order for a window, then an exact measurement is needed. Otherwise, an estimate is fine. **28.** $10mn + 5m$
29. $-2k^3 - k^2 - 14$ **30.** $96a^2$ **31.** $(3a)(12a) = 36a^2$
32. $40 + 90 + x = 180$ or $40 + x = 90$; $x = 50$
33. $x + 50 + x = 90$; $2x + 50 = 90$; $x = 20$ **34.** 105
35. -50 **36.** 4 **37.** $45.12 = 1.39n + 0.49n$; 24 people
38. $8.51 = 8y + 2.19$; $0.79 **39.** rational
40. 11 and -11 **41.** $4 < \sqrt[3]{72} < 5$ **42.** about 12.25 ft
43. about 4.33 mm

Unit 3

Pages 128–130 Talk it Over

1. 0.23; percent of 1999 participants who had some college **2.** No. **3.** Yes. Answers may vary depending on survey used. **4.** Answers may vary. An example is given. No. The percent measures the proportion of high school graduate participants to the total number of participants. It does not mean that the number of participants increased, but that a larger percentage of the total participants were high school graduates.
5. Answers may vary. An example is given. The trends are easier to see by looking at the graphs, because they show at a glance whether there has been an increase or decrease. **6.** row 1 and column A
7. 29,036; B4; Each number represents the amount of money the non-profit organization has each year from that particular source. For example, C5 represents interest income in 1999. **8.** B6 and C6; Formulas can use information from other cells of the spreadsheet directly to compute values and save time. **9.** rows 2, 3, 4, and 5 **10.** a column

Pages 131–134 Exercises and Problems
1. 4×4 **3.** tax, in dollars, per gallon of gas in Turkey
5. Answers may vary. An example is given. A stacked bar graph is better because it enables the reader to compare how the total cost of gas varies by country.
7. a. Answers may vary. An example is given. The tides occur later every day. High and low tides stay roughly the same distance apart. **b.** Answers may vary. An example is given: high tide—around 5 P.M., low tide—around 11 P.M. **11. a.** music videos
b. Answers may vary. Using the graph seems faster.
13. a. music videos had the highest value of shipments, followed by compact disc singles. Sales of albums and cassette singles were much lower.
b. The value of music video shipments increased from 1996 to 1998, and declined in the following year.
c. In part (a) you read the values vertically on the line representing 1998, while in part (b) you read the values horizontally, following the line representing music video shipments. **15.** 301.8; C3; D4 represents net income or loss in 1999 and C3 represents expenses in 1998. **17.** row 4 **19, 21.** Answers may vary. Examples are given. **19.** pictograph; shows the slight difference in numbers better **21.** circle graph; shows half the total much better **25.** 14 m **26.** Answers may vary. Example: 0.5 **27.** Answers may vary. Example: 0.75 **28.** 7 **29.** -30 **30.** 8

Pages 135–137 Talk it Over
1. Answers may vary. An example is given. The numbers are decimals that range from 0.3 to 5.1. **2.** Yes, 1.1 appears three times. **3.** Yes, the two types of muffins have much higher fat contents than the other breads and crackers. **4.** Estimates may vary.
5. The amounts 5.1 and 4.0 are very different from the other amounts. These amounts increase the total sum, which is used to find the mean, but their sizes do not affect the median or the mode. **6.** No. The mean is not necessarily greater than the median or the mode(s) in a data set. For example, in the data set 2, 5, 9, 12, 12, the median, 9, and the mode, 12, are both greater than the mean, 8; in the data set 5, 5, 5, 5, the mean, the median, and the mode all equal 5. **7.** Answers may vary. An example is given. The median appears most typical because it is close in value to 9 of the 11 values. **8.** corn and bran muffins; avoid eating these muffins **9. a.** No. 1.1 **b.** mean: about 0.85; median: 0.9; mode: 1.1; the mean

Pages 139–142 Exercises and Problems
1. Methods may vary. An example is given. Arrange the values in order from smallest to largest: 12, 15, 17, 23, 43, 56. There are 6 numbers in the list, so the median is the average of the third and fourth numbers, 17 and 23. The median is 20. **3.** Yes, if each entry appears the same number of times. **5.** Choices for most typical numbers and reasons may vary.

Examples are given. mean: about 134.4; median: 134.5; modes: 122, 144; The modes are most typical since they represent 6 of the 14 data values. The mean and median are 8 units away from the closest data value. **7.** Answers may vary. Examples are given. There are no outliers in Exercises 4 and 5; in Exercise 6 the outlier is 603. **9.** It is not possible to find the mean because the data are not numerical. If there were an odd number of sizes, then the middle size when the sizes are listed from smallest to largest would be the median. Since there are an even number of sizes and you cannot find the "average" of two sizes, there is no median. The mode is XL. **11.** about 75.7 **13. a–c.** Answers may vary. Examples are given. **a.** The mean gives equal importance to all her scores because it is the average. **b.** The median is in the middle and is not influenced by a single score that may not be representative of her work. **c.** The median is more typical of her scores. She has one poor grade which affects her average. **15. a.** Ad Pros: mean: $23,800; median: $25,000; mode: $25,000. Lunch Fare: mean: about $24,167; median: $19,000; modes: $12,000 and $25,000 **b.** Lunch Fare; Ad Pros; Ad Pros **19.** −33 **21.** 918; since $\frac{\text{sum}}{6} = 153$, sum = 6 · 153 = 918 **23.** No; reasons may vary. An example is given. She would need to get 108 on the last test to have a mean score of 90, and a score of 108 is impossible. **27.** No. The median age has nothing to do with the current year, but rather with population changes and life expectancy. **30.** Answers may vary. An example is given. A matrix would be a more useful tool for displaying this data, because I could easily use the data to estimate monthly fuel costs. **31.** 3^7 **32.** x^3

33. −5 −4 −3 −2 −1 0 1 2 3   −5 < 3
34. −5 −4 −3 −2 −1 0 1 2   −4 < −2

Pages 143, 145 Talk it Over
1. distance **2.** about 8.13 m **3.** 1928, 1961, 1964; 1962 and 1964, 1965 and 1967 **4.** The record jumps would have to be greater than or equal to 8.95 m. **5.** Long jumps before this date were less than 7.98 m. **6.** greatest increase: 1968; smallest increase: 1965; The biggest interval represents the greatest increase and the smallest interval represents the smallest increase. **7.** to include 8.96 m and show the record could be tied at a future date; The symbol > means "greater than," while the symbol ≥ means "greater than or equal to." The symbol < means "less than," while the symbol ≤ means "less than or equal to." **8.** If j is greater than 0, then 0 must be less than j.

9. Answers may vary. An example is given. Yes. No. In Sample 1, any and all numbers greater than or equal to 8.96 do represent a possible long jump

record, and this is what the graph shows. However, realistically speaking, the length of a long jump must be limited and cannot go into infinity. In Sample 2, there are an infinite number of points between 0 and 1.91, yet there are not an infinite number of past high jump records.

Pages 146–148 Exercises and Problems
3. B **5.** −2 0 2 4 6 8 10

x is greater than or equal to zero and less than 8.

7. −1.6   1.1   −2 −1.5 −1 −0.5 0 0.5 1 1.5

x is greater than or equal to −1.6 and less than or equal to 1.1.

9. $−2 \le t \le 30$, t = surface temperature
−2   30

11. $90 < d < 180$, d = degree measure of an obtuse angle   0 90 180

13. $40 \le s \le 55$, s = speed limit
15 40 55

25. mean: about 38.72; median: 35.5; mode: 37
26. 15 and −15; about 6.08
27.

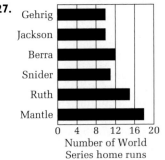

Number of World Series home runs

Page 149 Checkpoint
1. Answers may vary. An example is given. Hi! I decided to write to tell you how my grades have improved. Although the median (middle) score is theoretically 78, it was not one of my actual scores. My first four scores were 75 or lower, my last four scores were all higher than 80. Although my mean (average) score is about 79, my mode (most common) score is 84! The line graph shows the upward trend of my quiz grades.

My Quiz Grades

2. a.

	1978–1979	1988–1989	1998–1999
Men	52%	47%	44%
Women	48%	53%	56%

b. Women's share of awarded bachelor's degrees is increasing, while men's share is decreasing.
c. A series of circle graphs would best show the varying percentage of the whole for each gender, over time. One could see the trend quicker than by reading a table. **3. a.** mean: about 12.4; median: 12; modes: 12, 13; Choices and explanations may vary. An example is given. Since the data are closely grouped except for one value, the mean, median, and modes are almost equivalent. I think all of them are typical for the data set. **b.** range: 9 months, outlier: 18 months **c.** Answers may vary. Examples are given. (1) The mean is most affected, decreasing from about 12.4 to about 11.7. (2) The mode is most affected because there are now three modes, 11, 12, 13, instead of two modes. **4.** Answers may vary. An example is given. She needs a combined score of 196 or more on the two tests. For instance, scores of 98 and 98, 99 and 97, or 96 and 100 will give her a mean of at least 90.

5. $8 \leq d \leq 40$, where d = diameter in feet;

0 8 16 24 32 40 48

6. $t \leq 32$, where t = temperature at which water will freeze;

0°   32°

Pages 150–153 Talk it Over
1. the graph on the left; It includes persons of age 20, and all persons up to but not including 25.
2. $20 \leq a < 25$, a = age **3.** about 4500 **4.** Answers may vary. An example is given. Histograms and bar graphs are both ways to compare data in different categories. Each type of graph uses bars to show amounts. Each category in a histogram is an interval, the height of the bar shows the frequency in the interval, and there are no spaces between bars. A bar graph shows a specific value for a specific category, and has a space between bars to separate the categories. **5.** There are no spaces between bars of a histogram because they represent parts of a continuous interval on the number line. **6.** No. Both show data for intervals only, not for specific ages. **7.** Answers may vary. An example is given. The exact number was 8 over my estimate. **8. a.** 108 **b.** Answers may vary. Example: 225–249, 250–274, 275–299, 300–324, 325–349 **c.** Answers may vary . An example is given.

Number of *Galaxy* Copies Sold Each Week

Number sold	Frequency
225–249	4
250–274	5
275–299	7
300–324	6
325–349	3

9. Yes. The stem, "15," appears only once, but the leaf, "6," appears twice. **10.** Answers may vary. An example is given. Count from the first leaf and the last leaf at the same time until you get to the middle number (median) or numbers (median is average of two numbers). 155.5 **11.** No. 181 is an outlier, since on most days there are more than enough spaces.
12. Answers may vary. An example is given. They are alike in that they each divide the data into intervals, show the frequency in each interval, and the number of "leaves" in any entry corresponds to the height of the histogram bar. They are different in that the histogram shows only the frequency of values, while the stem-and-leaf plot also shows the actual values.

Pages 154–157 Exercises and Problems
3. Answers may vary. An example is given. This group covers the largest interval, 25 years, except for the "over 74" interval. It is expected that there are more people living that are under 25 than there are over 74. **5.** Estimates may vary by region. Examples are given. Northeast: about 50 million; West: about 50 million; Midwest: about 60 million; South: about 85 million **7.**

11. a.

Average Number of Days of Precipitation per Year

```
 3 | 5 6
 4 |
 5 | 1
 6 | 1
 7 |
 8 | 2 6 9
 9 | 0 0 6 7 8 9
10 | 1 4 4 4 7 9
11 | 2 3 4 5 5 6 7 9
12 | 2 4 4 5 5 5 6 6 7 8 9
13 | 4 4 5
14 |
15 | 2 4 4 6 6
16 | 9
17 |
18 |
19 |
20 | 9
```

b. 115.5 days

19. $v \geq 18$, v is voting age.
18

20. $2 \leq a \leq 9$, a is the increase in average global temperature from now until 2050.
2   9

21.   **22.**

130°   40°

23.

24. median: 184; range: 197; outlier: 279

Pages 159–160 Talk it Over
1. a. 28.5; 12 **b.** These ranges are shown by the lengths of the whiskers in the plot. **2. a.** 25%; 25%
b. No. Explanations may vary. An example is given. The percents will remain about the same because the lower and upper quartiles are the medians of the bottom 50% and top 50%, so it does not matter how many scores are in the data set. **3. a.** 50% **b.** These scores are where the box is drawn in the plot. **c.** No. Explanations may vary. An example is given. The quartiles and the median divide the data set into 4 parts with each part representing about 25% of the data, so the middle two parts represent about 50% for any number of scores in the data set. **4.** Answers may vary. An example is given. *Quartile* sounds like "quarter" or "quart," which refer to $\frac{1}{4}$ or 25% of a dollar and $\frac{1}{4}$ or 25% of a gallon, respectively. The quartiles help to divide the data into four parts, each part representing 25% of the data. **5.** No. Comparing where the boxes and whiskers start and end is enough to make those statements. **6.** Class I has a smaller box indicating a closer clustering of scores.
7. Estimates and statements may vary. An example is given. Class I: about 73; Class II: about 60; 75% of Class I scored above 73, whereas 75% of Class II scored above 60.

Pages 160–163 Exercises and Problems
3. Descriptions may vary. An example is given. When the 32 data values are listed from smallest to largest, the lower quartile is the average of the eighth and ninth numbers in the list, or 11.
5. a.   4   8   12   16   20

b. about 75% **c.** about 25%

7. a.
4   8   12   16   20   24
Kim
Jared

b. Statements may vary. Examples are given. The plot for Jared's class extends farther in both directions than the plot for Kim's class, so Jared's class has a wider range of ages than Kim's class. The median of Jared's data is greater than the upper extreme of Kim's data, so about 50% of the brothers and sisters of the students in Jared's class are older than all of the brothers and sisters of the students in Kim's class.
c. Answers may vary. An example is given. More of the brothers and sisters of students in Jared's class are at least 17 years old than are less than 17 years old. **d.** Answers may vary. An example is given. Yes, agree. The box portion of the plot for Jared's data lies completely to the right of the box portion of the plot for Kim's data. This shows that 75% of the brothers and sisters of Jared's classmates are older than 75% of the brothers and sisters of Kim's classmates. Also, if you choose an age at random from Jared's data, it is more than 50% likely that the age is greater than the upper extreme of Kim's data. **9. a.** 7 **b.** 15
c. Answers may vary. Examples are given. 15 > 7 (or 15 is about twice 7); the left whisker in Jared's plot is longer than (about twice as long as) the left whisker in Kim's plot. **11.** about $350; about $200
13. about 25% **15.** No. The median cost of repairs for the Facet is $350, so $300 is lower. **21.** about 59
22. 0–1.9. This means that most volunteers work 0–1.9 hours per week. **23.** You need to know the exact amount of hours that each volunteer has worked each week. **24.** $9a - 12b$ **25.** $3x^2$
26. Answers may vary. An example is given. A line graph would show specifically the change in tide over a 24-hour period.

Page 165 Talk it Over
1. Answers may vary. An example is given. You could use a table to display each state and percent of trash recycled by that state. **2.** Answers may vary. An example is given. A bar graph could be used to display these data. **3.** Answers may vary. An example is given. You could use a histogram or a stem-and-leaf plot.

Pages 166–169 Exercises and Problems
1. Answers may vary. Examples are given. The bar graph shows that the percentage of tires recycled is about the same as the percentage of paper recycled. The circle graph shows that almost half the landfill space is taken up by paper. The box-and-whisker plot shows that about 50% of Southerners contribute more tons of trash per person, per year, than 75% of Westerners. The histogram shows that about 30 states recycle 10% or less of their trash. **3.** a, c, d **5.** a, d

7. Answers may vary. Examples are given. A line graph can be used to show trends over time. A line graph can be used to compare two sets of data, especially over time. A line graph can be used to estimate an unknown data value between two known data values. **9, 11.** Answers may vary. Examples are given. **9. a.** Canada produces almost three times as much ice cream as Sweden. **b.** This graph gives a quick comparison of different nations' ice cream production. The ice cream cone makes the subject matter clear. **11. a.** Only 3 out of 17 Running Club members ran 20 or more times in October. **b.** The plot quickly displays this small data set, and allows each data value to be seen. **13, 15, 17.** Choices may vary. Examples are given. **13.** circle graph; shows parts of a whole **15.** box-and-whisker plot **17.** Answers may vary. Examples are given. **a.** A line plot shows outliers best. It shows exactly where the data fall and how they cluster so outliers can easily be seen. **b.** A histogram conceals outliers because it only shows an interval of data. How exact data values are grouped in the interval cannot be seen.

20.

21. about 8400 km^2 **22.** Record Place; about 20 more cassettes **23.** False.

Pages 170–171 Talk it Over

1. Answers may vary. An example is given. Yes. The steepness of the various graphs makes it appear that income increases either slowly or quite dramatically. **2. a.** $1000; $10,000; $1000 **b.** 1 year; 1 year; 4 years **c.** The bigger the interval between scale marks on the horizontal axis, the more vertical the graph; the bigger the interval between scale marks on the vertical axis, the more horizontal the graph. **3.** about 27.8%; Answers may vary. An example is given. Graph A; Graph B suggests no change, and Graph C suggests too dramatic a change for 27.8%. **4.** There were about twice as many calculators in 2000 as there were in 1999. **5.** The area of the 2000 calculator is about four times the area of the 1999 calculator. **6.** No. Answers may vary. An example is given. The 2000 calculator should have twice the area (same width, twice the height) of the 1999 calculator.

Pages 172–175 Exercises and Problems

5. False. **7.** True. **11.** Answers may vary. An example is given. The graph does not show the one hurricane in March. The table tells us exactly how many hurricanes occurred, but you would have to estimate this on the graph. **13.** No. Reasons may vary. For example, the data in the table are given per month, so one month is the smallest interval of time that could be used for a histogram. **15. a.** Graph B **b.** Graph A

c. Graph A **17.** The actual number of cable systems in 1975 and 1995, 3.51 million and 11.13 million, are indicated along the horizontal axis; 11.13 > 3.51, so there was an increase from 1975 to 1995. Also, the television symbol for 1995 is much larger than the symbol for 1975, indicating a big increase from 1975 to 1995. **19.** b **23–26.** Choices may vary. Examples are given. **23.** bar graph; Each jumper's bar would show the length of the jump and could be compared easily. **24.** histogram; It shows the frequency (number of visitors) in an interval (each day of a month). **25.** circle graph; It shows the percentage of total graduates for each age. **26.** 7×10^5 **27.** 2.34×10^7 **28.** 6×10^{-3} **29.** 4.61×10^{-5}

30–33.

Pages 177–178 Unit 3 Review and Assessment

1. 4×2 **2.** plastic caps and lids collected at state beaches in 1997 **3. a, b.** Answers may vary. Examples are given. **3. a.** More of each type of trash was collected in 1997 than in 1998. The biggest decrease was in the number of plastic caps and lids collected. **b.** My statements are more easily seen by the graph. **4.** mean: 24; median: 26; mode: 18; The mean and median are most typical because both are near the middle of the data set. **5.** 12 **6.** No. It is only 2 units from the next score. **7.** 28 or higher **8.** $35 \leq s \leq 55$, s = speed of Laurie Chin;

35   55

0 10 20 30 40 50 60

9. $a \geq 17$, a = necessary age to do a road test at a testing center

15 16 17 18 19 20

10. a, b. Answers may vary. Examples are given. **a.** Most VCR's sold cost between $101.00 and $150.00; the number of VCR's sold in the $50.00–$100.00 price range is the same as the number of VCR's sold in the $151.00–200.00 and the $251.00–$300.00 ranges. **b.** exact cost of VCR's and how many different models there are in each price range

11. a. Homeroom Class Sizes

1	2 4 5 7 7
2	1 3 3 3 3 4 6 6 6 8 9
3	0 1 4 4 8
4	3
5	1 6
6	7

b. 26 **c.** Statements may vary. An example is given. About half the class sizes were in the 20–30 student range. **12. a.**

Homeroom Class Sizes

First day
Last day

b. Answers may vary. Examples are given. There was a wider range of homeroom class sizes on the first day than on the last day. The median class size on the first day was the same as the median class size on the last day. **13–17.** Answers may vary. Examples are given. **13.** A box-and-whisker plot is an excellent way to compare two large sets of data. The plot allows you to compare the medians, quartiles, and ranges. **14.** A circle graph shows best what portion of Sara's total monthly income was spent on various items. **15.** line graph; It is best for showing change over time. **16.** The new graph is misleading because of the scale gap of 50,000 units. The new graph shows that $\frac{1}{3}$ fewer plastic caps/lids were collected from 1997–1998, when it was actually $\frac{1}{4}$ fewer.

It appears from the new graph that in 1997 twice as many metal beverage cans were collected as plastic caps and lids, which is false. **17.** Circle graphs show parts of a whole. Circle graphs are based on percentages. Angle measures are used to divide up the circle.

Unit 4

Pages 183–184 Talk it Over
1. Answers may vary but should include: Each square is labeled (N or S), (E or W), (1, 2, 3, or 4). The numbers increase as you move away from the common vertex of N1 W1, N1 E1, S1 E1, S1 W1. **2.** N = North, S = South, E = East, W = West **3.** crossbow or brass dividers **4.** N1 E1 **5.** (1, 4) **6.** point E **7.** point C or B **8.** quadrant II **9.** Start at the origin. Move 4 units to the right, then 3 units down and place a dot at that location. **10. a.** the point two units to the right and two units below the upper left-hand corner **b.** plates

Pages 185–186, 189 Exercises and Problems
1. No; reasons may vary. An example is given. (1, 3) is the point one unit to the right and three units above the origin. This is different from (3, 1) which is three units to the right and one unit above the origin. **3.** the U.S. Capitol **5.** Dept. of State **7.** C1, C2 **9.** C5, C6 **11.** northeast **13.** quadrant III **15.** about 0°, 78 W **34. a.** Answers may vary. For example, the highest costs for each item are found in Chicago or New York, while Dallas and San Francisco tend to have the lowest costs.

b. Answers may vary. For example, a combined bar graph using a single set of axes and color coding for the cities would make many comparisons easier. **35. a.**

b. rectangle

Pages 191, 192, 194 Talk it Over
1. Answers may vary. Examples are given. An equilateral triangle has all 60° angles; $\triangle ABC$ has one 90° angle. Also, $\overline{AC}$ is longer than $\overline{AB}$ or $\overline{BC}$, so $\triangle ABC$ is not equilateral. **2.** Yes; $\overline{FE}$ and $\overline{HJ}$; $\overline{GH}$ and $\overline{ED}$; $\overline{GF}$ and $\overline{JD}$. **3.** It has 4 right angles and the opposite sides are equal in length. **4.** The width 4 is the same as the difference between the first coordinates of X and Y. **5.** It is the difference of their second coordinates. **6. a.**

b. area of $\triangle RST$ = 10.5 square units **7.** Answers may vary. For example, another method would be to count the number of squares in rectangle $NSMR$. **8.** Add the areas of rectangle $LSNP$ and $\triangle NSM$ to get the area of trapezoid $LMNP$.

Pages 194–196 Exercises and Problems
1, 3. Answers may vary. Examples are given.
1. description; Describing a square is simple: a polygon with 4 right angles and 4 equal sides. **3.** coordinates; There are different types of parallelograms, so coordinates would probably be simpler than a description. **7.** pentagon; The figure has 5 sides.

9. square; The figure has 4 equal sides and 4 right angles.

11, 13, 15. Methods may vary. Examples are given.
11. 22.75 square units; I found the area of a rectangle with length 7 and width 6.5. Half this area is the area of the triangle. **13.** 17.5 square units; I found the

Selected Answers

area of a rectangle with length 5 and width 7. Half the area of the rectangle is the area of the triangle. **15.** 16.5 square units; I found the area of a rectangle with length 7 and width 3. Then I subtracted the areas of the two triangles that are not part of the trapezoid. **17.** Calvin **22.** 49 **23.** 13 **24.** $9x - 12$ **25.** $9a + 3ab$ **26. a.** Check graphs. **b.** $(4, -2)$ **c.** $(-2, -2)$ **d.** right triangle

Pages 197–198 Talk it Over
1. 4 units; right **2.** Yes. **3.** $B(-3, 1)$ and $B'(1, 1)$; They have the same y-coordinate. **4.** left or right **5.** up or down

Pages 199–201 Exercises and Problems
3. $T'(-3, -1)$, $E'(-2, 2)$, $D'(1, -2)$ **5.** $T'(-6, 3)$, $E'(-5, 6)$, $D'(-2, 2)$ **7.** not a translation **9.** $J'(-6, 1)$, $K'(0, 3)$, $L'(-1, 6)$ **17.** $P'(1, 7)$ **19.** $P'(2, 5)$
21. $(x, y) \rightarrow (x + 4, y - 6)$

25. a.

b. square; All angles are right angles and all 4 sides are congruent. **26.** 11 **27.** $-15\frac{2}{3}$ **28.** $-8\frac{1}{2}$ **29.** 90°
30. 180° **31.** 270°

Pages 203–204 Talk it Over
1. No. **2.** Answers may vary. An example is given. In order for someone to copy your rotation, you need to specify the center of the rotation and the amount and direction of the turn. Directions: Put your finger on a corner of the paper and turn it 30° clockwise.
3. A turn 180° clockwise moves points to the same place as a turn 180° counterclockwise. **4. a.** 270° clockwise **b.** 90° clockwise

Pages 206–209 Exercises and Problems
1. a–c. Answers may vary. Examples are given.
a. about a 90° rotation from a vertical to a horizontal position, with the center of rotation at the base of the trunk **b.** about a 40° rotation clockwise and counterclockwise, with the center of rotation at the hinge of the scissors **c.** The sun appears to rotate about 180° from east to west each day, with the center of rotation at my location. **3.** 90° counterclockwise or 270° clockwise **5.** 90° clockwise or 270° counterclockwise

7. a–b.

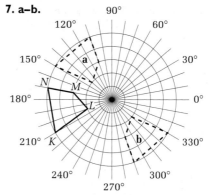

13. Yes. The design has symmetry at 60°, 120°, 180°, 240°, and 300°. **15.** Yes. The design has symmetry at about 26°, 52°, 78°, 104°, 130°, 156°, 182°, 208°, 234°, 260°, 286°, 312°, and 338°. **23.** $A'(5, -4)$, $B'(-2, -6)$
24.

Worst Day of the Week

Page 210 Checkpoint
1. Answers may vary. Two uses of coordinate systems are maps and computer screens. Both use horizontal and vertical distances for locations. Coordinates of a location on a map describe a square region, while the coordinates of a location on a computer screen indicate a pixel of light.
2. a.

b. quadrant III
c. The bowl of the Big Dipper is a quadrilateral. The lengths of opposite sides are not the same, so the bowl is not a parallelogram. **3.** origin or $(0, 0)$ **4.** 4.5 square units **5.**

6. 180°, either counterclockwise or clockwise
7. translational symmetry **8.** no symmetry
9. rotational symmetry

Pages 212–213 Talk it Over
1. Answers may vary. A positive correlation is expected. **2.** Answers may vary. One might reason there is no correlation or that there is a negative cor-

relation—girls, who tend to be shorter, tend to have longer fingernails than boys. **3.** No. 270 horsepower is a good prediction based on the data, but the actual car may have a different horsepower. **4.** about 2600 cc **5.** Answers may vary. Examples are given. **a.** No. All of the points lie below the line, so the line does not lie as close as it could to many of the points.

Pages 214–217 Exercises and Problems
1. a. One point would be directly above the other.
b. One point would lie to the left of the other.
3. a. Predictions may vary. **b.** Graphs may vary.
c. Answers may vary, based on graphs in part (b).
5. negative correlation **7.** positive correlation
13. no correlation

Precipitation and Latitude

15. positive correlation

Days of Rain and Average Precipitation

17, 19, 21. Answers may vary. Examples are given.
17. about 45°F **19.** about 15 in. **21.** c **24.** 180°
25. 90° **26.** 360°
27.

-4 -3 -2 -1 0 1 2 3

28.

-3 -2 -1 0 1 2 3 4 5 6

29.

-3 -2 -1 0 1 2 3 4 5 6 7 8

30. a. $17.25 **b.** $40.25 **c.** 5.75x dollars

Pages 218–219 Talk it Over
1. Answers may vary; for example, the change in temperature on a January morning in St. Paul, MN.
2. highest: 6°F; 12:00 noon; lowest: −5°F; 2:00 or 3:00 A.M. **3.** Temperature increased from 3:00 A.M. to 9:00 A.M. and from 11:00 A.M. to 12:00 noon. Temperature decreased from 12:00 midnight to 2:00 A.M. and from 10:00 A.M. to 11:00 A.M. **4.** Yes. **5.** No. **6.** box size; The control variable is usually put on the horizontal axis. **7.** dependent variable: height from the ground; control variable: time during the ride

Pages 222–224 Exercises and Problems
1. horizontal; vertical **3.** The time it takes Michael to run the 100 m dash is a function of his speed. dependent: Michael's time; control: Michael's speed
5. a. dependent: length; control: age
b.

Length of Lemon Shark

c. Yes; passes the vertical-line test **d.** about 115 cm
e. about 9 years **7.** b **9.** function; passes the vertical-line test

Year from Present

11. a. three **b.** one **c.** Graph B; There is only one y for each x. **17.** Answers may vary. The data points should be close to an upward-slanting line.

18. $\frac{1}{4}$ **19.** $-\frac{1}{4}$ **20.** 2 **21.** $-\frac{8}{3}$ **22.** −20; 0; −45 **23.** 10; 8; 11 **24.** 2; 0; −3 **25.** $-\frac{1}{2}$; undefined; $\frac{1}{3}$

Pages 227, 229, 230 Talk it Over
1, 2. Choices of variables may vary. **1.** control: the number of minutes you have already watched, w; dependent: the number of minutes left on the tape, t; $t = 108 - w$ **2.** control: number of tickets sold, t; dependent: profit earned by senior class, p; $p = 5t - 500$ **3.** Carmella cannot burn negative calories in negative minutes. Both calories and minutes have to be positive quantities and this is true only in quadrant I. **4.** Answers may vary, but the point should be of the form $(x, 5x)$. **5.** vertical; control
6. Each y-value is the same as its x-value. **7.** y is the reciprocal of x.

Pages 231–233 Exercises and Problems
1. table of values, equation, graph, verbal description
3. $y = \frac{x}{2}$ or $y = 0.5x$ **5, 7, 9.** Choices of variables may vary. **5. a.** control variable: total sales, s; dependent variable: total pay, p **b.** $p = 0.045s + 350$ **c.** $590.66
7. Let t = time (seconds); let d = distance (feet); $t = \frac{d}{1000}$ **9.** Let n = number of people; let c = amount each person pays; $c = \frac{800}{n}$

17. $y = 5.3x$ **19.** $y = 30x$

21. a. $5.24 **b.** $x + 0.05x = 1.05x$ **c.** Let x = total price before tax; let y = total cost; $y = x + 0.05x$ or $y = 1.05x$ **d.**

(4.99, 5.24)

e. Yes.

23. absolute value function or $y = |x|$ **25.** reciprocal function or $y = \frac{1}{x}$ **27.** No. **29.** Yes. **31.** quadrants I, II **33.** quadrants I, II **35, 37.** Answers may vary.

35. conjecture: line   **37.** conjecture: V-shaped

41. Answers may vary. There should be an x-value with two y-values. **42.** 21 **43.** 4 **44.** $\frac{-27}{7}$

Pages 235–236 Unit 4 Review and Assessment
1. Answers may vary. **2. a.** $A(-1, 1)$; $B(-1, -1)$; $C(1, -1)$ **b.** quadrant III **3. a.**

b. parallelogram **c.** 30 square units

4. $P'(-6, 6)$, $Q'(-1, 6)$, $R'(-1, 2)$, $S'(-6, 4)$ **5.** 180°
6. 90° clockwise **7.** 90° counterclockwise **8.** no symmetry **9.** translational **10.** rotational
11.

Type of Ball

12. positive correlation **13–14.** Estimates may vary. Examples are given. **13.** about 110 g **14.** about 8.5 cm **15.** No. **16.** Yes. **17.** No. **18. a.** The amount of money left is the dependent variable. The number of tapes bought is the control variable. **b.** The amount of money left is a function of the number of tapes bought. **c.** $a = 30 - 3.5t$, where a = amount of money left (in dollars) and t = number of tapes bought. **d.**

Buying Tapes

19. $y = x + 2$

20.

x	y
−2	7
−1	5
0	3
1	1
2	−1
3	−3

21. a parabola

x	y
−2	1
−1.5	−0.75
−1	−2
−0.5	−2.75
0	−3
0.5	−2.75
1	−2
1.5	−0.75
2	1

22. Answers may vary. An example is given. Coordinates can be used to show movement. By changing the coordinates you can move shapes up or down, to the left or to the right, and diagonally. Coordinates can be used to show locations on maps by identifying squares where buildings and other places can be found. Coordinates can be used to make graphs that show relationships between two quantities.

Pages 243–244 Talk it Over

1. Answers may vary. An example is given. A table is good, because you can make comparisons week by week until the exact answer is found.
2. $11 + 10w = 85$; $y = 11 + 10x$ **3, 4.** Situations may vary. Examples are given. **3.** Four copies of Shakespeare's *The Tempest* cost $15. How much does one copy cost? **4.** A 100-point quiz consists of a 50-point essay and two short-answer questions. If the short-answer questions are worth an equal number of points, how many points is each short-answer question worth?

Pages 244–246 Exercises and Problems

3. Twenty tickets must be sold.

Number of Tickets Sold	Value of Tickets	
16	$108.00	
17	$114.75	
18	$121.50	
19	$128.25	← < $131
20	$135.00	← > $131

5. The population was less than 35,000,000 in 1995.

	A	B	
1	Year	Population	
2	1998	36,096,000	
3	1997	B2 − 430,600	
4	1996	B3 − 430,600	
5	1995	B4 − 430,600	← < 35,000,000
⋮	⋮	⋮	

7. Solve $2(800) + 2x = 1950$. The lengths of the other sides are 800 ft, 175 ft, and 175 ft. **11, 13, 15.** Choice of variables may vary. **11.** $t = 7p$, where t = time in minutes and p = number of pounds of vegetables
13. $e = \frac{1}{20}f$ or $e = \frac{f}{20}$, where e = number of English words in a situation using everyday French and f = total number of words used **15.** $m = \frac{2.75p}{t}$, where m = number of minutes you wait in line, p = number of people ahead of you, and t = number of tellers
17. Ex. 14 (finding daily high temperatures)

19.

20.

21.

22. −7 **23.** 7 **24.** $-\frac{3}{5}$ **25.** 0 **26.** 0.75 **27.** 6.3 **28.** −3
29. −3 **30.** −2 **31.** −2 **32.** $2x + 8$ **33.** $-4k − 21$
34. $\frac{2}{3}t + 10$ **35.** $15x − 46$

Pages 247, 250 Talk it Over

1. a–d. oral exercises **2.** Answers may vary. An example is given. I think Alison's method makes more sense because Keith's method suggests that all opposites are negative. **3. a.** Yes. **b.** Yes. **c.** Yes.
d. Yes. **4.** Answers may vary. An example is given. Find the opposite of the first term. Next change the subtraction signs to addition signs and the addition signs to subtraction signs. Then evaluate the new expression.
5.
$$6 − x = −2$$
$$6 − x + x = −2 + x$$
$$6 = −2 + x$$
$$6 + 2 = −2 + x + 2$$
$$8 = x$$
6.
$$(n − 2)180 = 450$$
$$\frac{(n − 2)180}{180} = \frac{450}{180}$$
$$n − 2 = 2.5$$
$$n − 2 + 2 = 2.5 + 2$$
$$n = 4.5$$

Pages 250–251, 254 Exercises and Problems

3. $-x − 6$ **5.** $-5k − 3$ **7.** $-2x − 5$ **9.** 17 **11.** 10 **13.** 7
15. 11 **17.** −2 **19.** 5.7 **21.** Yes. If $n = 3$, then the polygon is a triangle. No. Since no polygon can have less than three sides. No. A polygon cannot have partial sides. Yes. n can be any whole number greater than 2. **23.** Yes. **32.** Choice of variables may vary. $T = 45 + 38h$, where T = total earnings, h = number of hours. If $h = 4$, then $T = 197. **33.** Answers may vary. Player 1 is more consistent in his or her scores. Player 2 received better scores than Player 1 on 5 of the 9 holes. **34.** −10 **35.** 13 **36.** −1

Pages 255–257 Talk it Over

1. tortoise: 2 mi; hare: 350 mi **2.** 17.5 mi
3. a. $(t − 12)$ h **b.** t h **c.** $35(t − 12)$ mi **d.** $0.2t$ mi
4. The distances are equal. **5.** $35(t − 12) = 0.2t$
6. You can find out how many hours the race lasted.
7. Use $t ≈ 12.1$ and $r = 0.2$ in $D = rt$ to get $D = r \cdot t ≈ 2.42$ mi. **8.** 6 min

Pages 258–260 Exercises and Problems

3. rate **5.** time **7.** tortoise: 0.2 mi/h, hare: 35 mi/h
9. −3 **11.** −36 **13.** 10 **15.** $\frac{2}{3}$ **17.** about 6 h 2 min
19. a. $25,000 + 1000y$ **b.** $20,000 + 1500y$ **c.** 10 years
21. a. 2 mi/h **b.** $10 = 3.75r + 1.25(4)$; $r = 1\frac{1}{3}$ mi/h
26. 3 **27.** −4 **28.** −6 **29.** 8^3 **30.** 5^2 **31.** 3^4 **32.** c
33. Let a = age in months of a dollar bill; $13 ≤ a ≤ 18$

1. a and d **2.** Answers may vary. An example is given. Adding –2 is the same as subtracting 2, subtracting –2 is the same as adding 2. **3.** No. –1 is not less than –1. Yes. –8(–5) ≤ 40 is true. **4.** There are an infinite number of points on the graph. **5.** Answers may vary. An example is given. $x < 11$ **6.** Answers may vary. An example is given. $25 < -5x$ **7.** Answers may vary. An example is given. Choose any x less than or equal to 16, for example, $x = 0$. Substitute this value into the original inequality. Simplify to see if the result is true. **8. a.** Divide by 5. **b.** Add 4. **c.** Divide by –3. **9.** In the third step, dividing both sides by –6 reversed the inequality symbol.
10. a. $t \le 12{,}000$; t = no. of tickets **b.** $w < 2$; w = weeks to complete report **c.** $8 + w \le s$; w = minimum wage, s = Claire's hourly wage **d.** $s > 10 + a$; a = average test score, s = Kwai's score
11. a. over: >; under: <; less than: <; more than: >; maximum: ≤; minimum: ≥ **b.** Answers may vary. An example is given. The maximum amount that she can spend is $100.

2.

Number of weeks	Total saved ($)
0	500
1	500 + 22(1) = 522
2	500 + 22(2) = 544
⋮	⋮
31	500 + 22(31) = 1182
32	500 + 22(32) = 1204

Alma needs 32 weeks.
3. Answers may vary. An example is given. On Saturday I bought a $29 jacket and three small plants and spent $47 in all. How much did each plant cost?
4. $3x + 2(x - 5) = 90$; $x = 20$; 60° and 30°
5. $2x + 4(x + 3) = 180$; $x = 28$; 56° and 124° **6.** –13
7. 3 **8.** 1.5 **9.** 2 **10.** $y \le 4$

11. $m < -3$

12. $c < -2$

13. $7(40) + 10x > 380$; $x > 10$; 11 h

3. C **5.** $q < -\frac{3}{2}$

7. $x \le -\frac{2}{5}$

9. $x \le 4.5$

11. $x \ge 2.5$

13. $t \le 15$

15. c **17.** b **19.** a **21.** $50{,}000 > 4.5t$; $t < 11{,}111\frac{1}{9}$; maximum temperature is about 11,111°F. **25.** up to 270 newsletters **27.** 100 ft or less **29.** at least 15 lawns **31.** no solution

33. 5 **34.** 9 **35.** –19 **36.** –5 **37.** –8 **38.** –6
39. D: distance; r: rate; t: time **40.** P: perimeter; l: length; w: width **41.** V: volume; l: length; w: width; h: height

1. Answers may vary. An example is given. First use the distributive property to get $5x - 25 + 2x = 17$. Then combine the like terms $5x$ and $2x$ to get $7x - 25 = 17$. Next, add 25 to both sides to undo the subtraction of 25; this gives $7x - 25 + 25 = 17 + 25$ or $7x = 42$. To undo the multiplication by 7, divide both sides by 7; this gives $\frac{7x}{7} = \frac{42}{7}$; $x = 6$.

1. $\frac{D}{t} = r$; Distance divided by time equals rate.
2. Answers may vary. An example is given. To solve $I = prt$ for r, divide each side by pt: $\frac{I}{pt} = r$.

1. $128 = r \cdot 32$ $D = rt$
Divide both sides by the coefficient of r.
$$\frac{128}{32} = \frac{r \cdot 32}{32} \qquad \frac{D}{t} = \frac{rt}{t}$$
$$4 = r \qquad\qquad \frac{D}{t} = r$$
r is a number. r is an algebraic expression.
3. $d = \frac{C}{\pi}$ **5.** $\frac{E}{c^2} = m$ **7.** $\frac{-r + 220p}{p} = a$ **9.** $s = b + c$
11. $y = 100 - x$ **13.** $y = 75 - 5x$ **15.** $y = \frac{c - ax}{b}$
17. a. $s = 200 + 0.12d$ **b.** $d = \frac{s - 200}{0.12}$ **c.** $3333.33
d. $1238.00 **24.** $x < -2$

25. $y \le -4$

26. $x > -2$

27. 80.6% **28.** $\frac{1}{3}$ **29.** $\frac{5}{2}$ **30.** $-\frac{6}{11}$ **31.** $\frac{7}{9}$

1. 12 **2.** Answers may vary. Examples are given. $\frac{2}{5}$ and $\frac{5}{2}$, –3 and $-\frac{1}{3}$, –1 and –1 **3.** 1 **4.** Division by zero is undefined. **5.** multiplying, reciprocal **6.** Explanations may vary. An example is given. Since the factors in a product can be grouped in any way,

$\frac{1}{6} \cdot 6h = \left(\frac{1}{6} \cdot 6\right)h$. Since $\frac{1}{6} \cdot 6 = 1$ and multiplying by 1 does not change a number, $\left(\frac{1}{6} \cdot 6\right)h = 1 \cdot h = h$.
7. Yes. $4(0.25) = 1$ **8.** No. The product is not 1, it is -1. **9.** Add 19 to both sides of the equation. Then multiply both sides by $-\frac{4}{3}$, the reciprocal of $-\frac{3}{4}$.
10. Methods may vary. Examples are given. (1) Subtract 12 from both sides and divide both sides by 0.4, or (2) subtract 12 from both sides, rewrite 0.4 as $\frac{4}{10}$ or $\frac{2}{5}$, and multiply both sides by the reciprocal $\frac{5}{2}$. I prefer (2), using the reciprocal, because dividing by decimals takes too long.

Pages 277–279 Exercises and Problems
1. The goal is to get the variable alone. **3.** 32 **5.** 16
7. 30 **9.** $y = \frac{18 - 9x}{-4}$ **11.** $y = \frac{15 - 7x}{2}$ **13.** $x = \frac{2}{5}y - 1$
15. Enter "1" and then press the $\boxed{\div}$ key. Then enter "2.5" and press the $\boxed{=}$ key. This gives 0.4, the reciprocal of 2.5. **22.** $\frac{P - b}{2} = s$ **23.** $\frac{46 - 5y}{-6} = x$
24. $2x - 14 = y$ **25.** $y = 2x$ **26.** 250 **27.** 25 **28.** 3
29. 14

Pages 281, 283 Talk it Over
1. a. $\frac{A}{b} = h$ **b.** Replace A with 25 and b with 10, then divide. **2.** Answers may vary. An example is given. I agree because the width of a rectangle is the perpendicular distance between two opposite sides. This is the same as the height of the parallelogram (the distance to the base from a point on the opposite side).
3. a. A height drawn from a vertex must be perpendicular to the base opposite the vertex. Sometimes the base must be extended in order to meet the height at a right angle. **b.** Yes. **c.** No.

Pages 285–288 Exercises and Problems
1. a. the segment drawn from P perpendicular to $\overline{AB}$ **b.** same as (a) **3.** 28 ft^2 **5.** 5.2 cm **7.** 9.5 cm
9. 69,882 cm^2 or 6.9882 m^2 **15. a.** 1912 ft^2 **b.** The perimeter of the square bandstand would be about 15 ft greater. **c.** Recommendations may vary. An example is given. The perimeter of the octagonal bandstand is less than that of a square bandstand. The octagonal shape will probably cost less. **17.** height: 10 units; area: 80 square units **19.** Explanations may vary. An example is given. Multiply both sides by 2, then divide both sides by $(b_1 + b_2)$ to get $h = \frac{2A}{b_1 + b_2}$
21. 75 **22.** −16 **23.** −16 **24.** (−3, 4), (−8, 1), (−4, −6), (−1, 4) **25.** $y = 20 - 2x$ **26.** $y = -6 - \frac{x}{6}$
27. $y = \frac{5}{4}(16 + 4x)$ or $y = 20 + 5x$

Pages 289, 291 Talk it Over
1. a. Their sum is 90°. **b.** $n + 30 = 90$ **c.** 60°
2. a. $w + z = 90$ **b.** No; reasons may vary. An example is given. The equation has two variables, and to find the unknown measures you need to write the equation in terms of only one variable. **c.** Answers may vary. An example is given. $w + w = 90$ or $2w = 90$; 45°, 45° **3.** The conditions cannot all be met at the same time. **4. a.** Cliff labeled the acute angles by using the definition of complementary. His equation relates the complement of the angle with four times the angle. **b.** Emma used x for one angle and the condition that the second angle is 4 times the first to label the angles. Her equation shows the sum of these two to be 90°. **c.** Answers may vary. An example is given. Emma's method; it seems more straightforward.

Pages 292–293 Exercises and Problems
3. correct **5.** $x = -9$, $y = -72$ **7.** $p = 6$, $m = 15$ **9.** 30° and 150° **11. a.**

b. 40°, 60°, and 80° **17.** Answers may vary. An example is given. $b = 2 - 3a$; $a = 1$, $b = -1$ **20.** The rectangle's area equals the parallelogram's area (24 units^2). The triangle's area is 12 units^2.
21. $q < 4$
22. $a \le -5$
23. $m \ge 9$
24. 78% **25.** 156% **26.** $43\frac{1}{3}\%$ **27.** $87\frac{1}{2}\%$

Pages 295–296 Unit 5 Review and Assessment
1. a.

Number of Pages	Total Charges
1	$6 + 2(1) = 8$
2	$6 + 2(2) = 10$
3	$6 + 2(3) = 12$
⋮	⋮
n	$6 + 2(n)$

b.

c. $6 + 2n = t$, where n = number of pages, t = total charges **d.** 12 pages **2.** Yes. The polygon would have 12 sides. **3.** 135 s **4.** Answers may vary.
5. −26 **6.** −5 **7.** 8 **8.** 12 **9.** −2 **10.** $\frac{1}{2}$
11. a. Explanations may vary. An example is given. John forgot to put a negative sign in front of the 5. He should have had $-5 = 4x$ and then $-\frac{5}{4} = x$.
b. Dwayne forgot to reverse the inequality sign when he multiplied by −1. The result should be $-5 < y$.

12. $x < -3$

13. $a \geq -4$

14. $x > 4$

15. 19 h   **16.** $\dfrac{I}{pr} = t$ **17.** $y = 180 - 4x$ **18.** $\dfrac{P}{T} + 2 = n$ or $\dfrac{P + 2T}{T} = n$ **19.** $x = \dfrac{21}{4}y + \dfrac{35}{4}$ **20.** $x = \dfrac{8}{3}(y - 6)$ or $x = \dfrac{8}{3}y - 16$ **21.** $y = \dfrac{4}{5}(1 - 5x)$ or $y = \dfrac{4}{5} - 4x$ **22.** $\dfrac{y}{4} = x$

23. Area of a parallelogram $= bh$ **24.** Area of a trapezoid $= \dfrac{1}{2}(b_1 + b_2)h$ **25.** about 105,000 mi^2
26. $x = 4$, $y = -1$ **27.** $y = 3x$, $y + 2x = 180$; two angles of 36°, 1 angle of 108°

Unit 6

Pages 301–302 Talk it Over
1. 20 in.   **2.** $\dfrac{16}{12}$ **3.** Yes. The aspect ratio, $\dfrac{16}{12}$, can be simplified to $\dfrac{4}{3}$.   **4.** about 15%   **5.** Answers may vary. Examples are given: discounts at stores, newspaper survey results, test grades.

Pages 303–305 Exercises and Problems
3. 1:4   **5.** 4:1   **13.** $a = 1$, $b = 3$ **14.** $r = -5$, $s = 5$
15. $d = 13$, $e = 2$ **16.** Answers may vary.

Pages 309–311 Talk it Over
1. Since the probability is a little more than 50%, it is just slightly more likely the person is a female than not.   **2.** $P(E) = \dfrac{\text{male residents at least 25 yr old with 1–3 years of college}}{\text{total residents at least 25 yr old}} = \dfrac{35{,}390}{287{,}275} \approx 0.123$. The probability is about 0.12 or 12%.
3. three   **4.** 0; Explanations may vary. An example is given. When a die is rolled, the side facing up indicates the number rolled. It is not possible to have two sides of a die facing up.   **5.** The largest value that a probability of an event can have is 1, which represents 100% probability. Most events have a probability less than one. The complement would then be 1 minus the probability of this event.
6. $P(\text{not } E) + P(E) = 1$

Pages 311–313 Exercises and Problems
1. impossible   **3.** certain   **7. a.** Answers and explanations may vary. An example is given. The probability of choosing a female is about 58%, and the probability of choosing a male is about 42%. Therefore, there is a slightly better probability of a female student being chosen.   **b.** about 0.42 or 42%   **9.** Answers may vary. An example is given. No, the probability for the event will remain at 50%. Tossing a fair coin in an example of theoretical probability and the prob-

ability of a tail is equally as likely as the probability of a head regardless of any previous outcomes.
11. a. about 0.24 or 24%   **b.** about 0.76 or 76%
13. thin crusts   **15.** $\dfrac{12}{52} = \dfrac{3}{13} \approx 0.23$ or 23%
17. $\dfrac{39}{52} = \dfrac{3}{4} = 0.75 = 75\%$ **19.** $\dfrac{26}{52} = \dfrac{1}{2} = 0.5 = 50\%$
21. $\dfrac{1}{52} \approx 0.02$ or 2%   **23.** red: 0.2; yellow: 0.2; green: 0.1; orange: 0.1; tan: 0.1   **25.** $\dfrac{8}{5}$ **26.** $\dfrac{37}{3}$ **27.** $\dfrac{3}{5}$
28. square roots ± 5; cube root 2.92
29. square roots ± 7.62; cube root 3.87
30. square roots ± 8.49; cube root 4.16   **31.** 721.5
32. -162 **33.** -5.74

Page 315 Talk it Over
1. Descriptions may vary. An example is given. The first ratio must equal the second ratio. Multiplying the denominator of the second ratio, 4, by 3 gives the denominator of the first ratio, 12. So multiply the numerator of the second ratio, 3, by 3 to get 9 as the numerator of the first ratio. Then $x = 9$.   **2. a.** 60
b. $4x = 45$ **c.** The factors of the left side of the equation in part (b), 4 and x, are the numerator of the first ratio and the denominator of the second ratio. The factors of the right side, 15 and 3 ($45 = 3 \cdot 15$), are the denominator of the first ratio and the numerator of the second ratio.   **3.** Descriptions may vary. An example is given. Multiply both sides by the LCD of the fractions, $6y$. This gives $5y = 72$. Divide both sides by 5; $y = 14.4$.   **4.** Yes. Explanations may vary. An example is given. Rewrite 5 as $\dfrac{5}{1}$ to get $\dfrac{5}{1} = \dfrac{12}{y}$. Then use cross products to solve.

Pages 316–317, 319 Exercises and Problems
1. 2, 3, 8, 12; $2 \cdot 12 = 3 \cdot 8$, $24 = 24$ **3.** 7.2   **5.** 1250
7. about 2.3   **9.** D   **11.** Answers may vary. Examples are given. $\dfrac{x}{7} = \dfrac{6}{84}$, $\dfrac{7}{x} = \dfrac{84}{6}$ **13.** $\dfrac{n}{36} = \dfrac{4}{9}$, $\dfrac{36}{n} = \dfrac{9}{4}$, $\dfrac{n}{4} = \dfrac{36}{9}$, $\dfrac{4}{n} = \dfrac{9}{36}$, $\dfrac{4}{9} = \dfrac{n}{36}$, $\dfrac{9}{4} = \dfrac{36}{n}$, $\dfrac{36}{9} = \dfrac{n}{4}$, $\dfrac{9}{36} = \dfrac{4}{n}$
15, 17, 19. Explanations may vary. Examples are given.   **15.** Proportional reasoning is not appropriate because people do not grow at a constant rate.
17. Proportional reasoning is not appropriate because many factors determine gasoline mileage, such as road surface, tire wear, and weather conditions.
19. Proportional reasoning is appropriate but the wrong proportion is used in the problem. The number of seconds depends on the number of cuts, not the number of pieces. Two cuts are needed to get 3 pieces. So $\dfrac{12 \text{ s}}{2 \text{ cuts}} = 6$ s/cut. To get 4 pieces, 3 cuts are needed. At 6 s/cut, 3 cuts take $3(6) = 18$ s. So, it would take 18 s (not 16 s) to saw a log into 4 pieces.

30. $\frac{2}{12} = \frac{1}{6} \approx 0.17$ or 17% **31.** $\frac{7}{12} \approx 0.58$ or 58%

32. $\frac{9}{12} = \frac{3}{4} = 0.75 = 75\%$ **33.** control variable: time; dependent variable: distance **34.** control variable: number of lawns cut; dependent variable: earnings **35.** 90 **36.** 1175 **37.** 62.5

Pages 320 Checkpoint

1. Answers may vary. An example is given. Two types of ratios I have studied in this unit are experimental probability and theoretical probability. For each ratio, the possible values are any number on a scale from 0 to 1, including 0 and 1. The ratios are alike because they describe the probability of an event. They are different because experimental probability describes events based on actual observations, and theoretical probability describes events based on outcomes that are likely to occur without doing an experiment. **2. a.** 65°, 25° **b.** 13:18 **3.** about 0.48 or 48% **4.** $\frac{1}{2} = 0.5 = 50\%$ **5.** $\frac{1}{5} = 0.2 = 20\%$

6. $\frac{4}{5} = 0.8 = 80\%$ **7.** 0.9 **8.** 4 **9.** 16 **10.** 450 mi

Pages 321, 325 Talk it Over

1. Answers may vary. An example is given. An ocean can be very large, which would make it difficult to be sure all the whales in every part are counted. Since whales are constantly in motion, it would be hard to tell if a whale had already been counted or not. Usually a city park has a very large squirrel population. Squirrels can move rapidly and easily climb trees, hiding above eye level. Also, the squirrel population is constantly changing as squirrels run in and out of the park. **2.** Answers may vary. Examples are given. **a.** Estimate the area that the crowd takes up. Count the number of people in one part of the area. Estimate how many of these parts are in the total area and multiply this number by the number of people who can fit in this part. **b.** It would be difficult to use this method. A deer moves among the trees, whereas crowds are usually still. **3.** Multiply $3 \cdot 2000$ and $50 \cdot x$. Then divide by 50. **4.** The estimate would be less certain due to the increased overall range of numbers of faulty bulbs. A larger margin gives more room for error.

Pages 325–327 Exercises and Problems

1. a. the second handful of dried beans **b.** all the dried beans **5. a.** about 3135 residents **b.** about 3010 to 3260 residents **7. a.** about 207,690 to 265,650 votes **b.** Answers may vary. An example is given. Johnson's and Rubinski's intervals overlap, so it is possible either could win, but the results of the exit poll show Johnson is favored. **c.** Reasons may vary. Examples are given. The margin of error may be larger than originally anticipated. The sample of 400 is so small compared to the population of 1,295,000 as to be insignificant. Only 483,000 or about 37% of reg-

istered voters voted, so perhaps the pre-election poll included people who did not end up voting at all. The pre-election poll counts changeable opinions, whereas the exit poll counts unchangeable votes.
11. 36 **12.** about 15.7 **13.** 30 **14.** R corresponds to X, S corresponds to Y, T corresponds to Z **15.** 14 **16.** 28

Pages 330–331 Talk it Over

1. pentagon **2.** $\angle J$ corresponds to $\angle P$, $\angle K$ corresponds to $\angle Q$, $\angle L$ corresponds to $\angle R$, $\angle M$ corresponds to $\angle S$, $\angle N$ corresponds to $\angle T$; $\overline{JK}$ corresponds to $\overline{PQ}$, $\overline{KL}$ corresponds to $\overline{QR}$, $\overline{LM}$ corresponds to $\overline{RS}$, $\overline{MN}$ corresponds to $\overline{ST}$, $\overline{NJ}$ corresponds to $\overline{TP}$ **3. a.** 1:1; the measures of the corresponding angles are equal. **b.** Yes. Since the corresponding angles are congruent and the corresponding sides are in proportion, the triangles are similar. **4.** Descriptions may vary. An example is given. Use a ruler to find the dimensions of store 18 on the drawing. Use the scale and the drawing dimensions to write proportions that can be solved to find the actual dimensions. Multiply the actual dimensions to find the area in square feet. **5.** The proportion would have 1 in. replaced with $\frac{3}{4}$ in. $\frac{\frac{3}{4}}{40} = \frac{1\frac{15}{16}}{a}$; $77.5 = \frac{3}{4}a$; $a \approx 103$ ft

Pages 332–336 Exercises and Problems

1. a. ~ **b.** Answers may vary. An example is given. Congruent figures have corresponding sides of equal length and corresponding angles of equal measure. Similar figure have corresponding angles of equal measure and corresponding sides in proportion, not necessarily equal. Congruent figures are always similar. Therefore, the symbol for congruence contains an equals sign and the symbol for similarity. Similar figures are not always congruent, so the symbol for similarity does not contain the equals sign. **3.** 74° **5.** 6 **7.** No. Explanations may vary. An example is given. Solving the proportion $\frac{1.5}{2} = \frac{x}{4}$, you get $x = 3$. The ball would reach the player 3 m above the floor. The player might catch the pass, but not easily. **11.** A distance of 2 units on the drawing represents a distance of 1 unit on an actual grasshopper. The drawing is twice as large as an actual grasshopper. **13.** Answers may vary. An example is given: about $\frac{1}{4}$ in. **15. a.** 2 **b.** 4 **19.** Explanations may vary. An example is given. Each triangle contains a 90° angle. The vertical angles are congruent. Since two pairs of corresponding angles are congruent, the triangles are similar. 50 m **29.** about 597,000 people **30.** mean: about 79; median: 81; mode: 84

31. parallelogram

Pages 337, 339 Talk it Over
1. Answers may vary. An example is given. The top right globe has the same height but twice the width. The bottom left globe has the same width but twice the height. The bottom globe has twice the height and twice the width. **2.** No. Yes, the bottom right graphic is similar to the original. **3.** Answers may vary. An example is given. $\frac{A'C'}{AC} = \frac{3}{1}$, $\frac{A'B'}{AB} = \frac{3}{1}$, $\frac{B'C'}{BC} = \frac{3}{1}$; $\angle A \cong \angle A'$, $\angle B \cong \angle B'$, $\angle C \cong \angle C'$; the triangles are similar. $\frac{J'K'}{JK} = \frac{1}{2}$, $\frac{K'L'}{KL} = \frac{1}{2}$, $\frac{L'M'}{LM} = \frac{1}{2}$, $\frac{M'J'}{MJ} = \frac{1}{2}$; $\angle J \cong \angle J'$, $\angle K \cong \angle L'K'J'$, $\angle L \cong \angle L'$, $\angle M \cong \angle L'M'J'$; the quadrilaterals are similar. **4. a.** The dilation in Sample 1 is an enlargement. **b.** The dilation in Sample 2 is a reduction. **c.** A scale factor that is greater than 1 results in an enlargement. **d.** A scale factor between 0 and 1 results in a reduction. **5.** Drawings may vary. An example is given. The center of dilation is at P and the scale factor is $\frac{1}{2}$.

Pages 340–342 Exercises and Problems
3. dilation **5. a.** (−1, 0) **b.** 2 **7. a.** (−3, 6) **b.** 2

9.

11.

17. $\angle A = \angle D = 63°$; $\angle B = 42°$; $\angle F = 75°$; $AB = 39$; $FE = 24$ **18.** 24 **19.** 11 **20.** −9 **21.** $\frac{1}{6}$ **22.** 2 to 3 **23.** 3 : 4

Pages 344–347 Talk it Over
1. a. sin 53° ≈ 0.79863551 **b.** Answers may vary. An example is given. If the calculator answer were rounded to the nearest hundredth, it would be the same as the ratio I found in the Exploration. The values may be slightly different due to small measuring errors in measuring the angle and rounding the lengths to the nearest half unit.
2. a. cos 53° ≈ 0.6018150232 **b.** Answers may vary. An example is given. If the calculator answer were rounded to the nearest hundredth, it would be the same as the ratio I found in the Exploration. The values may be slightly different due to small measuring errors in measuring the angle and rounding the lengths to the nearest half unit. **3.** $\overline{AC}$; $\overline{BC}$
4. cos K ≈ 0.89, sin K ≈ 0.44, cos L ≈ 0.44, sin L ≈ 0.89 Statements may vary. An example is given. The cosine of $\angle K$ is the same as the sine of $\angle L$, and the sine of $\angle K$ is the same as the cosine of $\angle L$.
5. Explanations may vary. An example is given. Question 4 suggests that the sine of one acute angle of a right triangle is equal to the cosine of the other acute angle. **6.** sin 37° = cos 53° ≈ 0.6018150232; cos 37° = sin 53° ≈ 0.79863551 **7.** No, the hypotenuse will always be the longest side and its value will always be in the denominator of the ratio.
8. closer to **9.** Answers may vary. An example is given. Let d be the distance between the foot of the ladder and the base of the building. You can find d by using the equation cos 75° = $\frac{d}{12}$. **10.** Answers may vary. An example is given. I would use the sine ratio since it is the ratio of the leg opposite the angle over the hypotenuse. The leg opposite has a length equal to the height of the ramp, and the hypotenuse has a value equal to the length of the ramp.

Pages 348–350 Exercises and Problems
3. 0.53 **5.** 0.98 **7.** $\frac{5}{13}$, 0.38 **9.** $\frac{5}{13}$, 0.38
11. a–d. Answers may vary.
13. Drawings may vary. An examples is given.

17. sin 50° = $\frac{x}{12}$, cos 40° = $\frac{x}{12}$; about 9.2

19, 21. Sketches may vary. Examples are given.
19. maximum height: **21.** about 96.4 m
about 14.5 ft

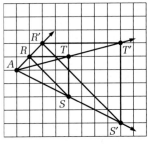

23. about 119.4 mi **26.**

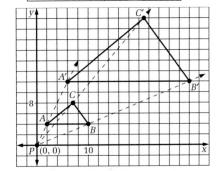

27. Yes. The broken scale gives the impression that station WRRR is much more popular than WSSS or WTTT when it actually only has about 3000 more listeners than WSSS and about 2000 more listeners than WTTT. **28.** $\frac{4}{12} = \frac{1}{3} \approx 0.33$

Pages 352–354 Unit 6 Review and Assessment
1. 6:1 **2.** \$.16/oz **3.** There are about 19,200 women attending the game. **4.** 0.2 or 20% **5.** 0.3 or 30% **6.** 0.65 or 65% **7.** Since 35 of 45 hits were against a right-handed pitcher, the probability of the next hit being against a right-handed pitcher is about 0.78 or 78%. **8.** 8 **9.** Yes. **10.** 3 **11.** No. **12.** $\frac{1}{6} \approx 0.17$ or 17% **13.** $\frac{1}{2} = 0.5 = 50\%$ **14.** $\frac{5}{6} \approx 0.83$ or 83%
15. $\frac{1}{2} = 0.5 = 50\%$ **16.** Answers may vary. An example is given. Probability has many important uses, from interpreting the results of polls to telling the fairness of games. There are two types of probability, experimental probability and theoretical probability. Both tell the chances that a certain event is likely to happen. However, experimental probability is based on observations and recorded results, while theoretical probability is based on the knowledge that the possible outcomes of an event are equally likely to happen without doing an experiment. You can use data from a table to find the probability of an event by using the formula for experimental probability:

$$P(E) = \frac{\text{number of times } E \text{ is observed to happen}}{\text{total number of observations}}.$$ **17.** 15

18. $\frac{4}{3}$ or about 1.33 **19.** 20 stacks **20.** Candidate A:

about 1,380,000 votes; Candidate B: about 1,120,000 votes; Candidate C: about 500,000 votes **21.** No.
22. Candidate A: 1,230,000 to 1,530,000 votes; Candidate B: 970,000 to 1,270,000 votes; Candidate C: 350,000 to 650,000 votes **23.** False; any two squares are similar, but one square may be smaller, so they would not be congruent. **24.** True. **25.** Answers may vary. An example is given. Christie's father wants to measure the ropes for a tree swing from a branch about halfway up a tree in the backyard. He needs to know the height of the tree. He is 6 ft tall and his shadow is 4 ft long. The tree's shadow is 12 ft long. How tall is the tree? **26. a.** Explanations may vary. An example is given. Both triangles have $\angle C$ in common, and each triangle has a right angle. Since two pairs of corresponding angles are congruent, the triangles are similar. **b.** 20 **c.** 10 **27.** $8\frac{1}{3}$ in.

28.

Vertices of Original	Vertices of Image
$A(2, 4)$	$A'(6, 12)$
$B(10, 4)$	$B'(30, 12)$
$C(7, 8)$	$C'(21, 24)$

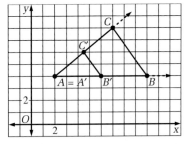

29.

Vertices of Original	Vertices of Image
$A(2, 4)$	$A'(2, 4)$
$B(10, 4)$	$B'(6, 4)$
$C(7, 8)$	$C'(4.5, 6)$

30. $\frac{1}{3}$ **31.** 60 **32.** $\frac{4}{5}$ **33.** $\frac{4}{5}$ **34.** $\frac{3}{5}$ **35.** $\frac{3}{5}$ **36. a.** The wires are about 2020 ft each. **b.** The distance from the base is about 917 ft.

Pages 359, 360, 362 Talk it Over

1. The heights of the posts increase by 1.5 ft as the distance from the eaves increases by 2 ft. **2.** For each triangle, the ratio $\frac{h}{d}$ equals 0.75.

Post	Horizontal distance d of posts from eaves (ft)	Height h of post (ft)	$\frac{h}{d}$
1	2	1.5	0.75
2	4	3	0.75
3	6	4.5	0.75
4	8	6	0.75
5	10	7.5	0.75

3. Explanations may vary. An example is given. Two triangles are similar when two pairs of corresponding angles are congruent. The triangles formed by the posts all have right angles and all have the angle formed with the eaves in common. Since the triangles are similar, corresponding sides are proportional, so the ratios $\frac{h}{d}$ are the same. **4.** Multiply both sides of the equation by d. **5.** Substitute 5 for h in the equation $h = 0.75d$; $5 = 0.75d$; divide both sides by 0.75; $\frac{5}{0.75} = \frac{0.75}{0.75}d$; $d = 6\frac{2}{3}$. **6.** larger **7.** $\frac{4}{3}$; The tangent ratio of $\angle B$ is the reciprocal of the tangent ratio of $\angle A$. **8. a.** about 0.7536 **b.** Answers may vary. An example is given. It is difficult with a protractor to find the exact angle measure. While 37° is close, the actual angle measure is slightly smaller. **9.** about 36.9°; This measure is smaller by one tenth of a degree. **10.** larger; Explanations may vary. An example is given. For a steeper roof, the height of the roof would be greater. This would make the tangent ratio, $\frac{\text{height}}{\text{horizontal distance}}$, larger.

Pages 363–366 Exercises and Problems

1. 1.25 **3.** 10 **5. a.** $h = \frac{4}{3}d$ **b.** $\frac{4}{3}$ **7. a.** rise = 3 ft, run = 4 ft **b.** slope = $\frac{3}{4}$ = 0.75; Yes. **c.** $\frac{1.5}{2}$ = 0.75 **d.** $\frac{3}{4}$ = 0.75 **13.** $\overline{RT}$ **15. a.** 2 **b.** about 1.963 **c.** No. Explanations may vary. An example is given. If a triangle is formed using the given lengths, the measure of $\angle T$ would be close to, but not exactly equal to, 63°.
17. a.

Angle	10°	20°	30°	40°	50°	60°	70°	80°
Tangent	0.1763	0.3640	0.5774	0.8391	1.1918	1.7321	2.7475	5.6713
Sine	0.1736	0.3420	0.5000	0.6428	0.7660	0.8660	0.9397	0.9848
Cosine	0.9848	0.9397	0.8660	0.7660	0.6428	0.5000	0.3420	0.1736

17. b. Answers may vary. Examples are given. The sine of an angle is equal to the cosine of the complement of the angle; sine and tangent values increase as the angle increases, whereas cosine values decrease;

sine and cosine values are numbers less than 1, whereas tangent values may be greater than 1; the tangent value is equal to the sine value divided by the cosine value.
19. a.

b. Explanations may vary. An example is given. To find the length of the adjacent leg, use the equation $\tan 20° = \frac{14}{\text{adjacent leg}}$. To find the hypotenuse, use the equation $\sin 20° = \frac{14}{\text{hypotenuse}}$. **c.** 38.5 cm, 40.9 cm
22. $\sin A \approx 0.9231$; $\cos A \approx 0.3846$ **23.** 2.4 **24.** 240 **25.** $0.41\overline{6}$, or $\frac{5}{12}$ **26.** $l = \frac{1}{3}h$

Pages 369–370 Talk it Over

1. about 33.6 in.; This answer is close to the prediction in Sample 2. **2.** Yes. Explanations may vary. An example is given. When you multiply each side of the equation $\frac{B}{D} = 0.8$ by D, you obtain the equivalent equation $B = 0.8D$. **3.** From the 12 in. mark on the vertical axis, draw a horizontal line across until it reaches the fitted line. Then draw a vertical line down until it reaches the horizontal axis. Estimate the drop height at the crossing point. **4.** Answers may vary. An example is given. Rashid could use the equation $\frac{B}{D} = 0.8$ or $B = 0.8D$; substitute 12 for B and then solve for D; $\frac{12}{D} = 0.8$; $12 = 0.8D$; $D = \frac{12}{0.8} = 15$; He should use a drop height of about 15 in. **5.** The variation constant, 0.8, and the slope, $0.81\overline{6}$, are close.
6. $\frac{4}{3} \approx 1.3$

Pages 370–374 Exercises and Problems

1. B and D; B represents the bounce height, D represents the drop height.
3. ➤ No. No.
 ➤ Answers may vary. Most balls display direct variation.
 ➤ Answers may vary. The variation constants should be nearly the same for the same type of ball. Differences among groups' results could be due to measurement errors or rounding differences.
 ➤ Variation constants depend on the balls used. The ball with the most bounce has the largest variation constant. The ball with the least bounce has the smallest variation constant.
5. Yes. For each data point, the ratio $\frac{\text{height}}{\text{width}}$ is close to 0.07. **7.** Yes. For each data point, the ratio $\frac{\text{cost}}{\text{errors}}$ is close to 21. **9.** Reasons may vary. An example is given. **9. a.** No. The water level does not change steadily over time. **b.** continuous

11. a. control: speed; dependent: stopping distance

b. $\frac{15}{10} = 1.5$, $\frac{40}{20} = 2$, $\frac{75}{30} = 2.5$, $\frac{120}{40} = 3$, $\frac{175}{50} = 3.5$, $\frac{240}{60} = 4$,

$\frac{315}{70} = 4.5$ **c.** No. Explanations may vary. An example is given. The graph is a curve, not a straight line, and the ratio $\frac{\text{dependent variable}}{\text{control variable}}$ increases steadily.

13. about $\frac{1}{33}$, or about 0.03 **15.** about 3.9 atm

17. a. Each ratio $\frac{D}{W}$ is equal to about 0.017. **b.** The dosage varies directly with the weight. about 0.017; $D = \frac{1}{60}W$ or $D \approx 0.017\,W$. **c.** 1.25 tablets; Methods may vary. For example, substitute 75 for W in the equation in part (b) and solve to find the value of D, or continue the pattern established in the table, noting that the values of W are increasing by 15 and the corresponding values of D are increasing by 0.25.

17. d.

Heartworm Medicine for Dogs

e. $\frac{1}{60}$ or about 0.017 **23. a.** 1 **b.** 45° **25.** about 1.22

26.

27.

28.

29. $P = 2l + 2w$ **30.** $P = 4s$ **31.** $P = 3s$

Page 377 Talk it Over

1.

	$\frac{45°}{360°}$	$\frac{135°}{360°}$	$\frac{60°}{360°}$	$\frac{30°}{360°}$	$\frac{90°}{360°}$
	$\frac{1}{8}$	$\frac{3}{8}$	$\frac{1}{6}$	$\frac{1}{12}$	$\frac{1}{4}$

2. 72°

---

5. about 50.2 ft (using $\pi \approx 3.14$) **7. a.** about 37.3 ft **9.** about 9 in. **11.** 4

$P = 4s$ s

13. a, b, and c

15. about 3.1 ft

23. slope $= \frac{2}{5}$

24. slope $= 2$

25. SAT Scores

26. 18 **27.** −1 **28.** 3

Page 382 Checkpoint

1. Answers may vary. An example is given. For one variable to vary directly with another, the two quantities must have a constant ratio. Find the ratio for each data pair. If the ratio is constant or almost constant, one variable varies directly with the other.

2. a. $\frac{7}{4}$ or 1.75 **b.** $\frac{4}{7}$ or about 0.571 **3.** about 13.9 ft

4. Estimates may vary. Examples are given. **a.** about 13 in. **b.** about 37 in. **5.** Estimates may vary; for example, about 0.7. **6. a.** about 1256 cm **b.** about 19.1 ft **c.** $C = \pi d$ **7. a.** about 44 in. (using $\pi \approx 3.14$) **b.** about 7.3 in. **c.** about 14.7 in.

Pages 383–387 Talk it Over

1. Answers may vary. An example is given. The equations are different because they involve different quantities, variables, and constants, and they have different solution pairs. They all have the form variable = constant × another variable, so each is a direct variation equation.

2.

equation	$h = 0.75d$	$B = 0.8D$	$C = \pi d$
control variable	d	D	d
dependent variable	h	B	C
variation constant	0.75	0.8	π

---

3. Method 1; Explanations may vary. An example is given. Method 1 is easier because you just need to multiply each time by the variation constant, 8.4, to find the amount earned, rather than setting up a proportion. **4. a.** 0 **b.** 3.14159; 0.75; 0.8 **c.** Point (2, 6.28318) is on the graph of $C = \pi d$; point (6, 4.5) is on the graph of $h = 0.75d$; point (4, 3.2) is on the graph of $B = 0.8D$. **5.** Answers may vary. An example is given. The three lines are similar because they all have the general form for direct variation, $y = kx$, and all pass through the origin. They are different because the three lines in question 4 have positive slopes or variation constants, while these three have negative slopes or variation constants. **6.** Lines with negative slope slant downward from left to right. Lines with positive slopes slant upward from left to right. **7.** −1 **8. a, b.** Explanations may vary. Examples are given. **a.** To go from (−1, 2) to (2, −4), you move 3 units to the right (a run of 3) and 6 units down (a rise of −6). **b.** To go from (2, −4) to (−1, 2), you move 3 units to the left (a run of −3) and 6 units up (a rise of 6). **c.** Regan: $\frac{\text{rise}}{\text{run}} = \frac{-6}{3} = -2$; Lianon: $\frac{\text{rise}}{\text{run}} = \frac{6}{-3} = -2$ **9.** Yes. The rise has a change of −2, which is down, for every run change of 1 to the right.

Pages 388–391 Exercises and Problems
1. 8.4 represents the hourly rate of pay, $8.40.
3. $12.93 **5. a.** 1875 words **b.** 320 min, or 5 h 20 min
7. a. 57.6 min **b.** Yes, the skater covers about 2.8 mi.
9. $y = \frac{1}{3}x$ **11. a.** Yes. All the points lie close to a fitted line passing through the origin. **b.** $y = \frac{1}{2}x$ **13. a.** No. The line connecting the points does not pass through the origin.

17. **19.**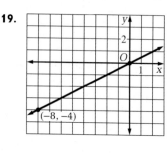

23. C **25.** B **27.** Explanations may vary. An example is given. A: $y = \frac{5}{3}x$; B: $y = -\frac{3}{5}x$; Graph A shows positive slope and Graph B shows negative slope.

29. **31.**

35. about 44.0 in. **36.** about 69.1 cm **37.** $-6x - 4y$
38. $-20a + 8b$ **39.** $7c - 35d$ **40.** $m + n$ **41.** $\frac{3}{25}$
42. $2\frac{1}{2}$

Pages 393, 394, 396 Talk it Over
1. Estimates may vary. An example is given.
$3 \times 1.4 = 4.2$, which is about equal to 6.85;
$5 \times 1.2 = 6$, which is about equal to 5.95. **2.** number of gallons of gasoline; the cost of the gasoline; 1.369
3. No. Reasons may vary. An example is given. Because the amounts in a conversion factor are equal, the ratio represents the number 1. So when you multiply by a conversion factor, you are changing the units of the expression but not the value. **4.** $\frac{1 \text{ in.}}{2.54 \text{ cm}}$; about 4.7 in. **5.** Answers may vary. Examples are given. $\frac{60 \text{ s}}{1 \text{ h}}, \frac{7 \text{ days}}{1 \text{ week}}, \frac{3 \text{ ft}}{1 \text{ yd}}, \frac{100 \text{ cm}}{1 \text{ m}}, \frac{36 \text{ in.}}{1 \text{ yd}}$ **6.** Answers may vary. An example is given. The conversion factor $\frac{1 \text{ mi}}{1.61 \text{ km}}$ is the same as the conversion factor $\frac{0.621 \text{ mi}}{1 \text{ km}}$ because $\frac{1}{1.61} \approx \frac{0.621}{1}$. **7. a.** $d = 44t$
b. 1320 ft

Pages 396–399 Exercises and Problems
3. $\frac{\text{h}}{\text{s}}$ **5.** $\frac{\text{ft}}{\text{min}}$ **7. a.** distance traveled, number of gallons **b.** 22 mi/gal **9.** about 80 km **11.** 38,016 ft
13. 3875 pesos **15. a.** 1.3 pesos **b.** $C = 1.3L$
c. 32.5 pesos **17. a.** The green line represents super unleaded gasoline. **b.** the cost of 10 gallons of each type of gasoline **c.** the number of gallons of each type of gasoline that can be bought for $8 **d.** In the graph on the left, the gray vertical segment represents the amount of money you save by buying 10 gal of regular unleaded rather than 10 gal of super unleaded gasoline. In the graph on the right, the gray horizontal segment represents the additional amount of gasoline you can afford by buying $8 worth of regular unleaded rather than $8 worth of super unleaded gasoline. **21.** about 0.513 mi **23.** about 47.2 mi/h

28.

29.

30. 80 **31.** $5\frac{5}{9}$ or about 5.6 **32.** 180 **33.** 135°
34. 120° **35.** 65°

Page 401 Talk it Over
1. The variable r represents the length of an irrigation arm; it cannot be a negative number. **2.** If you multiply both sides of $\frac{A}{\pi} = r^2$ by π, you get the equivalent equation $A = \pi r^2$.

Pages 404–407 Exercises and Problems
3. about 113.0 ft² (using $\pi \approx 3.14$) **5.** about 28.3 square units **7.** Answers may vary. An example is given. I agree. The circumference is 4π units and the area is 4π square units. The kinds of units are different, but the number of units is the same.

9. a.

$r\,(\text{cm})$	$r^2\,(\text{cm}^2)$	$A\,(\text{cm}^2)$	$\dfrac{A}{r^2}$
1	1	3.14	3.14
2	4	12.56	3.14
3	9	28.26	3.14
4	16	50.24	3.14
5	25	78.50	3.14
6	36	113.04	3.14

b. There is a constant ratio, 3.14. **c.** 3.14.
d. Answers may vary. An example is given. I predict a straight line through the origin with a slope equal to 3.14.

11. about 19.6 in.² **13.** about 20.4 cm² **15.** about 17.4 ft² **17. a.** about 18.8 in.² **b.** about 14.1 in.²
c. A slice of Tom's pizza is about $1\frac{1}{3}$ times as large as a slice of Vera's pizza. **19.** $1836.90 (using $\pi \approx 3.14$)

21. a. about 16.75 ft² (using $\pi \approx 3.14$) **b.** 17 marigolds **28.** 750 mi/h **29.** $198/yd² **30.** 90° clockwise or 270° counterclockwise **31.** −20 **32.** 63 **33.** −1

Pages 409–411 Unit 7 Review and Assessment
1. Answers may vary. An example is given. The slope, tangent ratio, and direct variation ratio are different ways to express the ratio of the length of a vertical leg to the length of a horizontal leg in a right triangle. The tangent can be thought of as the slope of the hypotenuse and the slope as the "rise" of the opposite leg over the "run" of the adjacent leg. A straight line passing through the origin can be expressed by an equation with a variation constant. This variation constant is the same as the slope. While the tangent ratio involves an angle, the slope is a rate and does not necessarily involve an angle. You might find the slope of the roof to determine its steepness, the tangent of an angle in order to find the length of a side or an angle measure for a triangle, and the variation constant to write an equation relating two variables. **2. a.** $h = s \tan 35°$ **b.** 0.700
c. about 14 ft **d.** about 60 ft **e.** $\tan 35°$ or 0.700
3. a. For each central angle, $\frac{M}{W} = 0.025$.
b. $\frac{M}{W} = 0.025$, or $M = 0.025W$ **c.** 7 m

4. a.

b. bounce height of 47 cm from a drop height of 100 cm **c.** Yes. Explanations may vary. An example is given. The remaining points are close to a straight line that passes through the origin. Also, for the remaining data each ratio $\frac{B}{D}$ is close to 0.4.
d. about 0.4 **e.** about 28 cm **5.** about 2,716,100 mi (using $\pi \approx 3.14$) **6.** 6 complete turns **7.** about 41.1 in. **8. a.** about 0.657; inches per pound **b.** about 3.3 in. **c.** about 4.6 lb **9. a.** C; The line slants down from left to right. **b.** B; Lines A and B have positive slope because they slant up from left to right. B has the smallest slope because it has a small rise compared to the run. **c.** A; The slope of line A is positive and greater than that of line B.

10. a.

b. −1.5

c. quadrants II and IV   **d.** 6

11. about 5840 days (4 to 5 more if you include an extra day for each leap year)   **12.** $y = \frac{1}{365}d$; $\frac{1}{365}$ or about 0.0027   **13.** about 42,190 m   **14.** about 4.17 h   **15.** about 95.3 ft/s   **16. a.** $51\frac{3}{7}°$, or about 51.4°   **b.**

b. about 16.1 in.^{2} (using $\pi \approx 3.14$)   **17. a.** about 42.1 in.^{2} **b.** about 0.27   **c.** No. Explanations may vary. For example, multiplying both parts of a ratio by 2 does not change the ratio.

Unit 8

Pages 417–419 Talk it Over

1.

Time in minutes (t)	Height of balloon in feet (h)
0	6000
1	6110
2	6220
3	6330
4	6440
5	6550
6	6660

2. $h = 6000 + 110t$ **3.** control: t; dependent: h

4. Graphs may vary. An example is given. The points lie on a straight line.

Balloon Heights

5. Answers may vary. Examples are given. *Linear* means in a straight line. In this situation, *growing* means increasing in height above the ground.   **6.** 110; The slope means that for every minute after the balloon takes off, the balloon rises 110 ft more above sea level.

7. (0, 6000); This point represents the height of the balloon above sea level before it begins rising.   **8.** Answers may vary. Examples are given. Both equations have the variables h for height and t for time and model rise of a balloon. The slope in the equation for question 2 is 110 and the vertical intercept is 6000, while the slope in the equation $h = 60t + 8200$ is 60 and the vertical intercept is 8200.   **9.** Explanations may vary. An example is given. If you redraw the graph so there is no gap in the scale, but still let two units on the scale equal 100 ft, the graph of the line will look the same (only higher up). If you decide to let one unit on the scale equal 100 ft, then the graph of the line rises more steeply. Either way, the slope will not change.   **10.** Yes. The graph passes the vertical-line test.   **11. a.** No. Reasons may vary. An example is given. The graph does not pass through the origin.   **b.** Explanations may vary. An example is given. The vertical intercept in the equation $h = 60t + 8200$ is 8200. The vertical intercept in a direct variation equation is always zero.   **12.** Yes; Yes.   **13.** y; x

Pages 421–424 Exercises and Problems
1. C   **3.** A

5. a.

Weight in tons (w)	Total cost in dollars (c)
0	25
1	44
2	63
3	82

Sand Sales at Better Building Supplies

b. slope: 19; vertical intercept: 25; Explanations may vary. An example is given. The slope shows that the cost increases $19 for each additional ton of sand sold. The vertical intercept is the delivery charge.   **c.** $c = 19w + 25$

7. a.

Distance driven in miles (m)	Gas remaining in gallons (g)
0	12
15	11
30	10
45	9
60	8

Gasoline Use

b. slope: $-\frac{1}{15}$; vertical intercept: 12; Explanations may vary. An example is given. The slope shows that for each 15 miles driven, 1 gallon of gasoline is used. The vertical intercept represents the amount of gasoline in the car, 12 gallons, before driving any distance.

28

Integrated Mathematics

c. $g = -\frac{1}{15}m + 12$ **9.** Answers and explanations may vary. An example is given. I agree with Nancy that the slope of the line is always the rate given in the situation because the rate shows how the dependent variable changes based on the control variable. This is the same as the slope or the ratio $\frac{rise}{run}$. I also agree that the vertical intercept is always the starting value. It is the point where the value of the control variable is zero. **11.** 3, −5 **13.** −1, −$\frac{1}{2}$ **19, 21.** Explanations may vary. Examples are given. **19.** Yes; Yes. The situation can be represented by the equation $c = 2.5m$, where c is the total cost and m is the number of movies attended. The equation has the general form of direct variation. The slope is positive, which indicates growth, and the graph is a line through the origin. **21.** No. The cost will not increase or decrease, so the the rate of growth is 0. Since the line does not pass through the origin, this is not an example of direct variation. **25. a.** $\frac{2}{3}$, 0 **b.** $y = \frac{2}{3}x$

c. linear growth **d.** Yes. The line goes through the origin. **27. a.** 4, −8 **b.** $y = 4x - 8$ **c.** linear growth **d.** No. The line does not go through the origin.
29, 31. Explanations may vary. Examples are given.
29. neither; The graph is not a straight line.
31. neither; The graph is not a line. **34.** about 26.2 in.^{2} **35.** −$\frac{3}{2}$ or −1.5 **36.** −11 **37.** 26 **38.** 26

39. −6 **40.** $y = \frac{c}{b}$ **41.** $y = 60 - x$ **42.** $y = b - ax$

43. $y = \frac{1}{3}x + 50$

Pages 426, 428, 429 Talk it Over
1. 4; by the circle around \$48 at the point (0, 4); by the point (0, 4) **2.** Yes; No. Explanations may vary. An example is given. It is not possible to buy a fraction of a tape. **3.** No. Explanations may vary. An example is given. The order of the coordinates is important because each coordinate represents a specific variable. If you change the order, the coordinates no longer represent the correct variable.
4. a, b. Answers may vary. Examples are given.
a. All the equations have the same slope, −$\frac{2}{3}$.

However, they all have different vertical intercepts.
b. All the equations have the same variable expression, $8t + 12d$, but they each equal different amounts of money. The equations in step 3 are in slope-intercept form, while the equations in step 5 (b) are not.
5. −$\frac{3}{2}$; linear decay **6.** 1; If $r = 0$, then Dynah does not spend any time running. She would spend 1 h walking the 4 mi. **7. a, b.** Explanations may vary. Examples are given. **a.** No. You cannot have a negative amount of time. **b.** Yes. It is possible to run or walk for part of an hour. **c.** $0 \le r \le \frac{2}{3}$

8. a. Substitute 0 for x and solve to find the value for y. **b.** Substitute 0 for y and solve to find the value for x. **c.** Substitute any value for x (or y) other than those for the intercepts and solve to find the value for y (or x).

Pages 429–432 Exercises and Problems
1. a. the cost of 1 tape **b.** the cost of 1 compact disc **c.** the number of compact discs bought **d.** the number of tapes bought **e.** the total cost of t tapes **f.** the total cost of d compact discs **3. a.** $r - \frac{1}{4}w + 0b$ or $r - \frac{1}{4}w$ **b.** $r - \frac{1}{4}w = 32$

5. a. Tables may vary. An example is given.

w	l
10	120
20	110
30	100
40	90
50	80
60	70

b. $2l + 2w = 260$ **c.** Graphs may vary. They should represent part of the line below.

Perimeter of a Pool

d. Explanations may vary. An example is given. The graph should not cross either axis because if $l = 0$ or $w = 0$, then you would have a line segment instead of a rectangle and a pool cannot be a line segment.
9, 11. Answers may vary. Examples are given.
9. (11, 0), $\left(0, \frac{11}{3}\right)$, (2, 3) **11.** $\left(-\frac{2}{5}, 0\right)$, (0, −1), (2, −6)

13. $y = -\frac{2}{3}x - 2$ **15.** $y = 12x - \frac{4}{3}$

17. horizontal intercept: 18; vertical intercept: 12
19. a. $0.054s + 0.072c = 18$
24. a. $c = 1.25m + 32$

Towing Charges

b. 1.25, 32; The slope indicates that the cost increases by \$1.25 for each mile towed. The vertical intercept is the cost of hooking up the car.

25. a.

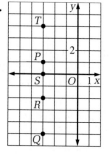

b. All the points lie on a horizontal line and have *y*-coordinate 4. **c.** Yes. Explanations may vary. An example is given. For each value of the control variable, there is only one value for the dependent variable.

26. a.

b. All the points lie on a vertical line and have *x*-coordinate –3. **c.** No. Explanations may vary. An example is given. There is more than one value for the dependent variable when the control variable equals –3.

Page 434 Talk it Over

1. The slope is undefined. **2.** The slope is 0.

3. The slope is 0.

4. Descriptions and explanations may vary. An example is given. The equation in question 3 is different from the other two because the variable, *y*, has a coefficient of 2 instead of a coefficient of 1 as the others do. This difference does not change the fact that the graph is a horizontal line. If you divide both sides by 2, you get $y = -\frac{3}{2}$.

Page 435, 437 Exercises and Problems

1, 3. Estimates may vary. Examples are given.
1. about 0 **3.** Since the line appears to be vertical, the slope is undefined. **5.** 0; $y = -2$ **7.** 0; $y = 4$

9. The slope is undefined.

11. The slope is 0.

13. $x = 4$ **15.** $y = 6$ **17.** Choices of coordinates may vary. An example is given: (0, –4), (0, –2), (0, 1), (0, 6). They each have *x*-coordinate 0. $x = 0$ **19.** True.

21. False. **28.** $y = -\frac{2}{3}x + 4$ **29.** $y = \frac{4}{9}x - 8$

30. $y = 0x + 5$ **31.** not possible; The slope is undefined, and the equation has no vertical intercept.

32. $12\frac{2}{3}$ **33.** –8 **34.** 378

35. –2; –3; $y = -2x - 3$

Page 438 Checkpoint

1. Answers may vary. An example is given. Linear growth and direct variation situations are alike because each can be represented by an equation in slope-intercept form. The graphs of both are straight lines. Linear growth can have a vertical intercept other than 0, while direct variation always passes through the origin. Linear growth never has negative slope, while direct variation can have a positive or negative slope. **2.** A, B **3.** A **4.** Equations and graphs may vary. Examples are given. $y = 0.5x + 2.5$

Costs for Plan B

5. 0 **6.** $15j + 10s$

7–9. Graphs, intercepts, and equations may vary depending on choices of control and dependent variables. Examples are given.

7.

Combinations of Jeans and Shirts that can be Bought with $60

Number of jeans

8. Yes. The vertical intercept represents buying only shirts, and the horizontal intercept represents buying only jeans.

9. a. $15j + 10s = 60$

b. $-\frac{3}{2}$; The number of shirts that Mark can buy decreases by 3 for every 2 pairs of jeans he buys.

10. vertical intercept: -4; horizontal intercept: 6 **11.** vertical intercept: 3; horizontal intercept: 6

12. The slope is 0.

13. $x = -3$

Pages 440, 441, 443 Talk it Over

1. Yes. **2.** No. Answers may vary. An example is given. Covering up the scales, it might seem as if each line on the graph represents 1 unit, making the slope appear to be $-\frac{1}{6}$. The unequal scales make the rate of change appear to be more gradual than it would appear with equal scales. **3. a.** 241 s; The prediction is 9.07 s more than the actual time. **b.** 209 s **4.** No, but the results should be close. **5.** substituting the values for the slope and the vertical intercept in the equation $y = mx + b$ **6.** $y = -\frac{3}{5}x + 8$ **7. a.** dependent variable **b.** (12, 41) **c.** a decrease of 7 dollars per week; negative; m; Explanations may vary. An example is given. The rate of change is the same as the slope. Since Kemitra is spending money every week, the amount she has decreases, so the slope is negative. **d.** $y = -7x + 125$

Amount of Money Left

Number of weeks

e. The vertical intercept represents the amount of money Kemitra is given for her birthday. The horizontal intercept represents the number of weeks it takes for her to spend all her money. **f.** $104

Pages 443–446 Exercises and Problems

3. $y = -x + 7$ **5.** $y = 2$ **7.** $y = 2x + 1$ **9. a.** $F = \frac{9}{5}C + 32$ or $C = \frac{5}{9}F - \frac{160}{9}$ **b.** 20°C **11. a–c.** Graphs, equations, and predictions may vary. Examples are given.

a.

Activity at Old Faithful

Length of eruption in minutes

b. $t = 13l + 31$ **c.** about 85.6 min **13. a.** $\overline{AB}$: $\frac{5}{2}$; $\overline{BC}$: 0; $\overline{CD}$: $\frac{5}{2}$; $\overline{AD}$: 0 **b.** $\overline{AB}$ and $\overline{CD}$; $\overline{BC}$ and $\overline{AD}$ **c.** $\overleftrightarrow{AB}$: $y = \frac{5}{2}x + 3$; $\overleftrightarrow{BC}$: $y = 3$; $\overleftrightarrow{CD}$: $y = \frac{5}{2}x - \frac{19}{2}$; $\overleftrightarrow{AD}$: $y = -2$ **15.** $y = \frac{4}{5}x + 11$ **17.** $y = -\frac{3}{2}x + 8$

19. $y = \frac{3}{4}x + 3$ **21.** $x = -3$ **23. a.** control variable

b. (10, 8.7) **c.** $.75 per mile **d.** $c = 0.75m + 1.2$

e.

Taxi Charges

Distance in miles

f. $4.95; $13.95; by the points (5, 4.95) and (17, 13.95) **g.** The vertical intercept represents the initial charge before driving any distance. **26.** $y = 5$ **27.** $x = 1$ **28.** $x = 5.5$, $y = 27.5$ **29.** $x = 4$, $y = 15$ **30.** $x = -2$, $y = -8$

Pages 449–450 Talk it Over

1. For any value of n that is greater than 20, the line representing Videobusters is below the line representing Movies Plus. This means that the cost at Videobusters is below or less than the cost at Movies Plus. **2.** For $c = 2.50n$, $50 = 2.5(20)$, and $50 = 50$. For $c = 2.00n + 10$, $50 = 2.00(20) + 10$, $50 = 40 + 10$, and $50 = 50$. **3.** No. Explanations may vary. An example is given. The graph shows diagonal lines because the distance increases as the time increases. This comparison of distance and time does not involve the direction in which they are running. **4.** Estimates may vary. An example is given. Rita; about 11 s; Sandy: about 12.5 s; Rita wins. **5.** Both equations have the same slope, 8. **6.** If the lines intersect, then the system has a solution. If the lines are parallel, then the system has no solution.

1. a. Group I **b.** No. **3.** Estimates may vary.
Examples are given. **a.** (2, 3) **b.** (2, 3)

7. Estimates may vary. An example is given: about
$\left(2\frac{1}{3}, \frac{1}{3}\right)$.

9. $(-6, -6)$

11. Descriptions may vary. An examples is given. The
dog chases the squirrel but never catches up with it
because they are both running at the same rate, and
the squirrel had a 5 m head start. **13.** solution

15. no solution **19.** $y = \frac{1}{3}x - \frac{2}{3}$, $y = \frac{1}{4}x - \frac{1}{2}$; solution

25. $y = \frac{5}{6}x - 3$ **26.** $y = \frac{5}{3}x - 11$

27. Yes. $x < 5.5$

28. Yes. $x \geq 5$

29. Yes. $x \geq 4$

1. Write the equations in slope-intercept form. If the
values for m are equal and the values for b are not,
then there is no solution. Graph the equations. If the
lines are parallel, then there are no solutions.

2. $y = 5x - 19$ **3.** $y = -\frac{1}{4}x + \frac{1}{4}$ **4.** solution **5.** no
solution **6.** solution **7.** Choices of variables may
vary. An example is given. Let c be the total cost in
dollars and let g be the number of gallons bought.
$c = g + 10$, $c = 1.5g$; $g = 20$, $c = 30$ (At 20 gallons, the
cost for either is $30.)

1. (a) $y \geq x$ **2.** First, graph the boundary line $y = 3$ as
a solid line. Then shade the region above the line.
3. a, b. Descriptions may vary. Examples are given.
a. The graph of $x = 2$ is a vertical line, parallel to the
y-axis, with all points having x-coordinate 2. **b.** The
graph of $x \leq 2$ includes the graph of $x = 2$, and the
region to the left of the line is shaded. **4.** solid;
below **5.** dashed; above **6.** solid; above **7.** dashed;
below **8.** Answers may vary. An example is given.
The coordinates of all the points in the shaded region
make the inequality $y \leq 4 - \frac{2}{3}x$ true. Since this
inequality is the slope-intercept form of the original
inequality, $8x + 12y \leq 48$, they both have the same

solutions. **9.** all points with whole-number coordinates in the region bounded by the x-axis, the y-axis,
and the line $y = 4 - \frac{2}{3}x$ **10.** No. Explanations may
vary. An example is given. If the inequality is in
slope-intercept form, then the symbol < means to
graph below the boundary line. However, if the
inequality is in standard form, you need to check a
point on one side of the boundary line to determine
which region to shade. **11.** If one point in the region
makes the inequality true, then all the points in the
region make the inequality true and this is the correct
region to shade. **12.** The boundary line is a boundary
for the solution region. A point on this line may be a
solution to the inequality, but it will not help you
determine which region is the solution region.

13. $y > \frac{2}{3}x - 4$; Yes.

3. C **5.** D

7.

9.

11.

13.

17. a. (8, 7), (7, 4), (7.5, 6), (5.5, 4)
b, c. The slope is 1.
d. below **e.** >; <
f. Explanations may
vary. An example is
given. If lines were
drawn from the origin to
each point on the graph,
the lines would lie
below the line $y = x$.
This means that each
line must have a slope
less than 1. Since the
slopes of these lines are
represented by the ratio

Right Triangle Lengths

$\frac{BC}{AB}$, which is also the cosine ratio for $\angle B$, $\cos B$ must
be less than 1.

19.

21.

13.

15. a, b.

23.

c. The lines are parallel.   **d.** The regions do not overlap. Explanations may vary. An example is given. The boundary lines do not overlap since they are parallel, so the only way the regions could overlap is if the region between the two parallel lines contained solution points and this does not happen.

23. Descriptions may vary. An examples is given. trapezoid

25. $x + 2y \le 6$

26.   **27.**

28.   **29.**

32. solution   **33.** no solution   **34.** no solution
35. about 188 books   **36.** $\frac{5}{6} \approx 83\%$

37.

38.

30. about 6 mm   **31.** about 17.5 cm   **32.** $a = 35°$; $b \approx 5.7$ m   **33.** angle a and 55°; Their sum is 90°.
34. $7 < \sqrt{50} < 8$ **35.** $7 < \sqrt{58} < 8$ **36.** $13 < \sqrt{193} < 14$
37. $0 < \sqrt{0.18} < 1$ **38.** $0 < \sqrt{0.0136} < 1$

Pages 464 Talk it Over
1. The boundary line is dashed because the graph represents only failing grades, and 60 is a passing grade. Also, 60 is not a solution of $x < 60$.   **2.** No.
3. at least 67 (assuming scores must be whole numbers)   **4.** Answers may vary. An example is given. (80, 10); none; 80 is the mid-year test score, and 10 is the year-end score. A student with these grades will not have a passing weighted average.

Pages 465–468 Exercises and Problems
3. No.   **5.** No.   **7.** Yes.

9.   **11.**

Pages 470–471 Unit 8 Review and Assessment
1. a. $\frac{2}{3}$; 2   **b.** $y = \frac{2}{3}x + 2$ **c.** linear growth   **d.** No. The line does not pass through the origin.

2. a.

Water Depth in the Levys' Pool

b. slope: –1.5; vertical intercept: 20; The slope means that the water level decreases 1.5 in. per minute. The vertical intercept is the height of the water before the pool is drained, 20 in. **c.** $h = -1.5t + 20$ **d.** $13\frac{1}{3}$ min; horizontal intercept **3. a–e.** Answers may vary depending on the choice of control variable. Examples are given. Let r = running distance and b = biking distance. **a.** $7.5r + 20b = 30$ **b.** $r = -2\frac{2}{3}b + 4$

c.

Completing a Triathlon

d. horizontal intercept: 1.5; vertical intercept: 4; The horizontal intercept means that Jim will spend 1.5 h biking the 30 mile trail if he does not run. The vertical intercept means that Jim will spend 4 h running the 30 mile trail if he does not ride his bicycle.
4. The slope is undefined.

5. The slope is 0.

6. a.

b. $y = 7$

7. Descriptions and explanations may vary. An example is given. To graph $y = 2x - 3$, I would graph the vertical intercept, –3, which is obvious in the equation because it is in slope-intercept form. I would then use the slope and move up 2 and right 1 to graph another point, $(1, -1)$. I'd check this point in the equation before drawing the line. To graph $5x - 4y = 12$, I would substitute 0 for x to find the vertical intercept, $(0, -3)$, and then substitute 0 for y to find the horizontal intercept, $\left(2\frac{2}{5}, 0\right)$. I would then draw a line through the two intercepts. I like the method for using intercepts because they are usually easy points to calculate.

8. $y = \frac{1}{2}x - 2$ **9.** $y = 2x + 11$ **10.** Equations may vary. An example is given. $y = -x - 11$
11. a. $y = 0.75x + 16.25$ **b.** slope: 0.75; vertical intercept: 16.25; The slope means that the fraction of the hourly pay (one hour per month) that goes towards union dues is 0.75. The vertical intercept is the fixed amount each member must pay toward union dues, \$16.25, regardless of the rate of hourly pay.
c. \$27.13 **12. a.** Estimates may vary. An example is given. $\left(2\frac{2}{3}, 3\frac{2}{3}\right)$ **b.** $\left(2\frac{1}{4}, 3\frac{3}{4}\right)$ **13.** no solution
14. solution **15.** solution **16. a.** Let c = total cost and w = weight of package in ounces. $c = w + 5$ and $c = 1.25w + 3.50$ **b.**

Shipping Charges

c. 6 oz **d.** for packages that weigh more than 6 oz

17.

18.

19.

20.

21. a. $x + y \le 65$ **b.** $20x + 25y \le 1200$

c.

Plants for Decoration

d. 48; This number is the vertical intercept of the boundary line $20x + 25y \le 1200$.

Integrated Mathematics

Page 480 Talk it Over

1. the definition of complementary angles; two angles whose measures add up to 90° **2.** No. Yes. Explanations may vary. An example is given. The inductive method shows that for only 6 right triangles, the acute angles are complementary. Maybe if Charles had tried a seventh triangle, he would have had a different result. The deductive method uses a general right triangle, not a specific one. Barbara uses known definitions and properties to show and prove that the acute angles of a right triangle are complementary.

Pages 481–484 Exercises and Problems

1. a–c. Drawings and tables may vary. The results should support the conjecture made in the Exploration. **3.** b and c **5.** making a sketch; Answers may vary. An example is given. Each problem gives measurements of figures. Making a sketch of each figure helps you understand the problem and makes it easier to solve. **7.** 12 in. **9.** about 21.8 mi **11.** $h = 12$ m; area = 60 m^2 **13.** about 127.3 ft **23.** deductive **25.** inductive

29. **30.**

31. 0.2 **32.** $\frac{1}{3}$ **33.** 8 **34.** 14 **35.** 20 ft

Pages 486, 488 Talk it Over

1. Arguments may vary. An example is given. Since the triangle is a right triangle, you can use the Pythagorean theorem to find the value of x. The hypotenuse is x, so $x^2 = 3^2 + 3^2 = 9 + 9 = 18$. $x^2 = 18$, so $x = \sqrt{18}$. **2.** Corresponding sides of similar triangles are in proportion; arguments may vary. An example is given. Since the triangles are similar, the corresponding sides have the same ratio. Therefore, $\frac{1}{3} = \frac{\sqrt{2}}{x}$. Using cross products, $x = 3\sqrt{2}$. **3. a.** They are equal. **b.** Yes; explanations may vary. An example is given. Since $18 = 9 \cdot 2$, $\sqrt{18} = \sqrt{9 \cdot 2}$. Also, $\sqrt{9} = 3$, so $\sqrt{9} \cdot \sqrt{2} = 3\sqrt{2}$. From part (a), $\sqrt{18} = 3\sqrt{2}$. Therefore, $\sqrt{9 \cdot 2} = \sqrt{9} \cdot \sqrt{2}$. **c.** They both equal about 4.24. **4.** The result is the number a. **5.** It is not efficient to rewrite $\sqrt{50}$ as $\sqrt{5} \cdot \sqrt{10}$ because neither 5 nor 10 has a perfect square factor. **6.** Martha's; She factored out the largest square root and avoided three steps.

Pages 489–491 Exercises and Problems

3. $2\sqrt{17}$ **5.** $6\sqrt{2}$ **7.** $\sqrt{21}$ **9.** $6\sqrt{10}$ **11.** 11 **13.** $60\sqrt{15}$ **15.** $4\sqrt{3}, -4\sqrt{3}$ **17.** $2\sqrt{3}, -2\sqrt{3}$ **19.** $a\sqrt{29}, -a\sqrt{29}$ **21.** $8\sqrt{2}$ **27.** 20 m **28.** $\sqrt{29}$ in. or about 5.4 in. **29.** 15 ft **30.** 12 cm

31.

32. 0 **33.** −11.5 **34.** 0 **35.** 3

Pages 493, 495 Talk it Over

1. Explanations may vary. An example is given. Statement (1) is false because all champions do not buy the same brand of shoes. Statement (2) is false because choosing a particular brand of shoes does not make someone a champion. **2. a, b.** Discussions may vary. Examples are given. **a.** The statement is false. It is possible for the sky to be partly cloudy with the sun shining through the clouds. **b.** The statement is true. A square is a particular kind of rectangle. **3.** Answers may vary. An example is given. Statement: If you can ice skate, then you are a hockey player. Hypothesis: You can ice skate. Conclusion: You are a hockey player. The if-then statement is false because someone who can ice skate may not skate well enough to be a hockey player. Also, the person may be a figure skater, a speed skater, or an entertainer in an ice show. **4.** Yes. **5. a.** −1.3 = 0 or $x = 0$; Since −1.3 ≠ 0, $x = 0$. **b.** Divide both sides by −1.3; $x = 0$. **6.** No. To use the property, you must start with a product equal to 0. The product given is equal to −1.

Pages 496–498 Exercises and Problems

1. Find a counterexample that contradicts the statement. **3, 5, 7, 9.** Counterexamples may vary. Examples are given. **3. a.** Hypothesis: You see an advertisement for a product. Conclusion: You will buy the product. **b.** False. I see many advertisements for products that I do not want to buy or that are too expensive for me to buy. **5. a.** Hypothesis: $x^2 = 25$ Conclusion: $x = \pm\sqrt{25}$ **b.** True. **7. a.** Hypothesis: a and b are non-negative integers. Conclusion: $\sqrt{ab} = \sqrt{a} \cdot \sqrt{b}$ **b.** True. **9. a.** Hypothesis: $2y = 0$ Conclusion: $y = 0$ **b.** True. **11, 13, 15, 17.** Counterexamples may vary. Examples are given.

11. a. If you are south of the equator, then you are in Zimbabwe. **b.** False. You could be in another country south of the equator, such as Uruguay. **13. a.** If $(m + n)$ is an even number, then m and n are even numbers. **b.** False. Suppose $(m + n) = 4$. The values for m and n could be 3 and 1, which are odd numbers.   **15. a.** If the area of a figure is half the area of some parallelogram with the same base and height, then the figure is a triangle.   **b.** True.   **17. a.** If an event is certain to happen, then the probability of the event is 1.   **b.** True.   **21.** 0   **23.** 0, −1   **25.** 0, 2   **27.** Yes; because $7^2 + 24^2 = 625$ and $25^2 = 625$ **29.** No; because $4^2 + 5^2 = 41$ and $6^2 = 36$.   **31.** No; because $2^2 + 7^2 = 53$ and $8^2 = 64$.   **33.** Yes.   **39.** $6\sqrt{2}$ **40.** $4\sqrt{3}$ **41.** 30   **42.** $240\sqrt{10}$ **43.** $\frac{1}{6}$ **44.** $\frac{1}{3}$ **45.** 0   **46.** $\frac{5}{6}$

Page 499 Checkpoint

1. Explanations may vary. An example is given. Suppose you start with $\sqrt{10} \cdot \sqrt{15}$. You can rewrite this product as $\sqrt{10 \cdot 15}$, or $\sqrt{150}$. See if you can find any perfect square factors for the number under the square root symbol. A perfect square factor of 150 is 25, so you can write $\sqrt{150}$ as $\sqrt{25 \cdot 6}$. Rewrite this as $\sqrt{25} \cdot \sqrt{6}$. Since $\sqrt{25} = 5$, the final answer is $5\sqrt{6}$.   **2.** 39 in.   **3.** 20 cm   **4.** deductive   **5.** $10\sqrt{3}$ **6.** $6\sqrt{7}$ **7.** $5\sqrt{2}$, $-5\sqrt{2}$ **8. a.** Hypothesis: A number is odd. Conclusion: It is a multiple of 3.   **b.** False. Counterexamples may vary. An example is given. The number 5 is odd, but it is not a multiple of 3.   **c.** If a number is a multiple of 3, then it is odd.   **9.** $0, -\frac{3}{2}$ **10.** No; because $45^2 + 14^2 = 2221$ and $50^2 = 2500$.

Page 503 Talk it Over

1. a. ratio of areas   **b.** ratio of lengths   **2.** Answers may vary. An example is given. I prefer Method 2, counting the number of minutes, not only because it is less work, but also because it makes more sense to me to compare minutes instead of line segments when dealing with time.

Page 504–506 Exercises and Problems

1. greater than; Explanations may vary. An example is given. If you draw the lines across the square, as shown at right, you can see that the area of the shaded region is greater than one fourth of the total area. Therefore, the probability that a disk will land in the shaded region is greater than $\frac{1}{4}$, or 0.25.

3. a. Answers may vary. The ratio should be about 0.75.   **b.** Answers may vary. The sum should be close to 1.   **5. a.** $\frac{1}{3}$ **b.** $\frac{1}{4}$; probability in part (a)   **7.** B   **9.** $\frac{1}{8}$ or 0.125   **16. a.** If Raymond lives in Canada, then he lives in Toronto.   **b.** False. Raymond may live somewhere else in Canada, such as Montreal.   **17.** Answers may vary. An example is given. The figure has four sides, opposite pairs of sides are congru-

ent and parallel and all angles measure 90°.   **18. a.** $A = \frac{1}{2}bh$ **b.** $C = \pi d$ or $C = 2\pi r$

Pages 507, 508, 510 Talk it Over

1. rectangle; top and bottom: 4.5 cm by 10 cm; sides: 4.5 cm by 16 cm; front and back: 10 cm by 16 cm   **2.** $A = lw$ **3.** 554 cm²   **4.** Explanations may vary. An example is given. All the faces make up the surface of the figure, so the total area of all the faces is the area of the surface of the figure.   **5.** Explanations may vary. An example is given. In step 1, the circular bases are cut out, and the curved surface is cut vertically. In step 2, the circular bases are laid flat, and the curved surface is opened. Step 3 shows the area for each part of the cylinder. The circular bases each have an area of πr^2. The curved surface flattens into a rectangle having an area of $2\pi rh$.   **6.** In the last step, $2\pi r$ represents the length of the rectangle, which is the same as the circumference of each base.   **7.** the slant height   **8.** Descriptions may vary. An example is given. Find the area of the base; $10 \times 10 = 100$ square units. Find the area of one face; $\frac{1}{2}(10)(13) = 65$ square units. Since there are four faces, multiply this area by 4; $4(65) = 260$ square units. Add the area of the base and the area of the faces to find the total surface area; $100 + 260 = 360$ square units.

Pages 512–514 Exercises and Problems

3. triangular prism; 432 cm²   **5.** trapezoidal prism; 352 cm²   **7. a.** Drawings may vary.   **b.** triangular prism   **11.** Descriptions may vary. An example is given. The two figures are alike because they are both space figures with congruent, parallel bases and have heights of 6 cm. They are different because the first figure is a hexagonal prism with a surface area of about 154.8 cm², while the second figure is a cylinder with a surface area of about 169.6 cm².   **13.** about 100.5 m²   **17.** square pyramid; 384 m²   **19.** square pyramid; about 289 in.²   **25.** about 0.29 or 29%   **26.** about 0.71 or 71%   **27.** 1 or 100%   **28.** Sketches may vary. You need to know the length of each base and the height.   **29.** 70 in.³   **30.** 54 in.³

Pages 516, 518 Talk it Over

1. Explanations may vary. An example is given. In the formula $A = \frac{1}{2}(b_1 + b_2)h$, h represents the height of the trapezoidal base of the prism, which is 6 in. In the formula $V = Bh$, h represents the height of the prism, which is 8 in. Although h represents a height in each formula, it represents different heights, so the values substituted are not the same.   **2. a.** triangular prism   **b.** First find the area of the triangular base using $A = \frac{1}{2}bh = \frac{1}{2}(6)(4) = 12$ ft². Next multiply its base area times the height: $V = Bh = 12 \cdot 7 = 84$ ft³.

3. Answers may vary. An example is given. The bases of the space figure are the two sides which are congruent and parallel. The front and back are the bases of the jukebox. The distance between the bases is the height of the space figure. The distance between the front and back of the jukebox is 25 in. Therefore, the 25 in. label is the height. **4.** Answers may vary. An example is given. The word *composite* is an adjective meaning "composed of" or "made out of." This means a space figure is made out of other space figures by putting them together. The jukebox is a space figure made out of a half cylinder and a rectangular prism.

Pages 519–521 Exercises and Problems
3. 4394 ft^3 **5.** 3.8 yd **7.** 4 m **9.** 9 fish **11.** about 157.1 cm^3 **13.** about 85.7 m^3 **15.** about 30.0 yd **23.** rectangular prism; 80 in.^{2} **24.** cylinder; about 291.3 m^2 **25.** triangular prism; about 104.3 ft^2 **26.** 20 m/s **27.** about 19.1 m **28.** $y = -\frac{8}{3}x + \frac{7}{3}$

Page 522 Checkpoint
1. Descriptions may vary. An example is given. The space figure is a triangular prism. To find the area of the bases you need to find the height of the triangles: $h = \sqrt{14^2 - 6^2} \approx 12.6$ yd. The area of the bases is $2\left(\frac{1}{2} \cdot 12 \cdot 12.6\right) = 151.2$. Find the area of the faces: $7.5 \cdot 14 = 105$; $7.5 \cdot 14 = 105$; $7.5 \cdot 12 = 90$. Add the areas to find the surface area: $151.2 + 105 + 105 + 90 = 451.2$ yd^2. **2.** $\frac{2}{9}$, or about 0.2 **3.** about 1224 mm^2 **4.** about 31.9 in.^{2}; about 12.4 in.^{3}

Pages 523, 525 Talk it Over
1. $V = Bh$ **2.** Answers may vary. An example is given. Divide the volume of the prism by 3. **3.** The volume of the cone is $\frac{1}{3}$ the volume of the cylinder. **4.** about 130.9 ft^3

Pages 526–529 Exercises and Problems
3. 360 mm^3 **5.** about 208.17 ft^3 **7.** Drawings may vary. **9.** about 78,698,448 ft^3 **15. a.** 864 m^3 **b.** about 678.6 m^3 **c.** about 78.5% **17.** cylinder; about 282.7 ft^3 **18.** triangular prism; about 17.1 m^3 **19.** 7.5 **20.** 15 **21.** 4:3 **22.** 2.5, −2.5

Pages 530–532 Talk it Over
1. No. Reasons may vary. An example is given. You would need more than 3 fronts of TV sets of the size representing 1975 to cover the area of the front of the TV set representing 1995. **2.** No. Reasons may vary. An example is given. You could fit more than 3 TV sets of the size representing 1975 into the TV set rep-

resenting 1995. **3.** Answers may vary. An example is given. The heights of the TV sets appear to be in the same ratio as the number of cable systems for each year. **4.** $\frac{3}{4}$ **5.** $\frac{9}{16}$ **6.** Yes. **7.** Since the scale factor is the ratio of corresponding lengths of similar figures, you can square the numerator and square the denominator of the scale factor to find the ratio of the areas. **8.** 7:6 **9.** The bases are similar rectangles. All corresponding lengths are in proportion: $\frac{12}{6} = \frac{8}{4} = \frac{5}{2.5} = \frac{2}{1}$. **10.** 2:1 **11.** 8:1 **12.** Yes. **13. a.** 1:40 **b.** 64,000

Pages 533–538 Exercises and Problems
1. 9:16 **3.** 49:100 **5.** 25:64; 76.8 mm^2 **7.** 4:9; 90 in.^{2} **11. a.** 25%; 56.25%; 36% **b.** 144% **13. a.** about $8\frac{1}{3}$ in. **b.** 27 ft^3:1 in.^{3}, or 46,656 in.^{3}:1 in.^{3} **19.** No. The ratio of the diameters is not the same as the ratio of the heights. **21.** Yes. The ratio of all corresponding sides is 2:3. **23.** 64:3375 **25.** 27:64; 13.5π in.^{3} **27.** 125:216; 691.2 cm^3 **30.** about 1340.4 yd^3 **31. a.** $A(0, 2)$; $B(-3, 0)$; $C(0, -5)$; $D(3, 0)$ **b.** $x = 0$ or y-axis **c.** $A'(4, 2)$; $B'(1, 0)$; $C'(4, -5)$; $D'(7, 0)$ **d.** $A''(0, -2)$; $B''(3, 0)$; $C''(0, 5)$; $D''(-3, 0)$

Pages 540–541 Unit 9 Review and Assessment
1. a. about 11.2 km **2.** inductive **3.** $4\sqrt{6}$ **4.** $16\sqrt{6}$ **5.** $3\sqrt{3}, -3\sqrt{3}$ **6. a.** Hypothesis: You have a fever. Conclusion: You stay home from school. **b.** If you stay home from school, you have a fever. **c.** False. You could stay home from school because you sprained your ankle. **7.** Answers may vary. An example is given. If the ground is wet in the morning, it rained last night; false; it might have snowed. If it rained last night, the ground is wet in the morning. **8.** 0, −4 **9.** 0, 2 **10.** Yes; the Pythagorean theorem applies: $(12)^2 + (16)^2 = (20)^2$. **11. a.** about 0.16 **b.** about 0.21 **12.** 150 in.^{2} **13.** 112 in.^{2} **14.** 72 ft^3 **15.** Can 1; Explanations may vary. An example is given. Can 1 and Can 2 have equal volumes, but Can 1 has less surface area than Can 2. This means that Can 1 holds as much as Can 2, but less materials are needed to make Can 1. Other factors that might influence the manufacturer's decision would be the information displayed on the label, the type of product, and the size and shape of shipping cartons. **16.** about 372.02 cm^3 **17.** 54 square units **18.** 125 times

Page 550 Talk it Over

1. the x-axis; $y = 0$ **2.** below; 3 units below
3. 2 units to the left of the line of reflection
4. Answers may vary. Examples are given. **a.** The whale's tail in the photo has symmetry because one half of the tail is a reflection of the other half.

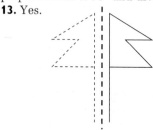

line of
reflection

original   image
(image)   (original)

b. Yes, if it has symmetry. An example is the whale's tail in part (a).

Pages 551–554 Exercises and Problems

1. The image is congruent to the original. The orientation is reversed. The line of reflection divides in half and is perpendicular to each segment connecting corresponding points on the image and the original.
3. a. raises its left arm **b.** walks towards me **c.** Yes, but the words and letters are backwards. **7.** $\overline{AB}$ is perpendicular to $\overline{PP'}$ and divides $\overline{PP'}$ in half.
13. Yes.

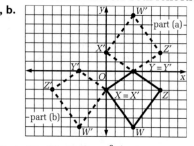

15. No. The image is not congruent to the original figure. This is a dilation combined with a reflection.
17. the line $y = -1$ **19.** the line $x = 2$ **21.** $WXYZ$ has clockwise orientation and $W'X'Y'Z'$ has counterclockwise orientation for both reflections.
a, b.

25. 4:25 **26.** 2430 cm^3

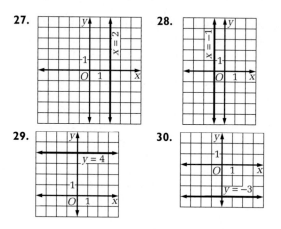

27. $x = 2$ **28.** $x = -1$ **29.** $y = 4$ **30.** $y = -3$

Pages 555, 557 Talk it Over

1. a. the y-axis, or the line $x = 0$ **b.** $(0, 0)$
2. a. the y-axis, or the line $x = 0$ **b.** $(0, 0)$ **c.** -2^2; Yes, it matters because $(-2)^2 = (-2)(-2) = 4$ and $-2^2 = -(2 \cdot 2) = -4$. **3.** Answers may vary. An example is given. When $x = 1$, the values of y are opposites (-1 and 1); when $x = 0$, the values of y are the same (0); when $x = -2$, they are opposites (-4 and 4). In general, for a given value $x \neq 0$ of x, the corresponding values of y are opposites. **4.** the x-axis, or the line $y = 0$ **5.** the parabolas in parts (a) and (b)
6. the parabolas in parts (c) and (d) **7.** (a) I, II; (b) I, II, III, IV; (c) I, II; (d) I, II **8.** Yes. The graph of the parabola in part (b) is in the III and IV quadrants. In these quadrants, the value of the y-coordinate for each point is negative.

Pages 558–561 Exercises and Problems

3. 18 ft **7.** B **9.** A **11.** A **13.** E **15.** Answers may vary. An example is given. Yes, I agree. The graph of $y = x^2 + 7$ is U-shaped. The path of water from a fountain would be shaped like an upside-down U, rising to a high point and then falling. **17.** Translate the graph of $y = x^2$ up 10 units. **19.** Translate the graph of $y = x^2$ left 11 units. **21.** Translate the graph of $y = -x^2$ up 10 units. **23.** Translate the graph of $y = -x^2$ left 6 units. **25.** Translate the graph of $y = x^2$ right 1 unit and up 2 units. **27.** none
29. the equations in Exercises 17, 18, 21, and 22
31. the equations in Exercises 17, 22, and 25
33. a. $x = 0$ **b.** $(0, 8)$ **35. a.** $x = 11$ **b.** $(11, 0)$
37. $y = x^2 - 9$ **39.** $y = (x + 10)^2$ **41.** $y = -(x + 5)^2$
43. False. The x-axis is the line of reflection.
44. True. **45.** False. The orientation of $\triangle A'B'C'$ is reversed. **46.** True. **47.** -3 **48.** 0 **49.** 2 **50.** 0
51. -4 **52.** 0 or 1

Pages 562–563 Talk it Over

1. Answers may vary. An example is given. The income increases. **2. a.** $9: \$20 - \$9 = \$11$; $30 + 5(9) = 75$; $\$11 \times 75 = \$825$; $\$10$: $\$20 - \$10 = \$10$; $30 + 5(10) = 80$; $\$10 \times 80 = \$800$
b. Answers may vary. An example is given. The

income decreases. **3. a.** 0 **b.** 0 **4. a.** the drop in price; the income **b.** Yes. There is only one income value for each drop in price. **5.** Explanations may vary. An example is given. values of x such that $0 \le x \le 20$; The price cannot drop more than \$20. (You could say $-6 \le x \le 20$ if negative values of x are viewed as price increases.) **6.** Answers may vary. An example is given. The highest point on the graph is the vertex at (7, 845), so dropping the price \$7 to \$13 maximizes income at \$845. **7.** The y-intercept is 600. **8. a.** Answers may vary. An example is given. The factor $20 - x$ equals 0 when $x = 20$, so $y = 0$. **b.** Answers may vary. An example is given. The factor $30 + 5x$ equals 0 when $x = -6$, so $y = 0$.

Pages 565, 567 Exercises and Problems

5.

7. x-intercepts: 0 and -7; y-intercept: 0
9. x-intercepts: -7 and 4; y-intercept: 28
11. x-intercepts: 4 and $-\frac{13}{3}$; y-intercept: -52
13. a. 0 and -9 **b.** 47 **18.** down 7 units
19. up 3 units **20.** right 1 unit **21.** 10^7 **22.** 10^2
23. 10^4 **24.** $\frac{1}{10^4}$, or 10^{-4}

Page 567 Checkpoint

1. Answers may vary. An example is given, using the parabola shown in Sample 1(c) on page 557. The equation of the line of symmetry is $x = -2$. The vertex is $(-2, 0)$. The x-intercept is -2. The y-intercept is 4.

2. a.

$A'(0, 3)$, $B'(-1, 1)$, $C'(-3, 1)$, $D'(-3, 3)$; $ABCD$ has counterclockwise orientation and $A'B'C'D'$ has clockwise orientation.

b.

$A'(0, -3)$, $B'(1, -1)$, $C'(3, -1)$, $D'(3, -3)$; $ABCD$ has counterclockwise orientation and $A'B'C'D'$ has clockwise orientation.

3. Translate the graph of $y = x^2$ up 8 units.
4. Translate the graph of $y = x^2$ right 1 unit.
5. Reflect the graph of $y = x^2$ over the x-axis.

6.

7. x-intercepts: -5 and -11; y-intercept: 55
8. x-intercepts: 0 and 12; y-intercept: 0

Pages 568–571 Talk it Over

1. a. 4^3 **b.** 4^2 **c.** $4^3 \cdot 4^2$ **d.** 4^5 **2. a.** x^3 **b.** x^2 **c.** $x^3 \cdot x^2$ **d.** x^5 **3. a.** 1024 **b.** 1024 **4.** Yes. Shortcuts may vary. An example is given. To write the product $3^6 \cdot 3^4$ as a power of 3, add the exponents: $3^{6+4} = 3^{10}$. **5.** Explanations may vary. An example is given. She noticed that 5^{12} contains 12 factors of 5 and 5^9 contains 9 factors of 5, so $5^{12} \cdot 5^9$ contains 12 + 9, or 21 factors of 5 in all. So she found that instead of writing out all the factors she could add the exponents and write $5^{12} \cdot 5^9$ as $5^{12+9} = 5^{21}$.
6. $(-3)^2 \cdot (-3)^3 = (-3)^?$
$(-3)^2 \cdot (-3)^3 =$
$\underbrace{(-3)(-3)}_{2 \text{ factors}} \cdot \underbrace{(-3)(-3)(-3)}_{3 \text{ factors}} = (-3)^{2+3}$
$\underbrace{}_{2 + 3 \text{ factors}}$
So $(-3)^2 \cdot (-3)^3 = (-3)^{2+3} = (-3)^5$
7. associative property of multiplication **8.** Yes. Reasons may vary. An example is given.
$y^2 \cdot y^3 \cdot y^4 = y^{2+3} \cdot y^4 = y^{(2+3)+4} = y^{2+3+4}$, since the way you group numbers being added doesn't change the sum. **9. a.** 3^8 **b.** a^6 **10.** Shortcuts may vary. An example is given. Multiply the exponents: $(a^2)^3 = a^{2 \cdot 3} = a^6$. **11.** Explanations may vary. An example is given. $(a^n)^n$ means that there are n factors of a^m. Using the product of powers rule, you add the exponents to get $a^{m+\dots+m}$. There are n terms in the sum, so $a^{n+\dots+m} = a^{m \cdot n}$. **12. a.** $8x^3$
b. $xy \cdot xy \cdot xy = x^3 y^3$ **c.** $xy^2 \cdot xy^2 \cdot xy^2 = x^3 y^6$
13. Shortcuts may vary. An example is given. Write each of the factors 2 and x to the third power: $2^3 \cdot x^3$, or $8x^3$. **14.** Explanations may vary. An example is given. $(ab)^n$ means that there are n factors of ab. Therefore, there are n factors of a and n factors of b. We write n factors of a as a^n and n factors of b as b^n, so $(ab)^n$ is the same as $a^n \cdot b^n$.

Pages 572–575 Exercises and Problems

1. To use the product of powers rule, the bases must be the same. **3.** t^{10} **5.** k^{10} **7.** $54a^6$ **9.** $-28z^5$
11. $a^4 b^2$ **13.** $-8m^6 n^2$ **15.** $\frac{1}{4}x^2$; one fourth the area of the original square **17. a.** $4 \cdot 4 = 4^2$
b. $x \cdot x \cdot x \cdot x \cdot x = x^5$ **c.** Yes. Shortcuts may vary. An example is given. Write $\frac{5^{12}}{5^9}$ as $5^{12-9} = 5^3$. The shortcut is to subtract the exponents.

19. $x^{0+b} = x^b$; x^0 is equal to 1. **21.** y^{24} **23.** d^{10}
25. $-243h^{15}$ **27.** $625y^{24}z^{12}$ **31.** Terry
36. x-intercepts: 5 and 2; y-intercept: 10
37. x-intercepts: 0 and -3; y-intercept: 0
38. a. $3(x + 2) = 3x + 3 \cdot 2$
b. $2\ \boxed{} = 2\ \boxed{} + 2\ \boxed{}$
$\quad\ \ \underbrace{}_{x+3} \qquad \underbrace{}_{x} \quad \underbrace{}_{3}$
39. $2n - 10$ **40.** $24r + 18$ **41.** $-3x - 36$ **42.** $8m + 8n$

Page 579 Talk it Over
1. a. List all the factors of 12 and all of the factors of
15, then select the largest factor that is common to
both numbers. **b.** $3x$ **2.** Answers may vary. An
example is given. Use the zero-product property and
set each factor equal to zero and solve for x: $5x = 0$,
$x = 0$; $x + 1 = 0$, $x = -1$.

Pages 580, 582 Exercises and Problems
1. $x(x + 4)$ **3.** $x(x + 2)$ **9.** $-x^2 + 15x$ **11.** $6x^2 - 42x$
13. $-20x^2 + 36x$ **15. a.** $x(x - 5)$ **b.** x-intercepts: 0
and 5; y-intercept: 0 **17. a.** $x(12 + x)$ **b.** x-intercepts:
0 and -12; y-intercept: 0 **19. a.** $-x(x - 10)$
b. x-intercepts: 0 and 10; y-intercept: 0
21. a. $8x(x - 5)$ **b.** x-intercepts: 0 and 5;
y-intercept: 0 **23. a.** $6x(2 - x)$ **b.** x-intercepts: 0 and
2; y-intercept: 0 **25.** binomial **27.** monomial
31. $2m^8$ **32.** $10x^5$ **33.** $27a^3c^3$ **34.** $9n^4$
35. $x^2 + 8x + 7$ **36.** $x^2 - 12x - 8$ **37.** $x^2 - x + 14$
38. $x = 0$; $(0, -13)$ **39.** $x = 0$; $(0, 42)$ **40.** $x = 11$; $(11, 0)$

Pages 583–585 Talk it Over
1. No, you will be left with a square "hole" in your
tile rectangle. **2. a.** 2 square units **b.** 2
c. $(x + 2)(x + 1)$ **d.** $x^2 + 3x + 2$ **3. a.** $(x + 5)(x + 2)$
b. $x^2 + 7x + 10$ **c.** Yes. **4.** Yes. **5.** $x = -2$
6. a. When the graph crosses the x-axis, the value of y
is zero: $(x + 3)(x + 1) = 0$. By the zero-product property, $x + 3 = 0$ or $x + 1 = 0$, so $x = -3$ or $x = -1$.
b. $(-2, 0)$ **c.** Yes.
7. a. $y = x^2 + 4x + 4$, $y = x^2 + 4x + 3$, $y = x^2 + 4x$
b. Answers may vary. **c.** Yes, since
$x = -\dfrac{b}{2a} = -\dfrac{4}{2(1)} = -2$, she got $x = -2$ **8.** The line of
symmetry of the given equations is a vertical line.
Changing the value of c moves the vertex up or down
along this line.

Pages 587–589 Exercises and Problems
5. $x^2 + 5x + 6$ **7.** $x^2 - 16$ **9.** $x^2 - 4x + 4$
11. $2x^2 - x - 10$ **17.** A; y-intercept is 6 and line of
symmetry is $x = -2.5$. **19.** C; y-intercept is -6 and
line of symmetry is $x = 2.5$. **21. a.** $x = -4$
b. $(-4, -4)$ **c.** 12 **23. a.** $x = -8$ **b.** $(-8, -49)$ **c.** 15
25. a. $x = 3$ **b.** $(3, -2)$ **c.** 7 **27.** a and g; b, d, e, f,
and h **31.** $x^2 + 3x$ **32.** $2x^2 - 3x$ **33.** $12x^2 + 15x$

34. $-2x^2 + 16x$ **35.** $-2x(x + 3)$; x-intercepts: 0 and -3;
y-intercept: 0 **36.** -11 and 20 **37.** 1 and 15, -1 and
-15, 3 and 5, -3 and -5 **38.** 1 and 17, -1 and -17
39. 1 and 24, -1 and -24, 2 and 12, -2 and -12,
3 and 8, -3 and -8, 4 and 6, -4 and -6 **40.** 1 and 21,
-1 and -21, 3 and 7, -3 and -7

Page 590 Checkpoint
1. $6x(x + 3)$; Explanations may vary. An example is
given. $6x^2 = 2 \cdot 3 \cdot x \cdot x$ and $18x = 2 \cdot 3 \cdot 3 \cdot x$. The
greatest common factor of $6x^2$ and $18x$ is $2 \cdot 3 \cdot x$, or
$6x$. Factor out $6x$. **2.** m^7 **3.** $-3a^5b^6$ **4.** y^{10}
5. $81m^8n^4$ **6.** $x^2 + 5x$ **7.** $x^2 - 10x$ **8.** $-2x^2 - 12x$
9. a. $x(x + 3)$ **b.** x-intercepts: 0 and -3; y-intercept: 0
10. a. $-5x(x - 2)$ **b.** x-intercepts: 0 and 2;
y-intercept: 0 **11.** $x^2 - x - 12$ **12. a.** $x = 4$ **b.** $(4, -10)$
c. 6

Pages 591–593 Talk it Over
1. a. Answers may vary. An example is given. The
number of small square tiles is the product of the
numbers of tall thin tiles in the two groups along
two sides of the large square tile. **b.** There are 8 tall
thin tiles and 15 small square tiles; $3 + 5 = 8$ and
$3 \cdot 5 = 15$.

	x	1	1	1	1	1
x	x^2	x	x	x	x	x
1	x	1	1	1	1	1
1	x	1	1	1	1	1
1	x	1	1	1	1	1

2. No rectangle can be built using 1 x^2-tile, 2 x-tiles,
and 3 unit tiles. **3. a.** $x^2 + 8x + 15$ **b.** $x^2 + 4x - 12$
c. $x^2 - 11x + 24$ **4, 5.** Answers may vary. An example is given. **4.** The coefficient of x in the expanded
form is equal to the sum of the two numbers in the
factored form, and the constant term in the expanded
form is equal to the product of the two numbers in
the factored form. **5.** I think that the integer b is
equal to the sum of the numbers in the factored form
and that the integer c is equal to the product of these
numbers. **6. a.** The coefficient of x is -7, not 7.
b. What two integers have the sum -7? What two
integers have the product 12? **c.** $x - 3$ and $x - 4$
7. Answers may vary. An example is given. The sum
of two negative integers is a negative integer, but the
sum of the factors must be 7, a positive integer.
8. Explanations may vary. An example is given. List
pairs of integers whose product is -12. Add the integers in each pair to find the pair whose sum is -4.
Then write the factored form $(x + 2)(x - 6)$.

Pages 595–597 Exercises and Problems
1. $x^2 + 4x + 3 = (x + 3)(x + 1)$ **7.** $(x + 6)(x + 3)$
9. $(x - 3)(x - 2)$ **11.** $(x - 12)(x - 1)$ **13.** cannot be factored; The only pairs of positive factors of 10 are 1,
10 and 2, 5. Neither pair has the sum 9. **15.** $x + 2$
17. $x - 6$ **19.** $(x - 4)(x + 2)$ **21.** $(x - 6)(x - 2)$

23. $(x + 8)(x - 2)$

25. **27.**

31. Answers may vary. An example is given. The x^2-term has a coefficient other than 1 or −1. $3(x - 2)(x - 1)$ **34.** $x^2 + 8x + 12$ **35.** $x^2 - 3x - 28$ **36.** $x^2 + 3x - 40$ **37.** $-\frac{8}{9}$ **38.** 12, −12 **39.** $2\sqrt{7}, -2\sqrt{7}$ **40.** 64 **41.** −4 **42.** 1

Pages 598, 599, 601, 602 Talk it Over

1. a. $d = \frac{15s}{10}$, or $d = 1.5s$, or $d = \frac{3s}{2}$ **b.** Yes. Reasons may vary. An example is given. The equation has the form $y = kx$, so it is an example of direct variation, which is a special kind of linear function. **c.** s **d.** d **2. a.** No. Reasons may vary. An example is given. A linear function has the variable raised to the first power and can be written in the form $y = mx + b$; since this equation does not have that form, it is not linear. **b.** s **c.** d **3. a.** $0 = 0.05s^2 + s - 60$ **b.** $a = 0.05, b = 1, c = -60$ **4.** Answers may vary. An example is given. A linear equation can be written in the form $ax + by = c$ and a quadratic equation can be written in the form $0 = ax^2 + bx + c$. **5.** No. Explanations may vary. An example is given. For a speed of 25 mi/h, the student-driver's rule of thumb gives $\frac{25 \text{ mi/h}}{10 \text{ mi/h}} \cdot 15 \text{ ft} = 37.5 \text{ ft}$, which underestimates stopping distance by more than a car length. **6. a.** $x = -10$ **b.** about 35 units **c.** $-45 = -10 - 35$ and $25 = -10 + 35$ **7.** because 26.1 and −46.1 are approximations obtained by using a rounded square root of a number that is not a perfect square **8.** Answers may vary. An example is given. 26.1;Yes, I think the estimate of 25 mi/h is good enough because it is very close to the more accurate answer of 26.1 mi/h. Also, the estimate is slightly low, which actually increases the margin of safety.

Pages 603–605 Exercises and Problems

3. 206.25 ft **5.** 30 mi/h **7. a.** at $x = -1$ and at $x = -5$ **b.** −1 and −5 **9.** Estimates may vary. An example is given: about 0.5 and about −1.75.

11. a. 0.4 m **b.** The dolphin will reach a height of 0.6 m twice: at 1 m on the way up and at 1.5 m on the way down. **13.** $x = 3$ **15. a.** $0 = x^2 + x - 20$ **b.** $0 = (x + 5)(x - 4)$ **c.** −5, 4 **17. a, b.** 4, −2 **c.** Answers may vary. An example is given. I think factoring is much easier than using the quadratic formula because factoring takes me less time. **19, 21, 23.** Estimates and methods may vary. Examples are given. **19.** −0.4, 1; graphing or quadratic formula **21.** 3, 7; factoring **23.** −4, 5; graphing or quadratic formula **27.** $(x - 7)(x - 1)$ **28.** $(x + 5)(x - 4)$ **29.** $(x - 6)(x + 4)$

30.

31. x-intercept: 0.5; y-intercept: 1 **32.** x-intercept: 0; y-intercept: 0 **33.** x-intercepts: 0 and 3; y-intercept: 0

Pages 607–608 Unit 10 Review and Assessment

1. a. $y = -1$ **b.** The line of reflection divides $\overline{BB'}$ in half and is perpendicular to $\overline{BB'}$. **c.** 2 units; 2 units **d.** The orientation of $\triangle ABC$ is clockwise. The orientation of $\triangle A'B'C'$ is reversed; it is counterclockwise. **2.** No. The image is not congruent to the original figure and the orientation is not reversed. **3.** Yes. **4.**

5. Translate the graph of $y = x^2$ down 15 units. **6.** $x = -8$; $(-8, 0)$

7.

8. x-intercepts: 2 and −6; y-intercept: −12 **9.** b^{10} **10.** $-30x^4y^3$ **11.** m^{28} **12.** $-125a^3b^6$ **13.** $6x^2 - 10x$ **14.** $y = 7x(x + 3)$; x-intercepts: 0 and −3; y-intercept: 0 **15.** Answers may vary. $y = x(x + 3)$ **16.** $x^2 - 9x + 18$ **17. a.** $x = 5$ **b.** $(5, -29)$ **c.** −4 **18.** $(x - 8)(x - 2)$ **19.** $(x - 6)(x + 3)$ **20.** cannot be factored; The only pairs of factors of −8 are these: 1, −8; −1, 8; 2, −4; and −2, 4. None of these pairs has the sum 6.

21.

22. Answers may vary. An example is given. With linear equations, we get the variable alone and produce one solution. With quadratic equations, we make one side of the equation zero and solve by factoring, graphing, or the quadratic formula. In either case, the solutions are the *x*-intercepts of the graph.
23. about 0.8, about −0.8; Methods may vary. An example is given. I used the quadratic formula.

Technology Handbook

Page 612 Try This
1. a. 2.25 **b.** 28 **c.** 1 **2. a.** (−15 + 29) ÷ 2 **b.** 19
3. 64

Page 614 Try This
4. a.

b.

c.

d.

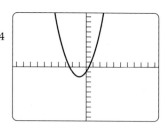

5. Graphs may vary. An example is given.

Page 616 Try This
6. approximate
x-intercepts:−2.4 and 0.4

Page 616 Try This
7. −2.42 and −2.41 **8.** 100 couples

Extra Practice

Pages 620–621 Extra Practice Unit 1
1. 4 **3.** 5 **5.** 30 **7.** 3 **9.** 25 **11.** 26 **13.** 10^3 **15.** 10^4
17. 10^8 **19.** 10^3 **21.** 10^0 **23.** 10^{34} **25.** 28 **27.** 60
29. 841 **31.** 35 **33.** 269 **35.** 832 **37.** $4a − 4b$
39. $4r + 2s$ **41.** $2x^2 − 4$ **43.** $12a$ **45.** $8d$ **47.** no like
terms **49.** $r^3 + 7r + 6$ **51.** no like terms **53.** $14x + 9$
55. $\triangle ABC \cong \triangle RST$; $\overline{AB} \cong \overline{RS}, \overline{BC} \cong \overline{ST}, \overline{CA} \cong \overline{TR}$
57. hexagon $PQRSTZ \cong$ hexagon $TUVWXY$;
$\overline{PQ} \cong \overline{TU}, \overline{QR} \cong \overline{UV}, \overline{RS} \cong \overline{VW}, \overline{ST} \cong \overline{WX}, \overline{TZ} \cong \overline{XY}$,
$\overline{ZP} \cong \overline{YT}$ **59.** pentagon $EFGHI \cong$ pentagon $ELKJI$;
$\overline{EF} \cong \overline{EL}, \overline{FG} \cong \overline{LK}, \overline{GH} \cong \overline{KJ}, \overline{HI} \cong \overline{JI}, \overline{IE} \cong \overline{IE}$
61. square **63.** rhombus **65.** kite **67.** parallelogram
69.

71.

73.

Pages 622–623 Extra Practice Unit 2
1. a. 15 **b.** −56 **3. a.** $\frac{7}{8}$ **b.** $\frac{7}{8}$ **5. a.** −32 **b.** 62

7. 5.7×10^{-2} **9.** 6.497×10^4 **11.** 4.8×10^{10}
13. 360,000,000 **15.** 0.001 **17.** 0.000048 **19.** 30°
21. 75° **23.** 75° **25.** 105° **27.** $x = 80°$ **29.** $x = y = 90°$
31. $4r^2$ **33.** $10s - 4st - 2t$ **35.** $4x^3 + 4x - 1$
37. $-3w - 2k + 3wk$ **39.** 7 **41.** 8 **43.** −10 **45.** 0
47. 7 **49.** 55 **51.** 18 **53.** 45 **55.** −40 **57.** 81
59. $\sqrt{30}$ is a number between 5 and 6; 5.48
61. $\sqrt[3]{70}$ is a number between 4 and 5; 4.12
63. $\frac{8}{7}, -\frac{8}{7}$ **65.** 25, −25 **67.** $\sqrt[3]{800}, \sqrt{87}, 9.4$

Pages 624–625 Extra Practice Unit 3
1. mean = 13.125; median = 12; mode = 11;
outlier = 19; range = 8 **3.** mean = 77.6; median = 73;
mode = 68; outlier = 108; range = 44 **5.** 62 **7.** 81
9. 2.5

11.
13.
15.

17. $-1 \le x < 1$ **19.** $x \ge 106$

21.

6	4 7 8 8 9
7	7 8
8	4
9	3
10	8

23.

NFL Touchdowns

25.
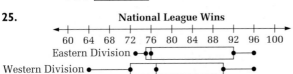
National League Wins

27. Answers may vary.
An examples is given.
I chose a circle graph.
This is a good way to
display data that
represents various
percentages of a whole.

1996 World Gemstone Sales

Pages 625–627 Extra Practice Unit 4
1.

obtuse triangle;
12.5 sq. units

3.

trapezoid; 14 sq. units

5. $R'(3, 5)$, $S'(-2, 5)$, $T'(-3, 0)$ **7.** $J'(4, -1)$, $K'(4, -6)$,
$L'(8, -5)$, $M'(8, -3)$ **9.** $(0, 1)$ **11.** 90° clockwise
13. 45° counterclockwise
15.

17.
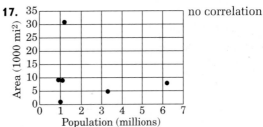
no correlation

19. Yes; passes vertical-line test. **21.** b **23.** $y = -\frac{1}{3}x$
25. $y = -x + 1$ **27.** $s = 0.8P$, where s is sale price, and
P is original price.

Pages 628–629 Extra Practice Unit 5
1. $-2x + 3$ **3.** $x + 3y$ **5.** $17 + 7m$ **7.** −8 **9.** −7 **11.** $\frac{4}{3}$
13. 27 **15.** 2 **17.** −3 **19.** −7.5 **21.** 4 **23.** −4 **25.** −2
27. $y \ge -7$
29. $a \le -\frac{3}{2}$
31. $j > 12$
33. $k > 4$
35. $s = \frac{P}{4}$ **37.** $E = \frac{I}{d^2}$ **39.** $a = \frac{h + 16t^2}{t}$ **41.** $-\frac{5}{2}$ **43.** 24

45. -6 **47.** -8 **49.** -12 **51.** $y = \dfrac{ax - c}{b}$ **53.** $y = \dfrac{4}{3}x - 16$

55. $y = -\dfrac{3}{2}x + 18$ **57.** 21 sq. units **59.** 45 m^2

61. 68 ft^2 **63.** 36 **65.** $x = 4, y = 12$ **67.** $r = -\dfrac{5}{3}, s = -\dfrac{5}{9}$

69. $a = 3, b = 7$ **71.** $a = \dfrac{2}{3}, b = 2\dfrac{2}{3}$ **73.** $x = 6, y = 12$

Pages 629–631 Extra Practice Unit 6

1. Yes. The experimental probability that a voter will be in favor is 0.514, which is more than 50%. **3.** 1
5. 0.5 **7.** 0.9 **9.** $x = 10$ **11.** $t = 10.24$ **13.** $a = 8.75$
15. $b = 2250$ **17.** $x = 0.3$ **19.** $k = 0.84$ **21.** $125°$
23. 8 **25.** 46.5 **27.** $150°$ **29.** 32 **31.** $\triangle PQR \sim \triangle PTS$; $\angle Q \cong \angle T$ and $\angle S \cong \angle R$, so the triangles are similar.

33.

35.

37. 0.97 **39.** 0.50 **41.** $\dfrac{21}{29}$; 0.72 **43.** $\dfrac{20}{29}$; 0.69

Pages 631–632 Extra Practice Unit 7

1. 1.60 **3.** 6.31 **5.** $\dfrac{3}{4}$; $\dfrac{4}{3}$ **7.** 4.4 cm **9.** about 9.4 mm
11. about 267 m **13.** about 12.6 m **15.** about 8.7 cm

17.

19.

21.

23.

25. $y = -\dfrac{1}{4}x$ **27.** km **29.** $\dfrac{\text{cycles}}{\text{s}}$ **31.** h **33.** 154 in.^{2}

35. 2.5 mm^2 **37.** 25.1 m^2 **39.** $\dfrac{9\pi}{8}$ cm^2, or about 3.5 cm^2

Pages 633–635 Extra Practice Unit 8

1. 2; 7 **3.** 0.7; -3.5 **5.** -1; 5 **7.** 2; -1; $y = 2x - 1$
9. $\dfrac{2}{3}$; $\dfrac{1}{3}$; $y = \dfrac{2}{3}x + \dfrac{1}{3}$ **11.** $y = 5x - 7$ **13.** $y = -\dfrac{1}{2}x - 4$
15. $y = -6x + 18$

17. $(0, -2), (-8, 0)$

19. $(0, -3), (10, 0)$

21. $\left(0, -\dfrac{5}{2}\right), (-2, 0)$

23. undefined; $x = -3$ **25.** 0; $y = -2.5$

27. Slope is undefined. **29.** Slope is undefined.
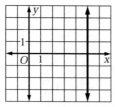

31. Slope is undefined. **33.** Slope is undefined.

35. $y = \dfrac{3}{5}x - 2$ **37.** $y = -2x + 19$ **39.** $y = \dfrac{2}{3}x + 4$

41. $y = -5x + 5$ **43.** $y = -1$
45, 47, 49. Estimates may vary. Examples are given.

45. $\left(-1\frac{2}{3}, -1\right)$

47. $\left(-2\frac{2}{3}, 3\frac{1}{3}\right)$

49. about $\left(\frac{1}{2}, \frac{1}{4}\right)$

51.

53.

55.

57.

59.

61.

63.

65.

67.

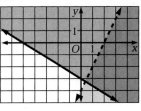

Pages 635–637 Extra Practice Unit 9
1. 25 **3.** 9 **5.** 30 **7.** $\sqrt{149} \approx 12.2$ **9.** $4\sqrt{3}$ **11.** $3\sqrt{10}$
13. 7 **15.** $6\sqrt{2}$ **17.** 6 **19.** $30\sqrt{3}$ **21.** $x = \pm 2\sqrt{14}$
23. $x = \pm 2\sqrt{5}$ **25.** $x = \pm 9\sqrt{2}$ **27.** If $m \times n$ is an even number, then m and n are even numbers. False; $3 \times 4 = 12$. **29.** If a pair of angles are congruent, then they are vertical angles. False; Two congruent angles in two different triangles are not vertical angles.
31. 0 **33.** 0, −3 **35.** 0, −9 **37.** No; $8^2 + 10^2 \neq 12^2$.
39. Yes; $20^2 + 21^2 = 29^2$. **41.** Yes; $9^2 + 40^2 = 41^2$.
43. $\frac{1}{3}$ **45.** $\frac{1}{6}$ **47.** 1 **49.** $\frac{1}{3}$ **51.** $\frac{1}{4}$ **53.** triangular prism; 96 in.^{2} **55.** pyramid; 1536 cm^2 **57.** pyramid; 576 ft^2
59. half-cylinder; about 173.7 m^2
61. trapezoidal prism; 216 in.^{2} **63.** about 35.3 m^3
65. about 84.8 in.^{3} **67.** 1200 ft^3 **69.** 3072 cm^3
71. about 2261.9 mm^3 **73.** 16:9; 18 m^2
75. 25:36; 86.4 m^2 **77.** 27:8; $53\frac{1}{3}\pi$ m^3

Pages 638–639 Extra Practice Unit 10
1. a.

$\triangle ABC$ has clockwise orientation, and $\triangle A'B'C'$ has counterclockwise orientation.

b. $\triangle ABC$ has clockwise orientation, and $\triangle A'B'C'$ has counterclockwise orientation.

3. a. Quadrilateral $PQRS$ has counterclockwise orientation, and quadrilateral $P'Q'R'S'$ has clockwise orientation.

3. b.

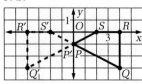

Quadrilateral *PQRS* has counterclockwise orientation, and quadrilateral *P'Q'R'S'* has clockwise orientation.

5. D **7.** A **9.**

11. 0 and 4; 0 **13.** −8 and 3; −24 **15.** $\frac{2}{3}$ and $-\frac{1}{4}$; −2

17. $6b^6$ **19.** $35x^4y^3$ **21.** t^{12} **23.** $3125a^{15}$ **25.** $-64a^3b^9$

27. $64r^{30}s^{12}$ **29.** $-a^2 - 4a$ **31.** $6x^2 - 15x$

33. $28x^2 + 63x$ **35.** $x(3 - x)$; 0 and 3; 0 **37.** $x(x - 4)$;
0 and 4; 0 **39.** $2x(x - 3)$; 0 and 3; 0 **41.** $x^2 - 3x - 10$

43. $x^2 - 12x + 36$ **45.** $x^2 + 12x + 36$

47. $4x^2 - 19x + 12$ **49.** $10x^2 + 43x + 28$

51. $21x^2 + 25x - 4$ **53. a.** $x = -1$ **b.** $(-1, 0)$ **c.** 1

55. a. $x = 5$ **b.** $(5, -30)$ **c.** −5 **57.** $(x + 14)(x - 2)$

59. $(x - 10)(x - 3)$ **61.** $(x - 6)(x + 5)$

63.

65.

67.

69, 71, 73, 75, 77. Methods and estimates may vary.
Answers are given. **69.** 9 and 5 **71.** 2 and 4

73. 3 and −1 **75.** −2 and $\frac{7}{3}$ **77.** 1 and $-\frac{1}{2}$

Toolbox Skills

Page 640 Skill 1

1. 76 **2.** 36 **3.** 49 **4.** 49 **5.** 300 **6.** 90 **7.** 60 **8.** 101
9. 1100 **10.** 6300 **11.** 55 **12.** 1200

Page 641 Skill 2

1. $7 < 10$

2. $-4 < 0$

3. $5 > -7$

4. $-5 > -7$

5. −1, 0, 2; −1 < 0 < 2 **6.** −5, −3, 0; −5 < −3 < 0
7. −7, 1, 3; −7 < 1 < 3 **8.** −6, −4, −2; −6 < −4 < −2
9. −19, −9, 12; −19 < −9 < 12 **10.** −27, −17, −7;
−27 < −17 < −7 **11.** −100, 0, 56; −100 < 0 < 56
12. −10, −1, 1, 10; −10 < −1 < 1 < 10

Page 642 Skill 3

1. 9 **2.** −9 **3.** 5 **4.** −5 **5.** 0 **6.** −8 **7.** 5 **8.** −6 **9.** −18
10. 1 **11.** 0 **12.** −10 **13.** −10 **14.** 9 **15.** −33 **16.** 0

Pages 643–644 Skill 4

1. 2 **2.** −1 **3.** 8 **4.** −5 **5.** 1 **6.** −6 **7.** 1 **8.** 10 **9.** 9
10. −8 **11.** 0 **12.** −10 **13.** 40 **14.** −8 **15.** 8 **16.** 0
17. −4 **18.** −9 **19.** 3 **20.** −25 **21.** 25 **22.** 25 **23.** 3
24. 0 **25.** −10 **26.** 1 **27.** −48 **28.** −6 **29.** 30 **30.** −18
31. −21

Page 645 Skill 5

1. Yes. **2.** No. **3.** Yes. **4.** No. **5.** No. **6.** Yes. **7.** 6
8. 4 **9.** −5 **10.** 10 **11.** 4 **12.** −1 **13.** −9 **14.** −24
15. −4 **16.** 5 **17.** 1 **18.** 32 **19.** 7 **20.** 48 **21.** −2
22. −12 **23.** −6 **24.** −2

Pages 646–647 Skill 6

1. a. $x + 2 = -1$ **b.** $x = -3$ ☐ = ■ ■ ■

2. 5 **3.** 4 **4.** −3 **5.** 2 **6.** −4 **7.** 0

8. a. $2x = 10$

b. (1) ⬭⬭ = ⬭⬭⬭⬭⬭ (2) $2x = 10$
$\frac{2x}{2} = \frac{10}{2}$
$x = 5$ $x = 5$

9. 4 **10.** −4 **11.** −6 **12.** 4 **13.** 6 **14.** −1 **15.** 8

Page 648 Skill 7

1. $2 \times 2 \times 2 \times 5$ **2.** 3×13 **3.** prime
4. $2 \times 2 \times 3 \times 7$ **5.** $2 \times 2 \times 2 \times 13$ **6.** $2 \times 3 \times 17$
7. $2 \times 5 \times 11$ **8.** $5 \times 5 \times 5$ **9.** prime **10.** $3 \times 7 \times 7$
11. $2 \times 2 \times 3 \times 3 \times 7$ **12.** $2 \times 2 \times 2 \times 2 \times 3 \times 3$
13. 7×19 **14.** 2×29 **15.** $2 \times 2 \times 2 \times 2 \times 11$

Page 649 Skill 8

1. 3; 18 **2.** 5; 110 **3.** 7; 210 **4.** 15; 90 **5.** 9; 27
6. 6; 144 **7.** 25; 50 **8.** 4; 60 **9.** 3; 210 **10.** 4; 32
11. 11; 110 **12.** 20; 300

Page 650 Skill 9

1. $\frac{5}{3}$ **2.** $-\frac{4}{7}$ **3.** $-\frac{1}{6}$ **4.** 1 **5.** $\frac{1}{6}$ **6.** $-\frac{4}{9}$ **7.** $\frac{6}{11}$ **8.** −9
9. $-\frac{3}{14}$ **10.** $\frac{10}{7}$

Pages 651–652 Skill 10

1. $\frac{7}{9}$ **2.** $\frac{1}{2}$ **3.** $\frac{7}{9}$ **4.** 1 **5.** $1\frac{5}{9}$ **6.** $\frac{7}{15}$ **7.** $\frac{1}{4}$ **8.** $\frac{7}{18}$ **9.** $-\frac{4}{15}$

10. $-\frac{37}{56}$ **11.** $-\frac{2}{9}$ **12.** $\frac{16}{25}$ **13.** $-\frac{7}{9}$ **14.** $\frac{1}{11}$ **15.** $1\frac{1}{24}$

16. $1\frac{11}{35}$ **17.** $\frac{3}{14}$ **18.** $-\frac{2}{5}$ **19.** $\frac{5}{18}$ **20.** $\frac{3}{25}$ **21.** $\frac{1}{15}$ **22.** 8

23. $-2\frac{1}{2}$ **24.** $\frac{3}{4}$ **25.** $\frac{27}{50}$ **26.** $\frac{5}{18}$ **27.** $-\frac{3}{8}$ **28.** -1 **29.** $1\frac{1}{2}$

30. $\frac{9}{20}$ **31.** $\frac{20}{27}$ **32.** $-\frac{25}{49}$

Pages 654 Skill 11

1. $0.7; \frac{7}{10}$ **2.** $0.32; \frac{8}{25}$ **3.** $1.25; \frac{5}{4}$ **4.** $0.0075; \frac{3}{400}$

5. $0.075; \frac{3}{40}$ **6.** $66\%; \frac{33}{50}$ **7.** $33\frac{1}{3}\%; \frac{1}{3}$ **8.** $0.9\%; \frac{9}{1000}$

9. $37.5\%; \frac{3}{8}$ **10.** $160\%; \frac{8}{5}$ **11.** $0.72; 72\%$

12. $0.029; 2.9\%$ **13.** $0.576; 57.6\%$ **14.** $1.35; 135\%$

15. $0.1\overline{6}; 16.\overline{6}\%$, or $16\frac{2}{3}\%$

Page 654 Skill 12

1. 40% **2.** 250% **3.** 4% **4.** 37.5% **5.** 7.5%

6. 125% **7.** 30% **8.** 18.75% **9.** 0.5% **10.** $33\frac{1}{3}\%$

Page 655 Skill 13

1. 8% decrease **2.** 10% increase **3.** 2.4% increase **4.** 26% decrease

Page 656 Skill 14

1. 1.8 **2.** 21 **3.** 26 **4.** 3.7 **5.** 98.7 **6.** 7.4 **7.** 110 **8.** 0.08 **9.** 45 **10.** $7.95; $18.55 **11.** Answers may vary. An example is given. 79% is almost 80%, so, if 80% of $50 is $40 (0.8($50) = $40), then 79% of $50 is a little less than $40. **12.** Answers may vary. An example is given. No; 250 items are half the items, not $\frac{1}{2}\%$; 1% of the items is 5 items, so a $\frac{1}{2}\%$ defective rate would yield about two or three defective items per 500 items.

Page 656 Skill 15

1. 80 **2.** 125 **3.** 950 **4.** 648 **5.** 21 **6.** 375 **7.** 800 **8.** 7.5 **9.** 500 **10.** 12.8 **11.** 62.5 **12.** 160 **13.** 150

Page 657 Skill 16

1. 45° **2.** 120° **3.** 90° **4.** 135°

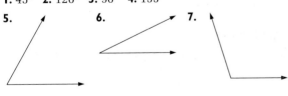

5. **6.** **7.**

8.

9. a. 88° **b.** $(125 - x)°$

Page 658 Skill 17

1. 27 **2.** 4.8 cm **3.** $2x + 12$

Page 659 Skill 18

1. 64 cm^2 **2.** 99 ft^2 **3.** 2.25 mm^2 **4.** $8t$ yd^2

5. 2.88 in.^{2}

Page 659 Skill 19

1. 2400 cm^3 **2.** 22.5 in.^{3} **3.** 4 ft^3 **4. a.** 343 yd^3

b. 0.125 ft^3

Page 660 Skill 20

1. $(3, -3)$ **2.** $(-2, 5)$ **3.** $(2, 4)$ **4.** $(-2, -5)$ **5.** $(-1, 4)$

6. $(-2, 0)$ **7.** $(2, -5)$ **8.** $(-5, -2)$ **9.** $(0, 2)$ **10.** $(4, 3)$

Page 660 Skill 21

1–6.

Page 661 Skill 22

1.

Fat (g) per Slice in Turkey Meats

2.

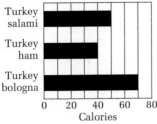

Calories per Slice in Turkey Meats

1.

Average Temperature
in Miami, Florida

2.

Average Temperature
in Peoria, Illinois

1.   National Football League
Longest Punts 1999–2000

Rouen

Berger

Miller

Tupa

= 10 yards

2.   National Football League
Punting Yardage 1999–2000

Rouen

Berger

Miller

Tupa

= 500 yards

1.   Bruins' Record
1999–2000

Wins
Ties
Losses

2.   Sabres' Record
1999–2000

Wins
Ties
Losses

1. 7 calculators   **2.** 2562 mi   **3.** 209 student tickets

1. $245   **2.** $4.75   **3.** 2400 items   **4.** 130 ft^2

Appendix 1

Pages 670, 671 Talk it Over

1. Control variable: minutes after tap is turned on; dependent variable: height of water   **2.** Control variable values: all amounts of time from 0 through 6 minutes; dependent variable values: all heights from 0 through 21 cm   **3.** Yes; both the control variable and the dependent variable are continuous quantities. **4.** Descriptions may vary. An example is given. The domain is the number of days: 0, 1, 2, 3.... The range is the dollar amounts 0, 0.10, 0.20, 0.30.... There may be an upper limit to the domain and the range. For example, once you owe more in fines than a book is worth, the library may charge you the cost of replacing the book.

Page 671 Exercises and Problems

1. The domain is the number of weeks: 0, 1, 2, 3, 4, 5, 6. The range is the dollar amounts 120, 100, 80, 60, 40, 20, 0.   **3.** The domain is the number of gallons from 0 through the total number of gallons his tank holds. If g is the total number of gallons his tank holds, then the range is the dollar amounts to the nearest penny from 0 through 1.69g.   **5.** The domain is the number of tickets sold: 0, 1, 2, …, 12. The range is the dollar amounts 0, 3.50, 7.00, …, 42.

Appendix 2

Pages 672, 673 Talk it Over

1. The slopes are the same; the slope is the amount Ilona charges per pin ($25).   **2.** The vertical intercept of the first line is 0; this is the amount of money made before any pins are sold, disregarding start-up costs. The vertical intercept of the second line is −300; Ilona needs to make $300 to pay off her start-up costs. **3.** A−m; B−k; C−n; D−l; You can match the graphs by checking the y-intercepts.   **4.** Descriptions may vary. An example is given. Changing the value of m changes the slope. When $m > 0$, the graph slopes up from left to right, and becomes steeper as m increases. When $m < 0$, the graph slopes down from left to right. It becomes steeper as $|m|$ increases. Changing the value of b changes the y-intercept. The graph crosses the y-axis at the origin when $b = 0$, above the origin when $b > 0$, and below the origin when $b < 0$.

Page 673 Exercises and Problems

1. The graph of $y = 3x$ will slope up from left to right and will be steeper than the graph of $y = x$. The graph of $y = -3x$ will slope down from left to right. All three graphs will pass through the origin.   **3. a.** $h = 55t + 10,152$ **b.** The graph of $h = 55t + 10,152$ will be less steep than the graph of $h = 110t + 6000$ because its slope is smaller. Its vertical intercept is greater, so it will cross the vertical axis at a higher point.